Lecture Notes in Computer Science   **11627**

Commenced Publication in 1973
Founding and Former Series Editors:
Gerhard Goos, Juris Hartmanis, and Jan van Leeuwen

More information about this series at http://www.springer.com/series/7410

Johannes Buchmann · Abderrahmane Nitaj ·
Tajjeeddine Rachidi (Eds.)

Progress in Cryptology – AFRICACRYPT 2019

11th International Conference on Cryptology in Africa
Rabat, Morocco, July 9–11, 2019
Proceedings

 Springer

Editors
Johannes Buchmann
Technical University of Darmstadt
Darmstadt, Germany

Abderrahmane Nitaj
Université de Caen
Caen, France

Tajjeeddine Rachidi
Al Akhawayn University
Ifrane, Morocco

ISSN 0302-9743   ISSN 1611-3349 (electronic)
Lecture Notes in Computer Science
ISBN 978-3-030-23695-3   ISBN 978-3-030-23696-0 (eBook)
https://doi.org/10.1007/978-3-030-23696-0

LNCS Sublibrary: SL4 – Security and Cryptology

This Springer imprint is published by the registered company Springer Nature Switzerland AG
The registered company address is: Gewerbestrasse 11, 6330 Cham, Switzerland

Preface

The 11th edition of the International Conference on the Theory and Applications of Cryptographic Techniques, Africacrypt 2019 was held in Rabat, Morocco, during July 9–11, 2019. The conference was organized by Al Akhawayn University in Ifrane (AUI), Morocco, in cooperation with the International Association for Cryptologic Research (IACR). Tajjeeddine Rachidi (AUI, Morocco) was responsible for the local organization, supported by a local organizing team consisting of Dr. Latifa ElMortaji, Ibtissam Latachi, and Bouchra Saad. We are indebted to them for their support and smooth collaboration.

The aim of Africacrypt 2019 was to provide an international forum for researchers from academia and practitioners from industry from all over the world, for discussions regarding all forms of cryptology, coding theory, and information security.

We had the privilege of chairing the Program Committee, which consisted of 35 members. There were 53 papers submitted to the conference. Each paper was assigned to at least three members of the Program Committee and was reviewed anonymously. The review process was challenging and the Program Committee, aided by reports from 59 external reviewers, produced a total of 166 reviews in all. In total, 22 papers were accepted on May 2, 2019. Authors then had the opportunity to update their papers until May 10, 2019. The present proceedings include all the revised papers. We are indebted to the members of the Program Committee and the external reviewers for their diligent work.

The conference was honored by the presence of two invited speakers, namely, Martin R. Albrecht, who spoke on "So How Hard Is Solving Hard Lattice Problems Anyway?" and Sebastian Faust with his talk "Scaling Blockchains with Off-chain Protocols." We are grateful to them.

We also would like to thank the authors of all submissions and all the speakers, as well all the participants. They all contributed to the success of the conference, and to making Africacrypt conference series an excellent forum for the advancement of cryptology.

We are also thankful to the staff at Springer for their help with producing the proceedings and to the staff of EasyChair for the use of their conference management system.

Last but not least, we thank Professor Driss Ouaouicha, President of Al Akhawayn University in Ifrane, Morocco, for his unconditional support of Africacrypt. We extend our gratitude to Group OCP and Les Eaux Minérales d'Oulmès, gold and bronze sponsors of the conference.

May 2019

Johannes Buchmann
Abderrahmane Nitaj
Tajjeeddine Rachidi

Organization

Africacrypt 2019 was organized by Al Akhawayn University in Ifrane, Morocco.

General Chair

Tajjeeddine Rachidi   Al Akhawayn University in Ifrane, Morocco

Program Chairs

Johannes Buchmann	TU Darmstadt, Germany
Abderrahmane Nitaj	University of Caen Normandie, France
Tajjeeddine Rachidi	Al Akhawayn University in Ifrane, Morocco

Invited Speakers

Martin R. Albrecht	Royal Holloway, University of London, UK
Sebastian Faust	TU Darmstadt, Germany

Organizing Committee

Tajjeeddine Rachidi (Chair)	Al Akhawayn University in Ifrane, Morocco
Latifa ElMortaji	Al Akhawayn University in Ifrane, Morocco
Ibtissam Latachi	FSDM, USMBA, Morocco
Bouchra Saad	Al Akhawayn University in Ifrane, Morocco

Program Committee

Elena Andreeva	Katholieke Universiteit Leuven, Belgium
Muhammad Rezal Kamel Ariffin	Institute for Mathematical Research, UPM, Malaysia
Hatem M. Bahig	Ain Shams University, Egypt
Magali Bardet	University of Rouen Normandie, France
Lejla Batina	Radboud University, The Netherlands
Hussain Ben-Azza	ENSAM, Meknes, Morocco
Olivier Blazy	University of Limoges, France
Colin Boyd	Norwegian University of Science and Technology, Norway
Sébastien Canard	Orange Labs, Caen, France
Sherman S. M. Chow	The Chinese University of Hong Kong, SAR China
Nicolas Courtois	University College London, UK
Joan Daemen	Radboud University, The Netherlands

Luca De Feo	University of Versailles, France
Sow Djiby	University Cheikh Anta Diop, Dakar, Senegal
Nadia El Mrabet	SAS - CGCP - EMSE, Saint Etienne, France
Javier Herranz	Universitat Politècnica de Catalunya, Spain
Sorina Ionica	University of Picardie, France
Tetsu Iwata	Nagoya University, Japan
Juliane Krämer	TU Darmstadt, Germany
Subhamoy Maitra	Indian Statistical Institute, India
Abderrahmane Nitaj	University of Caen Normandie, France
Yanbin Pan	Chinese Academy of Sciences, Beijing, China
Christophe Petit	University of Oxford, UK
Elizabeth Quaglia	Royal Holloway, University of London, UK
Tajjeeddine Rachidi	Al Akhawayn University of Ifrane, Morocco
Adeline Roux-Langlois	CNRS - IRISA, France
Palash Sarkar	Indian Statistical Institute, India
Alessandra Scafuro	North Carolina State University, USA
Ali Aydin Selcuk	TOBB University, Turkey
Pantelimon Stanica	Naval Postgraduate School, Monterey, USA
Noah Stephens-Davidowitz	Massachusetts Institute of Technology, USA
Joseph Tonien	University of Wollongong, Australia
Damien Vergnaud	Pierre and Marie Curie University/Institut Universitaire de France, Paris, France
Vanessa Vitse	University of Grenoble Alpes, France
Amr Youssef	Concordia University, Montreal, Canada

Additional Reviewers

Khalid Abdelmoumen	Saqib A. Kakvi	Constanza Riera
Alexandre Adomnicai	Orhun Kara	Yann Rotella
Guy Barwell	Robin Larrieu	Simona Samardjiska
Jean Belo Klamti	Rio LaVigne	Olivier Sanders
Pauline Bert	Ela Lee	Patrick Struck
Carl Bootland	Isis Lovecruft	Halil Kemal Taskin
Laura Brouilhet	Jack P. K. Ma	Yannick Teglia
Ahmet Burak Can	Ramiro Martínez	Oleksandr Tkachenko
Ilaria Chillotti	Pedro Maat Massolino	Jacques Traoré
Thomas Debris	Simon-Philipp Merz	Marloes Venema
Christoph Dobraunig	Romy Minko	Jorge Villar
Gautier Eberhart	Lina Mortajine	Jiafan Wang
Pierre-Alain Fouque	Suleyman Ozarslan	Xiuhua Wang
Ashley Fraser	Kostas Papagiannopoulos	Léo Weissbart
Ariel Gabizon	Albrecht Petzoldt	Weiqiang Wen
Lydia Garms	Robert Primas	Yang Yu
Chris Hicks	Chen Qian	Yongjun Zhao
Murat Ilter	Sebastian Ramacher	

Sponsoring Institutions

- OCP Group, Morocco (Gold sponsor)

- Les Eaux Minérales d'Oulmès, Morocco (Bronze sponsor)

Origin of Submissions

Australia
Austria
Belgium
Brazil
Canada
China
Cyprus
Estonia
Finland
France
Germany
Hong Kong
India

Italy
Japan
Morocco
The Netherlands
Norway
Spain
Switzerland
Tunisia
Turkey
United Arab Emirates
United Kingdom
United States

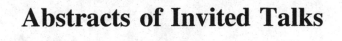

Abstracts of Invited Talks

So How Hard Is Solving Hard Lattice Problems Anyway?

Martin R. Albrecht

Information Security Group, Royal Holloway, University of London

Abstract. Establishing the cost of solving hard lattice problems is a pressing concern at the moment owing to schemes reliant on these problems being considered for deployment. In this talk, I discuss recent advances in this area in recent years, both in the classic and in the quantum world, to arrive at the current state of the art.

Keywords: Lattice-based cryptography · Post-quantum · Learning with errors

Scaling Blockchains with Off-Chain Protocols

Sebastian Faust

TU Darmstadt, Germany

Abstract. One of the main challenges of decentralized blockchain systems is scalability. For instance, in Bitoin – the most popular blockchain system – transactions can take up to 10 minutes until they are processed, and throughput is limited to five to seven transactions per second. A promising approach to improve scalability of blockchains is represented by off-chain protocols. Off-chain protocols work by building a second layer network over the blockchain, thereby allowing that the massive amount of transactions is carried out directly between the involved users. There has recently been a plethora of different constructions for off-chain protocols proposed by industry and academia. Examples of such systems are the Lightning network for Bitcoin, state channel constructions such as Counterfactual or Perun, and various types of Plasma systems for Ethereum. In this talk, we summarize some of the recent progress that has been made in the field of off-chain protocols.

Keywords: Blockchain · Off-chain protocols · State channels

Contents

New Schemes and Analysis

Block Ciphers

Side-Channel Attacks and Countermeasures

Signatures

Protocols

Tiny WireGuard Tweak

Jacob Appelbaum[(✉)], Chloe Martindale[(✉)], and Peter Wu[(✉)]

Department of Mathematics and Computer Science,
Eindhoven University of Technology, Eindhoven, Netherlands
jacob@appelbaum.net, chloemartindale@gmail.com, peter@lekensteyn.nl

Abstract. We show that a future adversary with access to a quantum computer, historic network traffic protected by WireGuard, and knowledge of a WireGuard user's long-term static public key can likely decrypt many of the WireGuard user's historic messages. We propose a simple, efficient alteration to the WireGuard protocol that mitigates this vulnerability, with negligible additional computational and memory costs. Our changes add zero additional bytes of data to the wire format of the WireGuard protocol. Our alteration provides transitional post-quantum security for any WireGuard user who does not publish their long-term static public key – it should be exchanged out-of-band.

Keywords: WireGuard · Post-quantum cryptography ·
Mass surveillance · Network protocol · Privacy · VPN · Security

1 Introduction

WireGuard [12] is a recently introduced Virtual Private Network (VPN) protocol which is both simple and efficient. It aims to replace other protocols such as IPsec [22] and OpenVPN [44] for point-to-point tunnels with a secure protocol design that rejects cryptographic agility. WireGuard uses a fixed set of sound cryptographic primitives and does not negotiate them – in stark contrast to nearly every other major VPN protocol. Unlike many protocols, WireGuard *requires* out-of-band peer configuration information to be exchanged before it may be used. All peers *must* exchange fixed pairwise-unique long-term static public keys as well as Internet host name or address information out-of-band. WireGuard optionally allows peers to fix a pairwise-unique static symmetric value known as a Pre-Shared Key (PSK). A well-known VPN provider, Mullvad, has a worldwide deployment [31] of WireGuard that uses this PSK [32] as

Author list in alphabetical order; see https://www.ams.org/profession/leaders/culture/CultureStatement04.pdf. This work was done when the third author was a master student at Eindhoven University of Technology under the supervision of Jacob Appelbaum and Tanja Lange. This work was supported in part by the Netherlands Organization for Scientific Research (NWO) under grants 639.073.005 and 651.002.004 (CHIST-ERA USEIT). Permanent ID of this document: tue-wireguard-africacrypt-2019. Date of this document: May 9, 2019.

© Springer Nature Switzerland AG 2019
J. Buchmann et al. (Eds.): AFRICACRYPT 2019, LNCS 11627, pp. 3–20, 2019.
https://doi.org/10.1007/978-3-030-23696-0_1

a method of adding post-quantum transitional security to the protocol. Wire-Guard does not require, nor use a PSK by default. A protocol is post-quantum transitionally secure when it is secure against a passive adversary with a quantum computer [40]. If this transitionally secure protocol is used today, it is not possible for a quantum attacker to decrypt today's network traffic, *tomorrow*.

If a future adversary has access to a quantum computer, historic network traffic protected by WireGuard, and knowledge of *one* WireGuard user's long-term static public key, this threatens the security of the protocol for all related WireGuard users, as explained in Sect. 5. In this paper we propose a tiny tweak to the WireGuard protocol that makes WireGuard traffic flows secure against such an adversary; if our alteration is incorporated into the WireGuard protocol, a user's historic traffic will not be able to be decrypted by such an adversary if they do not release their long-term static public key to the network, as explained in Sect. 6. We accomplish this with both extremely minimal costs and minimal changes to the original protocol, as detailed in Sect. 6.1.

Note that our analysis applies to the current version of WireGuard [14] as implemented in the Linux kernel [18] as opposed to the older version described in the NDSS paper [12]. A major difference exists in the application of the PSK during the handshake which results in two incompatible protocols.

Acknowledgements. We would like to thank Jason A. Donenfeld for WireGuard and for insightful discussions about possible ways to improve WireGuard against quantum adversaries including for suggesting hashing of public keys. We would like to thank various anonymous helpers for their reviews of earlier drafts of this paper. We would also like to thank those in the TU/e coding theory and cryptology group and the cryptographic implementations group including Gustavo Banegas, Daniel J. Bernstein, and especially Tanja Lange for their valuable feedback.

2   Realistic Adversary Concerns

It is well-documented and indisputable that a number of nation-state-sponsored adversaries are unilaterally conducting mass surveillance of the Internet as a whole. This has created new notions of realistic threat models [3,35,38] in the face of such pervasive surveillance adversaries. Some of these adversaries have an openly stated interest in *"collecting it all"* [25] and have directly stated that they use this data as actionable information, for example, for use in internationally contested drone strikes against unknown persons. The former director of the CIA, General Michael Hayden, famously said: *"We kill people based on metadata"* [9]. We additionally see that these adversaries target encrypted protocols and for example seek to exploit properties of handshakes, which may allow them to launch other subsequent attacks. These types of attacks are documented in the publication of numerous internal documents [1,29,30] that show attacks, claims, and results against a number of VPNs and other important cryptographic protocols. Development of quantum computers for attacking cryptographic protocols is explicitly a budget line item [4]. We consider it prudent to analyze WireGuard as a protocol that is, among others, of interest to these adversaries.

We consider nation-state mass surveillance adversaries (for example NSA [5, 7] using XKeyscore [26]) as one of the primary adversaries to users of encrypted network tunnels, and we find that WireGuard will be vulnerable when these adversaries gain access to a quantum computer (see Sect. 5 for details). This is primarily due to the fact that large-scale [27] surveillance data sets which contain logged encrypted traffic are explicitly kept for later attempts at decryption [23].

We also consider less powerful adversaries which are directly coercive, oppressive, or political (COPs). These adversaries are able to take possession of any endpoint, such as through theft or other ill-gotten means, which includes a long-term public static cryptographic key pair. This type of attack is regularly carried out against VPN providers and is commonly understood as a kind of compulsion [11] attack.

3 WireGuard Overview

In this section we present an overview of the WireGuard protocol, briefly consider relevant implementations, and discuss traffic analysis considerations.

3.1 WireGuard Implementations

WireGuard is implemented in multiple languages and is easy to understand. The primary implementation is available as a patch to the Linux kernel and is written in C [18]. Implementations targeting MacOS and iOS [19], Android [17], and Windows [20] use the wireguard-go [15] implementation which is written in the Go programming language. An experimental implementation in the Rust programming language is also available, wireguard-rs [16].

The first author has implemented a user space Python implementation for experimentation using Scapy [8] for use on GNU/Linux. The third author has implemented a protocol dissector [43] for WireGuard in Wireshark [10], a software program that can capture and analyze network traffic. Our implementations are based on the published WireGuard paper [12] and the evolving white paper [14].

3.2 WireGuard as a Tunneling Protocol

WireGuard is a point-to-point protocol for transporting IP packets. It uses the UDP protocol for transporting protocol messages. It is implemented as a device on common operating systems and users of WireGuard route IP packets into the WireGuard device to securely send those packets to their WireGuard peer. WireGuard does not have state for any IP packets that it transmits and It does not re-transmit packets if they are dropped by the network.

To start using the WireGuard protocol, a user must first generate a long-term static Curve25519 [6] key pair and acquire the long-term static public key of their respective peer. This precondition for running the WireGuard protocol is different from common Internet protocols as users *must* exchange these keys out of band. This is in contrast to services such as OpenVPN which may only need to exchange a user name or password for access control reasons. Example methods of distributing WireGuard keys include using a camera on a smart phone to import the peer public keys with a QR code, or by manually entering the data. This *must* be done before attempting to run the WireGuard protocol and the would-be agents running the protocol are designed to not emit packets to parties which do not have possession of previously exchanged public keys. Users are also required to exchange a DNS name or an IP address along with a UDP port number for at least one of the two parties. To use the WireGuard tunnel, the peers additionally have to exchange the expected *internal* IP addressing information for their respective WireGuard tunnel endpoints. This again is in contrast to other VPN solutions which usually include some sort of automatic IP addressing scheme to ease automatic configuration of internal tunnel endpoint addresses.

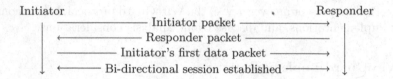

Fig. 1. Informal protocol narration of the 1.5 Round Trip Time (1.5-RTT) handshake valid for a ninety second session; parties may change roles in subsequent sessions; for additional information see Fig. 7 and Algorithm 1

After configuring the endpoints with the respective public keys and IP addresses, peers will be able to create new cryptographic WireGuard sessions with each other as shown in Fig. 1.

3.3   WireGuard's Cryptographic Handshake

The Noise Protocol framework [34] abstractly defines different Diffie-Hellman handshakes with different security, and privacy properties for use in cryptographic protocols. Protocol designers select a Noise Protocol pattern and then select the ideal abstract handshake properties. They must then select concrete objects such as an authenticated encryption scheme and a Diffie-Hellman primitive. WireGuard's cryptographic handshake [14] is a variant of IKpsk2 pattern from the Noise Protocol [34, Section 9.4] framework. A WireGuard handshake consists of the initiator sending an initiation message (see Fig. 3) and the responder replying with a corresponding responder message (see Fig. 4).

WireGuard selected Curve25519 [6] for Diffie-Hellman non-interactive key exchange messages, BLAKE2s [39] for hashing operations, HKDF [28] as the key derivation function (KDF), and ChaCha20Poly1305 [33] for authenticated encryption with additional data (AEAD).

WireGuard additionally augments the Noise protocol in certain areas that weaken conventional security assumptions relating to identity hiding; WireGuard reduces the identity hiding properties of the Noise IK protocol as part of a trade-off strategy to reduce computational costs and to resist detection by untargeted Internet-wide scanning. The popular Wireshark traffic analysis program displays a peer's identity and associates it with flows of traffic. We observe that preconditions of the protocol more closely resemble the Noise KK pattern; KK assumes that both parties know their peer's respective long-term static public key while IK assumes that only the responder's long-term static public key is known by the initiator. However, it is strictly weaker than the KK pattern in that the initiator always reveals their own long-term static public key identity to the responder, and thus to the network, encrypted to the responder's long-term public key. Unlike other protocols, the roles of initiator and responder do also reverse [14]. This happens automatically when the responder attempts to send a data packet without a valid session.

3.4 Handshake Details

The initiator's long-term static public key is encrypted using the ChaCha20Poly1305 AEAD using a key derived from the responder's long-term static public key and a per-session ephemeral Curve25519 key pair generated by the initiator. The resulting ciphertext is decrypted, and the public key of the initiator is found, and matched to a corresponding data structure previously initialized for cryptographic operations on the responder side; see Algorithm 1 for details. In Sect. 5.2, we describe an attack based on the transmission of the encrypted long-term static public key.

Notes on Algorithm 1:

- As in the WireGuard protocol, we use the following notation for symmetric encryption with a nonce and additional authenticated data (AEAD): ciphertext = aead-enc(key, nonce, message, associated data).
- Algorithm 1 gives a *simplified* version of the WireGuard key agreement process; the only fundamental simplifications that we have applied are:
  - We introduce Laura and Julian as parties in the role of Initiator and Responder.
  - Compressing the application of multiple hash function operations from $H(H(x)||y)$ to a single $H(x||y)$.
  - Omission of some constants in the initial hash and KDF salt.
  - Omission of details about construction of the 96-bit nonce. This value also serves as a counter for replay detection within a given session.
  - Compressing the application of multiple KDF's to a set of variables to the application of a single KDF to the set of variables.

4   Traffic Analysis

WireGuard traffic visible to a third party observer is subject to trivial finger-printing and confirmation that the WireGuard protocol is in use. The protocol is not designed to resist traffic analysis: session identifiers, sequence numbers, and other values are visible. For any surveillance adversary, writing a comprehensive network protocol dissector is quick work as evidenced in our Wireshark and Scapy implementations. There are four message types. Three of these types have a fixed length and each has static values which act as distinguishers or network

---

Algorithm 1. Simplified WireGuard key agreement process

Public Input: Curve25519 $E/\mathbb{F}_p$, base point $P \in E(\mathbb{F}_p)$, hash function H, an empty string ϵ, key derivation function KDF_n returning n derived values index by n, and a MAC function Poly1305.

Secret Input (Laura): secret key $\mathsf{sk}_L \in \mathbb{Z}$, public key $\mathsf{pk}_L = \mathsf{sk}_L \cdot P \in E(\mathbb{F}_p)$, Julian's pre-shared public key $\mathsf{pk}_J \in E(\mathbb{F}_p)$, shared secret $\mathsf{s} = \mathsf{DH}(\mathsf{sk}_L, \mathsf{pk}_J)$, message time, PSK $Q \in \{0,1\}^{256}$; $Q = 0^{256}$ by default.

Secret Input (Julian): secret key $\mathsf{sk}_J \in \mathbb{Z}$, public key $\mathsf{pk}_J = \mathsf{sk}_J \cdot P \in E(\mathbb{F}_p)$, Laura's pre-shared public key $\mathsf{pk}_L \in E(\mathbb{F}_p)$, shared secret $\mathsf{s} = \mathsf{DH}(\mathsf{sk}_J, \mathsf{pk}_L)$, PSK $Q \in \{0,1\}^{256}$; $Q = 0^{256}$ by default.

Output: Session keys.

1: Both parties choose ephemeral secrets: $\mathsf{esk}_L \in \mathbb{Z}$ for Laura, $\mathsf{esk}_J \in \mathbb{Z}$ for Julian.
2: Laura publishes $\mathsf{epk}_L \leftarrow \mathsf{esk}_L \cdot P$.
3: Laura computes $\mathsf{se}_{JL} \leftarrow \mathsf{esk}_L \cdot \mathsf{pk}_J$; Julian computes $\mathsf{se}_{JL} \leftarrow \mathsf{sk}_J \cdot \mathsf{epk}_L$.
4: Both parties compute $(\mathsf{ck}_1, \mathsf{k}_1) \leftarrow \mathsf{KDF}_2(\mathsf{epk}_L, \mathsf{se}_{JL})$.
5: Laura computes $\mathsf{h}_1 \leftarrow H(\mathsf{pk}_J \| \mathsf{epk}_L)$.
6: Laura computes and transmits $\mathsf{enc\text{-}id} \leftarrow \mathsf{aead\text{-}enc}(\mathsf{k}_1, 0, \mathsf{pk}_L, \mathsf{h}_1)$.
7: Julian decrypts $\mathsf{enc\text{-}id}$ with $\mathsf{aead\text{-}dec}(\mathsf{k}_1, 0, \mathsf{enc\text{-}id}, \mathsf{h}_1)$ and verifies that the resulting value (pk_L) is valid user's public key; aborts on failure.
8: Both parties compute $(\mathsf{ck}_2, \mathsf{k}_2) = \mathsf{KDF}_2(\mathsf{ck}_1, \mathsf{s})$.
9: Laura computes $\mathsf{h}_2 \leftarrow H(\mathsf{h}_1 \| \mathsf{enc\text{-}id})$.
10: Laura computes and transmits $\mathsf{enc\text{-}time} \leftarrow \mathsf{aead\text{-}enc}(\mathsf{k}_2, 0, \mathsf{time}, \mathsf{h}_2)$.
11: Both parties compute $\mathsf{pkt} \leftarrow \mathsf{epk}_L \| \mathsf{enc\text{-}id} \| \mathsf{enc\text{-}time}$.
12: Laura computes and transmits $\mathsf{mac1} \leftarrow \mathsf{MAC}(\mathsf{pk}_J, \mathsf{pkt})$.
13: Julian verifies that $\mathsf{mac1} = \mathsf{MAC}(\mathsf{pk}_J, \mathsf{pkt})$; aborts on failure.
14: Julian computes $\mathsf{time} = \mathsf{aead\text{-}dec}(\mathsf{k}_2, 0, \mathsf{enc\text{-}time}, \mathsf{h}_2)$; aborts on failure.
15: Julian transmits $\mathsf{epk}_J \leftarrow \mathsf{esk}_J \cdot P$.
16: Laura computes $\mathsf{se}_{LJ} \leftarrow \mathsf{sk}_L \cdot \mathsf{epk}_J$; Julian computes $\mathsf{se}_{LJ} \leftarrow \mathsf{esk}_J \cdot \mathsf{pk}_L$.
17: Laura computes $\mathsf{ee} \leftarrow \mathsf{esk}_L \cdot \mathsf{epk}_J$; Julian computes $\mathsf{ee} \leftarrow \mathsf{esk}_J \cdot \mathsf{epk}_L$.
18: Both parties compute $(\mathsf{ck}_3, \mathsf{t}, \mathsf{k}_3) \leftarrow \mathsf{KDF}_3(\mathsf{ck}_2 \| \mathsf{epk}_J \| \mathsf{ee} \| \mathsf{se}_{LJ}, Q)$.
19: Julian computes $\mathsf{h}_3 \leftarrow H(\mathsf{h}_2 \| \mathsf{enc\text{-}time} \| \mathsf{epk}_J \| \mathsf{t})$.
20: Julian computes and transmits $\mathsf{enc\text{-}e} \leftarrow \mathsf{aead\text{-}enc}(\mathsf{k}_3, 0, \epsilon, \mathsf{h}_3)$.
21: Laura verifies that $\epsilon = \mathsf{aead\text{-}dec}(\mathsf{k}_3, 0, \mathsf{enc\text{-}e}, \mathsf{h}_3)$.
22: Both parties compute shared secrets $(T_i, T_r) \leftarrow \mathsf{KDF}_2(\mathsf{ck}_3, \epsilon)$.
23: **return** (T_i, T_r).

---

selectors [36]. The fourth type has variable length, it additionally has static distinguishers and is linkable to other packets in any given flow. WireGuard does not attempt to hide that the WireGuard protocol is in use from a surveillance adversary, and it additionally does not attempt to hide information that allows sessions within network flows to be distinguished. WireGuard does attempt to resist active probing by requiring any initiating party to prove knowledge of the long-term static public key of the responder.

4.1 Example WireGuard Protocol Run

To create a WireGuard session, the protocol is broken into several phases. The initiating party is called an *initiator*, and the receiving party which must be reachable, is called the *responder*. The first phase is a handshake protocol described in detail in Sect. 3.3, and the second phase is a time-limited data-transfer window. The third phase is reached when a time limit or a data-transfer limit is reached, at which point a new cryptographic session is established. Unlike other cryptographic protocols, the WireGuard protocol has no session renegotiation, peers simply start again as if they have never had a session in the first place.

After a successful handshake, once the initiator has received a responder message, it may proceed to send transport data messages (see Fig. 6) which contain encrypted IP packets. The responder is only permitted to send data messages after successfully receiving and authenticating the transport data packet sent by the initiator. Data messages with an encrypted empty payload act as Keep-Alive messages. These are trivially distinguishable messages by their type and length as shown in Fig. 2.

Fig. 2. Flow graph between two WireGuard peers as seen in Wireshark

An example interaction taken from a packet capture between two WireGuard peers can be found in Fig. 2, and an informal protocol narration in Fig. 1.

If either initiator or responder are under heavy computational load, they may send a Cookie message (see Fig. 5) in response to an initiation or responder message without making further progress in completing the handshake. The recipient of a Cookie message should decrypt the cookie value and use it to calculate the MAC2 value for use in the next handshake attempt. It will not retransmit the same handshake message under any circumstances. If a handshake is unsuccessful, the initiator will try to start a new handshake.

There is no explicit error or session-tear-down signaling. A session is invalidated after a fixed duration of time; session lifetimes are currently around ninety seconds.

4.2 Packet Formats

We display the four packet formats. The protocol includes only these four wire message formats, though there is an implied fifth type: an empty data message may be used as keep alive message. Each message is encapsulated entirely inside of an IP packet with UDP payload.

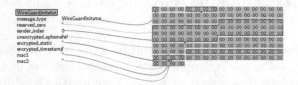

Fig. 3. 148 byte initiator packet payload

In Fig. 3, the initiator message is shown. It is a fixed-size frame of 148 bytes. The MAC2 field is set to zero unless the sender has received a Cookie message before. This message is larger than the responder's message intentionally to prevent misuse such as amplification attacks using forged source addresses.

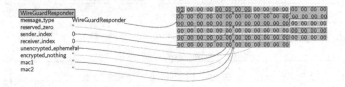

Fig. 4. 92 byte responder packet payload

In Fig. 4, the responder message is shown. It is a fixed-sized frame of 92 bytes. Unlike the initiator packet, it does not contain a long term static public key.

In Fig. 5, the cookie message is shown. It is a fixed-sized frame of 64 bytes. This is not used for each run of the WireGuard protocol. This message is only sent by the initiator or responder when they are "under load". The recipient must decrypt the cookie value and store it for inclusion in future handshake messages.

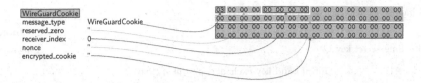

Fig. 5. 64 byte Cookie packet payload

While all handshake messages (Figs. 3, 4, 5) have fixed lengths, the Transport Data message (Fig. 6) has a variable length. At minimum it is 32 bytes in length. This includes the Transport Data message headers and the authentication tag for the encrypted payload. For any given WireGuard protocol run, the maximum size of a generated UDP packet depends on the maximum transmission unit (MTU) of the network interface. These are typically much smaller than the theoretical limits of an IP packet.

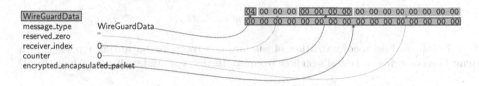

Fig. 6. Variable length (32 up to $\infty + 16$) byte data packet payload.

The UDP layer has a theoretical maximum length of $2^{16} - 1$, this length also includes eight bytes of the UDP header so the actual maximum length for the UDP payload is $2^{16} - 1 - 8$ bytes. While WireGuard itself does not impose a maximum length, implementations on various platforms might be constrained by their environment. For example, the Linux kernel does not support IPv6 Jumbograms [21] and FreeBSD currently does not support IPv6 Jumbograms with UDP due to the lack of a physical medium [24].

5 Security and Privacy Issues

We consider both the mass surveillance adversary and the less powerful local adversary conducting targeted attacks from Sect. 2.

5.1 Identity Hiding Weakening

Throughout this section, suppose, as was justified in Sect. 2 to be a realistic situation, that a WireGuard user has released its long-term static public key. We analyze a handshake involving this user with this user in the role of responder.

Initial handshake message creation and processing

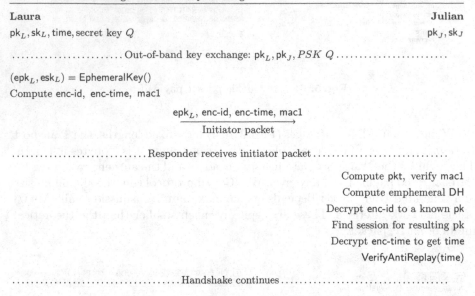

Fig. 7. Informal protocol narration of sending and receiving an initiator packet. (For definitions of terms and details on how to compute, decrypt, and verify, see Algorithm 1)

The initiation packet contains the static public key of the initiator and it is encrypted as previously described with an ephemeral key pair used in conjunction with the responder's static key pair. The initiation packet is augmented with what WireGuard's design describes as a MAC. Under our assumptions, the input, which is an initiator or a responder packet, and the MAC key, which is the static public key of the receiving party, are both *public* values.

Third party observers are able to passively confirm the identity of both peers when their public keys are known to the observer. This is strictly worse than NoiseIK's identity hiding properties and allows non-sophisticated attackers to link known static public keys to individual flows of traffic.

Ostensibly the additional MAC over the whole packet is done primarily as a verification step: to prevent arbitrary packets (e.g. from an adversary) from causing the responder to compute a Diffie-Hellman key-exchange. This is a known deficiency in OpenVPN [13].

The MAC check also prevents practical Internet-wide scans from finding *unknown* WireGuard responders. While a verification step may be necessary to prevent unknown parties from exhausting resources or forcing a responder message, this additional MAC verification method is strongly divergent from the identity hiding properties of the Noise IK pattern; because of this identity hiding property, it is easier for a quantum adversary to attack, as we show below.

A simple shared secret value, set either on a per-site or per-peer basis would provide a similar protection without revealing the identity of one or both of the peers.

5.2   Quantum Attack

Consider an attacker capable[1] of running Shor's algorithm [41]. Shor's algorithm breaks the discrete logarithm problem in any group in time polynomial in the size of the group; observe that this includes elliptic curve groups. Suppose that the long-term static public key of some WireGuard user U_0 is known to an adversary. We show in Algorithms 2 and 3 that in this situation, Shor's algorithm will apply to users of the WireGuard protocol, as given in Algorithm 1.

Recall from Sect. 4 that network traffic is visible to a third-party observer. In particular, an adversary can detect when a handshake takes place between U_0 and any other WireGuard user. We describe in Algorithm 2 how to extract the long-term static secret key of any initiator with a quantum computer when U_0 is the responder.

Of course after computing the ephemeral keys, an adversary who has access to the static secret and public keys of both the initiator and the responder of a WireGuard handshake can completely break the protocol (assuming the responder U_0 and the initiator use the default WireGuard settings, i.e. no PSK).

Now suppose an adversary wishes to attack some user U_n. Suppose also that there exists a *traceable path* from U_0 to U_n, that is, if by analyzing the traffic flow the adversary can find users $U_1, \ldots, U_{n-1}$ for which every pair of 'adjacent' users U_i and U_{i+1} have performed a WireGuard handshake. We show in Algorithm 3 how the adversary can then compute U_n's long-term static key pair. Recall from Sect. 4 that the information of which pairs of users have performed a WireGuard handshake is freely available; if such a path exists then an adversary can easily find it.

An important remark on this attack: if two WireGuard users do not publish their static public keys, and *both* users do not interact with any other WireGuard users, then this attack does not apply to those two users.

5.3   A Brief Comment on Extra Security Options

In Sect. 5.2 we analyzed the *default* use of the WireGuard protocol. There is an option open to WireGuard users to also preshare another secret key, i.e., to use a PSK Q as an additional input for the KDF in Step 18 of Algorithm 1. If the user does not configure a PSK, the default value ($Q = 0^{256}$) will be used.

Use of a secret PSK will not prevent a quantum adversary from computing sk_L, pk_L using the method described in Sect. 5.2. It does however prevent compromise of session keys T_i and T_r in Step 22 of Algorithm 1 as the adversary no longer has enough information to compute ck_3 in Step 18 of Algorithm 1.

---

[1] See [37] for a recent estimate of the resources needed by an attacker to carry out such an attack using Shor's algorithm.

Algorithm 2. Extract Initiator's Long-term Static Key Pair

Input: Long-term static public key pk_J of the responder; Ephemeral public key epk_L of the initiator (transmitted over the wire in Step 2 of Algorithm 1); enc-id as sent over the wire by the initiator in Step 6 of Algorithm 1.

Output: Long-term static key pair sk_L, pk_L of the initiator.

1: Using Shor's algorithm, compute esk_L from epk_L.
2: Compute k_1 and h_1 as in Steps 4 and Steps 5 respectively of Algorithm 1.
3: Compute $pk_L = \mathsf{aead\text{-}dec}(k_1, 0, \mathsf{enc\text{-}id}, h_1)$.
4: Compute sk_L from pk_L using Shor's algorithm.
   return sk_L, pk_L.

Algorithm 3. Extract User U_n's Long-term Static Key Pair

Input: Long-term static public key of some WireGuard User U_0; A traceable path from U_0 to WireGuard User of interest U_n.

Output: Long-term static key pair of WireGuard User U_n.

1: **for** $i := 0, \ldots, n-1$ **do**
2: $U_i \leftarrow$ Responder (without loss of generality, c.f. Section 3.3).
3: $U_{i+1} \leftarrow$ Initiator (also without loss of generality).
4: Compute long-term static key pair of U_{i+1} using Algorithm 2.
5: **end for**
   return Long-term static key pair of U_n.

A prudent user may still be concerned about an adversary stealing their PSK; the tiny protocol tweak presented in Sect. 6 addresses this concern as well as protecting those who use the default mode of the WireGuard protocol.

Of course our tweak cannot protect against an adversary who steals the static long-term public key of both the initiator and the responder in a WireGuard handshake.

6   Blinding Flows Against Mass Surveillance

We propose a tiny tweak to the Wireguard handshake which thwarts the quantum attack outlined in the previous section: In Step 6 and Step 7 of Algorithm 1, replace pk_L by $H(pk_L)$. We suggest to use BLAKE2s as the hash function H as it is already used elsewhere in WireGuard. Naturally, the unhashed static public key pk_L of the initiator has still been exchanged out-of-band, so the responder can still perform Diffie-Hellman operations with the initiator's static public key pk_L, and is able to compute the hash $H(pk_L)$. In Step 7 and Step 16 of Algorithm 1, the responder will use the decrypted value $H(pk_L)$ to look up the corresponding key pk_L.

The hashing process conceals the algebraic structure of the static public key of the initiator and replaces it with a deterministic, predictable identifier. This requires no extra configuration information for either of the peers. BLAKE2s is a one-way hashing function and a quantum adversary cannot easily [42] deduce the initiator's static public or secret key from this hash value unless the hash function is broken.

An attacker as described in Sect. 5.2 may confirm a guess of a known long-term static public key. If the guess is correct, they may carry out the attack as in the unchanged WireGuard protocol. However, the tweak protects sessions where the public keys are not known.

We claim only *transitional security* with this alteration. That is, that a future quantum adversary will not be able to decrypt messages sent before the advent of practical quantum computers, if the messages are encrypted via an updated version of WireGuard that includes our proposed tweak. The tweaked protocol is not secure against active quantum attacks with knowledge of both long-term static public keys and a known PSK value. With knowledge of zero or only one long-term static public key, the protocol remains secure. A redesign of the WireGuard protocol to achieve full post-quantum security is still needed.

There are of course other choices of values to replace the static public key in Step 6 and Step 7 of Algorithm 1 to increase security. One alternative choice of value is an empty string, as in the case with the message sent in response to initiator packets by the responder. This would change the number of trial decryptions for the responder for initiator messages to $\mathcal{O}(n)$ where n is the number of configured peers. This change would allow any would-be attacker to force the responder to perform many more expensive calculations. It would improve identity hiding immensely but at a cost that simply suggests using a different Noise pattern in the first place. A second alternative choice of value is a random string which is mapped at configuration time, similar to a username or a numbered account, which is common in OpenVPN and similar deployments. This provides $\mathcal{O}(1)$ efficiency in lookups of session structures but with a major loss in ease of use and configuration. It would also add a second identifier for the peer which does not improve identity hiding. Both alternative choices have drawbacks. The first method would create an attack vector for unauthenticated consumption of responder resources and the second method would require additional configuration. Both weaken the channel binding property of Noise [34, Chapter 14] as the encrypted public key of the initiator is no longer hashed in the handshake hash. The major advantage of our proposed choice is that it does not complicate configuration, nor does it require a wire format change for the WireGuard protocol. Assuming collision-resistance of the hash function, the channel binding property is also preserved. Our proposal concretely improves the confidentiality of the protocol without increasing the computation in any handshake. It increases the computation for peer configuration by only a single hash function for each configured public key.

This change does not prevent linkability of flows as it exchanges one static identifier for another, and it does preclude sharing that identifier in a known vulnerable context (Fig. 8).

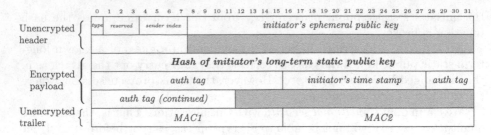

Fig. 8. Tweaked initiator packet (in bytes)

6.1 Modified Protocol Costs

Our modification obviously requires implementation changes. We study the effect on the proposed Linux kernel implementation as outlined in the WireGuard paper [14] as well as the effect on the alternative implementations.

The hash function input of the initiator's static public key and the output value have an identical length, thus the wire format and internal message structure definitions do not need to change to accommodate the additional hash operation.

Initiators only have a single additional computational cost, calculation of the hash over their own static public key. This could be done during each handshake at no additional memory cost, or during device configuration which only requires an additional 32 bytes of memory in the device configuration data structure to store the hash of the peer's long-term static public key.

Responders must be able to find the peer configuration based on the initiation handshake message since it includes the peer's static public key, optional PSK, permitted addresses, and so on. In the unmodified protocol, a hash table could be used to enable efficient lookups using the static public key as table key. At insertion time, a hash would be computed over the table key. The Linux kernel implementation uses SipHash2-4 [2] as hash function for this table key [14, Section 7.4]. Our modification increases the size of the per-peer data structure by 32 bytes and requires a single additional hash computation per long-term static public key at device configuration time. There are no additional memory or computational costs during the handshake.

The wireguard-go [15, device/device.go] implementation uses a standard map data type using the static public key as map key. Again, a single additional hash computation is required at configuration time with no additional memory usage.

Recall that WireGuard is based on the Noise protocol framework. Our modification is not compatible with the current version of this framework, and thus implementations that rely on a Noise library to create and process handshake messages must be changed to use an alternative Noise implementation. This affects the Rust implementation [16].

6.2   Alternative Designs and Future Work

In theory, an alternative WireGuard implementation could accept any initiator that connects to it and successfully completes the handshake. Additional authorization could then be performed after the handshake. Our modification would make it impossible to create such implementations as it ensures that the assumed pre-condition of requiring an out-of-band exchange of long-term static public key is not violated.

Our proposed modification is generic and also applies to other protocols based on the Noise IK pattern. A new *pattern modifier* could be defined in the Noise specification that enables new protocols to improve transitional post-quantum security in the case where static public keys have been exchanged before, and only an identity selector needs to be transmitted.

7   Conclusions

We show that a future adversary with access to a quantum computer, historic network traffic protected by WireGuard, and knowledge of a WireGuard user's long-term static public key can likely decrypt many WireGuard users' historic messages when the optional PSK was not used or was compromised. We present a simple solution to this problem: hashing the long-term static public key before it is sent encrypted over the wire, resulting in the destruction of the algebraic structure of the elliptic-curve point which otherwise could be exploited by quantum computers via Shor's algorithm. The resulting hashed public key is the same size as the original public key and does not increase the size of any of the protocol messages. The required input for a quantum adversary to run Shor's algorithm would not be available from the network flow alone and it would thwart such an attacker from using a database of network flows to decrypt those very same flows. Targeted quantum attacks would still be possible in the case that the long-term keys of both parties, initiator and responder, are known. Active quantum attacks may still be possible, but our alteration provides transitional security. Our improvement requires zero extra bytes of data transmitted on the wire, potentially zero or 32 extra bytes for each peer data structure in memory, and completely negligible computational costs for cooperating honest parties.

References

1. Adams, A.A.: Report of a debate on Snowden's actions by ACM members. SIGCAS Comput. Soc. 44(3), 5–7 (2014). https://doi.org/10.1145/2684097.2684099
2. Aumasson, J.-P., Bernstein, D.J.: SipHash: a fast short-input PRF. In: Galbraith, S., Nandı, M. (eds.) INDOCRYPT 2012. LNCS, vol. 7668, pp. 489–508. Springer, Heidelberg (2012). https://doi.org/10.1007/978-3-642-34931-7_28
3. Barnes, R.L., Schneier, B., Jennings, C., Hardie, T., Trammell, B., Huitema, C., Borkmann, D.: Confidentiality in the face of pervasive surveillance: a threat model and problem statement. RFC 7624, pp. 1–24 (2015). https://doi.org/10.17487/RFC7624

4. Gellman, B., Miller, G.: 'Black budget' summary details U.S. spy network's successes, failures and objectives (2013). https://www.washingtonpost.com/world/national-security/black-budget-summary-details-us-spy-networks-successes-failures-and-objectives/2013/08/29/7e57bb78-10ab-11e3-8cdd-bcdc09410972_story.html, news article

5. Bellare, M., Paterson, K.G., Rogaway, P.: Security of symmetric encryption against mass surveillance. In: Garay, J.A., Gennaro, R. (eds.) CRYPTO 2014. LNCS, vol. 8616, pp. 1–19. Springer, Heidelberg (2014). https://doi.org/10.1007/978-3-662-44371-2_1

6. Bernstein, D.J.: Curve25519: new Diffie-Hellman speed records. In: Yung, M., Dodis, Y., Kiayias, A., Malkin, T. (eds.) PKC 2006. LNCS, vol. 3958, pp. 207–228. Springer, Heidelberg (2006). https://doi.org/10.1007/11745853_14

7. Bieker, F.: Can courts provide effective remedies against violations of fundamental rights by mass surveillance? The case of the United Kingdom. In: Aspinall, D., Camenisch, J., Hansen, M., Fischer-Hübner, S., Raab, C. (eds.) Privacy and Identity 2015. IAICT, vol. 476, pp. 296–311. Springer, Cham (2016). https://doi.org/10.1007/978-3-319-41763-9_20

8. Biondi, P.: Scapy (2010). http://www.secdev.org/projects/scapy/, website

9. Cole, D.: Michael Hayden: "we kill people based on metadata" (2014). https://www.justsecurity.org/10311/michael-hayden-kill-people-based-metadata/, David Cole quoting former director of the CIA Michael Hayden

10. Combs, G., et. al.: Wireshark (1998–2019). https://www.wireshark.org/

11. Danezis, G., Clulow, J.: Compulsion resistant anonymous communications. In: Barni, M., Herrera-Joancomartí, J., Katzenbeisser, S., Pérez-González, F. (eds.) IH 2005. LNCS, vol. 3727, pp. 11–25. Springer, Heidelberg (2005). https://doi.org/10.1007/11558859_2. http://www.freehaven.net/anonbib/cache/ih05-danezisclulow.pdf

12. Donenfeld, J.A.: WireGuard: next generation kernel network tunnel. In: 24th Annual Network and Distributed System Security Symposium, NDSS 2017, San Diego, California, USA, 26 February–1 March 2017. The Internet Society (2017). https://www.ndss-symposium.org/ndss2017/ndss-2017-programme/wireguard-next-generation-kernel-network-tunnel/

13. Donenfeld, J.A.: Wireguard Black Hat 2018 talk slides (2018). https://www.wireguard.com/talks/blackhat2018-slides.pdf, see slide 41

14. Donenfeld, J.A.: WireGuard: next generation kernel network tunnel (2018). https://www.wireguard.com/papers/wireguard.pdf, version 416d63b 2018–06-30

15. Donenfeld, J.A.: Source code for the Go implementation of WireGuard (2019). https://git.zx2c4.com/wireguard-go, commit c2a2b8d739cb

16. Donenfeld, J.A.: Source code for the Rust implementation of WireGuard (2019). https://git.zx2c4.com/wireguard-rs, commit a7a2e5231571

17. Donenfeld, J.A.: WireGuard Android application source (2019). https://git.zx2c4.com/wireguard-android/

18. Donenfeld, J.A.: WireGuard Linux kernel source (2019). https://git.zx2c4.com/WireGuard, tag 0.0.20190227, commit ab146d92c353

19. Donenfeld, J.A.: WireGuard MacOS and iOS application source (2019). https://git.zx2c4.com/wireguard-ios/

20. Donenfeld, J.A.: WireGuard Windows application source (2019). https://git.zx2c4.com/wireguard-windows/

21. Dumazet, E.: Linux kernel patch: ipv6: Limit mtu to 65575 bytes (2014). https://git.kernel.org/linus/30f78d8ebf7f514801e71b88a10c948275168518

22. Dunbar, N.: IPsec networking standards – an overview. Inf. Sec. Techn. Report **6**(1), 35–48 (2001). https://doi.org/10.1016/S1363-4127(01)00106-6
23. Erwin, M.: The Latest Rules on How Long NSA Can Keep Americans' Encrypted Data Look Too Familiar (2015). https://www.justsecurity.org/19308/congress-latest-rules-long-spies-hold-encrypted-data-familiar/, blog entry
24. FreeBSD: Chapter 8. IPv6 Internals - Jumbo Payload. https://www.freebsd.org/doc/en/books/developers-handbook/ipv6.html#ipv6-jumbo
25. Greenwald, G.: The crux of the NSA story in one phrase: 'collect it all' (2013). https://www.theguardian.com/commentisfree/2013/jul/15/crux-nsa-collect-it-all, news article
26. Greenwald, G.: XKeyscore: NSA tool collects 'nearly everything a user does on the internet' (2013). https://www.theguardian.com/world/2013/jul/31/nsa-top-secret-program-online-data
27. Hogan, M.: Data flows and water woes: the Utah data center. Big Data Soc. **2**(2), 2053951715592429 (2015). https://journals.sagepub.com/doi/abs/10.1177/2053951715592429
28. Krawczyk, H., Eronen, P.: HMAC-based Extract-and-Expand Key Derivation Function (HKDF). RFC 5869, pp. 1–14 (2010). https://doi.org/10.17487/RFC5869
29. Landau, S.: Making sense from Snowden: what's significant in the NSA surveillance revelations. IEEE Secur. Priv. **11**(4), 54–63 (2013). https://doi.org/10.1109/MSP.2013.90
30. Landau, S.: Highlights from making sense of Snowden, Part II: what's significant in the NSA revelations. IEEE Secur. Priv. **12**(1), 62–64 (2014). https://doi.org/10.1109/MSP.2013.161
31. Mullvad: Introducing a post-quantum VPN, Mullvad's strategy for a future problem. https://mullvad.net/en/blog/2017/12/8/introducing-post-quantum-vpn-mullvads-strategy-future-problem/, blog post
32. Mullvad: mullvad-wg-establish-psk. https://github.com/mullvad/oqs-rs/tree/master/mullvad-wg-establish-psk, source code post
33. Nir, Y., Langley, A.: ChaCha20 and Poly1305 for IETF Protocols. RFC 8439, pp. 1–46 (2018). https://doi.org/10.17487/RFC8439
34. Perrin, T.: The Noise protocol framework (2018). https://noiseprotocol.org/noise.html
35. Preneel, B.: Post-Snowden threat models. In: Weippl, E.R., Kerschbaum, F., Lee, A.J. (eds.) Proceedings of the 20th ACM Symposium on Access Control Models and Technologies, Vienna, Austria, 1–3 June 2015, p. 1. ACM (2015). https://doi.org/10.1145/2752952.2752978
36. Privacy and Civil Liberties Oversight Board: Report on the Surveillance Program Operated Pursuant to Section 702 of the Foreign Intelligence Surveillance Act (2014). https://www.pclob.gov/library/702-Report.pdf, July 2nd, 2014; see page 12
37. Roetteler, M., Naehrig, M., Svore, K.M., Lauter, K.: Quantum resource estimates for computing elliptic curve discrete logarithms. In: Takagi, T., Peyrin, T. (eds.) ASIACRYPT 2017, Part II. LNCS, vol. 10625, pp. 241–270. Springer, Cham (2017). https://doi.org/10.1007/978-3-319-70697-9_9
38. Rogaway, P.: The moral character of cryptographic work. IACR Cryptology ePrint Archive 2015, p. 1162 (2015). http://eprint.iacr.org/2015/1162
39. Saarinen, M.O., Aumasson, J.: The BLAKE2 cryptographic hash and message authentication code (MAC). RFC 7693, pp. 1–30 (2015). https://doi.org/10.17487/RFC7693

40. Schanck, J.M., Whyte, W., Zhang, Z.: Circuit-extension handshakes for Tor achieving forward secrecy in a quantum world. Proc. Priv. Enhancing Technol. **4**, 219–236 (2016). https://eprint.iacr.org/2015/287.pdf
41. Shor, P.W.: Algorithms for quantum computation: discrete logarithms and factoring. In: 35th Annual Symposium on Foundations of Computer Science, Santa Fe, New Mexico, USA, 20–22 November 1994, pp. 124–134. IEEE Computer Society (1994). https://doi.org/10.1109/SFCS.1994.365700
42. Wiener, M.J.: The full cost of cryptanalytic attacks. J. Cryptol. **17**(2), 105–124 (2004). https://doi.org/10.1007/s00145-003-0213-5
43. Wu, P.: Bug 15011 - Support for WireGuard VPN protocol (2018). https://bugs.wireshark.org/bugzilla/show_bug.cgi?id=15011
44. Yonan, J.: OpenVPN. https://openvpn.net/. Accessed 11 Nov 2018

Extended 3-Party ACCE and Application to LoRaWAN 1.1

Sébastien Canard[1] and Loïc Ferreira[1,2(✉)]

[1] Orange Labs, Applied Crypto Group, Caen, France
{sebastien.canard,loic.ferreira}@orange.com
[2] Univ Rennes, INSA Rennes, CNRS, IRISA, Rennes, France

Abstract. LoRaWAN is an IoT protocol deployed worldwide. Whereas the first version 1.0 has been shown to be weak against several types of attacks, the new version 1.1 has been recently released, and aims, in particular, at providing corrections to the previous release. It introduces also a third entity, turning the original 2-party protocol into a 3-party protocol. In this paper, we provide the first security analysis of LoRaWAN 1.1 in its 3-party setting with a provable approach, and show that it suffers from several flaws. Based on the 3(S)ACCE model of Bhargavan et al., we then propose an extended framework that we use to analyse the security of LoRaWAN-like 3-party protocols, and describe a generic 3-party protocol provably secure in this extended model. We use this provable security approach to propose a slightly modified version of LoRaWAN 1.1. We show how to concretely instantiate this alternative, and formally prove its security in our extended model.

Keywords: Security protocols · Security model · Internet of Things · LoRaWAN

1 Introduction

Establishing a secure communication between two parties is a fundamental goal in cryptography as well as formally proving that such a protocol is secure. In their seminal paper, Bellare and Rogaway [3] propose a security model for the symmetric 2-party setting, and describe provably secure mutual authentication and key exchange protocols. Subsequent models have been proposed (e.g., [6,8,13,18] to cite a few). All these models consider protocols in a 2-party setting. However there exist concrete deployments making use of protocols defined or improperly seen as 2-party schemes, that involve, in fact, three (or more) entities, which different cryptographic operations are attributed to (e.g., the 3G/4G mobile phone technology).

Whereas the field of 2-party protocols has been intensively investigated, the 3-party case has received less attention so far. Yet (unsurprisingly) this does not prevent 3-party protocols from being deployed in real-life, despite the lack of a suitable security model that allows seizing precisely, and incorporating their specifics. An example of such a protocol is LoRaWAN 1.1.

© Springer Nature Switzerland AG 2019
J. Buchmann et al. (Eds.): AFRICACRYPT 2019, LNCS 11627, pp. 21–38, 2019.
https://doi.org/10.1007/978-3-030-23696-0_2

LoRaWAN 1.1. The LoRaWAN protocol has been designed to set up a Low-Power Wide-Area Network (LPWAN) based on a long range, low rate, and wireless technology dedicated to IoT and M2M. The version 1.0 [23] has been released in 2016. It has been shown to be weak against several types of attacks [2], hence its security is quite questionable. The last version, LoRaWAN 1.1 [22], has been published in 2017. This version aims, in particular, at providing corrections to the previous release, and is assumed to be more secure.

Whereas the version 1.0 of LoRaWAN describes a 2-party protocol between an end-device (ED) and a Network Server (NS), the version 1.1 introduces a third entity: the Join Server (JS). In this new version, the cryptographic operations of the authenticated key exchange are now shared among these three components. This change turns the previous 2-party protocol into a non-standard 3-party protocol with *unknown* security properties. Tampering with a 2-party protocol in order to turn it into a 3-party protocol should be done with care. This motivates a formal analysis in order to define the security goals, and to verify that the protocol meets the latter. In the remainder of this paper, "LoRaWAN" refers to "LoRaWAN 1.1".

Related Work. Alt, Fouque, Macario-Rat, Onete, and Richard [1] formally analyse the authenticated key exchange of the 3G/4G technology in its complete 3-party setting (with the addition of components from the core network), and show how to enhance the security with a small modification easily incorporated in the protocol. Regarding the same technology, Fouque, Onete, and Richard [12] use a 3-party security model, and show how to thwart end-device-tracking attacks while retaining most of the 3G/4G key exchange scheme structure.

Bhargavan, Boureanu, Fouque, Onete, and Richard [5] consider the use of TLS when it is proxied through an intermediate middlebox (such as a Content Delivery Network (CDN)). They propose the notion of 3(S)ACCE-security in order to analyse such a setting. This model extends the classical 2-party ACCE model of Jager, Kohlar, Schäge, and Schwenk [13] to the 3-party setting. They describe several attacks targeting a specific CDN architecture, and show that the latter does not meet its claimed security goals. In the same context, Bhargavan, Boureanu, Delignat-Lavaud, Fouque, and Onete [4] describe several types of attacks against *multi-context TLS* protocol (mcTLS) [19] which extends TLS to support middleboxes in order to offer in-network services. In contrast, they propose a proper security model called *Authenticated and Confidential Channel Establishment with Accountable Proxies* (ACCE-AP), and describe a generic 3-party construction secure in their model.

These works illustrate that 3-party protocols deserve suitable security models in order to be properly analysed, and to enlighten subtleties that, otherwise, would remain ignored at the cost of the security.

Contributions. In this context, our contributions are threefold:

1. We present an *improved security model* that we call 3-ACCE, based on that of Bhargavan et al. [5]. This meets the need of a general framework that

incorporates the subtleties of a LoRaWAN-like protocol, and allows expliciting the security requirements of such 3-party protocols. As additional enhancements, we add (i) ED authentication, (ii) the security operations done by NS during the channel establishment, and (iii) an extended "binding" property that links *all* the entities involved in the key exchange.

2. We describe a *generic 3-party protocol* that is provably secure in our enhanced model. That is, we provide a general theorem with its full proof in our 3-ACCE security notion. This generic protocol can be concretely instantiated with LoRaWAN but also other protocols.

3. We present the *first security analysis of LoRaWAN 1.1* using a provable approach. First, we describe several flaws that weaken the protocol. Next, we apply our generic result to LoRaWAN 1.1, and propose a slightly modified version of the protocol which achieves stronger security properties. We show how to concretely instantiate this alternative, and formally prove its security in our extended 3-party model.

Paper Outline. In Sect. 2, we describe the protocol LoRaWAN 1.1, and show that it suffers from several flaws that enable theoretical attacks. A general framework that we call 3-ACCE, and aiming at analysing the security of 3-party protocols is presented in Sect. 3. In addition, we propose a generic 3-party protocol that we formally prove to be secure in this extended model. We use this framework, in Sect. 4, to propose a slightly modified version of LoRaWAN 1.1 with stronger security properties, that we prove to be secure in our 3-ACCE model. Finally, we conclude in Sect. 5.

2 LoRaWAN 1.1

2.1 Overview of the Protocol

We recall the main lines of the LoRaWAN 1.1 protocol. Figure 1 depicts the protocol. A complete description can be found in the specification [22].

Three entities are involved in the key exchange and secure channel establishment: (i) ED (end-device): wireless sensor or actuator that communicates with NS through gateways, (ii) NS (Network Server): the entry point to the network, (iii) JS (Join Server): the server, located in the backend network, that owns the master keys of each ED. A fourth entity, the Application Server (AS), participates to the session once the authenticated key exchange is completed, and the secure channel is established. Exploiting a fleet of EDs, AS aims at collecting data or monitoring the EDs in order to provide some service.

LoRaWAN 1.1 is a protocol based on shared (static) master keys. All the cryptographic operations are based on the AES block cipher. Each ED stores two distinct 128-bit master keys MK_1, MK_2, and JS owns the list of all the master keys. Initiated only by ED, the key exchange is made of four main messages. The first two (*Join Request* and *Join Accept*) are used to mutually authenticate ED and JS, and to share the data used to compute the 128-bit session keys.

These messages are computed with MK_1. The other two (*RekeyInd* and *Rekey-Conf*) are used to validate the session keys. They are computed with the session keys, as any other post-accept messages (i.e., sent through the secure channel). In this paper, we focus on the standard method likely the most used to execute the protocol (the *Join procedure*), and leave the other methods (the emergency *Rejoin type 1 procedure*, and the *Rejoin type 0/2 procedure* that aims mainly at changing ED's radio parameters), much less used, as a future work.

Two counters cnt_E and cnt_J (unique per ED) are transmitted during the key exchange. They are initialised to 0 and monotonically increased (respectively by ED and JS) at each new session. From these two counters, JS's identifier id_J, and the master keys MK_1, MK_2, ED and JS compute four 128-bit session keys: integrity keys $K_c^{i_1}$ and $K_c^{i_2}$, and encryption keys K_c^e, and K_a^e. The session keys $K_c^{i_1}$, $K_c^{i_2}$, K_c^e are sent by JS to NS (through an undefined by the specification but allegedly secure protocol). K_a^e is sent by JS either to AS (through a protocol undefined by the specification), or to NS.

To that point, ED can send protected messages to the network. The messages are encrypted with AES-CTR and K_c^e or K_a^e depending on the message type. A *command* message is encrypted with K_c^e and exchanged between ED and NS. An *application* message is encrypted with K_a^e and exchanged between ED and AS. All these messages are MAC-ed with two different functions (depending on the direction) which are based on a tweaked version of AES-CMAC (a block is prefixed to the input), and output a 4-byte tag.

2.2 Cryptographic Flaws in LoRaWAN 1.1

Size of the Counters. The counters cnt_E, cnt_J are respectively 2-byte and 3-byte long. It is likely that so few values can be exhausted, which brings ED to be unable to initiate a new session and be lastly (if not for good) "disconnected" from the network. Note that there are two other methods that allow ED to initiate a session (the so-called Rejoin procedures). However the Rejoin type 0/2 procedure is available only if a session is *ongoing* (because the first request is sent through the current secure channel). As for the Rejoin type 1 procedure, it is invoked periodically based on a predefined frequency, which means that it is *not* available *at will*.

The specification states that if the cnt_E counter wraps around, then ED must use a different id_J value (parameter used in the Join Request and Join Accept messages, and in the session keys computation). In fact, $id_J \| cnt_E$ behaves as a counter where id_J corresponds to the most significant bits, and cnt_E to the least significant bits. Therefore it may not be enough to exhaust the cnt_E counter in order to stuck ED. However, we do think that, due to lack of clarity of the specification regarding the rationale in storing more than one id_J value into ED, and the fact that LoRaWAN 1.1 inherits from the previous version of the protocol, it is likely that only one id_J value will be stored into ED (as in the previous version, where cnt_E is a pseudo-random value). Moreover it has been shown [2] that it is possible to compel ED to repeatedly send Join Request

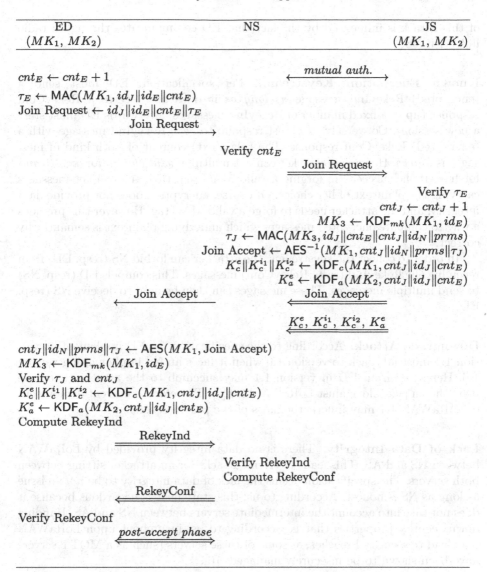

Fig. 1. Correct execution of LoRaWAN 1.1 Double line arrows indicate the use of secure channel keys. There two secure channels: ED-NS (LoRaWAN), and NS-JS (undefined).

messages, hence to likely use all the cnt_E values. Therefore exhausting ED's counter appears feasible.

Size of MAC Tags. The MAC's output is 4-byte long. Hence, MAC forgeries are made easier, and, in combination with the fact that data encryption is done in counter mode, so are attacks against data integrity. Note that the duration of this attack is influenced by the fact that ED communicates through a radio link with NS.

Known Encryption Keystream. Per specification, ED must send a (encrypted) RekeyInd message *as long as* it does not receive a RekeyConf response (up to a fixed number of RekeyInd messages, afterwards ED must start a new session). Conversely, NS must respond to *each* RekeyInd message with a (encrypted) RekeyConf response. The (plaintext) content of both kind of messages is *known*. Hence, an attacker can get multiple *valid encryption keystreams* for free. If she succeeds in forging a valid MAC tag, then she can get messages carrying the plaintext of her choice. Of course, encryption does not provide data integrity, and the attacker needs to forge a valid MAC tag. However this provides a way to compute encrypted messages which underlying plaintext is semantically correct.

In order to collect the keystreams, the attacker can forbid NS (resp. ED) from receiving the RekeyInd (resp. RekeyConf) messages. This compels ED (resp. NS) to send multiple messages. These messages can then be used to deceive NS (resp. ED).

Downgrade Attack. According to the specification, an ED implementing version 1.1 must fall back to version 1.0 when it faces an NS implementing version 1.0. Hence, even an ED in version 1.1 may succumb to the attacks that have been shown possible against LoRaWAN 1.0 [2]. Therefore, a current deployment of LoRaWAN 1.1 may inherit the flaws of the previous version.

Lack of Data Integrity. There is no data integrity provided by LoRaWAN between NS and AS. This leads to trivial attacks for an attacker sitting between both servers. The specification deems the lack of data integrity to be *not* an issue as long as NS is honest. According to us, this statement is hazardous because it does not take into account the intermediate servers between NS and AS. Handing down security properties that is, according to us, incumbent upon LoRaWAN may lead to security breaches, as some of these servers (such as a MQTT server) have been shown to be insecurely managed [16].

2.3 The Need for a Suitable Security Model

During the key exchange phase, the only cryptographic operation that NS does, in order to accept ED as partner, is verifying the RekeyInd message with keys received from JS. This allows the following theoretical attack. If the attacker, on the one hand, succeeds in sending keys of her choice to NS on behalf of JS, she can, on the other hand, provide a consistent RekeyInd message (computed under these keys), bringing NS to accept although no ED (and possibly no JS) is actually involved in the session. The attacker is then able to send valid messages to NS on behalf of ED (the same session keys are used to compute the RekeyInd message and the subsequent messages of the post-accept phase). This scenario implies being able either to impersonate JS to NS, or to break the channel security established (with a protocol undefined by the LoRaWAN specification) between NS and JS (see Fig. 1). This attack does *not* even need to target the core LoRaWAN protocol. It is conceivable because of the way the cryptographic operations in LoRaWAN are shared between ED, NS and JS, and interleaved with the undefined protocol used between NS and JS. This highlights how the security of LoRaWAN crucially depends on this additional protocol. Analysing LoRaWAN implies to take the latter into account.

LoRaWAN 1.1 is a 3-party protocol, not a 2-party protocol between a client (ED) and a backend network (NS-JS). Assessing its security (as a 3-party protocol) needs care. Therefore, it requires a suitable security model that incorporates all its subtleties, and makes explicit the security requirements which, for some of them (such as the protocol between NS and JS), are barely mentioned in the specification despite their crucial role in the overall security of a LoRaWAN network. In Sect. 3, we describe a 3-ACCE security model that aims at capturing the security goals of such 3-party protocols.

3 Extended 3-ACCE Model

3.1 Execution Environment

We describe the execution environment related to our model, using the notations of the ACCE model of Jager et al. [13], and Bhargavan et al. [5]. We use this execution environment to analyse our generic 3-party protocol Π. The security definitions of a secure pseudo-random function (PRF), and a secure pseudo-random permutation (PRP) can be found in Jager et al. [13]. We take the definition of a stateful authenticated encryption (sAE) scheme from that of a stateful length-hiding authenticated encryption scheme of Jager et al. [13] (without the length-hiding property).

Protocol Entities. Our model considers three sets of parties: a set $\mathcal{E}$ of end-devices, a set $\mathcal{N}$ of Network Servers, and a set $\mathcal{J}$ of Join Servers. Each party is given a long term key ltk.

Session Instances. Each party P_i maintains a set of instances Instances = $\{\pi_i^0, \pi_i^1, \ldots\}$ modeling several (sequential or parallel) executions of the 3-party protocol Π. Each instance π_i^n has access to the long term key ltk of its party parent P_i. Moreover, each instance π_i^n maintains the following internal state:

> The **instance parent** π_i^n.parent $\in \mathcal{E} \cup \mathcal{N} \cup \mathcal{J}$ indicating the party P_i that owns that instance: π_i^n.parent $= P_i$.

- The **partner-party** π_i^n.pid $\in \mathcal{E} \cup \mathcal{N} \cup \mathcal{J}$ indicating the party π_i^n.parent is presumably running the protocol with. $P_i \in \mathcal{E}$ can only be partnered with a party $P_k \in \mathcal{J}$. $P_k \in \mathcal{J}$ can only be partnered with a party $P_j \in \mathcal{N}$. $P_j \in \mathcal{N}$ can be partnered with either $P_i \in \mathcal{E}$ or $P_k \in \mathcal{J}$.

- The **role** $\pi_i^n.\rho \in \{\text{ed}, \text{ns-client}, \text{ns-server}, \text{js}\}$ of $P_i = \pi_i^n.\text{parent}$. If $P_i \in \mathcal{E}$, then $\pi_i^n.\rho = \text{ed}$. If $P_i \in \mathcal{J}$, then $\pi_i^n.\rho = \text{js}$. If $P_i \in \mathcal{N}$, then $\pi_i^n.\rho \in \{\text{ns-client}, \text{ns-server}\}$. In such a case, $\pi_i^n.\rho = \text{ns-client}$ if $\pi_i^n.\text{pid} \in \mathcal{J}$, and $\pi_i^n.\rho = \text{ns-server}$ if $\pi_i^n.\text{pid} \in \mathcal{E}$.
- The **session identifier** $\pi_i^n.\text{sid}$ of an instance.
- The **acceptance flag** $\pi_i^n.\alpha$ originally set to $\perp$ when the session is ongoing, and set to $1/0$ when the party accepts/rejects the partner's authentication.
- The **session keys** $\pi_i^n.\text{ck}$ set to $\perp$ at the beginning of the session, and set to a non-null bitstring corresponding to the encryption and decryption session keys once π_i^n computes the session keys.
- The **key material** $\pi_i^n.\text{km}$ set to $\perp$ if $\pi_i^n.\rho \in \{\text{ed}, \text{ns-server}\}$. Otherwise km is set to $\perp$ at the beginning of the session, and set to a non-null bitstring once π_i^n ends in accepting state.
- The **security bit** $\pi_i^n.\text{b}$ sampled at random at the beginning of the security experiments.
- The **partner-instances set** $\pi_i^n.\text{ISet}$ stores the *instances* that are involved in the same protocol run as π_i^n (including π_i^n itself).
- The **partner-parties set** $\pi_i^n.\text{PSet}$ stores the *parties* parent of the instances in $\pi_i^n.\text{ISet}$ (including $P_i = \pi_i^n.\text{parent}$ itself).

A correct execution of the protocol Π involves four instances π_i^n, π_j^u, π_j^v, π_k^ℓ such that

- $\pi_i^n.\text{parent} = P_i \in \mathcal{E}$, $\pi_j^u.\text{parent} = \pi_j^v.\text{parent} = P_j \in \mathcal{N}$, $\pi_k^\ell.\text{parent} = P_k \in \mathcal{J}$
- $\pi_j^u.\rho = \text{ns-server}$ and $\pi_j^v.\rho = \text{ns-client}$
- $\pi_i^n.\text{sid} = \pi_j^u.\text{sid} \neq \perp$ and $\pi_j^v.\text{sid} = \pi_k^\ell.\text{sid} \neq \perp$
- $\pi_i^n.\text{ck} = \pi_j^u.\text{ck} = \pi_j^v.\text{km} = \pi_k^\ell.\text{km} \neq \perp$

Then, the partner-instances set and the partner-parties set are defined as $\pi.\text{ISet} = \{\pi_i^n, \pi_j^u, \pi_j^v, \pi_k^\ell\}$ and $\pi.\text{PSet} = \{P_i, P_j, P_k\}$, $\forall \pi \in \{\pi_i^n, \pi_j^u, \pi_j^v, \pi_k^\ell\}$.

Adversarial Queries. An adversary may interact with the instances by issuing the following queries.

- NewSession(P_i, ρ, pid): this query creates a new session π_i^n with role ρ, executed by party P_i, and intended partner-party pid.
- Send(π_i^n, M): the adversary can send a message M to π_i^n, receiving a response M', or an error message $\perp$ if the instance does not exist or if $\pi_i^n.\alpha = 1$. (Send queries in an accepting state are handled by the Decrypt query.)
- Reveal(π_i^n): this query returns the session keys $\pi_i^n.\text{ck}$ and the key material $\pi_i^n.\text{km}$ of an instance π_i^n ending in accepting state.
- Corrupt(P_i): this query returns the long term key $P_i.\text{ltk}$ of P_i.
- Encrypt(π_i^n, M_0, M_1, H): it encrypts the message M_b, $b = \pi_i^n.\text{b}$, with header H, with the encryption session keys (stored within $\pi_i^n.\text{ck}$) of an *accepting* instance π_i^n (if $\pi_i^n.\alpha \neq 1$, then π_i^n returns $\perp$).
- Decrypt(π_i^n, C, H): this query decrypts the ciphertext C with header H, with the decryption session keys (stored within $\pi_i^n.\text{ck}$) of an *accepting* instance π_i^n (if $\pi_i^n.\alpha \neq 1$, then π_i^n returns $\perp$).

3.2   Security Definitions

Partnership. We define the 3-ACCE partnering with the sets ISet and PSet. π_i^n.ISet stores instances partnered with π_i^n, and π_i^n.PSet stores parties partnered with π_i^n. Moreover, we define sid to be the transcript, in chronological order, of all the (valid) messages sent and received by an instance during the key exchange, but, possibly, the last message. Therefore we use the 2-ACCE partnering notion (based on the definition of matching conversations initially proposed by Bellare and Rogaway [3], and modified by Jager et al. [13]) to define pairwise partnered instances, and we use the two sets ISet and PSet in order to identify all the instances that are partnered in the 3-ACCE model.

Correctness. The correctness in 3-ACCE is defined as follows. We demand that, for any instance π ending in an accepting state, the following conditions hold:

- $\forall \pi \in \{\pi_i^n, \pi_j^u, \pi_j^v, \pi_k^\ell\}$, π.ISet $= \{\pi_i^n, \pi_j^u, \pi_j^v, \pi_k^\ell\}$ and $|\pi.\text{ISet}| = 4$
- π_i^n.parent $= P_i \in \mathcal{E}$, π_j^u.parent $= \pi_j^v$.parent $= P_j \in \mathcal{N}$, π_k^ℓ.parent $= P_k \in \mathcal{J}$
- π.PSet $= \{P_i, P_j, P_k\}$
- π_i^n.ck $= \pi_j^u$.ck $= \pi_j^v$.km $= \pi_k^\ell$.km $\neq \bot$
- π_i^n.sid $= \pi_j^u$.sid $\neq \bot$
- π_j^v.sid $= \pi_k^\ell$.sid $\neq \bot$

Security of ACCE protocols is defined by requiring that (i) the protocol is a secure authentication protocol, and (ii) in the post-accept phase all data is transmitted over an authenticated and confidential channel in the sense of length-hiding sAE. Security of 3-ACCE protocols is defined in a similar way (but the length-hiding property), but we include an additional requirement in the entity authentication property in order to "bind" all the parties involved in a session. The adversary's advantage to win is defined with two games: the *entity authentication* game, and the *channel security* game. In both, the adversary can query all oracles NewSession, Send, Reveal, Corrupt, Encrypt, and Decrypt.

Entity Authentication (EA). This security property must guarantee that any instance π_i^n ending in accepting state is partnered with a unique instance. In addition to the two parties explicitly involved in the communication, we guarantee that a third party participate in the session (each one belonging to a different set $\mathcal{E}$, $\mathcal{N}$, $\mathcal{J}$). The purpose of this property, that we borrow from Bhargavan et al. [5], is to make sure that if some ED establishes a communication with some NS, there is a JS that is also involved. Conversely if a secure channel is established between an NS and a JS, we want to make sure that it is with the aim of establishing a communication between that NS and some ED. In this EA security experiment, the adversary is successful if, when it terminates, there exists an instance that *maliciously accepts* according to the following definition.

Definition 1 (Entity Authentication). *An instance is said to maliciously accept if the adversary succeeds in fulfilling one of the following winning conditions.*

ED adversary – *An instance π_i^n of parent $P_i \in \mathcal{E}$ is said to maliciously accept if*

- $\pi_i^n.\alpha = 1$ *and* $\pi_i^n.\mathsf{pid} = P_k \in \mathcal{J}$.
- *No instance in $\pi_i^n.\mathsf{ISet}$ was queried in Reveal queries.*
- *No party in $\pi_i^n.\mathsf{PSet}$ is corrupted.*
- *There is no unique $\pi_j^u \mid (\pi_j^u.\mathsf{parent} \in \mathcal{N} \wedge \pi_j^u.\mathsf{sid} = \pi_i^n.\mathsf{sid})$, or there is no $\pi_k^\ell \in P_k.\mathsf{Instances} \mid \pi_k^\ell.\mathsf{km} = \pi_i^n.\mathsf{ck}$.*

NS adversary – *An instance π_j^u of parent $P_j \in \mathcal{N}$ is said to maliciously accept if at least one of the following two conditions holds*

(a)
- $\pi_j^u.\alpha = 1$ *and* $\pi_j^u.\mathsf{pid} = P_i \in \mathcal{E}$.
- *No instance in $\pi_j^u.\mathsf{ISet}$ was queried in Reveal queries.*
- *No party in $\pi_j^u.\mathsf{PSet}$ is corrupted.*
- *There is no unique $\pi_i^n \mid (\pi_i^n \in P_i.\mathsf{Instances} \wedge \pi_j^u.\mathsf{sid} = \pi_i^n.\mathsf{sid})$, or there is no $\pi_k^\ell \mid (\pi_k^\ell.\mathsf{parent} = P_k \in \mathcal{J} \wedge \pi_i^n.\mathsf{pid} = P_k \wedge \pi_k^\ell.\mathsf{km} = \pi_j^u.\mathsf{ck})$.*

(b)
- $\pi_j^v.\alpha = 1$ *and* $\pi_j^v.\mathsf{pid} = P_k \in \mathcal{J}$.
- *No instance in $\pi_j^v.\mathsf{ISet}$ was queried in Reveal queries.*
- *No party in $\pi_j^v.\mathsf{PSet}$ is corrupted.*
- *There is no unique $\pi_k^\ell \in P_k.\mathsf{Instances} \mid (\pi_j^v.\mathsf{sid} = \pi_k^\ell.\mathsf{sid})$, or there is no $\pi_i^n \mid (\pi_i^n.\mathsf{parent} \in \mathcal{E} \wedge \pi_i^n.\mathsf{pid} = P_k \wedge \pi_i^n.\mathsf{ck} = \pi_j^v.\mathsf{km})$.*

JS adversary – *An instance π_k^ℓ of parent $P_k \in \mathcal{J}$ is said to maliciously accept if*

- $\pi_k^\ell.\alpha = 1$ *and* $\pi_k^\ell.\mathsf{pid} = P_j \in \mathcal{N}$.
- *No instance in $\pi_k^\ell.\mathsf{ISet}$ was queried in Reveal queries.*
- *No party in $\pi_k^\ell.\mathsf{PSet}$ is corrupted.*
- *There is no unique $\pi_j^v \in P_j.\mathsf{Instances} \mid (\pi_j^v.\mathsf{sid} = \pi_k^\ell.\mathsf{sid})$, or there is no $\pi_i^n \mid (\pi_i^n.\mathsf{parent} \in \mathcal{E} \wedge \pi_i^n.\mathsf{pid} = P_k \wedge \pi_k^\ell.\mathsf{km} = \pi_i^n.\mathsf{ck})$.*

The adversary's advantage is defined as its winning probability:

$$\mathsf{adv}_{\Pi}^{\mathsf{EA}}(\mathcal{A}) = \Pr[\mathcal{A} \text{ wins the EA game}].$$

Channel Security (CS). In the channel security game, the adversary can use all oracles. At some point, the adversary sends a challenge M_0, M_1 (issuing a query Encrypt) to some instance π_i^n, and gets C_b the encryption of M_b, $b = \pi_i^n.\mathsf{b}$. The adversary is successful if she guesses b. That is, she must output an instance π_i^n and its security bit. The security bit $\pi_i^n.\mathsf{b}$ is chosen at random at the beginning of the game.

Definition 2 (Channel Security). *An adversary $\mathcal{A}$ breaks the channel security if she terminates the channel security game with a tuple (π_i^n, b) such that*

- $\pi_i^n.\alpha = 1$
- *No instance in $\pi_i^n.\mathsf{ISet}$ was queried in Reveal queries.*
- *No party in $\pi_i^n.\mathsf{PSet}$ is corrupted.*
- $\pi_i^n.\mathsf{b} = b$

The adversary's advantage is defined as

$$\mathsf{adv}_\Pi^{\mathsf{CS}}(\mathcal{A}) = \left| \Pr[\mathcal{A} \text{ wins the } \mathsf{CS} \text{ game}] - \frac{1}{2} \right|.$$

Definition 3 (3-ACCE-security). *A 3-party protocol Π is 3-ACCE-secure if Π satisfies correctness, time adversaries $\mathcal{A}$, $\mathsf{adv}_\Pi^{\mathsf{EA}}(\mathcal{A})$ and $\mathsf{adv}_\Pi^{\mathsf{CS}}(\mathcal{A})$ are a negligible function of the security parameter.*

3.3 Building 3-ACCE from 2-ACCE

In this section we describe a generic 3-party protocol Π. Next, we show that protocol Π is generically secure in the 3-ACCE model described in Sects. 3.1 and 3.2.

Our Generic 3-Party Protocol. The Fig. 2 depicts our view of the 3-ACCE protocol Π between ED, NS and JS. It is composed of two distinct protocols denoted P and P' respectively. P is a 2-ACCE protocol between ED and NS, and P' is a 2-ACCE protocol between NS and JS. The details of the protocol Π are given in Fig. 3.

Protocol Π is generic in the sense that it depicts a whole class of protocols. Informally, this class corresponds to 3-party protocols where one entity behaves mostly as a key server (JS), whereas the post-accept phase is managed by the other two entities (ED, NS). Moreover, the P component has the following features. Its key exchange is made of four main messages: the first two with the major purpose of exchanging the material intended for the key derivation, and the last two in order to confirm the session keys or to authenticate the parties. For example, TLS-PSK [11], SRP [24], and SIGMA-R [15] can be instances of P. As we will see in Sect. 4, LoRaWAN is such another instance.

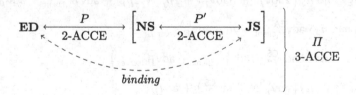

Fig. 2. 3-ACCE protocol Π

Main Theorem and Sketch Proof. Based on the security of P and P', we show that protocol Π is 3-ACCE-secure according to Definition 3.

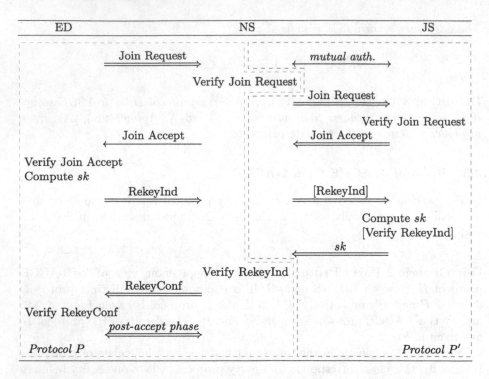

Fig. 3. Correct execution of protocol Π, made of P (left) and P' (right) components. Double line arrows indicate the use of the secure channel keys.

Theorem 1. *The protocol Π is a secure 3-ACCE protocol under the assumption that P is a secure 2-ACCE protocol, and P' is a secure 2-ACCE protocol, with the following reductions*

$$\mathsf{adv}_{\Pi}^{\mathsf{EA}} \leq n_{\mathsf{E}} \cdot n_{\mathsf{N}} \cdot n_{\mathsf{J}} \left(2\mathsf{adv}_{P}^{\mathsf{CS}} + 3\mathsf{adv}_{P'}^{\mathsf{CS}} + 2p_{jr} + 2p_{ja} + \mathsf{adv}_{P',\mathsf{client}}^{\mathsf{EA}} + \mathsf{adv}_{P',\mathsf{server}}^{\mathsf{EA}} \right)$$

$$+ n_{\mathsf{E}} \left(n_{\mathsf{J}} \cdot \mathsf{adv}_{P,\mathsf{client}}^{\mathsf{EA}} + n_{\mathsf{N}} \cdot \mathsf{adv}_{P,\mathsf{server}}^{\mathsf{EA}} \right)$$

$$+ n_{\mathsf{N}} \cdot n_{\mathsf{J}} \left(3\mathsf{adv}_{P'}^{\mathsf{CS}} + \mathsf{adv}_{P',\mathsf{client}}^{\mathsf{EA}} + \mathsf{adv}_{P',\mathsf{server}}^{\mathsf{EA}} \right)$$

$$\mathsf{adv}_{\Pi}^{\mathsf{CS}} \leq n_{\mathsf{E}} \cdot n_{\mathsf{N}} \cdot n_{\mathsf{J}} \left(\mathsf{adv}_{P}^{\mathsf{CS}} + 3\mathsf{adv}_{P'}^{\mathsf{CS}} \right) + \mathsf{adv}_{\Pi}^{\mathsf{EA}}$$

where n_{E}, n_{N}, and n_{J} are respectively the number of ED, NS, and JS parties.

We give here only a sketch of proof of Theorem 1. The extended proof is given in the full version of the paper [7]. Let us first consider the EA security property. We split the proof into three parts depending which party (ED, NS, JS) the adversary targets.

ED Adversary. Roughly speaking, the adversary can first try to impersonate NS to ED as in a 2-party execution of protocol P ($\mathsf{adv}_{P,\mathsf{client}}^{\mathsf{EA}}$). The adversary can also try to bypass the intermediate NS in order to get from JS all the necessary material (Join Accept message, session keys sk) in order for ED to accept. This implies necessarily that a server adversary be able to impersonate a legitimate NS to JS, that is to break the EA-security of P' ($\mathsf{adv}_{P',\mathsf{server}}^{\mathsf{EA}}$). Finally, the adversary can try to make ED and NS have different sid. In order to be successful, the adversary has to provide a valid RekeyInd message to NS different than the one computed by ED. This implies either forging such a message, or getting the keys used to compute it, and transmitted by JS to NS. We reduce both possibilities to the channel security w.r.t. P ($\mathsf{adv}_P^{\mathsf{CS}}$), and P' ($\mathsf{adv}_{P'}^{\mathsf{CS}}$).

Since we have ruled out the impersonation of NS to ED, and the impersonation of NS to JS, ED uses the Join Accept message sent by JS upon reception of the Join Request message computed by ED. Therefore, ED and JS compute the P-session keys with the same inputs (and the same function). Hence they output the same keys (i.e., $\pi_i^n.\mathsf{ck} = \pi_k^\ell.\mathsf{km}$). In addition, ED and NS have matching conversations (i.e., they share the same sid). Taking account of all parties adds a factor at most $n_\mathsf{E} \cdot n_\mathsf{N} \cdot n_\mathsf{J}$.

NS Adversary. First we deal with the winning condition (a). The adversary can first try to impersonate ED to NS. This implies breaking the EA-security of P when the server side is targeted ($\mathsf{adv}_{P,\mathsf{server}}^{\mathsf{EA}}$). Then the adversary can try to impersonate a legitimate JS to NS ($\mathsf{adv}_{P',\mathsf{client}}^{\mathsf{EA}}$).

The only cryptographic operation that NS does in order to accept is verifying the RekeyInd message it gets from ED with the keys provided by JS. Therefore the adversary is successful if, on the one hand, she provides some keys sk to NS (through the secure channel ensured by P'), and, on the other hand, she sends to NS a RekeyInd message computed under these keys sk. This can be reduced to the channel security w.r.t. P' ($\mathsf{adv}_{P'}^{\mathsf{CS}}$).

The remaining possibility in order for the adversary to win is to provide a RekeyConf message so that NS and ED do not share the same sid. This is possible either if the adversary forges such a message, or if she is able to get the keys used to compute the message (transmitted by JS to NS through a secure channel ensured by P'). We reduce either possibility respectively to the channel security w.r.t. P ($\mathsf{adv}_P^{\mathsf{CS}}$), and P' ($\mathsf{adv}_{P'}^{\mathsf{CS}}$). Furthermore, since we have ruled out the impersonation of JS to NS, and also the possibility to forge P' application messages, NS and JS share the same P session keys. That is $\pi_j^u.\mathsf{ck} = \pi_k^\ell.\mathsf{km}$.

Regarding condition (b), the adversary can first try to impersonate a legitimate JS to NS ($\mathsf{adv}_{P',\mathsf{client}}^{\mathsf{EA}}$). Then the adversary can proceed as under condition (a). That is, providing to NS some keys sk of her choice, and a RekeyInd message computed under sk. This implies forging a valid P' application message carrying the keys sk. We reduce such a possibility to the channel security w.r.t. P' ($\mathsf{adv}_{P'}^{\mathsf{CS}}$). Then, in order to have that NS and JS do not share the same sid, the adversary can try to forge a P' application message (carrying a Join Request or a RekeyInd message) intended to JS. We can reduce the latter to the channel security w.r.t. P' ($\mathsf{adv}_{P'}^{\mathsf{CS}}$).

Finally the adversary wins if NS and ED do not share the same P session keys. This is possible if the adversary forges either a Join Request message or a Join Accept message. These two possibilities are respectively bounded by the probabilities p_{jr} and p_{ja} (see Sect. 4.1).

JS Adversary. The adversary can first try to impersonate NS to JS ($\mathsf{adv}^{\mathsf{EA}}_{P',\mathrm{server}}$). Then, in order to have that NS and JS do not share the same sid, the adversary can try to forge one of the messages exchanged through the secure channel (in either direction), which can be reduced to the channel security w.r.t. P' ($\mathsf{adv}^{\mathsf{CS}}_{P'}$). Ruling out all these possibilities guarantees that JS and NS share the same sid (i.e., $\pi^\ell_k.\mathsf{sid} = \pi^v_j.\mathsf{sid}$).

Finally, the adversary can try to make ED and JS compute different P-session keys. Since these keys depend on the data carried in the Join Request and Join Accept messages, this implies forging either message (probability $p_{jr} + p_{ja}$). Ruling out both possibilities guarantees that $\pi^n_i.\mathsf{ck} = \pi^\ell_k.\mathsf{km}$.

Regarding the CS property of protocol Π, we first rule out the possibility that an instance maliciously accepts ($\mathsf{adv}^{\mathsf{EA}}_\Pi$). This leaves two possibilities: either the adversary targets directly the ED-NS secure channel, or the NS-JS secure channel. We can reduce the latter possibility to the CS-security of P' ($\mathsf{adv}^{\mathsf{CS}}_{P'}$). Regarding the former possibility, the adversary can try to get the P session keys (sk) sent by JS to NS ($\mathsf{adv}^{\mathsf{CS}}_{P'}$), or to break the channel security w.r.t. P ($\mathsf{adv}^{\mathsf{CS}}_P$). Finally, we have also to take into account that the session keys sk (which the CS-security of P relies on) are sent by JS to NS through the secure channel provided by P' ($\mathsf{adv}^{\mathsf{CS}}_{P'}$).

4 3-ACCE Security with LoRaWAN 1.1

In this section, we use the generic result of Sect. 3.3, and apply it to LoRaWAN. For this purpose, we have to (i) show that LoRaWAN 1.1 fulfills the structure of the protocol Π proved to be secure by Theorem 1, (ii) prove that the underlying protocol $P = P_{LoRaWAN}$ is 2-ACCE-secure, and (iii) choose a 2-ACCE-secure instantiation for the protocol $P' = P'_{LoRaWAN}$.

As described in Sect. 2.1, a typical LoRaWAN network involves four entities: ED, NS, JS, and AS. But only the first three are actually involved in the key exchange, and the channel establishment. Moreover, in actual deployments, AS is often co-localised with NS. That is, AS is in fact merely a functionality handled by NS, and the latter is given the four session keys K^e_a, K^e_c, $K^{i_1}_c$, $K^{i_2}_c$. Hence, we instantiate LoRaWAN accordingly: our protocol is made of three active entities (ED, NS, JS) which the different cryptographic operations are attributed to.

Since LoRaWAN is based on static symmetric keys, we define the long term key of each party to be $\mathsf{ltk} = (\mathsf{pk}, \mathsf{sk}, \mathsf{mk})$, made of (i) a private key sk, (ii) the corresponding certified public key pk, and (iii) a master symmetric key mk. If $P_k \in \mathcal{J}$, the three components of ltk are defined. Otherwise, $P_j.\mathsf{ltk} = (\mathsf{pk}, \mathsf{sk}, \perp)$ if $P_j \in \mathcal{N}$, and $P_i.\mathsf{ltk} = (\perp, \perp, \mathsf{mk})$ if $P_i \in \mathcal{E}$. Each party $P_i \in \mathcal{E}$ has a unique master key mk, shared with a party $P_k \in \mathcal{J}$.

4.1 2-Party Protocol P in LoRaWAN 1.1 is 2-ACCE Secure

Theorem for $P_{LoRaWAN}$. Let $P_{LoRaWAN}$ correspond to the messages exchanged, and the operations done between a client (ED) and a server (NS-JS). Let $StAE_{client}$ (resp. $StAE_{server}$) be the AEAD function used by the client (resp. server) to encrypt and MAC the messages.

Theorem 2. *Under the assumption that $StAE_{client}$ and $StAE_{server}$ are sAE-secure, $P_{LoRaWAN}$ is a secure 2-ACCE protocol with the following reductions:*

$$adv_P^{EA} \leq q \left[(n_C + n_S) \left(adv_{MAC}^{PRF} + 2adv_{AES}^{PRF} \right) + n_C \left(adv_{AES}^{PRP} + adv_{StAE_{server}}^{sAE} \right) \right.$$
$$\left. + n_S \cdot adv_{StAE_{client}}^{sAE} + 2^{-\mu} \left(n_C \cdot (1 - 2^{-\beta}) + n_S \right) \right]$$
$$adv_P^{CS} \leq q^2 \cdot n_C \cdot n_S \left(adv_{StAE_{client}}^{sAE} + adv_{StAE_{server}}^{sAE} + 2adv_{AES}^{PRF} \right) + adv_P^{EA}$$

where q is the number of instances per party, n_C (resp. n_S) is the number of client (resp. server) parties, μ is the bit length of the MAC tag, and β is the bit length of the counter cnt_J.

Sketch Proof of Theorem 2. We consider the ACCE security model of Jager et al. [13], and define the entity authentication and the channel security experiments accordingly, but we forbid any corruption of the party (and its presumed partner) involved in the security experiments (the entity authentication game and the channel security game). That is LoRaWAN does not provide forward secrecy, nor protects against key-compromise impersonation attacks [6]. We give here only a sketch of proof of Theorem 2. The extended proof is given in the full version of the paper [7].

As for the EA-security of $P_{LoRaWAN}$, we consider first a client (ED) adversary, and then a server (NS-JS) adversary.

Regarding a client adversary, we idealise each cryptographic function used to compute a Join Accept message: the KDF_{mk} function used to compute the MAC key MK_3 (adv_{AES}^{PRF}), the MAC function (adv_{MAC}^{PRF}), and the encryption function (adv_{AES}^{PRP}). To that point, the ability of an adversary to forge a valid Join Accept message lies on the ability to provide a valid counter (probability at most $\frac{2^{\beta}-1}{2^{\beta}}$), and a valid MAC tag (probability $2^{-\mu}$) carried in the Join Accept message. Hence $\Pr[\text{forgery Join Accept}] \leq p_{ja} = adv_{AES}^{PRF} + adv_{MAC}^{PRF} + adv_{AES}^{PRP} + 2^{-\mu}(1 - 2^{-\beta})$. Then the adversary is successful if the client and the server do not share the same sid. This is possible if the adversary succeeds in forging a valid RekeyConf message ($adv_{AES}^{PRF} + adv_{StAE_{server}}^{sAE}$). Taking account of all possible client instances adds a factor $q \cdot n_C$.

Regarding the server adversary, we first idealise each cryptographic function used to compute a Join Request and a RekeyInd message: the MAC function used to compute the Join Request's MAC tag (adv_{MAC}^{PRF}), and the KDF_c and KDF_a functions used to compute the session keys involved in the calculation of the RekeyInd message ($2adv_{AES}^{PRF}$). To this point, the probability to forge a valid

Join Request message corresponds to the probability to forge a valid MAC tag ($2^{-\mu}$). Hence Pr[forgery Join Request] $\leq p_{jr} = \mathsf{adv}_{\mathsf{MAC}}^{\mathsf{PRF}} + 2^{-\mu}$. Finally, the only remaining possibility for the adversary is that client and server do not share the same sid. This implies forging a valid RekeyInd message ($\mathsf{adv}_{\mathsf{StAE}_{client}}^{\mathsf{sAE}}$). Taking account of all possible server instances adds a factor $q \cdot n_\mathsf{S}$.

Regarding the CS experiment, we first abort if there exists an instance of some client or server party that maliciously accepts ($\mathsf{adv}_P^{\mathsf{EA}}$). Then we idealise the cryptographic functions used to compute the session keys K_c^e, $K_c^{i_1}$, $K_c^{i_2}$, and K_a^e ($2\mathsf{adv}_{\mathsf{AES}}^{\mathsf{PRF}}$). Finally we reduce the ability to win the CS experiment to the security of the underlying AEAD functions that are used to encrypt messages in either direction: StAE_{client} and StAE_{server} ($\mathsf{adv}_{\mathsf{StAE}_{client}}^{\mathsf{sAE}} + \mathsf{adv}_{\mathsf{StAE}_{server}}^{\mathsf{sAE}}$). Taking account of all possible instances adds a factor $q^2 \cdot n_\mathsf{C} \cdot n_\mathsf{S}$.

4.2   Meeting 3-ACCE Security

As exhibited by Theorem 2, the (too) short size of several parameters provides useless security bounds in Theorem 2. Therefore, we modify LoRaWAN 1.1 the following way.

- We demand that the size μ of the MAC output be high enough so that the security bounds $\mathsf{adv}_P^{\mathsf{EA}}$ and $\mathsf{adv}_P^{\mathsf{CS}}$ be tight.
- We slightly change the behaviour of JS as follows (the components surrounded with brackets in Fig. 3 depict these additional operations): JS verifies entirely the Join Request message (including ED's counter cnt_E), and the RekeyInd message. Only if the RekeyInd message is valid, JS sends the session keys sk to NS. This change aims at precluding an attack that allows the adversary to trivially win the EA experiment. Indeed, if JS does not verify the RekeyInd message, it accepts as soon as it sends the Join Accept message, without guarantee that ED completes the protocol run.
- The genuine LoRaWAN specification states that ED must send a RekeyInd message to NS as long as it does not receive a RekeyConf response. We demand that ED send only one message. Firstly in order to clearly separate the pre-accept and post-accept phases. Secondly, because sending multiple RekeyInd messages allows the adversary to trivially win the EA experiment. Indeed, the adversary has to merely forbid NS from receiving the first RekeyInd message, and this breaks the transcript equality. This aims also at reducing the impact of the flaw described in Sect. 2.2.
- We require that *all* entities implement version 1.1 (including NS) so that no fallback to LoRaWAN 1.0 be possible (and the vulnerabilities of that version be avoided [2]).

Hence our adapted version of LoRaWAN 1.1 fulfills the structure of protocol Π, and the protocol $P_{LoRaWAN}$ is 2-ACCE-secure.

Now we define the companion security protocol $P'_{LoRaWAN}$ that is used between NS and JS. As explained in Sect. 2.3, the careful choice of this protocol is crucial to the overall security of a LoRaWAN network. Therefore, we define the protocol $P'_{LoRaWAN}$ to be TLS 1.2 [9] in DHE, or RSA mode, with mutual authentication, and instantiated with AEAD encryption schemes such as AES-GCM, AES-CCM [17], or ChaCha20-Poly1305 [20]. TLS 1.2 is known to be 2-ACCE-secure [13,14]. Alternatively, $P'_{LoRaWAN}$ can be defined as TLS 1.3 [21] in (EC)DHE mode, with mutual authentication. We recall that TLS 1.3 uses only AEAD encryption schemes. TLS 1.3 is proved to be 2-AKE-secure [10]. Although this result applies to an earlier draft of the protocol, we may reasonably assume that the final version also guarantees 2-AKE-security. Since AEAD encryption schemes are used, this implies 2-ACCE-security for TLS 1.3.

Combining all the above with Theorem 1, we obtain the 3-ACCE-security of our adapted version of LoRaWAN 1.1.

5 Conclusion

Using a provable security approach, we have provided the first analysis of LoRaWAN 1.1, a dedicated IoT protocol that aims at replacing the previous 1.0 version currently deployed worldwide. Our results highlights several flaws that weaken the protocol, and show, in particular, that the security of LoRaWAN 1.1 crucially depends on the companion security protocol (undefined by the specification) used between two of the parties. This also reveals that analysing such a 3-party protocol requires a suitable security model that incorporates all its subtleties, and makes explicit the security requirements.

Consequently, we have extended the notion of 3-ACCE-security to provide a general framework that captures the security properties a 3-party protocol should guarantee, and allows assessing its security. We have described such a generic protocol provably secure in our model. Applying these results, we have proposed a slightly modified version of LoRaWAN 1.1 with stronger security properties, formally proved it to be secure in our security model, and described how to concretely instantiate it.

References

1. Alt, S., Fouque, P.-A., Macario-rat, G., Onete, C., Richard, B.: A cryptographic analysis of UMTS/LTE AKA. In: Manulis, M., Sadeghi, A.-R., Schneider, S. (eds.) ACNS 2016. LNCS, vol. 9696, pp. 18–35. Springer, Cham (2016). https://doi.org/10.1007/978-3-319-39555-5_2
2. Avoine, G., Ferreira, L.: Rescuing LoRaWAN 1.0. In: Financial Cryptography and Data Security (FC 2018) (2018).https://fc18.ifca.ai/preproceedings/13.pdf
3. Bellare, M., Rogaway, P.: Entity authentication and key distribution. In: Stinson, D.R. (ed.) CRYPTO 1993. LNCS, vol. 773, pp. 232–249. Springer, Heidelberg (1994). https://doi.org/10.1007/3-540-48329-2_21
4. Bhargavan, K., Boureanu, I., Delignat-Lavaud, A., Fouque, P., Onete, C.: A formal treatment of accountable proxying over TLS. In: 2018 IEEE Symposium on Security and Privacy (SP), pp. 339–356 (2018)
5. Bhargavan, K., Boureanu, I., Fouque, P.A., Onete, C., Richard, B.: Content delivery over TLS: a cryptographic analysis of keyless SSL. In: 2017 IEEE European Symposium on Security and Privacy (EuroS&P), pp. 1–16. IEEE, April 2017

6. Blake-Wilson, S., Johnson, D., Menezes, A.: Key agreement protocols and their security analysis. In: Darnell, M. (ed.) Cryptography and Coding 1997. LNCS, vol. 1355, pp. 30–45. Springer, Heidelberg (1997). https://doi.org/10.1007/BFb0024447
7. Canard, S., Ferreira, L.: Extended 3-Party ACCE and Application to LoRaWAN 1.1. Cryptology ePrint Archive (2019). http://eprint.iacr.org/2019/479
8. Canetti, R., Krawczyk, H.: Analysis of key-exchange protocols and their use for building secure channels. In: Pfitzmann, B. (ed.) EUROCRYPT 2001. LNCS, vol. 2045, pp. 453–474. Springer, Heidelberg (2001). https://doi.org/10.1007/3-540-44987-6_28
9. Dierks, T., Rescorla, E.: The Transport Layer Security (TLS) Protocol - Version 1.2 (August 2008), RFC 5246
10. Dowling, B., Fischlin, M., Günther, F., Stebila, D.: A cryptographic analysis of the TLS 1.3 handshake protocol candidates. In: Ray, I., Li, N., Kruegel: C. (eds.) ACM CCS 15. pp. 1197–1210. ACM Press, October 2015
11. Eronen, P., Tschofenig, H.: Pre-Shared Key Ciphersuites for Transport Layer Security (TLS) (December 2005), RFC 4279
12. Fouque, P.A., Onete, C., Richard, B.: Achieving better privacy for the 3GPP AKA protocol. Cryptology ePrint Archive, Report 2016/480 (2016)
13. Jager, T., Kohlar, F., Schäge, S., Schwenk, J.: On the security of TLS-DHE in the standard model. Cryptology ePrint Archive, Report 2011/219 (2011)
14. Kohlar, F., Schäge, S., Schwenk, J.: On the security of TLS-DH and TLS-RSA in the standard model. Cryptology ePrint Archive, Report 2013/367 (2013)
15. Krawczyk, H.: SIGMA: the 'SIGn-and-MAc' approach to authenticated Diffie-Hellman and its use in the IKE protocols. In: Boneh, D. (ed.) CRYPTO 2003. LNCS, vol. 2729, pp. 400–425. Springer, Heidelberg (2003). https://doi.org/10.1007/978-3-540-45146-4_24
16. Lundgren, L.: Taking over the world through MQTT - Aftermath. Black Hat USA (2017)
17. McGrew, D.: An Interface and Algorithms for Authenticated Encryption (January 2008), RFC 5116
18. Morrissey, P., Smart, N.P., Warinschi, B.: A modular security analysis of the TLS handshake protocol. In: Pieprzyk, J. (ed.) ASIACRYPT 2008. LNCS, vol. 5350, pp. 55–73. Springer, Heidelberg (2008). https://doi.org/10.1007/978-3-540-89255-7_5
19. Naylor, D., et al.: Multi-Context TLS (mcTLS): enabling secure in-network functionality in TLS. In: Proceedings of the 2015 ACM Conference on Special Interest Group on Data Communication, SIGCOMM 2015, pp. 199–212. ACM (2015)
20. Nir, Y., Langley, A.: ChaCha20 and Poly1305 for IETF Protocols (May 2015), RFC 7539
21. Rescorla, E.: The Transport Layer Security (TLS) Protocol Version 1.3 (August 2018), RFC 8446
22. Sornin, N.: LoRaWAN 1.1 Specification (June 2017), LoRa Alliance, version 1.1
23. Sornin, N., Luis, M., Eirich, T., Kramp, T.: LoRaWAN Specification (July 2016), LoRa Alliance, version 1.0
24. Wu, T.: The SRP Authentication and Key Exchange System (September 2000), RFC 2945

Post-quantum Cryptography

The Mersenne Low Hamming Combination Search Problem Can Be Reduced to an ILP Problem

Alessandro Budroni[✉] and Andrea Tenti

Department of Informatics, University of Bergen, Bergen, Norway
{alessandro.budroni,andrea.tenti}@uib.no

Abstract. In 2017, Aggarwal, Joux, Prakash, and Santha proposed an innovative NTRU-like public-key cryptosystem that was believed to be quantum resistant, based on Mersenne prime numbers $q = 2^N - 1$. After a successful attack designed by Beunardeau, Connolly, Géraud, and Naccache, the authors revised the protocol which was accepted for Round 1 of the Post-Quantum Cryptography Standardization Process organized by NIST. The security of this protocol is based on the assumption that a so-called Mersenne Low Hamming Combination Search Problem (MLHCombSP) is hard to solve. In this work, we present a reduction of MLHCombSP to an instance of Integer Linear Programming (ILP). This opens new research directions that are necessary to be investigated in order to assess the concrete robustness of such cryptosystem. We propose different approaches to perform such reduction. Moreover, we uncover a new family of weak keys, for whose our reduction leads to an attack consisting in solving $< N^3$ ILP problems of dimension 3.

Keywords: Post-Quantum Cryptography · Public-key cryptography · Integer Linear Programming · Mersenne-based cryptosystem

1 Introduction

In [2], Aggarwal, Joux, Prakash, and Santha introduced a new public-key encryption scheme similar to the NTRU cryptosystem [12] that employs the properties of Mersenne numbers.

A Mersenne number is an integer $q = 2^N - 1$ so that N is prime. One can associate to each element in the ring $\mathbb{Z}_q$ the binary string representing the unique representative $0 \le a < q$ of the class $[a] \in \mathbb{Z}_q$. The secret key is a pair of elements F and $G \in \mathbb{Z}_q$ so that their Hamming weight is $h < \sqrt{N/10}$ Let R be a random element of $\mathbb{Z}_q$; the public key is given by the pair $(R, T \equiv RF + G \mod q)$. The security assumption (and the mathematical problem that supports the robustness of this cryptosystem) is that it is hard to recover F and G, knowing only R and T. This assumption is called *Mersenne Low Hamming Combination Search Problem* (MLHCombSP).

© Springer Nature Switzerland AG 2019
J. Buchmann et al. (Eds.): AFRICACRYPT 2019, LNCS 11627, pp. 41–55, 2019.
https://doi.org/10.1007/978-3-030-23696-0_3

This version is actually the second iteration of the cryptosystem, first presented in [1]. The security assumptions were based on a problem similar to MLHCombSP called *Mersenne Low Hamming Ratio Search Problem* (MLHRatioSP). That has been attacked by Beunardeau et al. in [6]. There the attack is performed via a series of calls to an SVP-oracle. Its complexity has been estimated by de Boer et al. in [7]. They also showed that a Meet-in-the-Middle attack is possible using locality-sensitive hashing, which improves upon brute force. However, Beunardeau et al. turned out to be the most effective of the two. After the publications of these works, Aggarwal et al. revised the protocol [2] to prevent the above attacks from being effective against full-scale ciphers.

This protocol has been accepted to the Round 1 of the Post-Quantum Cryptography Standardization Process organized by NIST. However, it does not appear among the proposals for Round 2.

1.1 Our Contribution/Outline

In this work we present a non-trivial reduction to a relatively low-dimensional Integer Linear Programming (ILP) instance of the underlying mathematical problem of [2]. The resulting instance of ILP produces the right solution with probability p, that depends on the size of G. It is possible to perform a trade-off between the size of the ILP problem to solve and the success probability.

In Sect. 2 we introduce notation and related work. Furthermore, we recap the Beunardeau et al. attack against [1] with a generalization to the MLHCombSP. Section 3 describes our reduction together with the success probability analysis. There we describe variations in the description of the ILP to be solved, that allow some flexibility for the attacker. In particular, one can perform a trade-off between the success probability and the dimension of the resulting ILP. The application of this trade-off is shown for two examples. In Sect. 4 we describe a new family of weak keys and the probability of such a pair to appear. This family is obtained by performing two independent rotations on F and G so that, after these rotations, they become as small as possible. In this way the size of the set of the weak keys increases. For example, for $N = 1279$ and $h = 17$ (parameters used in [6]), a random key is weak in the sense of Beunardeau et al. with probability $\sim 2^{-34}$. It is possible to estimate that a random key becomes weak after rotations with probability $\sim 2^{-11}$.

2 Preliminaries

Definition 1. *Let N be a prime number and let $q = 2^N - 1$. Then q is called a Mersenne number. If q is also prime, then it is called Mersenne prime number.*

Let $\text{seq}_N : \{0, ..., q - 1\} \to \{0, 1\}^N$ be the map which associates to each A the corresponding N-bits binary representation $\text{seq}_N(A)$ with most-significant bit to the left.

Denote with $\mathbb{Z}_q$ the ring of integers modulo q. We extend the function seq_N also to elements in $\mathbb{Z}_q$. Let us consider an integer $0 \leq B < q$, seq_N maps $[B] \in \mathbb{Z}_q$

to the N-bits binary representation of B. We define the *Hamming weight* $w(F)$ of F as the Hamming weight of $\text{seq}_N(F)$, i.e. the number of 1s in $\text{seq}_N(F)$.

Lemma 1. *Let $k \geq 0$ be a positive integer, let A be an N-bits number, and let $q = 2^N - 1$. Then $\text{seq}_N(2^k A \bmod q)$ corresponds to a rotation of $\text{seq}_N(A)$ of k positions to the left and $\text{seq}_N(2^{-k} A \bmod q)$ corresponds to a rotation of k positions to the right.*

Proof. We prove it by induction on k. Write $\text{seq}_N(A) = (A_{N-1}, ..., A_1, A_0)$, where A_{N-1} is the most significant bit of A. Then we can represent A as

$$A = A_{N-1} \cdot 2^{N-1} + ... + A_1 \cdot 2 + A_0.$$

If we multiply A by 2 modulo q we obtain

$$2 \cdot A \equiv A_{N-1} \cdot 2^N + A_{N-2} \cdot 2^{N-1} + ... + A_1 \cdot 2^2 + A_0 \cdot 2 \quad \bmod q$$
$$\equiv A_{N-2} \cdot 2^{N-1} + ... + A_1 \cdot 2^2 + A_0 \cdot 2 + A_{N-1} \quad \bmod q.$$

Then $\text{seq}_N(2 \cdot A) = (A_{N-2}, ..., A_0, A_{N-1})$, i.e. the left rotation of 1 position of $\text{seq}_N(A)$.

By inductive hypothesis, $\text{seq}_N(2^k \cdot A)$ corresponds to the left rotation of k positions of $\text{seq}_N(A)$, then $\text{seq}_N(2^{k+1} \cdot A) = \text{seq}_N(2 \cdot 2^k \cdot A)$ corresponds to the left rotation of one position of $\text{seq}_N(2^k \cdot A)$, that is the left rotation of $k + 1$ positions of $\text{seq}_N(A)$. The case right rotations of $\text{seq}_N(A)$ follows trivially. □

The security of the Aggarwal et al. cryptosystem [2] relies on the assumption that the following two problems are hard to solve.

Mersenne Low Hamming Ratio Search Problem. Let $q = 2^N - 1$ be a Marsenne prime number, $h < N$ an integer, F and G two integers chosen at random from the set of N-bits numbers with Hamming weight h. Let $H < q$ be the non-negative integer such that

$$H \equiv \frac{F}{G} \bmod q \qquad (1)$$

The *Mersenne Low Hamming Ratio Search Problem* (MLHRatioSP) is to find (F, G) knowing h and H.

Mersenne Low Hamming Combination Search Problem. Let $q = 2^N - 1$ be a Marsenne prime number, $h < N$ an integer, R a random N-bits number, and F, G integers chosen at random from the set of N-bits numbers with Hamming weight h. Let $T < q$ be the non-negative integer such that

$$RF + G \equiv T \bmod q \qquad (2)$$

The *Mersenne Low Hamming Combination Search Problem* (MLHCombSP) is to find (F, G) knowing h and the pair (R, T).

In [1], the authors suggest to choose N and h to be such that $\binom{N-1}{h-1} \geq 2^\lambda$ and $4h^2 < N$, for a desired λ-bit security level. After the publications of the attacks by Beunardeau et al. [6] and De Boer et al. [7], the authors revised the choice of the parameters [2] to be such that $h = \lambda$ and $10h^2 < N$.

2.1 Previous Attacks

Brute Force Attack. In [1], Aggarwal et al. showed that a brute force attack to the MLHRatioSP would require $\binom{N-1}{h-1}$ trials. This attack consists in assuming that one of the two secret numbers, say F, has a 1 in the most significant bit (condition that can be obtained by a rotation of $\text{seq}_N(F)$). Then one should try, for every N-bits number with 1 as most significant bit and weight h, if the corresponding G through relation (1) has weight h. This approach does not apply to the MLHCombSP, which instead requires $\binom{N}{h}$ trials.

Meet-in-the-Middle Attack. De Boer et al. [7] showed that a Meet-in-the-Middle attack to MLHRatioSP is possible using locality-sensitive hashing with complexity $\tilde{O}\left(\sqrt{\binom{N-1}{h-1}}\right)$ on classical computers and $\tilde{O}\left(\sqrt[3]{\binom{N-1}{h-1}}\right)$ on quantum computers. This can be generalized to the MLHCombSP.

Weak Keys and Lattice Attack. Following the parameters' setting in [1], Beunardeau et al. found a weak key attack to the MLHRatioSP for the case when both F and G happen to have bits set to 1 only in their right halves, i.e. $F, G < \sqrt{2^N}$ [6]. This event happens with probability 2^{-2h}.

Following the above idea, Beunardeau et al. also presented a more general attack to the MLHRatioSP which consists in guessing a decomposition of F and G into windows of bits such that all the '1's are "close" to the right-most bit of such windows. Then F and G can be recovered through a lattice reduction algorithm such as LLL [13]. Even if Beunardeau et al. showed that this attack practically hits the security estimations in [1], they did not present any clear asymptotic analysis of its complexity. However, de Boer et al. [7], computed the complexity of this attack.

In [2], the authors stated that the above attack likely generalizes to the MLHCombSP case. Building directly on the work presented in [7], we show in the next subsection that this is true. However we refer the reader to [6] and [7] for a more detailed description.

2.2 The Beunardeau et al. Attack on MLHCombSP

Since F is taken at random among the N-bits numbers with Hamming weight h, w.h.p. the '1' valued bits of $\text{seq}_N(F)$ do not appear in big clusters along the N possible positions. One then computes an interval-like partition $\mathcal{P}$ of $\{0, \ldots, N-1\}$ at random, i.e. each set of $\mathcal{P}$ is of the form $\{a, a+1, \ldots, b-1, b\}$, with $0 \leq a < b < N$. If each '1' valued bit of $\text{seq}_N(F)$ falls in the right-half of one of the sets of $\mathcal{P}$, then each one of them corresponds to a binary substring of $\text{seq}_N(F)$, corresponding in turn to a "small" number. Therefore, the array of these numbers can be seen as a representation of F.

Let $\mathcal{P} = \{P_1, .., P_k\}$ and $\mathcal{Q} = \{Q_1, ..., Q_l\}$ be two interval-like partitions of $\{0, ..., N-1\}$ and $(R, T) \in \mathbb{Z}_q^2$ be public parameters of an MLHCombSP instance. Let p_i, q_i be the smallest elements of P_i, Q_i respectively. Let us consider the following integer lattice.

$$\mathcal{L}_{\mathcal{P},\mathcal{Q},R,T} = \left\{ (x_1, ..., x_k, y_1, ..., y_l, u) \mid R \cdot \sum_{i=1}^{k} 2^{p_i} \cdot x_i + \sum_{j=1}^{l} 2^{q_i} \cdot y_i - uT \equiv 0 \mod q \right\}$$

The above defined lattice $\mathcal{L}_{\mathcal{P},\mathcal{Q},R,T}$ has determinant $\det(\mathcal{L}_{\mathcal{P},\mathcal{Q},R,T}) = q$ and dimension $d = k + l + 1$. Let $(F, G) \in \mathbb{Z}_q^2$ be such that $w(F) = w(G) = h$ and $RF + G \equiv T$ as in a MLHCombSP instance. Define the vector

$$\mathbf{s} = (f_1, ..., f_k, g_1, ..., g_l, 1) \in \mathcal{L}_{\mathcal{P},\mathcal{Q},R,T},$$

where $0 \le f_i < 2^{|P_i|}$ and $0 \le g_j < 2^{|Q_j|}$ are the unique natural numbers such that $\sum_{i=1}^{k} f_i \cdot 2^{p_i} = F$ and $\sum_{j=1}^{l} g_j \cdot 2^{q_j} = G$, where $|\cdot|$ denotes the cardinality operator. One wishes to find the vector $\mathbf{s}$ through some lattice reduction algorithm applied to $\mathcal{L}_{\mathcal{P},\mathcal{Q},R,T}$.

The lattice $\mathcal{L}_{\mathcal{P},\mathcal{Q},R,T}$ is very similar to the one defined in [7] for the MLHRatioSP and their success probability analysis of the attack holds for this case too. Therefore the following conclusions follow directly from the work of de Boer et al.

Given two partitions $\mathcal{P}$ and $\mathcal{Q}$ of $\{0, ..., N-1\}$ with block size at least $N/d + \Theta(\log N)$, where $d = k + l + 1$ with $k = |P|$ and $l = |Q|$. The success probability of finding the vector $\mathbf{s} \in \mathcal{L}_{\mathcal{P},\mathcal{Q},R,T}$ using a SVP-oracle is $2^{-2h+o(1)}$.

Remark 1. *The above attack is actually a simplified version of the attack of Beunardeau et al. Indeed, a more general attack can be made by considering the variation of partition sizes and the fraction of each partition block. This variant of the attack has success probability $2^{-(2+\delta)h+o(1)}$, for some small constant $\delta > 0$ [7].*

Remark 2. *In practice, instead of an SVP-oracle, the LLL algorithm [13] which has polynomial complexity is used. This decreases the overall complexity of the attack, but the success probability is decreased too [7].*

The above attack was made against the parameters setting contained in the first version of Aggarwal et al. work. However, as already mentioned, in the most recent version of their work the authors revisited the protocol in order to withstand it.

2.3   Integer Linear Programming

An *Integer Linear Programming* (ILP) problem in his *canonical form* is defined as follows. Given a matrix $A \in \mathbb{Q}^{m \times n}$ and two vectors $\mathbf{c} \in \mathbb{Q}^n$ and $\mathbf{b} \in \mathbb{Q}^m$, minimize (or maximise) the quantity

$$\mathbf{c}^T \mathbf{x}$$

subject to

$$\begin{cases} A\mathbf{x} \le \mathbf{b}, \\ \mathbf{x} \ge 0, \\ \mathbf{x} \in \mathbb{Z}^n \end{cases}$$

An *ILP-oracle* is an oracle that solves any ILP instance.

Solving a general ILP is proved to be NP-hard [17]. Nevertheless, understanding the complexity of specific families of ILP problems is not an easy task: it can widely vary from case to case [18]. For example, when the number of variables is fixed, or when the problem can be reduced to a simple *Linear Programming* problem, it is proved that it has polynomial complexity [14,20].

Nowadays there exists families of ILP solving algorithms, for example *Branch and Bound* [16], *Lagrange relaxation* [10], *Column Generation* [3], and the *Cutting Planes* [15], whose implementations [9,11] are able to solve in practice relatively challenging instances.

3   ILP Reduction

Let R, T be two random elements of $\mathbb{Z}_q^*$. We define the map $\varphi : \mathbb{Z}_q \to \mathbb{Z}_q$ sending $X \mapsto -RX + T$. Any point on the graph of φ, namely $\{(X, \varphi(X))\}_{X \in \mathbb{Z}_q}$, satisfying the condition that both coordinates have Hamming weight equals to h is a solution to the MLHCombSP. We denote such condition as *the graph condition*.

We notice that φ is bijective, for it is the combination of two bijective functions (i.e. multiplication times a nonzero element of a field and sum with an element of the underlying group). This means that for any subset $\mathcal{U} \subseteq \mathbb{Z}_q$, the restriction $\varphi_{|\mathcal{U}}$ is injective. Hence, $|\operatorname{Im}(\varphi_{|\mathcal{U}})| = |\mathcal{U}|$. We assume that $\operatorname{Im}(\varphi_{|\mathcal{U}})$ is a random element of the family of subsets of cardinality $|\mathcal{U}|$ of $\mathbb{Z}_q$.

Let $\mathcal{V}$ be another subset of $\mathbb{Z}_q$. The probability that a random element of $\operatorname{Im}(\varphi_{|\mathcal{U}})$ is in $\mathcal{V}$ is given by $\frac{|\mathcal{V}|}{2^N - 1}$. Hence the expected size of $\operatorname{Im}(\varphi_{|\mathcal{U}}) \cap \mathcal{V}$ is given by the mean of the Hypergeometric distribution [8] in $|\mathcal{U}|$ draws, from a population of size $2^N - 1$ that contains $|\mathcal{V}|$ objects that yield a success. That is:

$$\mathbb{E}(|\operatorname{Im}(\varphi_{|\mathcal{U}}) \cap \mathcal{V}|) = \frac{|\mathcal{U}||\mathcal{V}|}{2^N - 1}. \tag{3}$$

Let E_G be the number of '0' valued bits before the first '1' valued bit in $\operatorname{seq}_N(G)$. In this case, one can set $\mathcal{V} = \{2^{N-E_G-1}, \ldots, 2^{N-E_G} - 1\}$ and $|\mathcal{V}| = 2^{N-E_G}$. With such a bound on G, given a $\mathcal{U}$ of size $< 2^{E_G}$, with $F \in \mathcal{U}$, there is only one expected solution to the system of constraints:

$$\begin{cases} T - Rx \equiv y \mod q, \\ x \in \mathcal{U}, \\ y \in \mathcal{V}. \end{cases} \tag{4}$$

and one solution is certainly $x = F$, $y = G$.

Our attack is meant to find solid choices for $\mathcal{U}$ and $\mathcal{V}$ to use to solve (4).

Remark 3. *For every fixed instance of $x \in \{0, \ldots, q-1\}$, there is exactly one $a \in \mathbb{Z}$ that satisfies $0 \leq T + aq - Rx < q$. In particular, this means that for every fixed instance of $x \in \{0, \ldots, q-1\}$ there exists at most one $a \in \mathbb{Z}$ satisfying $2^h \leq T + aq - Rx \leq 2^N - 2^{N-h}$.*

It is possible to represent (4) in terms of integers:

$$\begin{cases} T + qa - Rx = y, \\ x \in \mathcal{U}, \\ y \in \mathcal{V}. \end{cases} \qquad (5)$$

Here, there is an abuse of notation: we intend $\mathcal{U}$ as the intersection $\mathcal{U} \cap \{2^h - 1, \ldots, 2^N - 2^{N-h}\}$ and $\mathcal{V}$ as the intersection $\mathcal{V} \cap \{2^h - 1, \ldots, 2^N - 2^{N-h}\}$.

Remark 3 implies that the number of solutions of the system is smaller than or equal to $|\operatorname{Im}(\varphi_{|\mathcal{U}}) \cap \mathcal{V}|$. So the expected number of solutions to (5) is smaller than or equal to $\frac{|\mathcal{U}||\mathcal{V}|}{2^N - 1}$.

For some choices of $\mathcal{U}$ and $\mathcal{V}$, one can find solutions to (5) using an ILP-oracle.

Let $\mathcal{U} = \{l_{x_3}, l_{x_3} + 1, \ldots, u_{x_3} - 1, u_{x_3}\}$ for some l_{x_3} and u_{x_3} and let $\mathcal{V} = \{l_y, l_y + 1, \ldots, u_y - 1, u_y\}$ for some l_y and u_y. Assuming that (5) has a unique solution, then it is detected by the following ILP instance:

$$T x_1 + q x_2 - R x_3 = y, \qquad (6)$$

with constraints

$$\begin{cases} x_1 = 1, \\ l_{x_3} \leq x_3 \leq u_{x_3}, \\ l_y \leq y \leq u_y. \end{cases} \qquad (7)$$

Finding good choices on $\mathcal{U}$ and $\mathcal{V}$ (i.e. small and containing F and G with high probability) is difficult for the ILP instance (6). At the cost of increasing the dimension of the ILP problem to be solved, one can reduce the size of $\mathcal{U}$.

One such way is to fully exploit the fact that F has weight exactly h to establish the following ILP problem in the integer variables $x_1, x_2, x_3, n_1, \ldots, n_N$:

$$T x_1 + q x_2 - R x_3 + 0 n_1 + \cdots + 0 n_N = y, \qquad (8)$$

with constraints

$$\begin{cases} x_1 = 1, \\ x_3 = \sum_{i=1}^{N} n_i 2^{i-1}, \\ 0 \leq n_i \leq 1, \quad \text{for } i = 1, \ldots, N \\ \sum_{i=1}^{n} n_i = h, \\ l_y \leq y \leq u_y. \end{cases} \qquad (9)$$

Using these constraints results in having $\mathcal{U}$ of (5) of size $|\mathcal{U}| = \binom{N}{h}$. On the other hand, the dimension of the ILP to be solved moved from being 3 to being $N + 3$. In Subsects. 3.2 and 3.3, we explore ways to perform trade-offs in order to choose in advance either the number of variables of the ILP to be solved or the size of $\mathcal{U}$.

3.1   Cyclic Shifts

Consider the multiplication in both sides of (2) by 2^k, for some $k > 0$,

$$2^k RF + 2^k G \equiv 2^k T \mod q. \tag{10}$$

Define $\tilde{R} \equiv 2^k R \mod q$, $\tilde{T} \equiv 2^k T \mod q$, $\tilde{F} \equiv 2^k F \mod q$ and $\tilde{G} \equiv 2^k G \mod q$. Note that $w(\tilde{F}) = w(\tilde{G}) = h$. Through (10) we can define two new MLHCombSP instances:

$$R\tilde{F} + \tilde{G} \equiv \tilde{T} \mod q, \tag{11}$$

where both F and G are rotated by k positions to the left, and

$$\tilde{R}F + \tilde{G} \equiv \tilde{T} \mod q, \tag{12}$$

where only G is rotated. By combining (11) and (12) we can rotate independently F and G. At the cost of N^2 rotations we can always find the cyclic shifts that minimizes both F and G. Performing the shifts greatly improves the probability that for small $\mathcal{U}$ and $\mathcal{V}$ of the form $\{2^l, \ldots, 2^{l+1}\}$, F and G solve (5). This results in a family of weak keys not considered in [6]. A complete analysis of the improvements is reported in Sect. 4.

3.2   Portion of F

As mentioned above, it is possible to reduce the dimension of the ILP (8) to be solved at the cost of increasing the size of $\mathcal{U}$. One of such methods consists in considering only the most significant bits of F in the constraints. Let γ be in the real interval $(0, 1]$. Let $\tilde{h} = \lceil \gamma h \rceil$ and let $\tilde{N} = \lceil \gamma N \rceil$. It is possible to solve the following ILP problem instead of (8):

$$Tx_1 + qx_2 - Rx_3 + 0n_1 + \cdots + 0n_{\tilde{N}} = y, \tag{13}$$

with constraints

$$\begin{cases} x_1 = 1, \\ |\sum_{i=1}^{\tilde{N}} n_i \cdot 2^{i-1} - x_3/2^{N-\tilde{N}}| < 1, \\ 0 \leq n_i \leq 1, \quad \text{for } i = 1, \ldots, \tilde{N} \\ \tilde{h} - t \leq \sum_{i=1}^{n} n_i \leq \tilde{h} + t, \\ l_y \leq y \leq u_y. \end{cases} \tag{14}$$

for some $0 \leq t \leq \tilde{h}$.

Proposition 1. *For fixed $n_1, \ldots, n_{\tilde{N}}$ there exist exactly $2^{N-\tilde{N}}$ possible x_3 satisfying the first inequality in (14).*

Proof. Let write a general x_3 as $x_3 = F_{N-1}2^{N-1} + \cdots + F_0 2^0$. It follows that

$$x_3/2^{N-\tilde{N}} = F_{N-1}2^{\tilde{N}-1} + \cdots + F_{N-\tilde{N}}2^0 + F_{N-\tilde{N}-1}2^{-1} + \cdots + F_0 2^{\tilde{N}-N}.$$

We notice that $F_{N-1}, \ldots, F_{N-\tilde{N}}$ are set to be equal to $n_{\tilde{N}}, \ldots, n_1$ by (14), while the remaining coefficients can assume values in $\{0, 1\}$. There are exactly $2^{N-\tilde{N}}$ such x_3. □

Let us compute the size of $\mathcal{U}$ that arises from the given constraints. Thanks to Proposition 1, the size of $\mathcal{U}$ is determined only by the constraints on $n_1, \ldots, n_{\tilde{N}}$. The conditions to be satisfied are:

$$\begin{cases} 0 \leq n_i \leq 1, \text{ for } 1 \leq i \leq \tilde{N}, \\ \tilde{h} - t \leq \sum_{i=1}^{\tilde{N}} n_i \leq \tilde{h} + t, \end{cases}$$

for some $0 \leq t \leq \tilde{h}$. In this scenario, the solution to the MLHCombSP is not guaranteed to be a solution to the above system. Indeed, F satisfies the above constraints if and only if its most $\tilde{N}$ significant bits contain between $\tilde{h} - t$ and $\tilde{h} + t$ '1' valued bits. This probability is given by:

$$\mathbb{P}(F \in \mathcal{U}) = \frac{\sum_{i=\tilde{h}-t}^{\tilde{h}+t} \binom{h}{i}\binom{N-h}{\tilde{N}-i}}{\binom{N}{\tilde{N}}}. \tag{15}$$

Such an $\mathcal{U}$ has size

$$|\mathcal{U}| = \sum_{i=\tilde{h}-t}^{\tilde{h}+t} \binom{\tilde{N}}{i} 2^{N-\tilde{N}}.$$

3.3   Merging

A possible approach to reduce the dimension of the ILP (8) is to merge more than one bit in a single n_i. Say, for example, that we merge the bits in pairs; this means that each one of the n_i can assume values in $\{0, 1, 2, 3\}$ and that the total weight varies between h and $2h$, as we prove in Proposition 2.

Example 1. *Let us consider $F = (00010011)$. By merging bits in pairs and assuming the MILP gives the correct solution, one gets $n_1 = (00)$, $n_2 = (01)$, $n_3 = (00)$, $n_4 = (11)$. The total sum results in $n_1 + n_2 + n_3 + n_4 = 4 \leq 2h = 6$.*

Using this method, it is possible to merge an arbitrary number of bits together. Let $S = \lceil N/s \rceil$. The instance of ILP that emerges after merging bits in groups of s is the following:

$$Tx_1 + qx_2 - Rx_3 + 0n_1 + \cdots + 0n_S = y \tag{16}$$

under the conditions

$$\begin{cases} x_1 = 1, \\ l_{x_2} \leq x_2 \leq u_{x_2}, \\ 2^h - 1 < y < 2^N - 2^{N-h}, \\ 0 \leq n_i \leq 2^s - 1, \text{ for } 0 \leq i \leq S, \\ h \leq \sum_{i=1}^{S} n_i < 2^{s-1}h, \\ x_3 = \sum_{i=1}^{S} 2^{s(i-1)} n_i. \end{cases} \tag{17}$$

Hence the size of the ILP can be established a priori. The more bits one merges, the harder it is that the ILP will return the correct solution, for it is expected that the system of inequalities has more than one solution.

The following proposition shows that a solution $(X, \varphi(X))$ satisfying the graph condition is also a solution to the system of inequalities (17) and, therefore, it can be obtained via the ILP-oracle with the instance (16).

Proposition 2. *Let* $F, G \in \mathbb{Z}_q$ *so that* $\varphi(F) = G$ *and so that the Hamming weight of* $\text{seq}_N(F)$ *is* h. *Then there exists an instance* $(y, x_2, x_3, n_1, \ldots, n_S)$ *with* $x_3 = F$ *and* $y = G$ *that solves the system:*

$$\begin{cases} T + x_2 q - R x_3 = y, \\ 2^h - 1 < y < 2^N - 2^{N-h}, \\ x_3 = \sum_{i=1}^{S} 2^{s(i-1)} n_i, \\ 0 \le n_i \le 2^s - 1, \ for \ 0 \le i \le S, \\ h \le \sum_{i=1}^{S} n_i \le 2^{s-1} h. \end{cases} \tag{18}$$

Proof. The first equation and the first inequality are satisfied by the definition of φ. The second equation and the second inequality represent the fact that we are writing x_3 in base 2^s. Hence the only remaining thing to prove is that the last inequality holds.

Let $F = F(0)2^0 + \ldots + F(N-1)2^{N-1}$. We notice that $n_i = \sum_{j=0}^{s-1} F((i-1)s+j)2^j$. For the fact that $\sum_{i=0}^{N-1} F(i) = h$, we conclude that

$$\sum_{i=1}^{S} n_i = \sum_{i=1}^{S} \sum_{j=0}^{s-1} F((i-1)s+j)2^j \ge \sum_{i=1}^{S} \sum_{j=0}^{s-1} F((i-1)s+j) = h.$$

We prove the second inequality by induction on h. For $h = 1$, n_i is a string of weight 1 of s bits. That is at most 2^{s-1}.

Assuming that the inequality holds for $h - 1$. If $n_i \le 2^{s-1}$ for every i, the inequality is satisfied. Hence we assume that there exists one j for which $n_j > 2^{s-1}$. This means that the Hamming weight of $\text{seq}_s(n_j) \ge 2$. Then one gets:

$$\sum_i n_i \le 2^s + \sum_{i \ne j} n_i.$$

The sum of the Hamming weights of $\text{seq}_s(n_j)$, $j \ne i$ is at most $h-2$. By inductive hypothesis, it follows that

$$\sum_i n_i \le 2^s + 2^{s-1}(h-2) = 2^{s-1} h.$$

The Proposition is proved. $\square$

The following Proposition determines the size of $\mathcal{U}$ that one obtains from considering the ILP (17).

Proposition 3. *Let $\mathcal{U}$ be the set containing all $0 \leq F < q$, whose 2^s-ary representation satisfies $0 \leq n_i \leq 2^s - 1$, for $0 \leq i \leq S$ and $h \leq \sum_{i=1}^{S} n_i \leq 2^{s-1}h$. Then*

$$|\mathcal{U}| = \sum_{d=h}^{2^{s-1}h} l_{2^s}(S, d),$$

where $l_t(n, d)$ is the number of integer solutions to $z_1 + \ldots + z_n = d$, $0 \leq x_i < t$.

Proof. Let d be one of the values of $\sum_{i=1}^{S} n_i$. For each d, we consider all the possible configurations of $n_1, \ldots, n_S$. Since each of these is bounded by $2^s - 1$, the number of legitimate configurations is $l_{2^s}(S, d)$. $\qquad\square$

Examples

In the following table we present the size of the resulting ILP instances depending on the value of s and the corresponding success probability in two concrete cases. We selected different choices of s and set $\mathcal{V} = \{2^{N-t-1} + 2^{h-1}, \ldots, 2^{N-t} - 2^{N-t-h}\}$ for t satisfying $\log_2(|\mathcal{U}|) + t \geq N$. The probability of $G \in \mathcal{V}$ is reported and corresponds to the success probability. Indeed, if $G \in \mathcal{V}$ then (F, G) is a solution to the system of inequalities given by the intersection of (16) with (17) and we expect it is its unique solution.

Following the attack here presented, we computed the probability that, given a fixed s, E_G is so that $\log_2(|\mathcal{U}|) + E_G \geq N$. The random variable E_G is distributed according to the negative hypergeometric distribution [4], where we are looking for the probability that the first success (first '1' valued bit) happens at the E_G-th trial, given a random sample without replacement from a population of size N containing h successes.

The parameters chosen are $N = 1279$ and $h = 17$ (Table 1).

Table 1. Success probabilities for $N = 1279$ and $h = 17$

s	Probability of success	Number of variables in ILP
1	$2^{-2.56}$	1282
2	$2^{-3.97}$	643
3	$2^{-6.13}$	430
4	$2^{-9.13}$	323
5	$2^{-12.94}$	259
6	$2^{-17.33}$	217
7	$2^{-21.73}$	186
8	$2^{-26.07}$	163
9	$2^{-30.47}$	146
10	$2^{-34.06}$	131

We notice that for these parameters, $N < 10h^2$, so it violates the guidelines given in [2]. The reason for which these where chosen is to compare the success probability with the attack by Beunardeau et al. [6], which was performed against the previous version of the protocol.

The same experiments were reproduced with $N = 1279$ and $h = 11$ (Table 2).

Table 2. Success probabilities for $N = 1279$ and $h = 11$

s	Probability of success	Number of variables in ILP
1	$2^{-1.36}$	1282
2	$2^{-1.78}$	643
3	$2^{-2.80}$	430
4	$2^{-4.29}$	323
5	$2^{-6.26}$	259
6	$2^{-8.64}$	217
7	$2^{-11.18}$	186
8	$2^{-13.71}$	163
9	$2^{-16.27}$	146
10	$2^{-18.42}$	131

Remark 4. *While solving MLHRatioSP MLHCombSP for parameters $N = 1279$ and $h = 17$ is enough to break the cryptosystem described in [1], we remark that the new security parameters suggested in [2] are $h = 256$ and $N > 10h^2$.*

Remark 5. *It is possible to generalize all the presented approaches used to account for the weight of F to account also the weight of G. However this would result in an increasing of the dimension of the ILP problem. One would nonetheless significantly increase the probability of success.*

Remark 6. *The above work can be easily adjusted in order to solve the MLHRatioSP by taking $T = 0$ and eliminating the variable x_1.*

4   A New Family of Weak Keys

In [6] a family of weak keys was introduced for the MLHRatioSP. Those were the ones for which all the '1' valued bits appeared in the right hand side of $\text{seq}_N(F)$ and $\text{seq}_N(G)$. As noted in [2], one can break keys is this family by performing a rational reconstruction [19] of the quotient H. Aggarwal et al. also claim that the family of weak keys described in [6] extends to the MLHCombSP as well. A key in this family appears with probability 2^{-2h}.

Using the rotations described in Sect. 3.1 and the ILP instance (5), we show that this family can be extended. One can notice that many keys which have a long sequence of zeros in the middle of their bit-sequence representation are not considered as weak keys in [6]. However, we show that this is a weakness that can be exploited.

As mentioned above, one can perform up to N^2 shifts in order to get F and G as small as possible, so that it is more likely that $E_F + E_G \geq N$. Let $\mathcal{E}_F$ and $\mathcal{E}_G$ be respectively the length of the largest sequences of consecutive zeros of F and G. The distribution of such values of $\mathcal{E}_A$ is more difficult to compute and require recursion. Again, the problem is modelled as an urn problem with h white balls and $N - h$ black balls, where all the balls are samples without replacement. The probability $\mathbb{P}(\mathcal{E}_A \geq k)$ can be thought as the complementary of the probability that there are no sequences of consecutive black balls of length k. The latter, we call $\bar{p}(b, w, k)$ and is recursively defined as follows:

$$\bar{p}(b, w, k) = \begin{cases} 1 & \text{if } b \leq k, \\ 0 & \text{if } b > k \text{ and } w = 0, \\ \frac{w}{w+b-k}\bar{p}(b, w-1, k) + \\ + \sum_{i=1}^{k-1}\left(\prod_{j=0}^{i-1}\frac{b-j}{w+b-j}\right)\frac{w}{w+b-k}\bar{p}(b-i, w-1, k) & \text{otherwise.} \end{cases}$$

Remark 7. *The probability given here is actually slightly smaller than the actual probability that the best shift has $\mathcal{E}_A \geq k$, for the current formula does not consider that the sequences of consecutive zeros can run from one extreme to the other of $\mathrm{seq}_N(A)$. As an example, $\mathrm{seq}_{10}(A) = (0010001000)$ will give $\mathcal{E}_A = 5$, while the $\bar{p}$ distribution will consider for A that the longest sequence of zeros is 3.*

Computing this expression is challenging even for small numbers. The estimates that we used is the following. Let Ω be the family of multisets

$$\Omega = \left\{ \{0^{a_0}, \ldots, h^{a_h}\} | a_0 \geq a_i \geq 0 \text{ for } i > 0, \sum_{i=1}^{h} a_i = N - h \right\}.$$

This family represents all the possible sequences of zeroes and ones of length N and weight h after the best shift. Let $\psi : \mathcal{Z} \to \Omega$ be the function that assigns an element of weight h in $\mathbb{Z}_q$ to the corresponding multiset in Ω. Due to symmetries, there exist $A, B \in \Omega$ so that $|\psi^{-1}(A)| \neq |\psi^{-1}(B)|$, so the probability that for a random multiset $S \in \Omega$, $a_0 = k$ is different from $\bar{p}(h, N - h, k)$. Nevertheless, experiments show that the two distributions are very similar. Hence we used the former distribution, which is easier to compute, for the numerical examples.

These computations reveal a new family of weak keys: namely, if F and G are so that $\mathcal{E}_F + \mathcal{E}_G \geq N$. One can perform N^2 rotations and guess up to $N - \lceil N/h \rceil - h$ possible $\mathcal{E}_F$ to find a unique solution to the intersection of (6) and (7), where $\mathcal{U} = \{2^{N-\mathcal{E}_F-1} + 2^{h-1}, \ldots, 2^{N-\mathcal{E}_F} - 2^{\mathcal{E}_F-h+1} + 1\}$ and where $\mathcal{V} = \{2^{\mathcal{E}_G-1} + 2^{h-1}, \ldots, 2^{\mathcal{E}_G} - 2^{\mathcal{E}_G-h+1} + 1\}$. Such solution is obtained by asking the ILP-oracle to solve instances of dimension 3.

For $N = 1279$ and $h = 17$, the expected $\mathcal{E}_A$ is ≈ 256. For these parameters and using the described estimates, one gets that $\mathbb{P}(\mathcal{E}_F + \mathcal{E}_G \geq N) \approx 2^{-11}$.

This improves upon Beunardeau et al. work for which approximately 1 over 2^{34} keys is weak.

5 Conclusions and Future Work

We provide a generalization of the Beunardeu et al. attack to the case of MLH-CombSP that runs with the same time complexity, as conjectured by Aggarwal et al. in [2].

We also extend the family of weak keys that should be avoided when generating the private key (F, G). Those keys can be successfully attacked with $< N^3$ queries to an ILP-oracle that solves ILP instances of dimension 3.

Results in Table 1 show that, using an ILP-oracle, the success probability can be significantly higher compared to the one of the Beunardeu et al. attack [6,7]. In practice, we would need to replace the ILP-oracle with an ILP solver. Since many practical ILP algorithms do not provide the exact solution, we expect the success probability to decrease, in the sense that, even though the system of inequalities has exactly one solution, it is not detected by the ILP solver.

In general, it is not easy to determine the complexity of an ILP instance. Unlike Linear Programming, the dimension of ILP is not determinant in establishing whether an instance is feasible or not to solve [5]. Therefore the size of the ILPs emerging from our reduction is not necessarily related to their hardness.

Unfortunately, the vast majority of the ILP solvers available does not support big numbers arithmetic. This prevented us from performing noteworthy experiments since it is an essential requirement when considering parameters that are cryptographically relevant. With a dedicated implementation it would be possible to perform such experiments that would provide empirical hints about the real complexity of those ILP instances.

Anyhow, if one wanted to use the Aggarwal et al. cryptosystem, it is advisable to investigate the nature of those ILP instances, to be sure that they do not fall into any category that allows a fast solving algorithm. We remark that ILP problems in Sect. 3 have only one expected possible solution and large portions of the variables are bounded by relatively tight constraints.

Aknowledgments. The authors thank Igor Semeav and Qian Guo for useful suggestions in the early stages of this work, and greatly thank Phillippe Samer for insightful discussions on ILP. The authors are also grateful to anonymous reviewers for constructive comments.

References

1. Aggarwal, D., Joux, A., Prakash, A., Santha, M.: A new public-key cryptosystem via mersenne numbers. Cryptology ePrint Archive, Report 2017/481, version:20170530.072202 (2017)
2. Aggarwal, D., Joux, A., Prakash, A., Santha, M.: A new public-key cryptosystem via mersenne numbers. In: Shacham, H., Boldyreva, A. (eds.) CRYPTO 2018. LNCS, vol. 10993, pp. 459–482. Springer, Cham (2018). https://doi.org/10.1007/978-3-319-96878-0_16

3. Appelgren, L.: A column generation algorithm for a ship scheduling problem. Transp. Sci. **3**, 53–68 (1969). https://doi.org/10.1287/trsc.3.1.53

4. Berry, K.J., Mielke Jr., P.W.: The negative hypergeometric probability distribution: sampling without replacement from a finite population. Percept. Motor Skills **86**(1), 207–210 (1998). https://doi.org/10.2466/pms.1998.86.1.207

5. Bertsimas, D., Weismantel, R.: Optimization Over Integers. Dynamic Ideas, Belmont (2005)

6. Beunardeau, M., Connolly, A., Graud, R., Naccache, D.: On the hardness of the mersenne low hamming ratio assumption. Cryptology ePrint Archive, Report 2017/522 (2017)

7. de Boer, K., Ducas, L., Jeffery, S., de Wolf, R.: Attacks on the AJPS mersenne-based cryptosystem. In: Lange, T., Steinwandt, R. (eds.) PQCrypto 2018. LNCS, vol. 10786, pp. 101–120. Springer, Cham (2018). https://doi.org/10.1007/978-3-319-79063-3_5

8. Casella, G., Berger, R.L.: Statistical inference, vol. 2. Duxbury Pacific Grove, CA (2002)

9. CPLEX Optimizer, I.: IBM ILOG CPLEX optimization studio (2018)

10. Fisher, M.L.: The lagrangian relaxation method for solving integer programming problems. Manag. Sci. **27**(1), 1–18 (1981). https://doi.org/10.1287/mnsc.27.1.1

11. Gurobi Optimization, L.: Gurobi optimizer reference manual (2018)

12. Hoffstein, J., Pipher, J., Silverman, J.H.: NTRU: a ring-based public key cryptosystem. In: Buhler, J.P. (ed.) ANTS 1998. LNCS, vol. 1423, pp. 267–288. Springer, Heidelberg (1998). https://doi.org/10.1007/BFb0054868

13. Lenstra, A.K., Lenstra, H.W., Lovász, L.: Factoring polynomials with rational coefficients. Mathematische Annalen **261**(4), 515–534 (1982). https://doi.org/10.1007/BF01457454

14. Lenstra Jr., H.W.: Integer programming with a fixed number of variables. Math. Oper. Res. **8**(4), 538–548 (1983). https://doi.org/10.1287/moor.8.4.538

15. Marchand, H., Martin, A., Weismantel, R., Wolsey, L.: Cutting planes in integer and mixed integer programming. Discrete Appl. Math. **123**(1–3), 397–446 (2002). https://doi.org/10.1016/S0166-218X(01)00348-1

16. Morrison, D.R., Jacobson, S.H., Sauppe, J.J., Sewell, E.C.: Branch and bound algorithms. Discret. Optim. **19**(C), 79–102 (2016). https://doi.org/10.1016/j.disopt.2016.01.005

17. Papadimitriou, C.H.: On the complexity of integer programming. J. ACM **28**(4), 765–768 (1981). https://doi.org/10.1145/322276.322287

18. Schrijver, A.: Theory of Linear and Integer Programming. Wiley, New York (1986). https://doi.org/10.1002/net.3230200608

19. Wang, P.S.: A p-adic algorithm for univariate partial fractions. In: Proceedings of the Fourth ACM Symposium on Symbolic and Algebraic Computation, SYMSAC 1981, pp. 212–217. ACM, New York (1981). https://doi.org/10.1145/800206.806398

20. Wolsey, L.: Integer Programming. Wiley Series in Discrete Mathematics and Optimization. Wiley, New York (1998)

Simple Oblivious Transfer Protocols Compatible with Supersingular Isogenies

Vanessa Vitse[✉]

Univ. Grenoble Alpes, CNRS, Institut Fourier, 38000 Grenoble, France
vanessa.vitse@univ-grenoble-alpes.fr

Abstract. The key exchange protocol of Diffie and Hellman, which can be defined for any group, has the special feature of using only exponentiations. In particular, it can also be instantiated in Kummer varieties, which are not groups, and in the post-quantum isogeny-based setting.

In this article, we propose a new simple oblivious transfer (OT) protocol, based on Diffie–Hellman key exchange, that only uses exponentiations; we also revisit the older Wu–Zhang–Wang scheme. Both protocols can be directly instantiated on fast Kummer varieties; more importantly, they can also be transposed in the isogeny setting. The semantic security of our proposals relies on the hardness of non-standard versions of the (supersingular) DH problem, that are investigated within this article. To the best of our knowledge, these protocols are the simplest discrete-log based OT schemes using only exponentiations, and the first isogeny-based OT schemes.

Keywords: Oblivious transfer · Diffie–Hellman key exchange · Supersingular isogeny · Post-quantum cryptography

1 Introduction

The key exchange protocol of Diffie and Hellman is undoubtedly the single most influential concept in the history of modern cryptography, and though more than forty years old, it continues to see new developments. A convenient feature of the Diffie–Hellman protocol is that it can be instantiated in any group; current applications no longer use the multiplicative group of finite fields where it was first defined but rather the group of points of an elliptic curve or Jacobian variety. Interestingly, the key exchange does not use group products, but only *exponentiations*, or more precisely commuting exponentiation maps. This benign observation actually allows the generalization of the Diffie–Hellman protocol to non-group settings, two of which we will describe now.

The first one is Kummer varieties, which are formed from Jacobian varieties by identifying a point and its inverse. A Kummer variety is not a group, but nevertheless inherits some of the operations of its parent Jacobian: in particular, there are well-defined (in additive notations) multiplication maps $[D] \mapsto [a\,D]$ and differential addition $\{[D], [D']\} \mapsto \{[D+D'], [D-D']\}$. These operations are

© Springer Nature Switzerland AG 2019
J. Buchmann et al. (Eds.): AFRICACRYPT 2019, LNCS 11627, pp. 56–78, 2019.
https://doi.org/10.1007/978-3-030-23696-0_4

sufficient for implementing Diffie–Hellman key exchange, and more importantly, they are usually faster than their Jacobian counterparts. For elliptic curves, this corresponds to the famous x-only Montgomery ladder. The use of Kummer varieties in higher genus is more recent, and their performances in genus 2 make them competitive alternatives to elliptic curves [5,22].

The second setting is isogeny-based cryptography (first proposed in [11,23, 24]), whose main advantage over groups is its resistance against quantum attacks. The most prominent algorithm in this setting is the SIDH key exchange of De Feo, Jao and Plût [12], which is adapted from Diffie–Hellman: the group of points of a single elliptic curve is replaced by the set of all supersingular elliptic curves defined over a finite field $\mathbb{F}_{p^2}$, and exponentiation maps are replaced by isogenies of prescribed degrees. In this context, the analog of the discrete logarithm problem is the *computational supersingular isogeny problem*: given two supersingular elliptic curves E and E', and possibly additional information, find an isogeny ϕ from E to E'. There is currently no known subexponential quantum algorithm for solving this problem. A variant, called CSIDH, has been proposed recently by Castryck et al. [8]; it is currently slower than SIDH, and asymptotically weaker because it is subject to the subexponential quantum attack of [9], but it has smaller key sizes and relies on more natural security assumptions.

The analogy between the group setting and the supersingular isogeny setting is far from being an exact correspondence, though. Consequently, the adaptation of a DLP-based protocol using only exponentiations to this second setting can be quite challenging (while on the other hand, the adaptation to Kummer varieties is trivial). However, we believe that most exponentiation-only DLP-based protocols can be modified to work with supersingular isogenies. The goal of this article is to demonstrate this claim on two examples: the first is a new oblivious transfer protocol, while the second is an older scheme of Wu, Zhang and Wang [27]. Both protocols are exponentiation-only, and we explain how to convert them into (C)SIDH-based protocols.

Oblivious transfer is among the fundamental tools of cryptography. It can be presented quite simply: Alice knows two secrets, say s_0 and s_1. Bob wants to know one of these secrets, but he does not want Alice to know which one. Oblivious transfer protocols (more precisely here, $\binom{2}{1}$-oblivious tranfer) resolve exactly that, allowing Bob to learn the secret of his choice without learning anything about the other secret, and without divulging anything about his choice to Alice. Introduced by Rabin [21] and Even et al. [14], oblivious transfer is a universal building block for secure multiparty computations [16], and a number of constructions have been proposed. In many protocols, the security relies on the computational hardness of either the RSA problem or the Diffie–Hellman problem, or variants thereof. In this article, we are interested in the latter (DH-based protocols); the most well-known are Bellare–Micall's, Naor–Pinkas's and Chou–Orlandi's [4,10,17]. To the best of our knowledge, only Wu, Zhang and Wang's construction [27] relies solely on exponentiations, but it requires additional validation measures to be secure, see Sect. 2.1. And while several post-quantum OT schemes have been proposed (most notably by Peikert et al. [19]; see also [15] for more references), none of them are based on supersingular isogenies.

The first contribution of this article is the study and construction of DH-based oblivious transfer schemes that use only exponentiations (Sect. 2). We begin by reviewing the protocol of Wu, Zhang and Wang, explaining how to improve its security. We then propose a new, conceptually simple oblivious transfer scheme. Because it can be straightforwardly adapted to work on fast Kummer varieties, we believe this protocol to be interesting on its own, outside of the post-quantum setting. For its analysis (Sects. 2.3 and 2.4), we define a notion of semantic security of an oblivious transfer scheme, capturing the computational intractability for the receiver of gaining information on both of Alice's secrets. The security of our new protocol then relies on the hardness of a new variant of the Diffie–Hellman problem, the "2-inverse problem". We also analyze the Wu–Zhang–Wang protocol, showing that in the random oracle model (and only in this model), its security is equivalent to the hardness of a second variant of the Diffie–Hellman problem. Of course, these two problems deserve more scrutiny, but we give some arguments in favor of their intractability. Then after some background on the SIDH setting, we present in Sect. 3 the corresponding version of both OT protocols, raising some interesting open problems along the way. The last section deals with their security, which mainly relies on the hardness of the isogeny versions of the previous problems. It turns out that the security panorama is somewhat different in the group setting, the SIDH and the CSIDH setting, see Fig. 1.

Setting	Wu–Zhang–Wang protocol	New OT protocol
Groups	UC sec. (ROM) vs passive adv. [13] Semantic sec. (ROM) vs malicious adv. Not semantic sec. (IND-CPA) vs malicious adv.	UC sec. (ROM) vs passive adv. [13] Semantic sec. (IND-CPA) vs malicious adv.
SIDH [12]	UC sec. (ROM) vs passive adv. [13] Semantic sec. (IND-CPA) vs malicious adv.	UC sec. (ROM) vs passive adv. [13] Semantic sec. (IND-CPA) vs malicious adv.
CSIDH [8]	Semantic sec. (IND-CPA) vs malicious adv.	Semantic sec. (IND-CPA) vs passive adv. Not secure vs malicious adv.

Fig. 1. Security panorama, conditional on the hardness of the underlying problems. The underlying encryption scheme is either modeled as a random oracle (ROM) or assumed to be IND-CPA.

Related Works. Since the first version of this article, two preprints have been posted on the same topic. The first paper, by Barreto, Oliveira and Benits [2], proposes a supersingular isogeny oblivious transfer protocol that does not derive from an exponentiation-only algorithm. Instead, it is an adaptation of Chou–Orlandi's protocol [10]. The difficulty is to replace the group product appearing in the protocol; the solution of Barreto et al. requires the use by Alice and Bob of a secure coin-flipping mechanism. Their protocol is about as efficient as ours, but this extra mechanism makes it somewhat less natural.

The second paper is a recent preprint by Delpech de Saint Guilhem, Orsini, Petit and Smart [13]. Their work is quite similar to ours: realizing the importance of exponentiation-only algorithms, they independently arrived at the same protocol as the one proposed here, and seem to have rediscovered the Wu–Zhang–Wang OT scheme. Their focus, however, is more directed toward the definition of a general framework. Their security proofs are also quite different: they decided to consider UC security, but only for the case of passive adversaries. On the other hand, in this article we investigate a different security setting (semantic security), but more importantly we allow malicious adversaries; in particular, we show that against a malicious receiver, the Wu–Zhang–Wang protocol is not semantically secure in the group setting outside of the random oracle model, and the new OT protocol is not secure (even in the random oracle model) in the CSIDH setting. Both works rely on the hardness of somewhat different problems, and we believe their paper and ours to be complementary.

2 Simple Diffie–Hellman Based Oblivious Transfer Protocols

Because of its simplicity, Diffie–Hellman key exchange has served as a basis for several oblivious transfer methods (see [4,10,17]). However, all these schemes use some multiplications in the group G, besides exponentiations. To the best of our knowledge, the only existing exponentiation-only oblivious transfer construction is the 2003 protocol of Wu, Zhang and Wang [27]. We revisit this protocol below, before proposing in Sect. 2.2 a new scheme, conceptually close to Bellare and Micali's (and Chou and Orlandi's variant). Being based uniquely on exponentiations, both protocols can be directly adapted to work on fast Kummer varieties, but we will not delve further on the subject. More importantly, we will be able in Sect. 3 to turn them into quantum-resistant, isogeny-based protocols.

2.1 The Oblivious Transfer Protocol of Wu, Zhang and Wang

In the oblivious transfer setting, Alice has two secrets s_0, s_1 and Bob wants to learn one of them, without allowing Alice to know which one; and Alice does not want Bob to learn both secrets. Let $k \in \{0, 1\}$ be the index of Bob's choice. As published in [27], the Wu–Zhang–Wang protocol requires Alice's secrets to be (encoded as) elements of a cyclic group $G = \langle g \rangle$. It is based on the "double lock" principle, which in turn amounts to the commutativity of the exponentiation maps.

Alice picks an exponent a and "locks" her secrets s_0 and s_1 by computing $A_0 = (s_0)^a$ and $A_1 = (s_1)^a$, that she sends to Bob. Bob chooses his own exponent b; according to the index k of the secret he is interested in, he adds his lock to A_k by computing the group element $B' = (A_k)^b$, that he sends to Alice. Then Alice computes $B = (B')^{a^{-1}}$, thus removing her lock, and sends it to Bob. Finally, Bob unlocks his desired secret by computing $B^{b^{-1}}$. Correctness of the protocol follows from the identity $B^{b^{-1}} = ((((s_k)^a)^b)^{a^{-1}})^{b^{-1}} = s_k$; it can be interpreted in terms of the commutativity of the exponentiation maps $\phi_a : g \mapsto g^a$ and $\phi_b : g \mapsto g^b$, see Fig. 2.

Unfortunately, this protocol is unsecure against a malicious Bob (we will give more complete definitions in Sect. 2.4). Indeed, a dishonest Bob can send $B'' = (A_0^x A_1^y)^b$ for some x, y of his choice to Alice, instead of A_0^b or A_1^b. If he does that, at the end of the exchange he will learn not s_0 nor s_1, but the quantity $s_0^x s_1^y$, which is related to both (for instance, it will be their quotient s_0/s_1). A way to prevent this is to use a validation method, as discussed in [27], in order to ensure that Bob sends either A_0^b or A_1^b, but this adds to the complexity of the protocol.

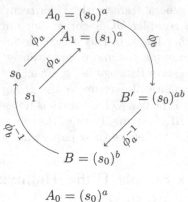

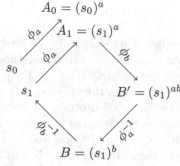

Fig. 2. Wu–Zhang–Wang protocol (top, $k = 0$; bottom, $k = 1$).

A more interesting possibility is to turn the protocol into a *random* oblivious transfer [3]. Instead of s_0 and s_1, Alice starts with two random elements r_0 and r_1 of G, and computes A_0 and A_1 as $(r_0)^a$ and $(r_1)^a$. At the end of the exchange, Bob knows either r_0 or r_1, but not both, and Alice does not know which one; at this point her secrets s_0 and s_1 have not been involved yet. Then r_0 and r_1 can be used as key seeds to encrypt s_0 and s_1 using a symmetric encryption function. Of course, a malicious Bob could still learn $r_0^x r_1^y$ instead of r_0 or r_1; but if the encryption function is secure enough, that does not help him to decrypt Alice's secrets. We give below the complete protocol.

1. Setup: Alice and Bob agree on a cyclic group G of prime order, such that the Diffie–Hellman problem is hard in G. They also agree on a symmetric encryption scheme Enc and a key derivation function KDF.
2. Alice picks two uniformly random, non-neutral elements $r_0, r_1 \in G$, and a uniformly random integer $a \in \{1, \ldots, \#G - 1\}$. She computes $A_0 = (r_0)^a$ and $A_1 = (r_1)^a$ with a fast exponentiation algorithm and sends them to Bob.
3. Bob performs elementary checks on Alice's values, then chooses a uniformly random integer $b \in \{1, \ldots, \#G - 1\}$. According to the index k of the secret he is interested in, he computes the group element $B' = (A_k)^b$ and sends it to Alice.
4. Alice encrypts her secrets s_0 and s_1 with the key derived from the random values r_0 and r_1 respectively. She checks Bob's values, computes $B = (B')^{a^{-1}}$ and sends it to Bob, together with the ciphertexts $S_0 = \text{Enc}(s_0, \text{KDF}(r_0))$ and $S_1 = \text{Enc}(s_1, \text{KDF}(r_1))$.
5. Bob decrypts S_k with the key derived from $B^{b^{-1}} = r_k$.

2.2   A New, Simple DH-Based Oblivious Transfer Protocol

We propose in this section a new random oblivious transfer protocol, also based on Diffie–Hellman key exchange scheme. We will see that it has some advantages compared to the Wu–Zhang–Wang protocol, with respect to security (Sect. 2.4) and complexity in the supersingular isogeny setting (Sect. 3.4). As above, Alice has two secrets s_0, s_1 and Bob wants to learn one of them, without allowing Alice to know which one; and Alice does not want Bob to learn both secrets. The index of Bob's choice is denoted by $k \in \{0, 1\}$.

1. Setup: Alice and Bob agree on a cyclic group G of prime order and a generator g of G, such that the Diffie–Hellman problem is hard in G. They also agree on a secure symmetric encryption function Enc and key derivation function KDF.
2. – Alice picks two different integers $a_0, a_1 \in \{1, \ldots, \#G - 1\}$, chosen independently and uniformly randomly.
   – For each $i \in \{0, 1\}$, she computes $A_i = g^{a_i}$; she sends Bob A_0, A_1.
3. Bob chooses a uniformly random integer $b \in \{1, \ldots, \#G - 1\}$.
   – He computes the group element $B = g^b$.
   – Bob performs elementary checks on A_0, A_1, then according to the index $k \in \{0, 1\}$ of the secret he is interested in, he computes $B' = (A_k)^b$ and sends it to Alice.
4. After checking Bob's values, for each $i \in \{0, 1\}$, Alice computes $B'^{a_i^{-1}}$ where a_i^{-1} is the inverse of a_i modulo $\#G$, and encrypts her secret s_i with the key derived from this computed value. She sends Bob the ciphertexts $S_0 = \text{Enc}(s_0, \text{KDF}(B'^{a_0^{-1}}))$ and $S_1 = \text{Enc}(s_1, \text{KDF}(B'^{a_1^{-1}}))$.
5. Bob computes $\text{Enc}^{-1}(S_k, \text{KDF}(B))$.

Correctness of the protocol follows from the identity $B'^{a_k^{-1}} = ((g^{a_k})^b)^{a_k^{-1}} = g^b = B$; it can be interpreted in terms of commuting maps ϕ_{a_0}, ϕ_{a_1} and ϕ_b, see Fig. 3. If we compare to a similar diagram for Diffie–Hellman key exchange, we see that the direction of the lower-right arrows have been reversed, and only one of them completes a commutative square; the second one points to a value that Bob should not be able to compute. As discussed above, this actually implements a *random* OT scheme: after the two first exchanges, Alice has two random (but related) elements $B'^{a_0^{-1}}$ and $B'^{a_1^{-1}}$, and only one of them is known to Bob, but at this point Alice's secrets have not yet been involved. The use of a symmetric encryption scheme together with a key derivation function gives the $\binom{2}{1}$-OT protocol.

2.3 Security Against a Malicious Sender

By definition, Alice should not be able
to discover the secret bit $k \in \{0,1\}$
of Bob. In both protocols, the only
information she has access to is Bob's
computed value $B' = (A_k)^b$. If Alice
is honest-but-curious, and the order of
the group G is indeed prime as specified, then A_0 and A_1, which are equal
to either $(r_0)^a$ and $(r_1)^a$ or g^{a_0} and
g^{a_1}, are both generators of the group
G. Since b is uniformly distributed in
$\{1, \ldots, \#G - 1\} \simeq (\mathbb{Z}/\#G\mathbb{Z})^*$, the element $B' = (A_k)^b$ is also uniformly dis-
tributed in $G \setminus \{e\}$ (where $e = g^0$ is the
neutral element) and therefore leaks no
information about k to Alice.

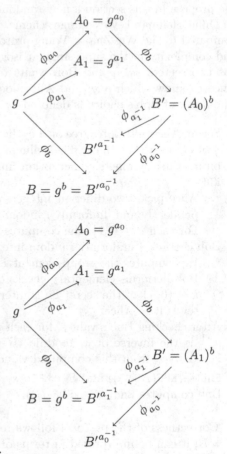

A malicious Alice could, however,
send Bob elements A_0, A_1 that are not
of the specified form. But for $B' =
(A_k)^b$ not to be uniformly distributed
she needs A_0 or A_1 not to be a generator
of G. As long as G is of prime order, this
means setting A_0 or A_1 to e, which Bob
can detect easily. Otherwise, Alice could
try working in a group G of composite
order. This is only possible if Bob does
not check the order of the agreed-upon
group G, or if Alice sends elements A_0
and A_1 that are not in G, in the spirit of
the invalid curve attack [6]. In any case,

Fig. 3. Another view of our DH-based
OT protocol (top, $k = 0$; bottom, $k = 1$)

as long as Bob performs some elementary checks—namely, that G has indeed
prime order, that A_0 and A_1 belong to G and are different from e—then Alice
obtains no information whatsoever about Bob's secret bit k.

Note that a malicious Alice could also tamper with the last part of the
protocol and replace one of her secrets (or one of her ciphertexts) with garbage,
and check whether Bob receives something meaningful or not. This weakness is
however inherent to any OT schemes; the only countermeasure is for Bob to stop
further communication with Alice.

2.4 Semantic Security Against a Malicious Receiver

By definition, Bob should not be able to decrypt, or at least gain information on,
both of Alice's secrets s_0 and s_1. A difficulty in the analysis is that Bob is not

constrained to follow the protocol: instead of sending $B' = (A_k)^b$, he can send Alice any element of his choice in G. As discussed above, Alice has little means of ensuring the validity of Bob's transmitted value, besides checking whether $B' \in G \setminus \{e\}$; doing otherwise would require expensive validation mechanisms, such as providing a zero-knowledge proof that Bob knows the logarithm of B' in basis either A_0 or A_1.

Because of this, we need a framework for the security of oblivious transfer protocols with respect to the sender's secrets. It is often defined in terms of an ideal functionality, but this makes for difficult proofs outside of the random oracle model. We prefer to define this security in terms of an indistinguishability property. Quite classically, in order to express that Bob obtains useful information on a secret or not, we consider a situation where the secret is selected randomly between two messages of his choice and ask if Bob can tell which one was selected. The following game is modeled on the definition of the IND-CPA property; in our $\binom{2}{1}$-oblivious transfer context, it makes no real sense to give Bob more power and to consider adaptative attacks (see however [7] for the security of $\binom{n}{k}$-OT).

Indistinguishability game for oblivious transfer:

Given a message length n:
- Bob sends Alice two pairs of distinct messages (m_0, m_0') and (m_1, m_1') of his choice, of the same length n;
- Alice chooses randomly, uniformly and independently two bits b_0 and b_1,

  then sets $s_0 = \begin{cases} m_0 & \text{if } b_0 = 0 \\ m_0' & \text{if } b_0 = 1 \end{cases}$ and $s_1 = \begin{cases} m_1 & \text{if } b_1 = 0 \\ m_1' & \text{if } b_1 = 1 \end{cases}$

- Alice and Bob perform the oblivious transfer protocol with s_0 and s_1;
- Bob must answer whether $b_0 = b_1$ or $b_0 \neq b_1$.

Definition 1. *An oblivious transfer protocol is* semantically secure *if for any polynomially-limited Bob, his advantage, defined as $P(\text{correct answer}) - 1/2$, is a polynomially-negligible function in the security parameter.*

The rationale behind this definition is that Bob should not be able to extract meaningful information about both s_0 and s_1, or equivalently about both b_0 and b_1. Since they are bits, this means being able to answer correctly whether $b_0 = b_1$ or $b_0 \neq b_1$ with probability greater than $1/2$. If Bob is honest-but-curious, he can learn either b_0 or b_1, and the semantic security implies that he does not learn non-negligible information on the second bit, as expected. If Bob is malicious, he could conceivably try to cheat during the protocol by sending invalid data, exchanging the complete knowledge of either b_0 or b_1 for a partial knowledge on both; this is for instance possible in Wu, Zhang and Wang's original protocol. Our definition of semantic security implies that only negligible information can be thus obtained. Overall, it captures the idea that any useful information gained by Bob on one of Alice's secrets forbids him to gain any useful information on the other secret.

Security of Our New Protocol. Obviously, the practical security of the random OT schemes we have presented depends on the underlying encryption and key derivation functions Enc and KDF, and they cannot provide a perfect secrecy as it is the case for Bob's secret k. A standard assumption is that Enc combined with KDF operates as a random oracle, meaning that Bob cannot gain any information on s_0 and s_1 if he does not know the encryption keys. For instance, as in [4,17], one can simply set $\text{Enc}(s, \text{KDF}(k)) = s \oplus H(k)$ where H is a random oracle (in practice, a cryptographic hash function). More realistically, we will rather assume that the combination of the encryption and key derivation functions is semantically secure, or more precisely satisfies the *indistinguishability under chosen-plaintext attack* (IND-CPA) property. Coming back to our indistinguishability game, under this assumption Bob cannot tell apart the encryptions of m_0 and m_0', resp. m_1 and m_1', with polynomially-limited resources if he does not have information on the respective encryption key.

The security of our protocol in the IND-CPA model consequently relies on the assumption that Bob cannot produce an element $B' \in G \setminus \{e\}$ such that he has information on both $B'^{a_0^{-1}}$ and $B'^{a_1^{-1}}$. This is made precise in the following decisional problem, presented in the form of a game between Bob and an oracle.

2-inverse decisional Diffie–Hellman problem (2-inv-DDHP):
Given a cyclic group $G = \langle g \rangle$, elements g^α, g^β:

- Bob sends the challenge oracle an element $X \in G \setminus \{e\}$ of his choice;
- the oracle samples two independently and uniformly random elements $R_0, R_1 \in G \setminus \{e\}$ and bits $b_0, b_1 \in \{0,1\}$.
- the oracle then outputs two pairs (Y, Y') and (Z, Z') such that

$$(Y,Y') = \begin{cases} (X^{\alpha^{-1}}, R_0) \text{ if } b_0 = 0 \\ (R_0, X^{\alpha^{-1}}) \text{ if } b_0 = 1 \end{cases} \quad \text{and} \quad (Z,Z') = \begin{cases} (X^{\beta^{-1}}, R_1) \text{ if } b_1 = 0 \\ (R_1, X^{\beta^{-1}}) \text{ if } b_1 = 1 \end{cases}$$

- Bob must answer whether $b_0 = b_1$ or $b_0 \neq b_1$.

As in the oblivious transfer indistinguishability game, if this problem is hard then Bob cannot gain any useful information on the pair $(X^{\alpha^{-1}}, X^{\beta^{-1}})$ that does not come from information on only one of them separately. Bob can of course identify either b_0 or b_1 by submitting $X = (g^\alpha)^x$ or $(g^\beta)^x$ for an x of his choice; if the 2-inv-DDHP is hard in G, he cannot do better with polynomially-limited resources.

Theorem 1. *The protocol of Sect. 2.2 is semantically secure if 2-inv-DDHP is hard and the underlying encryption scheme is IND-CPA.*

(Because of space limitation we cannot give a complete proof; the idea is that under the IND-CPA assumption, if a contestant has access to an algorithm solving the oblivious transfer indistinguishability game with a non-negligible advantage, then he can use it to obtain a non-negligible advantage against 2-inv-DDHP.)

There is an obvious reduction from the standard decisional Diffie–Hellman problem (DDHP) to 2-inv-DDHP. The decisional problem closest to ours is the inverse decisional Diffie–Hellman problem (inv-DDHP, see [1]): given g, g^α and h, determine if $h = g^{\alpha^{-1}}$. If Bob can solve inv-DDHP, he can solve 2-inv-DDHP by submitting $X = g$. However, there is no obvious reduction from 2-inv-DDHP to inv-DDHP (and neither from inv-DDHP to DDHP), because of the additional freedom in the choice of X, but we do not believe this freedom to be practically usable. As a matter of fact, even if Bob manages to obtain some partial information on both Alice's encryption keys $B'^{a_0^{-1}}$ and $B'^{a_1^{-1}}$, he will probably not be able to use it to gain partial information on both secrets s_0 and s_1, although this claim clearly depends on the encryption scheme used (he would need some kind of related key attacks). Nevertheless, it is safer to implement our oblivious transfer protocol in a group where the decisional Diffie–Hellman problem is hard, for instance on cryptographic elliptic curves that are not pairing-friendly.

Security of the Wu–Zhang–Wang Protocol. In the random oracle model, the security of the Wu–Zhang–Wang protocol against a malicious receiver relies on the hardness of yet another problem, that we dub the **one-more exponentiation problem** (1MEP): Given a cyclic group $G = \langle g \rangle$ of prime order, two non-neutral elements Y and Z, and a secret integer $\alpha \in \{1, \ldots, \#G - 1\}$,

- Bob submits an element $X \in G$ of his choice to an oracle, that outputs X^α;
- then Bob must produce Y^α and Z^α.

Clearly, Bob can solve 1MEP if he can solve the computational Diffie–Hellman problem (twice, with inputs X, X^α, Y and then X, X^α, Z). On the other hand, for an honest-but-curious Bob who follows the protocol and submits either Y or Z, solving 1MEP is equivalent to solving the CDHP with inputs Y, Z and either Y^α or Z^α. But a malicious Bob is not constrained in his choice of X; this freedom implies that there is no trivial equivalence between 1MEP and CDHP, even though it is not at all clear how to use this freedom meaningfully. In any case, there does not seem to be any practical way to solve these problems beyond computing discrete logarithms.

However, the decisional version of 1MEP is easy: by submitting Y/Z to the exponentiation oracle, Bob recovers Y^α/Z^α and therefore gains information on the pair (Y^α, Z^α). This means that the Wu–Zhang–Wang protocol is not semantically secure under the IND-CPA assumption, for the same reason that the original version was insecure and had to be transformed in a random OT scheme. In practice, this is an actual weakness only if Bob manages to mount a kind of related key attack. But in any case, achieving semantic security for this protocol would require not only the hardness of 1MEP, but also a form of non-standard indistinguishability property of the underlying encryption scheme.

2.5   Comparison Between the Two Schemes

From a complexity point of view, we can compare the two schemes by count-ing the number of group exponentiations, which are usually the most expensive operations. We can see that the Wu–Zhang–Wang protocol requires five expo-nentiations, against six for our proposal, and is thus slightly more efficient. This is however no longer true in the supersingular isogeny setting, as explained in Sect. 3.4.

From a security point of view, we have seen that the two schemes rely on distinct hardness assumptions. Still, outside of the random oracle model the Wu–Zhang–Wang protocol is weaker than ours, and cannot offer semantic security under standard indistinguishability assumptions on the underlying symmetric encryption scheme.

Note that the protocols, as presented above, actually implement $\binom{2}{1}$ (or 1-out-of-2) oblivious transfer. Turning them into $\binom{n}{1}$-OT can be done using the classical Naor–Pinkas transform [18]: it only requires $O(\ln(n))$ parallel executions of the first steps of the protocol, and thus only $O(\ln(n))$ exponentiations; but obviously, Alice must still send $O(n)$ encrypted messages in the final step. Achieving $\binom{n}{t}$-OT is a different task. The Wu–Zhang–Wang protocol admits a solution with $O(n+t)$ operations, as explained in the original paper [27], whereas our protocol still necessitates t executions of the $\binom{n}{1}$ scheme.

3   SIDH-based Oblivious Transfer

3.1   Background on (C)SIDH

Let E and E' be two elliptic curves defined over the same finite field $\mathbb{F}_q$. By a theorem of Tate, we know that there exists an isogeny $\phi : E \to E'$ defined over $\mathbb{F}_q$ if and only if E and E' have the same number of $\mathbb{F}_q$-rational points, and this can be checked quite efficiently. On the other hand, finding such an isogeny ϕ, or equivalently determining its kernel, is usually much more difficult.

Actually, this gives a construction of a one-way function. Starting from a subgroup G of $E(\mathbb{F}_q)$, Vélu's formulae allow one to compute the curve $E' \simeq E/G$ and the corresponding isogeny $\phi : E \to E'$ using $O(\#G)$ operations in E. But when the order of G is smooth (in applications we will have $\#G = 2^n$ or 3^m), then ϕ can be efficiently computed as a composition of small degree isogenies, and the cost drops to $\tilde{O}(\log(\#G))$; see [12] for more details. On the other hand, the inverse function, which consists of determining $G = \ker \phi$ from E, E' and potential other information such as $\#G = \deg \phi$, is harder to compute. How much harder depends on the setting; in the case of smooth degrees, the best known quantum attacks have exponential complexity for supersingular elliptic curves [25].

This one-way function can be used to construct a Diffie–Hellman-type key exchange. In this context, the exponentiation maps of the Diffie–Hellman proto-col are replaced by the computation of quotient curves E/G, and recovering G

from E and E/G becomes the analog of the discrete logarithm problem. The difficulty is that the analogy between exponentations and taking quotients of curves is not perfect. Indeed, Diffie–Hellman key exchange relies on the existence of a commutative, efficiently computable group action of $(\mathbb{Z}/\#G\mathbb{Z})^*$ on G, defined by $(a, g) \mapsto g^a$. In the isogeny setting, the corresponding group is the ideal class group $\mathcal{C}l(End(E))$ of the endomorphism ring, but $End(E)$ is not commutative when E is supersingular. CSIDH circumvents this difficulty by working with the commutative subring $End_{\mathbb{F}_p}(E)$ of endomorphisms defined over $\mathbb{F}_p$; adapting our group-based OT protocols to the CSIDH setting is therefore rather easy and we leave the details to the interested reader (but see Sect. 4.3).

The SIDH key exchange of De Feo, Jao and Plût is more complex and uses two different torsion subgroups of a supersingular curve E defined over $\mathbb{F}_{p^2}$. We assume that the full 2^n and 3^m torsion of E is defined over $\mathbb{F}_{p^2}$, where n and m are integers related to the security level (typically $100 \leq n \leq 500$) such that $2^n \approx 3^m$; actually, any pair of small prime numbers can be used intead of 2 and 3. The protocol works as follows:

- Alice and Bob agree on a basis $\langle U, V \rangle$ of $E[2^n]$ and $\langle P, Q \rangle$ of $E[3^m]$
- Alice samples randomly and uniformly $a \in \mathbb{Z}/2^n\mathbb{Z}$, sets $R_A = U + aV$, then computes the curve $E_A \simeq E/\langle R_A \rangle$ with corresponding isogeny $\phi_A : E \to E_A$. She sends Bob the triple $(E_A, \phi_A(P), \phi_B(Q))$.
- Bob computes similarly the curve $E_B \simeq E/\langle R_B \rangle$ and the corresponding isogeny $\phi_B : E \to E_B$ where $R_B = P + bQ$ and b is sampled from $\mathbb{Z}/3^m\mathbb{Z}$. He sends Alice $(E_B, \phi_B(U), \phi_B(V))$.
- Alice computes $E_{BA} \simeq E_B/\langle \phi_B(U) + a\phi_B(V) \rangle$; Bob computes $E_{AB} \simeq E_A/\langle \phi_A(P) + b\phi_A(Q) \rangle$

Now Alice and Bob can use the common j-invariant $j(E_{AB}) = j(E_{BA})$ as a shared secret; indeed, $E_{BA} \simeq E_B/\langle \phi_B(R_A) \rangle \simeq E/\langle R_A, R_B \rangle \simeq E_A/\langle \phi_A(R_B) \rangle \simeq E_{AB}$.

The security of this scheme corresponds to the hardness of the analog of the computational Diffie–Hellman problem (CDHP):

Supersingular Computational Diffie–Hellman Problem (SSCDH [12]):
Let E be a supersingular elliptic curve defined over $\mathbb{F}_{p^2}$ with rational 2^n and 3^m torsion, and let (U, V) and (P, Q) be bases of $E[2^n]$ and $E[3^m]$ respectively. Let $\phi_A : E \to E_A$ and $\phi_B : E \to E_B$ be isogenies such that $\ker \phi_A = \langle U + aV \rangle$ and $\ker \phi_B = \langle P + bQ \rangle$, where a, b are chosen randomly and uniformly in $\mathbb{Z}/2^n\mathbb{Z}$ and $\mathbb{Z}/3^m\mathbb{Z}$.
Given the curves E, E_A, E_B and the points $\phi_A(P), \phi_A(Q), \phi_B(U), \phi_B(V)$, find the j-invariant of $E/\langle U + aV, P + bQ \rangle$.

There is a similar decisional problem, the Supersingular Decisional Diffie–Hellman Problem (SSDDH); we refer to [12] for its formalization. Currently, the best approach to solve this problem is to recover $\ker \phi_A$ from the knowledge of E,

E_A and $\phi_A(P)$ and $\phi_A(Q)$ (CSSI, **Computational Supersingular Isogeny Problem**); this is the SIDH analog of the computation of discrete logarithms. Of course, we can swap the 2^n and 3^m torsion and obtain a similar problem. Compared to the one-way function described at the beginning of this section, here an attacker has access to the images of P and Q. However, currently there is no known algorithm that exploits meaningfully this extra information, at least when $2^n \approx 3^m$ (see however [20]).

3.2   Basic Outline

From SIDH to OT. Our goal in this section is to construct isogeny-based, post-quantum oblivious transfer protocols, that are the analog in the SIDH setting of the group-based OT protocols presented in Sect. 2. We start with our new protocol (Sect. 2.2), which is somehow simpler to adapt; the Wu–Zhang–Wang protocol will be treated in Sect. 3.4.

We follow closely the blueprint of the method presented in Sect. 2.2. Instead of computing only one curve E_A and the corresponding isogeny $\phi_A : E \to E_A$ as in the SIDH key exchange, Alice now computes two curves $E_{A,0} \simeq E/\langle R_0 \rangle$ and $E_{A,1} \simeq E/\langle R_1 \rangle$, and the corresponding isogenies $\phi_{A,i} : E \to E_{A,i}$ of degree 2^n. She transmits Bob the two curves, one for each of her secrets, together with auxiliary data (as above, the image of a fixed basis $\langle P, Q \rangle$ of $E[3^m]$). Then Bob computes his part, namely, the two curves $E_B \simeq E/\langle R_B \rangle$ and $E'_B \simeq E_{A,k}/\langle \phi_{A,k}(R_B) \rangle$, where $k \in \{0,1\}$ still stands for the index of the secret Bob is interested in, and the corresponding "parallel" isogenies $\phi_B : E \to E_B$ and $\phi'_B : E_{A,k} \to E'_B$.

In the key exchange protocol, Bob transmitted Alice the curve E_B together with the image by ϕ_B of a fixed basis of $E[2^n]$; this allowed Alice to compute the isogeny ϕ'_A "parallel" to ϕ_A, whose kernel is $\langle \phi_B(R_A) \rangle = \langle \phi_B(U) + a\phi_B(V) \rangle$. But for the oblivious transfer protocol, we want to proceed the other way round: Bob sends Alice the curve E'_B, which is 3^m-isogenous to $E_{A,0}$ or $E_{A,1}$, but Alice does not know to which one. Similarily to Sect. 2.2, the key point is thus to "reverse" the map $\phi'_{A,k}$ going from E_B to E'_B. In the isogeny setting, what we are interested in are actually the domain and codomain of the map $\phi'_{A,k}$, and our goal becomes to compute the dual isogeny $\widehat{\phi}'_{A,k} : E'_B \to E_B$.

Dual Isogenies. It is a standard fact about elliptic curves that for any isogeny $\phi : E \to E'$ between two elliptic curves there exists another isogeny $\widehat{\phi} : E' \to E$, called the dual isogeny of ϕ, such that $\widehat{\phi} \circ \phi$ (resp. $\phi \circ \widehat{\phi}$) is the multiplication-by-$\deg \phi$ endomorphism of E (resp. E').

If $\phi : E \to E'$ is an isogeny of degree d coprime to the characteristic, given by a cyclic kernel $\ker \phi = \langle R \rangle \subset E[d]$, then the kernel of $\widehat{\phi}$ can be easily described. Let $T \in E$ be such that $E[d] = \langle R, T \rangle$. Since $\ker(\widehat{\phi} \circ \phi) = E[d] = \langle R, T \rangle$ and ϕ is surjective, it follows that $\ker \widehat{\phi} = \phi(E[d]) = \langle \phi(R), \phi(T) \rangle = \langle \phi(T) \rangle$. When all the d-torsion is rational, it is not difficult to find such a complementary generator T of $E[d]$, after which $\phi(T)$ and $\widehat{\phi}$ can be computed using Vélu's formulae.

Completing the Oblivious Transfer. In order to complete the protocol, Alice will compute two isogenies: one which will be "parallel" to $\hat{\phi}_{A,k}$, and the other a bogus one, arriving at some unknown curve. As in De Feo–Jao–Plût construction, Alice needs extra information to compute efficiently these maps. What she can do easily is find a generator of the kernel of the dual isogeny $\hat{\phi}_{A,i} : E_{A,i} \rightarrow E_A$ (for each $i \in \{0,1\}$), by taking the image by $\phi_{A,i}$ of a generator T_i of a complement of $\ker\phi_{A,i} = \langle R_i \rangle$ in $E[2^n]$. Now she can compute $\hat{\phi}'_{A,k}$, even without knowing k, if she has access to $\phi'_B(\phi_{A,k}(T_k))$. But she cannot give Bob $\phi_{A,i}(T_i)$: this discloses $\ker\hat{\phi}_{A,i}$, from which Bob or any eavesdropper can recover $\ker\phi_{A,i}$, ruining the

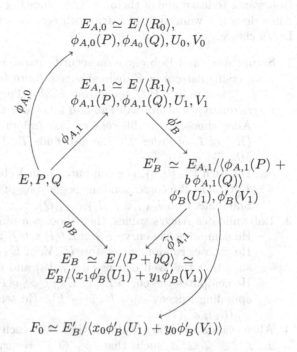

$$E_{A,0} \simeq E/\langle R_0 \rangle,$$
$$\phi_{A,0}(P), \phi_{A_0}(Q), U_0, V_0$$

$$E_{A,1} \simeq E/\langle R_1 \rangle,$$
$$\phi_{A,1}(P), \phi_{A,1}(Q), U_1, V_1$$

$$E'_B \simeq E_{A,1}/\langle \phi_{A,1}(P) + b\,\phi_{A,1}(Q) \rangle$$
$$\phi'_B(U_1), \phi'_B(V_1)$$

$$E, P, Q$$

$$E_B \simeq E/\langle P + bQ \rangle \simeq$$
$$E'_B/\langle x_1\phi'_B(U_1) + y_1\phi'_B(V_1) \rangle$$

$$F_0 \simeq E'_B/\langle x_0\phi'_B(U_1) + y_0\phi'_B(V_1) \rangle$$

Fig. 4. SIDH-based oblivious transfer, case $k = 1$

protocol. One way to achieve that, while preventing Bob from gaining useful information, is to ask him to compute and send Alice the image by ϕ'_B of a basis of $E_{A,k}[2^n]$; we will see however in Sect. 4.1 that some care must be taken in doing so.

More precisely, a basis (U_0, V_0) of $E_{A,0}[2^n]$ is chosen, as well as a basis (U_1, V_1) of $E_{A,1}[2^n]$, and Bob transmits Alice these bases together with $\phi'_B(U_k)$, $\phi'_B(V_k)$ and E'_B. Then Alice writes $\phi_{A,0}(T_0)$ and $\phi_{A,1}(T_1)$ as $x_0U_0 + y_0V_0$ and $x_1U_1 + y_1V_1$, and she computes the two curves $F_0 \simeq E'_B/\langle x_0\phi'_B(U_k) + y_0\phi'_B(V_k) \rangle$ and $F_1 \simeq E'_B/\langle x_1\phi'_B(U_k) + y_1\phi'_B(V_k) \rangle$. One of these two curves, F_k, corresponds to the quotient $E'_B/\langle \phi'_B(T_k) \rangle$, which is isomorphic to the curve E_B computed by Bob; the other one is random. Thus Alice has obtained two values $j(F_0)$ and $j(F_1)$, such that one of them, $j(F_k) = j(E_B)$, is known to Bob, but Alice does not know which one. They can be used as key seeds to encrypt Alice's secrets using a key derivation function and a symmetric cipher, as in the group-based setting. The complete construction is illustrated in Fig. 4.

3.3 A First Protocol

We now detail the protocol sketched above for the $\binom{2}{1}$-oblivious transfer; as in Sect. 2.5, it can be easily turned into a $\binom{n}{1}$-OT. Alice has two secrets s_0, s_1 and

Bob wants to learn one of them, without allowing Alice to know which one; and Alice does not want Bob to learn both secrets. Let $k \in \{0, 1\}$ be the index of Bob's choice.

1. Setup: Alice and Bob agree on security parameters n, m such that $2^n \approx 3^m$, a supersingular curve E defined over a finite field $\mathbb{F}_{p^2}$ such that $E[2^n 3^m] \subset E(\mathbb{F}_{p^2})$, and points P, Q generating $E[3^m]$. They also agree on a secure symmetric encryption protocol Enc and a key derivation function KDF.

2. – Alice chooses two different cyclic random subgroups $G_0 = \langle R_0 \rangle, G_1 = \langle R_1 \rangle$ of E of order 2^n. She also finds $T_0, T_1 \in E[2^n]$ such that $E[2^n] = \langle R_0, T_0 \rangle = \langle R_1, T_1 \rangle$.
   – For each $i \in \{0, 1\}$, she computes with Vélu's formulae the curve $E_{A,i} \simeq E/G_i$ and the corresponding isogeny $\phi_{A,i} : E \to E_{A,i}$. She sends Bob $E_{A,i}, \phi_{A,i}(P), \phi_{A,i}(Q)$.

3. Bob validates Alice's values, then chooses a uniformly random $b \in \mathbb{Z}/3^m\mathbb{Z}$.
   – He computes the curve $E_B \simeq E/\langle P + bQ \rangle$ and its j-invariant j_B.
   – He chooses random generators U_0, V_0 of $E_{A,0}[2^n]$, resp. U_1, V_1 of $E_{A,1}[2^n]$, such that the Weil pairings $w(U_0, V_0)$ and $w(U_1, V_1)$ are equal.
   – He computes the curve $E'_B \simeq E_{A,k}/\langle \phi_{A,k}(P) + b\,\phi_{A,k}(Q) \rangle$ and the corresponding isogeny $\phi'_B : E_{A,k} \to E'_B$. He sends Alice U_0, V_0, U_1, V_1, E'_B, $\phi'_B(U_k), \phi'_B(V_k)$.

4. Alice validates Bob's values, then for each $i \in \{0, 1\}$, she computes $x_i, y_i \in \mathbb{Z}/2^n\mathbb{Z}$ such that $\phi_{A,i}(T_i) = x_i U_i + y_i V_i$. She then computes $F_i \simeq E'_B/\langle x_i \phi'_B(U_k) + y_i \phi'_B(V_k) \rangle$. She computes the encryption $S_i = \mathrm{Enc}(s_i, \mathrm{KDF}(j(F_i)))$ of the secret s_i with the key derived from the j-invariant of F_i. She then sends Bob S_0, S_1.

5. Bob computes $\mathrm{Enc}^{-1}(S_k, \mathrm{KDF}(j_B))$.

The correctness of the algorithm follows from the identities

$$
\begin{aligned}
F_k &\simeq \Big((E/\langle R_k \rangle)/\langle \phi_{A,k}(P) + b\,\phi_{A,k}(Q) \rangle \Big)/\langle x_k \phi'_B(U_k) + y_k \phi'_B(V_k) \rangle \\
&\simeq \Big((E/\langle R_k \rangle)/\langle \phi_{A,k}(P + bQ) \rangle \Big)/\langle \phi'_B(x_k U_k + y_k V_k) \rangle \\
&\simeq \Big((E/\langle R_k \rangle)/\langle \phi_{A,k}(P + bQ) \rangle \Big)/\langle \phi'_B(\phi_{A,k}(T_k)) \rangle \\
&\simeq (E/\langle R_k, T_k \rangle)/\langle P + bQ \rangle \simeq (E/E[2^n])/\langle P + bQ \rangle \simeq E/\langle P + bQ \rangle \simeq E_B.
\end{aligned}
$$

The associated diagram, presented in Fig. 4 above, is the analog of Fig. 3 (except that for brevity only the case $k = 1$ is pictured), with supersingular curves and isogenies instead of group elements and exponentiation maps.

3.4 The Supersingular Isogeny Version of the Wu–Zhang–Wang Protocol

The exponentiation-only OT scheme of Wu, Zhang and Wang can also be modified to work in the supersingular isogeny setting. But this translation raises some very interesting points about isogeny-based crypto. We recall that in the original protocol (Sect. 2.1), Alice's secrets s_0 and s_1 are elements of the group G, whereas in the random-OT version, Alice chooses random elements $r_0, r_1 \in G$. Thus for its SIDH adaptation, we need to be able to answer one of the following problems.

- **Problem 1:** is possible to efficiently encode messages as (isomorphism classes of) supersingular elliptic curves over a given finite field?
- **Problem 2:** is it possible to efficiently sample random (isomorphism classes of) supersingular elliptic curves over a given finite field?

Both questions are not new, but satisfying answers would greatly improve the state-of-the-art in isogeny-based cryptography. Note that it is possible to efficiently construct supersingular elliptic curves over a finite field, but the resulting curves are always quite special (usually $j = 0$ or 1728). The difficulty with both problems is that supersingular elliptic curves form a very small proportion of all elliptic curves: over $\mathbb{F}_{p^2}$, approximately only one curve out of p is supersingular. Even though testing for supersingularity can be done efficiently, this small proportion means that the strategy of sampling random curves until a supersingular one is found is prohibitively expensive. Now, a standard solution to the second problem is to run a random isogeny walk, starting from a known supersingular curve. Because of the good mixing properties of the supersingular isogeny graph, only $O(\ln(p))$ steps are needed to reach an almost uniform distribution. But even if the reached curve is random, the entity running the isogeny walk always knows the path connecting it to the starting curve; this may be a problem in some applications.

The first problem is much more difficult and has currently no solution, even partial. Isogeny walks allow to map messages to supersingular curves, but this only yields one-way functions. For this reason, we just give below the SIDH translation of the random-OT version of the Wu–Zhang–Wang protocol.

1. Setup: Alice and Bob agree on security parameters n, m such that $2^n \approx 3^m$, and a finite field $\mathbb{F}_{p^2}$ such that $2^n 3^m | p \pm 1$.
2. – Alice chooses two random supersingular elliptic curves E_0 and E_1 defined over $\mathbb{F}_{p^2}$ with cardinality divisible by $2^{2n} 3^{2m}$. For each $i \in \{0, 1\}$, she chooses a random subgroup $\langle R_i \rangle \subset E_i[2^n]$ of order 2^n, as well as T_i such that $\langle R_i, T_i \rangle = E_i[2^n]$, and she computes with Vélu's formulae the curve $E_{A,i} \simeq E_i / \langle R_i \rangle$ and the corresponding isogeny $\phi_{A,i} : E_i \to E_{A,i}$.
   – Alice finds points $W_0 \in E_{A,0}$ and $W_1 \in E_{A,1}$ such that $(\phi_{A,0}(T_0), W_0)$ and $(\phi_{A,1}(T_1), W_1)$ are bases of $E_{A,0}[2^n]$ and $E_{A,1}[2^n]$ respectively, with equal Weil pairing. Using one random invertible matrix in $\mathrm{GL}_2(\mathbb{Z}/2^n\mathbb{Z})$, she computes new bases (U_0, V_0) and (U_1, V_1) of $E_{A,0}[2^n]$ and $E_{A,1}[2^n]$ respectively, with equal Weil pairing, and such that $\phi(T_0) = U_0 + aV_0$ and $\phi(T_1) = U_1 + aV_1$ for a given $a \in \mathbb{Z}/2^n\mathbb{Z}$. She keeps a secret and sends Bob $E_{A,0}, U_0, V_0, E_{A,1}, U_1, V_1$.
3. – According to the index k of the secret he is interested in, Bob chooses a random order 3^m subgroup $\langle P \rangle \subset E_{A,k}[3^m]$, as well as Q such that $\langle P, Q \rangle = E_{A,k}[3^m]$. He computes the curve $E'_B \simeq E_{A,k} / \langle P \rangle$ and the corresponding isogeny $\phi'_B : E_{A,k} \to E_{AB}$.

 – Bob chooses a random basis (P', Q') of $E'_B[3^m]$ and computes the coordinates x, y of $\phi'_B(Q)$ in this basis. He sends Alice E'_B, $\phi'_B(U_k)$, $\phi'_B(V_k)$, P', Q'.

4. Alice computes $E_B \simeq E'_B/\langle\phi'_B(U_k)+a\,\phi'_B(V_k)\rangle$ and the corresponding isogeny $\hat{\phi}'_{A,k} : E'_B \rightarrow E_B$. She sends Bob E_B, $\hat{\phi}'_{A,k}(P')$, $\hat{\phi}'_{A,k}(Q')$.

5. For each $i \in \{0, 1\}$, Alice computes $S_i = \texttt{Enc}(s_i, \texttt{KDF}(j(E_i)))$, the encryption of the secret s_i with the key derived from the j-invariant of E_i. She sends Bob S_0, S_1.

6. Bob computes $E'_k \simeq E_B/\langle x\,\hat{\phi}'_{A,k}(P')+y\,\hat{\phi}'_{A,k}(Q')\rangle$ and $\texttt{Enc}^{-1}(S_k, \texttt{KDF}(j(E'_k)))$.

The correctness of the protocol follows from the identities

$$E'_k \simeq E_B/\langle\hat{\phi}'_{A,k}(\phi'_B(Q))\rangle \simeq E'_B/\langle\phi'_B(T_k), \phi'_B(Q)\rangle$$

$$\simeq E_{A,k}/\langle P, T_k, Q\rangle \simeq (E_{A,k}/E_{A,k}[3^m])/\langle T_k\rangle \simeq E_{A,k}/\langle T_k\rangle \simeq E_k.$$

Compared to the DH-based protocol, we see in Fig. 5 that the exponentiations have been replaced by isogeny computations, and their inverses by taking dual isogenies. As in the De Feo–Jao–Plût protocol and our previous proposal, we need information on images of basis points to ensure commutativity. A difficulty comes from

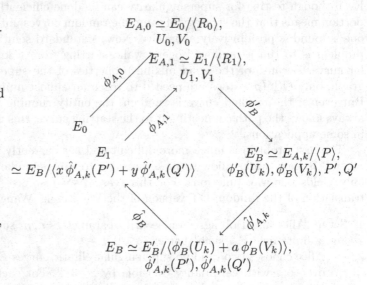

Fig. 5. SIDH version of the Wu–Zhang–Wang protocol, case $k = 1$

the fact that Alice must compute $\hat{\phi}'_{A,k}$, the dual to the isogeny parallel to $\phi_{A,k}$, without knowing k. For this reason, we need that $\phi_{A,0}(T_0)$ and $\phi_{A,1}(T_1)$, which generate the kernels of the duals $\hat{\phi}_{A,0}$ and $\hat{\phi}_{A,1}$, have the same coordinates in the bases (U_0, V_0) and (U_1, V_1) respectively. This, and the considerations of Sect. 4.1, explain the somewhat complicated second item of Step 2.

The most expensive operation in isogeny-based crypto is by far the computation of large degree isogenies. At first glance, it seems that the above protocol requires five such operations. However, as explained above, choosing the random supersingular curves E_0 and E_1 requires the computations of two additional large degree isogenies, for a total of seven operations. This is slightly more than with our first protocol, which only requires six isogeny computations.

4   Security Analysis

4.1   Malicious Alice

Contrarily to the group-based setting, our SIDH-based protocols do not provide perfect secrecy for Bob's secret bit k. In both protocols, Alice has access to Bob's answer E'_B, $\phi'_B(U_k)$, $\phi'_B(V_k)$, and she knows that E'_B is 3^m-isogenous to one of the curves $E_{A,0}$, $E_{A,1}$; recovering Bob's secret k amounts to finding to which curve E'_B is isogenous. This is the Decisional Supersingular Isogeny (DSSI) problem of [12]: given two supersingular elliptic curves defined over $\mathbb{F}_{p^2}$, determine if they are 3^m-isogenous. A simple cardinality argument shows that it is very unlikely that E'_B is 3^m-isogenous to both $E_{A,0}$ and $E_{A,1}$ (there are $\approx p/12$ supersingular curves defined over $\mathbb{F}_{p^2}$, while the number of 3^m-isogenies from E'_B is of the order of $3^m \leq \sqrt{p}$). So a brute-force approach can, in theory, succeed in finding k; nevertheless this problem is expected to be computationally intractable.

However Alice has more information than just E'_B: she knows $\phi'_B(U_k)$ and $\phi'_B(V_k)$, the images under Bob's isogeny of the basis points U_k, V_k. In particular, she can compute the Weil pairings (with respect to the 2^n-torsion) of $\phi'_B(U_k)$ with $\phi'_B(V_k)$, U_0 with V_0, and U_1 with V_1. Because of the property of the Weil pairing, it holds that

$$w(\phi'_B(U_k), \phi'_B(V_k)) = w(U_k, V_k)^{\deg \phi'_B} = w(U_k, V_k)^{3^m}.$$

Thus if $w(U_0, V_0) \neq w(U_1, V_1)$, Alice can find which one is equal to $w(\phi'_B(U_k), \phi'_B(V_k))$ when put to the 3^m-th power, and determine Bob's secret k.

For this reason, such values of U_0, V_0 and U_1, V_1 have been avoided in our protocols (one cannot simply choose $w(U_i, V_i) = 1$ since in that case (U_i, V_i) do not form a basis of $E_{A,i}[2^n]$). In the first protocol of Sect. 3.3, we tasked Bob with the responsibility of choosing U_i, V_i, see second item of step 3. It is not possible to do that in the second protocol of Sect. 3.4, because the points $\phi_{A,0}(T_0)$ and $\phi_{A,1}(T_1)$, which are known only to Alice, must have the same coordinates in bases (U_0, V_0) and (U_1, V_1) respectively. Consequently, Bob must imperatively check that the points sent by Alice have the same Weil pairing, and are indeed bases of $E_{A,0}[2^n]$, resp. $E_{A,1}[2^n]$.

With this extra condition, we see that our protocol requires the following extension of the DSSI problem to be computationally hard:

Extended decisional supersingular isogeny problem (XDSSI):
Given two supersingular elliptic curves E and E' defined over $\mathbb{F}_{p^2}$, together with points U, V, U', V' such that $\langle U, V \rangle = E[2^n]$, $\langle U', V' \rangle = E'[2^n]$, and $w(U, V)^{3^m} = w(U', V')$, determine if there exists an isogeny $\phi : E \to E'$ of degree 3^m such that $\phi(U) = U'$ and $\phi(V) = V'$.

It turns out that in our setting, the computational and decisional problems CSSI and XDSSI are basically equivalent, see [26]. Consequently, as long as the CSSI problem remains hard, with suitable parameters our constructions are secure with respect to Bob's choice.

As a final note, the above analysis actually holds for an honest-but-curious Alice. Conceivably, a malicious Alice could transmit Bob a pair of supersingular elliptic curves and basis points of her choice, that could help her discover Bob's secret. More precisely, she could send any pair of curves, although Bob can easily check that the curves he receives are indeed supersingular, and that (in our first protocol) the accompanying points form a basis of the 3^m-torsion satisfying $w(\phi_{A,i}(P), \phi_{A,i}(Q)) = w(P,Q)^{2^n}$. However, it is expected that the (extended) decisional supersingular isogeny problem is hard for any starting curve E, and thus a malicious Alice has no advantage over an honest-but-curious one.

4.2   Malicious Bob

Most of what has been said in Sect. 2.4 about the security of the oblivious transfer schemes in the group-based setting can be transposed to the supersingular isogeny setting; in particular, we can differentiate between the random oracle model and the IND-CPA property. The difference is in the formulation of the security assumptions — besides the obvious fact that they have been much less studied than their group counterparts.

More precisely, under the IND-CPA assumption the security of our first protocol relies on the hardness of the following problem:

2-inverse decisional supersingular isogeny problem (2-inv-DSSIP):
Let E, E_0, E_1 be three supersingular elliptic curves defined over $\mathbb{F}_{p^2}$ such that E_0 and E_1 are 2^n-isogenous to E, and let $\phi_0 : E \to E_0$, $\phi_1 : E \to E_1$ be the corresponding isogenies. Let (P,Q) be a basis of $E[3^m]$ and for each $i = 0, 1$, let (U_i, V_i) be a basis of $E_i[2^n]$ and (x_i, y_i) be the coordinates in this basis of a generator of the dual isogeny $\widehat{\phi}_i$.

Given E, E_0, E_1 and the points $P, Q, U_0, V_0, U_1, V_1, \phi_0(P), \phi_0(Q), \phi_1(P), \phi_1(Q)$:

- Bob sends the challenge oracle a supersingular elliptic curve E' and a basis (U', V') of $E'[2^n]$;
- the oracle computes the supersingular curves $F_0 \simeq E'/\langle x_0 U' + y_0 V' \rangle$, $F_1 \simeq E'/\langle x_1 U' + y_1 V' \rangle$, $F_0' \simeq E'/\langle W_0 \rangle$ and $F_1' \simeq E'/\langle W_1 \rangle$ where W_0 and W_1 are uniformly random points of E' of order 2^n;
- the oracle chooses randomly, uniformly and independently two bits b_0, b_1. Then it outputs two pairs (C_0, C_0') and (C_1, C_1') of supersingular curves such that

$$(C_0, C_0') = \begin{cases} (F_0, F_0') \text{ if } b_0 = 0 \\ (F_0', F_0) \text{ if } b_0 = 1 \end{cases} \quad \text{and} \quad (C_1, C_1') = \begin{cases} (F_1, F_1') \text{ if } b_1 = 0 \\ (F_1', F_1) \text{ if } b_1 = 1 \end{cases}$$

- Bob must answer whether $b_0 = b_1$ or $b_0 \neq b_1$.

The corresponding computational problem (2-inv-CSSIP), relevant in the random oracle model, is to find three supersingular elliptic curves E', F_0, F_1 and a basis (U', V') of $E'[2^n]$ such that $F_0 \simeq E'/\langle x_0 U' + y_0 V' \rangle$ and $F_1 \simeq E'/\langle x_1 U' + y_1 V' \rangle$.

If one can solve the CSSI Problem (see Sect. 3.1), i.e. if generators of $\ker \phi_0$ and $\ker \phi_1$ can be efficiently computed, then it is easy to obtain values for x_0, y_0, x_1, y_1 and solve the above problem. However, in contrast with the group setting, there is no obvious reduction to the SSCDH problem; this is because E, E_0, E_1 and the associated points do not form a SIDH triple (this would need one of E_0 and E_1 to be 3^m-isogenous to E instead of 2^n-isogenous). There is also no visible reduction from 2-inv-DSSIP to the SSDDH problem, nor even to the DSSI problem, and we expect it to be as difficult as 2-inv-CSSIP. Of course, Theorem 1 can be straightforwardly adapted.

Actually, it seems difficult to solve 2-inv-CSSIP or 2-inv-DSSIP without computing x_0, y_0, x_1, y_1, that is, solving the CSSI problem. It would require to find a curve E' and points U', V' such that U', resp. V', is related to both U_0 and U_1, resp. V_0 and V_1. This is possible for either U_0 and V_0 or U_1 and V_1, and it is precisely how the oblivious transfer protocol works, but we expect this to be computationally infeasible for both, even on a quantum computer. The only other way is to cheat and submit points U', V' that do not form a basis of $E'[2^n]$, thus limiting the possible values of $x_i U' + y_i V'$. In our protocol, Alice can easily detect if Bob does that and abort the communication if necessary; in any case she should always perform this safety check (step 4) before going any further.

For the supersingular isogeny version of the Wu–Zhang–Wang protocol, we can see that its security relies on the hardness of the analog of the one-more exponentiation problem.

One-more isogeny computational problem (1MICP)

Let E_0 and E_1 be two supersingular elliptic curves defined over $\mathbb{F}_{p^2}$. Let (U_0, V_0), resp. (U_1, V_1), be a basis of $E_0[2^n]$, resp. $E_1[2^n]$. Finally, let a be a random element of $\mathbb{Z}/2^n\mathbb{Z}$.

- Bob submits a supersingular elliptic curve of his choice E', together with a basis (U', V') of $E'[2^n]$ and a basis (P', Q') of $E'[3^m]$ to an oracle;
- the oracle outputs $E'' \simeq E'/\langle U' + aV' \rangle$, as well as the points $\phi'(P'), \phi'(Q')$, where ϕ' is the isogeny $E' \rightarrow E''$;
- then Bob must produce $E_0/\langle U_0 + aV_0 \rangle$ and $E_1/\langle U_1 + aV_1 \rangle$.

As with 2-inv-CSSIP, there is a clear reduction from this problem to the CSSI problem, but no obvious reduction to the SSCDH problem. Interestingly, in this supersingular isogeny setting the decisional version of this problem is not easy, as was the case in the group setting (we do not give its full definition, but it follows the same distinguishability game as 2-inv-DSSIP). Indeed, because of the lack of a group law, it is difficult for Bob to submit an elliptic curve E' that is related to both E_0 and E_1. Actually, if Bob can find such a curve E' isogenous both to

E_0 and E_1, then he can find an isogeny between E_0 and E_1; but this is supposed to be a quantum-hard problem. Consequently, and under reasonable hardness assumptions, the supersingular isogeny version of the Wu–Zhang–Wang protocol can offer a semantically secure oblivious transfer if coupled with an IND-CPA encryption scheme; this was not the case for the group-based protocol.

4.3   Security Overview in the CSIDH Setting

The security of our OT protocols in the CSIDH setting against a malicious receiver relies on the intractability of the corresponding versions of the above problems. While the decisional and computational forms of the One-more-isogeny problem seem as secure as in the SIDH setting, this is no longer the case for the 2-inverse problem.

Indeed, let E be a supersingular curve defined over $\mathbb{F}_p$, $[\mathfrak{a}]$ an element of the ideal class group of $End_{\mathbb{F}_p}(E)$, and $E' = [\mathfrak{a}] * E$. If E^t and E'^t stand for the quadratic twists of E and E', it holds that $E'^t = [\mathfrak{a}]^{-1} * E^t$. While this observation is used in [8] to speed up computations, it implies that the computational 2-inverse problem can be trivially solved in the CSIDH setting by answering $(E^t, ([\mathfrak{a}] * E)^t, ([\mathfrak{b}] * E)^t)$ to a challenge $(E, [\mathfrak{a}] * E, [\mathfrak{b}] * E)$. Thus the new OT protocol cannot be secure against a malicious receiver. For an honest-but-curious receiver, however, breaking the protocol amounts to solving the CSIDH version of the Diffie-Hellman problem, which is still considered hard.

5   Conclusion

We have studied in this article two Diffie–Hellman based oblivious transfer protocols: a rewriting of the 2003 scheme of Wu, Zhang and Wang, and an entirely new one. Besides their simplicity, their main advantage is that they give rise to post-quantum, supersingular isogeny based protocols; they can also be instantiated on fast Kummer surfaces. To the best of our knowledge, these are the only existing OT protocols with these features.

Our analysis introduces a new definition of semantic security for OT schemes, as well as several non-standard versions of the (SI)DH problem. We believe these problems to be intractable in general, and have given arguments in that direction; but obviously, further investigation by the cryptographic community is needed.

As importantly, we hope to have demonstrated the importance of being exponentiation-only for discrete-log based schemes. Finding such a simple DLP-based signature protocol is an open problem; this would provide a practical signature protocol for isogeny-based cryptography, which is currently lacking.

Acknowledgments. This work has been supported in part by the European Union's H2020 Programme under grant agreement number ERC-669891. The author would like to thank Luca de Feo, Charles Bouillaguet, Damien Vergnaud and Antoine Joux for their helpful discussions, and anonymous referees for their relevant remarks and for pointing us the article of Wu, Zhang and Wang.

References

1. Bao, F., Deng, R.H., Zhu, H.F.: Variations of Diffie-Hellman problem. In: Qing, S., Gollmann, D., Zhou, J. (eds.) ICICS 2003. LNCS, vol. 2836, pp. 301–312. Springer, Heidelberg (2003). https://doi.org/10.1007/978-3-540-39927-8_28
2. Barreto, P., Oliveira, G., Benits, W.: Supersingular isogeny oblivious transfer. Cryptology ePrint Archive, Report 2018/459 (2018). https://eprint.iacr.org/2018/459
3. Beaver, D.: Precomputing oblivious transfer. In: Coppersmith, D. (ed.) CRYPTO 1995. LNCS, vol. 963, pp. 97–109. Springer, Heidelberg (1995). https://doi.org/10.1007/3-540-44750-4_8
4. Bellare, M., Micali, S.: Non-interactive oblivious transfer and applications. In: Brassard, G. (ed.) CRYPTO 1989. LNCS, vol. 435, pp. 547–557. Springer, New York (1990). https://doi.org/10.1007/0-387-34805-0_48
5. Bernstein, D.J., Chuengsatiansup, C., Lange, T., Schwabe, P.: Kummer strikes back: new DH speed records. In: Sarkar, P., Iwata, T. (eds.) ASIACRYPT 2014. LNCS, vol. 8873, pp. 317–337. Springer, Heidelberg (2014). https://doi.org/10.1007/978-3-662-45611-8_17
6. Biehl, I., Meyer, B., Müller, V.: Differential fault attacks on elliptic curve cryptosystems. In: Bellare, M. (ed.) CRYPTO 2000. LNCS, vol. 1880, pp. 131–146. Springer, Heidelberg (2000). https://doi.org/10.1007/3-540-44598-6_8
7. Camenisch, J., Neven, G., Shelat, A.: Simulatable adaptive oblivious transfer. In: Naor, M. (ed.) EUROCRYPT 2007. LNCS, vol. 4515, pp. 573–590. Springer, Heidelberg (2007). https://doi.org/10.1007/978-3-540-72540-4_33
8. Castryck, W., Lange, T., Martindale, C., Panny, L., Renes, J.: CSIDH: an efficient post-quantum commutative group action. In: Peyrin, T., Galbraith, S. (eds.) ASIACRYPT 2018. LNCS, vol. 11274, pp. 395–427. Springer, Cham (2018). https://doi.org/10.1007/978-3-030-03332-3_15
9. Childs, A., Jao, D., Soukharev, V.: Constructing elliptic curve isogenies in quantum subexponential time. J. Math. Cryptol. 8(1), 1–29 (2014)
10. Chou, T., Orlandi, C.: The simplest protocol for oblivious transfer. In: Lauter, K., Rodríguez-Henríquez, F. (eds.) LATINCRYPT 2015. LNCS, vol. 9230, pp. 40–58. Springer, Cham (2015). https://doi.org/10.1007/978-3-319-22174-8_3
11. Couveignes, J.-M.: Hard homogeneous spaces. Cryptology ePrint Archive, Report 2006/291 (2006). https://eprint.iacr.org/2006/291
12. De Feo, L., Jao, D., Plût, J.: Towards quantum-resistant cryptosystems from supersingular elliptic curve isogenies. J. Math. Cryptol. 8(3), 209–247 (2014)
13. Delpech de Saint Guilhem, C., Orsini, E., Petit, C., Smart, N.P.: Secure oblivious transfer from semi-commutative masking. Cryptology ePrint Archive, Report 2018/648 (2018). https://eprint.iacr.org/2018/648
14. Even, S., Goldreich, O., Lempel, A.: A randomized protocol for signing contracts. In: Advances in cryptology–CRYPTO 1982. Plenum Press, New York (1983)
15. Kazmi, R.A.: Cryptography from post-quantum assumptions. Cryptology ePrint Archive, Report 2015/376 (2015). https://eprint.iacr.org/2015/376
16. Kilian, J.: Founding cryptography on oblivious transfer. In: Proceedings of the Twentieth Annual ACM Symposium on Theory of Computing–STOC 1988, pp. 20–31. ACM (1988)
17. Naor, M., Pinkas, B.: Efficient oblivious transfer protocols. In: Proceedings of the 12th Annual ACM-SIAM Symposium on Discrete Algorithms (SODA 2001), pp. 448–457. SIAM, ACM (2001)

18. Naor, M., Pinkas, B.: Computationally secure oblivious transfer. J. Cryptology **18**(1), 1–35 (2005)
19. Peikert, C., Vaikuntanathan, V., Waters, B.: A framework for efficient and composable oblivious transfer. In: Wagner, D. (ed.) CRYPTO 2008. LNCS, vol. 5157, pp. 554–571. Springer, Heidelberg (2008). https://doi.org/10.1007/978-3-540-85174-5_31
20. Petit, C.: Faster algorithms for isogeny problems using torsion point images. In: Takagi, T., Peyrin, T. (eds.) ASIACRYPT 2017. LNCS, vol. 10625, pp. 330–353. Springer, Cham (2017). https://doi.org/10.1007/978-3-319-70697-9_12
21. Rabin, M.O.: How to exchange secrets by Oblivious Transfer. Technical report TR-81. Harvard Aiken Computation Laboratory (1981)
22. Renes, J., Schwabe, P., Smith, B., Batina, L.: μKummer: efficient hyperelliptic signatures and key exchange on microcontrollers. In: Gierlichs, B., Poschmann, A.Y. (eds.) CHES 2016. LNCS, vol. 9813, pp. 301–320. Springer, Heidelberg (2016). https://doi.org/10.1007/978-3-662-53140-2_15
23. Rostovtsev, A., Stolbunov, A.: Public-key cryptosystem based on isogenies. Cryptology ePrint Archive, Report 2006/145 (2006). https://eprint.iacr.org/2006/145
24. Stolbunov, A.: Constructing public-key cryptographic schemes based on class group action on a set of isogenous elliptic curves. Adv. Math. Commun. **4**(2), 215–235 (2010)
25. Tani, S.: Claw finding algorithms using quantum walk. Theoret. Comput. Sci. **410**(50), 5285–5297 (2009)
26. Urbanik, D., Jao,D.: SoK: the problem landscape of SIDH. In: Proceedings of the 5th ACM on ASIA Public-Key Cryptography Workshop – APKC 2018, pp. 53–60. ACM, New York (2018)
27. Wu, Q.-H., Zhang, J.-H., Wang, Y.-M.: Practical t-out-n oblivious transfer and its applications. In: Qing, S., Gollmann, D., Zhou, J. (eds.) ICICS 2003. LNCS, vol. 2836, pp. 226–237. Springer, Heidelberg (2003). https://doi.org/10.1007/978-3-540-39927-8_21

An IND-CCA-Secure Code-Based Encryption Scheme Using Rank Metric

Hamad Al Shehhi[1], Emanuele Bellini[1], Filipe Borba[2], Florian Caullery[1], Marc Manzano[1], and Victor Mateu[1(✉)]

[1] Darkmatter LLC, Abu Dhabi, United Arab Emirates
{hamad.alshehhi,emanuele.bellini,florian.caullery,marcos.manzano,
victor.mateu}@darkmatter.ae
[2] Universidade Federal de Santa Catarina, Florianópolis, Brazil
filipeoborba@gmail.com

Abstract. The use of rank instead of Hamming metric has been proposed to address the main drawback of code-based cryptography: large key sizes. There exist several Key Encapsulation Mechanisms (KEM) and Public Key Encryption (PKE) schemes using rank metric including some submissions to the NIST call for standardization of Post-Quantum Cryptography. In this work, we present an IND-CCA PKE scheme based on the McEliece adaptation to rank metric proposed by Loidreau at PQC 2017. This IND-CCA PKE scheme based on rank metric does not use a hybrid construction KEM + symmetric encryption. Instead, we take advantage of the bigger message space obtained by the different parameters chosen in rank metric, being able to exchange multiple keys in one ciphertext. Our proposal is designed considering some specific properties of the random error generated during the encryption. We prove our proposal IND-CCA-secure in the QROM by using a security notion called disjoint simulatability introduced by Saito et al. in Eurocrypt 2018. Moreover, we provide security bounds by using the semi-oracles introduced by Ambainis et al.

Keywords: Post Quantum Cryptography ·
Code-based cryptography · Rank metric · IND-CCA · PKE · QROM

1 Introduction

The use of standard public key cryptography algorithms such as RSA and ECDH has been a model to secure information in the last decades. However, in the past few years, the threat of a quantum computer breaking the security of all the standard public key cryptosystems in feasible time has forced the community to look for quantum resistant cryptographic schemes which can be implemented on traditional electronic computers. This field of research is called Post-Quantum Cryptography (PQC) [5]. The NIST call for proposals [21] has increased the motivation of the research community towards this topic. By the time of writing, some proposals were withdrawn from the competition as some major flaws

© Springer Nature Switzerland AG 2019
J. Buchmann et al. (Eds.): AFRICACRYPT 2019, LNCS 11627, pp. 79–96, 2019.
https://doi.org/10.1007/978-3-030-23696-0_5

were discovered on their security. Some others had to modify their initial parameters to keep meeting the security requirements from NIST. This was caused by either a misconception on the security of some problems or by new attacks being presented. These challenges were expected given that the security assumptions on which these schemes rely are often not as well understood as the previous standard ones (e.g., discrete logarithm and integer factorization).

In 2017, a proposal from Loidreau [17] and its implementation [1], which is not part of the NIST competition, was presented. The scheme is a modification of the McEliece cryptosystem [18] using rank instead of Hamming metric. The advantage of which relies on the fact that the complexity of decoding with random codes in this metric is quadratic compared to the complexity of decoding in the Hamming metric. Therefore, code-based cryptosystems using rank metric require smaller key sizes. The first cryptosystem based on this metric was proposed by Gabidulin, Paramonov and Tretjakov (GPT) [12] and it used Gabidulin codes. It was broken by the Overbeck attack framework [23]. This attack on the GPT encryption scheme is able to, given a public key G, forge an alternative Gabidulin code able to decrypt the ciphertexts encrypted using G. To do this, it exploits the fact that the column scrambler matrix used to compute the public key in order to hide the structure of the private Gabidulin code is a matrix of elements over the base field $\mathbb{F}_q$. In Loidreau's scheme, this matrix is replaced by another one having coefficients in a random vectorial subset. That adaptation is enough to prevent Overbeck's attack framework.

Nowadays, many cryptographic protocols require to use a IND-CCA-secure cryptosystem in order to protect the privacy of the participants involved in it. Unfortunately, Loidreau's original proposal and its implementation [1] do not offer IND-CCA security, which implies no protection against malleability. Therefore, it cannot be used in many practical cases. The concept of ciphertext malleability was first introduced by Dolev et al. [9], and nowadays it is known that non-malleability against chosen ciphertext attacks is equivalent to IND-CCA-security. Furthermore, several techniques to turn a IND-CPA-secure cryptosystem into an IND-CCA-secure one have been presented. One of the most used solutions to turn an IND-CPA PKE scheme into a IND-CCA KEM is the Fujisaki-Okamoto transformation [10].

1.1   Our Contribution

In this paper we propose an IND-CCA-secure variant of Loidreau's rank based PKE scheme. We present a construction inspired by ideas from recent transformation techniques [10,15,24] used to obtain IND-CCA KEM, or the hybrid PKE construction using symmetric key. However, in our case the target is a non-hybrid PKE scheme with a message space large enough to fit more than just one symmetric key. Our construction takes advantage of the bigger error space from rank metric and uses it as a random value required for the decryption validations. As a result, the proposed decryption algorithm does not require any encryption operation. We prove the IND-CCA security of our proposal in the QROM with a security proof based on previous works by Nojima et al., [22] and Saito, Xagawa and Yamakawa [24] from which we borrow the central notion of *Disjoint Simulatability*.

Besides the theoretical description of the PKE scheme, we also prove our scheme suitable for real world scenarios by presenting new parameters and a performance comparison with the original implementation of Loidreau's scheme given in [1].

1.2 Structure

In the next section we recall some definitions needed to understand Loidreau's scheme and our modification such as *rank metric* and *Gabidulin codes* or the security requirements IND-CPA and IND-CCA. After that, we recall the original scheme in Sect. 3 and, in Sect. 4, we propose a new IND-CCA-secure PKE scheme and three parameter sets for different security levels. Section 5 is devoted to proving our proposal IND-CCA-secure in the QROM. Moreover, the performance of new algorithms and a comparison with the original ones and the resulting algorithms from applying SXY [24] transformation is provided in Sect. 5.2. Finally, Sect. 6 is devoted to the conclusions.

2 Preliminaries and Notations

We denote by $\mathbb{F}_{q^m}$ the finite field of q^m elements and by $\mathbb{F}_{q^m}^n$ the vectorial space of dimension n over the field $\mathbb{F}_{q^m}$. We denote by $GL_n(\mathbb{F}_q)$ the set of all invertible square matrices of n rows and n columns with elements in $\mathbb{F}_q$. Besides that, in the algorithms we use $a \leftarrow_\$ B$ to note that a is a random element from B.

Let $e = (e_1, \ldots, e_n) \in \mathbb{F}_{q^m}^n$. The rank weight of a vector e is denoted as $\mathsf{rk}(e)$, and is defined as the rank of the matrix

$$E = \begin{pmatrix} e_{1,1} & \cdots & e_{n,1} \\ e_{1,2} & \cdots & e_{n,2} \\ \vdots & \ddots & \vdots \\ e_{1,m} & \cdots & e_{n,m} \end{pmatrix}$$

where $e_{i,j}$ is the j-th component of e_i seen as a vector over $\mathbb{F}_q$. The rank weight of a vector was introduced by Gabidulin in [11] to propose the error correcting codes defined below which can correct errors with repeating patterns, regardless of their Hamming weight.

Definition 1 (Gabidulin codes). *Let $k < n \leq m$ be non-negative integers and let $g = (g_1, \ldots, g_n) \in \mathbb{F}_{q^m}$ be linearly independent over $\mathbb{F}_q$. Let $[i] = q^i$ such that $x \to x^{[i]}$ is the i-th power of the Frobenius automorphism $x \to x^q$. Given the generator matrix*

$$G = \begin{pmatrix} g_1 & \cdots & g_n \\ g_1^{[1]} & \cdots & g_n^{[1]} \\ \vdots & \ddots & \vdots \\ g_1^{[k-1]} & \cdots & g_n^{[k-1]} \end{pmatrix}.$$

a Gabidulin code is defined as

$$Gab_{k,n}(g) = \{xG \mid x \in \mathbb{F}_{q^m}^k\}.$$

Gabidulin Codes are the rank-metric equivalent of Reed Solomon Codes. These codes can correct errors of rank weight up to $\lfloor (n-k)/2 \rfloor$ in polynomial-time where k is the code dimension and n the code length [11].

2.1 Decisional Rank Syndrome Decoding (DRSD) Problem

Code-based cryptography using rank metric generally relies on the hardness of Rank Syndrome Decoding problem (RSD). In our security proof we use the decisional version of this problem to prove some properties of our proposal. Let us recall the definition.

Definition 2 (DRSD Problem). *Given G a full rank $k \times n$ matrix over $\mathbb{F}_{q^m}$, $x \in \mathbb{F}_{q^m}^k$, and $e \in \mathbb{F}_{q^m}^n$. Considering y a random value in $\mathbb{F}_{q^m}^n$, is it feasible to distinguish $(G, xG + e)$ from (G, y)?*

The hardness of the DRSD problem is proven in [13, Apendix B.2]

2.2 Hash Functions

In our constructions, we use two different kinds of hash functions. One is the classical hash that we use for correctness, and the other is a hash function with a rather large output which will be obtained by using an eXtended Output Function (XOF). An XOF is a hash function whose output can be extended to an arbitrary desired length. A requirement for our XOF and hash function is to be secure against any quantum computer-aided attack. Fortunately, the SHA-3 and SHAKE as defined in [20] are proved to be secure in such attack scenarios [8].

2.3 Public-Key Encryption

A public-key encryption scheme $\mathsf{PKE} = (\mathsf{KGen}, \mathsf{Enc}, \mathsf{Dec})$ is defined by three algorithms. The key generation algorithm KGen receives as input a security parameter and outputs a keypair $(\mathsf{pk}, \mathsf{sk})$. The encryption algorithm Enc takes as input a public key pk and a message x from a finite message space M, and outputs a ciphertext $c \in \mathcal{C}$ where $\mathcal{C}$ is the ciphertext space and c is the encryption of the message m with the public key pk. The decryption algorithm Dec takes as input a secret key sk and a ciphertext $c \in \mathcal{C}$, and outputs a message $x \in M$ or a rejection symbol $\perp \notin M$.

Definition 3 (Perfect correctness). *A PKE scheme $\mathsf{PKE} = (\mathsf{KGen}, \mathsf{Enc}, \mathsf{Dec})$ has perfect correctness if for any keypair $(\mathsf{pk}, \mathsf{sk})$ generated by KGen and for any message $x \in M$*

$$\Pr[\mathsf{Dec}_{\mathsf{sk}}(c) = x \mid c \leftarrow \mathsf{Enc}_{\mathsf{pk}}(x)] = 1$$

2.4   IND-CPA and IND-CCA notions

We finally recall, following [4], the definitions of security notions for indistinguishability under chosen plaintext attack (IND-CPA) and indistinguishability under chosen ciphertext attack (IND-CCA) for PKE schemes.

Definition 4 *Let $E = (\mathsf{KGen}, \mathsf{Enc}, \mathsf{Dec})$ be an encryption scheme. Let $\mathcal{A} = (\mathcal{A}_1, \mathcal{A}_2)$ be an adversary, i.e. a pair of probabilistic polynomial time algorithms responsible, respectively, to generate a pair of messages given the public key and access to an oracle, and a guess on which of the two messages has been encrypted given access to the encryption of one of the two messages and to another oracle[1]. Let $\mathrm{atk} \in \{\mathrm{cpa}, \mathrm{cca}\}$ and $\lambda \in \mathbb{N}$. For $b \in \{0,1\}$, consider the atk indistinguishability experiment defined by the following steps:*

$$
\begin{array}{ll}
\multicolumn{2}{l}{\mathrm{Exp}_{E,\mathcal{A}}^{\mathrm{ind-atk-}b}(\lambda)} \\
\hline
1: & (\mathsf{pk}, \mathsf{sk}) \leftarrow_{\$} \mathsf{KGen}(\lambda) \\
2: & (x_0, x_1, s) \leftarrow \mathcal{A}_1^{O_1(.)}(\mathsf{pk}) \\
3: & y \leftarrow \mathsf{Enc}_{\mathsf{pk}}(x_b) \\
4: & b' \leftarrow \mathcal{A}_2^{O_2(.)}(x_0, x_1, s, y) \\
5: & \textbf{return } b'
\end{array}
$$

where, if $\mathrm{atk} = \mathrm{cpa}$, the oracles functions $O_1(.)$ and $O_2(.)$ return the empty string, and if $\mathrm{atk} = \mathrm{cca}$, the oracles functions $O_1(.) = O_2(.) = \mathsf{Dec}_{\mathsf{sk}}(.)$. Then, the $\mathrm{ind - atk}$ *advantage of $\mathcal{A}$ over the encryption scheme is defined as*

$$
\mathsf{Adv}_{E,\mathcal{A}}^{\mathrm{ind-atk}}(\lambda) = \Pr\left[\mathrm{Exp}_{E,\mathcal{A}}^{\mathrm{ind-atk-}1}(\lambda) = 1\right] - \Pr\left[\mathrm{Exp}_{E,\mathcal{A}}^{\mathrm{ind-atk-}0}(\lambda) = 1\right].
$$

A PKE scheme is secure against atk attack *if* $\mathsf{Adv}_{E,\mathcal{A}}^{\mathrm{ind-atk}}(\lambda)$ *is a negligible function of the security parameter λ.*

Informally, we consider a PKE scheme to be *secure against chosen-ciphertext attack* if a "reasonable" adversary cannot obtain "significant" advantage in distinguishing the cases $b = 0$ and $b = 1$ given access to the oracles, where reasonable reflects its resources usage. Still informally, the main difference between the two types of attacks consist in which oracle the adversary can access and when. In the IND-CPA game, the adversary has no access to the decryption oracle. However, in the IND-CCA game, the adversary has access to the decryption oracle. There exists two notions of IND-CCA security: IND-CCA1 security refers to the situation when the adversary can access the decryption oracle only before seeing the challenge ciphertext, while in the IND-CCA2 setting the adversary can access the decryption oracle even after seeing the challenge ciphertext, with the obvious constraint that he cannot ask the oracle to decrypt the challenge y. In this paper, when we refer to IND-CCA security, we mean IND-CCA2.

---

[1] The idea is that $\mathcal{A}_1$, once given the public key, is responsible to generate a test instance composed by two messages of its choice, while $\mathcal{A}_2$ receives a challenge ciphertext generated as a probabilistic function of the test instance, and must output a guess of which of the two messages has been encrypted.

2.5   Quantum Random Oracle Model (QROM)

It is common to provide security analysis in the Random Oracle Model (ROM). However, this model has been proven [6] not to be accurate when the attackers have access to a quantum computer. To deal with this case, a new model was defined. In this model, an adversary can quantumly query a random oracle. Therefore, some well-known techniques that were applied on the ROM, such as adaptive programmability or extractability, cannot be used in the QROM.

In the security proofs presented hereby we are going to use the notion of semi-classical oracles. This concept was recently introduced in [2] with the idea of allowing a quantum-accessible oracle to somehow measure the input and output. With this concept, the authors provided better bounds for some well-known problems resulting from the One-way to Hide (O2H) lemmas.

3   Loidreau's Proposal

Loidreau's scheme chooses a randomly selected vector space of $\mathbb{F}_2^m$ of fixed dimension to scramble the codes. The idea can be interpreted as replacing the permutation matrix in a McEliece-like cryptosystem by a matrix multiplying the Hamming weight of the vectors.

Let us recall the original scheme $\mathrm{PKE}_{Lo} = (\mathsf{KGen}, \mathsf{Enc}, \mathsf{Dec})$ as defined in [17]:

$\mathsf{KGen}(1^\lambda)$	$\mathsf{Enc}_{pk}(x)$	$\mathsf{Dec}_{sk}(y)$
$k, n, m, \delta, t \leftarrow \mathrm{ParamSelect}(1^\lambda)$	$t \leftarrow \lfloor (n-k)/(2\delta) \rfloor$	$(x, e) \leftarrow \mathrm{decode}_{sk}(yP)$
$G \leftarrow \mathrm{GenGabCode}(k, n, m)$	$e \leftarrow_\$ \{z \in \mathbb{F}_{2^m}^n \mid \mathsf{rk}(z) = t\}$	**if** $(x, e) = \bot$
$S \leftarrow_\$ GL_k(\mathbb{F}_{2^m})$	$y \leftarrow xG_{pub} + e$	**return** $\bot$
$V \leftarrow_\$ \{\mathcal{V} \subset \mathbb{F}_{2^m} \mid \dim(\mathcal{V}) = \delta\}$	**return** y	**else**
$P \leftarrow_\$ GL_n(V)$		**return** x
return $\mathsf{sk} = (G, S, P),$		
$\qquad \mathsf{pk} = G_{pub} = SGP^{-1}$		

More precisely, in KGen algorithm, given a security parameter 1^λ the function $\mathrm{ParamSelect}(1^\lambda)$ provides appropriate values for k, n, m, δ, and t. After that, the function $\mathrm{GenGabCode}(k, n, m)$ randomly generates the generator matrix of a Gabidulin code as defined in Sect. 2. Then, S, V, and P are generated and the keypair is computed and returned.

In Dec algorithm, the function $\mathrm{decode}_{sk}(yP)$ performs the decoding operation to recover xS and eP, from which it is easy to obtain (x, e) by using S^{-1} and P^{-1}. In the case of a decoding failure this function would return $\bot$.

It is worth noticing that matrix P is chosen so that it has all its entries in a vectorial subspace of dimension δ, then $\mathsf{rk}(eP) \leq \delta\mathsf{rk}(e) \leq \lfloor \frac{n-k}{2} \rfloor$ (see [17, Prop. 1]) which is decodable by the Gabidulin code.

The proof of correctness of the cryptosystem is based on the rank multiplication property, the same one used to show that the Low Rank Parity Check (LRPC) codes decoding procedure works.

4 Our Proposal

Loidreau's scheme is One Way Encryption (OWE) as defined in [17]. It has the property that given a ciphertext it is hard to obtain the plaintext. However, it does not achieve IND-CPA security (and therefore not IND-CCA security either) which is a security notion often required on real-world scenarios and also the weakest security notion required in the NIST call for standardization of PQC [21].

In this section we propose a new scheme which we will prove IND-CCA-secure. The main idea is to use the randomly generated error from Loidreau's encryption scheme for multiple purposes:

1. As a source of randomness to generate a value to mask the codeword.
2. As the error used to hide the resulting codeword.
3. As a random parameter for a correctness validation during decryption.

Usually, in transformations such as Fujiaki-Okamoto, this validation is done in the decryption algorithm by re-computing the ciphertext given all the parameters obtained after decoding. Yet, in our proposal the correctness validation does not require the re-encryption using the public key.

Our PKE scheme $\text{PKE}_{new} = (\text{KGen}, \text{Enc}', \text{Dec}')$ maintains the same key generation algorithm so it does not add any new parameter. For the remaining two algorithms we need two additional functions H and H'. The first one is an XOF function, and the other is hash function, as introduced in Sect. 2.2. The PKE_{new} algorithms are presented below:

$\text{KGen}(1^\lambda)$	$\text{Enc}'_{pk}(x)$	$\text{Dec}'_{sk}(y)$
$k, n, m, \delta \leftarrow \text{ParamSelect}(1^\lambda)$	$t \leftarrow \lfloor (n-k)/(2\delta) \rfloor$	$(x', e') \leftarrow decode_{sk}(yP)$
$G \leftarrow \text{GenGabCode}(k, n, m)$	$e \leftarrow_\$ \{z \in \mathbb{F}_{2^m}^n \mid \text{rk}(z) = t\}$	**if** $(x', e') = \perp$
$S \leftarrow_\$ GL_k(\mathbb{F}_{2^m})$	$x^* \leftarrow x \| H'(e, x)$	**return** $\perp$
$V \leftarrow_\$ \{\mathcal{V} \subset \mathbb{F}_{2^m} \mid \dim(\mathcal{V}) = \delta\}$	$y \leftarrow (x^* + H(e))G_{pub} + e$	**else**
$P \leftarrow_\$ GL_n(V)$	**return** y	$x \| v = x' + H(e')$
return $\text{sk} = (G, S, P),$		**if** $H'(e', x) \neq v$ and
$\quad \text{pk} = G_{pub} = SGP^{-1}$		$\text{rk}(e') \neq t$
		return $\perp$
		else
		return x

Notice that the confirmation hash (i.e. $H'(e, x)$) must be of a size that accommodates the desired security level. Otherwise, the security level of the scheme would be reduced to the security of finding a pre-image in H'. In practice, this causes a reduction in the message space because of the padding required. Fortunately, there exist sets of parameters that allow a bigger message space which can accommodate this restriction easily.

The security bounds of the scheme are different than the ones presented in the original proposal [17]. We consider the newly proposed algorithm for solving the rank syndrome decoding problem from Aragon et al. [3]. However, the complexity of finding a decoder given a public key remain the same as originally published.

- Decoding a ciphertext in the public code corresponds to the complexity of solving Bounded Distance binary Rank decoding (BDR) problem which is NP-hard. In this setting, the decoding complexity for a classical computer in terms of binary operations is equal to

$$(n - k)^3 m^3 2^{\frac{t(k+1)m}{n} - m}.$$

However, the amount of operations required for a quantum computer is

$$(n - k)^3 m^3 2^{\frac{1}{2}(\frac{t(k+1)m}{n} - m)}.$$

- The complexity of finding a proper decoder given a public key G_{pub} is

$$2^{(\delta-1)m - (\delta-1)^2}.$$

- The complexity of distinguishing the public code from a random code is lower bounded by the complexity of recovering a proper decoder from a public key G_{pub}.

In [7], it is shown that a polynomial attack can be applied if $\delta = 2$ and $k \geq n/2$. The authors also claim that the attack can probably be applied more generally when $k/n \geq 1 - 1/\delta$.

Next, we propose a parameter set to provide three different security levels taking into consideration the message space and the known attacks to Loidreau's scheme [17], including [3] and [7]. In Table 1 the parameter set is presented as well as the resulting public key size (PK Size) in Kilo-bytes and message space in bytes. The table also includes the complexity of known attacks to the cryptosystem for the chosen parameters. These attacks are decoding a ciphertext in the public code, noted as *Dec. Cplx.* for traditional electronic computers, or as *Quantum Dec. Cplx.* for quantum computers, and finding a proper decoder given a public key, noted as *PK Dec. Cplx.*

Table 1. Proposed parameters for our IND-CCA-secure scheme

m	n	k	δ	t	PK size	Message Space	Dec. Cplx	Quantum Dec. Cplx	PK Dec. Cplx
64	58	28	3	5	6.56 KB	224B	2^{129}	2^{81}	2^{124}
96	62	32	3	5	11.25 KB	384B	2^{194}	2^{116}	2^{188}
128	64	28	3	6	15.75 KB	448B	2^{256}	2^{146}	2^{252}

5 Security

IND-CCA security is required for several applications in which the protocol security relies on this indistinguishability notion to protect the messages. Numerous works have proposed mechanisms to go from one construction with weaker security to another one meeting IND-CCA. In our security proof we take into consideration the concept of disjoint simulatability introduced in [24, Section 3] which helps on proving a Deterministic PKE (DPKE) to behave like a pseudorandom number generator. First, we recall the definition:

Definition 5 (Disjoint Simulatability). *Let $\mathcal{D}_M$ denote an efficiently sampleable distribution on a set M. A DPKE scheme* DPKE = (KGen, Enc, Dec), *with plaintext and ciphertext spaces M and C is $\mathcal{D}_M$-disjoint simulatable if it provides the following two properties:*

- *Statistical Disjointness: there exists a Probabilistic Polynomial Time (PPT) algorithm S such that:*

$$Disj_{DPKE,S}(\lambda) := \max_{(\mathsf{sk},\mathsf{pk}) \leftarrow \mathsf{KGen}(1^\lambda)} \Pr\left[c \in \mathsf{Enc}_{\mathsf{pk}}(M) | c \leftarrow S(\mathsf{pk})\right]$$

is negligible.
- *Ciphertext Indistinguishability: for any PPT adversary A there exists a PPT algorithm S such that:*

$$Adv_{DPKE,\mathcal{D}_M,A,S} := \left| \Pr\left[A(\mathsf{pk},c^\star) \to 1 \middle| \begin{array}{c} (\mathsf{sk},\mathsf{pk}) \leftarrow \mathsf{KGen}(1^\lambda), m^\star \leftarrow \mathcal{D}_M; \\ c^\star \leftarrow \mathsf{Enc}_{\mathsf{pk}}(m^\star) \end{array}\right] \right.$$
$$\left. - \Pr\left[A(\mathsf{pk},c^\star) \to 1 | (\mathsf{sk},\mathsf{pk}) \leftarrow \mathsf{KGen}(1^\lambda), c^\star \leftarrow S(\mathsf{pk})\right] \right|$$

is negligible.

Our proposal as defined in Sect. 4 is not a DPKE. The first step required is to make it deterministic by simply adding the error e as an input to the encryption algorithm, precisely defining $DPKE_{new} = (\mathsf{KGen}, \mathsf{Enc}'', \mathsf{Dec}'')$ as follows:

$\mathsf{KGen}(1^\lambda)$	$\mathsf{Enc}''_{\mathsf{pk}}(x,e)$	$\mathsf{Dec}''_{\mathsf{sk}}(y)$
$k,n,m,\delta,t \leftarrow \mathsf{ParamSelect}(1^\lambda)$	$x^* \leftarrow x\|H'(e,x)$	$(x',e') \leftarrow decode_{\mathsf{sk}}(yP)$
$G \leftarrow \mathsf{GenGabCode}(k,n,m)$	$y \leftarrow (x^* + H(e))G_{pub} + e$	if $(x',e') = \perp$
$S \leftarrow_{\$} GL_k(\mathbb{F}_{2^m})$	**return** y	**return** $\perp$
$V \leftarrow_{\$} \{\mathcal{V} \subset \mathbb{F}_{2^m} | \dim(\mathcal{V}) = \delta\}$		**else**
$P \leftarrow_{\$} GL_n(V)$		$x\|v = x' + H(e')$
return $\mathsf{sk} = (G,S,P),$		if $H'(e',x) \neq v$ and
$\qquad \mathsf{pk} = G_{pub} = SGP^{-1}$		$rk(e') \neq t$
		return $\perp$
		else
		return (x,e')

Now we assume the error received as input in the encryption function is of rank t, and the *ParamSelect* function chooses as defined before: $t = \lfloor (n-k)/(2\delta) \rfloor$.

Theorem 1. *The DPKE scheme* $\text{DPKE}_{new} = (\text{KGen}, \text{Enc}'', \text{Dec}'')$, *with message space* M *and ciphertext space* C, *is* $\mathcal{D}_M$-*disjoint simulatable.*

Proof (Theorem 1). From [24, Lemma 3.1], it is sufficient to prove sparseness and pseudorandomness. The first property is proved by showing the following value

$$\text{Sparse}_{\text{DPKE}} := \max_{(\text{sk},\text{pk}) \leftarrow \text{KGen}()} \frac{|\text{Enc}_{\text{pk}}(M)|}{|C|} \tag{1}$$

to be negligible. In order to show that, lets denote by E the set of vectors of rank weight less than or equal to t in $\mathbb{F}_{2^m}^n$. Every component e_i of a vector $e \in E$ is a vector of a vectorial subspace of $V \subset \mathbb{F}_2^m$ of dimension t. The number of vectorial subspaces of $\mathbb{F}_2^m$ of dimension t is $\prod_{i=0}^{t-1}(2^m - 2^i)/(2^t - 2^i)$. We now have 2^t choices for each of the n components of e. Thus, we deduce that

$$|E| = 2^{tn} \prod_{i=0}^{t-1} \frac{2^m - 2^i}{2^t - 2^i}.$$

The code generated by G_{pub} possesses 2^{km} different codewords. Hence,

$$|\text{Enc}_{\text{pk}}(M)| = 2^{km+tn} \prod_{i=0}^{t-1} \frac{2^m - 2^i}{2^t - 2^i}.$$

Notice that encryptions with an error of rank less than t are included in this computation of $|\text{Enc}_{\text{pk}}(M)|$. These errors are not part of the encrypted ciphertext space, but it simplifies the computation and gives a sufficient upper bound. Finally, it is easy to see that $|C| = 2^{nm}$, therefore

$$\text{Sparse}_{\text{DPKE}} \leq 2^{n(t-m)+km} \prod_{i=0}^{t-1} \frac{2^m - 2^i}{2^t - 2^i}.$$

Considering the parameter sets provided in Table 1 we obtain the upper bound $\text{Sparse}_{\text{DPKE}} < 2^{-1436}$, which is negligible.

To prove the second part of the claim, pseudorandomness, we need to prove that we can see a ciphertext as a random value. First, let us exhibit a probability distribution from which an error $e \in \mathbb{F}_{2^m}^n$ of a given rank $t > 0$ can be sampled. One way to construct such an e is: sample t vectors $b_1, \ldots, b_t \in \mathbb{F}_2^m$ uniformly at random and draw n different sets of coefficients $\gamma_{1,i}, \ldots, \gamma_{t,i} \in \mathbb{F}_2, i \in \{1, \ldots, n\}$, all equally likely to be 0 or 1. Then we define e as

$$e = (\gamma_{1,1}b_1 + \ldots + \gamma_{t,1}b_t, \ldots, \gamma_{1,n}b_1 + \ldots + \gamma_{1,n}b_t).$$

Note that e is simply given by scalar multiplications and linear combinations of random variables following the uniform distribution over $\mathbb{F}_{2^m}$ (for the b_is) or over $\{0,1\}$ (the $\gamma_{i,j}$). Hence, e can be efficiently sampled by a combination of those distributions which we will denote by $\mathcal{E}_t^n$.

From the discussion above, we can observe that, for $e \leftarrow \mathcal{E}_t^n$, $\mathrm{rk}(e) \leq t$. The case where $\mathrm{rk}(e) < t$ corresponds to the fact that $b_1, \ldots, b_t$ does not form a basis of the vector space of $\mathbb{F}_2^t$. That is, $b_{i+1} \in \mathrm{span}(b_1, \ldots, b_i)$, for some $i < t$. Then, the probability of $\mathrm{rk}(e) < t$ is bounded above by $1/2^m + \ldots + 2^{t-1}/2^m = 2^{t-1}/2^m$. That probability is negligible given that $m \gg t$, which is the case for the set of parameters of our scheme (at maximum 2^{-59}).

Now, we can proceed with the following transformation:

- We can replace $c = xG_{pub} + e$ by $c = xG' + e$ where G' is a random $k \times n$ matrix over $\mathbb{F}_{2^m}$ because of the complexity of distinguishing the public code from a random code makes it unfeasible for a PPT adversary.
- We replace e with a random e' following the distribution described above.
- Now we can replace c by a random vector assuming the hardness of DRSD.$\square$

Lemma 1. *The public-key encryption scheme* $\mathrm{DPKE}_{new} = (\mathsf{KGen}, \mathsf{Enc}'', \mathsf{Dec}'')$ *with message space M and ciphertext space $\mathcal{C}$ has perfect correctness.*

Proof. Let us assume

$$\exists c \in \mathcal{C} \mid c = \mathsf{Enc}''_{pk}(x, e) \wedge c = \mathsf{Enc}''_{pk}(x', e') \wedge (x \neq x' \vee e \neq e').$$

We can see $c = x_c G_{pub} + e$ where $x_c = \mathcal{F}(x, e) = (x \| H'(e, x)) + H(e)$. Given that decoding is a deterministic function where $decode_{sk}(c) = (x_c, e)$, then the values x_c and e are fixed for ciphertext c. Therefore, if such c exists, it means that $\exists x_c \in \mathbb{F}_{2^m}^k \mid x_c = \mathcal{F}(x, e) \wedge x_c = \mathcal{F}(x', e)$. Given that function $\mathcal{F}(x, e)$, as presented above, have, as leftmost bits, x XORed with $H(e)$, it is not possible for the output to be the same value when it receives the inputs (x, e) and (x', e) unless $x = x'$. Hence, the claim follows. $\square$

As a last note, in the decryption algorithm we check that $\mathrm{rk}(e')$ equals t or not, in order to avoid possible decryption failures who might cause reaction attacks.

5.1   Security Proof

In order to demonstrate our proposal to be IND-CCA-secure we use game-hopping proof technique. The first step for us is to define $\mathrm{Game}_0^{\mathcal{A}}(1^\lambda)$ by copying the description of the experiment $\mathrm{Exp}_{E,\mathcal{A}}^{\mathrm{ind-atk}-b}(\lambda)$ where atk = cca. Apart from it, we add the encryption and decryption algorithms from PKE_{new}, defined in Sect. 4, which are used by the challenger to respond adversary queries $\mathcal{A}^{\mathsf{Enc}'_{pk}(\cdot)}(x_b)$, $\mathcal{A}_1^{\mathsf{Dec}'_{sk}(\cdot)}(\mathrm{pk})$, and $\mathcal{A}_2^{\mathsf{Dec}'_{sk}(\cdot)}(x_0, x_1, s, y)$.

$\mathrm{Game}_0^{\mathcal{A}}(1^\lambda)$	$\mathsf{Enc}'_{\mathsf{pk}}(x)$	$\mathsf{Dec}'_{\mathsf{sk}}(y)$
$(\mathsf{pk},\mathsf{sk}) \leftarrow_\$ \mathsf{KGen}(1^\lambda)$	$e \leftarrow_\$ \{z \in \mathbb{F}_{2^m}^n | \mathsf{rk}(z)=t\}$	$(x',e') \leftarrow decode_{\mathsf{sk}}(yP)$
$(x_0,x_1) \leftarrow \mathcal{A}_1^{\mathsf{Dec}'_{\mathsf{sk}}(\cdot)}(\mathsf{pk})$	$x^* = x||H'(e,x)$	if $(x',e') = \perp$
$y \leftarrow \mathcal{A}^{\mathsf{Enc}'_{\mathsf{pk}}(\cdot)}(x_b)$	$y \leftarrow (x^* + H(e))G_{pub} + e$	return $\perp$
$b' \leftarrow \mathcal{A}_2^{\mathsf{Dec}'_{\mathsf{sk}}(\cdot)}(x_0,x_1,y)$		else
return b'		$x||v = x' + H(e')$
		if $H'(e',x) \neq v$ and
		$\mathsf{rk}(e') \neq t$
		return $\perp$
		else
		return x

The transition from $\mathrm{Game}_0^{\mathcal{A}}$ to $\mathrm{Game}_1^{\mathcal{A}}$ is basically a modification to show how Enc' and Dec' use Enc'' and Dec'' from the DPKE_{new}.

$\mathrm{Game}_1^{\mathcal{A}}(1^\lambda)$	$\mathsf{Enc}'_{\mathsf{pk}}(x)$	$\mathsf{Dec}'_{\mathsf{sk}}(y)$
$(\mathsf{pk},\mathsf{sk}) \leftarrow_\$ \mathsf{KGen}(1^\lambda)$	$e \leftarrow_\$ \{z \in \mathbb{F}_{2^m}^n | \mathsf{rk}(z)=t\}$	$(x',e') \leftarrow \mathsf{Dec}''_{\mathsf{sk}}(y)$
$(x_0,x_1) \leftarrow \mathcal{A}_1^{\mathsf{Dec}'_{\mathsf{sk}}(\cdot)}(\mathsf{pk})$	$y \leftarrow \mathsf{Enc}''_{\mathsf{pk}}(x,e)$	if $(x',e') \neq \perp$
$y \leftarrow \mathcal{A}^{\mathsf{Enc}'_{\mathsf{pk}}(\cdot)}(x_b)$		return x'
$b' \leftarrow \mathcal{A}_2^{\mathsf{Dec}'_{\mathsf{sk}}(\cdot)}(x_0,x_1,y)$		else
return b'		return $\perp$

$\mathrm{Game}_1^{\mathcal{A}}$ is the same as $\mathrm{Game}_2^{\mathcal{A}}$ except that

$\mathrm{Game}_2^{\mathcal{A}}(1^\lambda)$	$\mathsf{Enc}'_{\mathsf{pk}}(x)$	$\mathsf{Dec}'_{\mathsf{sk}}(y)$
$(\mathsf{pk},\mathsf{sk}) \leftarrow_\$ \mathsf{KGen}(1^\lambda)$	$e \leftarrow_\$ \{z \in \mathbb{F}_{2^m}^n | \mathsf{rk}(z)=t\}$	$(x',e') \leftarrow \mathsf{Dec}''_{\mathsf{sk}}(y)$
$(x_0,x_1) \leftarrow \mathcal{A}_1^{\mathsf{Dec}'_{\mathsf{sk}}(\cdot)}(\mathsf{pk})$	$y \leftarrow \mathsf{Enc}''_{\mathsf{pk}}(x,e)$	if $y = \mathsf{Enc}''_{\mathsf{pk}}(x',e')$
$y \leftarrow \mathcal{A}^{\mathsf{Enc}'_{\mathsf{pk}}(\cdot)}(x_b)$		return x'
$b' \leftarrow \mathcal{A}_2^{\mathsf{Dec}'_{\mathsf{sk}}(\cdot)}(x_0,x_1,y)$		else
return b'		return $\perp$

The transition from $\mathrm{Game}_2^{\mathcal{A}}$ to $\mathrm{Game}_3^{\mathcal{A}}$ consists on changing the interaction from the challenger $\mathcal{A}^{\mathsf{Enc}'_{\mathsf{pk}}(\cdot)}(x_b)$ for a random value in $\mathbb{F}_{2^m}^n$.

$\mathrm{Game}_3^{\mathcal{A}}(1^\lambda)$	$\mathsf{Enc}_{\mathsf{pk}}(x)$	$\mathsf{Dec}_{\mathsf{sk}}(y)$
$(\mathsf{pk},\mathsf{sk}) \leftarrow_\$ \mathsf{KGen}(1^\lambda)$	$e \leftarrow_\$ \{z \in \mathbb{F}_{2^m}^n | \mathsf{rk}(z)=t\}$	$(x',e') \leftarrow \mathsf{Dec}''_{\mathsf{sk}}(y)$
$(x_0,x_1,s) \leftarrow \mathcal{A}_1^{\mathsf{Dec}_{\mathsf{sk}}(\cdot)}(\mathsf{pk})$	$y \leftarrow \mathsf{Enc}''_{\mathsf{pk}}(x,e)$	if $y = \mathsf{Enc}''_{\mathsf{pk}}(x',e')$
$y \leftarrow_\$ \mathbb{F}_{2^m}^n$		return x'
$b' \leftarrow \mathcal{A}_2^{\mathsf{Dec}_{\mathsf{sk}}(\cdot)}(x_0,x_1,s,y)$		else
return b'		return $\perp$

Lemma 2. *The transition from $Game_0$ to $Game_1$ has*

$$\Pr[Game_0 = 1] = \Pr[Game_1 = 1]$$

Proof. The operations in Enc' algorithm are the same in both games. In the case of Dec', it uses the same operations but validates the information more times. Hence, the probability remains the same. □

Lemma 3. *The transition from $Game_1$ to $Game_2$ has*

$$\Pr[Game_1 = 1] = \Pr[Game_2 = 1]$$

Proof. Given that $DPKE_{new} = (\mathsf{KGen}, \mathsf{Enc}'', \mathsf{Dec}'')$ has perfect correctness, as proved in Lemma 1, checking if $(x', e') \neq \bot$ would have exactly the same result as checking if $y = \mathsf{Enc}''_{\mathsf{pk}}(x', e')$. Therefore, the probability remains the same. □

Lemma 4. *The adversary $\mathcal{A}$ would not be able to distinguish if she is playing in $Game_2$ or in $Game_3$ and*

$$\mathsf{Adv}^{game_3}_{PKE_{new},\mathcal{A}}(\lambda) = \mathsf{Adv}^{game_2}_{PKE_{new},\mathcal{A}}(\lambda) + Disj_{DPKE,S}(\lambda)$$

Proof. Given that $DPKE_{new} = (\mathsf{KGen}, \mathsf{Enc}'', \mathsf{Dec}'')$ with message space M is $\mathcal{D}_M$-disjoint simulatable as proved in Lemma 1, the encryption algorithm can be seen as a pseudorandom generator receiving as input $x \in M$ and $e \in E$. Given that $|M| \approx 2^{(k-2)m}$ and $|E| > 2^{661}$, the adversary $\mathcal{A}$ would not be able to distinguish if the oracle $\mathsf{Enc}'_{\mathsf{pk}}(.)$ retrieves $y = \mathsf{Enc}'_{\mathsf{pk}}(x_b)$ or $y \leftarrow_{\$} C$. Therefore, the additional advantage from the previous game is based on the probability of distinguishing between a valid and an invalid ciphertext which is $Disj_{DPKE,S}(\lambda)$. □

If an adversary is not able to distinguish between a random value and the result of the encryption algorithm, this basically means that regardless of the cleartext, the adversary does not learn anything from a ciphertext, not even if it is a proper encryption or not. However, there exist other attacks able to retrieve information from a code and, in these cases, adversary capabilities define the advantage to succeed in the IND-CCA experiment.

Theorem 2 (Security in the ROM). *Given the PKE scheme $DPKE_{new}$, for any IND-CCA adversary $\mathcal{A}$ without quantum capabilities*

$$\Pr\left[\mathsf{Exp}^{IND\text{-}CCA}_{PKE_{new},\mathcal{A}}(\lambda) = 1\right] \approx \frac{1}{2},$$

where $\mathsf{Exp}^{IND\text{-}CCA}_{PKE_{new},\mathcal{A}}(\lambda) = 1$ is the event in which $b' = b$.

Proof. As we have already seen, $\mathcal{A}$ could not distinguish between $\mathsf{Exp}^{IND\text{-}CCA}_{E,\mathcal{A}}(\lambda)$ and $Game_3$. This means

$$\Pr\left[\mathsf{Exp}^{IND\text{-}CCA}_{PKE_{new},\mathcal{A}}(\lambda) = 1\right] = \frac{1}{2} + \mathsf{Adv}^{Game_3}_{PKE_{new},\mathcal{A}}(\lambda)$$

where
$$\text{Adv}^{\text{game}_3}_{PKE_{new},\mathcal{A}}(\lambda) = \text{Adv}^{\text{game}_2}_{PKE_{new},\mathcal{A}}(\lambda) + \text{Disj}_{\text{DPKE},S}(\lambda).$$

Given the security parameters defined in Sect. 4 we have that, for the lowest security parameters, the best algorithm to obtain the cleartext without knowledge of sk has complexity 2^{124}. Therefore

$$\text{Adv}^{\text{game}_2}_{PKE_{new},\mathcal{A}}(\lambda) = 2^{-124}.$$

Hence,
$$\Pr\left[\text{Exp}^{\text{IND-CCA}}_{PKE_{new},\mathcal{A}}(\lambda) = 1\right] = \frac{1}{2} + 2^{-124} + 2^{-1436} \approx \frac{1}{2}$$

□

In order to provide proper bounds for a quantum adversary with access to semi-oracles as defined in [2], we need to recall the lemma for searching in an unstructured function [2, Lemma 2] based on the original O2H lemma [25] from Unruh.

Lemma 5 (Search in unstructured function). *Let H be a random function, drawn from a distribution such that $\Pr[H(x) = 1] \leq \lambda$ for all x. Let $\mathcal{B}$ be a q-query adversary with query depth d. Then*

$$\Pr\left[H(x) = 1 | b \leftarrow \mathcal{B}^{H()}\right] \leq 4(d+2)(q+1)\lambda.$$

The proof of this lemma is in [2, Section 4.1].

Theorem 3 (Security in the QROM). *Given the PKE scheme DPKE_{new}, for any IND-CCA q-query adversary $\mathcal{A}$ with query depth d and access to a quantum oracle*
$$\Pr\left[\text{Exp}^{\text{IND-CCA}}_{PKE_{new},\mathcal{A}}(\lambda) = 1\right] \approx \frac{1}{2},$$
where $\text{Exp}^{\text{IND-CCA}}_{PKE_{new},\mathcal{A}}(\lambda) = 1$ is the event in which $b' = b$.

Proof. As in the previous theorem, we first have that by indistinguishability from $\mathcal{A}$ perspective
$$\Pr\left[\text{Exp}^{\text{IND-CCA}}_{PKE_{new},\mathcal{A}}(\lambda) = 1\right] = \frac{1}{2} + \text{Adv}^{\text{game}_3}_{PKE_{new},\mathcal{A}}(\lambda)$$

where
$$\text{Adv}^{Game_3}_{PKE_{new},\mathcal{A}}(\lambda) = \text{Adv}^{Game_2}_{PKE_{new},\mathcal{A}}(\lambda) + \text{Disj}_{\text{DPKE},S}(\lambda).$$

Given that $\mathcal{A}$ now have access to a quantum oracle, then her advantage is given by the hardness of solving the BDR problem. As stated in Sect. 4 the minimum security level would achieve 78bits of security. Moreover, from the previous Lemma 5 we can also bound the probability of finding x from $\text{Enc}''_{\text{pk}}(x, e)$ because the encryption function can be seen as a pseudorandom number generator. So, given that x_0 and x_1 are fixed, the adversary would have a bound defined by

$$\Pr\left[\mathsf{Enc}'_{pk}(x_0, e) = y \mid y \leftarrow \mathcal{A}^{\mathsf{Enc}'()}\right] \leq 4(d+2)(q+1)2^{-661}.$$

Notice that, we consider only x_0 option and try to find a proper error. If it is not found, then the plaintext message would be x_1. Therefore, we have

$$\mathrm{Adv}^{Game_2}_{PKE_{new}, \mathcal{A}}(\lambda) \leq 2^{-78} + 4(d+2)(q+1)2^{-661}.$$

Hence,

$$\Pr\left[\mathrm{Exp}^{\mathrm{IND\text{-}CCA}}_{PKE_{new}, \mathcal{A}}(\lambda) = 1\right] = \frac{1}{2} + 2^{-78} + 2^{-1436} + 4(d+2)(q+1)2^{-661} \approx \frac{1}{2}$$

□

5.2   Performance and Comparison

We have implemented our IND-CCA-secure PKE scheme with the parameters of 128 bits of security. We use SHA-3-256 and SHAKE-128 implementations of the Open Quantum Safe project [19] for the functions H' and H respectively. All the tests have been run in a Macbook Pro with an Intel Core i7 processor at 2.9 Ghz. In Table 2, we compared the original implementation of [1] with both the original and the new parameters detailed in Sect. 4. This modification already provides a 50% increase on the amount of operations per second for encryption and a 100% for decryption. In the same table we also provide the performance information on our IND-CCA-secure version using our proposed parameters. We did not provide information about key generation as the algorithm has not been modified in our transformation.

Table 2. Performance comparison for 128 bits security against quantum attackers between original implementation, original implementation with our new parameters, and our IND-CCA proposal.

	[1]	[1] New params	Our proposal
Encryption	21587 ops/s	30478 ops/s	23619 ops/s
Decryption	1127 ops/s	2207 ops/s	2108 ops/s

Considering the same parameters for 128 bits of quantum security, the encryption operation is a bit slower than the non-IND-CCA-secure version. As a consequence, the number of encryptions per second are now reduced around 23%. This is because the encryption is a really fast operation, therefore, adding the computation of two hashes has a significant cost given that the rest of operations are a simple multiplication of two (small) matrices and several XOR operations.

On the other hand, the decryption is only affected by a 5% because the cost of the decryption operation is largely dominated by the decoding procedure so, the two hashes do not increase significantly the time taken by the operation.

Next, we would like to stress on the difference between our new scheme and the ones that could be obtained by using the generic transformation from OW-CPA to IND-CCA of [15] or from [24]. First, both transformations end up building an IND-CCA KEM instead of a PKE. These transformations require two extra hashes during the encapsulation and an additional re-encryption operation during the decapsulation. In the case of Loidreau's scheme, it would translate as a total of four extra hashes and a matrix multiplication for each encryption/decryption. Our scheme does not seem to need this additional matrix multiplication. Unfortunately, the available decoding algorithms for Gabidulin do not allow us to avoid this matrix multiplication. Indeed, the Welsh-Berlekamp [16] and Gao-like [26]) approaches directly output the message xS during the decryption procedure while the Berlekamp-Massey-like [14] algorithms outputs the error multiplied by the masking matrix eP. Hence, in both strategies, we have to compute a matrix multiplication to recover the original error which was added to the ciphertext during the encryption. Thus, the operations required for decryption in our scheme ended up having the same cost as in the generic transformations. However, this could change if a different decoding technique avoids these extra matrix multiplications.

Taking into consideration that our implementation is thread safe, and that we do not use the rest of the processors, these 23619 encryptions per second can easily be multiplied by 6. Therefore, the performance figures presented here make our scheme usable in practical applications. Moreover, our proposal can be used as a KEM like most of the proposals for NIST competition, but it can also be used for other purposes where the larger message space would allow to encrypt something bigger than just a key for each ciphertext. In fact, the message space is big enough to embed a few ciphertext from elliptic curve cryptography, and use our proposed scheme as a protection against quantum attacks. This way, many keys could be distributed using only one post quantum encryption.

6   Conclusions

We have presented an IND-CCA-secure version of Loidreau's public key encryption scheme. This proposal is usable for encrypting large messages as it can encrypt plaintexts of size 224, 384 or 448 bytes for a corresponding level of security of 128, 192 and 256 bits. Our proposal presents a overhead of 23% in the computational cost for encryption when compared to the original Loidreau's scheme. Thus, the new cryptosystem is still practical. Moreover, the transformation in the decryption has a similar cost as other transformations such as Hofheniz et al. [15] or Saito et al. [24]. Nevertheless, in our case, the cost of the decryption might be reduced by using an alternative decoding method able to retrieve both the codeword and error without requiring an additional matrix multiplication. As it is, the security proof relies on some properties which are specific for the Loidreau's scheme. Though, it is likely that our transformation might be adapted or generalized to other post-quantum schemes, even in different settings, such as lattices. We leave this generalization as a future work.

References

1. Al Abdouli, A., et al.: Drankula, a McEliece-like rank metric based cryptosystem implementation. In: Proceedings of the 15th International Joint Conference on e-Business and Telecommunications, ICETE 2018, vol. 2, SECRYPT, pp. 230–241 (2018)
2. Ambainis, A., Hamburg, M., Unruh, D.: Quantum security proofs using semi-classical oracles. Cryptology ePrint Archive, Report 2018/904 (2018). https://eprint.iacr.org/2018/904
3. Aragon, N., Gaborit, P., Hauteville, A., Tillich, J.: A new algorithm for solving the rank syndrome decoding problem. In: IEEE International Symposium on Information Theory, ISIT, pp. 2421–2425 (2018)
4. Bellare, M., Desai, A., Pointcheval, D., Rogaway, P.: Relations among notions of security for public-key encryption schemes. In: Krawczyk, H. (ed.) CRYPTO 1998. LNCS, vol. 1462, pp. 26–45. Springer, Heidelberg (1998). https://doi.org/10.1007/BFb0055718
5. Bernstein, D.J., Buchmann, J., Dahmen, E.: Post Quantum Cryptography, 1st edn. Springer, Heidelberg (2008)
6. Boneh, D., Dagdelen, Ö., Fischlin, M., Lehmann, A., Schaffner, C., Zhandry, M.: Random oracles in a quantum world. In: Lee, D.H., Wang, X. (eds.) ASIACRYPT 2011. LNCS, vol. 7073, pp. 41–69. Springer, Heidelberg (2011). https://doi.org/10.1007/978-3-642-25385-0_3
7. Coggia, D., Couvreur, A.: On the security of a Loidreau's rank metric code based encryption scheme. arXiv preprint arXiv:1903.02933 (2019)
8. Czajkowski, J., Groot Bruinderink, L., Hülsing, A., Schaffner, C., Unruh, D.: Post-quantum security of the sponge construction. In: Lange, T., Steinwandt, R. (eds.) PQCrypto 2018. LNCS, vol. 10786, pp. 185–204. Springer, Cham (2018). https://doi.org/10.1007/978-3-319-79063-3_9
9. Dolev, D., Dwork, C., Naor, M.: Non-malleable cryptography (extended abstract). In: Proceedings of the 23rd Annual ACM Symposium on Theory of Computing, pp. 542–552 (1991)
10. Fujisaki, E., Okamoto, T.: Secure integration of asymmetric and symmetric encryption schemes. In: Wiener, M. (ed.) CRYPTO 1999. LNCS, vol. 1666, pp. 537–554. Springer, Heidelberg (1999). https://doi.org/10.1007/3-540-48405-1_34
11. Gabidulin, E.M.: Theory of codes with maximum rank distance. Probl. Inf. Transm. (English translation of Problemy Peredachi Informatsii) 21(1), 3–16 (1985)
12. Gabidulin, E.M., Paramonov, A.V., Tretjakov, O.V.: Ideals over a non-commutative ring and their application in cryptology. In: Davies, D.W. (ed.) EUROCRYPT 1991. LNCS, vol. 547, pp. 482–489. Springer, Heidelberg (1991). https://doi.org/10.1007/3-540-46416-6_41
13. Gaborit, P., Hauteville, A., Phan, D.H., Tillich, J.-P.: Identity-based encryption from codes with rank metric. In: Katz, J., Shacham, H. (eds.) CRYPTO 2017. LNCS, vol. 10403, pp. 194–224. Springer, Cham (2017). https://doi.org/10.1007/978-3-319-63697-9_7

14. Gadouleau, M., Yan, Z.: Complexity of decoding Gabidulin codes. In: 42nd Annual Conference on Information Sciences and Systems. CISS 2008, pp. 1081–1085 (2008)
15. Hofheinz, D., Hövelmanns, K., Kiltz, E.: A modular analysis of the fujisaki-okamoto transformation. In: Kalai, Y., Reyzin, L. (eds.) TCC 2017. LNCS, vol. 10677, pp. 341–371. Springer, Cham (2017). https://doi.org/10.1007/978-3-319-70500-2_12
16. Loidreau, P.: A welch–berlekamp like algorithm for decoding gabidulin codes. In: Ytrehus, Ø. (ed.) WCC 2005. LNCS, vol. 3969, pp. 36–45. Springer, Heidelberg (2006). https://doi.org/10.1007/11779360_4
17. Loidreau, P.: A new rank metric codes based encryption scheme. In: Lange, T., Takagi, T. (eds.) PQCrypto 2017. LNCS, vol. 10346, pp. 3–17. Springer, Cham (2017). https://doi.org/10.1007/978-3-319-59879-6_1
18. McEliece, R.J.: A public-key cryptosystem based on algebraic coding theory. The Deep Space Network Progress Report, pp. 114–116, January and February 1978
19. Mosca, M., Stebila, D.: Contributors: Open quantum safe (2017). https://openquantumsafe.org/
20. NIST: Federal inf. process. stds. (nist fips) - 202 (2015). https://dx.doi.org/10.6028/NIST.FIPS.202
21. NIST: Submission requirements and evaluation criteria for the post-quantum cryptography standardization process (2016). https://csrc.nist.gov/CSRC/media/Projects/Post-Quantum-Cryptography/documents/call-for-proposals-final-dec-2016.pdf
22. Nojima, R., Imai, H., Kobara, K., Morozov, K.: Semantic security for the McEliece cryptosystem without random oracles. Des. Codes Crypt. **49**(1–3), 289–305 (2008)
23. Overbeck, R.: Structural attacks for public-key cryptosystems based on Gabidulin codes. J. Cryptol. **21**(2), 280–301 (2008)
24. Saito, T., Xagawa, K., Yamakawa, T.: Tightly-secure key-encapsulation mechanism in the quantum random oracle model. In: Nielsen, J.B., Rijmen, V. (eds.) EUROCRYPT 2018. LNCS, vol. 10822, pp. 520–551. Springer, Cham (2018). https://doi.org/10.1007/978-3-319-78372-7_17
25. Unruh, D.: Revocable quantum timed-release encryption. J. ACM **62**(6), 46:1–46:76 (2015)
26. Wachter-Zeh, A.: Decoding of block and convolutional codes in rankmetric.Ph.D. thesis, Université Rennes 1 (2013). https://tel.archives-ouvertes.fr/tel-0105674

Zero-Knowledge

UC-Secure CRS Generation for SNARKs

Behzad Abdolmaleki[1], Karim Baghery[1], Helger Lipmaa[1], Janno Siim[1(✉)], and Michał Zając[2]

[1] University of Tartu, Tartu, Estonia
jannosiim@gmail.com
[2] Clearmatics, London, UK

Abstract. Zero-knowledge SNARKs (zk-SNARKs) have recently found various applications in verifiable computation and blockchain applications (Zerocash), but unfortunately they rely on a common reference string (CRS) that has to be generated by a trusted party. A standard suggestion, pursued by Ben Sasson et al. [IEEE S&P, 2015], is to generate CRS via a multi-party protocol. We enhance their CRS-generation protocol to achieve UC-security. This allows to safely compose the CRS-generation protocol with the zk-SNARK in a black-box manner with the insurance that the security of the zk-SNARK is not influenced. Differently from the previous work, the new CRS-generation protocol also avoids the random oracle model which is typically not required by zk-SNARKs themselves. As a case study, we apply the protocol to the state-of-the-art zk-SNARK by Groth [EUROCRYPT, 2016].

Keywords: CRS model · SNARK · Subversion-security · UC security

1 Introduction

A zero-knowledge argument is a cryptographic protocol between a prover and a verifier where the objective is to prove the validity of some statement while not leaking any other information. In particular, such an argument should be *sound* (it should be impossible to prove false statements) and *zero-knowledge* (the only leaked information should be the validity of the statement). Practical applications often require a non-interactive zero-knowledge (NIZK) argument where the prover outputs a single message which can be checked by many different verifiers.

Zero-knowledge succinct non-interactive arguments of knowledge (zk-SNARKs) are particularly efficient instantiations of NIZK, and have thus found numerous application ranging from verifiable computation [29] to privacy-preserving cryptocurrencies [5] and privacy-preserving smart contracts [25]. In most of such zk-SNARKs (see, e.g., [13,15,19,20,26,29]), the verifier's computation is dominated by a small number of exponentiations and pairings in a bilinear group, while the argument consists of a small number of group elements. Importantly, a zk-SNARK exists for any NP-language.

One drawback in the mentioned pairing-based zk-SNARKs is their reliance on the strong common reference string (CRS) model. It assumes that in the

© Springer Nature Switzerland AG 2019
J. Buchmann et al. (Eds.): AFRICACRYPT 2019, LNCS 11627, pp. 99–117, 2019.
https://doi.org/10.1007/978-3-030-23696-0_6

setup phase of the protocol a trusted party publishes a CRS, sampled from some specialized distribution, while not leaking any side information. Subverting the setup phase can make it easy to break the security, e.g., leaking a CRS trapdoor makes it trivial to prove false statements. This raises the obvious question of how to apply zk-SNARKs in practice without completely relying on a single trusted party. The issue is further amplified since in all of the mentioned zk-SNARKs, one has to generate a new CRS each time the relation changes.

Reducing trust on CRS generation is indeed a long-standing open question. Several different approaches for this are known, but each one has its own problems. Some recent papers [6,8,9] have proposed efficient CRS-generation multi-party computation protocols, where only 1 out of N_p parties has to be honest, for a large class of known zk-SNARKs (in fact, most of the efficient pairing-based zk-SNARKs belong to this class, possibly after the inclusion of a small number of new elements to their CRSs) for which the CRS can be computed by a fixed well-defined class $\mathcal{C}^S$ of circuits. Following [6], we will call this class of zk-SNARKs $\mathcal{C}^S$-*SNARKs*. However, the CRS-generation protocols of [6,8,9] have the following two weaknesses:

1. They are not secure in the universal composability (UC) setting [10]. Hence, they might not be secure while running in parallel with other protocols, as is often the case in real life scenarios. Moreover, some systems require a UC-secure NIZK [22,25], but up to now their CRS is still be generated in a standalone setting. We note that [6,9] do prove some form of simulatability but not for full UC-security. Protocol of [8] is for one specific zk-SNARK.
2. All use the random oracle model and [8,9] additionally use knowledge assumption. Non-falsifiable assumptions [28] (e.g., knowledge assumptions) and the random oracle model are controversial (in particular, the random oracle model is uninstantiable [12,17] and thus can only be thought of as a heuristic), and it is desirable to avoid them in situations where they are not known to circumvent impossibility results. Importantly, construction of zk-SNARKs under falsifiable assumptions is impossible [16] and hence they do rely on non-falsifiable assumptions but usually not on the random oracle model. Relying on the random oracle model in the setup phase means that the complete composed system (CRS-generation protocol + zk-SNARK) relies on both random oracle model and non-falsifiable assumptions. Hence, we end up depending on two undesirable assumptions rather than one.

Updatable CRS [21] is another recent solution to the problem. Essentially, this can be viewed as a single round MPC protocol where each party needs to participate just once in the CRS computation. Current zk-SNARKs in updatable CRS model [21,27] are still less efficient, than the state-of-the-art non-updatable counterparts like the zk-SNARK by Groth [20].

As a different approach, in order to minimize the trust of NIZKs in the setup phase, Bellare *et al.* [4] defined the notion of subversion-resistance, which guarantees that a security property (like soundness) holds even if the CRS generators are all malicious. As proven in [4], achieving subversion-soundness and (even non-subversion) zero knowledge at the same time is impossible for NIZK arguments.

On the other hand, one can construct subversion-zero knowledge (Sub-ZK) and sound NIZK arguments. Abdolmaleki *et al.* [2] showed how to design efficient Sub-ZK SNARKs: essentially, a zk-SNARK can be made Sub-ZK by constructing an efficient public CRS-verification algorithm CV that guarantees the well-formedness of its CRS. In particular, [2] did this for the most efficient known zk-SNARK by Groth [20] after inserting a small number of new elements to its CRS. Fuchsbauer [14] proved that Groth's zk-SNARK (with a slightly different simulation) is Sub-ZK even without changing its CRS.

Our Contributions. We propose a new UC-secure multi-party CRS-generation protocol for $\mathcal{C}^S$-SNARKs that crucially relies only on *falsifiable assumptions* and *does not require a random oracle*. Conceptually, the new protocol follows similar ideas as the protocol of [6], but it does not use any proofs of knowledge. Instead, we use a discrete logarithm extractable (DL-extractable) UC commitment functionality $\mathcal{F}_{\mathsf{dlmcom}}$ that was recently defined by Abdolmaleki *et al.* [1]. A DL-extractable commitment scheme allows to commit to a field element x and open to the group element g^x. Since $\mathcal{F}_{\mathsf{dlmcom}}$ takes x as an input, the committer must know x and thus x can be extracted by the UC-simulator. As we will show, this is sufficient to prove UC-security of the new CRS-generation protocol.

In addition, we show that the Sub-ZK SNARK of [2] is a Sub-ZK $\mathcal{C}^S$-SNARK after just adding some more elements to its CRS. We also improve the efficiency of the rest of the CRS-generation protocol by allowing different circuits for each group, considering special multiplication-division gates, and removing a number of NIZK proofs that are used in [6]. Like in the previous CRS-generation protocols [6,8,9], soundness and zero-knowledge will be guaranteed as long as 1 out of N_p parties participating in the CRS generation is honest. If SNARK is also Sub-ZK [2,14], then zero-knowledge is guaranteed even if all N_p parties are dishonest, given that the prover executes a public CRS verification algorithm.

Since it is impossible to construct UC commitments in the standard model [11], the new UC-secure CRS-generation protocol necessarily relies on some trust assumption. The DL-extractable commitment scheme of [1] is secure in the registered public key (RPK) model[1] that is a weaker trust model than the CRS model. However, we stay agnostic to the concrete implementation of $\mathcal{F}_{\mathsf{dlmcom}}$, proving the security of the CRS-generation protocol in the $\mathcal{F}_{\mathsf{dlmcom}}$-hybrid model. Thus, the trust assumption of the CRS-generation protocol is directly inherited from the trust assumption of the used DL-extractable commitment scheme. Constructing DL-extractable commitment schemes in a weaker model like the random string model or the multi-string model is an interesting open question. Note that CRS-s of known *efficient* $\mathcal{C}^S$-SNARKs, with a few exceptions, contain $\Omega(\mathsf{n})$ group elements, where n is the circuit size (e.g., in the last CRS generation of Zcash [5], $\mathsf{n} \approx 2\,000\,000^2$). Hence, even a relatively

---

[1] In the RPK model, each party registers his public key with an authority of his choosing. It is assumed that even authorities of untrusted parties are honest to the extent that they verify the knowledge (e.g., by using a standalone ZK proof) of the corresponding secret key.

[2] See https://www.zfnd.org/blog/conclusion-of-powers-of-tau/.

inefficient DL-extractable commitment scheme (that only has to be called once per CRS trapdoor) will not be the bottleneck in the CRS-generation protocol.

We proceed as follows. First, we describe an ideal functionality $\mathcal{F}_{\mathsf{mcrs}}$, an explicit multi-party version of the CRS generation functionality. Intuitively (the real functionality is slightly more complicated), first, N_p key-generators $\mathcal{G}_i$ send to $\mathcal{F}_{\mathsf{mcrs}}$ their shares of the trapdoors, s.t. the shares of the honest parties are guaranteed to be uniformly random. Second, $\mathcal{F}_{\mathsf{mcrs}}$ combines the shares to create the trapdoors and the CRS, and then sends the CRS to each $\mathcal{G}_i$.

We propose a protocol $\mathsf{K}_{\mathsf{mcrs}}$ that UC-realizes $\mathcal{F}_{\mathsf{mcrs}}$ in the $\mathcal{F}_{\mathsf{dlmcom}}$-hybrid model, i.e., assuming the availability of a UC-secure realization of $\mathcal{F}_{\mathsf{dlmcom}}$. In $\mathsf{K}_{\mathsf{mcrs}}$, the parties $\mathcal{G}_i$ first $\mathcal{F}_{\mathsf{dlmcom}}$-commit to their individual share of each trapdoor. After opening the commitments, $\mathcal{G}_i$ compute crs by combining their shares with a variation of the protocol from [6]. The structure of this part of the protocol makes it possible to publicly check that it was correctly followed.

Next, we prove that a $\mathcal{C}^{\mathsf{S}}$-SNARK that is complete, sound, and Sub-ZK in the CRS model is also complete, sound, and Sub-ZK in the $\mathcal{F}_{\mathsf{mcrs}}$-hybrid model. Sub-ZK holds even if all CRS creators were malicious, but for soundness we need at least one honest party. We then show that the Sub-ZK secure version [2,14] of the most efficient known zk-SNARK by Groth [20] remains sound and Sub-ZK if the CRS has been generated by using $\mathsf{K}_{\mathsf{mcrs}}$. The main technical issue here is that since Groth's zk-SNARK is not $\mathcal{C}^{\mathsf{S}}$-SNARK (see Sect. 3), we need to add some new elements to its CRS and then reprove its soundness against an adversary who is given access to the new CRS elements. We note that Bowe et al. [9] proposed a different modification of Groth's zk-SNARK together with a CRS-generation protocol, but under strong assumptions of random beacon model, random oracle model, and knowledge assumptions. Role of the commitment in their case is substituted with a random beacon which in particular means that they do not need to fix parties in the beginning of the protocol.

We constructed a UC-secure CRS-generation protocol $\mathsf{K}_{\mathsf{mcrs}}$ in the $\mathcal{F}_{\mathsf{dlmcom}}$-hybrid model for any $\mathcal{C}^{\mathsf{S}}$-SNARK and in particular proved that a small modification of Groth's zk-SNARK secure when composed with $\mathsf{K}_{\mathsf{mcrs}}$. Moreover, the resulting CRS-generation protocol is essentially as efficient as the prior protocols from [6,8,9]. However, (i) we proved the UC-security of the new CRS-generation protocol, and (ii) the new protocol is falsifiable, i.e., it does not require either the random oracle model or any knowledge assumption.

2   Preliminaries

Let PPT denote probabilistic polynomial-time. Let $\lambda \in \mathbb{N}$ be the information-theoretic security parameter, in practice, e.g., $\lambda = 128$. All adversaries will be stateful. For an algorithm $\mathcal{A}$, let $\mathsf{im}(\mathcal{A})$ be the image of $\mathcal{A}$, i.e., the set of valid outputs of $\mathcal{A}$, let $\mathsf{RND}(\mathcal{A})$ denote the random tape of $\mathcal{A}$, and let $r \leftarrow_{\$} \mathsf{RND}(\mathcal{A})$ denote sampling of a randomizer r of sufficient length for $\mathcal{A}$'s needs. By $y \leftarrow \mathcal{A}(x; r)$ we denote that $\mathcal{A}$, given an input x and a randomizer r, outputs y. We denote by $\mathsf{negl}(\lambda)$ an arbitrary negligible function, and by $\mathsf{poly}(\lambda)$ an arbitrary polynomial function. $A \approx_c B$ means that distributions A and B are computationally indistinguishable. We write $x \leftarrow_\$ \mathcal{D}$ if x is sampled according to distribution $\mathcal{D}$ or uniformly in case $\mathcal{D}$ is a set. By $\mathrm{Supp}(\mathcal{D})$ we denote the set of all elements in $\mathcal{D}$ that have non-zero probability.

Assume that $\mathcal{G}_i$ are different parties of a protocol. Following previous work [6], we will make the following assumptions about the network and the adversary. It is possible that the new protocols can be implemented in the asynchronous model but this is out of scope of the current paper.

Synchronicity Assumptions: We assume that the computation can be divided into clearly divided rounds. As it is well-known, synchronous computation can be simulated, assuming bounded delays and bounded time-drift. For the sake of simplicity, we omit formal treatment of UC-secure synchronous execution, see [23] for relevant background.

Authentication: We assume the existence of an authenticated broadcast between the parties. In particular, (i) if an honest party broadcasts a message, we assume that all parties (including, in the UC-setting, the simulator) receive it within some delay, and (ii) an honest party $\mathcal{G}_j$ accepts a message as coming from $\mathcal{G}_i$ only if it was sent by $\mathcal{G}_i$.

Covertness: We assume that an adversary in the multi-party protocols is covert, i.e., it will not produce outputs that will not pass public verification algorithms. In the protocols we write that honest parties will abort under such circumstances, but in the proofs we assume that adversary will not cause abortions.

For pairing-based groups we will use additive notation together with the bracket notation, i.e., in group $\mathbb{G}_\iota$, $[a]_\iota = a[1]_\iota$, where $[1]_\iota$ is a fixed generator of $\mathbb{G}_\iota$. A deterministic *bilinear group generator* $\mathsf{Pgen}(1^\lambda)$ returns $\mathsf{p} = (p, \mathbb{G}_1, \mathbb{G}_2, \mathbb{G}_T, \hat{e}, [1]_1, [1]_2)$, where p (a large prime) is the order of cyclic abelian groups $\mathbb{G}_1$, $\mathbb{G}_2$, and $\mathbb{G}_T$, and $\hat{e} : \mathbb{G}_1 \times \mathbb{G}_2 \to \mathbb{G}_T$ is an efficient non-degenerate bilinear pairing, s.t. $\hat{e}([a]_1, [b]_2) = [ab]_T$. Denote $[a]_1 \bullet [b]_2 = \hat{e}([a]_1, [b]_2)$; this extends to vectors in a natural way. Occasionally we write $[a]_\iota \bullet [b]_{3-\iota}$ for $\iota \in \{1, 2\}$ and ignore the fact that for $\iota = 2$ it should be written $[b]_{3-\iota} \bullet [a]_\iota$. Let $[a]_\star := ([a]_1, [a]_2)$. As in [4], we will implicitly assume that p is generated deterministically from λ; in particular, the choice of p cannot be subverted.

UC Security. We work in the standard universal composability framework of Canetti [10] with static corruptions of parties. The UC framework defines a PPT environment machine $\mathcal{Z}$ that oversees the execution of a protocol in one of two worlds. The "ideal world" execution involves "dummy parties" (some of whom may be corrupted by an ideal adversary/simulator Sim) interacting with a functionality $\mathcal{F}$. The "real world" execution involves PPT parties (some of whom may be corrupted by a PPT real world adversary $\mathcal{A}$) interacting only with each other in some protocol π. We refer to [10] for a detailed description of the executions, and a definition of the real world ensemble $\mathsf{EXEC}_{\pi,\mathcal{A},\mathcal{Z}}$ and the ideal world ensemble $\mathsf{IDEAL}_{\mathcal{F},\mathsf{Sim}^\mathcal{A},\mathcal{Z}}$. A protocol π *UC-securely computes* $\mathcal{F}$ if there exists a PPT Sim such that for every non-uniform PPT $\mathcal{Z}$ and PPT $\mathcal{A}$, $\{\mathsf{IDEAL}_{\mathcal{F},\mathsf{Sim}^\mathcal{A},\mathcal{Z}}(\lambda, x)\}_{\lambda \in \mathbb{N}, x \in \{0,1\}^*} \approx_c \{\mathsf{EXEC}_{\pi,\mathcal{A},\mathcal{Z}}(\lambda, x)\}_{\lambda \in \mathbb{N}, x \in \{0,1\}^*}$.

The importance of this definition is a composition theorem that states that any protocol that is universally composable is secure when run concurrently with many other arbitrary protocols; see [10] for discussions and definitions.

CRS Functionality. The CRS model UC functionality $\mathcal{F}_{crs}^{\mathcal{D},f}$ parameterized by a distribution $\mathcal{D}$ and a function f intuitively works as follows. Functionality samples a trapdoor tc from $\mathcal{D}$, computes crs $= f(\text{tc})$, and stores crs after a confirmation from the simulator. Subsequently on each retrieval query $(\texttt{retrieve}, \text{sid})$ it responds by sending $(\texttt{CRS}, \text{sid}, \text{crs})$. For full details see Fig. 1.

$\mathcal{F}_{crs}^{\mathcal{D},f}$ is parametrized by a distribution $\mathcal{D}$ and a function f. It proceeds as follows, running with parties $\mathcal{G}_i$ and an adversary Sim.

CRS generation: Sample tc $\leftarrow_\$ \mathcal{D}$; Set crs $\leftarrow f(\text{tc})$; Send $(\texttt{crsOK?}, \text{sid}, \text{crs})$ to Sim; If Sim returns $(\texttt{crsOK}, \text{sid})$ then store (sid, crs).

Retrieval: upon receiving $(\texttt{retrieve}, \text{sid})$ from $\mathcal{G}_i$: If (sid, crs) is recorded for some crs then send $(\texttt{CRS}, \text{sid}, \text{crs})$ to $\mathcal{G}_i$. Otherwise, ignore the message.

Fig. 1. Functionality $\mathcal{F}_{crs}^{\mathcal{D},f}$

DL-extractable UC Commitment. Abdolmaleki et al. [1] recently proposed a discrete logarithm extractable (DL-extractable) UC-commitment scheme. Differently from the usual UC-commitment, a committer will open the commitment to $[m]_1$, but the functionality also guarantees that the committer knows x. Hence, in the UC security proof it is possible to extract the discrete logarithm of $[m]_1$. Formally, the ideal functionality $\mathcal{F}_{\text{dlmcom}}$ takes m as a commitment input (hence the user must know m), but on open signal only reveals $[m]_1$. See Fig. 2. We refer to [1] for a known implementation of $\mathcal{F}_{\text{dlmcom}}$ in the RPK model.

$\mathcal{F}_{\text{dlmcom}}$, parametrized by $\mathcal{M} = \mathbb{Z}_p$ and group $\mathbb{G}_\iota$, interacts with $\mathcal{G}_1, \ldots, \mathcal{G}_{N_p}$ as follows.

- Upon receiving $(\texttt{commit}, \text{sid}, \text{cid}, \mathcal{G}_i, \mathcal{G}_j, m)$ from $\mathcal{G}_i$, where $m \in \mathbb{Z}_p$: if a tuple $(\text{sid}, \text{cid}, \cdots)$ with the same (sid, cid) was previously recorded, do nothing. Otherwise, record $(\text{sid}, \text{cid}, \mathcal{G}_i, \mathcal{G}_j, m)$ and send $(\texttt{rcpt}, \text{sid}, \text{cid}, \mathcal{G}_i, \mathcal{G}_j)$ to $\mathcal{G}_j$ and Sim.
- Upon receiving $(\texttt{open}, \text{sid}, \text{cid})$ from $\mathcal{G}_i$, proceed as follows: if a tuple $(\text{sid}, \text{cid}, \mathcal{G}_i, \mathcal{G}_j, m)$ was previously recorded then send $(\texttt{open}, \text{sid}, \text{cid}, \mathcal{G}_i, \mathcal{G}_j, y \leftarrow [m]_\iota)$ to $\mathcal{G}_j$ and Sim. Otherwise do nothing.

Fig. 2. Functionality $\mathcal{F}_{\text{dlmcom}}$ for $\iota \in \{1, 2\}$

Non-interactive Zero-Knowledge. Let $\mathcal{R}$ be a relation generator, such that $\mathcal{R}(1^\lambda)$ returns a polynomial-time decidable binary relation $\mathbf{R} = \{(x, w)\}$. Here, x is the statement and w is the witness. We assume that λ is explicitly deducible from the description of $\mathbf{R}$. The relation generator also outputs auxiliary information $\xi_{\mathbf{R}}$ that will be given to the honest parties and the adversary. As in [2,20], $\xi_{\mathbf{R}}$ is the value returned by $\mathsf{Pgen}(1^{\lambda})$. Because of this, we also give $\xi_{\mathbf{R}}$ as an input to the honest parties; if needed, one can include an additional auxiliary input to the adversary. Let $\mathbf{L_R} = \{x : \exists w, (x, w) \in \mathbf{R}\}$ be an **NP**-language.

A (subversion-resistant) *non-interactive zero-knowledge argument system* [2] Ψ for $\mathcal{R}$ consists of six PPT algorithms:

CRS trapdoor generator: $\mathsf{K_{tc}}$ is a PPT algorithm that, given $(\mathbf{R}, \xi_{\mathbf{R}}) \in \mathrm{im}(\mathcal{R}(1^{\lambda}))$, outputs a *CRS trapdoor* tc. Otherwise, it outputs $\perp$.

CRS generator: $\mathsf{K_{crs}}$ is a *deterministic* algorithm that, given $(\mathbf{R}, \xi_{\mathbf{R}}, \mathsf{tc})$, where $(\mathbf{R}, \xi_{\mathbf{R}}) \in \mathrm{im}(\mathcal{R}(1^{\lambda}))$ and $\mathsf{tc} \in \mathrm{im}(\mathsf{K_{tc}}(\mathbf{R}, \xi_{\mathbf{R}})) \setminus \{\perp\}$, outputs crs. Otherwise, it outputs $\perp$. We distinguish three parts of crs: $\mathsf{crs_P}$ (needed by the prover), $\mathsf{crs_V}$ (needed by the verifier), and $\mathsf{crs_{CV}}$ (needed by CV algorithm).

CRS verifier: CV is a PPT algorithm that, given $(\mathbf{R}, \xi_{\mathbf{R}}, \mathsf{crs})$, returns either 0 (the CRS is ill-formed) or 1 (the CRS is well-formed).

Prover: P is a PPT algorithm that, given $(\mathbf{R}, \xi_{\mathbf{R}}, \mathsf{crs_P}, x, w)$, where $(x, w) \in \mathbf{R}$, outputs an argument π. Otherwise, it outputs $\perp$.

Verifier: V is a PPT algorithm that, given $(\mathbf{R}, \xi_{\mathbf{R}}, \mathsf{crs_V}, x, \pi)$, returns either 0 (reject) or 1 (accept).

Simulator: Sim is a PPT algorithm that, given $(\mathbf{R}, \xi_{\mathbf{R}}, \mathsf{crs}, \mathsf{tc}, x)$, outputs an argument π.

We also define the CRS generation algorithm $\mathsf{K}(\mathbf{R}, \xi_{\mathbf{R}})$ that first sets $\mathsf{tc} \leftarrow \mathsf{K_{tc}}(\mathbf{R}, \xi_{\mathbf{R}})$ and then outputs $\mathsf{crs} \leftarrow \mathsf{K_{crs}}(\mathbf{R}, \xi_{\mathbf{R}}, \mathsf{tc})$.

Ψ is *perfectly complete for* $\mathcal{R}$, if for all λ, $(\mathbf{R}, \xi_{\mathbf{R}}) \in \mathrm{im}(\mathcal{R}(1^{\lambda}))$, $\mathsf{tc} \in \mathrm{im}(\mathsf{K_{tc}}(\mathbf{R}, \xi_{\mathbf{R}})) \setminus \{\perp\}$, and $(x, w) \in \mathbf{R}$,

$$\Pr\left[\mathsf{crs} \leftarrow \mathsf{K_{crs}}(\mathbf{R}, \xi_{\mathbf{R}}, \mathsf{tc}) : \mathsf{V}(\mathbf{R}, \xi_{\mathbf{R}}, \mathsf{crs_V}, x, \mathsf{P}(\mathbf{R}, \xi_{\mathbf{R}}, \mathsf{crs_P}, x, w)) = 1\right] = 1 \ .$$

Ψ is *computationally adaptively knowledge-sound for* $\mathcal{R}$ [20], if for every non-uniform PPT $\mathcal{A}$, there exists a non-uniform PPT extractor $\mathsf{Ext}_{\mathcal{A}}$, s.t. $\forall \lambda$,

$$\Pr\left[\begin{array}{l} (\mathbf{R}, \xi_{\mathbf{R}}) \leftarrow \mathcal{R}(1^{\lambda}), (\mathsf{crs}, \mathsf{tc}) \leftarrow \mathsf{K}(\mathbf{R}, \xi_{\mathbf{R}}), r \leftarrow_r \mathsf{RND}(\mathcal{A}), \\ (x, \pi) \leftarrow \mathcal{A}(\mathbf{R}, \xi_{\mathbf{R}}, \mathsf{crs}; r), w \leftarrow \mathsf{Ext}_{\mathcal{A}}(\mathbf{R}, \xi_{\mathbf{R}}, \mathsf{crs}; r) : \\ (x, w) \notin \mathbf{R} \wedge \mathsf{V}(\mathbf{R}, \xi_{\mathbf{R}}, \mathsf{crs_V}, x, \pi) = 1 \end{array}\right] \approx_{\lambda} 0 \ .$$

Here, $\xi_{\mathbf{R}}$ can be seen as a common auxiliary input to $\mathcal{A}$ and $\mathsf{Ext}_{\mathcal{A}}$ that is generated by using a benign [7] relation generator; we recall that we just think of $\xi_{\mathbf{R}}$ as being the description of a secure bilinear group.

Ψ is *statistically unbounded ZK for* $\mathcal{R}$ [18], if for all λ, all $(\mathbf{R}, \xi_{\mathbf{R}}) \in \mathrm{im}(\mathcal{R}(1^{\lambda}))$, and all computationally unbounded $\mathcal{A}$, $\varepsilon_0^{unb} \approx_{\lambda} \varepsilon_1^{unb}$, where

$$\varepsilon_b^{unb} = \Pr[(\mathsf{crs}, \mathsf{tc}) \leftarrow \mathsf{K}(\mathbf{R}, \xi_{\mathbf{R}}) : \mathcal{A}^{O_b(\cdot, \cdot)}(\mathbf{R}, \xi_{\mathbf{R}}, \mathsf{crs}) = 1] \ .$$

Here, the oracle $O_0(x, w)$ returns $\perp$ (reject) if $(x, w) \notin \mathbf{R}$, and otherwise it returns $\mathsf{P}(\mathbf{R}, \xi_{\mathbf{R}}, \mathsf{crs_P}, x, w)$. Similarly, $O_1(x, w)$ returns $\perp$ (reject) if $(x, w) \notin \mathbf{R}$, and otherwise it returns $\mathsf{Sim}(\mathbf{R}, \xi_{\mathbf{R}}, \mathsf{crs}, \mathsf{tc}, x)$. Ψ is *perfectly unbounded ZK for* $\mathcal{R}$ if one requires that $\varepsilon_0^{unb} = \varepsilon_1^{unb}$.

Ψ is *statistically unbounded Sub-ZK for* $\mathcal{R}$, if for any non-uniform PPT subverter X there exists a non-uniform PPT Ext_X, such that for all λ, $(\mathbf{R}, \xi_\mathbf{R}) \in \mathrm{im}(\mathcal{R}(1^\lambda))$, and computationally unbounded $\mathcal{A}$, $\varepsilon_0^{unb} \approx_\lambda \varepsilon_1^{unb}$, where

$$\varepsilon_b^{unb} = \Pr \left[\begin{array}{l} r \leftarrow_r \mathsf{RND}(X), (\mathsf{crs}, \xi_X) \leftarrow X(\mathbf{R}, \xi_\mathbf{R}; r), \mathsf{tc} \leftarrow \mathsf{Ext}_X(\mathbf{R}, \xi_\mathbf{R}; r) : \\ \mathsf{CV}(\mathbf{R}, \xi_\mathbf{R}, \mathsf{crs}) = 1 \wedge \mathcal{A}^{O_b(\cdot, \cdot)}(\mathbf{R}, \xi_\mathbf{R}, \mathsf{crs}, \mathsf{tc}, \xi_X) = 1 \end{array} \right].$$

Here, the oracle $O_0(x, w)$ returns $\bot$ (reject) if $(x, w) \notin \mathbf{R}$, and otherwise it returns $P(\mathbf{R}, \xi_\mathbf{R}, \mathsf{crs}_P, x, w)$. Similarly, $O_1(x, w)$ returns $\bot$ (reject) if $(x, w) \notin \mathbf{R}$, and otherwise it returns $\mathsf{Sim}(\mathbf{R}, \xi_\mathbf{R}, \mathsf{crs}, \mathsf{tc}, x)$. Ψ is *perfectly unbounded Sub-ZK for* $\mathcal{R}$ if one requires that $\varepsilon_0^{unb} = \varepsilon_1^{unb}$.

Intuitively the previous definition says that an argument is Sub-ZK when for any untrusted (efficient) CRS generator X, some well-formedness condition $\mathsf{CV}(\mathbf{R}, \xi_\mathbf{R}, \mathsf{crs}) = 1$ implies that X knows a trapdoor which would allow him to simulate the proof. Hence, to protect privacy from malicious CRS generators, the prover just needs to verify that the CRS satisfies the CV algorithm.

Finally, a non-interactive argument system is *succinct* if the argument length is polynomial in λ and the verifier runs in time polynomial in $\lambda + |x|$.

3   Multi-party CRS Generation

Recently, [6,8,9] proposed several multi-party CRS-generation protocols for SNARKs. In particular, [6] proposes a specific class of arithmetic circuits $\mathcal{C}^S$, shows how to evaluate $\mathcal{C}^S$-circuits in an MPC manner, and claims that $\mathcal{C}^S$-circuits can be used to compute CRS-s for a broad class of SNARKs, in this paper called $\mathcal{C}^S$-SNARKs. The CRS of each $\mathcal{C}^S$-SNARK is an output of some $\mathcal{C}^S$-circuit taken into exponent. The input of such circuit is the CRS trapdoor. In the following, we review and modify the framework of [6] redefining slightly the class $\mathcal{C}^S$ and the CRS-generation protocol.

$\mathcal{C}^S$**-Circuits.** For an arithmetic circuit C over a field $\mathbb{F}$, denote by $\mathsf{wires}(C)$ and $\mathsf{gates}(C)$ the set of wires and gates of C (each gate can have more than one output wire), and by $\mathsf{inputs}(C), \mathsf{outputs}(C) \subset \mathsf{wires}(C)$ the set of input and output wires of C. There can also be wires with hard-coded constant values, but these are not considered to be part of $\mathsf{inputs}(C)$. The size of C is $|\mathsf{inputs}(C)| + |\mathsf{gates}(C)|$. For a wire w we denote the value on the wire by $\bar{w}$; this notation also extends to tuples, say, $\overline{\mathsf{inputs}}(C)$ denotes the tuple of values of $\mathsf{inputs}(C)$.

For a gate g, $\mathsf{output}(g) = w$ is the output wire and the tuple of all input wires is denoted by $\mathsf{inputs}(g)$. Let g_w be the gate with $w = \mathsf{output}(g_w)$. We consider circuits with *addition* and *multiplication-division* gates. For an addition gate ($\mathsf{type}(g) = \mathsf{add}$), $\mathsf{inputs}(g) = (w_1, \ldots, w_f)$, $\mathsf{coeffs}(g) = (a_0, a_1, \ldots, a_f)$, and it outputs a value $\bar{w} = a_0 + \sum_{j=1}^{f} a_j \bar{w}_j$. For a multdiv gate ($\mathsf{type}(g) = \mathsf{multdiv}$), $\mathsf{inputs}(g) = (w_1, w_2, w_3)$, $\mathsf{L\text{-}input}(g) = w_1$ is the left multiplication input, $\mathsf{R\text{-}input}(g) = w_2$ is the right multiplication input, $\mathsf{D\text{-}input}(g) = w_3$ is the division input, and $\mathsf{coeffs}(g) = a$. The output wire w contains the value $\bar{w} = a\bar{w}_1\bar{w}_2/\bar{w}_3$.

Previous works either only considered multiplication gates [6] or separate multiplication and division gates [9]. Using multdiv gates can, in some cases, reduce the circuit size compared to separate multiplication and division gates.

Class $\mathcal{C}^S$ contains $\mathbb{F}$-arithmetic circuits $C : \mathbb{F}^t \to \mathbb{F}^h$, such that:

(1) For any $w \in \mathsf{inputs}(C)$, there exists $g \in \mathsf{gates}(C)$ such that $\mathsf{type}(g) = \mathsf{multdiv}$, $\overline{\mathsf{inputs}}(g) = (1, \bar{w}, 1)$, and $\mathsf{coeffs}(g) = 1$. That is, each trapdoor itself should be a part of the output of the circuit. Adding those multdiv gates corresponds to the MPC protocol combining the shares of trapdoor ts of each party to get $[\mathsf{tc}]_\iota$.

(2) For any $g \in \mathsf{gates}(C)$:
   (a) $\mathsf{output}(g) \in \mathsf{outputs}(C)$. Hence, each gate output is a CRS element.
   (b) If $\mathsf{type}(g) = \mathsf{multdiv}$ then $\mathsf{L\text{-}input}(g) \notin \mathsf{inputs}(C)$, $\mathsf{R\text{-}input}(g), \mathsf{D\text{-}input}(g) \in \mathsf{inputs}(C)$. That is, the left multiplication input can be a constant or an output of a previous gate, the right multiplication and division inputs have to be one of the inputs of the circuit. This allows to easily verify the computation in the MPC. For convenience, we require further that constant value of $\mathsf{L\text{-}input}(g)$ can only be 1; from computational point of view nothing changes since $\mathsf{coeffs}(g)$ can be any constant.
   (c) If $\mathsf{type}(g) = \mathsf{add}$ then $\mathsf{inputs}(g) \cap \mathsf{inputs}(C) = \emptyset$. Addition is done locally in MPC (does not require additional rounds) with the outputs of previous gates, since outputs correspond to publicly known CRS elements.

The *sampling depth* depth_S of a gate $g \in \mathsf{gates}(C)$ is defined as follows:

1. $\mathsf{depth}_S(g) = 1$ if g is a multdiv gate and $\overline{\mathsf{L\text{-}input}}(g)$ is a constant.
2. $\mathsf{depth}_S(g) = \max\{\mathsf{depth}_S(g') : g' \text{ an input of } g\}$ for other multdiv gates,
3. $\mathsf{depth}_S(g) = b_g + \max\{\mathsf{depth}_S(g') : g' \text{ an input of } g\}$ for any add gate, where (i) $b_g = 0$ iff all the input gates of g are add gates. (ii) $b_g = 1$, otherwise.

Denote $\mathsf{depth}_S(C) := \max_g\{\mathsf{depth}_S(g)\}$. We again defined depth_S slightly differently compared to [6]; our definition emphasizes the fact that addition gates can be executed locally. Essentially, $N_p \cdot \mathsf{depth}_S(g_w)$ will be the number of rounds that it takes to compute $[\bar{w}]_\iota$ with our MPC protocol. The *multiplicative depth* of a circuit (denoted by $\mathsf{depth}_M(C)$) is the maximum number of multiplication gates from any input to any output. An exemplary $\mathcal{C}^S$-circuit is given in Fig. 3.

Multi-party Circuit Evaluation Protocol. We describe the circuit evaluation protocol, similar to the one in [6], that allows to evaluate any $\mathcal{C}^S$-circuits "in the exponent". We assume there are N_p parties $\mathcal{G}_i$, each having published a share $[\mathsf{ts}_{i,s}]_* \in \mathbb{F}^*$, for $s \in [1..t]$. The goal of the evaluation protocol is to output $([C_1(\mathsf{tc})]_1, [C_2(\mathsf{tc})]_2)$ where C_1, C_2 are $\mathcal{C}^S$-circuits and $\mathsf{tc} = (\prod_j \mathsf{ts}_{j,1}, \ldots, \prod_j \mathsf{ts}_{j,t})$. This protocol constructs a well-formed CRS, given that tc is the CRS trapdoor and $[C_1(\mathsf{tc})]_1$, $[C_2(\mathsf{tc})]_2$ are respectively all the $\mathbb{G}_1$ and $\mathbb{G}_2$ elements of the CRS. In Sect. 4, we combine the circuit evaluation protocol with a UC-secure commitment scheme to obtain a UC-secure CRS-generation protocol. Each step in the circuit evaluation protocol is publicly verifiable and hence, no trust is needed at all; except that to get the correct distribution we need to trust one party.

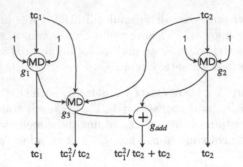

Fig. 3. Example $\mathcal{C}^S$ circuit with inputs tc_1 and tc_2

$C_{md}([b]_\iota, a, ts_{i,s}, ts_{i,k})$	$V_{md}([b']_\iota, [b]_\iota, a, [ts_{i,s}]_{3-\iota}, [ts_{i,k}]_{3-\iota})$
return $(a \cdot (ts_{i,s}/ts_{i,k}))[b]_\iota;$	**return** $((([b']_\iota = [0]_\iota) \vee$
	$([b']_\iota \bullet [ts_{i,k}]_{3-\iota} \neq a[b]_\iota \bullet [ts_{i,s}]_{3-\iota}))?\,0:1;$

$Eval_{md}(a, b, s, k)$

$[b_0]_\iota \leftarrow a[b]_\iota;$ // Multiplication with a is done by $\mathcal{G}_1$
for $i \in [1..N_p]$ **do** $\mathcal{G}_i$ broadcasts $[b_i]_\iota \leftarrow C_{md}([b_{i-1}]_\iota, 1, ts_{i,s}, ts_{i,k});$
return $[b_{N_p}]_\iota;$

Fig. 4. Algorithms C_{md}, V_{md} and the protocol $Eval_{md}$ for $\iota \in \{1, 2\}$.

We make two significant changes to the circuit evaluation protocol compared to [6]: (i) we do not require that $C_1 = C_2$, allowing CRS elements in $\mathbb{G}_1$ and $\mathbb{G}_2$ to be different, and (ii) instead of multiplication gates we evaluate multdiv gates.

Let us first describe the computation of $[\bar{w}]_\iota$ for a single gate g_w. For an add gate, given that all input gates have already been computed, that is, $[\bar{w}_1, \dots, \bar{w}_f]_\iota$ are already public, each $\mathcal{G}_i$ computes $[\bar{w}]_\iota = a_0 + \sum_{j=1}^{f} a_j[\bar{w}_j]_\iota$ locally. A multdiv gate g, with $\overline{inputs}(g) = (b, tc_s, tc_k)$ and $coeffs(g) = a$, can be implemented by the N_p-round protocol $Eval_{md}$ from Fig. 4. Here, each party $\mathcal{G}_i$ takes as input $[b]_\iota$ (the output of the preceding gate or just $[1]_\iota$ if there is none), runs C_{md} procedure on $ts_{i,s} \in \mathbb{F}$, $ts_{i,k} \in \mathbb{F}$ (her shares of the trapdoor that are also g's inputs), and broadcasts its output. Note that $[b]_\iota$ corresponds to the left multiplication, $ts_{i,s}$ to the right multiplication, and $ts_{i,k}$ to the division input of g.

Importantly, since each party $\mathcal{G}_i$ published $[\{ts_{i,j}\}_{j=1}^t]_\star$, everybody can verify that $\mathcal{G}_i$ executed C_{md} correctly by checking if $V_{md}([b_i]_\iota, [b_{i-1}]_\iota, a,$ $[ts_{i,s}, ts_{i,k}]_{3-\iota}) = 1$, where $[b_i]_\iota$ is $\mathcal{G}_i$'s output and $[b_{i-1}]_\iota$ is her input (the output of the party $\mathcal{G}_{i-1}$). We assume $[b_0]_\iota = [1]_\iota$ to allow the parties to check the computations of $\mathcal{G}_1$. Just running $Eval_{md}$ to evaluate each multdiv gate in C would require $\approx N_p \cdot depth_M(C)$ rounds. Next we see that computation can be parallelized to obtain $N_p \cdot depth_S(C)$ rounds.

Optimised Multi-party Circuit Evaluation Protocol. Before presenting the complete (parallelised) circuit evaluation protocol, we provide an illustrative example of how $\mathcal{C}^{\mathsf{S}}$-circuits can be evaluated efficiently using multiple parties. The idea behind this approach is to allow parties to evaluate the circuit not gate-by-gate but all the gates of the same sampling depth. We say that gates are in the same *layer* if they have the same depth$_{\mathsf{S}}$. Following the definition of depth$_{\mathsf{S}}$, layers are separated by add gates. That is, two gates, say g_1 and g_2 are in different layers if there is an add gate g_{add} such that g_1 (or g_2) depends on g_{add}'s output, while the other gate does not. In each layer, each gate is computed using only trapdoor elements and outputs from gates of some preceding layer. Parties evaluate the layer in a round-robin manner broadcasting intermediate values which allows other parties to verify the computation.

This is how the optimised protocol and the naive MPC protocol differ. Since naive protocol evaluates circuit gate-by-gate, one gate's output can be another's input even if both share the same layer. For instance, consider gates g_1 and g_3 from Fig. 3. There, g_1's output is g_3's input and they are both in the same layer. Since the output of g_1 is computed before g_3 is evaluated, it can be used in the computation. On the other hand, in the optimised version of circuit evaluation all gates in the same layer are evaluated at the same time, thus g_3 is computed at the same time when g_1 is computed.

Example 1. Suppose we have parties $\mathcal{G}_1$, $\mathcal{G}_2$, $\mathcal{G}_3$ that wish to compute $\mathsf{crs} = \{[\mathsf{tc}_1]_\star, [\mathsf{tc}_2]_\star, [\mathsf{tc}_1^2/\mathsf{tc}_2]_1, [\mathsf{tc}_1^2/\mathsf{tc}_2 + \mathsf{tc}_2]_1\}$. Let us only focus on the computation of $\mathbb{G}_1$ elements. This is represented by a $\mathcal{C}^{\mathsf{S}}$-circuit in Fig. 3 where we have (i) a multdiv gate g_1 with input values $(1, \mathsf{tc}_1, 1)$, (ii) a multdiv gate g_2 with input values $(1, \mathsf{tc}_2, 1)$, (iii) a multdiv gate g_3 that takes the output of g_1 as L-input, the circuit's inputs tc_1 as R-input, and tc_2 as D-input, that is, the input values of g_3 are $(\mathsf{tc}_1, \mathsf{tc}_1, \mathsf{tc}_2)$, and (iv) an add gate g_{add} that adds outputs of g_2 and g_3. The parties respectively publish shares $[\mathsf{ts}_{1,1}, \mathsf{ts}_{1,2}]_\star$, $[\mathsf{ts}_{2,1}, \mathsf{ts}_{2,2}]_\star$, $[\mathsf{ts}_{3,1}, \mathsf{ts}_{3,2}]_\star$.

- *In the first round*, $\mathcal{G}_1$ broadcasts $[b_{g_1}^1]_1 \leftarrow [\mathsf{ts}_{1,1}]_1$ for gate g_1, $[b_{g_2}^1]_1 \leftarrow [\mathsf{ts}_{1,2}]_1$ for gate g_2, and $[b_{g_3}^1]_1 \leftarrow [\mathsf{ts}_{1,1}^2/\mathsf{ts}_{1,2}]_1$ for gate g_3.
- *In the second round*, $\mathcal{G}_2$ broadcasts $[b_{g_1}^2]_1 \leftarrow \mathsf{ts}_{2,1} \cdot [b_{g_1}^1]_1$ for gate g_1, $[b_{g_2}^2]_1 \leftarrow \mathsf{ts}_{2,2} \cdot [b_{g_2}^1]_1$ for gate g_2, and $[b_{g_3,1}^2]_1 \leftarrow \mathsf{ts}_{2,1} \cdot [b_{g_3}^1]_1$, $[b_{g_3,2}^2]_1 \leftarrow (\mathsf{ts}_{2,1}/\mathsf{ts}_{2,2}) \cdot [b_{g_3,1}^2]_1$ for g_3 (note that g_3 required two computations rather than one).
- *In the third round*, $\mathcal{G}_3$ broadcasts $[b_{g_1}^3]_1 \leftarrow \mathsf{ts}_{3,1} \cdot [b_{g_2}^2]_1$ for gate g_1, $[b_{g_2}^3]_1 \leftarrow \mathsf{ts}_{3,2} \cdot [b_{g_2}^2]_1$ for gate g_2, and $[b_{g_3,1}^3]_1 \leftarrow \mathsf{ts}_{3,1} \cdot [b_{g_3,2}^2]_1$, $[b_{g_3,2}^3]_1 \leftarrow (\mathsf{ts}_{3,1}/\mathsf{ts}_{3,2}) \cdot [b_{g_3,1}^3]_1$ for g_3. For g_{add} each party computes $[b_{g_{add}}]_1 \leftarrow [b_{g_2}^3]_1 + [b_{g_3,2}^3]_1$.

Finally, if we define $\mathsf{tc}_1 := \mathsf{ts}_{1,1} \cdot \mathsf{ts}_{2,1} \cdot \mathsf{ts}_{3,1}$ and $\mathsf{tc}_2 := \mathsf{ts}_{1,2} \cdot \mathsf{ts}_{2,2} \cdot \mathsf{ts}_{3,2}$, then the outputs of $\mathcal{G}_3$ contain $[b_{g_1}^3]_1 = [\mathsf{tc}_1]_1$, $[b_{g_2}^3]_1 = [\mathsf{tc}_2]_1$, and $[b_{g_3,2}^3]_1 = [\mathsf{tc}_1^2/\mathsf{tc}_2]_1$; moreover, $[b_{g_{add}}]_1 = [\mathsf{tc}_2 + \mathsf{tc}_1^2/\mathsf{tc}_2]_1$. Besides addition, each element is built up one share multiplication at a time and hence the computation can be verified with pairings, e.g, the last output $[b_{g_3,2}^2]_1$ of $\mathcal{G}_2$ is correctly computed exactly when $[b_{g_3,2}^2]_1 \bullet [\mathsf{ts}_{2,2}]_2 = [b_{g_3,1}^2]_1 \bullet [\mathsf{ts}_{2,1}]_2$. □

Motivated by the example above, we give the full and formal description of the circuit evaluation protocol. Let $\mathsf{C}_\iota \in \mathcal{C}^{\mathsf{S}}$, for $\iota \in \{1, 2\}$, and $\mathsf{C}_{\iota,d} \subseteq \mathsf{gates}(\mathsf{C})$ be a circuit layer that contains all multdiv gates g at sampling depth d. For any

$g \in C_{\iota,d}$ let $\mathsf{ExtractPath}(g, C_{\iota,d})$ output the longest path $(g_1, \ldots, g_q = g)$ such that each $g_j \in C_{\iota,d}$, and, for $j < q$, $\mathsf{output}(g_j) = \mathsf{L\text{-}input}(g_{j+1})$. Intuitively, this is the path of gates in $C_{\iota,d}$ that following only the left inputs lead up to the gate g, say, $\mathsf{ExtractPath}(g_3, C_{1,1}) = (g_1, g_3)$ for the circuit C in Fig. 3. For simplicity, we describe a multdiv gate g by a tuple $([b]_{\iota}, a, s, k)$ where $[b]_{\iota} = [\mathsf{L\text{-}input}(g)]_{\iota}$ is the left input value, assumed already to be known by the parties, $a = \mathsf{coeffs}(g)$, $\overline{\mathsf{R\text{-}input}}(g) = \mathsf{tc}_s$, and $\overline{\mathsf{D\text{-}input}}(g) = \mathsf{tc}_k$.

The parties evaluate multdiv gates of the circuit in order $C_{\iota,1}, C_{\iota,2}, \ldots, C_{\iota,D_\iota}$, where D_ι is the sampling depth of C_ι. After each layer $C_{\iota,d}$ each party locally evaluates all the addition gates at depth $d + 1$. The evaluation of $C_{\iota,d}$ proceeds in a round-robin fashion. First, $\mathcal{G}_1$ evaluates $C_{\iota,d}$ with her input shares $\mathsf{ts}_{1,k}$ alone. Next, $\mathcal{G}_2$ multiplies her shares $\mathsf{ts}_{2,k}$ to each output of $\mathcal{G}_1$. However, to make computation verifiable, if $\mathcal{G}_2$ is supposed to compute $[b_g^1 \cdot \mathsf{ts}_{2,\alpha_1} \cdots \mathsf{ts}_{2,\alpha_q}]_\iota$, where $[b_g^1]_\iota$ is some output of $\mathcal{G}_1$, then it is done one multiplication at a time. Namely, she outputs $[b_{g,1}^2]_\iota = [b_g^1 \cdot \mathsf{ts}_{2,\alpha_1}]_\iota$, $[b_{g,2}^2]_\iota = [b_{g,1}^2 \cdot \mathsf{ts}_{2,\alpha_2}]_\iota$, $\ldots$, $[b_{g,q}^2]_\iota = [b_{g,q-1}^2 \cdot \mathsf{ts}_{2,\alpha_q}]_\iota$. Each multiplication would correspond to exactly one gate in $\mathsf{ExtractPath}(g, C_{\iota,d})$. The elements $[b_{g,1}^2, \ldots, b_{g,q-1}^2]_\iota$ are used only for verification; $[b_{g,q}^2]_\iota$ is additionally used by $\mathcal{G}_3$ to continue the computation. Each subsequent party $\mathcal{G}_i$ multiplies her shares to the output of $\mathcal{G}_{i-1}$ in a similar fashion. This protocol requires only $\mathsf{N}_p \cdot \mathsf{depth}_{\mathsf{S}}(C_\iota)$ rounds.

Let $\mathsf{cert}^\iota = (\mathsf{cert}_1^\iota, \ldots, \mathsf{cert}_{D_\iota}^\iota)$ be the total transcript (certificate) in $\mathbb{G}_\iota$ corresponding to the output of the multi-party evaluation of C_ι where cert_r^ι is the transcript in round r. Denote $\mathsf{cert} := (\mathsf{cert}^1, \mathsf{cert}^2)$. All gates of depth r of C_ι are evaluated by a uniquely fixed party $\mathcal{G}_i$. In what follows, let $i = \mathsf{rndplayer}(r)$ be the index of this party.

The complete description of evaluation and verification of a layer $C_{\iota,d}$ is given in Fig. 5 with function $\mathsf{C}_{\mathsf{layer}}$ and $\mathsf{V}_{\mathsf{layer}}$ that have the following interface. First, for $i = \mathsf{rndplayer}(r)$ and for both $\iota \in \{1, 2\}$, in round r to compute $[C_{\iota,d}(\mathsf{tc})]_\iota$, $\mathcal{G}_i$ computes $\mathsf{cert}_r^\iota \leftarrow \mathsf{C}_{\mathsf{layer}}(C_{\iota,d}, \iota, i, r, \{\mathsf{ts}_{i,k}\}_{k=1}^t, \{\mathsf{cert}_j^\iota\}_{j=1}^{r-1})$, given a circuit layer $C_{\iota,d}$, the shares $\mathsf{ts}_{i,k}$ for all t trapdoors of tc_k, and the transcript $\{\mathsf{cert}_j^\iota\}_{j=1}^{r-1}$ of all previous computation. Second, any party can verify, by using the algorithm $\mathsf{V}_{\mathsf{layer}}(C_{\iota,d}, \iota, i, r, \{[\mathsf{ts}_{i,k}]_{3-\iota}\}_{k=1}^t, \{\mathsf{cert}_j^\iota\}_{j=1}^r)$, that the computation of the circuit layer $C_{\iota,d}$ in round r has been performed correctly by $\mathcal{G}_i$. In particular, $\mathcal{G}_i$ checks that $\mathsf{V}_{\mathsf{layer}}$ outputs 1 for all rounds since $\mathcal{G}_i$'s previous round before executing $\mathsf{C}_{\mathsf{layer}}$ for her new round. Importantly, executing $\mathsf{V}_{\mathsf{layer}}$ does not assume the knowledge of any trapdoors.

4   UC-Secure CRS Generation

We propose a functionality $\mathcal{F}_{\mathsf{mcrs}}$ for multi-party CRS generation of any $\mathcal{C}^{\mathsf{S}}$-SNARK. Finally, we construct a protocol $\mathsf{K}_{\mathsf{mcrs}}$ that UC-realizes $\mathcal{F}_{\mathsf{mcrs}}$ in the $\mathcal{F}_{\mathsf{dlmcom}}$-hybrid model.

New Ideal Functionality. In Fig. 6, we define the new ideal functionality $\mathcal{F}_{\mathsf{mcrs}} = \mathcal{F}_{\mathsf{mcrs}}^{\mathsf{p},\mathsf{N}_p,\mathsf{C},\mathcal{D},\mathsf{comb}}$ for pairing-based (since it outputs elements from $\mathbb{G}_\iota$)

$\underline{\mathsf{C}_{\mathsf{layer}}(\mathsf{C}_{\iota,d}, \iota, i, r, \{\mathsf{ts}_{i,k}\}_{k=1}^{t}, \{\mathsf{cert}_j^{\iota}\}_{j=1}^{r-1})}$ // The following is executed by $\mathcal{G}_i$

1 :   Assert $i = \mathsf{rndplayer}(r)$; $\mathsf{cert}_r^{\iota} \leftarrow \epsilon$;
2 :   **for** $g = ([b]_{\iota}, a, s, k) \in \mathsf{C}_{\iota,d}$ **do**// In topological order
3 : $\mathsf{cert}_{g,i} \leftarrow \epsilon$; $(g_1, \ldots, g_q) \leftarrow \mathsf{ExtractPath}(g, \mathsf{C}_{\iota,d})$;
4 :   **if** $i = 1$ **then**
5 :   **if** $q = 1$ **then** $[b']_{\iota} \leftarrow \mathsf{C}_{\mathsf{md}}([b]_{\iota}, a, \mathsf{ts}_{1,s}, \mathsf{ts}_{1,k})$;
6 :   **else** Parse $\mathsf{cert}_{g_{q-1},1} = [b_L]_{\iota}$;
7 : $[b']_{\iota} \leftarrow \mathsf{C}_{\mathsf{md}}([b_L]_{\iota}, a, \mathsf{ts}_{1,s}, \mathsf{ts}_{1,k})$;
8 : $\mathsf{cert}_{g,1} \leftarrow [b']_{\iota}$;
9 :   **else** Parse $\mathsf{cert}_{g,i-1} = [b_1, \ldots, b_q]_{\iota}$; $[b']_{\iota} \leftarrow [b_q]_{\iota}$;
10 :   **for** $j = 1, \ldots, q$ **do**
11 :   Parse $g_j = ([b^*]_{\iota}, a^*, s^*, k^*)$;
12 : $[b']_{\iota} \leftarrow \mathsf{C}_{\mathsf{md}}([b']_{\iota}, 1, \mathsf{ts}_{i,s^*}, \mathsf{ts}_{i,k^*})$; Append $[b']_{\iota}$ to $\mathsf{cert}_{g,i}$;
13 :   Append $\mathsf{cert}_{g,i}$ to cert_r^{ι};
14 : **return** cert_r^{ι};

$\underline{\mathsf{V}_{\mathsf{layer}}(\mathsf{C}_{\iota,d}, \iota, i, r, \{[\mathsf{ts}_{i,k}]_{3-\iota}\}_{k=1}^{t}, \{\mathsf{cert}_j^{\iota}\}_{j=1}^{r})}$

1 :   Assert $i = \mathsf{rndplayer}(r)$;
2 :   **for** each evaluation of $[b']_{\iota} \leftarrow \mathsf{C}_{\mathsf{md}}([b]_{\iota}, a, \mathsf{ts}_{i,s}, \mathsf{ts}_{i,k})$ in round r by $\mathcal{G}_i$ **do**
3 :   Extract $[b']_{\iota}, [b]_{\iota}$ from $\{\mathsf{cert}_j^{\iota}\}_{j=1}^{r}$;
4 :   **if** $\mathsf{V}_{\mathsf{md}}([b']_{\iota}, [b]_{\iota}, a, [\mathsf{ts}_{i,s}]_{3-\iota}, [\mathsf{ts}_{i,k}]_{3-\iota}) = 0$ **then return** 0;
5 :   **return** 1;

Fig. 5. $\mathsf{C}_{\mathsf{layer}}$ and $\mathsf{V}_{\mathsf{layer}}$ for $\iota \in \{1, 2\}$

multi-party CRS-generation protocol. The CRS is described by a t-input arithmetic circuits $\mathbf{C} := (C_1, C_2)$ over a field $\mathbb{F} = \mathbb{Z}_p$ such that $\mathsf{crs} = ([C_1(\mathsf{tc})]_1, [C_2(\mathsf{tc})]_2)$ for $\mathsf{tc} \leftarrow_{\$} \mathcal{D}$, where $\mathcal{D}$ is a samplable distribution over $\mathbb{Z}_p^t$.

The trapdoor tc is constructed by combining shares $\mathsf{ts}_i \in \mathsf{Supp}(\mathcal{D})$ of each party $\mathcal{G}_i$ by a function comb. For each honest party $\mathcal{G}_i$, the ideal functionality picks $\mathsf{ts}_i \leftarrow_{\$} \mathcal{D}$, whereas for malicious parties we only know $\mathsf{ts}_i \in \mathsf{Supp}(\mathcal{D})$. The function comb should be defined so that if there exists at least one honest party then $\mathsf{tc} \leftarrow \mathsf{comb}(\mathsf{ts}_1, \ldots, \mathsf{ts}_{\mathsf{N}_p})$ is also distributed accordingly to $\mathcal{D}$. In such case we say that $\mathcal{D}$ is comb-*friendly*. It is true for example when comb is point-wise multiplication and $\mathcal{D}$ is a uniform distribution over $(\mathbb{Z}_p^*)^t$ as, e.g., in [6,8,9]. This guarantees the correct distribution of crs if at least one party is honest.

We believe $\mathcal{F}_{\mathsf{mcrs}}$ captures essentially any reasonable pairing-based multi-party CRS-generation protocol, where the trapdoor is shared between N_p parties. Note that specifying distinct honest and corrupted inputs to the functionality is common in the UC literature, [3,24]. In Theorem 2, we will establish the relation between $\mathcal{F}_{\mathsf{crs}}$ and $\mathcal{F}_{\mathsf{mcrs}}$.

New Protocol. We define the new multi-party CRS-generation protocol $\mathsf{K}_{\mathsf{mcrs}} = \mathsf{K}_{\mathsf{mcrs}}^{p, \mathsf{N}_p, \mathsf{C}, \mathcal{D}, \mathsf{comb}}$ (see Fig. 7) in the $\mathcal{F}_{\mathsf{dlmcom}}$-hybrid model. This allows us to instantiate the protocol with any DL-extractable commitment and, moreover, the only trust assumption that the protocol needs is the one inherited from the

---

Parameters: p defines a bilinear pairing, $C = (C_1, C_2)$ contains t-input arithmetic circuits over the field $\mathbb{Z}_p$, $\mathcal{D}$ is a distribution of trapdoor elements, and comb : $(\mathbb{Z}_p^t)^{N_p} \to \mathbb{Z}_p^t$. We have parties $\mathcal{G}_i$ for $i \in [1 .. N_p]$.

Share collection phase:
1. Upon receiving $(\text{sc}, \text{sid}, \mathcal{G}_i)$ from an honest $\mathcal{G}_i$, store $\text{ts}_i \leftarrow_\$ \mathcal{D}$ and send $(\text{sc}, \text{sid}, \mathcal{G}_i)$ to Sim.
2. Upon receiving $(\text{sc}, \text{sid}, \mathcal{G}_i, \text{ts}_i)$ from a dishonest $\mathcal{G}_i$, if $\text{ts}_i \in \text{Supp}(\mathcal{D})$, then store ts_i, else abort. Only one message from each $\mathcal{G}_i$ is accepted.

CRS generation phase: Once ts_i is stored for each $\mathcal{G}_i$:
1. Compute tc $\leftarrow$ comb$(\text{ts}_1, \ldots, \text{ts}_{N_p})$.
2. Set crs $\leftarrow ([C_1(\text{tc})]_1, [C_2(\text{tc})]_2)$ and send $(\text{CRS}, \text{sid}, \text{crs})$ to Sim.
3. If Sim returns (CRS, ok) then send $(\text{CRS}, \text{sid}, \text{crs})$ to every party $\mathcal{G}_i$ for $i \in [1 .. N_p]$.

Fig. 6. Ideal functionality $\mathcal{F}_{\text{mcrs}}$

commitment scheme, e.g., using construction from [1] gives security in the RPK model. Given that D_ι is the sampling depth of C_ι, then $R = N_p \cdot \max(D_1, D_2)$ is the number of rounds needed to evaluate both circuits in parallel. For the sake of simplicity, we assume cert_r^ι is the empty string for $r > N_p \cdot D_\iota$.

K_{mcrs} proceeds in rounds: (i) In round 1, each $\mathcal{G}_i$ gets a signal $(\text{sc}, \text{sid}, \mathcal{G}_i)$; parties commit to their shares of trapdoor tc. (ii) In round 2, each party $\mathcal{G}_i$ gets a signal $(\text{mcrsopen}, \text{sid})$; parties open their shares. (iii) In round $r \in [3 .. R + 2]$, $(\text{mcrscertok}, \text{sid}, \mathcal{G}_i, r)$ is triggered, where $i = \text{rndplayer}(r)$; parties jointly compute crs from the trapdoor shares; before party $\mathcal{G}_i$ performs her computation, she checks if previous computation were done correctly. (iv) In round $R + 3$, each party $\mathcal{G}_i$ gets the signal $(\text{mcrsfinal}, \text{sid}, \mathcal{G}_i)$ and extracts the crs from cert. The CRS will be output by $\mathcal{G}_i$ only if all the verifications succeeded. The signals sc, mcrsopen, mcrscertok, and mcrsfinal can be sent either by a controller server or by the internal clock of $\mathcal{G}_i$. The construction uses a secure broadcast channel; thus, if a message is broadcast, then all parties are guaranteed to receive the same message. Note that after $\mathcal{G}_j$ obtains $(\text{rcpt}, \text{lbl}_{ijk})$, for $i \in [1 .. N_p], j \neq i, k \in [1 .. t]$, she broadcasts $(\text{mcrsreceipt}, \text{lbl}_{ijk})$ since rcpt is not broadcast.

Security. To prove UC-security of K_{mcrs}, we restrict $\mathcal{F}_{\text{mcrs}}$ as follows: (i) $C = (C_1, C_2)$ such that $C_\iota \in \mathcal{C}^S$ for $\iota \in \{1, 2\}$. Note that this means that for any trapdoor element $\text{tc}_k \in \text{tc}$, $[\text{tc}_k]_\star \in \text{crs}$. (ii) $\mathcal{D}$ is the uniform distribution on $(\mathbb{Z}_p^*)^t$, (iii) comb$(\text{ts}_1, \ldots, \text{ts}_{N_p}) := \text{ts}_1 \circ \ldots \circ \text{ts}_{N_p}$, where $\circ$ denotes point-wise multiplication, and ts_{ik} is $\mathcal{G}_i$'s share of tc_k.

Theorem 1. K_{mcrs} *UC-realizes* $\mathcal{F}_{\text{mcrs}}$ *in the* $\mathcal{F}_{\text{dlmcom}}$-*hybrid model with perfect security against a static adversary. Formally, there exits a PPT simulator* $\text{Sim}^\mathcal{A}$ *such that for every static (covert) PPT adversary* $\mathcal{A}$ *and for any non-uniform PPT environment* $\mathcal{Z}$, $\mathcal{Z}$ *cannot distinguish* K_{mcrs} *composed with* $\mathcal{F}_{\text{dlmcom}}$ *and* $\mathcal{A}$ *from* Sim *composed with* $\mathcal{F}_{\text{mcrs}}$. *That is,* $\text{HYBRID}_{K_{\text{mcrs}}, \mathcal{A}, \mathcal{Z}}^{\mathcal{F}_{\text{dlmcom}}} = \text{IDEAL}_{\mathcal{F}_{\text{mcrs}}, \text{Sim}^\mathcal{A}, \mathcal{Z}}$.

Proof (Sketch). To prove UC-security, we have to construct an algorithm Sim that is able to simulate behaviour of honest parties for $\mathcal{Z}$ in the ideal world without knowing their real inputs. Since we are in $\mathcal{F}_{\text{dlmcom}}$-hybrid model, Sim simulates $\mathcal{F}_{\text{dlmcom}}$ for the malicious parties and hence learns their shares. At first, Sim

---

Share collection phase: *Round 1:* upon receiving $(\mathsf{sc}, \mathsf{sid}, \mathcal{G}_i)$, $\mathcal{G}_i$ does the following.

for $k \in [1 \mathinner{.\,.} t]$ do

  1. $\mathsf{ts}_{ik} \leftarrow\!\!\$\; \mathbb{Z}_p^*$;

  2. for $j \neq i$ do

     – Send $(\mathsf{commit}, \mathsf{sid}, \mathsf{cid}_{ijk}, \mathcal{G}_i, \mathcal{G}_j, \mathsf{ts}_{ik})$ to $\mathcal{F}_{\mathsf{dlmcom}}$;

     – Upon receiving $(\mathsf{rcpt}, \mathsf{lbl}_{ijk} = (\mathsf{sid}, \mathsf{cid}_{ijk}, \mathcal{G}_i, \mathcal{G}_j))$, $\mathcal{G}_j$ broadcasts $(\mathsf{mcrsreceipt}, \mathsf{lbl}_{ijk})$;

     – Store $\mathsf{st}_{ij} \leftarrow (\mathsf{lbl}_{ijk}, \mathsf{ts}_{ik})_{k=1}^t$;

If by the end of the round 1, $\mathcal{G}_i$ does not receive $(\mathsf{mcrsreceipt}, \mathsf{sid}, \mathsf{cid}_{jj'k}, \mathcal{G}_j, \mathcal{G}_{j'})$ for $k \in [1 \mathinner{.\,.} t]$, $j \neq i$, $j' \neq i$, and $j' \neq j$ then $\mathcal{G}_i$ aborts.

Round 2: upon receiving $(\mathsf{mcrsopen}, \mathsf{sid})$, $\mathcal{G}_i$ does:

for $k \in [1 \mathinner{.\,.} t]$ do

  1. for $j \neq i$ do

     – Send $(\mathsf{open}, \mathsf{sid}, \mathsf{cid}_{ijk})$ to $\mathcal{F}_{\mathsf{dlmcom}}$;

     – After receiving $(\mathsf{open}, \mathsf{lbl}_{ijk}, [\mathsf{ts}'_{ijk}]_1)$, where $\mathsf{lbl}_{ijk} = (\mathsf{sid}, \mathsf{cid}_{ijk}, \mathcal{G}_i, \mathcal{G}_j)$, from $\mathcal{F}_{\mathsf{dlmcom}}$, $\mathcal{G}_j$ stores $(\mathsf{lbl}_{ijk}, [\mathsf{ts}'_{ijk}]_1)$; // If $\mathcal{G}_i$ is honest then $\mathsf{ts}_{ik} = \mathsf{ts}'_{ijk}$

  2. Broadcast $(\mathsf{sbroadc}, \mathcal{G}_i, k, [\mathsf{ts}_{ik}]_1)$.

  3. Upon receiving $(\mathsf{sbroadc}, \mathcal{G}_i, k, [\mathsf{ts}_{ik}]_1)$ broadcast by $\mathcal{G}_i$, $\mathcal{G}_j$ does the following.

     – If $(\mathsf{lbl}_{ijk}, [\mathsf{ts}'_{ijk}]_1)$ is not stored for some $[\mathsf{ts}'_{ijk}]_1$ then abort.

     – Abort unless $[\mathsf{ts}_{ik}]_1 = [\mathsf{ts}'_{ijk}]_1 \neq [0]_1$.

     – If by the end of round 2, $\mathcal{G}_j$ has not received $(\mathsf{sbroadc}, \ldots)$, $\forall j \neq i$, $\forall k$, then $\mathcal{G}_j$ aborts.

CRS generation phase: *Round $r = 3$ to $R + 2$:*

upon receiving $(\mathsf{mcrscertok}, \mathsf{sid}, \mathcal{G}_i, r)$, $\mathcal{G}_i$ does the following, for $i = \mathsf{rndplayer}(r)$.

  1. Extract $\mathsf{C}_{1,d}$, $\mathsf{C}_{2,d}$ corresponding to round r from C_1, C_2;

  2. for $\iota \in \{1, 2\}$ do $\mathsf{cert}_r^\iota \leftarrow \mathsf{C}_{\mathsf{layer}}(\mathsf{C}_{\iota,d}, \iota, i, r, \{\mathsf{ts}_{i,k}\}_{k=1}^{r-1}, \{\mathsf{cert}_j^\iota\}_{j=1}^{r-1})$;

  3. $\mathsf{cert}_r \leftarrow (\mathsf{cert}_r^1, \mathsf{cert}_r^2)$; broadcast $(\mathsf{mcrscert}, \mathsf{sid}, \mathsf{cid}, \mathcal{G}_i, r, \mathsf{cert}_r)$;

  4. Any $j \neq i$ does after receiving $(\mathsf{mcrscert}, \mathsf{sid}, \mathsf{cid}, \mathcal{G}_i, r, \mathsf{cert}_r)$ from $\mathcal{G}_i$:

    (a) if $j \neq \mathsf{rndplayer}(r)$, $\mathsf{V}_{\mathsf{layer}}(\mathsf{C}_{1,d}, \iota, i, r, \{[\mathsf{ts}_{i,k}]_{3-\iota}\}_{k=1}^t, \{\mathsf{cert}_k^1\}_{k=1}^r)) = 0$, or $\mathsf{V}_{\mathsf{layer}}(\mathsf{C}_{2,d}, \iota, i, r, \{[\mathsf{ts}_{i,k}]_{3-\iota}\}_{k=1}^t, \{\mathsf{cert}_j^2\}_{j=1}^r)) = 0$ then abort;

    (b) Replace stored $(\mathsf{sid}, \mathsf{cid}, r-1, \{\mathsf{cert}_j^\iota\}_{j=1}^{r-1})$ with $(\mathsf{sid}, \mathsf{cid}, r, \{\mathsf{cert}_j^\iota\}_{j=1}^r)$;

If by the end of round r, for any i, $\mathcal{G}_i$ has not stored $(\mathsf{mcrscert}, \mathsf{sid}, \mathsf{cid}, \mathcal{G}_i, r, \mathsf{cert}_r)$ then $\mathcal{G}_i$ aborts.

Round $R + 3$: upon receiving $(\mathsf{mcrsfinal}, \mathsf{sid}, \mathcal{G}_i)$, $\mathcal{G}_i$ does the following.

  1. If $\mathcal{G}_i$ has already received this message then ignore;

  2. Extract crs from $\{\mathsf{cert}_k^1, \mathsf{cert}_k^2\}_{k=1}^R$. Write $(\mathsf{CRS}, \mathsf{crs})$ on the output tape.

Fig. 7. The protocol $\mathsf{K}_{\mathsf{mcrs}}$ in the $\mathcal{F}_{\mathsf{dlmcom}}$-hybrid model

picks random shares ts'_{ik} to simulate all the honest parties. Once the ideal functionality has received $(\mathsf{sc}, \mathsf{sid}, \mathcal{G}_i)$ from all the honest parties and $(\mathsf{sc}, \mathsf{sid}, \mathcal{G}_i, \mathsf{ts}_i)$ for all the dishonest parties (forwarded by Sim), then Sim receives $(\mathsf{CRS}, \mathsf{sid}, \mathsf{crs})$ from the ideal functionality. Now, Sim fixes one honest party $\mathcal{G}_h$ and opens its commitments to $[\mathsf{ts}_{hk}^*]_1 \leftarrow [\mathsf{tc}_k]_1 / (\prod_{i \in [1 \mathinner{.\,.} \mathsf{N}_p] \setminus \{h\}} \mathsf{ts}'_{ik})$ for $[\mathsf{tc}_k]_1 \in \mathsf{crs}$ and ts'_{ik} collected through $\mathcal{F}_{\mathsf{dlmcom}}$. Since $[\mathsf{tc}_k]_1$ is uniformly random, then so is $[\mathsf{ts}_{hk}^*]_1$ (the same distribution as in the real protocol). With a similar strategy Sim simulates each gate output for $\mathcal{G}_h$ such that the final output of the simulated protocol is crs, matching the output of the ideal functionality.

We discuss challenges of adaptive security and give the full proof of this theorem in the full version of the paper. $\qquad\qquad\qquad\qquad\qquad\qquad\square$

5   Secure MPC for NIZKs

Next, we show that $\mathsf{K}_{\mathsf{mcrs}}$ can be used to generate the CRS of any $\mathcal{C}^{\mathsf{S}}$-SNARK without harming the completeness, soundness, or (subversion) zero-knowledge properties. It could also be used to generate CRS of other primitives which can be represented by $\mathcal{C}^S$-circuits, but it is especially well suited for the intricate structure of SNARK CRS. Finally, we apply the protocol to the Sub-ZK secure version [2,14] of the most efficient zk-SNARK by Groth [20].

NIZK in the MCRS Model. Let Ψ be a NIZK argument system secure in the $\mathcal{F}_{crs}$-hybrid model. We show that by instantiating $\mathcal{F}_{crs}$ with $\mathcal{F}_{mcrs}$, the NIZK remains complete, sound, and zero-knowledge, provided that the adversary $\mathcal{A}$ controls up to $N_p - 1$ out of N_p parties. Here we require that $\mathcal{D}$ is comb-friendly. See Fig. 8 for the high-level description of MPC protocol for the CRS generation.

$K_{crs}^{\mathcal{F}_{mcrs}}$ proceeds as follows, running with a set $\{P_1, \ldots, P_{N'_p}\}$ of parties, designated set $\{\mathcal{G}_1, \ldots, \mathcal{G}_{N_p}\}$ of CRS generators, and an adversary Sim.
CRS generation: Send a signal to each $\mathcal{G}_i$ to execute the functionality $\mathcal{F}_{mcrs}$. If $\mathcal{F}_{mcrs}$ returns crs then $\mathcal{G}_i$ stores (sid, crs).
Retrieval: P_i sends (retrieve, sid) to each $\mathcal{G}_j$: If (sid, crs) is recorded for some crs then $\mathcal{G}_j$ sends (CRS, sid, crs). If all N_p responses from $\mathcal{G}_j$ are the same, then P_i outputs (CRS, sid, crs). Else P_i aborts.

Fig. 8. Protocol $K_{crs}^{\mathcal{F}_{mcrs}}$

Theorem 2. *Let $\mathcal{D}$ and* comb $: (\text{Supp}(\mathcal{D}))^{N_p} \to \text{Supp}(\mathcal{D})$ *be such that $\mathcal{D}$ is comb-friendly. $K_{crs}^{\mathcal{F}_{mcrs}}$ securely realizes $\mathcal{F}_{crs}^{\mathcal{D},f}$ in the $\mathcal{F}_{mcrs}$-hybrid model given (covert) $\mathcal{A}$ corrupts up to $N_p - 1$ out of N_p parties (i.e. CRS generators).*

The proof of this theorem is given in the full version of the paper. Next corollary immediately follows from the universal composition theorem [10].

Corollary 1. *Let Ψ be a NIZK argument that is complete, sound, computationally ZK, and computationally Sub-ZK in the $\mathcal{F}_{crs}^{\mathcal{D},f}$-hybrid model. By instantiating $\mathcal{F}_{crs}^{\mathcal{D},f}$ with $K_{crs}^{\mathcal{F}_{mcrs}}$, the following holds:*

1. *Ψ is complete, sound, and computationally zero-knowledge in the $\mathcal{F}_{mcrs}$-hybrid model, given that (covert) $\mathcal{A}$ corrupts up to $N_p - 1$ out of N_p parties.*
2. *Ψ is Sub-ZK in the $\mathcal{F}_{mcrs}$-hybrid model, even if (covert) $\mathcal{A}$ corrupts all N_p parties.*
3. *If $\mathcal{D}$ is a uniform distribution over $(\mathbb{Z}_p^*)^t$,* comb *the point-wise multiplication and the CRS can be computed by $\mathcal{C}^S$-circuits, then properties 1 and 2 hold in the $\mathcal{F}_{dlmcom}$-hybrid model since K_{mcrs} realizes $\mathcal{F}_{mcrs}$ in that setting.*

Applying K_{mcrs} to Groth's zk-SNARK. Figure 9 contains the description of the CRS for the Sub-ZK version of Groth's zk-SNARK $\mathcal{Z}^*$ as was proposed in [2]. We have omitted the element $[\alpha\beta]_T$ that can be computed from $[\alpha]_1$ and $[\beta]_2$. The CRS from [2] differs from the original CRS for Groth's zk-SNARK [20] by the entries in crs_{CV} which make the CRS verifiable using a CV algorithm. Here, $\ell_i(X)$ are Lagrange basis polynomials and $\ell(X) = X^n - 1$, $u_j(X)$, $v_j(X)$, $w_j(X)$

CRS / trapdoor: $\mathsf{tc} \leftarrow (\alpha, \beta, \gamma, \delta, \chi)$ and $\mathsf{crs} = (\mathsf{crs_P}, \mathsf{crs_V}, \mathsf{crs_{CV}})$, where

$$\mathsf{crs_P} \leftarrow \left(\begin{array}{c} \left[\alpha, \beta, \delta, \left((u_j(\chi)\beta + v_j(\chi)\alpha + w_j(\chi)) / \delta \right)_{j=m_0+1}^{m} \right]_1, \\ \left[(\chi^i \ell(\chi)/\delta)_{i=0}^{n-2}, (u_j(\chi), v_j(\chi))_{j=0}^{m} \right]_1, \left[\beta, \delta, (v_j(\chi))_{j=0}^{m} \right]_2 \end{array} \right)$$

$$\mathsf{crs_V} \leftarrow \left(\left[\left((u_j(\chi)\beta + v_j(\chi)\alpha + w_j(\chi)) / \gamma \right)_{j=0}^{m_0} \right]_1, [\gamma, \delta]_2 \right)$$

$$\mathsf{crs_{CV}} \leftarrow \left([\gamma, (\chi^i)_{i=1}^{n-1}, (\ell_i(\chi))_{i=1}^{n}]_1, [\alpha, \chi, \chi^{n-1}]_2 \right)$$

Fig. 9. CRS of Z^* Sub-ZK SNARK from [2]

are publicly-known circuit-dependent polynomials. Due to the lack of space, we do not present other algorithms of Z^*.

We recall that to use the algorithm $\mathsf{K}_{\mathsf{crs}}^{\mathcal{F}_{\mathsf{mcrs}}}$ the CRS has to be of the form $\mathsf{crs} = ([\mathsf{C}_1(\mathsf{tc})]_1, [\mathsf{C}_2(\mathsf{tc})]_2)$, where $\mathsf{C}_\iota \in \mathcal{C}^\mathsf{S}$. In Fig. 9, the highlighted entries cannot be computed from trapdoors by a $\mathcal{C}^\mathsf{S}$-circuit unless we add $\mathsf{crs_{TV}} = ([(w_j(\chi), \beta u_j(\chi), \alpha v_j(\chi))_{j=0}^{m}, \chi^n]_1, [(\ell_i(\chi))_{i=1}^{n}, (\chi^k)_{k=1}^{n-1}]_2)$ to the CRS. To obtain better efficiency we additionally add $[(\ell_i(\chi))_{i=1}^{n}]_2$ to the CRS, although they can be computed from the existing elements $[(\chi^k)_{k=1}^{n-1}]_2$. However, since we are adding elements to the CRS, we also need to reprove the soundness. We do this in the full version of the paper.

We give a brief description of the CRS-generation protocol for Z^* without explicitly describing the circuits C_1 and C_2. Without directly saying it, it is assumed that parties verify all the computations as shown in Fig. 7.

Share Collection Phase. Parties proceed as is in Fig. 7 to produce random and independent shares $[\mathsf{ts}_i]_\star = [\alpha_i, \beta_i, \gamma_i, \delta_i, \chi_i]_\star$ for each $\mathcal{G}_i$.

CRS Generation Phase. (i) On layers $\mathsf{C}_{1,1}, \mathsf{C}_{2,1}$ parties jointly compute $[\alpha, \beta, \gamma, \delta]_\star$, $[(\chi^k)_{k=1}^{n-1}]_\star$ and $[\chi^n]_1$. (ii) Each $\mathcal{G}_i$ locally computes $[(\ell_k(\chi))_{k=1}^{n}]_\star$, $[(w_j(\chi), u_j(\chi))_{j=0}^{m}]_1$, and $[(v_j(\chi))_{j=0}^{m}]_\star$ using $[(\chi^k)_{k=1}^{n-1}]_\star$; and also computes $[\ell(\chi)]_1 = [\chi^n]_1 - [1]_1$. (iii) On layer $\mathsf{C}_{1,2}$, from input $[\ell(\chi)]_1$, parties jointly compute $[(\chi^k \ell(\chi)/\delta)_{k=0}^{n-2}]_1$ using $\mathsf{n} - 1$ multdiv gates. Moreover, they compute $[(\beta u_l(\chi), \alpha v_l(\chi))_{l=0}^{m}]_1$. (iv) Each party computes locally $[(\beta u_l(\chi) + \alpha v_l(\chi) + w_l(\chi))_{l=0}^{m}]_1$. (v) On layer $\mathsf{C}_{1,3}$ parties compute jointly $[(\beta u_l(\chi) + \alpha v_l(\chi) + w_l(\chi)/\gamma)_{l=0}^{m_0}]_1$ and $[(\beta u_l(\chi) + \alpha v_l(\chi) + w_l(\chi)/\delta)_{l=m_0+1}^{m}]_1$.

The cost of the CRS generation for Z^* can be summarised as follows: the circuits C_1 and C_2 have both sampling depth 3; the multi-party protocol for computing the crs takes $3\mathsf{N}_p + 6$ rounds and requires $3\mathsf{m} + 3\mathsf{n} + 9$ multdiv gates. Note that with separate multiplication and division gates one would need $2\mathsf{m} + 3\mathsf{n} + 8$ multiplication gates and $\mathsf{m} + \mathsf{n}$ division gates which would be less efficient.

Acknowledgement. The authors were supported by the European Union's Horizon 2020 research and innovation programme under grant agreements No. 653497 (project PANORAMIX) and No. 780477 (project PRIViLEDGE), and by the Estonian Research Council grant (PRG49).

References

1. Abdolmaleki, B., Baghery, K., Lipmaa, H., Siim, J., Zajac, M.: DL-Extractable UC-Commitment Schemes. Technical Report 2019/201, IACR (2019). https://eprint.iacr.org/2019/201
2. Abdolmaleki, B., Baghery, K., Lipmaa, H., Zając, M.: A subversion-resistant SNARK. In: Takagi, T., Peyrin, T. (eds.) ASIACRYPT 2017. LNCS, vol. 10626, pp. 3–33. Springer, Cham (2017). https://doi.org/10.1007/978-3-319-70700-6_1
3. Barak, B., Canetti, R., Nielsen, J.B., Pass, R.: Universally composable protocols with relaxed set-up assumptions. In: 45th FOCS, pp. 186–195
4. Bellare, M., Fuchsbauer, G., Scafuro, A.: NIZKs with an untrusted CRS: security in the face of parameter subversion. In: Cheon, J.H., Takagi, T. (eds.) ASIACRYPT 2016. LNCS, vol. 10032, pp. 777–804. Springer, Heidelberg (2016). https://doi.org/10.1007/978-3-662-53890-6_26
5. Ben-Sasson, E., et al.: Zerocash: Decentralized anonymous payments from bitcoin. In: 2014 IEEE Symposium on Security and Privacy, pp. 459–474 (2014)
6. Ben-Sasson, E., Chiesa, A., Green, M., Tromer, E., Virza, M.: Secure sampling of public parameters for succinct zero knowledge proofs. In: 2015 IEEE Symposium on Security and Privacy, pp. 287–304 (2015)
7. Bitansky, N., Canetti, R., Paneth, O., Rosen, A.: On the existence of extractable one-way functions. In: 46th ACM STOC, pp. 505–514
8. Bowe, S., Gabizon, A., Green, M.D.: A multi-party protocol for constructing the public parameters of the pinocchio zk-SNARK. Cryptology ePrint Archive, Report 2017/602 (2017). http://eprint.iacr.org/2017/602
9. Bowe, S., Gabizon, A., Miers, I.: Scalable multi-party computation for zk-SNARK parameters in the random beacon model. Cryptology ePrint Archive, Report 2017/1050 (2017). http://eprint.iacr.org/2017/1050
10. Canetti, R.: Universally composable security: a new paradigm for cryptographic protocols. In: 42nd FOCS, pp. 136–145
11. Canetti, R., Fischlin, M.: Universally composable commitments. In: Kilian, J. (ed.) CRYPTO 2001. LNCS, vol. 2139, pp. 19–40. Springer, Heidelberg (2001). https://doi.org/10.1007/3-540-44647-8_2
12. Canetti, R., Goldreich, O., Halevi, S.: The random oracle methodology, revisited (preliminary version). In: 30th ACM STOC, pp. 209–218
13. Danezis, G., Fournet, C., Groth, J., Kohlweiss, M.: Square span programs with applications to succinct NIZK arguments. In: Sarkar, P., Iwata, T. (eds.) ASIACRYPT 2014. LNCS, vol. 8873, pp. 532–550. Springer, Heidelberg (2014). https://doi.org/10.1007/978-3-662-45611-8_28
14. Fuchsbauer, G.: Subversion-zero-knowledge SNARKs. In: Abdalla, M., Dahab, R. (eds.) PKC 2018. LNCS, vol. 10769, pp. 315–347. Springer, Cham (2018). https://doi.org/10.1007/978-3-319-76578-5_11
15. Gennaro, R., Gentry, C., Parno, B., Raykova, M.: Quadratic span programs and succinct NIZKs without PCPs. In: Johansson, T., Nguyen, P.Q. (eds.) EUROCRYPT 2013. LNCS, vol. 7881, pp. 626–645. Springer, Heidelberg (2013). https://doi.org/10.1007/978-3-642-38348-9_37
16. Gentry, C., Wichs, D.: Separating succinct non-interactive arguments from all falsifiable assumptions. In: 43rd ACM STOC, pp. 99–108
17. Goldwasser, S., Kalai, Y.T.: On the (in)security of the Fiat-Shamir paradigm. In: 44th FOCS, pp. 102–115

18. Groth, J.: Simulation-sound NIZK proofs for a practical language and constant size group signatures. In: Lai, X., Chen, K. (eds.) ASIACRYPT 2006. LNCS, vol. 4284, pp. 444–459. Springer, Heidelberg (2006). https://doi.org/10.1007/11935230_29

19. Groth, J.: Short pairing-based non-interactive zero-knowledge arguments. In: Abe, M. (ed.) ASIACRYPT 2010. LNCS, vol. 6477, pp. 321–340. Springer, Heidelberg (2010). https://doi.org/10.1007/978-3-642-17373-8_19

20. Groth, J.: On the size of pairing-based non-interactive arguments. In: Fischlin, M., Coron, J.-S. (eds.) EUROCRYPT 2016. LNCS, vol. 9666, pp. 305–326. Springer, Heidelberg (2016). https://doi.org/10.1007/978-3-662-49896-5_11

21. Groth, J., Kohlweiss, M., Maller, M., Meiklejohn, S., Miers, I.: Updatable and universal common reference strings with applications to zk-SNARKs. In: Shacham, H., Boldyreva, A. (eds.) CRYPTO 2018. LNCS, vol. 10993, pp. 698–728. Springer, Cham (2018). https://doi.org/10.1007/978-3-319-96878-0_24

22. Juels, A., Kosba, A.E., Shi, E.: The ring of Gyges: investigating the future of criminal smart contracts. In: ACM CCS 16, pp. 283–295 (2016)

23. Katz, J., Maurer, U., Tackmann, B., Zikas, V.: Universally composable synchronous computation. In: Sahai, A. (ed.) TCC 2013. LNCS, vol. 7785, pp. 477–498. Springer, Heidelberg (2013). https://doi.org/10.1007/978-3-642-36594-2_27

24. Kidron, D., Lindell, Y.: Impossibility results for universal composability in public-key models and with fixed inputs. J. Cryptol. 24(3), 517–544 (2011)

25. Kosba, A.E., Miller, A., Shi, E., Wen, Z., Papamanthou, C.: Hawk: the blockchain model of cryptography and privacy-preserving smart contracts. In: 2016 IEEE Symposium on Security and Privacy, pp. 839–858 (2016)

26. Lipmaa, H.: Progression-free sets and sublinear pairing-based non-interactive zero-knowledge arguments. In: Cramer, R. (ed.) TCC 2012. LNCS, vol. 7194, pp. 169–189. Springer, Heidelberg (2012). https://doi.org/10.1007/978-3-642-28914-9_10

27. Maller, M., Bowe, S., Kohlweiss, M., Meiklejohn, S.: Sonic: zero-knowledge snarks from linear-size universal and updateable structured reference strings. Cryptology ePrint Archive, Report 2019/099 (2019). https://eprint.iacr.org/2019/099

28. Naor, M.: On cryptographic assumptions and challenges. In: Boneh, D. (ed.) CRYPTO 2003. LNCS, vol. 2729, pp. 96–109. Springer, Heidelberg (2003). https://doi.org/10.1007/978-3-540-45146-4_6

29. Parno, B., Howell, J., Gentry, C., Raykova, M.: Pinocchio: Nearly practical verifiable computation. In: 2013 IEEE Symposium on Security and Privacy, pp. 238–252 (2013)

On the Efficiency of Privacy-Preserving Smart Contract Systems

Karim Baghery$^{(\boxtimes)}$

University of Tartu, Tartu, Estonia
karim.baghery@ut.ee

Abstract. Along with blockchain technology, smart contracts have found intense interest in lots of practical applications. A smart contract is a mechanism involving digital assets and some parties, where the parties deposit assets into the contract and the contract redistributes the assets among the parties based on provisions of the smart contract and inputs of the parties. Recently, several smart contract systems are constructed that use zk-SNARKs to provide privacy-preserving payments and interconnections in the contracts (e.g. Hawk [KMS+16] and Gyges [JKS16]). Efficiency of such systems severely are dominated by efficiency of the underlying UC-secure zk-SNARK that is achieved using CØCØ framework [KZM+15] applied on a non-UC-secure zk-SNARK. In this paper, we show that recent progresses on zk-SNARKs, allow one to simplify the structure and also improve the efficiency of both systems with a UC-secure zk-SNARK that has simpler construction and better efficiency in comparison with the currently used ones. More precisely, with minimal changes, we present a variation of Groth and Maller's zk-SNARK from Crypto 2017, and show that it achieves UC-security and has better efficiency than the ones that currently are used in Hawk and Gyges. We believe, new variation can be of independent interest.

Keywords: Privacy-preserving smart contracts · zk-SNARKs · UC-security · CRS model

1 Introduction

Eliminating the need for a trusted third party in monetary transactions, consequently enabling direct transactions between individuals is one of the main achievements in the cryptocurrencies such as Bitcoin. Importantly, it is shown that the technology behind cryptocurrencies has more potential than what only is used in direct transactions. Different blockchain-based systems such as smart contracts [KMS+16, JKS16], distributed cloud storages [WLB14], digital coins such as Ethereum [Woo14] are some evidence that why blockchain technology offers much more functionalities than what we can see in Bitcoin. Smart contracts are one of popular applications that along with blockchain technology, have found intense interest recently. A smart contract is a generic term denoting programs written in Turing-complete cryptocurrency scripting languages,

© Springer Nature Switzerland AG 2019
J. Buchmann et al. (Eds.): AFRICACRYPT 2019, LNCS 11627, pp. 118–136, 2019.
https://doi.org/10.1007/978-3-030-23696-0_7

that involves digital assets and some parties. The parties deposit assets into the contract and the contract redistributes the assets among the parties based on provisions of the smart contract and inputs of the parties.

Different research have shown that even if payments (e.g. in Bitcoin) or interconnections (e.g. in smart contracts) are conducted between pseudorandom addresses, but still they lack privacy of end-users. Indeed, this mostly arises from the nature of technology that a decentralized publicly shared ledger records list of transactions along with related information (e.g. addresses of parties, transferred values, etc), and long-time monitoring and some data analysis (e.g. transaction graph analysis) on this ledger usually reveals some information about the identity of end-users. To address these concerns and provide strong privacy for end-users, several alternatives to Bitcoin protocol and smart contract systems have been proposed; e.g. confidential assets [PBF+18], privacy-preserving auditing [NVV18], privacy-preserving cryptocurrencies such as Zerocash [BCG+14] and Monero [Noe15], privacy-preserving smart contract systems such as Hawk [KMS+16] and Gyges [JKS16].

Zerocash and Monero are two known anonymous cryptocurrencies that provide strong privacy for end-users. Each of them uses different cryptographic tools to guarantee strong privacy. Monero uses ring signatures that allow for an individual from a group to provide a signature such that it is impossible to identify which member of that group made the signature. On the other side, Zerocash uses zero-knowledge Succinct Non-interactive Arguments of Knowledge (zk-SNARKs [Gro10, Lip12, PHGR13, BCTV13, Gro16, GM17]) to prove the correctness of all computations inside a direct transaction, without revealing the source, destination and values of the transferred coins. In a similar technique, privacy-preserving smart contract system Hawk [KMS+16] and criminal smart contract system Gyges [JKS16] use universally composable zk-SNARKs to provide anonymous interconnection and payment in a smart contract.

zk-SNARKs. Among various Non-Interactive Zero-Knowledge (NIZK) arguments, zk-SNARKs are one of the most popular ones in practical systems. This is happened because of their succinct proofs, and consequently very efficient verification. A zk-SNARK proof allows one to efficiently verify the veracity of statements without learning extra information about the prover. The proofs can be verified offline very quickly (in few milliseconds) by possibly many independent verifiers. This can be very effective in efficiency of large-scale distributed systems. Efficiency of zk-SNARKs mainly comes from the fact that their construction relies on non-falsifiable assumptions (e.g. knowledge assumptions [Dam91]) that allow succinct proofs and non-black-box extraction in security proofs. On the other hand, a zk-SNARK with non-black-box extraction cannot achieve Universally Composable Security (UC-security) which is imperative and necessary in constructing larger cryptographic systems [Can01]. Du to this fact, zk-SNAKRs cannot be directly adopted in larger systems that should guarantee UC-security.

Privacy-Preserving Smart Contract Systems. Recently, some elegant UC-based frameworks are presented that allow to construct privacy-preserving smart contracts, including Hawk [KMS+16] and Gyges [JKS16] for criminal smart contracts. These systems record zk-SNARK proofs on ledger, instead of public transactions between pseudonyms, which brings stronger transactional privacy. Strictly speaking, Hawk is a system that gets a program and compiles it to a cryptographic protocol between the contract correspondents (including users and a manager) and the blockchain. It consists of two main blocks, where one is responsible for *private money transfers* and uses a variation of Zerocash [BCG+14], while the second part handles other contract-defined operations of the system. Similar to Zerocash, operations such as *Mint*, that is required in minting a new coin, and *Pour*, that enables anonymous transactions, are located in the first block. On the other side, contract-related operations such as *Freeze*, *Compute* and *Finalize*, that are three necessary operations defined by Hawk for each smart contract, are addressed in the second block. More details regard to the mentioned operations can be found in [KMS+16][1]. To achieve anonymity in the mentioned operations and payments, Hawk widely uses zk-SNARKs to prove different statements. As the whole system intended to achieve UC-security, so they needed to use a UC-secure zk-SNARK in the system. Additionally, since Zerocash also uses a non-UC-secure zk-SNARK and it is not proved to satisfy UC-security, so to make it useable in Hawk, they needed a variation of Zerocash that uses a UC-secure zk-SNARK and also guarantees UC-security. To this aim, designers of Hawk have used C∅C∅ framework [KZM+15] (a framework to lift a non-UC-secure sound NIZK to a UC-secure one; C∅C∅ stands for *Composable 0-knowledge, Compact 0-knowledge*) to lift the non-UC-secure zk-SNARK used in Zerocash [BCTV13], to a UC-secure zk-SNARK, such that the lifted scheme can be securely used in composition with the rest of system [Can01]. Then, due to using a UC-secure zk-SNARK in Zerocash, designer of Hawk modified the structure of original Zerocash and used the customized version in their system, which also guarantees UC-security. The lifted UC-secure zk-SNARK frequently is used in the system and plays an essential role in the efficiency of entire system.

Problem Statement. In the performance evaluation of Hawk [KMS+16] authors show that the efficiency of their system severely depend on efficiency of the lifted UC-secure zk-SNARK (which is the case in Gyges [JKS16] as well). In fact, computational complexity of both systems are dominated with complexity of the underlying UC-secure zk-SNARK. Particularly, Kosba et al. [KMS+16] emphasize that practical efficiency is a permanent goal of Hawk's design, so to get the best, they also propose various optimizations. By considering this, one may ask, can we improve efficiency of the underlying UC-secure zk-SNARKs such that the efficiency of complete systems will be improved?

Our Contribution. As the main contribution, we show that one can improve efficiency of Hawk (and similarly Gyges) smart contract system by improving the efficiency of underlying UC-secure zk-SNARK. We will see that one can use

---

[1] A tutorial about the system can be found in http://cryptowiki.net/index.php?title=Privacy_preserving_smart_contracts:_Hawk_project.

a similar approach used by Kosba et al. (in Hawk [KMS+16]) and Juels et al. (in Gyges [JKS16]) and construct a UC-secure version of Groth and Maller's zk-SNARK [GM17] (refereed as GM zk-SNARK in the rest), that has simpler construction and better efficiency than the ones that currently are used in the systems. To do so, we slightly modify the construction of GM zk-SNARK by enforcing the prover to send encryption of witnesses along with the proof, and then show that it achieves black-box simulation extractability, equivalently UC-security, which allows to deploy in both systems to improve their efficiency.

Both Hawk and Gyges have used C∅C∅ framework to lift a variation of Pinocchio zk-SNARK [PHGR13] which is deployed in Zerocash (proposed by Ben Sasson et al. [BCTV13]). Later it details we show that, as GM zk-SNARK [GM17] has better efficiency than the mentioned variation of Pinocchio zk-SNARK, and as our changes are lighter than the changes that are applied on Ben Sasson et al.'s zk-SNARK in Hawk [KMS+16] and Gyges [JKS16], so we get a UC-secure zk-SNARK that has simpler construction and better efficiency than the ones that currently are deployed in the systems. Indeed, we will see that our changes are a small part of their changes, which leads to have less overload.

In the modified construction, we do the changes in CRS circuit level and try to keep the prover and verifier procedure as original one that both are considerably optimized in the original construction [GM17]. We believe, new constructed UC-secure zk-SNARK can be of independent interest and it can be deployed in any large cryptographic system that aims to guarantee UC-security and needs to use zk-SNARKs. From a different perspective, new construction also can be used as a commit-and-proof system, as prover can send encryption (sort of commitment) of witnesses earlier than the proof elements. In such cases, one can consider linear commitment size and succinct proof size (proof would be 2 elements in $\mathbb{G}_1$ and 1 element in $\mathbb{G}_2$). We note that in UC-secure zk-SNARKs, the proofs are linear in witness size but still independent of size of the circuit that encodes language.

Discussion of UC-secure NIZKs. Most of efficient zk-SNARKs only guarantee *knowledge soundness*, meaning that if an adversary can come up with a valid proof, there exists an extractor that can extract the witness from the adversary. But in some cases, e.g. in signatures of knowledge SoKs [CL06], *knowledge soundness* is not enough, and one needs more security guarantee. More accurately, most of zk-SNARKs are vulnerable to the malleability attack which allows an adversary to modify an old proof to a new valid one, that is not desired in some cases. To address this, the notion of *simulation extractability* is defined which ensures that an adversary cannot come with a new acceptable proof (or an argument), even if he already has seen arbitrary simulated proofs, unless he knows the witness. In other words, simulation extractability implies that if an adversary, who has obtained arbitrary number of simulated proofs, can generate an acceptable new proof for a statement, there exists an extractor that can extract the witness. Based on extraction procedure which is categorized as Black-Box (BB) or non-Black-Box (nBB), there are various notions of simulation extractibility [Gro06, KZM+15, GM17]. In BB extraction, there exists a black-box (universal) extractor which can extract the witness from

all adversaries, however in the nBB extraction, for each adversary there exists
a particular extractor that can extract only if it has access to the adversary's
source code and random coins. It is already observed and proven that a NIZK
system that achieves simulation extractibility with BB extraction, can guarantee
the UC-security [CLOS02,Gro06,GOS06].Therefore, constructing a simulation-
extractable zk-SNARK with BB extraction is equivalent to constructing a UC-
secure zk-SNARK (which the proof will be only circuit succinct). Strictly speaking, in a UC-secure NIZK the simulator of *ideal-world* should be able to extract
witnesses without getting access to the source code of environment's algorithm,
which this is guaranteed by BB extraction.

A known technique to achieve a simulation-extractable NIZK with BB extraction is to enforce the prover to send the encryption of witnesses (with a public
key given in the CRS) along with proof, so that in security proofs the extractor can use the pair secret key for extraction [Gro06]. Using this technique, the
proof (communication) size will not be succinct anymore, as impossibility result
in [GW11] confirms, but the verification will be efficient yet and the extraction
issue that zk-SNARKs have in the UC framework [Can01] will be solved.

2   Preliminaries

Let PPT denote probabilistic polynomial-time, and NUPPT denote non-uniform
PPT. Let $\lambda \in \mathbb{N}$ be the security parameter, say $\lambda = 128$. All adversaries will be
stateful. For an algorithm $\mathcal{A}$, let $\text{im}(\mathcal{A})$ be the image of $\mathcal{A}$, i.e., the set of valid outputs of $\mathcal{A}$, let $\mathsf{RND}(\mathcal{A})$ denote the random tape of $\mathcal{A}$, and let $r \leftarrow_\$ \mathsf{RND}(\mathcal{A})$ denote
sampling of a randomizer r of sufficient length for $\mathcal{A}$'s needs. By $y \leftarrow \mathcal{A}(x; r)$
we mean given an input x and a randomizer r, $\mathcal{A}$ outputs y. For algorithms $\mathcal{A}$
and $\mathsf{Ext}_{\mathcal{A}}$, we write $(y \,\|\, y') \leftarrow (\mathcal{A} \,\|\, \mathsf{Ext}_{\mathcal{A}})(x; r)$ as a shorthand for "$y \leftarrow \mathcal{A}(x; r)$,
$y' \leftarrow \mathsf{Ext}_{\mathcal{A}}(x; r)$". An arbitrary negligible function is shown with $\mathsf{negl}(\lambda)$. Two
computationally indistinguishable distributions A and B are shown with $A \approx_c B$.

In pairing-based groups, we use additive notation together with the bracket
notation, i.e., in group $\mathbb{G}_\mu$, $[a]_\mu = a\,[1]_\mu$, where $[1]_\mu$ is a fixed generator of $\mathbb{G}_\mu$. A
bilinear group generator $\mathsf{BGgen}(1^\lambda)$ returns $(p, \mathbb{G}_1, \mathbb{G}_2, \mathbb{G}_T, \hat{e}, [1]_1, [1]_2)$, where p
(a large prime) is the order of cyclic abelian groups $\mathbb{G}_1$, $\mathbb{G}_2$, and $\mathbb{G}_T$. Finally, $\hat{e} :$
$\mathbb{G}_1 \times \mathbb{G}_2 \to \mathbb{G}_T$ is an efficient non-degenerate bilinear pairing, s.t. $\hat{e}([a]_1, [b]_2) =$
$[ab]_T$. Denote $[a]_1 \bullet [b]_2 = \hat{e}([a]_1, [b]_2)$.

We bellow review Square Arithmetic Programs (SAPs) that defines NP-
complete language specified by a quadratic equation over polynomials [GM17].

Square Arithmetic Program: Any quadratic arithmetic circuit with fan-in 2 gates
over a finite field $\mathbb{Z}_p$ can be lifted to a SAP instance over the same finite field (e.g.
by considering $ab = ((a + b)^2 - (a - b)^2)/4$) [GM17]. A SAP instance contains
$\mathcal{S}_p = (\mathbb{Z}_p, m_0, \{u_j, w_j\}_{j=0}^m)$. This instance defines the following relation:

$$
\mathbf{R}_{\mathcal{S}_p} = \left\{ \begin{array}{l} (\mathsf{x}, \mathsf{w}) : \mathsf{x} = (A_1, \ldots, A_{m_0})^\top \wedge \mathsf{w} = (A_{m_0+1}, \ldots, A_m)^\top \wedge \\[2mm] \left(\sum_{j=0}^m A_j u_j(X)\right)^2 \equiv \sum_{j=0}^m A_j w_j(X) \pmod{\ell(X)} \end{array} \right\}
$$

where $\ell(X) := \prod_{i=1}^{n}(X - \omega^{i-1}) = X^n - 1$ is the unique degree n monic polynomial such that $\ell(\omega^{i-1}) = 0$ for all $i \in [1..n]$. Alternatively, $(\mathsf{x}, \mathsf{w}) \in \mathbf{R}_{\mathcal{S}_p}$ if there exists a (degree $\leq n-2$) polynomial $h(X)$, s.t. $\left(\sum_{j=0}^{m} A_j u_j(X)\right)^2 - \sum_{j=0}^{m} A_j w_j(X) = h(X)\ell(X)$.

2.1 Definitions

We use the definitions of NIZK arguments from [Gro06, Gro16, GM17, KZM+15]. Let $\mathcal{R}$ be a relation generator, such that $\mathcal{R}(1^\lambda)$ returns a polynomial-time decidable binary relation $\mathbf{R} = \{(\mathsf{x}, \mathsf{w})\}$. Here, x is the statement and w is the witness. We assume one can deduce λ from the description of $\mathbf{R}$. The relation generator also outputs auxiliary information $\xi_{\mathbf{R}}$ that will be given to the honest parties and the adversary. As in [Gro16, ABLZ17], $\xi_{\mathbf{R}}$ is the value returned by $\mathsf{BGgen}(1^\lambda)$. Due to this, we also give $\xi_{\mathbf{R}}$ as an input to the honest parties; if needed, one can include an additional auxiliary input to the adversary. Let $\mathbf{L}_{\mathbf{R}} = \{\mathsf{x} : \exists \mathsf{w}, (\mathsf{x}, \mathsf{w}) \in \mathbf{R}\}$ be an **NP**-language.

A *NIZK argument system* Ψ for $\mathcal{R}$ consists of tuple of PPT algorithms, s.t.:

CRS generator: K is a PPT algorithm that given $(\mathbf{R}, \xi_{\mathbf{R}})$, where $(\mathbf{R}, \xi_{\mathbf{R}}) \in \mathrm{im}(\mathcal{R}(1^\lambda))$ outputs $\mathsf{crs} = (\mathsf{crs}_\mathsf{P}, \mathsf{crs}_\mathsf{V})$ and stores trapdoors of crs as ts. We distinguish crs_P (needed by the prover) from crs_V (needed by the verifier).
Prover: P is a PPT algorithm that, given $(\mathbf{R}, \xi_{\mathbf{R}}, \mathsf{crs}_\mathsf{P}, \mathsf{x}, \mathsf{w})$, where $(\mathsf{x}, \mathsf{w}) \in \mathbf{R}$, outputs an argument π. Otherwise, it outputs $\bot$.
Verifier: V is a PPT algorithm that, given $(\mathbf{R}, \xi_{\mathbf{R}}, \mathsf{crs}_\mathsf{V}, \mathsf{x}, \pi)$, returns either 0 (reject) or 1 (accept).
Simulator: Sim is a PPT algorithm that, given $(\mathbf{R}, \xi_{\mathbf{R}}, \mathsf{crs}, \mathsf{ts}, \mathsf{x})$, outputs an argument π.
Extractor: Ext is a PPT algorithm that, given $(\mathbf{R_L}, \xi_{\mathbf{R_L}}, \mathsf{crs}, \mathsf{x}, \pi, \mathsf{te})$ extracts the w; where te is extraction trapdoor (e.g. a secret key).

We require an argument system Ψ to be complete, computationally knowledge-sound and statistically ZK, as in the following definitions.

Definition 1 (Perfect Completeness [Gro16]). *A non-interactive argument* Ψ *is perfectly complete for* $\mathcal{R}$, *if for all* λ, *all* $(\mathbf{R}, \xi_{\mathbf{R}}) \in \mathrm{im}(\mathcal{R}(1^\lambda))$, *and* $(\mathsf{x}, \mathsf{w}) \in \mathbf{R}$,

$$\Pr\left[\mathsf{crs} \leftarrow \mathsf{K}(\mathbf{R}, \xi_{\mathbf{R}}) : \mathsf{V}(\mathbf{R}, \xi_{\mathbf{R}}, \mathsf{crs}_\mathsf{V}, \mathsf{x}, \mathsf{P}(\mathbf{R}, \xi_{\mathbf{R}}, \mathsf{crs}_\mathsf{P}, \mathsf{x}, \mathsf{w})) = 1\right] = 1 .$$

Definition 2 (Computational Knowledge-Soundness [Gro16]). *A non-interactive argument* Ψ *is computationally (adaptively) knowledge-sound for* $\mathcal{R}$, *if for every NUPPT* $\mathcal{A}$, *there exists a NUPPT extractor* $\mathsf{Ext}_{\mathcal{A}}$, *s.t. for all* λ,

$$\Pr\left[\begin{array}{l}(\mathbf{R}, \xi_{\mathbf{R}}) \leftarrow \mathcal{R}(1^\lambda), (\mathsf{crs} \| \mathsf{ts}) \leftarrow \mathsf{K}(\mathbf{R}, \xi_{\mathbf{R}}), \\ r \leftarrow_r \mathsf{RND}(\mathcal{A}), ((\mathsf{x}, \pi) \| \mathsf{w}) \leftarrow (\mathcal{A} \| \mathsf{Ext}_{\mathcal{A}})(\mathbf{R}, \xi_{\mathbf{R}}, \mathsf{crs}; r) : \\ (\mathsf{x}, \mathsf{w}) \notin \mathbf{R} \wedge \mathsf{V}(\mathbf{R}, \xi_{\mathbf{R}}, \mathsf{crs}_\mathsf{V}, \mathsf{x}, \pi) = 1\end{array}\right] \approx_\lambda 0 .$$

Here, $\xi_{\mathbf{R}}$ can be seen as a common auxiliary input to $\mathcal{A}$ and $\mathsf{Ext}_{\mathcal{A}}$ that is generated by using a benign [BCPR14] relation generator; A knowledge-sound argument system is called an *argument of knowledge*.

Definition 3 (Statistically Zero-Knowledge [Gro16]). *A non-interactive argument Ψ is statistically ZK for $\mathcal{R}$, if for all λ, all $(\mathbf{R}, \xi_{\mathbf{R}}) \in \mathrm{im}(\mathcal{R}(1^{\lambda}))$, and for all NUPPT $\mathcal{A}$, $\varepsilon_0^{unb} \approx_{\lambda} \varepsilon_1^{unb}$, where*

$$\varepsilon_b = \Pr[(\mathbf{crs} \,\|\, \mathbf{ts}) \leftarrow \mathsf{K}(\mathbf{R}, \xi_{\mathbf{R}}) : \mathcal{A}^{\mathsf{O}_b(\cdot,\cdot)}(\mathbf{R}, \xi_{\mathbf{R}}, \mathbf{crs}) = 1] \ .$$

Here, the oracle $\mathsf{O}_0(\mathsf{x}, \mathsf{w})$ returns $\bot$ (reject) if $(\mathsf{x}, \mathsf{w}) \notin \mathbf{R}$, and otherwise it returns $\mathsf{P}(\mathbf{R}, \xi_{\mathbf{R}}, \mathbf{crs}_\mathsf{P}, \mathsf{x}, \mathsf{w})$. Similarly, $\mathsf{O}_1(\mathsf{x}, \mathsf{w})$ returns $\bot$ (reject) if $(\mathsf{x}, \mathsf{w}) \notin \mathbf{R}$, and otherwise it returns $\mathsf{Sim}(\mathbf{R}, \xi_{\mathbf{R}}, \mathbf{crs}, \mathsf{x}, \mathsf{ts})$. Ψ is perfect ZK for $\mathcal{R}$ if one requires that $\varepsilon_0 = \varepsilon_1$.

Intuitively, a non-interactive argument Ψ is zero-knowledge if it does not leak extra information besides the truth of the statement. Beside the mentioned properties defined in Definitions 1–3, a zk-SNARK has *succinctness* property, meaning that the proof size is $\mathrm{poly}(\lambda)$ and the verifier's computation is $\mathrm{poly}(\lambda)$ and the size of instance. In the rest, we recall the definitions of simulation soundness and simulation extractability that are used in construction of UC-secure zk-SNARKs.

Definition 4 (Simulation Soundness [Gro06]). *A non-interactive argument Ψ is simulation sound for $\mathcal{R}$ if for all NUPPT $\mathcal{A}$, and all λ,*

$$\Pr\left[\begin{matrix} (\mathbf{R}, \xi_{\mathbf{R}}) \leftarrow \mathcal{R}(1^{\lambda}), (\mathbf{crs} \,\|\, \mathbf{ts}) \leftarrow \mathsf{K}(\mathbf{R}, \xi_{\mathbf{R}}), (\mathsf{x}, \pi) \leftarrow \mathcal{A}^{\mathsf{O}(\cdot)}(\mathbf{R}, \xi_{\mathbf{R}}, \mathbf{crs}) : \\ (\mathsf{x}, \pi) \notin Q \wedge \mathsf{x} \notin \mathbf{L} \wedge \mathsf{V}(\mathbf{R}, \xi_{\mathbf{R}}, \mathbf{crs}_\mathsf{V}, \mathsf{x}, \pi) = 1 \end{matrix}\right] \approx_{\lambda} 0 \ .$$

Here, Q is the set of simulated statement-proof pairs generated by adversary's queries to O, that returns simulated proofs.

Definition 5 (Non-Black-Box Simulation Extractability [GM17]). *A non-interactive argument Ψ is non-black-box simulation-extractable for $\mathcal{R}$, if for any NUPPT $\mathcal{A}$, there exists a NUPPT extractor $\mathsf{Ext}_{\mathcal{A}}$ s.t. for all λ,*

$$\Pr\left[\begin{matrix} (\mathbf{R}, \xi_{\mathbf{R}}) \leftarrow \mathcal{R}(1^{\lambda}), (\mathbf{crs} \,\|\, \mathbf{ts}) \leftarrow \mathsf{K}(\mathbf{R}, \xi_{\mathbf{R}}), \ \cdot \\ r \leftarrow_r \mathsf{RND}(\mathcal{A}), ((\mathsf{x}, \pi) \,\|\, \mathsf{w}) \leftarrow (\mathcal{A}^{\mathsf{O}(\cdot)} \,\|\, \mathsf{Ext}_{\mathcal{A}})(\mathbf{R}, \xi_{\mathbf{R}}, \mathbf{crs}; r) : \\ (\mathsf{x}, \pi) \notin Q \wedge (\mathsf{x}, \mathsf{w}) \notin \mathbf{R} \wedge \mathsf{V}(\mathbf{R}, \xi_{\mathbf{R}}, \mathbf{crs}_\mathsf{V}, \mathsf{x}, \pi) = 1 \end{matrix}\right] \approx_{\lambda} 0 \ .$$

Here, Q is the set of simulated statement-proof pairs generated by adversary's queries to O that returns simulated proofs. It is worth to mention that *non-black-box simulation extractability* implies *knowledge soundness* (given in Definition 2), as the earlier is a strong notion of the later which additionally the adversary is allowed to send query to the proof simulation oracle. Similarly, one can observe that *non-black-box simulation extractability* implies *simulation soundness* (given in Definition 4) that is discussed in [Gro06] with more details.

Definition 6 (Black-Box Simulation Extractability [KZM+15]). *A non-interactive argument Ψ is* black-box simulation-extractable *for $\mathcal{R}$ if there exists a black-box extractor* Ext *that for all NUPPT $\mathcal{A}$, and all λ,*

$$\Pr \left[\begin{array}{l} (\mathbf{R}, \xi_{\mathbf{R}}) \leftarrow \mathcal{R}(1^\lambda), (\mathsf{crs} \parallel \mathsf{ts} \parallel \mathsf{te}) \leftarrow \mathsf{K}(\mathbf{R}, \xi_{\mathbf{R}}), \\ (\mathsf{x}, \pi) \leftarrow \mathcal{A}^{O(\cdot)}(\mathbf{R}, \xi_{\mathbf{R}}, \mathsf{crs}), \mathsf{w} \leftarrow \mathsf{Ext}(\mathbf{R}, \xi_{\mathbf{R}}, \mathsf{crs}, \mathsf{te}, \mathsf{x}, \pi) : \\ (\mathsf{x}, \pi) \notin Q \wedge (\mathsf{x}, \mathsf{w}) \notin \mathbf{R} \wedge \mathsf{V}(\mathbf{R}, \xi_{\mathbf{R}}, \mathsf{crs}_\mathsf{V}, \mathsf{x}, \pi) = 1 \end{array} \right] \approx_\lambda 0 \ .$$

Similarly, Q is the set of simulated statement-proof pairs, and **te** is the extraction trapdoor. A key note about Definition 6 is that the extraction procedure is black-box and unlike the non-black-box case, the extractor Ext works for all adversaries.

2.2   CØCØ : A Framework for Constructing UC-Secure zk-SNARKs

Kosba et al. [KZM+15] have constructed a framework with several converters which the most powerful one gets a sound NIZK and lifts to a NIZK that achieves *black-box simulation extractability* (defined in Definition 6), or equivalently UC-security [Gro06]. Here we review construction of the most powerful converter that is used by both Hawk and Gyges to construct a UC-secure zk-SNARK.

Construction. Given a sound NIZK, to achieve a UC-secure NIZK, CØCØ framework applies several changes in all setup, proof generation and verification procedures of the input NIZK. Initially the framework defines a new language $\mathbf{L}'$ based on the language $\mathbf{L}$ in underlying NIZK and some new primitives that are needed for the transformation. Let $(\mathsf{KGen}_e, \mathsf{Enc}_e, \mathsf{Dec}_e)$ be a set of algorithms for a semantically secure encryption scheme, $(\mathsf{KGen}_s, \mathsf{Sig}_s, \mathsf{Vfy}_s)$ be a one-time signature scheme and $(\mathsf{Com}_c, \mathsf{Vfy}_c)$ be a perfectly binding commitment scheme. Given a language $\mathbf{L}$ with the corresponding **NP** relation $\mathbf{R_L}$, define a new language $\mathbf{L}'$ such that $((\mathsf{x}, c, \mu, \mathsf{pk}_s, \mathsf{pk}_e, \rho), (r, r_0, \mathsf{w}, s_0)) \in \mathbf{R_{L'}}$ iff:

$$(c = \mathsf{Enc}_e(\mathsf{pk}_e, \mathsf{w}; r)) \wedge ((\mathsf{x}, \mathsf{w}) \in \mathbf{R_L} \vee (\mu = f_{s_0}(\mathsf{pk}_s) \wedge \rho = \mathsf{Com}_c(s_0; r_0))) ,$$

where $\{f_s : \{0,1\}^* \to \{0,1\}^\lambda\}_{s \in \{0,1\}^\lambda}$ is a pseudo-random function family. Now, a sound NIZK argument system Ψ for $\mathcal{R}$ constructed from PPT algorithms $(\mathsf{K}, \mathsf{P}, \mathsf{V}, \mathsf{Sim}, \mathsf{Ext})$ can be lifted to a UC-secure NIZK Ψ' with PPT algorithms $(\mathsf{K}', \mathsf{P}', \mathsf{V}', \mathsf{Sim}', \mathsf{Ext}')$ as follows.

CRS and trapdoor generation $\mathsf{K}'(\mathbf{R_L}, \xi_{\mathbf{R_L}})$: Sample $(\mathsf{crs} \parallel \mathsf{ts}) \leftarrow \mathsf{K}(\mathbf{R_{L'}}, \xi_{\mathbf{R_{L'}}})$; $(\mathsf{pk}_e, \mathsf{sk}_e) \leftarrow \mathsf{KGen}_e(1^\lambda)$; $s_0, r_0 \leftarrow_\$ \{0,1\}^\lambda$; $\rho := \mathsf{Com}_c(s_0; r_0)$; and output $(\mathsf{crs}' \parallel \mathsf{ts}' \parallel \mathsf{te}') := ((\mathsf{crs}, \mathsf{pk}_e, \rho) \parallel (s_0, r_0) \parallel \mathsf{sk}_e)$.

Prover $\mathsf{P}'(\mathbf{R_L}, \xi_{\mathbf{R_L}}, \mathsf{crs}, \mathsf{x}, \mathsf{w})$: Parse $\mathsf{crs}' := (\mathsf{crs}, \mathsf{pk}_e, \rho)$; Abort if $(\mathsf{x}, \mathsf{w}) \notin \mathbf{R_L}$; $(\mathsf{pk}_s, \mathsf{sk}_s) \leftarrow \mathsf{KGen}_s(1^\lambda)$; sample $z_0, z_1, z_2, r_1 \leftarrow_\$ \{0,1\}^\lambda$; compute $c = \mathsf{Enc}_e(\mathsf{pk}_e, \mathsf{w}; r_1)$; generate $\pi \leftarrow \mathsf{P}(\mathbf{R_{L'}}, \xi_{\mathbf{R_{L'}}}, \mathsf{crs}, (\mathsf{x}, c, z_0, \mathsf{pk}_s, \mathsf{pk}_e, \rho), (r_1, z_1, w, z_2))$; sign $\sigma \leftarrow \mathsf{Sig}_s(\mathsf{sk}_s, (\mathsf{x}, c, z_0, \pi))$; and output $\pi' := (c, z_0, \pi, \mathsf{pk}_s, \sigma)$.

Verifier $V'(R_L, \xi_{R_L}, crs', x, \pi')$: Parse $crs' := (crs, pk_e, \rho)$ and $\pi' := (c, \mu, \pi, pk_s, \sigma)$; Abort if $\mathsf{Vfy}_s(pk_s, (x, c, \mu, \pi), \sigma) = 0$; call $V(R_{L'}, \xi_{R_{L'}}, crs, (x, c, \mu, pk_s, pk_e, \rho), \pi)$ and abort if it outputs 0.

Simulator $\mathsf{Sim}'(R_L, \xi_{R_L}, crs', ts', x)$: Parse $crs' := (crs, pk_e, \rho)$ and $ts' := (s_0, r_0)$; $(pk_s, sk_s) \leftarrow \mathsf{KGen}_s(1^\lambda)$; set $\mu = f_{s_0}(pk_s)$; sample $z_3, r_1 \leftarrow_\$ \{0,1\}^\lambda$; compute $c = \mathsf{Enc}_e(pk_e, z_3; r_1)$; generate $\pi \leftarrow P(R_{L'}, \xi_{R_{L'}}, crs, (x, c, \mu, pk_s, pk_e, \rho), (r_1, r_0, z_3, s_0))$; sign $\sigma \leftarrow \mathsf{Sig}_s(sk_s, (x, c, \mu, \pi))$; and output $\pi' := (c, \mu, \pi, pk_s, \sigma)$.

Extractor $\mathsf{Ext}'(R_L, \xi_{R_L}, crs', te', x, \pi')$: Parse $\pi' := (c, \mu, \pi, pk_s, \sigma)$, $te' := sk_e$; extract $w \leftarrow \mathsf{Dec}_e(sk_e, c)$; output w.

On input a SAP instance $\mathcal{S}_p = (\mathbb{Z}_p, m_0, \{u_j, w_j\}_{j=0}^m, \ell)$.

$K(R_{\mathcal{S}_p}, \xi_R)$: Pick $g_1 \leftarrow_r \mathbb{G}_1^*, g_2 \leftarrow_r \mathbb{G}_2^*, (\alpha, \beta, \gamma, \chi) \leftarrow_r (\mathbb{Z}_p^*)^4$ (such that $\ell(\chi) \neq 0$), generate $crs \leftarrow (crs_P, crs_V)$ and return (crs, ts); where $ts = (\alpha, \beta, \gamma, \chi)$ and

$$crs_P \leftarrow \begin{pmatrix} R_{\mathcal{S}_p}, \left[\alpha, \gamma\ell(\chi), \gamma^2\ell(\chi)^2, (\alpha+\beta)\gamma\ell(\chi), (\gamma\chi^i, \gamma^2\ell(\chi)\chi^i)_{i=0}^{n-1}\right]_1, \\ \left[(\gamma^2 w_i(\chi) + (\alpha+\beta)\gamma u_i(\chi))_{i=m_0+1}^m\right]_1, \left[\gamma\ell(\chi), (\gamma\chi^i)_{i=0}^{n-1}\right]_2 \end{pmatrix},$$

$$crs_V \leftarrow \left([\alpha, \gamma, (\gamma w_i(\chi) + (\alpha+\beta)u_i(\chi))_{i=0}^{m_0}]_1, [1, \beta, \gamma]_2\right).$$

$P(R_{\mathcal{S}_p}, \xi_R, crs_P, x = (A_1, \ldots, A_{m_0}), w = (A_{m_0+1}, \ldots, A_m))$:
1. Let $a^\dagger(X) \leftarrow \sum_{j=0}^m A_j u_j(X)$,
2. Let $c^\dagger(X) \leftarrow \sum_{j=0}^m A_j w_j(X)$,
3. Set $h(X) = \sum_{i=0}^{n-2} h_i X^i \leftarrow (a^\dagger(X)^2 - c^\dagger(X))/\ell(X)$,
4. Set $\left[\gamma^2 h(\chi)\ell(\chi)\right]_1 \leftarrow \sum_{i=0}^{n-2} h_i \left[\gamma^2 \chi^i \ell(\chi)\right]_1$,
5. Pick $r \leftarrow_r \mathbb{Z}_p$; Set
   - $\mathfrak{a} \leftarrow \left(\sum_{j=0}^m A_j \left[\gamma u_j(\chi)\right]_1 + r \left[\gamma\ell(\chi)\right]_1\right)$
   - $\mathfrak{b} \leftarrow \left(\sum_{j=0}^m A_j \left[\gamma u_j(\chi)\right]_2 + r \left[\gamma\ell(\chi)\right]_2\right)$
   - $\mathfrak{c} \leftarrow \sum_{j=m_0+1}^m A_j \left[(\gamma^2 w_j(\chi) + (\alpha+\beta)\gamma u_j(\chi)\right]_1 + r^2 \left[\gamma^2\ell(\chi)^2\right]_1 + r \left[(\alpha+\beta)\gamma\ell(\chi)\right]_1 + \left[\gamma^2\ell(\chi)\left(h(\chi) + 2r\sum_{j=0}^m A_j u_j(\chi)\right)\right]_1$
6. Return $\pi \leftarrow (\mathfrak{a}, \mathfrak{b}, \mathfrak{c})$.

$V(R_{\mathcal{S}_p}, \xi_R, crs_V, x = (A_1, \ldots, A_{m_0}), \pi = (\mathfrak{a}, \mathfrak{b}, \mathfrak{c}))$: assuming $A_0 = 1$, check

$$\mathfrak{a} \bullet [\gamma]_1 = [\gamma]_2 \bullet \mathfrak{b},$$

$$(\mathfrak{a} + [\alpha]_1) \bullet (\mathfrak{b} + [\beta]_2) = [\alpha]_1 \bullet [\beta]_2 +$$

$$+ \left(\sum_{j=0}^{m_0} A_j \left[(\gamma w_j(\chi) + (\alpha+\beta)u_j(\chi)\right]_1\right) \bullet [\gamma]_2 + \mathfrak{c} \bullet [1]_2.$$

$\mathsf{Sim}(R_{\mathcal{S}_p}, \xi_R, crs, x = (A_1, \ldots, A_{m_0}), ts)$: Pick $\mu \leftarrow \mathbb{Z}_p^*$, and compute $\pi = (\mathfrak{a}, \mathfrak{b}, \mathfrak{c})$ such that

$$\mathfrak{a} \leftarrow [\mu]_1, \quad \mathfrak{b} \leftarrow [\mu]_2, \quad \mathfrak{c} \leftarrow \left[\mu^2 + (\alpha+\beta)\mu - \gamma\sum_{j=0}^{m_0} A_j(\gamma w_j(\chi) + (\alpha+\beta)u_j(\chi))\right]_1$$

Fig. 1. Structure of GM zk-SNARK [GM17]

2.3   Groth and Maller's zk-SNARK

This section presents the construction of GM zk-SNARK that is presented by Groth and Maller in [GM17][2]. It is the first SAP-based zk-SNARK that achieves non-black-box simulation extractability, which makes the scheme secure against the malleability attacks. The structure of GM zk-SNARK is shown in Fig. 1.

3   An Efficient UC-Secure zk-SNARK

We present a variation of GM zk-SNARK [GM17] and show that it achieves black-box simulation extractability, and equivalently UC-security. GM zk-SNARK is the only scheme that guarantees non-black-box simulation extractablity which is stronger than knowledge-soundness that is usually achieved in most of pairing-based zk-SNARKs. We show that due to this strong security, with minimal changes we can achieve a UC-secure version of GM zk-SNARK.

Intuition. The goal is to present a UC-secure version of GM zk-SNARK but efficient than UC-secure zk-SNARKs that are lifted by CØCØ framework; especially more efficient than the ones that are deployed in [KMS+16,JKS16]. To do so, we slightly modify GM zk-SNARK and enforce prover P to encrypt its witnesses with a public key given in the CRS and send the ciphertext along with the proof. In this scenario, in security proof, the secret key of encryption scheme is given to the Ext which allows to extract witnesses in black-box manner, that is more realistic indeed. Actually this is an already known technique to achieve black-box extraction that also is used in CØCØ framework. It is undeniable that sending encryption of witnesses leads to have non-succinct proofs in witness size but still they are succinct in the size of circuit that encodes the language and it is simpler and more efficient than the ones that are lifted by CØCØ .

3.1   Construction

While modifying we keep internal computation of both prover and verifier as original one, that considerably are optimized for a SAP relation. Instead we define a new language L' based on the language L in GM zk-SNARK that is embedded with encryption of witness. Strictly speaking, given a language L with the corresponding **NP** relation $\mathbf{R_L}$, we define the following new language L' such that $((x, c, pk_e), (w, r)) \in \mathbf{R_{L'}}$ iff:

$$(c = \mathsf{Enc}_e(pk_e, w; r)) \wedge ((x, w) \in \mathbf{R_L}),$$

---

[2] We use original construction of GM zk-SNARK that is published in Crypto 2017 [GM17] and implemented in `Libsnark` library https://github.com/scipr-lab/libsnark. But one also can use the variation of GM zk-SNARK that recently is provided in full version of paper.

where $(\mathsf{KGen}_e, \mathsf{Enc}_e, \mathsf{Dec}_e)$ is a set of algorithms for a semantically secure encryption scheme with keys $(\mathsf{pk}_e, \mathsf{sk}_e)$. Accordingly, the modified version of GM zk-SNARK is given in Fig. 2. It is worth to mention that, due to the particular structure of new language $\mathbf{L}'$, all verifications will be done inside the circuit, and interestingly verifier and prover's internal computations are the same as before, just prover needs to send encryption of witnesses along with the proof. This is the key modification in removing nBB extraction (particularly knowledge-assumption based in zk-SNARKs) and achieving BB extraction.

CRS and trapdoor generation $\mathsf{K}'(\mathbf{R_L}, \xi_{\mathbf{R_L}})$: Generate key pair $(\mathsf{pk}_e, \mathsf{sk}_e) \leftarrow \mathsf{KGen}_e(1^\lambda)$; execute CRS generator of GM zk-SNARK and sample $(\mathsf{crs} \,\|\, \mathsf{ts}) \leftarrow \mathsf{K}(\mathbf{R_{L'}}, \xi_{\mathbf{R_{L'}}})$; output $(\mathsf{crs}' \,\|\, \mathsf{ts}' \,\|\, \mathsf{te}') := ((\mathsf{crs}, \mathsf{pk}_e) \,\|\, \mathsf{ts} \,\|\, \mathsf{sk}_e)$; where ts' are simulation trapdoors and te' is the extraction key.

Prover $\mathsf{P}'(\mathbf{R_L}, \xi_{\mathbf{R_L}}, \mathsf{crs}', \mathsf{x}, \mathsf{w})$: Parse $\mathsf{crs}' := (\mathsf{crs}, \mathsf{pk}_e)$; Abort if $(\mathsf{x}, \mathsf{w}) \notin \mathbf{R_L}$; sample $r \leftarrow_{\!\$} \{0,1\}^\lambda$; compute encryption of witnesses $c = \mathsf{Enc}_e(\mathsf{pk}_e, \mathsf{w}; r)$; execute prover P of GM zk-SNARK and generate $\pi \leftarrow \mathsf{P}(\mathbf{R_{L'}}, \xi_{\mathbf{R_{L'}}}, \mathsf{crs}, (\mathsf{x}, c, \mathsf{pk}_e), (\mathsf{w}, r))$; and output $\pi' := (c, \pi)$.

Verifier $\mathsf{V}'(\mathbf{R_L}, \xi_{\mathbf{R_L}}, \mathsf{crs}', \mathsf{x}, \pi')$: Parse $\mathsf{crs}' := (\mathsf{crs}, \mathsf{pk}_e)$ and $\pi' := (c, \pi)$; call verifier $\mathsf{V}(\mathbf{R_{L'}}, \xi_{\mathbf{R_{L'}}}, \mathsf{crs}, (\mathsf{x}, c, \mathsf{pk}_e), \pi)$ of GM zk-SNARK and abort if it rejects.

Simulator $\mathsf{Sim}'(\mathbf{R_L}, \xi_{\mathbf{R_L}}, \mathsf{crs}', \mathsf{x}, \mathsf{ts}')$: Parse $\mathsf{crs}' := (\mathsf{crs}, \mathsf{pk}_e)$ and $\mathsf{ts}' := \mathsf{ts}$; sample $z, r \leftarrow_{\!\$} \{0,1\}^\lambda$; compute $c = \mathsf{Enc}_e(\mathsf{pk}_e, z; r)$; execute simulator of GM zk-SNARK and generate $\pi \leftarrow \mathsf{Sim}(\mathbf{R_{L'}}, \xi_{\mathbf{R_{L'}}}, \mathsf{crs}, (\mathsf{x}, c, \mathsf{pk}_e), \mathsf{ts})$; and output $\pi' := (c, \pi)$.

Extractor $\mathsf{Ext}'(\mathbf{R_L}, \xi_{\mathbf{R_L}}, \mathsf{crs}', \mathsf{te}', \mathsf{x}, \pi')$: Parse $\pi' := (c, \pi)$ and $\mathsf{te}' := \mathsf{sk}_e$; extract $\mathsf{w} \leftarrow \mathsf{Dec}_e(\mathsf{sk}_e, c)$; output w.

Fig. 2. GM zk-SNARK with black-box simulation extractability

3.2   Efficiency

In the modified scheme, as the original one, proof is 2 elements in $\mathbb{G}_1$ and 1 element in $\mathbb{G}_2$, but along with c that is encryption of witnesses. So, proof size is dominated with size of c that is linear in witness size.

As verifier is untouched, so similar to GM zk-SNARK, the verification procedure consists of checking that the proof contains 3 appropriate group elements and checking 2 pairing product equations which in total it needs a multi-exponentiation $\mathbb{G}_1$ to m_0 exponents and 5 pairings.

In the setup, in result of our change, the arithmetic circuit will be slightly extended, but due to minimal changes (a more detailed comparison is provided in Fig. 3), the extension is less than the case that one uses $\mathsf{C} \emptyset \mathsf{C} \emptyset$ framework.

3.3   Security Proof

Theorem 1 (Perfect Completeness). *The protocol constructed in Sect. 3, is a non-interactive argument of knowledge that guarantees perfect completeness.*

Proof. We emphasizes that in the modified version, the internal computations of P and V are the same as original one, just they need to perform the computation for new SAP instance that has slightly larger size (e.g. $n = n_{old} + n_{new}$, where n is number of squaring gates in the new circuit, and n_{new} is the number of squaring gates that are added in result of new changes) and prover needs to output some new elements that are encryption of witnesses and will be used inside the unchanged verification equations. So by considering this fact, one can see that the completeness of modified protocol follows the original protocol. □

Theorem 2 (Computationally Zero-Knowledge). *The protocol constructed in Sect. 3, is a non-interactive argument of knowledge that guarantees computational zero-knowledge.*

Proof. To prove the theorem, we write a series of hybrid experiments that start from an experiment that encrypts a random value and uses the simulator, and finally gets to an experiment that uses the procedure of real prover. We show that all experiments are indistinguishable two-by-two. Before going through the games, recall that GM zk-SNARK scheme guarantees zero-knowledge and its simulation procedure is given in Fig. 1. So, consider the following experiment,

---

EXP_1^{zk}

– Setup: $(\mathsf{pk}_e, \mathsf{sk}_e) \leftarrow \mathsf{KGen}_e(1^\lambda)$; $(\mathbf{crs} \parallel \mathbf{ts}) \leftarrow \mathsf{K}(\mathbf{R}_{L'}, \xi_{\mathbf{R}_{L'}})$; $\mathbf{crs}' = (\mathbf{crs}, \mathsf{pk}_e)$

– $\mathsf{O}(\mathsf{x}, \mathsf{w})$: Abort **if** $(\mathsf{x}, \mathsf{w}) \notin \mathbf{R}_L$; Sample $z, r \leftarrow \{0,1\}^\lambda$; $c = \mathsf{Enc}_e(\mathsf{pk}_e, z; r)$;

$\qquad \pi \leftarrow \mathsf{Sim}(\mathbf{R}_{L'}, \xi_{\mathbf{R}_{L'}}, \mathbf{crs}, (\mathsf{x}, c, \mathsf{pk}_e), \mathbf{ts})$;

– $b \leftarrow \mathcal{A}^{\mathsf{O}(\mathsf{x},\mathsf{w})}(\mathbf{crs}')$;

return b; **fi**

EXP_2^{zk}

– Setup: $(\mathsf{pk}_e, \mathsf{sk}_e) \leftarrow \mathsf{KGen}_e(1^\lambda)$; $(\mathbf{crs} \parallel \mathbf{ts}) \leftarrow \mathsf{K}(\mathbf{R}_{L'}, \xi_{\mathbf{R}_{L'}})$; $\mathbf{crs}' = (\mathbf{crs}, \mathsf{pk}_e)$

– $\mathsf{O}(\mathsf{x}, \mathsf{w})$: Abort **if** $(\mathsf{x}, \mathsf{w}) \notin \mathbf{R}_L$; Sample $\boxed{r \leftarrow \{0,1\}^\lambda}$; $\boxed{c = \mathsf{Enc}_e(\mathsf{pk}_e, \mathsf{w}; r)}$;

$\qquad \pi \leftarrow \mathsf{Sim}(\mathbf{R}_{L'}, \xi_{\mathbf{R}_{L'}}, \mathbf{crs}, (\mathsf{x}, c, \mathsf{pk}_e), \mathbf{ts})$;

– $b \leftarrow \mathcal{A}^{\mathsf{O}(\mathsf{x},\mathsf{w})}(\mathbf{crs}')$;

return b; **fi**

Lemma 1. *If the used cryptosystem in the above games is semantically secure, then for two experiments* EXP_2^{zk} *and* EXP_1^{zk}, *we have* $\Pr[\mathsf{EXP}_2^{zk}] \approx \Pr[\mathsf{EXP}_1^{zk}]$.

Proof. By considering the fact that the cryptosystem $\Pi_{enc} = (\mathsf{KGen}_e, \mathsf{Enc}_e, \mathsf{Dec}_e)$ is a semantically secure, so no polynomial-time algorithm can distinguish an oracle that encrypts randomly chosen value z and uses simulator Sim from the case that it encrypts witness w and again uses Sim. □

$$\begin{array}{l} \mathsf{EXP}_3^{zk} \\ \hline \end{array}$$

- Setup: $(\mathsf{pk}_e, \mathsf{sk}_e) \leftarrow \mathsf{KGen}_e(1^\lambda); (\mathsf{crs} \| \mathsf{ts}) \leftarrow \mathsf{K}(\mathbf{R}_{\mathbf{L'}}, \xi_{\mathbf{R_{L'}}}); \mathsf{crs}' = (\mathsf{crs}, \mathsf{pk}_e)$
- $\mathsf{O}(\mathsf{x}, \mathsf{w})$: Abort if $(\mathsf{x}, \mathsf{w}) \notin \mathbf{R_L}$; Sample $r \leftarrow \{0,1\}^\lambda; c = \mathsf{Enc}_e(\mathsf{pk}_e, \mathsf{w}; r)$;

$$\pi \leftarrow \mathsf{P}(\mathbf{R}_{\mathbf{L'}}, \xi_{\mathbf{R_{L'}}}, \mathsf{crs}, (\mathsf{x}, c, \mathsf{pk}_e), (\mathsf{w}, r));$$

- $b \leftarrow \mathcal{A}^{\mathsf{O}(\mathsf{x}, \mathsf{w})}(\mathsf{crs}')$;

return b; **fi**

Lemma 2. *For experiments* EXP_3^{zk} *and* EXP_2^{zk} *we have* $\Pr[\mathsf{EXP}_3^{zk}] \approx \Pr[\mathsf{EXP}_2^{zk}]$.

Proof. As GM zk-SNARK guarantees zero-knowledge, so one can conclude that the real proof (generated by prover) in experiment EXP_3^{zk} is indistinguishable from the the simulated proof (generated by simulator) in experiment EXP_2^{zk}. □

This completes the proof of theorem.   □

Theorem 3 (Black-Box Simulation Extractability). *Assuming the encryption scheme is semantically secure and perfectly correct, the modified version of GM zk-SNARK in Sect. 3, satisfies black-box simulation extractability.*

Proof. Similarly, we go through a sequence of hybrid experiences. The proof uses a similar approach that is used in CØCØ framework and consequently in Hawk and Gyges, but with considerable simplifications. As the first experiment, consider the following experiment,

$$\begin{array}{l} \mathsf{EXP}_1^{SimExt} \\ \hline \end{array}$$

- Setup: $(\mathsf{pk}_e, \mathsf{sk}_e) \leftarrow \mathsf{KGen}_e(1^\lambda); (\mathsf{crs} \| \mathsf{ts}) \leftarrow \mathsf{K}(\mathbf{R}_{\mathbf{L'}}, \xi_{\mathbf{R_{L'}}}); \mathsf{crs}' = (\mathsf{crs}, \mathsf{pk}_e)$
- $\mathsf{O}(\mathsf{x})$: Sample $r, z \leftarrow \{0,1\}^\lambda; c = \mathsf{Enc}_e(\mathsf{pk}_e, z; r)$;

$$\pi \leftarrow \mathsf{Sim}(\mathbf{R}_{\mathbf{L'}}, \xi_{\mathbf{R_{L'}}}, \mathsf{crs}, (\mathsf{x}, c, \mathsf{pk}_e), \mathsf{ts}); \text{output } \pi' := (c, \pi)$$

- $(\mathsf{x}, \pi') \leftarrow \mathcal{A}^{\mathsf{O}(\mathsf{x})}(\mathsf{crs}', \mathsf{sk}_e)$;
- Parse $\pi' := (c, \pi)$; extract witness $\mathsf{w} \leftarrow \mathsf{Dec}_e(c, \mathsf{sk}_e)$;

return 1 iff $((\mathsf{x}, \pi') \notin Q) \wedge (\mathsf{V}(\mathbf{R}_{\mathbf{L'}}, \xi_{\mathbf{R_{L'}}}, \mathsf{crs}, (\mathsf{x}, c, \mathsf{pk}_e), \pi) = 1) \wedge ((\mathsf{x}, \mathsf{w}) \notin \mathbf{R_L})$;

where Q shows the set of statment-proof pairs generated by $\mathsf{O}(\mathsf{x})$. **fi**

$$\begin{array}{l} \mathsf{EXP}_2^{SimExt} \\ \hline \end{array}$$

- Setup: $(\mathsf{pk}_e, \mathsf{sk}_e) \leftarrow \mathsf{KGen}_e(1^\lambda); (\mathsf{crs} \| \mathsf{ts}) \leftarrow \mathsf{K}(\mathbf{R}_{\mathbf{L'}}, \xi_{\mathbf{R_{L'}}}); \mathsf{crs}' = (\mathsf{crs}, \mathsf{pk}_e)$
- $\mathsf{O}(\mathsf{x})$: Sample $r \leftarrow \{0,1\}^\lambda; c = \mathsf{Enc}_e(\mathsf{pk}_e, \mathsf{w}; r)$;

$$\pi \leftarrow \mathsf{Sim}(\mathbf{R}_{\mathbf{L'}}, \xi_{\mathbf{R_{L'}}}, \mathsf{crs}, (\mathsf{x}, c, \mathsf{pk}_e), \mathsf{ts}); \text{output } \pi' := (c, \pi)$$

- $(\mathsf{x}, \pi') \leftarrow \mathcal{A}^{\mathsf{O}(\mathsf{x})}(\mathsf{crs}', \mathsf{sk}_e)$;
- Parse $\pi' := (c, \pi)$; extract witness $\mathsf{w} \leftarrow \mathsf{Dec}_e(c, \mathsf{sk}_e)$;

return 1 iff $((\mathsf{x}, \pi') \notin Q) \wedge (\mathsf{V}(\mathbf{R}_{\mathbf{L'}}, \xi_{\mathbf{R_{L'}}}, \mathsf{crs}, (\mathsf{x}, c, \mathsf{pk}_e), \pi) = 1) \wedge ((\mathsf{x}, \mathsf{w}) \notin \mathbf{R_L})$;

where Q shows the set of statment-proof pairs generated by $\mathsf{O}(\mathsf{x})$. **fi**

Lemma 3. *If the used cryptosystem in the above games is semantically secure, then for two experiments* EXP_2^{SimExt} *and* EXP_1^{SimExt} *we have* $\Pr[\mathsf{EXP}_2^{SimExt}] \approx \Pr[\mathsf{EXP}_1^{SimExt}]$.

Proof. By the fact that the used cryptosystem is semantically secure, so no polynomial-time algorithm can distinguish an oracle that encrypts randomly chosen value z and uses simulator Sim' from the one that encrypts true witness w and again uses simulator Sim'. □

EXP_3^{SimExt}

- Setup:$(\mathsf{pk}_e, \mathsf{sk}_e) \leftarrow \mathsf{KGen}_e(1^\lambda)$; $(\mathbf{crs} \,\|\, \mathbf{ts}) \leftarrow \mathsf{K}(\mathbf{R}_{\mathbf{L}'}, \xi_{\mathbf{R}_{\mathbf{L}'}})$; $\mathbf{crs}' = (\mathbf{crs}, \mathsf{pk}_e)$

- $\mathsf{O}(\mathsf{x})$: Sample $r \leftarrow \{0,1\}^\lambda$; $c = \mathsf{Enc}_e(\mathsf{pk}_e, \mathsf{w}; r)$;

$\qquad \pi \leftarrow \mathsf{P}(\mathbf{R}_{\mathbf{L}'}, \xi_{\mathbf{R}_{\mathbf{L}'}}, \mathbf{crs}, (\mathsf{x}, c, \mathsf{pk}_e), (\mathsf{w}, r))$; output $\pi' := (c, \pi)$

- $(\mathsf{x}, \pi') \leftarrow \mathcal{A}^{\mathsf{O}(\mathsf{x})}(\mathbf{crs}', \mathsf{sk}_e)$;

- Parse $\pi' := (c, \pi)$; extract witness $\mathsf{w} \leftarrow \mathsf{Dec}_e(c, \mathsf{sk}_e)$;

   return 1 iff $((\mathsf{x}, \pi') \notin Q) \wedge (\mathsf{V}(\mathbf{R}_{\mathbf{L}'}, \xi_{\mathbf{R}_{\mathbf{L}'}}, \mathbf{crs}, (\mathsf{x}, c, \mathsf{pk}_e), \pi) = 1) \wedge ((\mathsf{x}, \mathsf{w}) \notin \mathbf{R}_{\mathbf{L}})$;

   where Q shows the set of statment-proof pairs generated by $\mathsf{O}(\mathsf{x})$. **fi**

Lemma 4. *If the underlying NIZK is simulation sound, then for two experiments* EXP_3^{SimExt} *and* EXP_2^{SimExt} *we have* $\Pr[\mathsf{EXP}_3^{SimExt}] \approx \Pr[\mathsf{EXP}_2^{SimExt}]$.

Proof. We note that if $(\mathsf{x}, \pi') \notin Q$, then the (x, c, π) (from (x, π')) is a valid message pair. By simulation soundness property of GM zk-SNARK, that prevents mallability attacks, we know that $(\mathsf{x}, \pi') \notin Q$.

On the other hand, since the decrypted w is unique for all valid witnesses, so due to the soundness of GM zk-SNARK (note that the definition of simulation soundness implies standard soundness) the probability that some witness is valid for $\mathbf{L}'$ and $(\mathsf{x}, \mathsf{w}) \notin \mathbf{R}_{\mathbf{L}}$ is $\mathsf{negl}(\lambda)$. □

We note that in all above experiments, extraction of witnesses is done universally, independent of adversarial prover's code, that is a critical issue in constructing the UC simulator that extracts witness form the proof sent by environment and the adversarial prover. So, this results that the modified scheme satisfies *black-box simulation extractability*. Consequently, following previous result (shown in [CLOS02, Gro06, GOS06]) that a NIZK argument system with black-box simulation extractability guarantees UC-security, we conclude that the modified construction of GM zk-SNARK in Fig. 2 achieves UC-security. □

4   On the Efficiency of Smart Contract Systems

Hawk and Gyges [KMS+16, JKS16] frequently generate CRS and use a UC-secure zk-SNARK to prove different statements. In Hawk author discuss that their system is dominated by efficiency of the underlying UC-secure zk-SNARK that are achieved from a variation of Pinocchio zk-SNARK [PHGR13] lifted by

CØCØ framework (the same is done in Gyges as well). In the rest, we discuss how UC-secure construction in Sect. 3 can improve efficiency of both smart contract systems. Our evaluation is focused precisely on Hawk, but as Gyges also have used CØCØ framework, so the same evaluation can be considered for Gyges.

Improving Efficiency of Hawk. We begin evaluation on Hawk by reviewing the changes that are applied on Ben Sasson et al.'s zk-SNARK (to get UC-security) before using it in Hawk. As discussed in Sect. 2.2, in order to lift any NIZK to a UC-secure NIZK, CØCØ applies several changes in setup, proof generation and proof verification of input NIZK. For instance, each time prover needs to generate a pair of signing/verifying keys for a one-time secure signature scheme, encrypt the witnesses using a given public-key, and sign the generated proof using the mentioned one-time signing key. On the other side, verifier needs to do extra verifications than the NIZK verification.

As we discussed in Sect. 3, to achieve a UC-secure version of GM zk-SNARK, we added a key generation procedure for a public-key cryptosystem in the setup phase, and prover only needed to encrypt the witnesses using the public-key in CRS and then generate a proof for new language as the original zk-SNARK. We did not add new checking to the verifier side and it is as the non-UC-secure version.

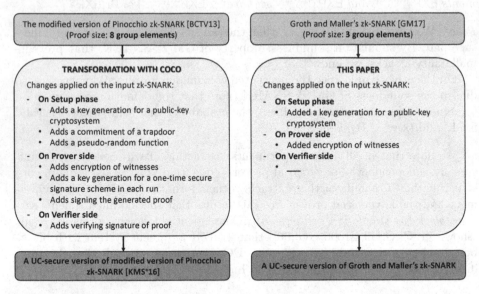

Fig. 3. The modifications applied by CØCØ transformation on the modified version of Pinocchio zk-SNARK [BCTV13] before using in Hawk system versus our changes on GM zk-SNARK (shown in Fig. 2) to get a UC-secure version.

Left side of Fig. 3 summarizes the modifications applied (by using CØCØ) on a variation of Pinocchio zk-SNARK before using in Hawk; and right side summarizes our changes on GM zk-SNARK to get BB simulation extractability and equivalently UC-security. As both use encrypting of witnesses, it seems having linear proof size on witness size currently is an undeniable issue to get black-box extraction. So, except this unavoidable modification, we applied minimal changes in the structure of GM zk-SNARK to achieve a UC-secure version of it.

Table 1. Comparison of Ben Sasson et al.'s [BCTV13] and GM [GM17] zk-SNARKs for arithmetic circuit satisfiability with m_0 element instance, m wires, n multiplication gates. Since [GM17] uses squaring gates, so n multiplication gates translate to $2n$ squaring gates. Implementations are done on a PC with 3.40 GHz Intel Core i7-4770 CPU, in single-threaded mode, for an R1CS instance with $n = 10^6$ constraints and $m = 10^6$ variables, of which $m_0 = 10$ are input variables. $\mathbb{G}_1$ and $\mathbb{G}_2$: group elements, E: exponentiations and P: pairings.

	CRS Leg., Time	Proof Size	Prover Comp	Verifier Comp	Ver. Equ
[BCTV13] & in libsnark	$6m + n - m_0\ \mathbb{G}_1$ $m\ \mathbb{G}_2$	$7\ \mathbb{G}_1$ $1\ \mathbb{G}_2$	$6m + n - m_0\ E_1$ $m\ E_2$	$m_0\ E_1$ $12\ P$	5
	104.8 s	287 bytes	128.6 s	4.2 millisec	—
[GM17] & in libsnark	$m + 4n + 5\ \mathbb{G}_1$ $2n + 3\ \mathbb{G}_2$	$2\ \mathbb{G}_1$ $1\ \mathbb{G}_2$	$m + 4n - m_0\ E_1$ $2n\ E_2$	$m_0\ E_1$ $5\ P$	2
	100.4 s	127 bytes	116.4 s	2.3 millisec	—

Additionally, Table 1 compares efficiency and practical performance of Ben Sasson et al.'s [BCTV13] and GM [GM17] zk-SNARKs from various perspectives before applying any changes. Empirical performance reported in libsnark library for a particular instance[3]. The experiments are done on a machine equipped with 3.40 GHz Intel Core i7-4770 CPU, in single-threaded mode, using the BN128 curve. Following Pinocchio scheme, Ben Sasson et al.'s zk-SNARK [BCTV13] is constructed for the QAP relation, while Groth and Maller's scheme works for the SAP relation by default. As discussed in [Gro16, GM17], a SAP instance can be constructed based on a simplification of systems on arithmetic constraints, such that all multiplication gates are replaced with squaring gates, but with at most two times gates.

Table 1 shows that GM zk-SNARK outperforms Ben Sasson et al.'s zk-SNARK in all metrics. Beside faster running times in all algorithms, GM zk-SNARK has only 2 verification equations, instead of 5 in [BCTV13]. By considering efficiency report in Table 1, and the fact that our modifications (summarized in Fig. 3) are lighter than what are applied on Ben Sasson et al.'s zk-SNARK before deploying in Hawk system, one can observe that new UC-secure zk-SNARK will simplify the system and would be more efficient than the one that currently is used in Hawk (similarly in Gyges). Indeed our changes are a small part of their already applied changes, so they will have less overload.

---

[3] Based on reported implementation on https://github.com/scipr-lab/libsnark.

Hawk needs to generate CRS of zk-SNARK for each smart contract and as the UC-secure zk-SNARK is widely deployed in various operations of the system, so substituting current UC-secure zk-SNARK with the new one in Sect. 3, can simplify the system and improve the efficiency of whole system, specially in larger scales. Moreover, in the construction of Hawk system, authors applied various effective optimizations to maximize the efficiency of underlying UC-secure zk-SNARK (Sec. V in [KMS+16]). The same techniques can work with new construction. For instance, it is shown that in the *Finalize* operation of a smart contract in Hawk, one may use non-UC-secure zk-SNARK, which similarly in new case one can use non-UC-secure version of GM zk-SNARK that is more efficient than the one that currently is used (compared in Table 1) and additionally it ensures non-block-box simulation extractability. In another noticeable optimization, Kosba et al. used some independently optimized primitives in the lifted UC-secure zk-SNARK, that had considerable effect in the practical efficiency of Hawk. Again,.by reminding that our changes are a small part of the changes applied by CØCØ , so a part of their optimized primitives (for encryption scheme) can be used in this case as well, but the rest can be ignored. Based on their experiences, such optimizations lead to have a gain of more than $10\times$ in the arithmetic circuit that is required for *Finalize* operation. We predict it should be even more with new scheme.

5   Open Discussions

In Hawk and Gyges [KMS+16, JKS16], authors used the fact that Pinocchio zk-SNARK and its variation by Ben-Sasson et al. [BCTV13] satisfies *knowledge soundness* and consequently *soundness*, and then used CØCØ framework and lifted a variation of Pinocchio zk-SNARK to a UC-secure one. On the other hand, *knowledge soundness* of the mentioned zk-SNARKs are proven under some knowledge assumptions, that are not clear how to use such assumptions in the UC framework. We used a similar technique and corollary in our security proofs. We considered the fact that *simulation extracability* implies *simulation-soundness* [Gro06], because if we can extract a witness from the adversary's proof, then the statement must belong the language. So, an interesting future direction might be reproving the soundness of Pinocchio zk-SNARK [PHGR13] (or the variation by Ben-Sasson et al. [BCTV13]), or simulation-soundness of GM zk-SNARK [GM17] under some different non-falsifiable assumptions (different from knowledge assumptions).

Acknowledgement. The author were supported by the European Union's Horizon 2020 research and innovation programme under grant agreement No 780477 (project PRIViLEDGE), and by the Estonian Research Council grant (PRG49).

References

ABLZ17. Abdolmaleki, B., Baghery, K., Lipmaa, H., Zając, M.: A subversion-resistant SNARK. In: Takagi, T., Peyrin, T. (eds.) ASIACRYPT 2017, Part III. LNCS, vol. 10626, pp. 3–33. Springer, Cham (2017). https://doi.org/10.1007/978-3-319-70700-6_1

BCG+14. Ben-Sasson, E., et al.: Zerocash: decentralized anonymous payments from bitcoin. In: 2014 IEEE Symposium on Security and Privacy, pp. 459–474. IEEE Computer Society Press, May 2014

BCPR14. Bitansky, N., Canetti, R., Paneth, O., Rosen, A.: On the existence of extractable one-way functions. In: Shmoys, D.B. (ed.) 46th ACM STOC, pp. 505–514. ACM Press, May/June 2014

BCTV13. Ben-Sasson, E., Chiesa, A., Tromer, E., Virza, M.: Succinct non-interactive arguments for a von neumann architecture. Cryptology ePrint Archive, Report 2013/879 (2013). http://eprint.iacr.org/2013/879

Can01. Canetti, R.: Universally composable security: a new paradigm for cryptographic protocols. In: 42nd FOCS, pp. 136–145. IEEE Computer Society Press, October 2001

CL06. Chase, M., Lysyanskaya, A.: On signatures of knowledge. In: Dwork, C. (ed.) CRYPTO 2006. LNCS, vol. 4117, pp. 78–96. Springer, Heidelberg (2006). https://doi.org/10.1007/11818175_5

CLOS02. Canetti, R., Lindell, Y., Ostrovsky, R., Sahai, A.: Universally composable two-party and multi-party secure computation. In: 34th ACM STOC, pp. 494–503. ACM Press, May 2002

Dam91. Damgård, I.: Towards practical public key systems secure against chosen ciphertext attacks. In: Feigenbaum, J. (ed.) CRYPTO 1991. LNCS, vol. 576, pp. 445–456. Springer, Heidelberg (1992). https://doi.org/10.1007/3-540-46766-1_36

GM17. Groth, J., Maller, M.: Snarky signatures: minimal signatures of knowledge from simulation-extractable SNARKs. In: Katz, J., Shacham, H. (eds.) CRYPTO 2017, Part II. LNCS, vol. 10402, pp. 581–612. Springer, Cham (2017). https://doi.org/10.1007/978-3-319-63715-0_20

GOS06. Groth, J., Ostrovsky, R., Sahai, A.: Perfect non-interactive zero knowledge for NP. In: Vaudenay, S. (ed.) EUROCRYPT 2006. LNCS, vol. 4004, pp. 339–358. Springer, Heidelberg (2006). https://doi.org/10.1007/11761679_21

Gro06. Groth, J.: Simulation-sound NIZK proofs for a practical language and constant size group signatures. In: Lai, X., Chen, K. (eds.) ASIACRYPT 2006. LNCS, vol. 4284, pp. 444–459. Springer, Heidelberg (2006). https://doi.org/10.1007/11935230_29

Gro10. Groth, J.: Short pairing-based non-interactive zero-knowledge arguments. In: Abe, M. (ed.) ASIACRYPT 2010. LNCS, vol. 6477, pp. 321–340. Springer, Heidelberg (2010). https://doi.org/10.1007/978-3-642-17373-8_19

Gro16. Groth, J.: On the size of pairing-based non-interactive arguments. In: Fischlin, M., Coron, J.-S. (eds.) EUROCRYPT 2016, Part II. LNCS, vol. 9666, pp. 305–326. Springer, Heidelberg (2016). https://doi.org/10.1007/978-3-662-49896-5_11

GW11. Gentry, C., Wichs, D.: Separating succinct non-interactive arguments from all falsifiable assumptions. In: Fortnow, L., Vadhan, S.P. (eds.) 43rd ACM STOC, pp. 99–108. ACM Press, June 2011

JKS16. Juels, A., Kosba, A.E., Shi, E.: The ring of gyges: investigating the future of criminal smart contracts. In: Weippl, E.R., Katzenbeisser, S., Kruegel, C., Myers, A.C., Halevi, S. (eds.), ACM CCS 16, pp. 283–295. ACM Press, October 2016

KMS+16. Kosba, A.E., Miller, A., Shi, E., Wen, Z., Papamanthou, C.: Hawk: the blockchain model of cryptography and privacy-preserving smart contracts. In: 2016 IEEE Symposium on Security and Privacy, pp. 839–858. IEEE Computer Society Press, May 2016

KZM+15. Kosba, A.E., et al.: CØCØ: A Framework for Building Composable Zero-Knowledge Proofs. Technical Report 2015/1093, IACR, 10 November 2015. http://eprint.iacr.org/2015/1093. Accessed 9 Apr 2017

Lip12. Lipmaa, H.: Progression-free sets and sublinear pairing-based non-interactive zero-knowledge arguments. In: Cramer, R. (ed.) TCC 2012. LNCS, vol. 7194, pp. 169–189. Springer, Heidelberg (2012). https://doi.org/10.1007/978-3-642-28914-9_10

Noe15. Noether, Shen: Ring signature confidential transactions for monero. IACR Cryptology ePrint Archive 2015:1098 (2015)

NVV18. Narula, N., Vasquez, W., Virza, M.: zkledger: privacy-preserving auditing for distributed ledgers. In: 15th {USENIX} Symposium on Networked Systems Design and Implementation ({NSDI} 18), pp. 65–80 (2018)

PBF+18. Poelstra, A., Back, A., Friedenbach, M., Maxwell, G., Wuille, P.: Confidential assets. In: Zohar, A., et al. (eds.) FC 2018. LNCS, vol. 10958, pp. 43–63. Springer, Heidelberg (2019). https://doi.org/10.1007/978-3-662-58820-8_4

PHGR13. Parno, B., Howell, J., Gentry, C., Raykova, M.: Pinocchio: nearly practical verifiable computation. In: 2013 IEEE Symposium on Security and Privacy, pp. 238–252. IEEE Computer Society Press, May 2013

WLB14. Wilkinson, S., Lowry, J., Boshevski, T.: Metadisk a blockchain-based decentralized file storage application. Storj Labs Inc., Technical Report, hal, pp. 1–11 (2014)

Woo14. Wood, G.: Ethereum: a secure decentralised generalised transaction ledger. Ethereum Project Yellow Paper **151**, 1–32 (2014)

Lattice Based Cryptography

Ring Signatures Based on Middle-Product Learning with Errors Problems

Dipayan Das[1]([⊠]), Man Ho Au[2], and Zhenfei Zhang[3]

[1] National Institute of Technology, Durgapur, India
dasdipayan.crypto@gmail.com
[2] The Hong Kong Polytechnic University, Hung Hom, China
mhaau@polyu.edu.hk
[3] Algorand, Boston, USA
zhenfei@algorand.com

Abstract. Lattice-based (linkable) ring signatures are an important notion to cryptography since it protects signer anonymity against quantum computers. In this paper, we proposed a new lattice-based linkable ring signature scheme using a variant of Learning with Errors problem called Middle-Product Learning with Errors (MPLWE). The proposed scheme follows a framework from [10,12] with the following improvements. Firstly, this scheme relies on a much weaker assumption. Secondly, our approach relies on a decisional problem, thus, the security analysis does not require the Forking Lemma which has been a fundamental obstacle for provable security under the quantum random oracle model (QROM).

1 Introduction

The concept of ring signature was initially introduced in [21]. It is a special type of signature where a signer can sign on behalf of an ad-hoc group (ring) while keeping himself anonymous. In addition, in a ring signature scheme, there is not a (centralized, trusted) manager who can reveal the identity of the signer. Each member is associated with a public key, and the ad-hoc group can be created spontaneously by collecting member's public keys.

In practise, it is desirable to have some additional features, where although the identity of the signer remains anonymous, signatures that are from the same signer can be identified. This type of ring signature is called linkable ring signatures [22]. This property is rigorous in the construction of cryptocurrencies to prevent double spending while preserving the anonymity of a spender [23]. The features of linkability and signer anonymity are also advantageous in other

Part of this work was supported by the Innovation and Technology Support Programme of Innovation and Technology Fund of Hong Kong (Grant No. ITS/356/17). The majority of the work of the first author was done while visiting The Hong Kong Polytechnic University.

J. Buchmann et al. (Eds.): AFRICACRYPT 2019, LNCS 11627, pp. 139–156, 2019.
https://doi.org/10.1007/978-3-030-23696-0_8

real-life applications, including, but not limited to, e-cash, e-voting, and ad-hoc authentication.

Classical cryptography is built on number theoretical problems, which will be broken by quantum adversaries using Shor's algorithm [36]. To mitigate the thread, NIST announced their plan to migrate to post-quantum cryptography [40]. To date, lattice-based solutions contributed to the majority of candidates to NIST's PQC process.

The linkable ring signature schemes are in an identical situation. There has been a sequence of work which proposes linkable ring signatures based on the traditional number theoretic problems [22,24–27], where anonymity and/or authenticity will be broken once quantum computer arrives. Recently, some lattice-based linkable signature schemes have been proposed. In [12], the authors proposed a one-time linkable ring signature based on the module SIS and module LWE problem. In [10], the authors also presented a one-time linkable ring signature based on the ring SIS problem. The scheme can be seen as a generalisation of BLISS [28] which is currently one of the compact lattice signatures known in the literature. In Raptor [29], a compact one-time linkable ring signature is proposed which claim to have the first lattice-based solution of linkable ring signature that is implementable. The main building block of Raptor is a Chameleon Hash Plus function. Raptor is the generalisation of the lattice-based signature Falcon [31] submitted to NIST PQC process. It should be noted that the underlying hardness assumption of the optimized version for Raptor [29] is NTRU, unlike module SIS/LWE problem for [12] and ring SIS problem for [10]. In [30] the authors also proposed a similar signature scheme based on hash-then-one-way signatures, where the underlying signature also relies on NTRU lattices.

It is worth noting that the above lattice-based solutions are provably secure in the random oracle model (ROM). The main ingredient for the proofs is the Forking Lemma [32,33] and its "rewind" method. Proofs using Forking Lemma are not tight. The loss in tightness is known to be intrinsic [34,35]. Also, the rewind method does not apply to a quantum random oracle, which has been a major obstacle to provable security under quantum random oracle model (QROM) [17,37].

1.1   Our Contribution

We proposed a new lattice-based one-time linkable ring signature parallel to [10,12]. The construction is based on the middle-product learning with errors problem (MPLWE) [7], a variant of learning with errors problem [38]. Our approach to obtaining a security proof in the random oracle model can be easily modified to the ring-LWE or LWE setting. We opt to instantiate our scheme with MPLWE since the construction is non-trivial, and the MPLWE problem enjoys a few advantages over the ring-LWE and LWE problem.

- It is more efficient than the LWE problem;
- it is as hard as ring-LWE problem for a broad set of polynomial rings.

Concretely, we prove the unforgeability, anonymity, linkability, and non-slanderability of our scheme based on the MPLWE problem. We introduce new techniques that bypass the Forking lemma in the context of ring signatures. The main ingredient of the new proof technique is to use "lossy" public keys (as defined in [16]) over actual public keys in the proof such that the lossy keys are computationally indistinguishable from the actual public keys. The hardness of distinguishing the two keys (lossy and real) comes from the hardness of the decisional MPLWE problem. This technique may have independent research interest in proving the security of ring signature in the quantum random oracle model.

2 Preliminaries

2.1 Notations

We will use $\mathbb{Z}^{<n}[x]$ to denote the set of all polynomials in $\mathbb{Z}[x]$ with degree less than n. In this paper, we will treat a polynomial and a vector as the same data type.

For a vector a, $\|a\|_\infty := \max_i |a_i|$; $a \xleftarrow{\$} \mathbb{Z}^{<n}[x]$ is to sample uniformly at random from $\mathbb{Z}^{<n}[x]$. For a distribution D, $x \xleftarrow{\$} D$ is to sample x according to D. Elements in $\mathbb{Z}_q$ are represented with integers lying in the interval $\left[\frac{-(q-1)}{2}, \frac{(q-1)}{2}\right]$ for some odd integer q. Typically, coefficients of elements in $\mathbb{Z}_{2t}$ lie in the interval $[-t, t]$. Whenever dealing with elements that are in $\mathbb{Z}_q$, we always explicitly assume that all operations in which they are involved end with a modulo q operation, unless stated otherwise. All logarithms used will have base 2.

For positive integers d, k and a polynomial $a \in \mathbb{Z}^{<k}[x]$, $\mathsf{Toep}^{d,k}(a)$ is defined as the matrix in $\mathbb{Z}$ of order $d \times (d + k - 1)$ such that the i-th row is given by the coefficients of the polynomial $x^{i-1} \cdot a$ for $i \in [1, d]$.

2.2 The Middle-Product Operation

Definition 1 (Middle-Product). *Let* d_1, d_2, d, k *be integers such that* $d_1 + d_2 - 1 = d + 2k$. *The middle-product* $\odot_d$ *is the mapping*

$$\mathbb{Z}^{<d_1}[x] \times \mathbb{Z}^{<d_2}[x] \mapsto \mathbb{Z}^{<d}[x]$$

$$(a, b) \to a \odot_d b := \lfloor \frac{a \cdot b \mod x^{k+d}}{x^k} \rfloor$$

Concretely, the mapping can be realized as follows. For a pair of polynomials $(a, b) \in \mathbb{Z}^{<d_1}[x] \times \mathbb{Z}^{<d_2}[x]$, their product over $\mathbb{Z}[x]$ is a polynomial of degree less than $d_1 + d_2 - 1$. Then, the middle-product of size d for a and b is obtained by firstly setting the coefficients of the monomials with exponent $0, 1, \ldots, k-1$ and $k + d, k + d + 1, \ldots, d + 2k - 1$ to 0, and then dividing the remaining by x^k.

For simplicity, unless otherwise specified, for the rest of the paper we will use d_1 and d_2 to denote the degree of the input polynomials to a middle production operation, d to denote the degree of the output polynomial, and $k = \frac{d_1 + d_2 - d - 1}{2}$.

For simplicity, we also assume $d_1 + d_2 - d - 1$ is even. This can be achieved by simply padding the input polynomials with leading 0s.

The middle-product is an additive homomorphism when either of its inputs is fixed. We have the following lemmas for middle-product.

Lemma 1 (Lemma 3.2 of [7]). *Let* $d, k > 0$. *Let* $r \in \mathbb{Z}^{<k+1}[x]$ *and* $a \in \mathbb{Z}^{<k+d}[x]$ *and* $b = r \odot_d a$. *Then* $\bar{b} = \mathsf{Toep}^{d,k+1}(r) \cdot \bar{a}$.

Lemma 2 (Lemma 3.3 of [7]). *Let* $d, k, n > 0$. *For all* $r \in \mathbb{Z}^{<k+1}[x], a \in \mathbb{Z}^{<n}[x], s \in \mathbb{Z}^{<n+d+k-1}[x]$ *we have* $r \odot_d (a \odot_{d+k} s) = (r \cdot a) \odot_d s$.

2.3 Middle-Product Learning with Errors Problem

In the literature, learning with errors (LWE) [38] and short integer solution (SIS) [39] problems are the primary tool to enable lattice-based cryptography. They enjoy a worst-case/average-case reduction to some hard lattice problems. In practise, we often resort to their ring variants, known as ring-LWE and ring-SIS problems, for better efficiency. Those ring variants rely on structured lattices (ideal lattices); exploiting the structure has been a minor concern for the community [4–6].

The middle product learning with errors problem (MPLWE) [7] is in a sense a combination of LWE and ring-LWE: it is more efficient than LWE; meanwhile, it is hard as long as ring-LWE is hard for a broader set of polynomial rings.[1] This allows us to hedge against the threat of relying on a single polynomial ring that may be potentially broken later.

Informally speaking, the decisional MPLWE problem is to distinguish (arbitrary many) samples $(a_i, b_i := a_i \odot_d s + e_i) \in \mathbb{Z}_q^{<n}[x] \times \mathbb{Z}_q^{<d}[x]$, where $s \xleftarrow{\$} \mathbb{Z}_q^{<n+d-1}[x]$ and $e_i \xleftarrow{\$} \chi$ for some χ over $\mathbb{Z}_q^{<d}[x]$; from the same number of samples $(a_i', b_i') \xleftarrow{\$} \mathbb{Z}_q^{<n}[x] \times \mathbb{Z}_q^{<d}[x]$ with non-negligible probability.

In terms of the hardness of this problem, it has been shown in [7] that if e_i is chosen from a rounded Gaussian distribution, then solving the MPLWE problem is as hard as solving ring-LWE problem for many rings. Meanwhile, if both s and e_i follow a discrete Gaussian distributions, then the MPLWE problem is also hard, based on the hardness of the "normal" ring-LWE problem for a set of rings [43]. Note that a normal (ring) LWE problem [11] is a problem where the secret and errors are sampled from a same distribution.

Let us give the formal definition of the problems.

Definition 2 (MPLWE distribution). *Assume* χ_1, χ_2 *be two narrow distributions over* $\mathbb{Z}_q^{<n+d-1}[x]$ *and* $\mathbb{Z}_q^{<d}[x]$ *respectively.* $\mathsf{MPLWE}_{q,n,d,\chi_1,\chi_2}(s)$ *is the distribution obtained by firstly sampling* $a_i \xleftarrow{\$} \mathbb{Z}_q^{<n}[x], e_i \xleftarrow{\$} \chi_2$ *and then outputting* $(a_i, b_i = a_i \odot_d s + e_i) \in \mathbb{Z}_q^{<n}[x] \times \mathbb{Z}_q^{<d}[x]$, *where* $s \xleftarrow{\$} \chi_1$.

---

[1] In this paper, we use ring-LWE to mean polynomial ring-LWE. In literature, ring-LWE is often used to define LWE over ring of integer instead of polynomial ring. Nevertheless, for many polynomials these two problems are equivalent. We refer to [42] for a detailed analysis.

In this paper, we instantiate both χ_1 and χ_2 from uniform distributions of small norm instead of discrete Gaussian distributions, due to the recent growing concerns on the side channel resistance of efficient Gaussian samplers [3,8]. We note that, to date, there isn't a hardness result on the MPLWE problem with uniform small secret and errors. However, from the past experience on other LWE variants, it is very likely this problem is also hard. We leave this to future work and focus on the fundamental design of the ring signature itself. In addition, in practice it is common to derive parameters from best-known attacks. We use BKZ with core quantum sieving model [1,2] to evaluate the security of our scheme.

Definition 3. *The (decisional)* MPLWE *problem is said to have distinguishing advantage ϵ, if for any polynomial time distinguisher $\mathcal{D}$ the distinguishing advantage of* $\mathrm{MPLWE}_{q,n,d,\chi_1,\chi_2}(s)$ *distribution from the uniform distribution is less than or equal to ϵ. That is*

$$| \Pr\left[\mathcal{D}(a, b = a \odot_d s + e \in \mathbb{Z}_q^{<n}[x] \times \mathbb{Z}_q^{<d}[x]) = 1\right]$$
$$- \Pr\left[\mathcal{D}(a, b \xleftarrow{s} \mathbb{Z}_q^{<n}[x] \times \mathbb{Z}_q^{<d}[x]) = 1\right] | \ \leq \epsilon$$

2.4 One Time Linkable Ring Signatures

The Framework. A one-time linkable ring signature consists of four efficient algorithms:

- **Parameter Generation Algorithm** (λ): It takes the security parameter λ as input, and outputs public parameter $\mathcal{P}$.
- **Key Generation Algorithm** $(\mathcal{P})$: It takes the public parameter $\mathcal{P}$ as input, and output a pair of keys (pk, sk), where pk is called the public key (or verification key), and sk is called the secret key (or signing key).
- **Signature Generation Algorithm** $((\mu, sk^i), L)$: It takes the message μ to be signed, secret key sk^i, and the list L of public keys in the ring as input such that $pk^i \in L$, and output a signature $\sigma_L(\mu)$.
- **Signature Verification Algorithm** $(\mu, \sigma_L(\mu), L)$: It takes the message μ, signature $\sigma_L(\mu)$, and the list L of public keys in the ring as input, and output either Accept or Reject.
- **Signature Linking Algorithm** $(\sigma_L(\mu_1), \sigma_{L'}(\mu_2))$: It takes two signatures $\sigma_L(\mu_1), \sigma_{L'}(\mu_2)$ as input and output either Linked or Unlinked.

The Correctness. The correctness of a one-time linkable ring signature is two-fold.

- **Correctness in Signature Verification Algorithm:** The algorithm should output "accept" when a signature is constructed by a member of the list L with overwhelming probability.
- **Correctness in Signature Linking Algorithm:** The algorithm should output "linked" if the two signatures are from the same signer, regardless of the rest of the lists.

2.5   Security of Linkable Ring Signatures

A linkable ring signature is secure if the following security notions hold.

- **One-time Unforgeability:** It is computationally infeasible for an adversary, who does not possess secret keys to any public keys in the list L to create a signature $\sigma_L(\mu)$ for any chosen message μ that will output "accept" by the Signature Verification Algorithm.
- **Anonymity:** It is computationally infeasible for an adversary to guess the identity of a signature $\sigma_L(\mu)$ for the message μ with probability non-negligibly better than a random guess.
- **Linkability:** It is computationally infeasible for a signer with the same key pair to create two signatures that will output "unlinked" by the signature linking algorithm.
- **Non-slanderability:** It is computationally infeasible for an adversary to create a valid signature that outputs "linked" by the signature linking algorithm for a signature created by an honest signer.

For the game-based definitions of the above security notion, we refer to Sect. 4.3 of [10].

3   The Proposed One-Time Linkable Ring Signature

3.1   Parameter Generation Algorithm

On inputting the security parameter, the Parameter Generation Algorithm outputs

- q: a large modulus;
- n, d, k: degree of all defining polynomials;
- κ: defining norm of the Hash function H;
- α, β: defining small norm distribution of secret and error respectively;
- γ, η: Rejection sampling parameter.

The Parameter Generation Algorithm also chooses two cryptographic Hash function:

- $\mathcal{H} : \mathbb{Z}_q^{<n}[x] \times \mathbb{Z}_q^{<d+k}[x] \mapsto \mathbb{Z}_q^{<d+k}[x]$
- $H : \{0,1\}^* \mapsto D_H := \{c \in \mathbb{Z}_2^{<k+1}[x] \text{ and } \|c\|_1 \leq \kappa\}$

Looking ahead, we will require H to behave as a random oracle; and $\mathcal{H}$ to be collision resistant. The Parameter Generation Algorithm also generates a pair of the public parameter $(a, h) \xleftarrow{\$} \mathbb{Z}_q^{<n}[x] \times \mathbb{Z}_q^{<n}[x]$. It is crucial that (a, h) are sampled uniform from the space to avoid any malicious trapdoors. We remark that our ring signature does not require a trusted set up or a common reference string. In our instantiation, (a, h) are chosen randomly. Those parameters can be obtained from random oracles/hash functions, with a "nothing-up-my-sleeve" type of seed, for instance, the first 256 bits of π or e, etc. This is a common practise in the literature.

3.2 Key Generation Algorithm

For the π-th user, the algorithm takes as follows:

1. Sample $s_\pi \xleftarrow{\$} \mathbb{Z}_{2\alpha}^{<n+d+k-1}[x]$, $e_\pi \xleftarrow{\$} \mathbb{Z}_{2\beta}^{<d+k}[x]$, $e'_\pi \xleftarrow{\$} \mathbb{Z}_{2\beta}^{<d+k}[x]$;
2. Compute $b_\pi = a \odot_{d+k} s_\pi + e_\pi$, $\tilde{h}_\pi = h \odot_{d+k} s_\pi + e'_\pi$;
3. Set $b'_\pi = b_\pi + \mathcal{H}(h, \tilde{h}_\pi)$;
4. Output $pk = b'_\pi$ and $sk = (s_\pi, e_\pi, e'_\pi, \tilde{h}_\pi)$.

3.3 Signature Generation Algorithm

To sign a message μ on behave of a list L the signer π does the following:

1. It firstly obtains the public keys b'_i for the rest of users in the list;
2. Compute $b''_i = b'_i - \mathcal{H}(h, \tilde{h}_\pi)$ for $i \in [1, w]$;
3. Sample $y_1 \xleftarrow{\$} \mathbb{Z}_{2\gamma}^{<n+d-1}[x]$, $y_2 \xleftarrow{\$} \mathbb{Z}_{2\eta}^{<d}[x]$, $y_3 \xleftarrow{\$} \mathbb{Z}_{2\eta}^{<d}[x]$;
4. Compute $c_{\pi+1} = H(L, \tilde{h}_\pi, \mu, a \odot_d y_1 + y_2, h \odot_d y_1 + y_3)$;
5. For $i \neq \pi$, choose $z_i \xleftarrow{\$} \mathbb{Z}_{2(\gamma-\kappa\alpha)}^{<n+d-1}[x]$, $z'_i \xleftarrow{\$} \mathbb{Z}_{2(\eta-\kappa\beta)}^{<d}[x]$, $z''_i \xleftarrow{\$} \mathbb{Z}_{2(\eta-\kappa\beta)}^{<d}[x]$, then
   evaluates $c_{i+1} = H(L, \tilde{h}_\pi, \mu, a \odot_d z_i + z'_i - c_i \odot_d b''_i, h \odot_d z_i + z''_i - c_i \odot_d \tilde{h}_\pi)$;
6. Compute $z_\pi = c_\pi \odot_{n+d-1} s_\pi + y_1$, $z'_\pi = c_\pi \odot_d e_\pi + y_2$, $z''_\pi = c_\pi \odot_d e'_\pi + y_3$;
7. If $\|z_\pi\|_\infty > \gamma - \kappa\alpha$ or $\|z'_\pi\|_\infty > \eta - \kappa\beta$ or $\|z''_\pi\|_\infty > \eta - \kappa\beta$, go to step 3;
8. Output signature as $(c_1, \{z_i, z'_i, z''_i\}_{i=1}^w, \tilde{h}_\pi)$.

It is to be noted that for $i \in [1, w]$, $b''_i = b_i$ when $i = \pi$. In step 6, we don't need to perform modulo q operation. The term $\tilde{h}_\pi$ is called the tag of the signer π which is a part of the signature.

Note that step 7 is known as "rejection sampling" in the literature [13,20]. This method is used to seal the transcript leakage and defeat common attacks such as learning parallelepiped type attacks from [18,19].

3.4 Signature Verification Algorithm

In the Verification algorithm, the verifier has the message μ, the signature $(c_1, \{z_i, z'_i, z''_i\}_{i=1}^w, \tilde{h}_\pi)$ the list L of w public keys $\{b'_i\}_{i=1}^w$.

1. Compute $b''_i = b'_i - \mathcal{H}(h, \tilde{h}_\pi)$ for $i \in [1, w]$;
2. Compute $c_{i+1 \bmod w} = H(L, \tilde{h}_\pi, \mu, a \odot_d z_i + z'_i - c_i \odot_d b''_i, h \odot_d z_i + z''_i - c_i \odot_d \tilde{h}_\pi)$
   for $i \in [1, w]$;
3. Output Accept if
   - For $i \in [1, w]$, $\|z_i\|_\infty \leq \gamma - \kappa\alpha$, $\|z'_i\|_\infty \leq \eta - \kappa\beta$, $\|z''_i\|_\infty \leq \eta - \kappa\beta$;
   - $c_1 = H(L, \tilde{h}_\pi, \mu, a \odot_d z_w + z'_w - c_w \odot_d b''_w, h \odot_d z_w + z''_w - c_w \odot_d \tilde{h}_\pi)$;
4. Output Reject otherwise.

3.5 Signature Linking Algorithm

In the Linking algorithm, it takes two signatures $\sigma_L(\mu), \sigma_{L'}(\mu')$ and outputs "linked" if the signatures outputs verified in the verification algorithm and generated by the same signer. Given two valid signatures $\sigma_L(\mu) = (c_1, \{z_i, z_i', z_i''\}_{i=1}^w, \tilde{h})$ and $\bar{\sigma}_L(\mu') = (\bar{c}_1, \{\bar{z}_i, \bar{z}_i', \bar{z}_i''\}_{i=1}^w, \bar{\tilde{h}})$, the algorithm outputs linked if $\tilde{h} = \bar{\tilde{h}}$.

4 Analysis of the Scheme

4.1 Correctness of Signature Generation Algorithm

The Signature generation algorithm is correct if $c_{\pi+1}$ in the signature generation algorithm is equal to $c_{\pi+1}$ in the signature verification algorithm. That is we have to show

$$H(L, \tilde{h}_\pi, \mu, a \odot_d y_1 + y_2, h \odot_d y_1 + y_3) = H(L, \tilde{h}_\pi, \mu, a \odot_d z_\pi$$
$$+ z_\pi' - c_\pi \odot_d b_\pi'', h \odot_d z_\pi + z_\pi'' - c_\pi \odot_d \tilde{h}_\pi)$$

Observe that,

$$a \odot_d z_\pi + z_\pi' - c_\pi \odot_d b_\pi'' = a \odot_d z_\pi + z_\pi' - c_\pi \odot_d b_\pi$$
$$= a \odot_d (c_\pi \odot_{n+d-1} s_\pi + y_1) +$$
$$(c_\pi \odot_d e_\pi + y_2) - c_\pi \odot_d (a \odot_{d+k} s_\pi + e_\pi)$$
$$= (a \cdot c_\pi) \odot_d s_\pi + a \odot_d y_1 + y_2 -$$
$$(c_\pi \cdot a) \odot_d s_\pi \ [\text{Using Lemma 2}]$$
$$= a \odot_d y_1 + y_2$$

Similarly, $h \odot_d z_\pi + z_\pi'' - c_\pi \odot_d \tilde{h}_\pi = h \odot_d y_1 + y_3$

4.2 Correctness of Signature Linking Algorithm

The Linking algorithm is correct if the tag generated by the same signer always gets linked. Note that the tag generated in the key generation algorithm is deterministic and the signer with secrets (s_π, e_π, e_π') always generates the same tag $\tilde{h}_\pi = h \odot_{d+k} s_\pi + e_\pi'$.

5 Security Analysis

Before giving the security results, let us first present the following three lemmas (adapted from [43]), which will be used in the security analysis.

The following lemma will be necessary for the simulation of the random oracle H in the security analysis of the scheme.

Lemma 3. *Let q be any large odd integer. Let η be any integer satisfying $\eta < \frac{q-1}{2}$ and d be any integer. For any given $w \in \mathbb{Z}_q^{<d}[x]$, we have*

$$\Pr_{y_1, y_2} [a \odot_d y_1 + y_2 = w] \leq \frac{1}{(2\eta + 1)^d}$$

for any polynomial a in $\mathbb{Z}_q^{<n}[x]$.

Proof. Note that

$$\Pr_{y_1, y_2} [a \odot_d y_1 + y_2 = w] \leq \Pr_{y_2} [y_2 = w - a \odot_d y_1] \leq \frac{1}{(2\eta + 1)^d}$$

The last inequality is due to the fact that if we choose y_2 from the correct distribution, the probability that for a fixed $w' := w - a \odot_d y_1$, the probability of $y_2 = w'$ is less than $\frac{1}{(2\eta+1)^d}$.

The next lemma shows if we choose (a, b) uniformly at random, then with negligible probability (a, b) follows MPLWE distribution.

Lemma 4. *Let q be any large odd integer. Let α, β, n, d, k are integers satisfying $\beta < \alpha$ and α is sufficiently smaller than $\frac{q-1}{2}$, $d \leq k < n$. If $(a, b) \xleftarrow{\$} \mathbb{Z}_q^{<n}[x] \times \mathbb{Z}_q^{<d+k}[x]$, the probability that there exists $s \in \mathbb{Z}_{2\alpha}^{<n+d+k-1}[x]$ and $e \in \mathbb{Z}_{2\beta}^{<d+k}[x]$ such that $b = a \odot_{d+k} s + e$ is at-most $\frac{(2\alpha+1)^{n+d+k-1}(2\beta+1)^{d+k}}{q^{d+k}}$.*

Proof. For a fixed $(s, e) \in \mathbb{Z}_{2\alpha}^{<n+d+k-1}[x] \times \mathbb{Z}_{2\beta}^{<d+k}[x]$, we have

$$\Pr_{a,b} [b = a \odot_{d+k} s + e] \leq \frac{1}{q^{d+k}}$$

Using Union bound, for all $(s, e) \in \mathbb{Z}_{2\alpha}^{<n+d+k-1}[x] \times \mathbb{Z}_{2\beta}^{<d+k}[x]$

$$\Pr_{a,b} [b = a \odot_{d+k} s + e] \leq \frac{(2\alpha + 1)^{n+d+k-1}(2\beta + 1)^{d+k}}{q^{d+k}}.$$

The following lemma bridges the connection between the adversary's random oracle queries and the probability of successfully forging signatures.

Lemma 5. *Let q be any large odd integer. Let $\alpha, \beta, n, d, k, \delta', \delta''$ are integers satisfying $\beta < \alpha < \delta'' < \delta'$ and $d \leq k < n$. Let $(a, b) \xleftarrow{\$} \mathbb{Z}_q^{<n}[x] \times \mathbb{Z}_q^{<d+k}[x]$ such that $b \neq a \odot_{d+k} s + e$ for any $s \in \mathbb{Z}_{2\alpha}^{<n+d+k-1}[x]$, $e \in \mathbb{Z}_{2\beta}^{<d+k}[x]$. Then for any $w \in \mathbb{Z}_q^{<d}[x]$ and any $c \xleftarrow{\$} D_H = \{c \in \mathbb{Z}_3^{<k+1}[x] \text{ and } \|c\|_1 \leq \kappa\}$, probability that there exists $z_1 \in \mathbb{Z}_{2\delta'}^{<n+d-1}[x]$, $z_2 \in \mathbb{Z}_{2\delta''}^{<d}[x]$ such that $w = a \odot_d z_1 + z_2 - c \odot_d b$ is at-most $\frac{1}{|D_H|} + \frac{(4\delta'+1)^{n+d-1}(4\delta''+1)^d |D_H|^2}{q^d}$.*

Proof. Let us denote S to be the set of all $(a, b) \in \mathbb{Z}_q^{<n}[x] \times \mathbb{Z}_q^{<d+k}[x]$ such that there exists at-most one $c \in D_H$ for which there exists $z_1 \in \mathbb{Z}_{2\delta'}^{<n+d-1}[x], z_2 \in \mathbb{Z}_{2\delta''}^{<d}[x]$ satisfying $a \odot_d z_1 + z_2 - c \odot_d b = w$. So

$$\Pr_{a,b,c}[\exists z_1 \in \mathbb{Z}_{2\delta'}^{<n+d-1}[x], z_2 \in \mathbb{Z}_{2\delta''}^{<d}[x] \text{ s.t } a \odot_d z_1 + z_2 - c \odot_d b = w]$$

$$\leq \Pr_{a,b}[(a,b) \in S] \frac{1}{|D_H|} + \Pr_{a,b}[(a,b) \notin S]$$

$$\leq \frac{1}{|D_H|} + \Pr_{a,b}[(a,b) \notin S]$$

Now $(a, b) \notin S$ implies there exists (z_1, z_2, c) and (z_1', z_2', c') with $c \neq c'$ such that

$$a \odot_d z_1 + z_2 - c \odot_d b = w$$
$$a \odot_d z_1' + z_2' - c' \odot_d b = w$$

Subtracting the above two equations, we get $a \odot_d d_1 + d_2 - d_c \odot_d b = 0$ where $d_1 = (z_1 - z_1'), d_2 = (z_2 - z_2'), d_c = (c - c')$.

Since $c \neq c'$, so $d_c \neq 0$. For fixed d_1, d_2, d_c, we have $d_c \odot_d b$ is uniform in $\mathbb{Z}_q^{<d}[x]$ for $b \xleftarrow{\$} \mathbb{Z}_q^{<d}[x]$ (since for $d_c \neq 0$, $\mathsf{Toep}(d_c)$ has full rank d). So we can write

$$\Pr_{a,b}[a \odot_d d_1 + d_2 - d_c \odot_d b = 0] \leq \frac{1}{q^d}$$

Thus using the Union bound for all d_1, d_2, d_c we have

$$\Pr_{a,b}[(a,b) \notin S] \leq \frac{(4\delta' + 1)^{n+d-1}(4\delta'' + 1)^d |D_H|^2}{q^d}$$

5.1   One-Time Unforgeability

The One-time Unforgeability result in the previous ring signatures [10,12,29] are proved using the Forking lemma. This is the generalisation of the technique introduced in [13]. But the proof is known to be not tight based on the underlying hard problems and also lacks the generalisation when the adversary is given the quantum access to the random oracle. To bridge this gap, we introduce the generalisation of lossy key technique, which was introduced in the context of signature scheme on the classical number theoretical problem by Katz and Wang [14], to prove the hardness of One-time Unforgeability in Ring Signatures. In lattice-based signature schemes, the technique proposed in [14] has been used to investigate the unforgeability result in [15–17] which are proved to have a tight reduction based on the underlying "decisional" problems.

At a high level, we use a sequence of games which are computationally indistinguishable to each other. Then we will show that probability for any polynomial time adversary's forgery output is negligible in the modified game.

Theorem 1. *Assume that the* MPLWE *problem has a distinguishing advantage* ϵ. *Then for any polynomial time adversary* $\mathcal{A}$ *who makes public key queries of* w *users,* q_h *hash queries of* H *and* q_s *signature queries of his choice (on the condition that* $\mathcal{A}$ *can not query signature more than once for each user) to the simulator* $\mathcal{S}$, *the advantage of winning the unforgeability game is less than or equal to* $\frac{q_s(q_s+q_h)}{(2\eta+1)^d} + w\epsilon + q_h(\frac{1}{|D_H|} + \frac{(4(\gamma-\kappa\alpha)+1)^{n+d-1}(4(\eta-\kappa\beta)+1)^d|D_H|^2}{q^d}) + \frac{w(2\alpha+1)^{n+d+k-1}(2\beta+1)^{d+k}}{q^{d+k}}$.

Proof. **Game 0:** During the forgery, $\mathcal{A}$ expects as input the public keys of the w users as the list $L = \{b'_i\}_{i=1}^w$. The simulator $\mathcal{S}$ runs the key generation algorithm and outputs L. The response to the hash and sign queries of $\mathcal{A}$ are obtained by outputting H and signature generation algorithm respectively on the queried input. $\mathcal{A}$ wins the unforgeability game if the advantage of winning this game is non-negligible.

Game 1: In this game, the $\mathcal{S}$ simulates the response to the hash and sign queries of $\mathcal{A}$ as follows:

Hash queries: $\mathcal{S}$ answers with $c \xleftarrow{\$} D_H$ for any hash queries to H made by $\mathcal{A}$. If an input repeats, $\mathcal{S}$ has to be consistent and reply with the same hash values as previously.

Sign queries: Upon receiving μ and signer's index $\pi \in [1, w]$, $\mathcal{S}$ simulates the signature $(c_1, \{z_i, z'_i, z''_i\}_{i=1}^w)$ for π as given below

1. It firstly obtains the public keys b'_i for the rest of users in the list;
2. Compute $b''_i = b'_i - \mathcal{H}(h, \tilde{h}_\pi)$ for $i \in [1, w]$;
3. Choose $c_{\pi+1} \xleftarrow{\$} D_H$;
4. For $i \neq \pi$, choose $z_i \xleftarrow{\$} \mathbb{Z}_{2(\gamma-\kappa\alpha)}^{<n+d-1}[x]$, $z'_i \xleftarrow{\$} \mathbb{Z}_{2(\eta-\kappa\beta)}^{<d}[x]$, $z''_i \xleftarrow{\$} \mathbb{Z}_{2(\eta-\kappa\beta)}^{<d}[x]$, then evaluates $c_{i+1} = H(L, \tilde{h}_\pi, \mu, a \odot_d z_i + z'_i - c_i \odot_d b''_i, h \odot_d z_i + z''_i - c_i \odot_d \tilde{h}_\pi)$;
5. Choose $z_\pi \xleftarrow{\$} \mathbb{Z}_{2(\gamma-\kappa\alpha)}^{<n+d-1}[x]$, $z'_\pi \xleftarrow{\$} \mathbb{Z}_{2(\eta-\kappa\beta)}^{<d}[x]$, $z''_\pi \xleftarrow{\$} \mathbb{Z}_{2(\eta-\kappa\beta)}^{<d}[x]$;
6. Program $c_{\pi+1} = H(L, \tilde{h}_\pi, \mu, a \odot_d z_\pi + z'_\pi - c_\pi \odot_d b''_\pi, h \odot_d z_\pi + z''_\pi - c_\pi \odot_d \tilde{h}_\pi)$;
7. Output signature as $(c_1, \{z_i, z'_i, z''_i\}_{i=1}^w, \tilde{h}_\pi)$.

The difference between the true signature response and the simulated response is that in the simulated one $c_{\pi+1} \xleftarrow{\$} D_H$ and then programmed as $c_{\pi+1} = H(L, \tilde{h}_\pi, \mu, a \odot_d z_\pi + z'_\pi - c_\pi \odot_d b''_\pi, h \odot_d z_\pi + z''_\pi - c_\pi \odot_d \tilde{h}_\pi) = H(L, \tilde{h}_\pi, \mu, a \odot_d z_\pi + z'_\pi - c_\pi \odot_d b_\pi, h \odot_d z_\pi + z''_\pi - c_\pi \odot_d \tilde{h}_\pi)$ without checking if $(L, \tilde{h}_\pi, \mu, a \odot_d z_\pi + z'_\pi - c_\pi \odot_d b_\pi, h \odot_d z_\pi + z''_\pi - c_\pi \odot_d \tilde{h}_\pi) = (L, \tilde{h}_\pi, \mu, a \odot_d y_1 + y_2, h \odot_d y_1 + y_3)$ was already set. So the difference will be in the time collision. Since the random oracle and signature queries are allowed to query q_h and q_s times respectively, so the distinguishing advantage between Game 0 and Game 1 is less than or equal to $\frac{q_s(q_s+q_h)}{(2\eta+1)^d}$ (by Lemma 3).

Game 2: In this game, $\mathcal{S}$ replaces true b_1 with a uniformly random b_1 and then set $b'_1 = b_1 + \mathcal{H}(h, \tilde{h}_1)$ in L. The rest of the public keys are unchanged. The distribution of the true b_1 with the uniform b_1 is computationally indistinguishable based on the MPLWE assumption. So the distinguishing advantage of $\mathcal{A}$ between Game 1 and Game 2 is less than or equal to ϵ.

Game 3: In this game, S replaces true $\{b_1, b_2\}$ with uniformly random $\{b_1, b_2\}$ and then set $b_i' = b_i + \mathcal{H}(h, \tilde{h}_i)$ for $i \in [1, 2]$. The rest of the public keys are unchanged. The distinguishing advantage of A between Game 2 and Game 3 is less than or equal to ϵ.

Approaching similarly,

Game w+1: In this game, S replaces all true $\{b_1, b_2, \ldots, b_w\}$ with uniformly random $\{b_1, b_2, \ldots, b_w\}$ and then set $b_i' = b_i + \mathcal{H}(h, \tilde{h}_i)$ for $i \in [1, w]$. The distinguishing advantage of A between Game w (where only b_w is true and the remaining public keys are uniform) and Game $w + 1$ is less than or equal to ϵ.

Now, if possible, let A outputs a forgery $(\bar{c}_1, \{\bar{z}_i, \bar{z}_i', \bar{z}_i''\}_{i=1}^w, \tilde{h})$ on the message $\bar{\mu}$ that was not queried to the Signing oracle. We also assume that A did make the hash query on some $(L, \tilde{h}, \bar{\mu}, a \odot_d \bar{z}_i + \bar{z}_i' - \bar{c}_i \odot_d b_i'', h \odot_d \bar{z}_i + \bar{z}_i'' - \bar{c}_i \odot_d \tilde{h})$. Since, otherwise, A has only $\frac{1}{|D_H|}$ chance of producing the right c. We will show that with negligible probability, A can produce such a signature in this case.

Since each b_i is uniformly random, the probability that there exists $s_i \in \mathbb{Z}_{2\alpha}^{<n+d+k-1}[x]$ and $e_i \in \mathbb{Z}_{2\beta}^{<d+k}[x]$ such that $b_i = a \odot_{d+k} s_i + e_i$ is at-most $\frac{(2\alpha+1)^{n+d+k-1}(2\beta+1)^{d+k}}{q^{d+k}}$ (by Lemma 4). So we assume that each b_i is not of this form.

Since we already assumed that A during his forgery has queried on some $(L, \tilde{h}, \bar{\mu}, a \odot_d \bar{z}_i + \bar{z}_i' - \bar{c}_i \odot_d b_i'', h \odot_d \bar{z}_i + \bar{z}_i'' - \bar{c}_i \odot_d \tilde{h})$, it is sufficient to show that when $c \xleftarrow{\$} D_H$, for a fixed $p \in \mathbb{Z}_q^{<d}[x]$, $p = a \odot_d z + z' - c \odot_d b_i''$ with $z \in \mathbb{Z}_{2(\gamma-\kappa\alpha)}^{<n+d-1}[x]$ and $z' \in \mathbb{Z}_{2(\eta-\kappa\beta)}^{<d}[x]$ is negligible. By Lemma 5, this happens with probability at-most $q_h(\frac{1}{|D_H|} + \frac{(4(\gamma-\kappa\alpha)+1)^{n+d-1}(4(\eta-\kappa\beta)+1)^d|D_H|^2}{q^d})$.

Thus A outputs a signature in this case with probability less than or equal to $q_h(\frac{1}{|D_H|} + \frac{(4(\gamma-\kappa\alpha)+1)^{n+d-1}(4(\eta-\kappa\beta)+1)^d|D_H|^2}{q^d}) + \frac{w(2\alpha+1)^{n+d+k-1}(2\beta+1)^{d+k}}{q^{d+k}}$.

5.2 Anonymity

In proving the anonymity result, we approach to the method similar to [10]. Though we have approached similar to [10], we could only prove computational anonymity instead of statistical/unconditional anonymity. The reason is due to the different underlying hardness assumption. In [10], the authors have used the SIS instances as the underlying hardness assumption and could prove statistical/unconditional anonymity based on the Leftover Hash Lemma (LHL)[2] which is not applicable in our case since we have used LWE instances.

We use a sequence of games which are computationally indistinguishable and different from each other. Then we will show that any polynomial time adversary's guess is close to the random guess.

Theorem 2. *Assume that the MPLWE problem has a distinguishing advantage ϵ. Then for any polynomial time adversary A who makes public key queries of w*

---

[2] LHL states that the SIS distribution is statically close to the uniform distribution. See [13] for a detailed discussion between SIS and LWE distribution.

users and q_h hash queries of H to the simulator S, the advantage of winning the anonymity game is less than or equal to $\frac{1}{w} + 2\epsilon + (w-1)\epsilon + \frac{q_h}{(2\eta+1)^d} + \frac{q_h w}{(2\eta+1)^d}$.

Proof. Game 0: In this game, $\mathcal{A}$ is allowed to query the list $L = \{b'_i\}_{i=1}^w$ of public keys of w users and q_h hash queries to the random oracle H. The simulator S runs the key generation algorithm and outputs L which consists of the public keys of the w users. Then S chooses $\pi \xleftarrow{\$} [1, w]$ and outputs signature $\sigma_L(\mu)$ on the message μ which is the output of the signature generation algorithm. $\mathcal{A}$ wins the anonymity game if he can guess the signer's index π, with probability non negligibly better than $\frac{1}{w}$.

Game 1: In this game, S makes some changes on the public key b'_π in the list L and tag $\tilde{h}_\pi$ of π. Instead of choosing the output of the key generation algorithm, he chooses $(b_\pi, \tilde{h}_\pi) \xleftarrow{\$} \mathbb{Z}_q^{<d+k}[x] \times \mathbb{Z}_q^{<d+k}[x]$ and set $b'_\pi = b_\pi + \mathcal{H}(h, \tilde{h}_\pi)$. The difference between Game 0 and Game 1 is that in the later, b_π and $\tilde{h}_\pi$ are chosen uniformly at random. The distribution of the true $(b_\pi, \tilde{h}_\pi)$ with the new $(b_\pi, \tilde{h}_\pi)$ are computationally indistinguishable based on the MPLWE assumption. So the distinguishing advantage between Game 0 and Game 1 is less than or equal to 2ϵ.

Game 2: In this game, for each $i \neq \pi$ in L, S replaces the original key generation algorithm with $b_i \xleftarrow{\$} \mathbb{Z}_q^{<d+k}[x]$ and set $b'_i = b_i + \mathcal{H}(h, \tilde{h}_i)$. The distinguishing advantage between Game 1 and Game 2 is less than or equal to $(w-1)\epsilon$.

Game 3: In this game, $c_{\pi+1} \xleftarrow{\$} D_H$ in the signature generation algorithm and then programs the oracle as $c_{\pi+1} = H(L, \tilde{h}_\pi, \mu, a \odot_d z_\pi + z'_\pi - c_\pi \odot_d b''_\pi, h \odot_d z_\pi + z''_\pi - c_\pi \odot_d \tilde{h}_\pi)$ instead of $c_{\pi+1} = H(L, \tilde{h}_\pi, \mu, a \odot_d y_1 + y_2, h \odot_d y_1 + y_3)$. The difference between the above two cases is that here S chooses $c_{\pi+1} \xleftarrow{\$} D_H$ without checking whether $c_{\pi+1} = H(L, \tilde{h}_\pi, \mu, a \odot_d y_1 + y_2, h \odot_d y_1 + y_3)$ was already set. Since q_h oracle query is allowed to $\mathcal{A}$, by Lemma 3 the distinguishing advantage between Game 2 and Game 3 is less than or equal to $\frac{q_h}{(2\eta+1)^d}$.

Game 4: In this game, the modification is done in (z_π, z'_π, z''_π). These are now chosen uniformly at random from $\mathbb{Z}_{2(\gamma-\kappa\alpha)}^{<n+d-1}[x] \times \mathbb{Z}_{2(\eta-\kappa\beta)}^{<d}[x] \times \mathbb{Z}_{2(\eta-\kappa\beta)}^{<d}[x]$ instead of $z_\pi = c_\pi \odot_{n+d-1} s_\pi + y_1$, $z'_\pi = c_\pi \odot_d e_\pi + y_2$, $z''_\pi = c_\pi \odot_d e'_\pi + y_3$ and applying rejection sampling. Since z_π, z'_π, z''_π in both the cases follow the same distribution, the distinguishing advantage between Game 3 and Game 4 is 0.

Game 5: In this game, S changes the index π. Here, instead of choosing the index $\pi + 1$ in signing, S chooses an index $l \xleftarrow{\$} [1, w]$. When π is replaced by some fixed l, it might cause some collisions with previous queries to the random oracle. Since the adversary $\mathcal{A}$ is allowed to make q_h queries to the random oracle, the distinguishing advantage between Game 4 and Game 5 is less than or equal to $\frac{q_h w}{(2\eta+1)^d}$, using Lemma 3.

It is to be noted that in Game 5, π is statistically independent. Thus the advantage of winning Game 5 is $\frac{1}{w}$. Thus the advantage of guessing the true signer (that is π) in Game 0 is less than or equal to

$$\frac{1}{w} + 2\epsilon + (w-1)\epsilon + \frac{q_h}{(2\eta+1)^d} + \frac{q_h w}{(2\eta+1)^d}.$$

5.3 One-Time Linkability

Theorem 3. *If there exists an adversary $\mathcal{A}$, who makes public key queries of w users and q_h hash queries of H, can break the linkability game in the ring signature, then there exists an algorithm to find a collision for the cryptographic Hash function $\mathcal{H}$ in the same time of $\mathcal{A}$.*

Proof. During forgery, $\mathcal{A}$ expects the list L of public keys, one secret key and q_h random oracle queries of the random oracle H from the simulator $\mathcal{S}$. $\mathcal{S}$ run the true key generation algorithm and outputs $L = \{b'_i\}_{i=1}^{w}$ and secret key $(s_\pi, e_\pi, e'_\pi, \tilde{h}_\pi)$ corresponding to some index $\pi \in [1, w]$. For random oracle queries of $\mathcal{A}$, $\mathcal{S}$ outputs $c \xleftarrow{\$} D_H$. If an input repeats, $\mathcal{S}$ has to be consistent and reply with the same hash values as previously.

Let $\mathcal{A}$ output a tag $\tilde{h}$ along with a signature $(c_1, \{z_i, z'_i, z''_i\}_{i=1}^{w})$ on some message μ which is "accepted" by the verification algorithm with non-negligible probability, but "unlinked" by the linking algorithm. That is $\tilde{h} \neq \tilde{h}_\pi$, where $\tilde{h}_\pi = h \odot_{d+k} s_i + e'_i$ is the original tag of $\mathcal{A}$.

Now, with $\mathcal{A}$'s tag, $\mathcal{S}$ computes $b'''_i = b'_i - \mathcal{H}(h, \tilde{h})$ for $i \in [1, w]$. Also with the original tag, $\mathcal{S}$ computes $b''_i = b'_i - \mathcal{H}(h, \tilde{h}_\pi)$ for $i \in [1, w]$.

Case 1. If for any i, $b''_i = b'''_i$, then $\mathcal{S}$ gets a collision on the cryptographic hash function $\mathcal{H}$ such that $\mathcal{H}(h, \tilde{h}) = \mathcal{H}(h, \tilde{h}_\pi)$.

Case 2. If for all $i \in [1, w]$, $b''_i \neq b'''_i$ then we will show that $\mathcal{A}$ can output a signature which will be accepted by the verification algorithm with negligible probability, which contradicts the hypothesis.

Note that for each i, $b'''_i = b'_i - \mathcal{H}(h, \tilde{h})$ is uniformly distributed in $\mathbb{Z}_q^{<d+k}[x]$, assuming $\mathcal{H}$ outputs uniformly random elements in $\mathbb{Z}_q^{<d+k}[x]$. So using Lemma 4, for each i probability that there exists $(s, e) \in \mathbb{Z}_{2\alpha}^{<n+d+k-1}[x] \times \mathbb{Z}_{2\beta}^{<d+k}[x]$ such that $b'''_i = a \odot_{d+k} s + e \leq \frac{(2\alpha+1)^{n+d+k-1}(2\beta+1)^{d+k}}{q^{d+k}}$.

Since during $\mathcal{A}$'s signature output $(c_1, \{z_i, z'_i, z''_i\}_{i=1}^{w}, \tilde{h})$, he has to query the random oracle H on some $(L, \tilde{h}, \mu, a \odot_d z_i + z'_i - c_i \odot_d b'''_i, h \odot_d z_i + z''_i - c_i \odot_d \tilde{h})$. So it is sufficient to show that when $c \xleftarrow{\$} D_H$, for a fixed $p \in \mathbb{Z}_q^{<d}[x]$, $p = a \odot_d z + z' - c \odot_d b'''_i$ with $z \in \mathbb{Z}_{2(\gamma-\kappa\alpha)}^{<n+d-1}[x]$ and $z' \in \mathbb{Z}_{2(\eta-\kappa\beta)}^{<d}[x]$ is negligible. By Lemma 5, this happens with probability at-most $q_h(\frac{1}{|D_H|} + \frac{(4(\gamma-\kappa\alpha)+1)^{n+d-1}(4(\eta-\kappa\beta)+1)^d|D_H|}{q^d})$. Hence the probability of $\mathcal{A}$ outputting a signature which is verified by the verification algorithm is less than or equal to $q_h(\frac{1}{|D_H|} + \frac{(4(\gamma-\kappa\alpha)+1)^{n+d-1}(4(\eta-\kappa\beta)+1)^d|D_H|^2}{q^d}) + \frac{w(2\alpha+1)^{n+d+k-1}(2\beta+1)^{d+k}}{q^{d+k}}$ which is negligible for sufficiently large q.

5.4 Non-Slanderability

It is known that for any linkable ring signature, if the notion of unforgeability and linkability holds, then it meets the notion of non-slanderability [10]. So the winning advantage of any polynomial adversary in the Non-Slanderability game is negligible based on the advantage of winning the unforgeability game and one-time linkability game.

6   Parameter Selection

The parameters of lattice-based constructions generally rely on a quantity called "root Hermite factor" [41]. In brief, this signifies the quantity which a lattice reduction algorithm must accomplish to break the construction. For calculating the root Hermite factor, we use the approach of [9]. The root Hermite factor is estimated by the root of the ratio of the Gaussian expected shortest vector in the kernel lattice and the expected length of the target vector. We set our parameters in Table 1 so that the root Hermite factor is beyond the scope of the known lattice reduction algorithms.

Table 1. Parameters of the ring signature

Parameters	
q	$\approx 2^{40}$
n	500
d	250
k	250
κ	17
α	100
β	80
γ	2^{20}
η	2^{19}
Expected number of repetitions to output a signature	≈ 12
Signature size ($w = 1$)	≈ 19.5 kb
Signature size ($w = 5$)	≈ 19.8 kb
Signature size ($w = 10$)	≈ 20.1 kb
Root Hermite factor required to break the key	1.002

The rejection sampling parameters γ, η play a crucial role in the security of the scheme (and signature size). If these parameters are too small, though breaking the scheme becomes harder (and signature size decreases), but the expected number of repetitions to output a potential signature becomes too large. These parameters are chosen carefully so that both the scheme is hard and repetition is optimal.

The signature size will mainly depend on the size of $\left(\{z_i, z'_i, z''_i\}_{i=1}^{w}, \tilde{h}_\pi\right)$. The approximate signature size is calculated by the sum of bit lengths of $\{z_i, z'_i, z''_i\}_{i=1}^{w}$ and $\tilde{h}_\pi$. Since $z_i \in \mathbb{Z}_{\gamma-\kappa\alpha}^{<n+d-1}[x]$, so we can represent each z_i by $(n+d-1)\log(2(\gamma-\kappa\alpha)+1)$ bits. Similarly, each of z'_i and z''_i can be represented by $d\log(2(\eta-\kappa\beta)+1)$ bits. And $\tilde{h}_\pi$ can be represented by $(d+k)\log q$ bits. Hence the approximate signature size is equal to $w(n+d-1)\log(2(\gamma-\kappa\alpha)+1) + 2wd\log(2(\eta-\kappa\beta)+1) + (d+k)\log q$ bits.

7   Conclusion

We proposed a new (one-time) linkable ring signature based on the assumed hardness of the decisional MPLWE problems. The construction is simple and efficient. We want to emphasize that we can easily replace the distributions of secret and errors from uniform to discrete Gaussian and set parameters that support the reduction from exponentially many ring-LWE to MPLWE. We choose the alternative to get better parameter estimates. Thus we do encourage cryptanalysis for our precise parameters because they are somewhat smaller than what is required for the reduction to go work.

Unlike lattice-based signature schemes, lattice-based ring signature schemes still lack the right model to prove the security when an adversary has access to a quantum random oracle. The new security reduction introduced in this paper is tight which can also motivate to analyse the security of a ring signature in the quantum random oracle model.

References

1. Chen, Y., Nguyen, P.Q.: BKZ 2.0: better lattice security estimates. In: Lee, D.H., Wang, X. (eds.) ASIACRYPT 2011. LNCS, vol. 7073, pp. 1–20. Springer, Heidelberg (2011). https://doi.org/10.1007/978-3-642-25385-0_1
2. Alkim, E., Ducas, L., Pöppelmann, T., Schwabe, P.: Post-quantum key exchange - a new hope. In: Proceedings of USENIX Security Symposium, pp. 327–343 (2016)
3. Groot Bruinderink, L., Hülsing, A., Lange, T., Yarom, Y.: Flush, gauss, and reload – a cache attack on the BLISS lattice-based signature scheme. In: Gierlichs, B., Poschmann, A.Y. (eds.) CHES 2016. LNCS, vol. 9813, pp. 323–345. Springer, Heidelberg (2016). https://doi.org/10.1007/978-3-662-53140-2_16
4. Ducas, L., Plançon, M., Wesolowski, B.: On the Shortness of Vectors to be found by the Ideal-SVP Quantum Algorithm. Cryptology ePrint Archive (2019). https://eprint.iacr.org/2019/234
5. Pellet-Mary, A., Hanrot, G., Stehlé, D.: Approx-SVP in Ideal Lattices with Preprocessing. Cryptology ePrint Archive (2019). https://eprint.iacr.org/2019/215
6. Cramer, R., Ducas, L., Peikert, C., Regev, O.: Recovering short generators of principal ideals in cyclotomic rings. In: Fischlin, M., Coron, J.-S. (eds.) EUROCRYPT 2016. LNCS, vol. 9666, pp. 559–585. Springer, Heidelberg (2016). https://doi.org/10.1007/978-3-662-49896-5_20
7. Roşca, M., Sakzad, A., Stehlé, D., Steinfeld, R.: Middle-product learning with errors. In: Katz, J., Shacham, H. (eds.) CRYPTO 2017. LNCS, vol. 10403, pp. 283–297. Springer, Cham (2017). https://doi.org/10.1007/978-3-319-63697-9_10
8. Ducas, L., et al.: CRYSTALS-Dilithium: a lattice-based digital signature scheme. IACR Trans. Cryptographic Hardware Embedded Syst. (TCHES) **2018**(1), 238–268 (2018)
9. Bai, S., Galbraith, S.D.: An improved compression technique for signatures based on learning with errors. In: Proceedings of CT-RSA, pp. 28–47 (2014)
10. Torres, W.A.A., et al.: Post-quantum one-time linkable ring signature and application to ring confidential transactions in blockchain (Lattice RingCT v1.0). In: Proceedings of ACISP, pp. 558–576 (2018)

11. Applebaum, B., Cash, D., Peikert, C., Sahai, A.: Fast cryptographic primitives and circular-secure encryption based on hard learning problems. In: Halevi, S. (ed.) CRYPTO 2009. LNCS, vol. 5677, pp. 595–618. Springer, Heidelberg (2009). https://doi.org/10.1007/978-3-642-03356-8_35
12. Baum, C., Lin, H., Oechsner, S.: Towards practical lattice-based one-time linkable ring signatures. In: Naccache, D., et al. (eds.) ICICS 2018. LNCS, vol. 11149, pp. 303–322. Springer, Cham (2018). https://doi.org/10.1007/978-3-030-01950-1_18
13. Lyubashevsky, V.: Lattice signatures without trapdoors. In: Pointcheval, D., Johansson, T. (eds.) EUROCRYPT 2012. LNCS, vol. 7237, pp. 738–755. Springer, Heidelberg (2012). https://doi.org/10.1007/978-3-642-29011-4_43
14. Katz, J., Wang, N.: Efficiency improvements for signature schemes with tight security reductions. In: Proceedings of ACM CCS, pp. 155–164 (2003)
15. Alkim, E., Bindel, N., Buchmann, J., Dagdelen, Ö.: TESLA: Tightly-Secure Efficient Signatures from Standard Lattices. Cryptology ePrint Archive (2015). https://ia.cr/2015/755
16. Abdalla, M., Fouque, P., Lyubashevsky, V., Tibouchi, M.: Tightly secure signatures from lossy identification schemes. J. Cryptol. 29(3), 597–631 (2016)
17. Kiltz, E., Lyubashevsky, V., Schaffner, C.: A concrete treatment of fiat-shamir signatures in the quantum random-oracle model. In: Nielsen, J.B., Rijmen, V. (eds.) EUROCRYPT 2018. LNCS, vol. 10822, pp. 552–586. Springer, Cham (2018). https://doi.org/10.1007/978-3-319-78372-7_18
18. Nguyen, P.Q., Regev, O.: Learning a parallelepiped: cryptanalysis of GGH and NTRU signatures. J. Cryptol. 22(2), 139–160 (2009)
19. Ducas, L., Nguyen, P.Q.: Learning a zonotope and more: cryptanalysis of NTRUSign countermeasures. In: Wang, X., Sako, K. (eds.) ASIACRYPT 2012. LNCS, vol. 7658, pp. 433–450. Springer, Heidelberg (2012). https://doi.org/10.1007/978-3-642-34961-4_27
20. Lyubashevsky, V.: Fiat-shamir with aborts: applications to lattice and factoring-based signatures. In: Matsui, M. (ed.) ASIACRYPT 2009. LNCS, vol. 5912, pp. 598–616. Springer, Heidelberg (2009). https://doi.org/10.1007/978-3-642-10366-7_35
21. Rivest, R.L., Shamir, A., Tauman, Y.: How to leak a secret. In: Boyd, C. (ed.) ASIACRYPT 2001. LNCS, vol. 2248, pp. 552–565. Springer, Heidelberg (2001). https://doi.org/10.1007/3-540-45682-1_32
22. Liu, J.K., Wei, V.K., Wong, D.S.: Linkable spontaneous anonymous group signature for ad hoc groups. In: Wang, H., Pieprzyk, J., Varadharajan, V. (eds.) ACISP 2004. LNCS, vol. 3108, pp. 325–335. Springer, Heidelberg (2004). https://doi.org/10.1007/978-3-540-27800-9_28
23. Noether, S., Mackenzie, A.: Ring confidential transactions. Ledger 1, 1–18 (2016)
24. Tsang, P.P., Wei, V.K.: Short linkable ring signatures for e-voting, e-cash and attestation. In: Deng, R.H., Bao, F., Pang, H.H., Zhou, J. (eds.) ISPEC 2005. LNCS, vol. 3439, pp. 48–60. Springer, Heidelberg (2005). https://doi.org/10.1007/978-3-540-31979-5_5
25. Au, M.H., Chow, S.S.M., Susilo, W., Tsang, P.P.: Short linkable ring signatures revisited. In: Atzeni, A.S., Lioy, A. (eds.) EuroPKI 2006. LNCS, vol. 4043, pp. 101–115. Springer, Heidelberg (2006). https://doi.org/10.1007/11774716_9
26. Liu, J.K., Au, M.H., Zhou, J.: Linkable ring signature with unconditional anonymity. IEEE Trans. Knowl. Data Eng. 26(1), 157–165 (2014)

27. Sun, S.-F., Au, M.H., Liu, J.K., Yuen, T.H.: RingCT 2.0: A compact accumulator-based (linkable ring signature) protocol for blockchain cryptocurrency monero. In: Foley, S.N., Gollmann, D., Snekkenes, E. (eds.) ESORICS 2017. LNCS, vol. 10493, pp. 456–474. Springer, Cham (2017). https://doi.org/10.1007/978-3-319-66399-9_25

28. Ducas, L., Durmus, A., Lepoint, T., Lyubashevsky, V.: Lattice signatures and bimodal gaussians. In: Canetti, R., Garay, J.A. (eds.) CRYPTO 2013. LNCS, vol. 8042, pp. 40–56. Springer, Heidelberg (2013). https://doi.org/10.1007/978-3-642-40041-4_3

29. Lu, X., Au, M.H., Zhang, Z.: Raptor: a practical lattice-based (linkable) ring signature. In: Deng, R., Gauthier-Umaña, V., Ochoa, M., Yung, M. (eds.) ACNS 2019. LNCS, vol. 11464, pp. 110–130. Springer, Cham (2019). https://doi.org/10.1007/978-3-030-21568-2_6

30. Lu, X., Au, M.H., Zhang, Z.: (Linkable) Ring signature from hash-then-one-way signature. In: Proceedings of IEEE TrustCom (2019)

31. Fouque, P., et al.: Falcon: Fast-Fourier Lattice-based compact Signatures over NTRU (2018). https://www.di.ens.fr/prest/Publications/falcon.pdf

32. Bellare, M., Neven, G.: Multi-signatures in the plain Public-Key Model and a general forking lemma. In: Proceedings of ACM CCS, pp. 390–399 (2006)

33. Pointcheval, D., Stern, J.: Security arguments for digital signatures and blind signatures. J. Cryptol. 13(3), 361–396 (2000)

34. Paillier, P., Vergnaud, D.: Discrete-log-based signatures may not be equivalent to discrete log. In: Roy, B. (ed.) ASIACRYPT 2005. LNCS, vol. 3788, pp. 1–20. Springer, Heidelberg (2005). https://doi.org/10.1007/11593447_1

35. Kiltz, E., Masny, D., Pan, J.: Optimal security proofs for signatures from identification schemes. In: Robshaw, M., Katz, J. (eds.) CRYPTO 2016. LNCS, vol. 9815, pp. 33–61. Springer, Heidelberg (2016). https://doi.org/10.1007/978-3-662-53008-5_2

36. Shor, P.W.: Polynominal time algorithms for discrete logarithms and factoring on a Quantum computer. In: Proceedings of ANTS, p. 289 (1994)

37. Zhandry, M.: Secure identity-based encryption in the quantum random oracle model. In: Safavi-Naini, R., Canetti, R. (eds.) CRYPTO 2012. LNCS, vol. 7417, pp. 758–775. Springer, Heidelberg (2012). https://doi.org/10.1007/978-3-642-32009-5_44

38. Regev, O.: On lattices, learning with errors, random linear codes, and cryptography. In: Proceedings of ACM STOC, pp. 84–93 (2005)

39. Ajtai, M.: Generating hard instances of lattice problems (extended abstract). In: Proceedings of ACM STOC, pp. 99–108 (1996)

40. NIST: Post-Quantum Cryptography-Round 1 Submissions. https://csrc.nist.gov/Projects/Post-Quantum-Cryptography/Round-1-Submissions

41. Gama, N., Nguyen, P.Q.: Predicting lattice reduction. In: Smart, N. (ed.) EUROCRYPT 2008. LNCS, vol. 4965, pp. 31–51. Springer, Heidelberg (2008). https://doi.org/10.1007/978-3-540-78967-3_3

42. Rosca, M., Stehlé, D., Wallet, A.: On the ring-LWE and polynomial-LWE problems. In: Nielsen, J.B., Rijmen, V. (eds.) EUROCRYPT 2018. LNCS, vol. 10820, pp. 146–173. Springer, Cham (2018). https://doi.org/10.1007/978-3-319-78381-9_6

43. TBA: A digital signature from Middle-Product Learning with Errors

Sampling the Integers with Low Relative Error

Michael Walter[✉]

IST Austria, Klosterneuburg, Austria
michael.walter@ist.ac.at

Abstract. Randomness is an essential part of any secure cryptosystem, but many constructions rely on distributions that are not uniform. This is particularly true for lattice based cryptosystems, which more often than not make use of discrete Gaussian distributions over the integers. For practical purposes it is crucial to evaluate the impact that approximation errors have on the security of a scheme to provide the best possible trade-off between security and performance. Recent years have seen surprising results allowing to use relatively low precision while maintaining high levels of security. A key insight in these results is that sampling a distribution with low *relative error* can provide very strong security guarantees. Since floating point numbers provide guarantees on the relative approximation error, they seem a suitable tool in this setting, but it is not obvious which sampling algorithms can actually profit from them. While previous works have shown that inversion sampling can be adapted to provide a low relative error (Pöppelmann *et al.*, CHES 2014; Prest, ASIACRYPT 2017), other works have called into question if this is possible for other sampling techniques (Zheng *et al.*, Eprint report 2018/309). In this work, we consider all sampling algorithms that are popular in the cryptographic setting and analyze the relationship of floating point precision and the resulting relative error. We show that all of the algorithms either natively achieve a low relative error or can be adapted to do so.

Keywords: Sampling · Discrete Gaussians · Lattice-based cryptography

1 Introduction

A key building block in many lattice based constructions is discrete Gaussian sampling over the integers. This is the distribution over the integers that is proportional to the standard continuous Gaussian distribution. Accordingly, it also has two parameters: a center c and a noise parameter σ. Sampling this

---

Supported by the European Research Council, ERC consolidator grant (682815 - TOC-NeT).

J. Buchmann et al. (Eds.): AFRICACRYPT 2019, LNCS 11627, pp. 157–180, 2019.
https://doi.org/10.1007/978-3-030-23696-0_9

distribution is one of the more complex operations in many lattice-based schemes and can be challenging to implement efficiently and securely.[1]

Recent years have seen increasing interest in implementations of lattice-based cryptography, which may be attributed to two of its properties. First, lattice problems are believed to be resistant to attacks involving quantum computers. While building a large scale computer that would threaten most of the cryptography currently in use is still an open problem, progress in that area has already led to an enormous effort in the search for *post-quantum* cryptography and compelled NIST to initiate the Post Quantum Standardization process[2]. In this process NIST is seeking to identify post-quantum secure key exchange/key encapsulation mechanisms and signature schemes. Not surprisingly, a large share of the first round submissions can be classified as lattice-based schemes. When such schemes employ discrete Gaussian sampling, it is usually in a setting where the parameters of the Gaussian are fixed once and for all, i.e. after initialization the sampling algorithm does not accept any parameters and generates samples from one fixed distribution.

A second reason for the rising interest in implementations of lattice-based cryptography is its versatility. Beginning with the breakthrough result of Gentry [9] on fully homomorphic encryption, a number of other advanced primitives have been realized from lattices, like identity based or attribute based encryption. What sounded like futuristic science fiction 15 years ago, is now making its way into practical implementations [4,11,12]. When discrete Gaussian sampling is used in such implementations, it is almost always in the context of trapdoor sampling [8,10,14]. Here, the parameters of the distribution can change per query, i.e. for each query the algorithm expects the parameters as input.

The two settings make for different challenges. For examples, the simpler primitives mentioned first are often expected to run in constrained environments and to be side-channel resistant, both of which are challenging to achieve for discrete Gaussian sampling with reasonable performance. On the other hand, in this context the distribution is fixed, which allows for precomputation and several time-memory trade-offs. The challenge in the second setting is that the distribution changes per query, which makes it harder to obtain time-memory trade-offs to increase performance (although some results are known, e.g. [1, 16]). What the two settings have in common is that the distribution is usually approximated rather than sampled exactly. However, the corresponding security proofs usually assume the exact distribution. This naturally leads to the question how accurately the distribution needs to be approximated in order to maintain the security level. This is a crucial question since the quality of approximation has a large impact on the performance of the sampling algorithms. Classically, the statistical distance was used to evaluate this trade-off between approximation

---

[1] Technically, this distribution has infinite support, but it is folklore that the support can be truncated to size $O(\sigma)$ without hurting security, so in this entire work we consider the truncated version only.

[2] https://csrc.nist.gov/Projects/Post-Quantum-Cryptography/Post-Quantum-Cryptography-Standardization.

and security level. This lead to the common believe that a statistical distance of less than 2^{-k}, achievable with k-bit fixed or floating point arithmetic, is required to maintain a security level of k bits.

Surprisingly, a recent line of research [3,16–19] has shown that sampling a distribution with a relative error of 2^{-k} can preserve up to $2k$ bits of security, or more. For example, a typical theorem in this context can be informally summarized as follows.

Theorem (informal). *Let S be a cryptographic primitive with access to a probability distribution $\mathcal{P}$, and let $\mathcal{Q}$ be a probability distribution such that the relative error between $\mathcal{P}$ and $\mathcal{Q}$ is bounded by $\delta_{\mathrm{RE}}(\mathcal{P}, \mathcal{Q}) \leq 2^{-\kappa/2}$. If S is κ-bit secure, then S is still $(\kappa - O(1))$-bit secure if $\mathcal{P}$ is replaced with $\mathcal{Q}$.*

Since floating point numbers with k bits guarantee a relative approximation error of less than 2^{-k}, this suggests that one can use k-bit floating point numbers to achieve security levels as large as $2k$ or more, as demonstrated in [18,19]. In many settings this can lead to a significant improvement, much larger than a factor two, over the classical approach of using approximations of about $k = \lambda$ bits of precision to achieve λ bits of security. This is because the common IEEE (extended) double precision standard with its 53 (64, resp.) bits of precision now allows for meaningful security guarantees. Using arbitrary precision libraries instead would be orders of magnitude slower than arithmetic with the common data types, which is often supported in hardware. Previous works, such as [16,18, 19], make use of different measures between distributions, e.g. Rényi divergences of different orders, and achieve some stronger results under certain conditions then abovementioned theorem. We point out that the starting point of these analyses is still the relative error between distributions, which is then used to prove bounds on other measures. We are not aware of any analysis of this type that is not based on the relative error.

Due to the guarantees provided by floating point numbers, it is tempting to assume that simply approximating all probabilities/numbers in your favorite sampling algorithm using k-bit floating point numbers is sufficient to preserve $2k$ bits of security. Unfortunately, this is not true in general. For example, [18] already pointed out that blindly using FP approximations in a sampling algorithm (in this case inversion sampling applied to the discrete Gaussian) can lead to catastrophic errors. A recent work [23] demonstrated that there are distributions for which one cannot even find a set of floating point numbers that approximate all the probabilities of the given distribution with small relative error and sum to 1 (thus representing a probability distribution). The authors claim that their result implies that sampling with small (in the sense needed for the results in [3,16–19] to apply) floating point error is impossible using "methods such as rejection sampling". On the other hand, this question has been addressed in the context of inversion (CDT) sampling [18,19]. The proposed algorithms use k-bit floating point numbers (during the online phase) only and the resulting relative error of the distribution is only $O(n2^{-k})$, where n is the number of elements in the support. The key point here is that at least in the case of inversion sampling, storing all probabilities of a distribution approximating the desired one is not necessary. This naturally raises the question if this is also the case for other samplers that are popular in the cryptographic context. This strikes us as a very important question for practical implementations of schemes like, for example, some of the ones submitted to the NIST Post Quantum Standardization process or the PALISADE project[3], due to the large potential improvement. This is amplified by the fact that the performance of sampling algorithms can vary widely on different platforms due to different time-memory-randomness trade-offs they achieve. So different samplers will be more suitable in different settings and it is useful to investigate, which samplers provide a low relative error and thus achieve strong security guarantees.

Overview of Samplers. In this work, we will survey several samplers and show how to adapt them (if necessary) in order to ensure that the relative error does not significantly outgrow 2^{-k} when working with k-bit floating point numbers. To the best of our knowledge our survey includes all samplers that are popular and/or useful in context of discrete Gaussian sampling.

The first and simplest algorithm that has been used for discrete Gaussian sampling is plain *rejection sampling* [10]. In this algorithm, a sample from the support is chosen uniformly at random and accepted with probability proportional to the desired distribution. This algorithm is very simple and generic and requires little memory, but it is not very suitable for discrete Gaussian sampling due to a high rejection rate and the requirement to compute irrational probabilities. Nonetheless, we consider it first due to its generality and our observations will be useful in later sections.

In settings where the distribution is fixed and known in advance, there are a number of generic algorithms that allow for faster sampling by performing distribution dependent precomputation and using additional memory. Probably the most popular one in the context of discrete Gaussian sampling is *inversion (CDT) sampling* [18]. Inversion sampling requires to precompute and store the cumulative distribution table, after which the sampling step becomes a binary search for a random element in this table. While this is much faster than rejection sampling, it requires a large amount of memory if the desired distribution has a large support (i.e. the noise parameter σ is very large).

Less well known in the cryptographic community seems to be the *alias method*, but we include it in our survey, because we believe it deserves more attention. The alias method requires a little more precomputation, but the memory is roughly the same as for inversion sampling. In contrast to inversion sampling, the online phase only requires a Bernoulli trial using a bias randomly chosen from a precomputed set. This has the potential of being even faster and easier to implement securely (e.g. in constant time) than inversion sampling.

A third algorithm along similar lines is *Knuth-Yao sampling* [7,20]. It also requires to precompute the probabilities from the entire support of the distribution. To generate a sample, it traverses a tree structure, which is based on the

---

[3] https://git.njit.edu/palisade/PALISADE.

binary expansion of these probabilities. This tree structure can either be precomputed explicitly, which requires an even larger memory overhead than inversion or alias sampling, or locally on-the-fly, in which case the memory requirement is equivalent to that of the previous two methods. However, the latter is also naturally less efficient. Knuth-Yao sampling is often recommended for environments where randomness is expensive, since it is provably nearly randomness optimal.

The three generic algorithms discussed above all have the advantage that they avoid any arithmetic with reals during the online phase, which seems to make them suitable for constraint environments. Unfortunately, they all suffer from memory requirements that can be prohibitive, especially on constrained devices. To mitigate this, [5] proposed an algorithm (which we denote by the *BLISS sampler*) that provides a different time-memory trade-off. This algorithm cleverly tailors rejection sampling to the discrete Gaussian to reduce the rejection rate and breaks the rejection step into a logarithmic number of Bernoulli trials with precomputed bias. Accordingly, it requires only logarithmic memory and no rational arithmetic, which makes it much more suitable for constrained devices.

With the exception of the rather slow rejection sampling, all algorithms described so far only allow to sample from a distribution that is fixed and known in advance, since they require distribution dependent precomputation. In more advanced settings, where the distribution is not fixed in advance, one is left with much fewer options. One of these options is Karney's algorithm [13]. It resembles the BLISS sampler insofar as it is also a rejection sampler that is tailored to the discrete Gaussian (albeit in a different way), but it is also able to perform the rejection step using no precomputation and using only integer arithmetic, assuming the parameters of the distribution are given as rationals. As such, it performs well in settings where the parameters of the desired distribution may vary per query [16].

Contribution. We distinguish between generic samplers that are not specific to discrete Gaussian sampling and algorithms that are specialized to discrete Gaussians.

We start with generic samplers and first make a rather simple observation that shows that rejection sampling does not require any modification and its output distribution will have small relative error if used with floating point numbers. Results from [16,18] then show that the error in terms of KL divergence is only the square of the relative error. This directly contradicts the aforementioned claim made in [23]. We also include a section about inversion sampling and demonstrate that the solution provided in [18] applies more generally than only to discrete Gaussians. Then we show that alias sampling can be easily adapted to achieve small relative error with almost no overhead. In Sect. 2.4, we consider a specific version of Knuth-Yao sampling and show that there are different ways to adapt it leading to different trade-offs in output quality versus running time.

We will then move on to the two specialized algorithms. We first address the BLISS sampler, where we show that above observation w.r.t. rejection sampling easily implies similar results for the BLISS sampler. Finally, we will consider Karney's algorithm, which is originally an exact algorithm, but for implementation purposes it is convenient to consider a floating point version of it, e.g. in the context of trapdoor sampling. While the observation about rejection sampling is useful also in this context, Karney's algorithm requires much more work to convert to a correct floating point algorithm due to some arithmetic that is required during the online phase. This part contains the bulk of our technical work. We remark that our floating point version introduces a lot of new conditionals to guard against numerical errors, which can hurt performance on standard CPUs significantly due to its detrimental effect on pipelining. To evaluate this effect and compare our algorithm to a high precision variant, we provide an implementation of our algorithm. Our experimental results on a standard PC suggest that at least for such architectures the slow down introduced by the conditionals is very acceptable compared to the speed up achievable in comparison with a high precision variant of Karney's algorithm. However, note that the performance of samplers depends strongly on the platform characteristics and the final choice should be made on a case-by-case consideration with a specific target platform in mind. We will release our implementation to the public.

Applications. The algorithms considered in this work can be used as building blocks in many kinds of cryptographic primitives. The results shown here on the relative error can be combined with results from [3,16–19] to prove strong security (since [17] even for distinguishing primitives like encryption). Furthermore, the approximate samplers as surveyed in this work can be used as a basis for convolution samplers [16,18]. These were first introduced to mitigate the large memory overhead of generic sampling techniques [5] and then shown to also yield a reduction from variable sampling to the fixed setting [16]. Such constructions ensure low relative error if instantiated with base samplers with low relative error. In this context, the results on alias sampling, inversion sampling and Knuth-Yao are particularly relevant, as their characteristics are very desirable for convolution sampling.

Previous Work. In this work we carry out some basic numerical analysis of some generic discrete sampling algorithms with a focus on the resulting relative error. Most previous work in the cryptographic context has focused on ensuring small statistical distances [5,6,21], or only considered the special case of inversion sampling [18,19]. More specifically, [18] shows that by reordering the probabilities, inversion sampling is able to achieve a bounded relative error at least in the special case of discrete Gaussians. [19] presents a version of inversion sampling – conditional CDT sampling – that works for any discrete distribution and achieves similar bounds but is less efficient, since it requires multiple iterations per sample.

The work of [3] analyzed the BLISS sampler using Rényi divergences, and specifically the divergence of order infinity is closely related to the relative error discussed in this work. We will briefly revisit this analysis in Sect. 3.1. Finally, a very recent work [22] showed that one can perform the rejection step in the BLISS sampler using polynomial approximations, which allows for much easier and faster constant-time implementation.

Preliminaries. In this work we make heavy use of the notation $(a\pm b)$ for $a, b \in \mathbb{R}$. By this we mean the interval $[\min(a+b, a-b), \max(a+b, a-b)]$. We will also do arithmetic with intervals and write $A \circ B$ for intervals A, B and $\circ \in \{+, -, \cdot, /\}$. We define this to be the interval $[\min_{\alpha \in A, \beta \in B}(\alpha \circ \beta), \max_{\alpha \in A, \beta \in B}(\alpha \circ \beta)]$. Finally, we define arithmetic of intervals with reals by viewing any constant $c \in \mathbb{R}$ as the interval $[c, c]$.

A k-bit floating point (FP) approximation $\hat{x}$ of a real x stores the k most significant bits of x as the mantissa $m \in \mathbb{Z}_{2^k}$ together with a binary exponent $e \in \mathbb{Z}$ and a sign $s \in \{-1, 1\}$. The value of an FP number (s, m, e) is $sm2^e$. This guarantees that the relative error is bounded by $\delta_{\mathrm{RE}}(x, \hat{x}) = |x - \hat{x}|/|x| \leq 2^{-k}$, or, equivalently, that $\hat{x} \in (1 \pm 2^{-k})x$. For simplicity, we assume that there is no limit on the size of the exponent, i.e. there are no overflows or underflows. The standard guarantee provided by most FP systems is that an arithmetic operation on two FP numbers yields the closest FP number to the true result. This generally holds for the four basic operations $\{+, -, \cdot, /\}$. Two values that already contain an approximation error, the operations $\{\cdot, /\}$ do not increase the error in the result by much, while the operations $\{+, -\}$ can have a very detrimental effect on the approximation error.

We use calligraphic letters to denote distributions. The Bernoulli distribution with bias p is denoted by $\mathcal{B}_p$. We extend the notion of relative error to any two distributions $\mathcal{P}$ and $\mathcal{Q}$

$$\delta_{\mathrm{RE}}(\mathcal{P}, \mathcal{Q}) = \max_{x \in S} \delta_{\mathrm{RE}}(\mathcal{P}(x), \mathcal{Q}(x)) = \max_{x \in S} \frac{|\mathcal{P}(x) - \mathcal{Q}(x)|}{\mathcal{P}(x)},$$

where S is the support of $\mathcal{P}$.

In this note, we will be interested in samplers that use only FP numbers of a given precision k (during the online phase) and output a distribution $\hat{\mathcal{D}}$ such that $\delta_{\mathrm{RE}}(\mathcal{D}, \hat{\mathcal{D}}) \leq O(2^{-k})$. Note that this necessarily implies that $\hat{\mathcal{D}}$ has the same support as the original distribution $\mathcal{D}$.

2   Generic Samplers

Not surprisingly, the literature on discrete Gaussian sampling borrows heavily from known generic sampling techniques. In the following we analyze some popular sampling methods. The results of this section, while technically simple, could be of interest in other contexts than discrete Gaussian sampling.

2.1   Rejection Sampling

The following lemma describes the basic principle of rejection sampling specialized to the setting of discrete probability distributions, which we prove for completeness.

Lemma 1 (Rejection Sampling). *Let $\mathcal{P}$ be a discrete probability distribution, called the* source *distribution, with support $S_\mathcal{P}$ and $f : S \mapsto \mathbb{R}_+$ a function* with domain $S \subset S_{\mathcal{P}}$ defining the target distribution $\mathcal{Q}(x) = \frac{f(x)}{\sum_{x \in S} f(x)}$. Let $M \geq \max_{x \in S} \frac{f(x)}{\mathcal{P}(x)}$. Given a sampler for $\mathcal{P}$ it is easy to generate a sample from $\mathcal{Q}$ by repeatedly drawing a sample $x \leftarrow \mathcal{P}$ and accepting it with probability $\frac{f(x)}{M\mathcal{P}(x)}$, until the first sample is accepted.

Proof. Accepting a sample x with probability $\frac{f(x)}{M\mathcal{P}(x)}$ is equivalent to generating a uniform value $u \in [0, M\mathcal{P}(x)]$ and accepting x if $u \leq f(x)$. In other words, this generates a pair $(x, u) \in S \times \mathbb{R}_+$ s.t. $u \leq M\mathcal{P}(x)$, which is distributed uniformly random among such pairs. Accepting x only if $u \leq f(x)$ amounts to a Monte-Carlo method of producing a pair $(x, u) \in S \times \mathbb{R}_+$ s.t. $u \leq f(x)$ uniformly at random and thus the marginal relative probability of x is exactly $f(x)$. $\square$

A particularly simple case is when $\mathcal{P}$ is the uniform distribution and $f(x) \leq 1$ for all $x \in S$. Then M can be chosen as $|S_{\mathcal{P}}|$, which means the acceptance probability is simply $f(x)$ for each x and no further floating point operation is necessary.

We now observe that rejection sampling naturally allows for FP approximations.

Lemma 2. *Let $f, \widehat{f} : S \mapsto \mathbb{R}_+$ be two functions with domain S and let $\mathcal{D}, \widehat{\mathcal{D}}$ be the corresponding distributions obtained by normalization. If $\delta_{\mathrm{RE}}(f(x), \widehat{f}(x)) \leq \mu$ for all $x \in S$, then $\delta_{\mathrm{RE}}(\mathcal{D}, \widehat{\mathcal{D}}) \leq 2\mu + O(\mu^2)$.*

Proof. It is easy to see that $\sum_{x \in S} \widehat{f}(x) \in (1 \pm \mu) \sum_{x \in S} f(x)$. So for any $x \in S$ we have

$$\widehat{\mathcal{D}}(x) = \frac{\widehat{f}(x)}{\sum_{x \in S} \widehat{f}(x)} \in \frac{(1 \pm \mu)f(x)}{(1 \pm \mu)\sum_{x \in S} f(x)} = (1 \pm (2\mu + O(\mu^2)))\mathcal{D}(x).$$

$\square$

Combining the two lemmas easily shows that at least the simple version of rejection sampling as described above can be safely used with FP approximations.

Remark 1. An important observation is that approximating the acceptance probability $\frac{f(x)}{M\mathcal{P}(x)}$ with a certain relative error is equivalent to approximating f with the same relative error. This makes Lemma 2 also applicable to algorithms that approximate the acceptance probability. I.e., if two rejection samplers use the same source distribution and only differ by a relative error $\leq \mu$ in the acceptance probability for all x, their output distributions will have relative error of at most $2\mu + O(\mu^2)$. Implications of this will be discussed in Sect. 3.

2.2 Inversion Sampling

While rejection sampling is very simple and versatile, for many distributions it can be rather slow in its simple form due to a large rejection rate. If the distribution is known in advance and has moderately sized support, one can use inversion sampling as a way to trade precomputation and memory for faster performance. For a discrete distribution $\mathcal{P}$ one computes the cumulative distribution table (CDT) of the desired distribution and stores it. The CDT consists of $n+1$ numbers (where n is size of the support) $0 = T[0] < T[1] < \cdots < T[n] = 1$ such that $\mathcal{P}(i) = T[i] - T[i-1]$ for all $i \in [n]$. When queried for a sample, a number $u \in [0,1)$ is drawn uniformly at random and the smallest value i with $T[i] \geq u$ is output. Clearly, the probability for any output i is $\Pr[u \leq T[i] \wedge u > T[i-1]] = T[i] - T[i-1] = \mathcal{P}(i)$. The question that we are concerned with is whether a bound can put on the relative error of the output distribution when storing k-bit FP approximations of the values $T[i]$. In [18] it was shown that in the special case of discrete Gaussians, the error can grow arbitrarily when applying inversion sampling in the obvious way, but is bounded by $O(n2^{-k})$ when reversing the order of the probabilities. We now demonstrate that this is in fact a very general technique that works for any finite discrete distribution.

Lemma 3. *Let $\mathcal{P}$ be discrete probability distribution of n elements with $\mathcal{P}(1) \leq \mathcal{P}(2) \leq \cdots \leq \mathcal{P}(n)$. Let $\widehat{\mathcal{P}}$ be the distribution output by an inversion sampler that approximates the entries in the CDT using k-bit FP numbers. Then $\delta_{\mathrm{RE}}(\mathcal{P}, \widehat{\mathcal{P}}) \leq n2^{-k+1}$.*

Proof. The inversion sampler stores the values $\widehat{T[i]} \in (1 \pm \mu)T[i]$, where $\mu = 2^{-k}$. So

$$
\begin{aligned}
\frac{\widehat{\mathcal{P}}(i)}{\mathcal{P}(i)} &= \frac{\widehat{T}[i] - \widehat{T}[i-1]}{\mathcal{P}(i)} \\
&\in \frac{(1 \pm \mu)T[i] - (1 \pm \mu)T[i]}{\mathcal{P}(i)} \\
&= \frac{(1 \pm \mu)\sum_{j \leq i}\mathcal{P}(j) - (1 \pm \mu)\sum_{j < i}\mathcal{P}(j)}{\mathcal{P}(i)} \\
&= 1 \pm \left(\frac{\mu \sum_{j \leq i}\mathcal{P}(j)}{\mathcal{P}(i)} + \frac{\mu \sum_{j < i}\mathcal{P}(j)}{\mathcal{P}(i)} \right).
\end{aligned}
$$

Due to the ordering of the probabilities we have $\mathcal{P}(j) \leq \mathcal{P}(i)$ for all $j \leq i$ and so the result follows. $\qquad\square$

Since inversion sampling as described above is only useful for distributions with polynomial support, the lemma shows that we can use inversion sampling for any such discrete distribution and achieve a small relative error by ordering the elements in the support according to their probabilities.

Application to Bernoulli Sampling. Assume we are given a bias p and want to sample from the respective Bernoulli distribution, i.e. the distribution over $\{0, 1\}$ with $p_0 = p$ and $p_1 = 1 - p$. The straight forward way of implementing this is to store p and during the online phase one draws a uniform number u in $[0, 1)$ and outputs 0 iff $u \leq p$. It should be clear that this can be viewed as a special case of inversion sampling with two element, i.e. $n = 2$. Applying the result from above shows that we can perform Bernoulli sampling and preserve a relative error of 2^{-k+2} if we reorder the probabilities. In this special case, this means we store an approximation of p or $1 - p$, whichever one is smaller. In fact, a direct calculation shows that this results in a relative error of at most 2^{-k}.

We also remark that [3] already observed that in the context of Bernoulli sampling one can assume w.l.o.g. that $p \leq \frac{1}{2}$ and that in this case an FP-approximation of p results in a small Rényi divergence of order infinity, which is essentially equivalent to the relative error.

2.3   Alias Method

Another popular method of using precomputation to speed up sampling for a known distribution is the alias method. Let $\mathcal{P}$ be a given probability distribution with support $S_{\mathcal{P}}$, where $|S_{\mathcal{P}}| = n$. The idea of alias sampling is to reduce sampling from $\mathcal{P}$ to sampling from a Bernoulli sampler randomly chosen from a carefully crafted set of Bernoulli samplers. To get an intuitive understanding of the algorithm, picture a set of buckets, one for each element in $S_{\mathcal{P}}$. These buckets have size $\frac{1}{n}$ and are filled with the probability mass of the corresponding element. Of course, some buckets are not full, while others are overflowing. In order to smooth things out, pick a bucket i that is not full, i.e. assume $p_i < \frac{1}{n}$. Mark its current filling level and then fill it up by moving probability mass from some overfull bucket, for example bucket j (where we assume $p_j > \frac{1}{n}$). The top of the now exactly full bucket i is labeled with j (so j is i's *alias*). Note that bucket j might now still be overflowing or not be full. Continue this procedure with a different i' and j' until every bucket is filled to exactly $\frac{1}{n}$. This is the offline/precomputation phase. In order to sample from $\mathcal{P}$, we select one of the buckets uniformly at random. Say we selected bucket i, which has a mark at p_i and alias j. We now draw a number r uniformly at random in $[0, \frac{1}{n})$. If $r \leq p_i$, we output i, otherwise we output the alias j. This is equivalent to drawing a Bernoulli sample with bias np_i and outputting i if the sample is 1 and j otherwise. The reason this works is that we did not change the amount of probability mass corresponding to a value. E.g., in the example of i and j above, assume that after moving mass from bucket j to bucket i, both buckets happen to be full. (In particular, this means that j does not have an alias and when selecting bucket j during sampling, we always output j.) Then the probability of obtaining i as a sample is exactly $\frac{1}{n}np_i = p_i$ and for j it is $\frac{1}{n}(1 + 1 - np_i) = \frac{2}{n} - p_i$. Since we assume bucket j was exactly full after moving $\frac{1}{n} - p_i$ mass to bucket i, we have $p_j = \frac{2}{n} - p_i$, which shows that alias sampling works correctly here. In summary, t he alias method works by constructing and storing n Bernoulli samplers B_j in the offline phase. In the online phase, one of the samplers is selected uniformly at random, a sample is obtained and depending on the result, one of two values is output. In our setting we assume that the bias of each sampler is computed exactly during the offline phase and the Bernoulli sampler is then approximated as described in Sect. 2.2.

Lemma 4. *The alias method can be implemented using only k-bit FP numbers during its online phase and guarantee a relative error of 2^{-k}.*

Proof. In the following we view the Bernoulli samplers as directly outputting one of the two values in the table, i.e. let $x_j, y_j \in [n]$ be the two values associated with the j-th Bernoulli sampler via the alias table and let b_j be the bias of that sampler. Then define

$$p_{B_j}(i) = \begin{cases} b_j & \text{if } i = x_j \\ 1 - b_j & \text{if } i = y_j \\ 0 & \text{otherwise.} \end{cases}$$

The probability that a value i is output by the alias sampler is then $p_i = \frac{1}{n} \sum_{j=1}^{n} p_{B_j}(i)$. From Sect. 2.2 we know that we can sample each Bernoulli sampler up to a relative error of $\mu = 2^{-k}$, so the probability of i under the approximate sampler is $\widehat{p}_i \in \frac{1}{n} \sum_{j=1}^{n} (1 \pm \mu) p_{B_j}(i) = \frac{(1 \pm \mu)}{n} \sum_{j=1}^{n} p_{B_j}(i)$, which shows that the relative error is at most 2^{-k}. □

It is noteworthy that alias sampling actually allows to achieve the optimal bound of 2^{-k} for the relative error using k-bit FP numbers only. This is in contrast to inversion sampling, where the relative error can be larger by a factor $O(n)$.

2.4   Knuth-Yao Sampling

Yet another way to spend precomputation and storage in order to speed up sampling from a known distribution is Knuth-Yao sampling. Knuth-Yao sampling constructs a binary tree, known as the distribution generating tree (DGT), during initialization from the given probabilities p_i. During the online phase, a random path from the root is traversed to the end, at which point the label of the leaf determines the sample that is output. Note that a leaf on level t of the tree has a probability of 2^{-t} of being sampled. So if for a sample i there are l leafs, where each is on a distinct level t_j, then the probability of outputting i is exactly $\sum_j^l 2^{-t_j}$. The tree is constructed from p_i such that for every '1' in position t in the fixed point binary expansion of p_i there is a leaf for i on level t. Then it is easy to see that the probability of i is exactly p_i. The fact that $\sum_i p_i = 1$ ensures that the tree can be easily constructed from the binary representation of the p_i and that there is a label for every leaf.

Knuth-Yao is often praised for its randomness efficiency, which is close to the entropy of the distribution and thus close to optimal. We point out though that at least in the context of discrete Gaussians, which have entropy[4] $\sim \log \sigma$, both inversion sampling and alias sampling can also be implemented to only require $\log n + O(1) = \log \sigma + O(1)$ random bits.

There are several ways to implement Knuth-Yao:

---

[4] Here, σ is the noise parameter of the discrete Gaussian. See Definition 1.

1. Construct the tree structure and traverse it as described above. This incurs a significant memory overhead, so this version seems only applicable if memory is not an issue.
2. In order to reduce the memory overhead, one can construct each level of the tree on-the-fly during the traversal using a table [7]. This table requires less storage than the tree itself, but still leaves a significant overhead. (In essence, the table contains a number in $[n]$ for every '1' in the binary expansions of the p_i, which means this table still requires larger storage than the probabilities itself by a factor $O(\log n)$.)
3. Finally, [20] introduced a variant that constructs the tree entirely on-the-fly only using the probability table. In this case the storage requirement essentially matches the one of inversion sampling and alias sampling.

Floating point numbers can be used to reduce the storage requirement in all three variants. When using FP approximations $\widehat{p}_i$ of p_i for all i, the difficulty is to deal with the fact that $\sum_i \widehat{p}_i \neq 1$. Note that we can easily ensure that $\sum_i \widehat{p}_i \leq 1$ by requiring that $\widehat{p}_i \leq p_i$ by always rounding down the approximations, which will increase the relative error by at most a factor 2. In this case, the DGT tree is not well defined and the result is that the algorithm might not ever encounter a leaf. However, this case is easily detected since the depth of the tree is bounded by $k - \min \log \widehat{p}_i$, where k is the precision of the FP numbers. In that case, one can simply restart the algorithm, which essentially turns this algorithm into a rejection sampler. We demonstrate this approach in Algorithm 1, where the subroutine $\mathrm{BIT}(p = (s, m, e), c)$ gives access to the c'th bit of the fixed point representation of the number represented by the k-bit FP number p.

Algorithm 1. Floating point version of Knuth-Yao, adapted from [20]. The list $(p_i)_i$ consists of k-bit FP numbers.

$\mathrm{SAMPLEKY}((p_i)_i, k)$		$\mathrm{BIT}((p = (s, m, e), c)$	
1	$c_{\max} = \lceil -\log \min_i p_i \rceil + k$	1	**if** $c < -e - k$ or $c > -e$
2	$d \leftarrow 0$	2	**return** 0
3	**while** true	3	**return** $m[c + e + k]$
4	$\quad$ **for** $c = 0$ to $c_{\max}$		
5	$\quad\quad b \leftarrow \{0, 1\}$		
6	$\quad\quad d \leftarrow 2d + 1 - b$		
7	$\quad\quad$ **for** $r = n$ down to 0		
8	$\quad\quad\quad d \leftarrow d - \mathrm{BIT}(p_r, c)$		
9	$\quad\quad\quad$ **if** $d = -1$		
10	$\quad\quad\quad\quad$ **return** r		

Theorem 1. *Let $\mathcal{P}$ be a discrete distribution over a finite set with probabilities p_i. If given $k \in \mathbb{Z}$ and a list of k-bit FP numbers $(\widehat{p}_i)_i$ such that $\widehat{p}_i \leq p_i$ and $\delta_{\mathrm{RE}}(p_i, \widehat{p}_i) \leq \mu$ for all i, then the output distribution $\widehat{\mathcal{P}}$ of Algorithm 1 satisfies $\delta_{\mathrm{RE}}(\mathcal{P}, \widehat{\mathcal{P}}) \leq 2\mu + (O(\mu^2))$. Furthermore, the expected running time and expected randomness consumption is $(1 + \mu)H(\mathcal{P}) + O(1)$.*

Proof. Since Algorithm 1 corresponds to a randomized walk on a truncated DGT (see [20] for details), the relative probability of each sample i is $\widehat{p}_i$. Now the first part of the theorem follows from Lemma 2.

For the second part notice that Algorithm 1 behaves, up to rejection, exactly like an exact implementation of Knuth-Yao, which has running time and randomness consumption $H(\mathcal{P})$. The result follows from the fact that the rejection probability is $\leq \mu$. □

Remark 2. If the rejection step is undesirable for some reason, there is another way to deal with the situation where no leaf is encountered: simply always output $j = \arg\max_i p_i$. Note that $p_j > 1/n$ and so

$$\widehat{p}_j + \mu \in (1 \pm \mu)p_j + \mu \in \left(1 \pm \left(\mu + \frac{\mu}{p_j}\right)\right)p_j \in (1 \pm (\mu + n\mu))p_j.$$

This shows that this solution leads to a relative error of $\leq 2n\mu$.

3   Specialized Algorithms

We now consider two algorithms that are specialized to discrete Gaussians. They are both based on rejection sampling and differ in the source distribution and the way the rejection step is carried out to achieve high efficiency. We start by defining the distribution we are interested in.

Definition 1. *We denote by $\mathcal{D}_{\mathbb{Z},\sigma,c}$ the distribution over $\mathbb{Z}$ that is proportional to $\rho_{\sigma,c}(x) = \exp(-\frac{(x-c)^2}{2\sigma^2})$. Furthermore, we define the distribution $\mathcal{D}_{\mathbb{Z},\sigma,c}^+$ to be the distribution proportional to $\mathcal{D}_{\mathbb{Z},\sigma,c}$ restricted to non-negative integers $\mathbb{Z}_{\geq 0}$. In either case, if the parameter c is omitted, it is understood to be 0.*

Note that sampling $\mathcal{D}_{\mathbb{Z},\sigma}$ is easily reduced to sampling $\mathcal{D}_{\mathbb{Z},\sigma}^+$: draw a sample $x \leftarrow \mathcal{D}_{\mathbb{Z},\sigma}^+$ and a uniform bit $s \leftarrow \mathcal{U}(\{0,1\})$. If $x = s = 0$, reject x and try again. Otherwise, return $(-1)^s \cdot x$. It is folklore that for cryptographic purposes one can view $\mathcal{D}_{\mathbb{Z},\sigma,c}$ as a $[c - t\sigma, c + t\sigma]$ bounded distribution for some constant t due to its exponential decay in the tails. This follows from known bounds on the so called *smoothing parameter* [15] and a simple hybrid argument. Furthermore, from an algorithmic perspective we can assume w.l.o.g. that $c \in [0,1)$ since the distribution can easily be shifted by an arbitrary integer. Finally, in all applications in the cryptographic context that we are aware of one can safely assume that $\sigma \geq 1$.

3.1   BLISS Sampler

The BLISS sampler was proposed in [5] as a way to achieve another trade-off between memory requirements and sampling performance for a known distribution. In particular, while plain rejection sampling is very slow, in many settings the memory required to apply any of the generic algorithms described in

Sect. 2 is prohibitively large, especially on constraint devices. The BLISS sampler addresses this issue by only requiring precomputed storage of $O(\log n)$ instead of $O(n)$, while still yielding much better performance than rejection sampling.

The BLISS sampler is a rejection sampler with two main differences to plain rejection sampling. First, it uses a different source distribution, which is still easy to sample, but better adapted to the target distribution, which reduces the rejection rate. Second, a list of logarithmically many precomputed values is used to perform the rejection step through a set of Bernoulli samples. This has the advantage that no FP arithmetic has to be performed during sampling.

The algorithm assumes that $\sigma = k \cdot \sigma_2$ for $\sigma_2 = \sqrt{1/(2 \ln 2)}$ and some $k \in \mathbb{Z}$. This is justified since in many settings σ is a parameter of the scheme and can be chosen accordingly. The source distribution is defined as $k \cdot \mathcal{D}_{\mathbb{Z},\sigma_2}^+ + \mathcal{U}(\{0, \ldots, k-1\})$, which can be easily sampled if there is an efficient way to sample $\mathcal{D}_{\mathbb{Z},\sigma_2}^+$. By the choice of σ_2 this can be done using inversion sampling, where the CDT is computed on-the-fly. To see this, note that $\rho_{\sigma_2}(x) = \exp(-\frac{x^2}{2\sigma_2^2}) = \exp(-x^2 \ln 2) = 2^{-x^2}$. So $\sum_{x=0}^{j} \rho(x) = \sum_{x=0}^{j} 2^{-x^2}$ which converges to a constant $\alpha < 2$ as $j \to \infty$. Furthermore, the entries of the CDT correspond exactly to the sums $\sum_{x=0}^{j} 2^{-x^2}$ for $j \in \mathbb{Z}$, which exhibits their binary expansion: the expansion has a one in positions that correspond to squares. Since $(a+1)^2 - a^2 = 2a + 1$, there are exactly $2a$ zeros between the a-th one and the $a + 1$-st one for $a < j$. This structure can be exploited by sampling a uniformly random number r in $[0, 2)$ one bit at a time (or in chunks) and checking if $r \in \left[\sum_{x=0}^{j} \rho_{\sigma_2}(x), \sum_{x=0}^{j+1} \rho_{\sigma_2}(x) \right]$ for some j. (Note that one can also easily check if $r > \alpha$ and reject r in that case). See [5] for details.

To sample from $\mathcal{D}_{\mathbb{Z},k\sigma_2}^+$, a sample from the source distribution is chosen by sampling $x \leftarrow \mathcal{D}_{\mathbb{Z},\sigma_2}^+$ and $y \leftarrow \mathcal{U}(\{0, \ldots, k-1\})$, which represent the sample $z = kx + y$. This sample is now accepted with probability $\exp(-\frac{y(y+2kx)}{2\sigma^2})$. Correctness follows from the fact that the probability of outputting a sample $z = kx + y$ is proportional to

$$
\rho_{\sigma_2}(x) \exp\left(-\frac{y(y+2kx)}{2\sigma^2}\right) = \exp\left(-\frac{x^2}{2\sigma_2^2} - \frac{y(y+2kx)}{2\sigma^2}\right) = \rho_\sigma(z).
$$

It remains to show how to perform the rejection step without FP arithmetic and little precomputed memory. For this, recall that an integer sample $z \in \{0, \ldots, \tau\sigma\}$ that is output by the source distribution, is accepted with probability $\exp(-\frac{f(z)}{2\sigma^2})$ for some integer $f(z) \leq z^2$, where As seen above, $f(z)$ is easily computable from z using only small integer arithmetic and τ can be considered a constant. The corresponding Bernoulli trial is realized by storing the numbers $c_i = \exp(-\frac{2^i}{2\sigma^2})$ for all $i \in [[2\log(\tau\sigma)]]$ in memory. Then the Bernoulli trial is performed by considering the binary representation of $f(z) = \sum_i z_i 2^i$ and rewriting

$$
\exp\left(-\frac{f(z)}{2\sigma^2}\right) = \exp\left(-\frac{\sum_i z_i 2^i}{2\sigma^2}\right) = \prod_i \exp\left(-\frac{z_i 2^i}{2\sigma^2}\right) = \prod_{i:z_i=1} \exp\left(-\frac{2^i}{2\sigma^2}\right).
$$

This shows that this trial can be carried out by a series of at most $l = \lceil 2\log(\tau\sigma) \rceil$ Bernoulli trials with bias of the form c_i for some i. It is clear that this works if storing the numbers c_i exactly, but this is clearly impossible in practice. The next lemma shows that we can approximate the biases c_i and achieve small relative error.

Lemma 5. *Let $\mathcal{D}$ be the output distribution of the BLISS sampler with biases c_i, and $\widehat{\mathcal{D}}$ be the same algorithm with biases $\widehat{c}_i$. If $\delta_{\mathrm{RE}}(c_i, \widehat{c}_i) \leq \mu$ for all i then $\delta_{\mathrm{RE}}(\mathcal{D}, \widehat{\mathcal{D}}) \leq 2l\mu + O(l^2\mu^2)$.*

Proof. Since $\widehat{c}_i \in (1 \pm \mu)c_i$, the rejection probability for any x is

$$\prod_{i:z_i=1} \widehat{c}_i \in \prod_{i:z_i=1} (1 \pm \mu)c_i \in (1 \pm \mu)^l \prod_{i:z_i=1} c_i \in (1 \pm (l\mu + O(\mu^2))) \prod_{i:z_i=1} c_i.$$

The result follows from Lemma 2 (cf. Remark 1). □

Lemma 5 shows that the BLISS sampler preserves the relative error up to a multiplicative loss of $\sim 2l = O(\log\sigma)$ if using FP numbers to approximate the biases c_i.

Remark 3. The work of [3] analyzed the required precision for the biases of the BLISS sampler by viewing the cryptosystem as using samples from the respective Bernoulli samplers, rather than from the discrete Gaussian. This requires fixing the number of Bernoulli samples a priori, which is possible in security analyses because one is usually only interested in bounded adversaries and it is reasonable to charge the adversary resources for obtaining Bernoulli samples. In comparison, our result is of a statistical nature and thus slightly stronger: the relative error of the distribution is bounded independently of the number of times the Bernoulli samplers are invoked, which is unbounded in the worst case. Furthermore, our approach has the advantage of being simpler and more modular.

3.2 Karney's Algorithm

Karney's algorithm is a type of rejection algorithm that efficiently samples from the discrete Gaussian. (In fact, the work [13] also shows how to sample from the continuous Gaussian, but we are only interested in discrete distributions here.) We give a description of Karney's algorithm in Algorithm 2. Sampling from the non-negative unit discrete Gaussian in Step 2 can be done using only uniform Bernoulli trials. Similarly, the Bernoulli trial in Step 12 is also done by cleverly dividing it up into a series of uniform Bernoulli trials. How exactly these two steps are carried out is not important here.

Algorithm 2. Karney's Algorithm

$\text{KARNEY}(\sigma, c)$

```
 1        while true
 2            t ← 𝒟⁺_{ℤ,1}
 3            s ← {−1, 1}
 4            j ← {0, …, ⌈σ⌉ − 1}
 5            i ← ⌈tσ + sc⌉
 6            x̄ ← i − (tσ + sc)
 7            x ← (x̄+j)/σ
 8            if x ≥ 1
 9                continue // reject
10            if t = 0 and x = 0 and s < 0
11                continue // reject
12            b ← ℬ_p where p = exp(−½x(2t + x))
13            if b = 1
14                return s(i + j)
```

Karney presented his algorithm as an exact algorithm using only integer arithmetic. The algorithm assumes that the parameters are given as rationals. However, a common use case is to apply this sampler on a regular PC using floating point numbers, for example during trapdoor sampling. In this context the parameters are given as floating point numbers, not as rationals. While floating point numbers can be naturally viewed as rationals, doing so in the straightforward manner leads to relatively large integers. Inspecting the algorithm, it is clear that the integers involved can have roughly twice the size of the mantissa of the floating point numbers of the input parameters. So if working with regular double precision floating point numbers ($k = 53$), the numbers may be larger than 100 bits, which exceeds the length of integers on most architectures (a reasonable target could be 64 bits).

A Floating Point Version. We are interested in a floating point version of Karney's algorithm. We will assume that the input is given as floating point numbers and that we only have floating point numbers of the same precision available. Furthermore, we assume that we have integers available with a specific bit size. This immediately puts an upper bound on the noise parameter, since we need to be able to represent samples from a discrete Gaussian that have more than negligible probability.

We want to bound the relative error achieved by the modified algorithm. We will show that we can perform all the steps in Karney's algorithm exactly, even with low precision numbers, except step 12 as this requires to compute x. Instead, we will approximate x, which allows to carry out an approximate Bernoulli trial (in the same way as in Karney's algorithm). The main observation is that Lemma 2 now applies: this approximation of the bias in the last rejection step only leads to a small difference in the relative probability for each potential sample $s(i + j)$ and thus a small relative error.

We will require a little background on floating point numbers, in particular we identify a set of operations on FP numbers with fixed precision that can be carried out exactly without resorting to FP numbers with higher precision.

Fact 1. *Given two k-bit FP numbers a and b we can easily compute*

- $a \le b$, $a < b$, $a = b$
- $(a)_{\%1}$, *the reduction* $\mod 1$, *i.e. separating out the fractional part of* a
- $2^t a$ *for any* $t \in \mathbb{Z}$
- $\lfloor a \rfloor$ *and* $\lceil a \rceil$

exactly as k-bit FP numbers.

Lemma 6 (Sterbenz Lemma). *Given two k-bit FP numbers a and b with* $\frac{1}{2} \le \frac{a}{b} \le 2$, *their difference* $a - b$ *is also a k-bit FP number.*

Corollary 1. *Given three positive FP numbers a, b, and c, we can check if* $(a + b) \circ c$ *for any* $\circ \in \{\le, \ge, <, >, =\}$.

Proof. Algorithm 3 performs the check for $\le$. Its correctness follows from Sterbenz lemma. The same approach works for any other comparison operator. $\square$

Algorithm 3. An exact algorithm to check if $a + b \le c$ for given FP numbers a, b, c

---

COMPARESUM$_{\text{FP}}(a, b, c)$

```
1      if a > c or b > c
2          return false
3      if a > c/2
4          return b ≤ c − a
5      if b > c/2
6          return a ≤ c − b
7      return true
```

Lemma 7. *Given a k-bit FP number* $a \ge 1$ *and an integer t, we can compute* $(ta)_{\%1}$ *and* $\lfloor ta \rfloor$ *using* $\lceil \log t \rceil$ *operations, assuming integer data types that are capable of representing* $\lfloor ta \rfloor$.

Proof. First note that $(a)_{\%1}$ is a $(k-1)$-bit fixed point number. Using simple peasant multiplication with k-bit fixed point arithmetic (e.g. emulated using k-bit FP arithmetic with fixed exponent) we can compute $(ta)_{\%1}$ and $\lfloor t(a)_{\%1} \rfloor$. Finally, compute $\lfloor ta \rfloor = t \lfloor a \rfloor + \lfloor t(a)_{\%1} \rfloor$. $\square$

We remark that in the case where the available integer type has bit size larger than the mantissa of the FP numbers plus $\lceil \log t \rceil$, the task in Lemma 7 can be achieved in a much simpler way: multiply t with the mantissa of a, which allows to directly read off the two desired values. This case is common on standard CPUs, where the FP numbers have 53 bits of precision and the common integer type has 63 bits. Furthermore, in our setting $\log t < 4$ with overwhelming probability. On the other hand, if working with 80-bit extended precision, where FP numbers commonly have a 63-bit mantissa, this is not the case anymore.

Algorithm 4. Rewrite of Karney's Algorithm
___

KARNEYREWRITE(σ, c)

1	**while true**
2	$t \leftarrow \mathcal{D}_{\mathbb{Z},1}^+$
3	$s \leftarrow \{-1, 1\}$
4	$j \leftarrow \{0, \ldots, \lceil \sigma \rceil - 1\}$
5	**if** CHECKREJECTA(σ, c, t, s, j)
6	**continue** // reject
7	**if** CHECKREJECTB(σ, c, t, s, j)
8	**continue** // reject
9	$i \leftarrow$ COMPUTEI(σ, c, t, s)
10	$x \leftarrow$ COMPUTEX(σ, c, t, s, j)
11	$b \leftarrow \mathcal{B}_p$
	where $p = \exp(-\frac{1}{2}x(2t + x))$
12	**if** $b = 1$
13	**return** $s(i + j)$

COMPUTEI(σ, c, t, s)

1	**return** $\lceil t\sigma + sc \rceil$

COMPUTEX(σ, c, t, s, j)

1	$i \leftarrow$ COMPUTEI(σ, c, t, s)
2	**return** $\frac{i - (t\sigma + sc) + j}{\sigma}$

CHECKREJECTA(σ, c, t, s, j)

1	$x \leftarrow$ COMPUTEX(σ, c, t, s, j)
2	**return** $x \geq 1$

CHECKREJECTB(σ, c, t, s, j)

1	$x \leftarrow$ COMPUTEX(σ, c, t, s, j)
2	**return** ($t = 0$ and $x = 0$ and $s < 0$)

We begin our analysis by rewriting Algorithm 2 using auxiliary procedures that encapsulate the critical steps (see Algorithm 4). Then we will present alternative procedures that can be implemented with FP numbers such that the entire procedure is guaranteed to yield a small relative error in the output distribution.

In the following, we show how to implement COMPUTEI, CHECKREJECTA and CHECKREJECTB exactly using FP numbers. Finally, we will introduce a procedure that approximates x such that the computed bias p has small relative error. Then the result follows from Lemma 2.

Lemma 8. *For any set of inputs* $(t, s, \sigma, c) \in \mathbb{Z}_+ \times \{-1, 1\} \times \mathbb{R}_+ \times [0, 1)$

$$\text{COMPUTEI}_{\text{FP}}(\sigma, c, t, s) = \text{COMPUTEI}(\sigma, c, t, s)$$

where σ *and* c *are given as FP numbers and* COMPUTEIFP(t, s, σ, c) *is implemented using FP numbers of the same precision.*

Proof. Let $a = \lfloor t\sigma \rfloor$ and $b = (t\sigma)_{\%1}$. Then $\lceil t\sigma + sc \rceil = a + \lceil b + sc \rceil$. Since $c \in [0, 1)$, there are only 3 possible values: $\lceil t\sigma + sc \rceil \in \{a, a + 1, a + 2\}$. We can split this up into the cases where $s = -1$ and $s = 1$. In the former case, we have

$$\lceil t\sigma + sc \rceil = \begin{cases} a & \text{if } b \leq c \\ a + 1 & \text{otherwise} \end{cases}$$

In the case $s = 1$ we have three cases:

$$\lceil t\sigma + sc \rceil = \begin{cases} a & \text{if } b = c = 0 \\ a+1 & \text{if } b + c \leq 1 \\ a+2 & \text{otherwise} \end{cases}$$

Recall that the second case can be checked using Corollary 1.   □

Algorithm 5. An exact algorithm to compute $i = \lceil t\sigma + sc \rceil$ using FP numbers, where $t \in \mathbb{Z}$, $s \in \{-1, 1\}$ and $c \in [0, 1)$

$\text{COMPUTEI}_{\text{FP}}(\sigma, c, t, s)$

```
1     i ← ⌊tσ⌋
2     b ← (tσ)%1
3     if s < 0 and b > c
4         i ← i + 1
5     if s > 0 and (b > 0 or c > 0)
6         if b + c ≤ 1        // cf. Corollary 1
7             i ← i + 1
8         else
9             i ← i + 2
10    return i
```

Lemma 9. *For any set of inputs* $(t, s, \sigma, c, j) \in \mathbb{Z}_+ \times \{-1, 1\} \times \mathbb{R}_+ \times [0, 1) \times \mathbb{Z}_+$

$$\text{CHECKREJECTA}_{\text{FP}}(\sigma, c, t, s, j) = \text{CHECKREJECTA}(\sigma, c, t, s, j)$$

where σ and c are given as FP numbers and $\text{CHECKREJECTA}_{\text{FP}}$ is implemented using FP numbers of the same precision.

Proof. As in the original algorithm, denote with $\bar{x} = i - \lceil t\sigma + sc \rceil$. Then this check is equivalent to $\bar{x} + j \geq \sigma$. If $\bar{x} = 0$ this must always be false by the choice of j so by correctness of ISXBARZERO (see below) we can assume $\bar{x} \in (0, 1)$. Furthermore, the check can only be true if $j = \lfloor \sigma \rfloor$, because $c \in [0, 1)$. In this case this is equivalent to $\bar{x} \geq (\sigma)\%1$. Note that $\bar{x} = 1 - (t\sigma + sc)\%1$, so this is the same as

$$1 \geq (t\sigma + sc)\%1 + (\sigma)\%1. \tag{1}$$

We consider the case $s > 0$. Then we have

$$(t\sigma + c)\%1 = \begin{cases} (t\sigma)\%1 + c - 1 & \text{if } (t\sigma)\%1 + c \geq 1 \\ (t\sigma)\%1 + c & \text{else} \end{cases}$$

Plugging this into (1)

$$1 \geq (t\sigma + sc)\%1 + (\sigma)\%1 = \begin{cases} (t\sigma)\%1 + (\sigma)\%1 + c - 1 & \text{if } (t\sigma)\%1 + c \geq 1 \\ (t\sigma)\%1 + (\sigma)\%1 + c & \text{else} \end{cases}$$

Note that we can distinguish the cases using Corollary 1. In each case we can compute $(t\sigma)_{\%1} + (\sigma)_{\%1}$ exactly and invoke Corollary 1, with the left-hand side being either 2 or 1, respectively.

Next consider the case $s < 0$. Then (1) is equivalent to $1 \geq (t\sigma - c)_{\%1} + (\sigma)_{\%1}$. Note that

$$(t\sigma - c)_{\%1} = \begin{cases} (t\sigma)_{\%1} - c & \text{if } (t\sigma)_{\%1} \geq c \\ (t\sigma)_{\%1} - c + 1 & \text{else.} \end{cases}$$

Again we can rewrite

$$1 \geq (t\sigma - c)_{\%1} + (\sigma)_{\%1} = \begin{cases} (t\sigma)_{\%1} + (\sigma)_{\%1} - c & \text{if } (t\sigma)_{\%1} \geq c \\ (t\sigma)_{\%1} + (\sigma)_{\%1} - c + 1 & \text{else.} \end{cases}$$

Again we can compute $(t\sigma)_{\%1} + (\sigma)_{\%1}$ exactly. Note that in the latter case the 1 cancels and we can directly check the inequality. In the former case, we check if $(t\sigma)_{\%1} + (\sigma)_{\%1} < 1$ in which case the inequality is obviously true. Otherwise, we subtract 1 from both sides which yields $0 \geq ((t+1)\sigma)_{\%1} - c$, which we can obviously check with $c \geq ((t+1)\sigma)_{\%1}$. $\qquad\square$

It remains to prove correctness of IsXBARZERO$_{\mathrm{FP}}$.

Lemma 10. *Algorithm 7 returns* **true** *iff* $t\sigma + sc$ *is integral.*

Proof. The value $t\sigma + sc$ is integral iff $(t\sigma)_{\%1} + (sc)_{\%1} \in \{0, 1\}$. If $s < 0$, this simply reduces to $(t\sigma)_{\%1} = c$. Otherwise we need to check if $(t\sigma)_{\%1} + c = 1$, which we can do by Corollary 1, or if $t\sigma = c = 0$. $\qquad\square$

Performing CHECKREJECTB exactly is straightforward, since $x = 0$ iff $j = 0$ and $\bar{x} = 0$. Conditioned on $t = 0$, the latter is the case iff $c = 0$ (cf. Algorithm 8).

The above shows that Algorithm 4 behaves identical if we replace COMPUTEI, CHECKREJECTA and CHECKREJECTB with COMPUTEI$_{\mathrm{FP}}$, CHECKREJECTA$_{\mathrm{FP}}$ and CHECKREJECTB$_{\mathrm{FP}}$, respectively. Clearly, we cannot hope to implement COMPUTEX exactly, since the result might not even be a k-bit FP number (where k is the precision of the parameters). However, it is sufficient to approximate x well enough in order to maintain a small relative error in the output distribution. We begin with the observation that it is sufficient to approximate x with a small *absolute or relative* error μ. Standard calculations show that in either case the term $\exp(-\frac{1}{2}\hat{x}(2t + \hat{x}))$ will be off by a multiplicative factor $\sim \exp(t\mu) \approx 1 + t\mu$, which shows that the relative error is only about $t\mu$.

Algorithm 6. An exact algorithm to check if $x \geq 1$	**Algorithm 7.** An exact algorithm to check if $t\sigma + sc$ is integral
$\text{CHECKREJECTA}_{\text{FP}}(\sigma, c, t, s, j)$	$\text{ISXBARZERO}_{\text{FP}}(\sigma, c, t, s)$

$\text{CHECKREJECTA}_{\text{FP}}(\sigma, c, t, s, j)$

```
1    if  j  <  ⌊σ⌋  or
     IsXBarZeroFP(σ, c, t, s)
2        return false
3        b ← (tσ)%1
4        a ← (σ)%1
5        z ← a + b
6        if s > 0
7            if b + c ≥ 1
8                return (z + c ≤ 2)
9            else
10               return (z + c ≤ 1)
11       else
12           if b > c
13               if z ≤ 1
14                   return true
15               else
16                   return (c ≥ (z)%1)
17           else
18               return (c ≥ z)
```

$\text{ISXBARZERO}_{\text{FP}}(\sigma, c, t, s)$

```
1    b ← (tσ)%1
2    if s > 0
3        if [(b = 0 and c = 0) or (b + c = 1)]
4            return true
5        if s < 0 and b = c
6            return true
7    return false
```

Algorithm 8. An exact algorithm to perform CHECKREJECTB using FP numbers

$\text{CHECKREJECTB}_{\text{FP}}(\sigma, c, t, s, j)$

```
1    return (c = 0 and t = 0 and j = 0
         and s < 0)
```

The problematic part is computing $\bar{x} = i - (t\sigma + sc)$ with low error. Recall that we can check if $\bar{x} = 0$, so assume that $\bar{x} \in (0, 1)$, which means $\bar{x} = 1 - (t\sigma + sc)_{\%1}$. While we can compute $b = (t\sigma)_{\%1}$ and sc exactly, the sum $a = b + sc$ is computed up to an approximation. Naively extracting the fractional part of a could cause catastrophic errors if $(b + sc)_{\%1}$ is very close to 1 and a is rounded to an integer. In that case, $(a)_{\%1} = 0$, which is very far from $(b + sc)_{\%1}$. This would result in a bad approximation of $\bar{x}$. To avoid this problem, we forgo the $(\cdot)_{\%1}$ computation and check explicitly if $b + sc < 0$ or $b + sc \geq 1$ and adjust $\bar{x}$ accordingly through appropriate additions and subtractions.

To prove a good approximation for Algorithm 9, we need a technical fact that can be easily verified using standard calculations.

Fact 2. *Let $\hat{a}$ and b be k-bit FP numbers such that $|a - \hat{a}| \leq \mu$. Then*

$$\left| \widehat{\hat{a} + b} - (a + b) \right| \leq \mu + 2^{-k}(a + b) + 2^{-k}\mu \lesssim \mu + 2^{-k}(a + b).$$

Lemma 11. *For any set of inputs $\sigma, c, t, s, j \in \mathbb{R}_+ \times [0, 1) \times \mathbb{Z}_+ \times \{-1, 1\} \times \mathbb{Z}_+$ given as k-bit FP numbers, if Algorithm 9 is implemented with k-bit FP numbers, then its output value x' will satisfy at least one of*

$$- \; |x' - x| = O(2^{-k})$$
$$- \; \delta_{\text{RE}}(x', x) = O(2^{-k}).$$

Proof. Multiple applications of Lemma 2 show that $\bar{x}$, as computed in line 4 to 8 of Algorithm 9, has low absolute error of $O(2^{-k})$, since all the numbers involved have small absolute value. We now make a case distinction: first consider the case $j = 0$. In that case, $x = \frac{\bar{x}}{\sigma}$ will have also small absolute error of $O(2^{-k}/\sigma)$. On the other hand, if $j \geq 1$, $\bar{x} + j$ will actually have relative error $O(2^{-k}/(x+j)) = O(2^{-k})$. Division by σ can increase this by at most a factor 2, which shows that also x has relative error of $O(2^{-k})$.   □

We are now ready to prove the main theorem of this section.

Theorem. *If Algorithm 4 is implemented using Algorithms 5, 6, 8, and 9 with k-bit numbers and the exponentiation in step 11 is computed with low relative error, the relative error between its output distribution and the one of Karney's algorithm is $O(2^{-k})$.*

Proof. Recall that Algorithm 4 behaves identical to its FP variant up to step 9. Denote the distribution of (s, i, j) that are not rejected up to that point as *source distribution*. The probability that such a sample is rejected has relative error $O(2^{-k})$ compared to the exact variant by Lemma 11. We can now apply Lemma 2 (cf. Remark 1) to finish the proof.   □

We note that the rejection step with value $\exp(-\frac{1}{2}x(2t + x))$ can be either carried out exactly as in Karney's original algorithm or using a fast procedure to approximate $\exp(\cdot)$ with small relative error, if it is available.

Algorithm 9. An algorithm to approximately compute x

$\textsc{ComputeX}_{\text{FP}}(\sigma, c, t, s, j)$

  1   **if** $\textsc{IsXbarZero}_{\text{FP}}(\sigma, c, t, s)$
  2   **return** $\frac{j}{\sigma}$
  3     $b \leftarrow (t\sigma)_{\%1}$
  4     $\bar{x} \leftarrow 1 - (b + sc)$
  5   **if** $s < 0$ and $b < c$
  6       $\bar{x} \leftarrow \bar{x} - 1$
  7   **if** $s > 0$ and $b + c \geq 1$
  8       $\bar{x} \leftarrow \bar{x} + 1$
  9   **return** $\frac{\bar{x}+j}{\sigma}$

3.3 Experimental Results

We implemented our FP version of Karney's algorithm (which we denote by $\textsc{Karney}_{\text{FP}}$ in this section) using standard IEEE double precision floating point numbers and compared it to a public implementation of Karney's algorithm [2], where we set the precision to 100 bits, such that the two algorithms offer similar security guarantees when used in cryptographic primitives. Our implementation uses the same source of randomness as [2], is also written in C and compiled with the same parameters. During our experimentation on a standard PC we found that KARNEY_FP is about 20 times faster than the high precision variant in [2] on typical parameters. We stress though that this is highly platform dependent and caution that this comparison is merely an indication that the relative performance of KARNEY_FP can be very good.

We note that [2] also provides an implementation using double precision FP numbers. While this version cannot guarantee a low relative error and thus guarantees a much lower level of security (if any), we point out that our implementation was only roughly 25% slower than the low precision version in [2]. This indicates that on standard PC's the penalty for the additional conditionals required to guarantee low relative error is very acceptable. The source code of our implementation will be made public with the publication of this work.

References

1. Aguilar-Melchor, C., Albrecht, M.R., Ricosset, T.: Sampling from arbitrary centered discrete Gaussians for lattice-based cryptography. In: Gollmann, D., Miyaji, A., Kikuchi, H. (eds.) ACNS 2017. LNCS, vol. 10355, pp. 3–19. Springer, Cham (2017). https://doi.org/10.1007/978-3-319-61204-1_1
2. Albrecht, M.R., Walter, M.L.: dgs, Discrete Gaussians over the Integers (2018). https://bitbucket.org/malb/dgs
3. Bai, S., Langlois, A., Lepoint, T., Stehlé, D., Steinfeld, R.: Improved security proofs in lattice-based cryptography: using the Rényi divergence rather than the statistical distance. In: Iwata, T., Cheon, J.H. (eds.) ASIACRYPT 2015, Part I. LNCS, vol. 9452, pp. 3–24. Springer, Heidelberg (2015). https://doi.org/10.1007/978-3-662-48797-6_1
4. Cousins, D.B., et al.: Implementing conjunction obfuscation under entropic ring LWE. In: 2018 IEEE Symposium on Security and Privacy, pp. 354–371. IEEE Computer Society Press, May 2018
5. Ducas, L., Durmus, A., Lepoint, T., Lyubashevsky, V.: Lattice signatures and bimodal Gaussians. In: Canetti, R., Garay, J.A. (eds.) CRYPTO 2013, Part I. LNCS, vol. 8042, pp. 40–56. Springer, Heidelberg (2013). https://doi.org/10.1007/978-3-642-40041-4_3
6. Ducas, L., Nguyen, P.Q.: Faster Gaussian lattice sampling using lazy floating-point arithmetic. In: Wang, X., Sako, K. (eds.) ASIACRYPT 2012. LNCS, vol. 7658, pp. 415–432. Springer, Heidelberg (2012). https://doi.org/10.1007/978-3-642-34961-4_26
7. Dwarakanath, N.C., Galbraith, S.D.: Sampling from discrete Gaussians for lattice-based cryptography on a constrained device. Appl. Algebra Eng. Commun. Comput. **25**(3), 159–180 (2014)
8. Genise, N., Micciancio, D.: Faster Gaussian sampling for trapdoor lattices with arbitrary modulus. In: Nielsen, J.B., Rijmen, V. (eds.) EUROCRYPT 2018, Part I. LNCS, vol. 10820, pp. 174–203. Springer, Cham (2018). https://doi.org/10.1007/978-3-319-78381-9_7
9. Gentry, C.: Fully homomorphic encryption using ideal lattices. In: Mitzenmacher, M. (ed.) 41st Annual ACM Symposium on Theory of Computing, pp. 169–178. ACM Press, May/June 2009
10. Gentry, C., Peikert, C., Vaikuntanathan, V.: Trapdoors for hard lattices and new cryptographic constructions. In: Ladner, R.E., Dwork, C. (eds.) 40th Annual ACM Symposium on Theory of Computing, pp. 197–206. ACM Press, May 2008

11. Gür, K.D., Polyakov, Y., Rohloff, K., Ryan, G.W., Savas, E.: Implementation and evaluation of improved Gaussian sampling for lattice trapdoors. In: Proceedings of the 6th Workshop on Encrypted Computing & Applied Homomorphic Cryptography, WAHC 2018, pp. 61–71. ACM, New York (2018)

12. Hallman, R.A., et al.: Building applications with homomorphic encryption. In: Lie, D., Mannan, M., Backes, M., Wang, X. (eds.) ACM CCS 18: 25th Conference on Computer and Communications Security, pp. 2160–2162. ACM Press, October 2018

13. Karney, C.F.F.: Sampling exactly from the normal distribution. ACM Trans. Math. Softw. **42**(1), 3:1–3:14 (2016)

14. Micciancio, D., Peikert, C.: Trapdoors for lattices: simpler, tighter, faster, smaller. In: Pointcheval, D., Johansson, T. (eds.) EUROCRYPT 2012. LNCS, vol. 7237, pp. 700–718. Springer, Heidelberg (2012). https://doi.org/10.1007/978-3-642-29011-4_41

15. Micciancio, D., Regev, O.: Worst-case to average-case reductions based on Gaussian measures. In: 45th Annual Symposium on Foundations of Computer Science, pp. 372–381. IEEE Computer Society Press, October 2004

16. Micciancio, D., Walter, M.: Gaussian sampling over the integers: efficient, generic, constant-time. In: Katz, J., Shacham, H. (eds.) CRYPTO 2017, Part II. LNCS, vol. 10402, pp. 455–485. Springer, Cham (2017). https://doi.org/10.1007/978-3-319-63715-0_16

17. Micciancio, D., Walter, M.: On the bit security of cryptographic primitives. In: Nielsen, J.B., Rijmen, V. (eds.) EUROCRYPT 2018, Part I. LNCS, vol. 10820, pp. 3–28. Springer, Cham (2018). https://doi.org/10.1007/978-3-319-78381-9_1

18. Pöppelmann, T., Ducas, L., Güneysu, T.: Enhanced lattice-based signatures on reconfigurable hardware. In: Batina, L., Robshaw, M. (eds.) CHES 2014. LNCS, vol. 8731, pp. 353–370. Springer, Heidelberg (2014). https://doi.org/10.1007/978-3-662-44709-3_20

19. Prest, T.: Sharper bounds in lattice-based cryptography using the Rényi divergence. In: Takagi, T., Peyrin, T. (eds.) ASIACRYPT 2017, Part I. LNCS, vol. 10624, pp. 347–374. Springer, Cham (2017). https://doi.org/10.1007/978-3-319-70694-8_13

20. Sinha Roy, S., Vercauteren, F., Verbauwhede, I.: High precision discrete Gaussian sampling on FPGAs. In: Lange, T., Lauter, K., Lisoněk, P. (eds.) SAC 2013. LNCS, vol. 8282, pp. 383–401. Springer, Heidelberg (2014). https://doi.org/10.1007/978-3-662-43414-7_19

21. Saarinen, M.-J.O.: Gaussian sampling precision in lattice cryptography. Cryptology ePrint Archive, Report 2015/953 (2015). http://eprint.iacr.org/2015/953

22. Zhao, R.K., Steinfeld, R., Sakzad, A.: FACCT: FAst, compact, and constant-time discrete Gaussian sampler over integers. Cryptology ePrint Archive, Report 2018/1234 (2018). https://eprint.iacr.org/2018/1234

23. Zheng, Z., Wang, X., Xu, G., Zhao, C.: Error estimation of practical convolution discrete Gaussian sampling with rejection sampling. Cryptology ePrint Archive, Report 2018/309 (2018). https://eprint.iacr.org/2018/309

A Refined Analysis of the Cost for Solving LWE via uSVP

Shi Bai[1], Shaun Miller[1(✉)], and Weiqiang Wen[2]

[1] Department of Mathematical Sciences, Florida Atlantic University,
Boca Raton, USA
shih.bai@gmail.com, shaunmiller2014@fau.edu
[2] Univ Rennes, CNRS, IRISA, Rennes, France
weiqiang.wen@inria.fr

Abstract. The learning with errors (LWE) problem (STOC'05) introduced by Regev is one of the fundamental problems in lattice-based cryptography. One standard strategy to solve the LWE problem is to reduce it to a unique SVP (uSVP) problem via Kannan's embedding and then apply a lattice reduction to solve the uSVP problem. There are two methods for estimating the cost for solving LWE via this strategy: the first method considers the largeness of the gap in the uSVP problem (Gama-Nguyen, Eurocrypt'08) and the second method (Alkim et al., USENIX'16) considers the shortness of the projection of the shortest vector to the Gram-Schmidt vectors. These two estimates have been investigated by Albrecht et al. (Asiacrypt'16) who present a sound analysis and show that the lattice reduction experiments fit more consistently with the second estimate. They also observe that in some cases the lattice reduction even behaves better than the second estimate perhaps due to the second intersection of the projected vector with the Gram-Schmidt vectors. In this work, we revisit the work of Alkim et al. and Albrecht et al. We first report further experiments providing more comparisons and suggest that the second estimate leads to a more accurate prediction in practice. We also present empirical evidence confirming the assumptions used in the second estimate. Furthermore, we examine the gaps in uSVP derived from the embedded lattice and explain why it is preferable to use $\mu = 1$ for the embedded lattice. This shows there is a coherent relation between the second estimate and the gaps in uSVP. Finally, it has been conjectured by Albrecht et al. that the second intersection will not happen for large parameters. We will show that this is indeed the case: there is no second intersection as $\beta \to \infty$.

Keywords: Lattice-based cryptography · LWE · uSVP ·
Lattice reduction

This work is in part supported through NATO SPS Project G5448 and through NIST awards 60NANB18D216 and 60NANB18D217, as well as the European Union PROMETHEUS project (Horizon 2020 Research and Innovation Program, grant 780701).

© Springer Nature Switzerland AG 2019
J. Buchmann et al. (Eds.): AFRICACRYPT 2019, LNCS 11627, pp. 181–205, 2019.
https://doi.org/10.1007/978-3-030-23696-0_10

1   Introduction

A lattice is a discrete additive subgroup of $\mathbb{R}^n$. A lattice $\mathcal{L}$ of dimension n (of full-rank) can be described using a basis $\mathbf{B}$ consisting of linearly independent vectors $\mathbf{b}_1, \cdots, \mathbf{b}_n \in \mathbb{R}^n$ through integral combinations $\mathcal{L}(\mathbf{B}) = \sum_{i=1}^{n} \mathbb{Z}\mathbf{b}_i$. Given a lattice basis $\mathbf{B}$ as input, one can apply lattice reduction algorithms such as [20,22,26,29,39,43] to find new bases made of relatively short and more orthogonal vectors. One quality measurement for a lattice basis $\mathbf{B}$ is the so-called Hermite factor $\mathrm{HF}(\mathbf{B}) = \|\mathbf{b}_1\|/(\mathrm{Vol}(\mathcal{L}(\mathbf{B})))^{1/n}$. Lattice reduction algorithms output reduced lattice bases with $\mathrm{HF}(\mathbf{B}) = \delta^n$ where δ is a function of the input parameter to the reduction algorithm. The number δ is also known as the root Hermite factor.

Lattices have attracted considerable interest in recent years as they can be used to construct cryptographic constructions (so-called lattice-based cryptography) which are believed to be quantum-resistant. Two fundamental computation problems in lattice-based cryptography are the short integer solution problem (SIS) [1,38] and the learning with errors problem (LWE) [17,37,40,41]. With parameters (m, n, q, B), the SIS problem is defined as follows: sample $\mathbf{A} \hookleftarrow U(\mathbb{Z}_q^{n \times m})$ (typically, $n \le m$), the goal is to find non-zero $\mathbf{x} \in \mathbb{Z}^m$ such that $\mathbf{A}\mathbf{x} \equiv \mathbf{0} \pmod{q}$ and $\|\mathbf{x}\| \le B$. Ajtai's seminal work [1] first established a worst-to-average connection for lattice-based primitives using the SIS problem. It then serves as a security foundation for numerous cryptographic primitives, including, among many others, hash functions [1] and signatures [25,35]. The LWE problem is introduced by Regev [40,41] and has been extensively used as a security foundation, for encryption schemes [25,41], fully homomorphic encryption schemes [18], signatures [10,21,25,35] and pseudo-random functions [15], and many others. The search version of the LWE problem with parameters (m, n, q, χ) is: sample $\mathbf{A} \hookleftarrow U(\mathbb{Z}_q^{m \times n})$ (typically $n \le m$), the goal is to find the vector $\mathbf{s} \in \mathbb{Z}^n$ given samples $\mathbf{b}$ where $\mathbf{b} \equiv \mathbf{A}\mathbf{s} + \mathbf{e} \pmod{q}$ and $\mathbf{e} \in \mathbb{Z}_q^m$ is a "short" error vector sampled from the given distribution χ. In this paper, we focus on χ which is a discrete Gaussian distribution of deviation αq. χ returns a vector $\mathbf{x} \in \mathbb{Z}_q^m$ with probability proportional to $\exp(-\|\mathbf{x}\|^2/(2\alpha^2 q^2))$.

Using lattice reduction, a standard method to solve the LWE problem is to first reduce it to an Unique Shortest Vector Problem (uSVP) via Kannan's embedding technique [30] and then apply a lattice reduction algorithm to solve the uSVP problem. For example, we describe the so-called primal lattice attack [2,5,7]. Given the matrix LWE instance $(\mathbf{A}, \mathbf{b} \equiv \mathbf{A}\mathbf{s} + \mathbf{e} \pmod{q})$, we construct the lattice $\mathcal{L} = \{\mathbf{x} \in \mathbb{Z}^{m+n+1} \mid (\mathbf{A} \mid \mathbf{I}_m \mid \mathbf{b}) \cdot \mathbf{x} \equiv \mathbf{0} \bmod q\}$. This is a lattice of rank $d = m + n + 1$ and volume q^m. It is expected that $(\mathbf{s}, \mathbf{e}, -1)$ is the unique shortest vector in the lattice. Thus it boils down to find the shortest vector in the lattice which can be done by a lattice reduction algorithm. The goal is to estimate the cost of lattice reduction for solving the uSVP problem constructed from LWE.

There are two methods for estimating the cost for solving LWE using the aforementioned LWE-to-uSVP strategy. The first method is proposed by Gama and Nguyen [23] and further investigated in subsequent works [2,6,28]. The main idea is to estimate the gap (between the first and second minima) in the uSVP lattice. As it is expected that $(\mathbf{s}, \mathbf{e}, -1)$ is the unique shortest vector in the lattice, the first minimum λ_1 of the uSVP lattice is about $\sqrt{\|\mathbf{e}\|^2 + \|\mathbf{s}\|^2}$. The second minimum λ_2 of the uSVP lattice is estimated from the Gaussian heuristic on random lattices: the expected first minimum of a lattice $\mathcal{L}$ of full rank d is about $\sqrt{d/(2\pi e)}\mathrm{Vol}(\mathcal{L})^{1/d}$. One assumes that the λ_2 of the uSVP lattice is about the same as the λ_1 of a random lattice with the same determinant and rank. Suppose a lattice reduction algorithm produces a reduced basis of root Hermite factor δ: for example, if a Block-Korkine-Zolotarev (BKZ) [20,26,42–44] algorithm of blocksize β is used, the root Hermite factor is about [19]:

$$\delta(\beta) \approx \left(\frac{\beta}{2\pi e} \cdot (\pi\beta)^{1/\beta} \right)^{\frac{1}{2(\beta-1)}}. \tag{1}$$

For large β, this is about $\beta^{1/(2\beta)}$ which we will use for asymptotic analysis. It then requires the uSVP gap $\gamma := \lambda_2/\lambda_1 \geq \tau \cdot \delta^d$ for a successful attack where τ is an experimental constant depending on the algorithm (and parameters). Finally, the running-time can be derived from the required δ given the gap γ which depends on the lattice reduction algorithm used. For the BKZ example, one can work out the blocksize β required and hence the running-time which is asymptotically $2^{O(\beta)}$ using the core-SVP model [3,7].

A second method is given in the New Hope key exchange paper [7]. Instead of looking at the gap of the uSVP directly, it considers the evolution of the Gram-Schmidt coefficients of the unique shortest vector in the BKZ tours. More precisely, it compares the expected length of the projection of the shortest vector orthogonally to the first $d - \beta$ Gram-Schmidt vectors with the length of $\mathbf{b}^*_{d-\beta+1}$ estimated using the GSA assumption. The justification is that, if this happens, the last β Gram-Schmidt coefficients of the shortest vector can be recovered during the local SVP of the last block.

These two estimates have been investigated extensively by Albrecht et al. in work [5]. They show that the lattice reduction experiments fits more consistently with the second estimate. They also present a sound analysis to show that, after the last β Gram-Schmidt coefficients of the shortest vector is recovered, a further size reduction is often sufficient to recover the complete secret. Interestingly, they also observe that in several cases the lattice reduction even behaves better than the second estimate for certain parameters. It is outlined that this may be caused by the occurrence of a second intersection of the projected vector with the Gram-Schmidt vectors.

1.1   Contribution

In this work, we revisit the analysis and experiments on estimating the cost for solving LWE via the uSVP approach. The experimental results are derived using the open-source lattice reduction libraries FPLLL and FPYLLL [46,47].

In Sect. 3, we first recall the two estimates from [7,23] and the analysis in [5]. Compared to [5], we expand the comparison of the two estimates with a larger set of LWE parameters (q, n, α). This complements the analysis and comparison in the Fig. 1 of [5]. Furthermore, we verify the accuracy of the second estimate on the smaller dimension regime (Subsect. 3.3), where the first estimate could lead to a smaller blocksize. For the second contribution (Subsect. 3.4), we examine the projection length of the shortest vector on the reduced bases with different BKZ blocksize. This confirms that the assumption on the projection length is valid. Our third contribution (Sect. 4) is a concrete investigation of the uSVP gap in the embedded lattices with $\mu = 1$ and $\mu = \text{dist}(\mathbf{t}, \mathcal{L}(\mathbf{B}))$, given BDD instance $(\mathbf{B}, \mathbf{t})$ as input. It has been a common practice (e.g. [2,7]) to use $\mu = 1$ in the embedded lattice, albeit the reduction of BDD to uSVP [36] works only with $\mu = \text{dist}(\mathbf{t}, \mathcal{L}(\mathbf{B}))$ in theory. We show that the gap in the uSVP instances on average behaves much better than the worst-case guarantee. Finally, it has been observed in [5] that in several cases the lattice reduction even behaves better than the second estimate for some parameters. It is conjectured that the second intersection will not happen for large parameters. We show in Sect. 5 that this is true: we provide numerical experiments to confirm the impacts of the second intersection and present an analysis that the position/length of the second intersection approaches 0 as $\beta \to \infty$.

2 Preliminaries

In this section, we recall some basic facts on lattices, lattice reduction, and computational problems based on lattices. We first introduce the notations used throughout the paper.

Notations. We let lower-case bold letters denote column vectors and upper-case bold letters denote matrices. For a vector $\mathbf{x}$, we use $\|\mathbf{x}\|$ to denote its ℓ_2-norm. Similarly, a matrix $\mathbf{B} = (\mathbf{b}_1, \cdots, \mathbf{b}_n)$ is also presented in a column-wise way.

2.1 Euclidean Lattices

Let $\mathbf{B} \in \mathbb{R}^{n \times n}$ be a full rank matrix. The lattice $\mathcal{L}$ generated by $\mathbf{B}$ is defined as $\mathcal{L}(\mathbf{B}) = \{\mathbf{B}\mathbf{x} \mid \mathbf{x} \in \mathbb{Z}^n\}$, and the matrix $\mathbf{B}$ is called a basis of $\mathcal{L}$ (or $\mathcal{L}(\mathbf{B})$). We let $\mathbf{B}^* = (\mathbf{b}_1^*, \cdots, \mathbf{b}_n^*)$ denote the Gram–Schmidt orthogonalization of $\mathbf{B}$. The determinant of a lattice $\mathcal{L}(\mathbf{B})$ is defined as $\text{Vol}(\mathcal{L}(\mathbf{B})) = \prod_{i \le n} \|\mathbf{b}_i^*\|$. The ℓ_2-norm of a shortest non-zero vector in a lattice $\mathcal{L}$ is denoted by $\lambda_1(\mathcal{L})$ which is called the minimum of $\mathcal{L}$. This can be extended successively:

Definition 1 (Successive minima). *For any lattice $\mathcal{L}$, the i-th minimum $\lambda_i(\mathcal{L})$ is the radius of the smallest ball with center the origin and containing i linearly independent lattice vectors:*

$$\lambda_i(\mathcal{L}) = \inf\{r : \dim(\text{span}(\mathcal{L} \cap \mathcal{B}(\mathbf{0}, r))) \ge i\}.$$

In subsequent sections, we will consider the ratio between λ_2 and λ_1. Minkowski's convex body theorem states that $\lambda_1(\mathcal{L}) \le 2 \cdot v_n^{-1/n} \cdot \text{Vol}(\mathcal{L})^{1/n}$ where v_n is the volume of an n-dimensional Euclidean ball of radius 1. The average version of the Minkowski's theorem is often known as the Gaussian heuristic: the λ_1 of a random n-dimensional lattice is asymptotically

$$\mathrm{GH}(\mathcal{L}) = v_n^{-1/n} \cdot \mathrm{Vol}(\mathcal{L})^{1/n}. \tag{2}$$

For $i \leq n$, we let $\pi_i(\mathbf{v})$ denote the orthogonal projection of $\mathbf{v}$ onto the linear subspace $(\mathbf{b}_1, \cdots, \mathbf{b}_{i-1})^\perp$. For $i < j \leq n$, we let $\mathbf{B}_{[i,j]}$ denote the local block $(\pi_i(\mathbf{b}_i), \cdots, \pi_i(\mathbf{b}_j))$, and $\mathcal{L}_{[i,j]}$ denote the lattice generated by $\mathbf{B}_{[i,j]}$.

2.2   Lattice Problems

Two fundamental computation problems in lattice-based cryptography are the short integer solution problem (SIS) [1,38] and the learning with errors problem (LWE) [17,37,40,41]. They are defined as follows.

Definition 2 (Search LWE$_{m,n,q,\chi}$). *With input parameters $n \geq 1$, modulus $q \geq 2$ and distribution χ, the search version of LWE$_{m,n,q,\chi}$ problem consists of m samples of the form $(\mathbf{a}, b) \in \mathbb{Z}_q^n \times \mathbb{Z}_q$, with $\mathbf{a} \hookleftarrow U(\mathbb{Z}_q^n)$, $b = \langle \mathbf{a}, \mathbf{s} \rangle + e \pmod{q}$ and $e \hookleftarrow \chi$. Typically $m \geq n$. We say that an algorithm solves the search LWE$_{n,q,\chi}^m$ if it outputs $\mathbf{s}$ with probability $\mathrm{poly}(1/(n \log q))$ in time $\mathrm{poly}(n \log q)$.*

If the number of samples is not restricted, we denote it as the LWE$_{n,q,\chi}$ problem. In this work, χ is a discrete Gaussian of deviation αq. For convenience, we will also present the LWE in its the matrix form $(\mathbf{A}, \mathbf{b})$ where $\mathbf{b} \equiv \mathbf{As} + \mathbf{e} \pmod{q}$.

A dual problem of LWE is the so-called short integer solution problem (SIS) [1,38]. We will mainly use its inhomogeneous version (ISIS) in this work.

Definition 3 (Search ISIS$_{m,n,q,B}$). *Given $\mathbf{A}$ uniformly sampled from $\mathbb{Z}_q^{n \times m}$ and a vector $\boldsymbol{b} \in \mathbb{Z}^n$, find non-zero $\mathbf{x} \in \mathbb{Z}^m$ such that $\mathbf{Ax} \equiv \boldsymbol{b} \pmod{q}$ and $\|\mathbf{x}\| \leq B$. Typically $m \geq n$. If $\boldsymbol{b} = 0$, it is the SIS$_{m,n,q,B}$ problem.*

Note that one can view the LWE problem $(\mathbf{A}, \mathbf{As} + \mathbf{e})$ as an SIS-like problem by writing $\mathbf{A}' \cdot (\mathbf{s}|\mathbf{e}) \equiv \mathbf{0} \pmod{q}$ where $\mathbf{A}' = (\mathbf{A}|\mathbf{I})$. This also provide an alternative method for analyzing LWE via the SIS-like problem. The learning with errors problem (LWE) can be considered as an average version of the BDD problem:

Definition 4 (Bounded Distance Decoding: BDD$_\alpha$). *Let $0 < \alpha < \frac{1}{2}$. Given a lattice basis $\mathbf{B}$ and a vector $\mathbf{t}$ such that $\mathrm{dist}(\mathbf{t}, \mathcal{L}(\mathbf{B})) \leq \alpha \cdot \lambda_1(\mathbf{B})$, find a lattice vector $\mathbf{v} \in \mathcal{L}(\mathbf{B})$ closest to $\mathbf{t}$. We will denote the α as the gap of the BDD$_\alpha$ problem.*

A dual problem of BDD is the so-called Unique Shortest Vector Problem (uSVP).

Definition 5 (Unique Shortest Vector Problem: uSVP$_\gamma$). *Let $\gamma \geq 1$. Given as input a lattice basis $\mathbf{B}$ such that $\lambda_2(\mathcal{L}(\mathbf{B})) \geq \gamma \cdot \lambda_1(\mathcal{L}(\mathbf{B}))$, the goal is to find a non-zero vector $\mathbf{v} \in \mathcal{L}(\mathbf{B})$ of norm $\lambda_1(\mathcal{L}(\mathbf{B}))$. We will denote the γ as the gap of the uSVP$_\gamma$ problem.*

In some cryptographic applications (e.g., lattice-based signatures [10,21,35]), it is preferred to use LWE problems where the secret **s** comes from the same distribution as the error **e**. This is known as the *normal form LWE*. We will assume this is the case in this work. Notice that there exists a polynomial time reduction from LWE with secret from arbitrary distribution to LWE in normal form [8].

2.3   Lattice Reduction

The security of lattice-based cryptography relies on the assumed hardness of solving the aforementioned geometric problems such as BDD and uSVP on high-dimensional lattices. The lattice reduction algorithms such as Block-Korkine-Zolotarev (BKZ) [20,27,42–44] are the most efficient methods for solving such problems currently known. Lattice reduction aims to compute a basis made of relatively short vectors from an arbitrary input basis. Quantitatively, one measure of quality is the so-called Hermite factor $\mathrm{HF}(\mathbf{B}) = \|\mathbf{b}_1\|/\mathrm{Vol}^{1/n}(\mathcal{L}(\mathbf{B}))$. Lattice reduction algorithms output reduced lattice bases with $\mathrm{HF}(\mathbf{B}) = \delta^n$ where δ is a function of the input parameter to the reduction algorithm. The δ is also known as the root Hermite factor (RHF).

We review some notions on lattice reduction. A lattice basis **B** is called size-reduced, if it satisfies $|\mu_{i,j}| \leq 1/2$ for $j < i \leq n$ where $\mu_{i,j} = \langle \mathbf{b}_i, \mathbf{b}_j^* \rangle / \langle \mathbf{b}_j^*, \mathbf{b}_j^* \rangle$. A basis **B** is HKZ-reduced if it is size-reduced and further satisfies:

$$\|\mathbf{b}_i^*\| = \lambda_1(\mathcal{L}_{[i,n]}), \ \forall i \leq n.$$

A basis **B** is BKZ-β reduced for blocksize $\beta \geq 2$ if it is size-reduced and satisfies:

$$\|\mathbf{b}_i^*\| = \lambda_1(\mathcal{L}_{[i,\min(i+\beta-1,n)]}), \ \forall i \leq n.$$

The work [19] shows that a BKZ-β reduced basis **B** satisfies $\|\mathbf{b}_1\| = \delta^n \mathrm{Vol}(\mathcal{L}(\mathbf{B}))$ where

$$\delta(\beta) \approx \left(\frac{\beta}{2\pi e} \cdot (\pi\beta)^{1/\beta} \right)^{\frac{1}{2(\beta-1)}}.$$

The Schnorr-Euchner BKZ algorithm [42–44] takes as inputs a blocksize β and a basis $\mathbf{B} = (\mathbf{b}_1, \cdots, \mathbf{b}_n)$ of a lattice $\mathcal{L}(\mathbf{B})$, and outputs a basis which is approximately BKZ-β-reduced, up to numerical inaccuracies. BKZ starts by LLL-reducing the input basis, then calls an SVP-solver of dimension β on consecutive local blocks $\mathbf{B}_{[k,\min(k+\beta-1,n)]}$ for $k = 1, \cdots, n-1$. This is referred to as one *BKZ tour*. Right after the local SVP at index k, if the found vector $\lambda_1(\mathcal{L}_{[k,\min(k+\beta-1,n)]}) < \|\mathbf{b}_k^*\|$, then BKZ updates the block $\mathbf{B}_{[k,\min(k+\beta-1,n)]}$ by inserting the vector found between indices $k-1$ and k and does an LLL reduction. Otherwise, it moves to the next block. The procedure terminates when no change occurs at all during a tour. In practice, one prefers to terminate the BKZ when the changes between tours becomes less significant. This is called the early-abort BKZ [27]: Hanrot et al. showed that BKZ can be terminated long before its completion, while still providing bases of good quality.

It remains to estimate the running-time of BKZ-β given β. In the literature [3,6,7,20], there are several approaches to estimate the running-time of BKZ. The main differences come from two aspects: is sieving or enumeration used for the local SVP? and how many calls to the local SVP oracle are expected? For convenience, we will use the "core-sieving" model of [3,7]. Essentially it considers a single SVP call of dimension β using sieving, which can be modeled by a running-time of $2^{O(\beta)}$.

Heuristics. Lattice reduction algorithms and their analyses often rely on heuristic assumptions. A common heuristic is the aforementioned Gaussian heuristic (see Eq. (2)). Let $\mathcal{L}$ be an n-dimensional lattice and $\mathcal{S}$ a measurable set in the real span of $\mathcal{L}$. The *Gaussian Heuristic* states that the number of lattice points in $\mathcal{S}$, denoted $|\mathcal{L} \cap \mathcal{S}|$, is about $\mathrm{vol}(\mathcal{S})/\mathrm{Vol}(\mathcal{L})$. In particular, taking $\mathcal{S}$ as a centered n-ball of radius R, the number of lattice points contained in the n-ball is about $V_n(R)/\mathrm{Vol}(\mathcal{L})$. Thus by setting $V_n(R) \approx \mathrm{Vol}(\mathcal{L})$, we see that $\lambda_1(\mathcal{L})$ is about $\mathrm{GH}(\mathcal{L}) = v_n^{-1/n} \cdot \mathrm{Vol}(\mathcal{L})^{1/n}$. Note that this is a factor of 2 smaller than the rigorous upper bound provided by Minkowski's theorem.

Another useful heuristic is the so-called *Geometric Series Assumption* (GSA) introduced in [45], which states that the Gram-Schmidt norms $\{\|\mathbf{b}_i^*\|\}_{i \leq n}$ of a BKZ-reduced basis behave as a geometric series, i.e., there is a constant $r > 1$ such that $\|\mathbf{b}_i^*\|/\|\mathbf{b}_{i+1}^*\| \approx r$ for all $i < n$.

2.4   Lattice Attack for LWE

In this subsection, we recall several methods that are used to solve the LWE problem using lattices. In these methods, the main idea is to treat the LWE problem as a BDD/uSVP problem and then apply a lattice reduction algorithm to solve the BDD/uSVP problem.

The first method is to view the LWE problem as an ISIS-like problem: given $(\mathbf{A}, \mathbf{b} \equiv \mathbf{As} + \mathbf{e} \pmod{q})$ one can form an ISIS-like instance

$$(\mathbf{A}|\mathbf{I}_m) \begin{pmatrix} \mathbf{s} \\ \mathbf{e} \end{pmatrix} \equiv \mathbf{b} \pmod{q}$$

where $\mathbf{I}_m$ is the $m \times m$ identity matrix. We can then solve this ISIS instance using either a BDD solver or uSVP solver via embedding. For example, we may use the lattice generated by

$$\mathbf{B} = \begin{pmatrix} \mathbf{I}_n & \mathbf{0} \\ \mathbf{A} & q\mathbf{I}_m \end{pmatrix}.$$

This is often known as the "primal attack". Usually matrix $\mathbf{A}$ has rank n. The $\mathcal{L}(\mathbf{B})$ is a lattice of rank $m + n$ and has volume q^m. We can then solve the BDD of $\mathcal{L}(\mathbf{B})$ with respect to the target point $\begin{pmatrix} \mathbf{0} \\ \mathbf{b} \end{pmatrix}$ which reveals $\begin{pmatrix} \mathbf{s} \\ -\mathbf{e} \end{pmatrix}$. Alternatively, we can reduce this BDD to uSVP; we will describe this method later.

The second method is to consider the lattice $\mathcal{L}_q(\mathbf{A}) = \{\mathbf{y} \in \mathbb{Z}^m : \mathbf{y} \equiv \mathbf{Ax} \pmod{q}, \forall \mathbf{x} \in \mathbb{Z}^n\}$. Note that the lattice $\mathcal{L}_q(\mathbf{A})$ contains a point which is close to the target point $\mathbf{b}$ within distance $\|\mathbf{e}\|$. One can hence solve the BDD of the lattice $\mathcal{L}_q(\mathbf{A})$ to the target point $\mathbf{b}$. The lattice $\mathcal{L}_q(\mathbf{A})$ has rank m and has volume q^{m-n}. This is equivalent to the "dual attack" where we multiply the left-kernel $\mathbf{A}^{\perp}$ of $\mathbf{A}$ on both sides of the equation $\mathbf{b} \equiv \mathbf{As} + \mathbf{e} \pmod{q}$. This leads to an ISIS-like problem of the form $\mathbf{A}^{\perp}\mathbf{b} \equiv \mathbf{A}^{\perp}\mathbf{e} \pmod{q}$ which we can solve using a BDD/uSVP solver.

These methods are sometimes equivalent, but not always, depending on the parameters given. For example, it has been investigated in [5,11] that for the binary secret LWE case, the first method leads to a better result since it uses the information about the smallness of $\mathbf{s}$. Furthermore, the allowed samples in cryptanalytic effort varies depending on the scheme considered. When there are not sufficiently enough samples, the first method might lead to a better complexity since it provides more "dimensions" for the lattice.

Reducing BDD to uSVP

We can solve the BDD using Kannan's embedding technique [30], Babai's nearest plane algorithm [9], or Lindner-Peikert's randomized nearest plane algorithm [33]. These algorithms have been further investigated by Liu and Nguyen [34] who show they can be considered as cases of pruned enumeration algorithms.

For the analysis of this paper we use Kannan's embedding technique. We describe it as follows. Given a BDD instance $(\mathbf{B}, \mathbf{t})$ where $\mathcal{L}(\mathbf{B})$ has rank d and $\mathbf{e}$ is the "shift", we consider the following basis matrix

$$\mathbf{B}' = \begin{pmatrix} \mathbf{B} & \mathbf{t} \\ \mathbf{0} & 1 \end{pmatrix}.$$

This is a lattice of rank $d+1$ and volume $\mathrm{Vol}(\mathcal{L}(\mathbf{B}))$. Observe that

$$\mathbf{B}' \begin{pmatrix} \mathbf{x} \\ -1 \end{pmatrix} = \begin{pmatrix} \mathbf{Bx} - \mathbf{t} \\ -1 \end{pmatrix} = \begin{pmatrix} \mathbf{e} \\ -1 \end{pmatrix}.$$

Hence, the lattice generated by the columns of $\mathbf{B}'$ contains a short vector related to the potential solution of the BDD problem. Usually the lattice $\mathcal{L}(\mathbf{B}')$ derived from embedding is a uSVP problem of sufficiently large gap, albeit there is no theoretical proof for this. To solve this problem, we can use the aforementioned lattice reduction algorithms such as the BKZ algorithm.

In [36], Lyubashevsky and Micciancio provide a reduction, which can reduce any $\mathrm{BDD}_{1/\gamma}$ instance $(\mathbf{B}, \mathbf{t})$ to an $\mathrm{uSVP}_{\gamma/2}$ instance with basis:

$$\mathbf{B}' = \begin{pmatrix} \mathbf{B} & \mathbf{t} \\ \mathbf{0} & \mu \end{pmatrix} \in \mathbb{Q}^{n+1},$$

with μ set to be the distance $d = \mathrm{dist}(\mathbf{t}, \mathcal{L}) \leq \lambda_1(\mathcal{L})/(2\gamma)$, where $\mathcal{L}$ is the lattice spanned by $\mathbf{B}$. In more detail, if $\mathbf{c}$ denotes a closest vector to $\mathbf{t}$ in $\mathcal{L}$ then it is shown that the vector $\mathbf{s}' = ((\mathbf{c} - \mathbf{t})^{\mathrm{T}}, -d)^{\mathrm{T}}$ is a shortest non-zero vector of lattice $\mathcal{L}'$ of basis $\mathbf{B}'$.

Later, Bai et al. [13] propose to preprocess the lattice $\mathcal{L}(\mathbf{B})$ using Khot's sparsification technique [31] before resorting to the Kannan's embedding: the component μ is decreased to be $\mathcal{O}(d/n)$, and the losing factor in the reduction is improved from 2 to $\sqrt{2}$.

However, on the practical side [2,5,7], one usually sets $\mu = 1$ in the embedded lattice and assumes there is no losing factor in the reduction. To be more precise, one assume that the first minimum and the second minimum of the embedded lattice are $\approx d$ and $\lambda_1(\mathcal{L}(\mathbf{B}))$, respectively. We assume this is true for the moment, but will have a detailed investigation on this topic in subsequent sections.

Other Attacks

In this work, we focus on the expected cost of solving LWE by regarding it as BDD and then reducing it to uSVP. There are other types of algorithms for solving LWE such as the combinatorial attacks. These algorithms usually require exponential memory and a large number of LWE samples. We do not consider these attacks in this work but refer the reader to [4, 12, 16, 32].

3   Revisiting the Cost of Solving uSVP

In this section, we first revisit the two approaches of [7, 23] for estimating the cost of solving uSVP and the analysis in [5]. Then we expand the comparison in [5] of the two estimates with a larger set of LWE parameters. Furthermore, we verify the accuracy of the second estimate on the smaller dimension regime, where the first estimate could lead to a smaller blocksize.

3.1   Two Estimates

Recall that we can view the LWE problem as a BDD problem. For simplicity, we will use the lattice $\mathcal{L}_q(\mathbf{A}) = \{\mathbf{y} \in \mathbb{Z}^m : \mathbf{y} \equiv \mathbf{A}\mathbf{x} \pmod{q}, \forall \mathbf{x} \in \mathbb{Z}^n\}$ defined in Subsect. 2.4. The lattice $\mathcal{L}_q(\mathbf{A})$ with the target point $\mathbf{b}$ defines a BDD instance: note this is a $\mathrm{BDD}_{1/\gamma}$ instance with $\gamma = \lambda_1(\mathcal{L}_q(\mathbf{A}))/\|\mathbf{e}\|$. The lattice $\mathcal{L}_q(\mathbf{A})$ has rank m and volume q^{m-n}. By Gaussian Heuristic, we have $\lambda_1(\mathcal{L}_q(\mathbf{A})) \approx \sqrt{\frac{m}{2\pi e}} \, q^{(m-n)/m}$. On the other hand, the LWE error $\mathbf{e}$ has length about $\sqrt{m}\alpha q$. Thus we obtain a $\mathrm{BDD}_{1/\gamma}$ instance where

$$\gamma \approx \frac{\min\left(q, \sqrt{\frac{m}{2\pi e}} \, q^{(m-n)/m}\right)}{\sqrt{m}\alpha q}. \tag{3}$$

For convenience, we assume that q is not too small and hence $\gamma \approx q^{-n/m}/\alpha$.

We first recall the estimate for solving uSVP by Gama and Nguyen [23] (we will refer to it as the *first estimate* or the *2008 estimate*). First, one assumes that the above $\mathrm{BDD}_{1/\gamma}$ reduces to uSVP_γ, where $\gamma \approx q^{-n/m}/\alpha$. Then Gama and Nguyen [23] show that the shortest vector in the uSVP_γ problem can be recovered as soon as $\gamma \geq \tau \cdot \delta^m$ where δ is root Hermite factor of the algorithm used. Here $\tau < 1$ is an empirical constant determined by experiments: it has been investigated that τ lies in between 0.3 and 0.4 when using the BKZ algorithm [2,5]. For simplicity, we will omit the constant τ in the asymptotic analysis (but set it to be 0.3 in actual experiments). As noted in Eq. (1), the $\delta(\beta)$ is a decreasing function of β and therefore we want to maximize δ. The optimal m is asymptotically $\frac{2n \log q}{\log(1/\alpha)}$ which leads to maximum $\delta \approx \alpha^{\log \alpha/(4n \log q)}$. The running time of BKZ-β is $2^{O(\beta)}$ using the core-SVP model. In terms of LWE parameters this is asymptotically

$$\exp\left(c_t \cdot \frac{n \log q}{\log^2 \alpha} \cdot \log\left(\frac{n \log q}{\log^2 \alpha}\right)\right) \tag{4}$$

for some constant c_t.

In the New Hope key exchange paper [7], another method for estimating the cost for solving LWE is given. We will refer to it as the *second estimate* or the *2016 estimate*. Instead of looking at the gap of the USVP directly, it considers the evolution of the Gram-Schmidt coefficients of the unique shortest vector in the BKZ tours. More precisely, it compares the expected length of the projected (expected) shortest vector $\mathbf{v} = (\mathbf{e}, -1)$ with the Gram-Schmidt lengths estimated by the GSA assumption. The key observation is that partial information of shortest vector $\mathbf{v}$ will be recovered in the last block, when the orthogonal projection of $\mathbf{v}$ to the first $d - \beta$ Gram-Schmidt vectors is shorter than the expected $\mathbf{b}^*_{d-\beta+1}$ predicated by the GSA assumption. Thus the success condition for recovering $(\mathbf{e}, -1)$ can be formulated as follows.

$$\sqrt{\beta}\alpha q \leq \delta^{2\beta-m} q^{(m-n)/m} \tag{5}$$

where δ depends on β. Here we simply take the rank of the lattice to be $m \approx d$.

These two estimates have been investigated extensively by Albrecht et al. in work [5]. They show that the lattice reduction experiments largely follow the behaviour expected from the second estimate. Furthermore, they also present a sound analysis to show that, after the last β Gram-Schmidt coefficients of the shortest vector is recovered, a further size reduction is often sufficient to recover the complete secret immediately. In fact, this can happen at indices smaller than the $d - \beta + 1$. As noted in [5], they observe an interesting phenomenon that in several cases the lattice reduction even behaves better than the second estimate for some parameters: the BKZ algorithm recovers a projection $\pi_i(\mathbf{v})$ at index following a distribution with a center smaller than $d - \beta + 1$. It is outlined in [5] that this may be caused by the occurrence of a second intersection of the projected vector with the Gram-Schmidt vectors.

3.2   Comparison of Estimates with Various (n, Q, α)

In this subsection, we expand the comparison in [5] on the two estimates with a larger set of LWE parameters. Note that a numerical comparison of two estimates is already given in the work [5]. Here we expand the range of the LWE parameters to the single-exponential regime: observe that the comparison in the

Fig. 1 of [5] fixes q, α and increases n. This compares the two estimates for LWE parameters in the super-exponential regime because of the estimate in Eq. (4). Here we assumed that the optimal m in the 2006 estimate is asymptotically the same as the 2008 estimate. Note that the 2008 estimate (e.g. Eq. (5)) can be re-formulated as

$$\beta^{1/(2\beta)} \leq \left(\frac{q^{-n/m}}{\alpha} \right)^{1/m} \beta^{1/(2m)}.$$

This can be compared to the uSVP gap argument in the 2008 estimate [23] where we have $\beta^{1/(2\beta)} \leq (q^{-n/m}/\alpha)^{1/m}$ instead. We want to minimize the β in Eq. (5). This is a constraint optimization problem which seems tedious. Instead we find the optimal m and β numerically. In setting the LWE parameters (n, q, α), we maintain the relation that

$$\log q / \log^2 \alpha \cdot \log(n \log q / (\log^2 \alpha)) \tag{6}$$

being a constant c. Note that this corresponds to the multiplier in front of n in the Eq. (4). This roughly means the running-time for solving LWE is asymptotically single-exponential.

We describe the parameters we used in the comparison. We set $c = 0.25$ and 0.35 respectively. For each c, we take $q = n^2$ and $q = n^4$ (thus four sets of parameters). Such parameters simulate commonly used conservative parameters (e.g. q not too large). Then we compute the corresponding α. For each set of parameters (n, q, α), we find the optimal m that leads to the smallest β using the 2016 estimate and the 2008 estimate (we set the empirical constant $\tau = 0.3$) respectively. We denote the smallest blocksize required from the two estimates as β_{2008} and β_{2016}. For each set of parameters, we plot the blocksize β required as an (increasing) function of n; we also plot the normalised blocksize difference which records $(\beta_{2008} - \beta_{2016})/\beta_{2008}$: this roughly illustrates the "improvement percentage". If this value is negative, we simply denote it by 0 but we will further consider these cases later. We plot the comparison on the four sets of parameters in Figs. 1, 2, 3, 4, 5, 6, 7 and 8.

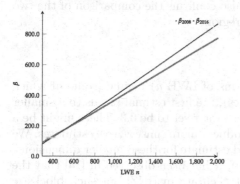

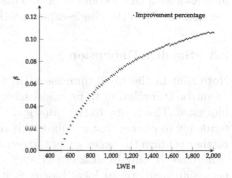

Fig. 1. Comparison of blocksize β of two estimates when $c = 0.25$ and $q = n^2$.

Fig. 2. Same as left hand side, but compares the improvement percentage of the blocksize.

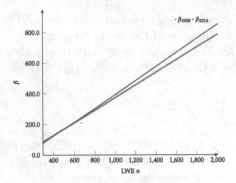

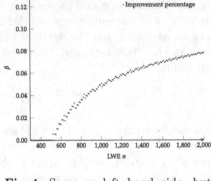

Fig. 3. Comparison of blocksize β of two estimates when $c = 0.25$ and $q = n^4$.

Fig. 4. Same as left hand side, but compares the improvement percentage of the blocksize.

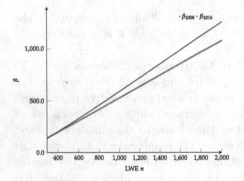

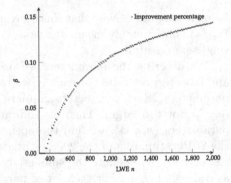

Fig. 5. Comparison of blocksize β of two estimates when $c = 0.35$ and $q = n^2$.

Fig. 6. Same as left hand side, but compares the improvement percentage of the blocksize.

It can be observed that the impacts of (the difference of) the two methods increases with the decrement of q. Similarly, the difference of the two methods increases with the decrement of α. This also confirms the comparison of the two methods in [5] in the single-exponential region.

3.3 Smaller Dimension

Note that in the small dimension (in terms of LWE n) regime (some of which might be still relevant to practical schemes), the first estimate leads to a smaller blocksize. This is due to the empirical constant τ set to be 0.3. There might be a tendency to use the first estimate as it produces more conservative estimates. We further confirm the accuracy of the second estimate for these smaller dimensions. Note that for tiny blocksizes (e.g. $\beta \leq 30$), it has been observed in [14] that the Gaussian heuristic in local blocks is not accurate in BKZ; nor such blocksize matter the running-time of BKZ too much. Thus we do not consider these tiny blocksizes. We choose parameters n, q, α such that the blocksizes are ≥ 40 and

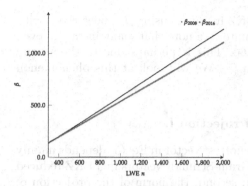

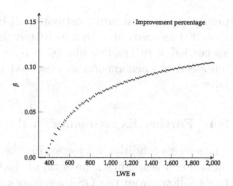

Fig. 7. Comparison of blocksize β of two estimates when $c = 0.35$ and $q = n^4$.

Fig. 8. Same as left hand side, but compares the improvement percentage of the blocksize.

compare the two methods in such region. Using the same approach as the last subsection, we set $c = 0.5$ and $q = n^2$. Then we find the corresponding α for the error rate. For each (n, q, α), we find the optimal m that leads to the smallest β using the 2016 estimate and the 2008 estimate respectively. For the 2008 estimate, we set the empirical constant $\tau = 0.3$: approximately we are comparing the two estimates in terms of $\delta^d \approx q^{-n/m}/(0.3\alpha)$ with $\delta^m \approx q^{-n/m}/\alpha\sqrt{\beta}$.

In Fig. 9 we can observe, for small LWE dimension n, the first estimate gives a smaller blocksize due to the empirical constant 0.3. Then we look at the concrete experiments with LWE parameters $n = 110$, $q = 12101$, $\sigma = \alpha q = 7.2$ of 100 instances. Using the 2008 estimate, the optimal $m = 277$ which leads to the $\beta = 39$. Using the 2016 estimate, the optimal $m = 294$ which leads to the $\beta = 66$. In Fig. 10, the experiments using BKZ of various blocksize as well as different number of samples are tabulated. It can be seen that the 2016 estimate indeed

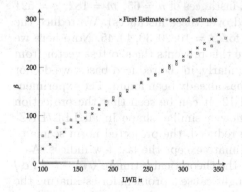

LWE parameters: $n = 110$, $q = 12101$, $\sigma = 7.21$			
2008 estimate	Sample m	Blocksize β	Succ. prob.
(smallest $\beta = 39$	277	40	0%
with $m = 277$)	277	50	0%
2016 estimate	optimal m	blocksize β	Succ. prob.
(smallest $\beta = 66$	294	50	0%
with $m = 294$)	294	60	52%
	294	66	100%

Fig. 9. Comparison of blocksize β of two estimates when $c = 0.5$ and $q = n^2$ for small n region.

Fig. 10. Experimental comparison of two estimate for small n region.

provides a more accurate estimate: all BKZ instances using $\beta = 66$ succeed with $m = 294$ as predicated by the 2016 estimate. We note that many instances even succeeded with smaller blocksize $\beta = 60$. This is perhaps due to the second intersection phenomenon as observed in [5]. We will look at this phenomenon later.

3.4 Further Experiments on the Projection Length

The success condition for recovering the shortest vector in Eq. (5) depends mainly on two heuristics: first, the norm of the Gram-Schmidt vectors in a BKZ reduced basis follows from the GSA assumption; second, the norm of the projection of the shortest vector onto the vector space spanned by the last β Gram-Schmidt vector is about $\alpha q \sqrt{\beta}$.

In practice, it is known [14;23] that the GSA assumption does not quite fit the BKZ experiments. However, the GSA assumption is optimistic from an attacker's point of view, which leads to a more conservative estimate. Hence we will assume this is the case. We will look at the second heuristic on the projection length. Denote the shortest vector to be $\mathbf{v}$. The heuristic on the project length essentially requires that $\mathbf{v}$, when expanded in terms of Gram-Schmidt vectors, have similar length on all components. This follows true if the Heuristic 2 described in work [24] is true: The distribution of the coordinates of the target vector $\mathbf{v}$, when written in the normalized Gram-Schmidt basis $(\mathbf{b}_1^*/\|\mathbf{b}_1^*\|, \mathbf{b}_2^*/\|\mathbf{b}_2^*\|, \cdots, \mathbf{b}_m^*/\|\mathbf{b}_m^*\|)$ of the input basis, looks like a uniformly distributed vector of norm $\|\mathbf{v}\|$. Observe that the heuristic depends on the shape of the input basis. For example, when the input basis is strongly reduced, the shortest vector $\mathbf{v}$ may already appear in the basis and hence the heuristic will not be true.

An experimental study has been presented in Fig. 2 of [5] using 16 LLL reduced bases. We conduct further experiments on the length of projected shortest vector on BKZ reduced bases of various blocksizes. We use the same parameters as Fig. 2 of [5]: we generate 200 LWE instances of $n = 65$, $m = 182$, $q = 521$ and $\sigma = 8/\sqrt{2\pi}$ (the results are averaged over these instances). We reduce the embedded bases using LLL and BKZ-β for $\beta = 10, 20, 30, 40, 45$. Note here we choose the largest blocksize to be 45 since this prevents the shortest vector from being recovered with high probability. Similarly, in the reduced bases, we do not consider those where the shortest vector has already been found. The experimental results are illustrated in Figs. 11 and 12. It can be seen that the projection norms of the shortest vector indeed follow a similar shape in all LLL/BKZ-reduced bases. When the lattice is more reduced, the projected norm seems to follow more closely to the theoretical estimate except the last few indices. As a conclusion, it seems even plausible to use the theoretical estimate $\sqrt{m - i + 1}\,\alpha q$ except for the last several indices. This might cause a problem for estimating the γ for the second intersection. We will consider such problem in a later section.

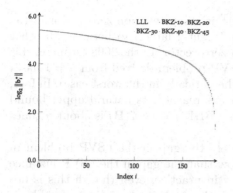

Fig. 11. Logarithmic norm of the projection of **v** on BKZ-β reduced bases for $\beta = 10, 20, 30, 40, 45$.

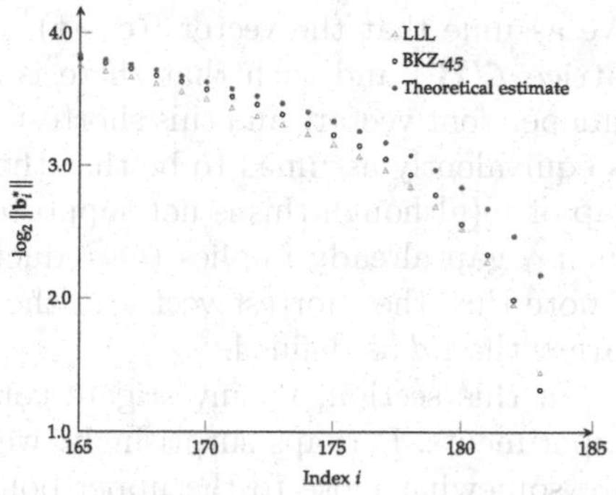

Fig. 12. Same as left hand side, but zoomed-in for only LLL and BKZ-45. Furthermore, theoretical estimate $\log_2(\sqrt{m-i+1}\,\alpha q)$ is plotted.

4 Gap in uSVP from LWE

In this section, we study the practical behavior of the reduction from the BDD problem to the uSVP problem. Note that in practice, we usually use the Kannan's embedding with $\mu = 1$. However, in theory, it is not known that whether the gap γ of the embedded uSVP lattice in this case is optimal. But this seems to be the preferable setting in practice. In this section, we aim to understand the relation between theory and practice (that can also be viewed as worst-case and average-case), and explain why it is preferable to use $\mu = 1$.

Let the BDD problem arise from LWE be $\mathrm{BDD}_{1/\gamma}$. We recall the reduction from $\mathrm{BDD}_{1/\gamma}$ to $\mathrm{uSVP}_{\gamma/2}$ by Lyubashevsky and Micciancio [36]. Given the $\mathrm{BDD}_{1/\gamma}$ instance $(\mathbf{B}, \mathbf{t})$, the following embedded lattice is constructed

$$\mathbf{B}' = \begin{pmatrix} \mathbf{B} & \mathbf{t} \\ \mathbf{0} & \mu \end{pmatrix} \in \mathbb{Q}^{n+1},$$

where μ is set to be the distance $d = \mathrm{dist}(\mathbf{t}, \mathcal{L}(\mathbf{B}))$. Since this is a $\mathrm{BDD}_{1/\gamma}$ instance, we know that $d \leq \lambda_1(\mathcal{L})/\gamma$. Let $\mathbf{c} \in \mathcal{L}(\mathbf{B})$ denote a closest vector to the target point $\mathbf{t}$. Lyubashevsky and Micciancio [36] show that the vector $\mathbf{s}' = ((\mathbf{c}-\mathbf{t})^{\mathrm{T}}, -\mu)^{\mathrm{T}}$ is a shortest non-zero vector in the lattice $\mathcal{L}(\mathbf{B}')$ and other independent vectors are at least γ times larger than this. The reduction cares about the worst-case behaviors. In practice, it may be quite possible that all other independent vectors are more than $\gamma/2$ times larger and hence leads to a uSVP problem with larger gap. In fact, we will show that this is indeed the case in practice and investigate to what extent it is better than the $\gamma/2$-gap. Note that there is a natural upper-bound for the reduction. Precisely, the gap in the uSVP problem cannot be larger than $\sqrt{2}\gamma/2$ since a shortest vector in the BDD lattice also resides in the embedded lattice and $\mathbf{s}'$ has length $\sqrt{2}d/2$. On the other hand, in practice, we just take $\mu = 1$ in the embedded lattice.

We assume that the vector $((\mathbf{c} - \mathbf{t})^T, -1)^T$ is a shortest non-zero vector in the lattice $\mathcal{L}(\mathbf{B}')$ and such that there is a sufficiently large gap between all other independent vectors and this shortest non-zero vector. In the 2008 estimate, this is equivalently assumed to be that the USVP problem derived from $\mu = 1$ has a gap of γ (although this is not supported theoretically in the worst case). In fact, such γ-gap already implies the reduction has reached its natural upper bound – note that the shortest vector in the given BDD lattice $\mathcal{L}(\mathbf{B})$ is about γ times larger than d as defined.

In this section, we investigate concretely the gap in the USVP problem in experiments. Perhaps surprisingly, we show that the gap in the USVP instance are somewhat close to the upper-bound γ in practice, even though this is not guaranteed in the worst-case. This also explains that why it is preferable to use $\mu = 1$ in practice. We set up the following experiments to investigate the gap in the resulted USVP instance in practice. For each set of parameters, we generate 100 LWE instances. For each instance, we construct the embedded lattices in two ways, with $\mu = 1$ and $\mu = d$ where $d = \lfloor \|\mathbf{e}\| \rfloor$. In experiments, we compute and compare the gaps in the resulted USVP instances.

Table 1. Experimental comparison on the gap of USVP derived from two embeddings.

n	m	q	BDD lattice		USVP lattice $\mu = 1$			USVP lattice $\mu = \|\mathbf{e}\|$		
			Theory	Experiment	Theoretical upper	Experiment	Ratio	Theoretical upper	Experiment	Ratio
16	32	1031	2.71	2.78	2.78	$\lesssim 2.55$	0.92	1.97	$\lesssim 1.96$	0.71
16	48	1031	8.40	8.49	8.49	$\lesssim 7.81$	0.92	6.00	$\lesssim 5.99$	0.71
32	48	8101	1.65	1.68	1.68	$\lesssim 1.58$	0.94	1.19	$\lesssim 1.19$	0.71
32	64	8101	7.23	7.33	7.33	$\lesssim 6.95$	0.94	5.18	$\lesssim 5.16$	0.70

We explain the notations in Table 1. For each parameter n, m, q in LWE, we use error deviation $\sigma = 3.1925 \approx \frac{8}{\sqrt{2\pi}}$. For each LWE/BDD instance, we calculate the theoretical gap in the BDD problem from $\min \left(q, (\Gamma(1 + m/2)^{1/m})/\sqrt{\pi} \cdot q^{(m-n)/m} \right)/(\sigma\sqrt{m})$. Note that we can measure in a better way: since we know the errors, we use the average norm of the errors in the denominator (instead of the estimate $\sigma\sqrt{m}$). This is tabulated in the **"Theory"** sub-column under "BDD". Then we use BKZ_m to find the $\lambda_1(\mathcal{L}(\mathbf{B}))$ and divide that by the norm of error in LWE. This is recorded in the **"Experiment"** sub-column under "BDD". Note that the experimental values obtained is slightly larger than the theory; this is perhaps due to the solver only finding the approximate shortest vector in practice. Then we construct the embedded USVP lattices with $\mu = 1$ and $\mu = d$, respectively. The sub-columns **"Theoretical upper"** under "USVP lattice" denote the upper bound of the gap in the USVP instances one can achieve using the values in the **"Experiment"** (not "Theory") sub-column under "BDD", for each type of embedding, respectively. For example, the experiment value 2.78 under $n = 16, m = 32, q = 1031$ implies that the corresponding USVP instances with $\mu = \|\mathbf{e}\|$ can at most have a gap of 1.97. The sub-column **"Experiment"** under "uSVP lattice" gives the experimental values for the gaps between the norm of a second shortest vector and $\|(\mathbf{e}^T, -\mu)^T\|$. Note that here we approximate the norm of a second shortest vector by considering the second shortest vector in a reduced basis using BKZ of blocksize m. This is not necessarily the λ_2 but hopefully a close approximation. Thus we denote "$\lesssim$" in the table. For the lattice reduction, we use BKZ in FPLLL until exhaustion with full enumeration for $m = 32$ and pruned enumeration for other m. The sub-column **"Ratio"** under "uSVP lattice" computes the ratio between the uSVP gap and the BDD gap. That is, it reflects the practical behavior of the reduction from $\text{BDD}_{1/x}$ to uSVP_y where the sub-column "Ratio" is computed as y/x. The larger the ratio, the better (larger gap) the uSVP instance is. All the figures in the table are averaged over 100 instances.

From a theoretical perspective, it is perhaps surprising to see that the BDD-uSVP reduction works pretty well in practice with both μ. In particular, with $\mu = 1$, it seems that $\text{BDD}_{1/\gamma}$ already reduces to $\text{uSVP}_{0.9\gamma}$ in practice. In theory for such case ($\mu = 1$), it is possible that there exists a lattice point $\mathbf{c}' \in \mathcal{L}(\mathbf{B})$ that is closer to $k \cdot \mathbf{t}$ for some multiple k, and therefore $(\mathbf{c}' - k \cdot \mathbf{t}, -k)$ decreases the desirable gap. However, experiments in Table 1 seems to imply that such bad points are rare in practice. Note that such cases can be provably eliminated by setting a larger $\mu = \|\mathbf{e}\|$ as shown in [36]. Specifically for such μ, it is guaranteed that the uSVP gap is $\gamma/2$ (from $\text{BDD}_{1/\gamma}$) in the worst case. Similarly, the practical/average behavior seems to be much better: with $\mu = \|\mathbf{e}\|$, the $\text{BDD}_{1/\gamma}$ problem reduces to $\text{uSVP}_{0.7\gamma}$ in practice.

We do not know how to explain such average behavior in theory. It may be related to the difference on the natural upper-bounds in two embeddings: with $\mu = 1$, the natural upper-bound of the gap in the uSVP problem is γ. This is larger than that (e.g. $\gamma/\sqrt{2}$) derived from the lattice using $\mu = \|\mathbf{e}\|$. Thus it may be due to a larger upper-bound providing larger "room" for the reduction, together with annoying "extremely close" lattice points (to multiple of target vector $\mathbf{t}$) being rare in practice. It may be interesting to further investigate this, e.g. by trying more μ between 1 and $\|\mathbf{e}\|$ and observe the impacts to the uSVP gap. We leave more investigations on this for future work.

So far, we've only discussed the gap appeared in the embedded uSVP instance under different embedding parameters. We further look at the impacts on the cost estimate under different embedding heights. In the 2008 estimate, it is assumed that given as input a $\text{BDD}_{1/\gamma}$ problem, one can reduce to a uSVP_γ problem. Then the root Hermite factor δ can be derived from the gap γ and hence the blocksize & running-time. It is also natural to see that when using the 2008 estimate, it is preferable to use $\mu = 1$ since it leads to a larger gap in the uSVP problem. In the 2016 estimate, the gap of the uSVP problem is not used explicitly. But one can see that the estimate is asymptotically equivalent to $\delta^m \leq \sqrt{\beta} \frac{\sqrt{m}q^{(m-n)/m}}{\|(\mathbf{e}|\mu)\|}$. The fractional part of the equation corresponds to the gap in the uSVP problem. Note that the difference on the gap using $\mu = 1$

and $\mu = \|\mathbf{e}\|$ is at most a scaling factor of $\sqrt{2}$. It seems to be a small factor however it may affect the concrete security level of schemes with moderate size.

5 Second Intersection

An interesting phenomenon observed in [5] shows that in several cases the lattice reduction behaves even better than the 2016 estimate for some parameters. First, the BKZ algorithm recovers a projection $\pi_i(\mathbf{v})$ at index following a distribution with a center below $d - \beta + 1$. After that, a size reduction usually immediately recovers the full secret. It is outlined in [5] that this may be caused by the occurrence of a second intersection of the projected vector with the Gram-Schmidt vectors. For example, to solve LWE parameter $n = 65, m = 182, q = 521$ and $\alpha q = 8/\sqrt{2\pi}$, it runs BKZ with blocksize $\beta = 56$ according to Eq. (5). Since $\beta = 56$ satisfies Eq. (5), a projection of our error should be found at index $d - \beta + 1 = 128$, recovering the last 56 coefficients of the error which leads to size reduction recovering the rest. In experiments the projection is found earlier (at index ≈ 124.76) and the coefficients of the error are found after one more call to size reduction. Second, the blocksize required to recover the secret (on average) is actually smaller than that estimated from Eq. (5). For the LWE parameter mentioned above, it requires to run BKZ using blocksize 56 according to Eq. (5). However, as noted in [5], using blocksize 51 is sufficient to recover more than half of the instances. Some justification has been outlined in Subsect. 4.3 of [5], mainly on the size reduction at index $\leq d - \beta + 1$. We will provide a refined analysis of why a smaller blocksize may work.

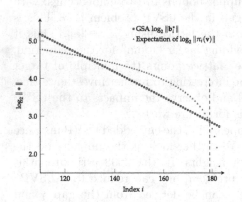

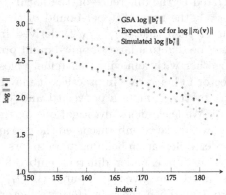

Fig. 13. Comparison between G-S norms of BKZ_{56} under GSA and the expected length of $\pi_i(\mathbf{v})$.

Fig. 14. Same as LHS, but zoomed-in to the last several indices. Furthermore, a BKZ simulator is used to estimate the $\log \|\mathbf{b}_i^*\|$.

We first recall the phenomenon in more detail as well as a brief explanation given in [5]. According to Eq. (5), the projection of the shortest vector should be recovered at position $d - \beta + 1$ when running the BKZ with block-size β on the USVP instance over a d-dimensional lattice (recall that in our description, the $d = m + 1$). However, it is observed that the existence of a second intersection on the expected projection length of the shortest vector and the Gram-Schmidt norms under GSA assumption may speed-up the recovery of $\mathbf{v}$. For example, Fig. 13 compares the (logarithmic) Gram-Schmidt norms of BKZ_{56} reduced basis under GSA assumption and the expected length of $\pi_i(\mathbf{v})$. Note there are 5 indexes in which $\|\pi_i(\mathbf{v})\|$ is smaller than the Gram-Schmidt norms, thus in this case, we denote $\kappa = 5$. In particular, after the second intersection, the expected length of $\pi_i(\mathbf{v})$ will be less than the $\|\mathbf{b}_i^*\|$ for κ indexes in the end. Hence the projection is likely to be the smallest vector of the projected lattice $\mathcal{L}(\pi_{d-\kappa+1}(\mathbf{b}_{d-\kappa+1}), \cdots, \pi_{d-\kappa+1}(\mathbf{b}_d))$ of dimension κ. The SVP oracle will find this projection and the BKZ algorithm will then insert it at index $d - \kappa + 1$. As a result, $\mathbf{b}_{d-\kappa+1}$ is updated to be (the lifted vector of) the projection of the vector $\mathbf{v}$ over the last κ Gram-Schmidt vectors. Further, it is likely that $\pi_{d-\beta-\kappa+1}(\mathbf{v})$ is the shortest vector of the projected lattice $\mathcal{L}(\pi_{d-\beta-\kappa+1}(\mathbf{b}_{d-\beta-\kappa+1}), \cdots, \pi_{d-\beta-\kappa+1}(\mathbf{b}_{d-\kappa+1}))$ of size β after which $\mathbf{v}$ can be recovered by a size reduction according to [5]. Therefore, assuming a projection of our vector $\pi_{d-\kappa+1}(\mathbf{v})$ has already been found, an SVP oracle will find $\pi_{d-\beta-\kappa+1}(\mathbf{v})$ in the lattice $\mathcal{L}(\pi_{d-\beta-\kappa+1}(\mathbf{b}_{d-\beta-\kappa+1}), \cdots, \pi_{d-\beta-\kappa+1}(\mathbf{b}_{d-\kappa+1}))$.

5.1   On Smaller Blocksize

A related interesting phenomenon is that often a smaller blocksize may be already sufficient to solve the USVP problem. This has been observed in [5] where a blocksize of $\beta' = \beta - \kappa$ is sufficient to recover the secret with high probability. We give a heuristic justification of this based on the second intersection. Suppose now β is the smallest blocksize that satisfies Eq. (5) with a nonzero κ depending on β.

Denote $\beta' = \beta - \kappa$. Suppose $BKZ_{\beta'}$ is run (instead of BKZ_β). For convenience, let δ_β denote the value of δ given blocksize β. Let κ' be the amount of indices where the projection of $\mathbf{v}$ is smaller than the GSA predicated Gram-Schmidt norm. Due to the second intersection, a projection of $\mathbf{v}$ is likely to be found at index $d - \kappa' + 1$ so after SVP the vector $\mathbf{b}_{d-\kappa'+1}$ will contain the last κ' coefficients of $\mathbf{v}$. Therefore the norm of $\mathbf{v}$, if decomposed in terms of the Gram-Schmidt vectors $\mathbf{b}_i$, will concentrate on the first $d - \kappa' + 1$ components. More precisely, $\|\mathbf{v}\|^2 = \sum_{i=1}^{d-\kappa'+1} c_i^2 \|\mathbf{b}_i^*\|^2$ where c_i are the coefficients in the decomposition. Following the same reasoning as in [5], we look at the β' dimensional lattice $\mathcal{L}(\pi_{d-\beta'-\kappa'+1}(\mathbf{b}_{d-\beta'-\kappa'+1}), \dots, \pi_{d-\beta'-\kappa'+1}(\mathbf{b}_{d-\kappa'+1}))$. If the projected shortest vector has a smaller norm than the GSA predicated norm of blocksize β', then we would be able to recover the last $\beta' + \kappa$ coefficients. The success condition can be phrased as

$$\sqrt{\beta' + \kappa'} \alpha q \leq \delta_{\beta'}^{2\beta'-d+2\kappa'} \mathrm{Vol}(\mathcal{L})^{1/d}. \tag{7}$$

Eq. (7) is sometimes satisfied, but not always, depending on the relation between κ and κ'. It seems plausible to assume that $\kappa' \approx \kappa$ for the analysis, albeit this may not be true in practice. (This can be seen from experiments the newly found β' will not recover as many error vectors as the original β. For example, $\beta' = 51$ in the aforementioned LWE parameters can only recover half of the instances.) Note that if $\kappa \approx \kappa'$, the left-hand side of Eq. (7) is the same as $\sqrt{\beta}\alpha q$ and the right-hand side is larger, hence $\pi_{d-\beta'-\kappa'+1}(\mathbf{v})$ is the shortest vector in the local lattice. By recovering $\beta' + \kappa$ coefficients of $\mathbf{v}$, a following size reduction will find the rest with a high probability.

5.2   Experiments on κ

In the experiments to follow, we consider the last projection of our vector $\mathbf{v}$ that was found before it is completely recovered in the next tour by size reduction. This confirms the existence of κ in practice. With LWE parameters $n = 65, m = 182, q = 521$ in both parameter sets, we consider two different choices of αq that produces different κ. The first is $\alpha q = 3.192$ and requires $\beta = 56$ while the second is $\alpha q = 2.469$ and requires $\beta = 42$. We run 800 instances in total and take the average for both parameter sets. The distribution of κ found are plotted in Figs. 15 and 16. The y axis represents the counts over 800 where a projection of $\mathbf{v}$ was found at index $d - \kappa + 1$ before the tour it was completely recovered and the x axis is the value κ. In both cases, we did not consider projections of $\mathbf{v}$ that were found at an index less than or equal to $d - \beta + 1$ as this will probably be where $\mathbf{v}$ is recovered by size reduction. The experiment that required $\beta = 56$ was allowed to run for at most 20 tours while the experiment requiring $\beta = 42$ is allowed 60 tours.

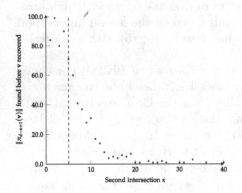
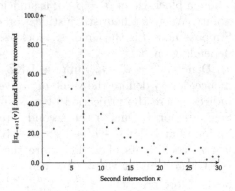

Fig. 15. Blocksize $\beta = 56$ required in Eq. (5) and $\kappa = 5$.

Fig. 16. Blocksize $\beta = 42$ required in Eq. (5) and $\kappa = 7$.

We notice that the experimental values for κ indeed follow approximately from the theoretical predicate from Eq. (5). However, we also notice that the experimental value for κ seems to be slightly less than the predicted value. This could be due to the inaccuracy of GSA when predicting the length of the last few projections. It is known that the simulator-based approach [14,23] provides a better estimation for the behavior of the lengths $\|\mathbf{b}_i^*\|$. We considered the average simulated $\|\mathbf{b}_i^*\|$ over 1000 instances with blocksize 56 and 200 tours. By comparing the simulator to the expected length of our projection (see Fig. 14), we see that fewer projections of $\mathbf{v}$ are below the simulator after the second intersection: There are 3 (resp. 5) indexes in which $\|\pi_i(\mathbf{v})\|$ is smaller than the simulator's (resp. GSA's) value for $\|\mathbf{b}_i^*\|$ (comparing Fig. 15 with Fig. 14).

5.3 Convergence of κ

It has been conjectured [5] that the second intersection will not happen for cryptographic meaningful parameters. We first show that the position of the second intersection approaches 0 as $\beta \to \infty$. We will also provide a numerical analysis for the index of the second intersection using both GSA assumption and simulator. We first take the logarithm of both the Gram-Schmidt norm at index x and the norm of $\pi_x(\mathbf{v})$:

$$\log(\pi_x(\|\mathbf{v}\|)) \approx \log(\sqrt{d-x+1} \cdot \alpha q),$$
$$\log(\|\mathbf{b}_x^*\|) \approx (x-1)\log(\alpha) + \log(\|\mathbf{b}_1\|)$$

where $\alpha \approx \delta^{-2}$ is the constant ratio in GSA. Note that $\|\mathbf{b}_1\| \approx \delta^d \mathrm{Vol}(\mathcal{L})^{1/d}$. Assuming Eq. (5) is satisfied so that $\alpha q \approx \delta^{2\beta-d}\mathrm{Vol}(\mathcal{L})^{1/d}/\beta^{1/2}$, the inequality can be represented as

$$\log(\frac{\kappa}{\beta}) \leq -4\log(\delta)(-\kappa + \beta) \tag{8}$$

where $\kappa = d - x + 1$. If there a nontrivial second intersection, the above relation has to be true for at least $\kappa = 1$. Using $\delta \approx v_\beta^{-1/(\beta(\beta-1))}$, one could see that for large enough blocksize, this relation can not be satisfied and hence the second intersection will not happen for large blocksize. This shows that the second intersection approaches 0 as $\beta \to \infty$. Further, we numerically investigate the evolution of κ in terms of β using relation (8). Figure 17 considers the values of κ given by relation (8) for different values of β. Notice that Fig. 17 shows that $\beta = 278$ is the smallest blocksize where κ already becomes 0. This suggests there is no second intersection when $\beta \geq 278$ is needed to satisfy Eq. (5). However, this could be an over-estimate from the attacker's point of view since the GSA assumption is used here.

To get a more accurate estimation of the value κ, we further compare that with the BKZ simulator. The next figure considered several different parameter sets ($n = 65, m = 182, q = 521$) only varying in αq and necessary β (averaged over α and LWE instances). We simulate 200 tours of BKZ-β using the BKZ simulator and averaged 1000 instances of each parameter set. Figure 18 shows that the value of κ derived by comparing the simulated $\|\mathbf{b}_i^*\|$ to $\|\pi_i(\mathbf{v})\|$ suggests there is no second intersection for blocksizes larger than 120. One can also see this produces slightly smaller κ for a given β than the comparison assuming GSA. This seems reasonable since the GSA assumption is known to be optimistic from

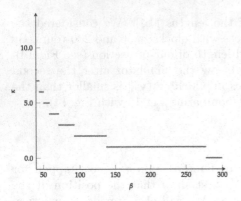

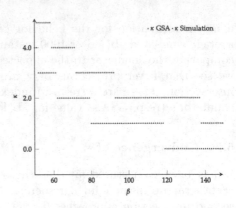

Fig. 17. Maximal κ satisfying Eq. (8) given β.

Fig. 18. Maximal κ satisfying Eq. (8) given β.

an attacker's point of view. In conclusion, this further suggests that a second intersection will only affect the results of running BKZ-β on smaller parameter sets.

Acknowledgments. We thank the reviewers for their valuable comments and suggestions. The authors would like to acknowledge the use of the services provided by Research Computing at the Florida Atlantic University.

References

1. Ajtai, M.: Generating hard instances of lattice problems (extended abstract). In: 28th Annual ACM Symposium on Theory of Computing, pp. 99–108. ACM Press, May 1996

2. Albrecht, M.R., Fitzpatrick, R., Göpfert, F.: On the efficacy of solving LWE by reduction to unique-SVP. In: Lee, H.-S., Han, D.-G. (eds.) ICISC 2013. LNCS, vol. 8565, pp. 293–310. Springer, Cham (2014). https://doi.org/10.1007/978-3-319-12160-4_18

3. Albrecht, M.R., Curtis, B.R., Deo, A., Davidson, A., Player, R., Postlethwaite, E.W., Virdia, F., Wunderer, T.: Estimate all the LWE, NTRU schemes!. In: Catalano, D., De Prisco, R. (eds.) SCN 2018. LNCS, vol. 11035, pp. 351–367. Springer, Cham (2018). https://doi.org/10.1007/978-3-319-98113-0_19

4. Albrecht, M.R., Faugère, J.-C., Fitzpatrick, R., Perret, L.: Lazy modulus switching for the BKW algorithm on LWE. In: Krawczyk, H. (ed.) PKC 2014. LNCS, vol. 8383, pp. 429–445. Springer, Heidelberg (2014). https://doi.org/10.1007/978-3-642-54631-0_25

5. Albrecht, M.R., Göpfert, F., Virdia, F., Wunderer, T.: Revisiting the expected cost of solving uSVP and applications to LWE. In: Takagi, T., Peyrin, T. (eds.) ASIACRYPT 2017, Part I. LNCS, vol. 10624, pp. 297–322. Springer, Cham (2017). https://doi.org/10.1007/978-3-319-70694-8_11

6. Albrecht, M.R., Player, R., Scott, S.: On the concrete hardness of learning with errors. J. Math. Cryptol. **9**(3), 169–203 (2015)

7. Alkim, E., Ducas, L., Pöppelmann, T., Schwabe, P.: Post-quantum key exchange - a new hope. In: Holz, T., Savage, S. (eds.) USENIX Security 2016: 25th USENIX Security Symposium, pp. 327–343. USENIX Association, August 2016
8. Applebaum, B., Cash, D., Peikert, C., Sahai, A.: Fast cryptographic primitives and circular-secure encryption based on hard learning problems. In: Halevi, S. (ed.) CRYPTO 2009. LNCS, vol. 5677, pp. 595–618. Springer, Heidelberg (2009). https://doi.org/10.1007/978-3-642-03356-8_35
9. Babai, L.: On Lovász lattice reduction and the nearest lattice point problem. Combinatorica 6, 1–13 (1986)
10. Bai, S., Galbraith, S.D.: An improved compression technique for signatures based on learning with errors. In: Benaloh, J. (ed.) CT-RSA 2014. LNCS, vol. 8366, pp. 28–47. Springer, Cham (2014). https://doi.org/10.1007/978-3-319-04852-9_2
11. Bai, S., Galbraith, S.D.: Lattice decoding attacks on binary LWE. In: Susilo, W., Mu, Y. (eds.) ACISP 2014. LNCS, vol. 8544, pp. 322–337. Springer, Cham (2014). https://doi.org/10.1007/978-3-319-08344-5_21
12. Bai, S., Galbraith, S.D., Li, L., Sheffield, D.: Improved combinatorial algorithms for the inhomogeneous short integer solution problem. J. Cryptol. 32(1), 35–83 (2019)
13. Bai, S., Stehlé, D., Wen, W.: Improved reduction from the bounded distance decoding problem to the unique shortest vector problem in lattices. In: Proceedings of ICALP, pp. 76:1–76:12 (2016)
14. Bai, S., Stehlé, D., Wen, W.: Measuring, simulating and exploiting the head concavity phenomenon in BKZ. In: Peyrin, T., Galbraith, S. (eds.) ASIACRYPT 2018, Part I. LNCS, vol. 11272, pp. 369–404. Springer, Cham (2018). https://doi.org/10.1007/978-3-030-03326-2_13
15. Banerjee, A., Peikert, C., Rosen, A.: Pseudorandom functions and lattices. In: Pointcheval, D., Johansson, T. (eds.) EUROCRYPT 2012. LNCS, vol. 7237, pp. 719–737. Springer, Heidelberg (2012). https://doi.org/10.1007/978-3-642-29011-4_42
16. Blum, A., Kalai, A., Wasserman, H.: Noise-tolerant learning, the parity problem, and the statistical query model. In: 32nd Annual ACM Symposium on Theory of Computing, pp. 435–440. ACM Press, May 2000
17. Brakerski, Z., Langlois, A., Peikert, C., Regev, O., Stehlé, D.: Classical hardness of learning with errors. In: Boneh, D., Roughgarden, T., Feigenbaum, J. (eds.) 45th Annual ACM Symposium on Theory of Computing, pp. 575–584. ACM Press, June 2013
18. Brakerski, Z., Vaikuntanathan, V.: Fully homomorphic encryption from ring-LWE and security for key dependent messages. In: Rogaway, P. (ed.) CRYPTO 2011. LNCS, vol. 6841, pp. 505–524. Springer, Heidelberg (2011). https://doi.org/10.1007/978-3-642-22792-9_29
19. Chen, Y.: Réduction de réseau et sécurité concrète du chiffrement complètement homomorphe. Ph.D. thesis, Université Paris Diderot (2009)
20. Chen, Y., Nguyen, P.Q.: BKZ 2.0: better lattice security estimates. In: Lee, D.H., Wang, X. (eds.) ASIACRYPT 2011. LNCS, vol. 7073, pp. 1–20. Springer, Heidelberg (2011). https://doi.org/10.1007/978-3-642-25385-0_1
21. Ducas, L., Durmus, A., Lepoint, T., Lyubashevsky, V.: Lattice signatures and bimodal Gaussians. In: Canetti, R., Garay, J.A. (eds.) CRYPTO 2013. LNCS, vol. 8042, pp. 40–56. Springer, Heidelberg (2013). https://doi.org/10.1007/978-3-642-40041-4_3
22. Fincke, U., Pohst, M.: Improved methods for calculating vectors of short length in a lattice, including a complexity analysis. Math. Comput. 44(170), 463–471 (1985)

23. Gama, N., Nguyen, P.Q.: Predicting lattice reduction. In: Smart, N. (ed.) EURO-CRYPT 2008. LNCS, vol. 4965, pp. 31–51. Springer, Heidelberg (2008). https://doi.org/10.1007/978-3-540-78967-3_3

24. Gama, N., Nguyen, P.Q., Regev, O.: Lattice enumeration using extreme pruning. In: Gilbert, H. (ed.) EUROCRYPT 2010. LNCS, vol. 6110, pp. 257–278. Springer, Heidelberg (2010). https://doi.org/10.1007/978-3-642-13190-5_13

25. Gentry, C., Peikert, C., Vaikuntanathan, V.: Trapdoors for hard lattices and new cryptographic constructions. In: Ladner, R.E., Dwork, C. (eds.) 40th Annual ACM Symposium on Theory of Computing, pp. 197–206. ACM Press, May 2008

26. Hanrot, G., Pujol, X., Stehlé, D.: Algorithms for the shortest and closest lattice vector problems. In: Chee, Y.M., Guo, Z., Ling, S., Shao, F., Tang, Y., Wang, H., Xing, C. (eds.) IWCC 2011. LNCS, vol. 6639, pp. 159–190. Springer, Heidelberg (2011). https://doi.org/10.1007/978-3-642-20901-7_10

27. Hanrot, G., Pujol, X., Stehlé, D.: Analyzing blockwise lattice algorithms using dynamical systems. In: Rogaway, P. (ed.) CRYPTO 2011. LNCS, vol. 6841, pp. 447–464. Springer, Heidelberg (2011). https://doi.org/10.1007/978-3-642-22792-9_25

28. Herold, G., Kirshanova, E., May, A.: On the asymptotic complexity of solving LWE. Des. Codes Cryptogr. $86(1)$, 55–83 (2018)

29. Kannan, R.: Improved algorithms for integer programming and related lattice problems. In: 15th Annual ACM Symposium on Theory of Computing, pp. 193–206. ACM Press, April 1983

30. Kannan, R.: Minkowski's convex body theorem and integer programming. Math. Oper. Res. $12(3)$, 415–440 (1987)

31. Khot, S.: Hardness of approximating the shortest vector problem in high L_p norms. In: Proceedings of FOCS, pp. 290–297. IEEE Computer Society Press (2003)

32. Kirchner, P., Fouque, P.-A.: An improved BKW algorithm for LWE with applications to cryptography and lattices. Cryptology ePrint Archive, Report 2015/552 (2015). http://eprint.iacr.org/2015/552

33. Lindner, R., Peikert, C.: Better key sizes (and attacks) for LWE-based encryption. In: Kiayias, A. (ed.) CT-RSA 2011. LNCS, vol. 6558, pp. 319–339. Springer, Heidelberg (2011). https://doi.org/10.1007/978-3-642-19074-2_21

34. Liu, M., Nguyen, P.Q.: Solving BDD by enumeration: an update. In: Dawson, E. (ed.) CT-RSA 2013. LNCS, vol. 7779, pp. 293–309. Springer, Heidelberg (2013). https://doi.org/10.1007/978-3-642-36095-4_19

35. Lyubashevsky, V.: Lattice signatures without trapdoors. In: Pointcheval, D., Johansson, T. (eds.) EUROCRYPT 2012. LNCS, vol. 7237, pp. 738–755. Springer, Heidelberg (2012). https://doi.org/10.1007/978-3-642-29011-4_43

36. Lyubashevsky, V., Micciancio, D.: On bounded distance decoding, unique shortest vectors, and the minimum distance problem. In: Halevi, S. (ed.) CRYPTO 2009. LNCS, vol. 5677, pp. 577–594. Springer, Heidelberg (2009). https://doi.org/10.1007/978-3-642-03356-8_34

37. Lyubashevsky, V., Peikert, C., Regev, O.: On ideal lattices and learning with errors over rings. In: Gilbert, H. (ed.) EUROCRYPT 2010. LNCS, vol. 6110, pp. 1–23. Springer, Heidelberg (2010). https://doi.org/10.1007/978-3-642-13190-5_1

38. Micciancio, D., Regev, O.: Worst-case to average-case reductions based on Gaussian measures. In: 45th Annual Symposium on Foundations of Computer Science, pp. 372–381. IEEE Computer Society Press, October 2004

39. Micciancio, D., Walter, M.: Fast lattice point enumeration with minimal overhead. In: Indyk, P. (ed.) 26th Annual ACM-SIAM Symposium on Discrete Algorithms, pp. 276–294. ACM-SIAM, January 2015

40. Regev, O.: On lattices, learning with errors, random linear codes, and cryptography. In: Gabow, H.N., Fagin, R. (eds.) 37th Annual ACM Symposium on Theory of Computing, pp. 84–93. ACM Press, May 2005
41. Regev, O.: Lattice-based cryptography (invited talk). In: Dwork, C. (ed.) CRYPTO 2006. LNCS, vol. 4117, pp. 131–141. Springer, Heidelberg (2006). https://doi.org/10.1007/11818175_8
42. Schnorr, C.: A hierarchy of polynomial time lattice basis reduction algorithms. Theor. Comput. Sci. **53**(2–3), 201–224 (1987)
43. Schnorr, C.P., Euchner, M.: Lattice basis reduction: improved practical algorithms and solving subset sum problems. In: Budach, L. (ed.) FCT 1991. LNCS, vol. 529, pp. 68–85. Springer, Heidelberg (1991). https://doi.org/10.1007/3-540-54458-5_51
44. Schnorr, C.P.: A more efficient algorithm for lattice basis reduction. In: Kott, L. (ed.) ICALP 1986. LNCS, vol. 226, pp. 359–369. Springer, Heidelberg (1986). https://doi.org/10.1007/3-540-16761-7_85
45. Schnorr, C.P.: Lattice reduction by random sampling and birthday methods. In: Alt, H., Habib, M. (eds.) STACS 2003. LNCS, vol. 2607, pp. 145–156. Springer, Heidelberg (2003). https://doi.org/10.1007/3-540-36494-3_14
46. The FPLLL development team. fplll, a lattice reduction library (2019). https://github.com/fplll/fplll
47. The FPYLLL development team. fpylll, a python wrapper for fplll (2019). https://github.com/fplll/fplll
48. Wang, Y., Aono, Y., Takagi, T.: Hardness evaluation for search LWE problem using progressive BKZ simulator. IEICE Trans. Fundam. Electron. Commun. Comput. Sci. **101**(12), 2162–2170 (2018)

New Schemes and Analysis

Memory-Efficient High-Speed Implementation of Kyber on Cortex-M4

Leon Botros$^{(\boxtimes)}$, Matthias J. Kannwischer$^{(\boxtimes)}$, and Peter Schwabe$^{(\boxtimes)}$

Radboud University, Nijmegen, The Netherlands
l.botros@student.ru.nl, matthias@kannwischer.eu, peter@cryptojedi.org

Abstract. This paper presents an optimized software implementation of the module-lattice-based key-encapsulation mechanism Kyber for the ARM Cortex-M4 microcontroller. Kyber is one of the round-2 candidates in the NIST post-quantum project. In the center of our work are novel optimization techniques for the number-theoretic transform (NTT) inside Kyber, which make very efficient use of the computational power offered by the "vector" DSP instructions of the target architecture. We also present results for the recently updated parameter sets of Kyber which equally benefit from our optimizations.

As a result of our efforts we present software that is 18% faster than an earlier implementation of Kyber optimized for the Cortex-M4 by the Kyber submitters. Our NTT is more than twice as fast as the NTT in that software. Our software runs at about the same speed as the latest *speed-optimized* implementation of the other module-lattice based round-2 NIST PQC candidate Saber. However, for our Kyber software, this performance is achieved with a much smaller RAM footprint. Kyber needs less than half of the RAM of what the considerably slower *RAM-optimized* version of Saber uses. Our software does not make use of any secret-dependent branches or memory access and thus offers state-of-the-art protection against timing attacks.

Keywords: ARM Cortex-M4 · Number-theoretic transform · Lattice-based cryptography · Kyber

1 Introduction

In 2016, NIST issued a call for proposals of new post-quantum cryptographic schemes including digital signatures and key encapsulation schemes (KEM) for future standardization [26]. In late 2017, 69 different proposals were accepted for a first round of evaluation. On January 30, 2019, NIST announced the second-round candidates which include 17 KEMs and 9 signature schemes. The report accompanying NIST's decision [1] states that the main criteria of selection were cryptanalytic attacks and message sizes. Implementation characteristics such as

This work has been supported by the European Commission through the ERC Starting Grant 805031 (EPOQUE). Date: May 10, 2019.

© Springer Nature Switzerland AG 2019
J. Buchmann et al. (Eds.): AFRICACRYPT 2019, LNCS 11627, pp. 209–228, 2019.
https://doi.org/10.1007/978-3-030-23696-0_11

speed, memory consumption, or code size on various platforms was not the main reason for not selecting any of the schemes to the second round evaluation. However, NIST stated that *"performance will play a larger role in the second round"* which is estimated to last for at least one year. Since only minor tweaks to submitted schemes are allowed it is likely that, unless there are major cryptanalytic advances, implementation performance will be a main criterion for schemes being considered beyond round two.

While many first-round submissions already include an implementation optimized for large Intel processors, most do not come with optimized implementations for other platforms. Yet, some of the schemes have been optimized for ARM Cortex-M microcontrollers and also FPGAs. One particularly important target platform is the ARM Cortex-M4 since a variety of schemes have been optimized for it and NIST recommended it to submission teams. Implementations of NIST candidates optimized for the Cortex-M4 are collected in pqm4 [21] which also provides a testing and benchmarking framework for fair comparison.

7 out of 17 round-two candidates[1] for key encapsulation are based on structured lattices and as such heavily rely on arithmetic in polynomial rings. Recent work [20] optimized multiplication on Cortex-M4 in the polynomial ring $\mathbb{Z}_{2^k}[X]/(f(X))$ using the decomposition algorithms of Karatsuba [22] and Toom-Cook [12,32]. Having fast arithmetic in $\mathbb{Z}_{2^k}[X]/(f(X))$ allows to speed up the two second-round candidates Saber and NTRU[2].

Even though multiplication in $\mathbb{Z}_{2^k}[X]/(f(X))$ can be fast for practical values of n and k, it comes at a major cost: Toom and Karatsuba require additional memory to store intermediate results. For the NTRU-HRSS-KEM parameters $n = 701$ and $k = 13$, [20] achieve the fasted multiplication using Toom-4 and 4 layers of Karatsuba, which requires 11 208 bytes of additional stack space. Even for the smaller polynomials with $n = 256$ in Saber, the fastest multiplication routine described in [20] requires 3800 bytes of RAM. In case this memory is not available, one has to fall back to considerably slower multiplication algorithms.

The situation is very different for Kyber (and also the round-2 NIST candidate NewHope [2,3]), which are designed to support very efficient multiplication in the underlying polynomial ring *without* additional memory. The idea is to use fast number-theoretic transforms (NTTs), which are even part of the specification of these two schemes. The use of fast NTT-based multiplication is not new in those schemes and there exists a large body of work on optimizing this operation on a variety of platforms. The most recent works on optimizing the NTT on large Intel and AMD processors are by Seiler [30] and by Lyubashevsky and Seiler [24]. The fastest implementation so far on our target architecture, the ARM Cortex-M4, is presented by Alkım, Jakubeit, and Schwabe in [4]. Earlier works on the same architecture include [11] and [27].

Contribution. The main contribution of this paper is to present improved optimization techniques for the NTTs in Kyber. In comparison to the performance presented in [4], our NTT is more than a factor of 1.8 faster (when applying

---

[1] see https://www.safecrypto.eu/pqclounge/round-2-candidates/.
[2] the second round merger of NTRU-HRSS-KEM [19] and NTRUEncrypt [33].

the same scaling to accommodate for the different dimension that was also used in [4]). Most of the techniques we present also apply to the NewHope parameters targeted in [4], but some of the speedup we achieve is specific to the smaller value of $q = 7681$ (NewHope uses $q = 12289$). We also optimize the other performance-critical routines in Kyber and describe how to reduce RAM usage in Kyber without significantly sacrificing performance. As a result we present the software, that at the same time has the smallest RAM footprint across all NIST PQC KEM candidates that have been optimized for the Cortex-M4, and has the lowest cycle count for the sum of key generation, encapsulation and decapsulation.

Kyber v2. While this paper was in submission, the Kyber team published various round-2 tweaks including the change of q from 7681 to 3329 which requires changing the NTT. All the optimizations presented in this paper still apply to Kyber v2. We have updated our software to support the new parameter sets and present the performance results for both versions.

Availability of Software. We place all the software described in this paper into the public domain. It is available at https://github.com/mupq/nttm4. The implementations using the round-2 parameter sets have also been merged into pqm4 [21].

Organization of this Paper. Section 2 gives the necessary background on the key encapsulation scheme Kyber and the NTTs used within Kyber. Section 3 presents the speed optimizations we applied to the NTT which yields a significantly faster implementation of Kyber. Section 4 describes how the fast implementation of Kyber can be gradually modified to use less stack space with minor and moderate computational overhead. Finally, Sect. 5 presents the performance results for our implementations and compares them to previous implementations of Kyber and other second round candidates in the NIST post-quantum competition.

2   Preliminaries

In this section we establish notation, briefly recall Kyber and the NTT used within Kyber, and then proceed to describe our target platform, the ARM Cortex-M4.

Notation. We refer to polynomials by regular font lower-case letters (a), vectors of polynomials by bold lower-case letters ($\mathbf{a}$) and matrices of polynomials by bold upper-case letters ($\mathbf{A}$). For a polynomial a we use $\hat{a}$ to denote the representation of a in NTT-domain and similarly $\hat{\mathbf{a}}$ and $\hat{\mathbf{A}}$ are the results of element-wise application of the NTT to the entries of $\mathbf{a}$ and $\mathbf{A}$. (Random) bitstrings are referred to by the lower-case Greek letters ρ, σ, and μ. We abstract away from seed expansion to polynomials following a uniform or centered binomial distribution by just calling SampleUniform or SampleCBD. Let q be prime and let $\mathbb{Z}_q$ denote the field $\mathbb{Z}/q\mathbb{Z}$. We define polynomial rings of the form $\mathcal{R}_q = \mathbb{Z}_q/(X^n + 1)$ over this field

Algorithm 1. CPA KeyGen (v1)

   Output: public key $pk = (\rho, \mathbf{t}')$
   Output: secret key $sk = \hat{\mathbf{s}}$
1: $\rho, \sigma \xleftarrow{\$} \{0,1\}^{256} \times \{0,1\}^{256}$
2: $\hat{\mathbf{A}} \in \mathcal{R}_q^{k \times k} \leftarrow \mathtt{SampleUniform}(\rho)$
3: $\mathbf{s}, \mathbf{e} \in \mathcal{R}_q^k \leftarrow \mathtt{SampleCBD}(\sigma)$
4: $\hat{\mathbf{s}} \leftarrow \mathtt{NTT}(\mathbf{s})$
5: $\mathbf{t} \leftarrow \mathtt{NTT}^{-1}(\hat{\mathbf{A}} \circ \hat{\mathbf{s}}) + \mathbf{e}$
6: **return** $pk = (\rho, \mathtt{Compress}(\mathbf{t})), sk = \hat{\mathbf{s}}$

Algorithm 3. CPA Decryption (v1)

   Input: secret key $sk = \hat{\mathbf{s}}$
   Input: compressed ciphertext $(\mathbf{u}', v')$
   Output: message $m \in \mathcal{R}_q$
   $\mathbf{u} \leftarrow \mathtt{Decompress}(\mathbf{u}')$
   $v \leftarrow \mathtt{Decompress}(v')$
   return $m \leftarrow v - \mathtt{NTT}^{-1}(\hat{\mathbf{s}}^T \circ \mathtt{NTT}(\mathbf{u}))$

Algorithm 2. CPA Encryption (v1)

   Input: public key $pk = (\rho, \mathbf{t}')$
   Input: message $m \in \mathcal{R}_q$
   Input: randomness $\mu \in \{0,1\}^{256}$
   Output: ciphertext $(\mathbf{u}', v')$
1: $\hat{\mathbf{A}} \in \mathcal{R}_q^{k \times k} \leftarrow \mathtt{SampleUniform}(\rho)$
2: $\mathbf{r}, \mathbf{e}_1 \in \mathcal{R}_q^k \leftarrow \mathtt{SampleCBD}(\mu)$
3: $e_2 \in \mathcal{R}_q \leftarrow \mathtt{SampleCBD}(\mu)$
4: $\hat{\mathbf{r}} \leftarrow \mathtt{NTT}(\mathbf{r})$
5: $\mathbf{u} \leftarrow \mathtt{NTT}^{-1}(\hat{\mathbf{A}}^T \circ \hat{\mathbf{r}}) + \mathbf{e}_1$
6: $\mathbf{t} \leftarrow \mathtt{Decompress}(\mathbf{t}')$
7: $v \leftarrow \mathtt{NTT}^{-1}(\mathtt{NTT}(\mathbf{t})^T \circ \hat{\mathbf{r}}) + e_2 + m$
8: **return** $(\mathtt{Compress}(\mathbf{u}), \mathtt{Compress}(v))$

where n is a power of two. We denote by $\circ$ the coefficient-wise multiplication of two polynomials in NTT domain with the natural extension to vectors and matrices. Similarly, let $c \in \mathcal{R}_q = \mathbf{a} \circ \mathbf{b}$ be the inner product of $\mathbf{a} \in \mathcal{R}_q^k$ and $\mathbf{b} \in \mathcal{R}_q^k$.

2.1 Kyber v1

Kyber [6,9], which is part of the Cryptographic Suite for Algebraic Lattices (CRYSTALS), is built on the hardness of the Module-LWE (MLWE) problem. Different from Ring-LWE, MLWE uses a matrix of polynomials in $\mathcal{R}_q$ as the public information $\hat{\mathbf{A}}$, whereas $\mathbf{s}$ and $\mathbf{e}$ become vectors of polynomials. For Kyber $\hat{\mathbf{A}}$ is a square $k \times k$ matrix and $\mathbf{s}$ and $\mathbf{e}$ are k-dimensional vectors. MLWE therefore presents a generalization of the Ring-LWE and the standard LWE problem. While this might have benefits in terms of security [9], it is also an advantage for implementations: One can change the security level by changing the dimension of the matrix, i.e., by changing k. Kyber uses the prime $q = 7681 = 2^{13} - 2^9 + 1$ and $\mathcal{R}_q = \mathbb{Z}_{7681}/(X^{256} + 1)$ for all security levels. Since $\mathcal{R}_q$ remains the same for all security levels it is possible to optimize all security levels of Kyber by optimizing arithmetic in $\mathcal{R}_q$. Kyber specifies three security levels: Kyber-512, Kyber-768, and Kyber-1024 which use $k = 2, 3, 4$, respectively. Besides k, the security levels only differ in the centered binomial distribution of the secret and error polynomials which is $\eta = 5, 4, 3$ respectively.

Kyber uses a two stage-construction to obtain a CCA-secure KEM: First, build an IND-CPA secure encryption scheme, which is called Kyber.CPA and then use a variant of the Fujisaki-Okamoto transform [15] to build the CCA-secure KEM. Algorithms 1, 2, and 3 illustrate key-generation, encryption, and decryption of the CPA-secure encryption scheme. For the details of the CCA transform, we refer the reader to [6, Alg. 7–9] for the pseudocode description. Since the public matrix $\mathbf{A}$ is sampled from a uniform distribution and since the number-theoretic transform of uniform randomness is again uniformly distributed, the NTT of $\mathbf{A}$ is omitted and $\hat{\mathbf{A}}$ is instead sampled directly in NTT domain. However, this is not possible for the secrets and errors, since those need to be small in normal domain.

Aside from symmetric cryptography used for randomness generation and hashing (in particular in the CCA transform), the main cost in Kyber is arithmetic in $\mathcal{R}_q$ and even more specifically multiplications. The main cost of these multiplications are the (forward and inverse) NTT. The number of NTT operations depends on the parameter k and is $2k$, $3k+1$, and $k+1$ for Kyber.CPA key generation, encryption, and decryption, respectively. Decapsulation of the CCA-secure KEM includes both Kyber.CPA encryption and Kyber.CPA decryption and thus requires $4k + 2$ NTTs.

The Number Theoretic Transform. The number-theoretic transform is a Fourier transform in a finite field, i.e., a multi-point evaluation of a polynomial at powers of a root of unity. In the specific setting of Kyber, the NTT of a polynomial $g = \sum_{i=0}^{n-1} g_i X^i \in \mathcal{R}_q$ is defined as

$$\mathrm{NTT}(g) = \hat{g} = \sum_{i=0}^{n-1} \hat{g}_i X^i, \text{ with}$$

$$\hat{g}_i = \sum_{j=0}^{n-1} \psi^j g_j \omega^{ij},$$

where $\omega = 3844$ and $\psi = \sqrt{\omega} = 62$. The inverse of this operation is given through

$$\mathrm{NTT}^{-1}(\hat{g}) = g = \sum_{i=0}^{n-1} g_i X^i, \text{ with}$$

$$g_i = n^{-1} \psi^{-i} \sum_{j=0}^{n-1} \hat{g}_j \omega^{-ij}.$$

With these definitions of NTT and NTT^{-1}, the multiplication of two polynomials $f, g \in \mathcal{R}_q$ can be computed as $f \cdot g = \mathrm{NTT}^{-1}(\mathrm{NTT}(f) \circ \mathrm{NTT}(g))$.

The FFT algorithm to compute Fourier transforms with only $\Theta(n \log n)$ operations was introduced by Cooley and Tukey in [13]; only several years later it was pointed out by Goldstine [16] that a similar algorithm had already been described by Gauss in the early 19th century. For a discussion also see [18]. The big picture is that the algorithm iterates through $\log_2 n$ levels, each level performs $n/2$ so-called *butterfly operations*, and each butterfly operation performs a multiplication by a power of ω, one addition, and one subtraction in $\mathbb{Z}_q$. The powers of the root of unity ω are often referred to as the "twiddle factors".

Note that in NTT and NTT^{-1}, polynomials are transformed *inplace* and without any additional temporary storage. This comes at a small price: the coefficients

Algorithm 4. CPA KeyGen (v2)	**Algorithm 5.** CPA Encryption (v2)
Output: public key $pk = (\rho, \hat{\mathbf{t}})$ **Output:** secret key $sk = \hat{\mathbf{s}}$ 1: $\rho, \sigma \xleftarrow{\$} \{0,1\}^{256} \times \{0,1\}^{256}$ 2: $\hat{\mathbf{A}} \in \mathcal{R}_q^{k \times k} \leftarrow \texttt{SampleUniform}(\rho)$ 3: $\mathbf{s}, \mathbf{e} \in \mathcal{R}_q^k \leftarrow \texttt{SampleCBD}(\sigma)$ 4: $\hat{\mathbf{t}} \leftarrow \hat{\mathbf{A}} \circ \texttt{NTT}(\mathbf{s}) + \texttt{NTT}(\mathbf{e})$ 5: **return** $pk = (\rho, \hat{\mathbf{t}}), sk = \hat{\mathbf{s}}$	**Input:** public key $pk = (\rho, \hat{\mathbf{t}})$ **Input:** message $m \in \mathcal{R}_q$ **Input:** randomness $\mu \in \{0,1\}^{256}$ **Output:** ciphertext $(\mathbf{u}', v')$ 1: $\hat{\mathbf{A}} \in \mathcal{R}_q^{k \times k} \leftarrow \texttt{SampleUniform}(\rho)$ 2: $\mathbf{r}, \mathbf{e}_1 \in \mathcal{R}_q^k \leftarrow \texttt{SampleCBD}(\mu)$ 3: $e_2 \in \mathcal{R}_q \leftarrow \texttt{SampleCBD}(\mu)$ 4: $\hat{\mathbf{r}} \leftarrow \texttt{NTT}(\mathbf{r})$ 5: $\mathbf{u} \leftarrow \texttt{NTT}^{-1}(\hat{\mathbf{A}}^T \circ \hat{\mathbf{r}}) + \mathbf{e}_1$ 6: $v \leftarrow \texttt{NTT}^{-1}(\hat{\mathbf{t}}^T \circ \hat{\mathbf{r}}) + e_2 + m$ 7: **return** $(\texttt{Compress}(\mathbf{u}), \texttt{Compress}(v))$

of polynomials in NTT domain are in so-called bit-reversed order. This issue can either be addressed by permuting coefficients or by implementing separate algorithms for NTT and NTT^{-1}, one that expects input in bitreversed order and produces output in normal order and the other one working the other way round. Kyber follows the second approach, i.e., avoids overhead of extra bitreversal operations. For a discussion of the different options, see also [28, Sec. 3.2].

2.2 Kyber V2

In the process of writing this paper, the second round of NIST began and the Kyber team published an updated Kyber specification [7]. We will in the following refer to this updated version as Kyber v2.

The main design decision for round 2 of the NIST competition was to remove the compression of the public key. To compensate for the increased bandwidth requirement, the Kyber team decided to reduce the value of q from 7681 to 3329, a choice that was enabled by the observation from [24] that also this value of q supports very fast NTT-based multiplication of polynomials. Another consequence of the decision to not compress public keys is that public keys can now be transmitted in NTT domain, which saves an NTT operation in encryption (and in the re-encryption during decapsulation of the CCA-secure KEM). Finally, the smaller value of q also requires smaller noise to achieve the same security level. This is why the parameter η of the centered binomial distribution changed to $\eta = 2$ for all security levels; note that this change is hidden by our high-level view of SampleCBD. The resulting key-generation and encryption algorithms are given in Algorithms 4 and 5; decapsulation is the same as for the round-1 version in this high-level perspective.

From a computational point of view, the most interesting aspect of the changes is the change of the definition of the NTT. In the round-1 version of Kyber, q was chosen such that $\mathbb{Z}_q$ contains 512-th roots of unity. As a consequence, the negacyclic NTT of elements of $\mathcal{R}_q$ is a vector of 256 degree-zero polynomials (i.e., scalars). In the round-2 version of Kyber, q is chosen such that $\mathbb{Z}_q$ contains 256-th roots of unity, but not 512-th roots of unity. As a consequence, the NTT of a polynomial $f \in \mathcal{R}_q$ is a vector of 128 polynomials of degree at most 1, i.e., with 2 coefficients each. Specifically, [7, Sec. 1.1] defines the NTT of a polynomial $f \in \mathcal{R}_q$ as

$$NTT(f) = \hat{f} = (\hat{f}_0 + \hat{f}_1 X, \hat{f}_2 + \hat{f}_3 X, \ldots, \hat{f}_{254} + \hat{f}_{255} X),$$

where coefficients $\hat{f}_i$ are defined as

$$\hat{f}_{2i} = \sum_{j=0}^{127} f_{2j} \zeta^{(2\mathrm{br}_7(i)+1)j}, \text{ and}$$

$$\hat{f}_{2i+1} = \sum_{j=0}^{127} f_{2j+1} \zeta^{(2\mathrm{br}_7(i)+1)j}.$$

In this definition $\zeta = 17$ is the first primitive 256th root of unity and br_7 reverses the bits in a 7-bit integer.

Note that with this definition of the NTT, the "pointwise" multiplication of two polynomials denoted by $\circ$ now consists of performing 128 multiplications of linear polynomials modulo $X^2 - \zeta^{2\mathrm{br}_7(i)+1}$.

2.3 ARM Cortex-M4

Our target platform is the ARM Cortex-M4, which NIST recommended as the reference platform for evaluation of post-quantum candidates on microcontrollers. It implements the ARMv7E-M instruction set which features 16 general purpose 32-bit registers of which 14 are usable by the developer; the other two are used for program counter and stack pointer. Unlike the ARMv7-M, the ARMv7E-M provides powerful DSP instructions that perform arithmetic operations on two 16-bit halfwords in parallel, which proved to be very beneficial for the other post-quantum KEMs Saber and NTRU-HRSS-KEM [20,23]. While Kyber does not benefit from the smlad instruction, we make use of parallel additions and subtractions using uadd16, usub16, sasx, and ssax. Another feature that we extensively use throughout our optimization is the barrel-shifter which allows to shift or rotate one of the arguments in arithmetic instructions without increasing the cycle count.

Specifically, we use the STM32F4DISCOVERY that is also used by a large number of previous optimization papers and the benchmarking and testing framework pqm4 [21]. It comes with 192 KiB of memory, 1 MiB of flash, and can operate at frequencies of up to 168 MHz. Compared to other ARM platforms like the Cortex-M0, our target platforms can be considered at the higher end of microcontrollers. The RAM and flash are sufficient to implement and evaluate almost all of the second round NIST candidates.

3 Optimizing for Speed

In this section we describe the optimizations we apply to speed up the computation of Kyber on the ARM Cortex-M4. Optimizations targeting the reduction of RAM usage will be presented in Sect. 4. The starting point of our optimization efforts is the optimized implementation for the Cortex-M4 by the Kyber authors [5], which is the same as the C reference implementation except for a hand-optimized NTT operation and which is included in the pqm4 framework [21].

3.1 Link-Time Optimization

While experimenting with the Kyber implementation from [5], we realized that its performance is heavily penalized in pqm4 because a number of small functions (in particular modular reductions) are implemented in different files than where they are used. Since pqm4 compiles all source files separately to object files, the compiler cannot inline those functions, which creates a large overhead from function calls. A simple, but not very elegant solution would be to place all source code in one large file and this indeed results in a speedup of about 5%.

A similar behaviour can be achieved by adding the link-time optimization compiler flag -flto, which adds additional information in object files to allow optimization when those are linked together. Since -flto consistently improves performance for implementations of Kyber, we use it throughout our experiments.

We contacted the authors of pqm4 [21] to include -flto as a default option. However, their benchmarks show that not all schemes benefit from -flto. Some schemes get significantly slower, while others have a up to 60% increase in stack consumption. Therefore, -flto was not turned on by default in pqm4.

3.2 Speeding up the NTT

In the following we describe our optimization strategy for the NTT, which includes a careful combination of known techniques with new micro-architecture specific improvements.

Representation of Polynomials. Polynomials in $\mathcal{R}_q$ have 256 coefficients in $\mathbb{Z}_q$, where q is the 13-bit prime 7681 (or 3329 for Kyber v2). Is is natural to represent polynomials as an array of length 256 of 16-bit integers. Inspired by [30] and unlike the implementation by the Kyber authors or the optimized NewHope implementation described in [4], we use an array of *signed* 16-bit integers to represent elements of $\mathcal{R}_q$. We will later discuss the effect of this choice on modular reductions; one immediate advantage of using signed representation is that during subtractions in $\mathbb{Z}_q$ we do not have to worry about underflows. Compared to using unsigned integers we thus trivially save an addition of a multiple of q before subtractions.

Merging NTT Layers. Similar to, e.g., [17] and [4], we merge several layers of the NTT transformation, i.e., we load four coefficients into registers at once, perform four butterfly operations on them, and store them back. This drastically reduces the number of loads and stores. However, it turns out that merging three layers of the NTT as proposed in [4] is not optimal, since there are not enough

Algorithm 6. Original unsigned Montgomery reduction [5]; using Montgomery factor $\beta = 2^{18}$.	**Algorithm 7**. Signed Montgomery reduction (this work, adapted from [30]); using Montgomery factor $\beta = 2^{16}$.
Input: a (32 bit)	
Output: reduced a (16 bit)	**Input:** a (32 bit)
1: mul t, a, q^{-1}	**Output:** reduced a (16 bit)
2: and t, #0x3fff	1: smulbb t, a, q^{-1} ▷ $t \leftarrow (a \mod \beta) \cdot q^{-1}$
3: mla a, t, q, a ▷ $a \leftarrow a + t \cdot q$	2: smulbb t, t, q ▷ $t \leftarrow (t \mod \beta) \cdot q$
4: lsr a, #18	3: usub16 a, a, t ▷ $a_{top} \leftarrow \left\lfloor \frac{a}{2^{16}} \right\rfloor - \left\lfloor \frac{t}{2^{16}} \right\rfloor$

registers to fit the constants required in the Montgomery and Barrett reductions (see below). In [4] this is solved by reloading the constants for each butterfly, but the cost for these loads is larger than the savings from fewer loads and stores of coefficients. We instead merge only two layers which allows us to still keep all constants in registers and still save 50% of load and store operations.

Precomputation of Twiddle Factors. Like most speed-optimized NTT implementations before, we precompute all powers of ω and store those in flash. For more efficient modular reduction after multiplication by the twiddle factors, we follow an approach first introduced in [3] and store twiddle factors in Montgomery representation [25]. More specifically, our optimizations are largely inspired by the refined approach described in [30] and we use the same Montgomery factor $\beta = 2^{16}$. We then reorder the twiddle factors in our table such that they can be picked up sequentially in the NTT computation; increasing the pointer to the twiddle factors after each load is free in ARMv7E-M. Since we need three twiddle factors per two (merged) layers, we pack two of them into one register, which saves one load operation and one register. The twiddle factors are only used in multiplications with 16-bit coefficients which allows to use smulbb and smulbt to multiply by the upper or the lower twiddle factor inside that register.

Montgomery Reductions. After the multiplication in each butterfly, we need to reduce the 32-bit product to 16-bit. This is done using a signed Montgomery reduction tailored to q. It turns out that the signed Montgomery reduction as proposed in [30] can be implemented in three clock cycles (Algorithm 7) on the ARM Cortex-M4 and as such is one clock cycle faster than the unsigned Montgomery reduction in [5] (Algorithm 6).

Unrolling. As usual we fully unroll the outer loop of the NTT iterating over the NTT levels. Additionally, to save an additional register, we unroll one of the inner loops as well. Depending on the current level, we unroll the loop with the least iterations to minimize the code-size increase. While this is also saving a small number of cycles, the performance gains by having an additional registers are much more significant.

Packing. Since q is well below 16-bits, polynomials are usually stored as `int16_t` arrays. Since our target platform is a 32-bit architecture it seems wasteful to only load one 16-bit coefficient into 32-bit registers. Loading and storing two coefficients at once saves half of the load and store operations. However, the available vector instruction in `ARMv7E-M` are quite limited. For example, there is no dedicated instruction performing two 16-bit multiplications yielding two 32-bit results. Still some operations can be performed in parallel. Therefore, we implement "double" butterflies, i.e., butterflies which operate on packed arguments and return a packed result. By doing this, we can for example perform two additions and subtractions in one clock cycles using `uadd16` and `usub16`. Unfortunately, some operations (e.g., the Barrett reduction) are more than twice as expensive to implement on packed arguments. Nonetheless, we achieve a speed-up in every butterfly by using packing.

Instruction Alignment. Since some instructions available in `ARMv7E-M` are 16-bit Thumb instructions, it is possible that a single Thumb instruction unaligns many following 32-bit ARM instructions which results in a vast performance penalty. Therefore, we make sure our code is as aligned as possible. This can be done by aligning the start of the function using `.align 2` (`.align n` aligns to 2^n bytes) and padding each sole Thumb instruction to 32-bit using the `.w` suffix.

Recent Improvements Proposed in [24]. Very recent work proposed yet another more efficient NTT in AVX2 [24] which can also be adapted to Kyber. The major speed-up that [24] achieved over [30] in the NTT stems form further optimizing the Montgomery reduction. Lyubashevsky and Seiler save an additional multiplication by avoiding the multiplication by q^{-1} and instead multiplying each of the precomputed twiddle factors by q^{-1}. This is possible since each product of a polynomial coefficient a_i by a twiddle factor is implemented through two separate multiplication instructions, one computing the low half and one computing the high half of the product. Since the low half of the product is multiplied by q^{-1} mod β inside the Montgomery reduction, one can precompute the product of q^{-1} and the corresponding twiddle factor and use this constant for the low product. This saves another multiplication instruction in the Montgomery reduction, but requires to store twice as many precomputed twiddles. Unfortunately, this does not carry over to our Cortex-M4 implementation since the low and high product are not computed separately, but in a single instruction. Doing these multiplications separately with different constants would be possible, but require an additional clock cycle and thus not save anything.

3.3   Optimizing Matrix-Vector Multiplication

Besides the NTT, another fairly expensive operation in Kyber is the matrix-vector multiplication in line 5 of Algorithm 1 and line 5 of Algorithm 2. We also optimize this operation in C. Since this optimization depends on the stack-reduction strategy, we describe it in Sect. 4.

3.4 Optimized Keccak

As we will see in Subsect. 5.3, even before our optimization of the NTT and matrix-vector multiplication, most of the cycles of the Kyber computation are spent in hashing and pseudorandom-number generation, which both boil down to the Keccak permutation [8]. For all derivatives of Keccak inside Kyber (i.e., SHA3-256, SHA3-512, SHAKE-128, and SHAKE-256) we use the highly optimized code from the eXtended Keccak Code Package [14], which is also included in the pqm4 framework.

3.5 Kyber V2

Various changes in the updated Kyber specification have an impact on performance, but all the optimizations presented above still apply with minor modifications: The smaller q allows to be more lazy with Barrett reductions in the NTT and NTT^{-1} which improves performance. Additionally, both the NTT and NTT^{-1} only require 7 instead of 8 layers of butterfly operations which saves roughly 1/8 of the cycles. However, the multiplication of polynomials in the NTT domain is no longer a pointwise multiplication and consequently becomes more expensive. These two changes approximately cancel each other out.

4 Decreasing Stack Usage

In addition to being fast, NTT-based multiplication provides the additional benefit of being entirely in-place; no additional stack space is needed. This presents a major advantage compared to for example $\mathbb{Z}_{2^k}[X]/(f(X))$, where the fastest multiplication methods use a combination of Toom-Cook [12,32] and Karatsuba's [22] algorithm which comes with a rather large memory footprint. The existing implementation of the NTT in Kyber were already in-place and the changes we applied to them did not change this. Therefore, we also optimized the C-code implementing the remainder of the scheme to use less stack space, making this implementation of Kyber particularly suitable for memory constrained devices. We analyzed which stack space requirements can be eliminated at no or very little computational cost, i.e., without recomputations.

Changes to Kyber.CCAKEM. Kyber uses a FO-transformation to transform a CPA-secure PKE into a CCA-secure KEM. The reference implementation of decapsulation does so by first decrypting the ciphertext and then re-encrypting the obtained plaintext. This produces a ciphertext which is then compared to the original. Only if they are equal, the shared secret key is returned. We eliminate this additional ciphertext on the stack by inlining the comparison into CPA encryption in a constant-time manner. This function is only used for re-encrypting and does not return a ciphertext, but rather a boolean value that indicates the ciphertexts were equal. The actual re-encrypted ciphertext is computed and compared byte per byte. This not only saves a considerable amount of stack space, but also slightly improves the speed.

Changes to Kyber.CPAPKE. The remaining changes were made in the C code of Kyber's CPA key generation (Algorithm 1), encryption (Algorithm 2) and decryption (Algorithm 3), where we reduced the number of polynomials that are kept in memory at the same time. In the reference implementation of key generation and encryption, firstly, the public matrix $\hat{\mathbf{A}}$ of $k \times k$ polynomials is sampled directly in NTT domain and stored in memory. Then, vectors of noise polynomials are sampled from a centered binomial distribution. Finally, all computations are performed. We optimize this by merging the sampling and the computations, i.e., we sample the required arguments on the fly where possible.

Generating and Multiplying $\hat{\mathbf{A}}$. Since a polynomial in Kyber has 256 coefficients each represented by 16 bits, storing one polynomial consumes 512 bytes of memory. Because the size of the matrix $\hat{\mathbf{A}}$ grows quadratically with k, its k^2 polynomials account for the majority of Kyber's stack usage. However, the matrix $\hat{\mathbf{A}}$ is only required once for matrix-vector pointwise multiplication and accumulation (see e.g., line 4 of Algorithm 1). The memory footprint can be reduced using an approach that reduces the storage requirements of $\hat{\mathbf{A}}$ to only the state of the extendable output function for one polynomial of $\hat{\mathbf{A}}$ at a time, allowing to generate a small number of coefficients for multiplication.

In this approach, the polynomials of output vectors **t** and **u** are serialized one at a time. The vector operands $\hat{\mathbf{s}}$ and $\hat{\mathbf{r}}$ are used k times in the matrix-vector multiplication. Therefore, we decided to keep those in memory throughout the computation. Only maintaining one polynomial of those in memory would require re-sampling and transforming them to NTT domain k times which would introduce a significant performance penalty.

For key generation we require $k + 1$ polynomials, for encryption we require $k + 1$ polynomials, and for decryption we only use 3 polynomials regardless of k, but since decapsulation calls both CPA encryption and decryption, the stack usage is determined by encryption.

Adding Noise. The noise polynomials $\mathbf{e}$, $\mathbf{e}_1$, and e_2 are only used once and are sampled from a centered binomial distribution using an extendable output function (XOF). We sample the coefficients of those polynomials on-the-fly without having to store the entire polynomials.

Kyber v2. Our stack optimizations are mostly unaffected by the algorithmic tweaks made by the Kyber team in round-2. However, in key generation (Algorithm 4), the noise vector **e** needs to be in NTT domain. Since the NTT transformation requires the entire polynomial **e** in memory; the on-the-fly sampling is no longer possible. Therefore, key generation requires an additional polynomial, i.e., $k + 2$ in total.

5   Results

For our experiments we use the STM32F4DISCOVERY together with an extended version of the pqm4 [21] benchmarking framework. Particularly all cycles counts and stack measurements are those reported by pqm4, i.e., running the schemes

Table 1. Cycle counts for NTT, NTT^{-1}, and the full polynomial multiplication $(\text{NTT}^{-1}(\text{NTT}(a) \circ \text{NTT}(b)))$. We outperform the current speed record by more than a factor of two for NTT and NTT^{-1}. The parameter changes in Kyber v2 further speed-up the polynomial multiplication.

	Implementation	NTT [cycles]	NTT^{-1} [cycles]	polymul [cycles]
Kyber v1	[5]	21 855	23 622	
	This work	9 452 (−56.8%)	10 373 (−56.1%)	32 576
Kyber v2	This work	7 725	9 347	27 873

at a low frequency of 24 MHz to not be impacted by memory wait states due to a slow memory controller. This allows to compare those numbers to boards different from the STM32F4DISCOVERY. We extend pqm4 to also report cycles spent in hashing. Similar as pqm4 we use arm-none-eabi-gcc at version 8.2.0[3] and set the optimization option to -O3.

We noticed that pqm4 suffered a serious performance penalty due to how it is using the 128 KiB memory of STM32F4DISCOVERY. pqm4 down-clocks the STM32F4DISCOVERY, such that all accesses to RAM should take the same number of cycles. However, according to [31] the 128 KiB of RAM are divided into SRAM1 which consists of 112 KiB and SRAM2 consisting of 16 KiB. In our experiments we noticed that memory accesses to SRAM2 are slower than to SRAM1, i.e., SRAM2 memory accesses cause wait states even at the low bench-marking frequency. At the time of writing pqm4 places the stack into SRAM2 which eventually grows into SRAM1. As a consequence of this, reducing memory consumption leads to the entire scheme fitting in SRAM2 introducing vast performance penalty. To account for this effect, we consistently place the stack in SRAM1 for all benchmarks. Consequently, the numbers in the following differ from this reported in pqm4. For fair comparison we re-benchmarked all implementations that were integrated pqm4 and indicate which benchmark results from related work were not performed using this way of benchmarking. We reported the problem to the authors of pqm4 and it is going to be resolved in a future version of pqm4.

In this section we present our results for Kyber. We start by benchmarking the NTT and polynomial multiplication in isolation and then report results for key generation, encapsulation, and decapsulation for all parameter sets of Kyber. All numbers reported in this section refer to the CCA-secure Kyber.

5.1   NTT and Polynomial Multiplication

Table 1 presents our new speed records for the computation of the NTT. Our optimized Kyber v1 NTT and NTT^{-1} are more than a factor two faster than the

---

[3] We also benchmarked our code using the February 2019 release of arm-none-eabi-gcc (8.3.0) which produced the same results.

speed records [5] Combining NTT and NTT^{-1} to perform a full polynomial multiplication in $\mathcal{R}_q$, i.e., computing $\text{NTT}^{-1}(\text{NTT}(a) \circ \text{NTT}(b))$ requires 32 576 clock cycles.

In Kyber v2 only 7 out of 8 layers of the NTT are computed, which reduces the run-time to roughly 7/8 of the cycles. Computing $\text{NTT}^{-1}(\text{NTT}(a) \circ \text{NTT}(b))$ is considerably (14%) faster even though $\circ$ becomes more expensive.

The fastest multiplication in $\mathbb{Z}_{2^{13}}/(X^{256} + 1)$, which has the same dimension as $\mathcal{R}_q$, using Toom–Cook [12,32] and Karatsuba [22] reported by Kannwischer–Rijneveld–Schwabe [20] requires 38 215 clock cycles. We outperform this by 27%. More importantly, Toom–Cook and Karatsuba multiplication require a significant amount of additional memory for intermediate values. For $\mathbb{Z}_{2^{13}}/(X^{256} + 1)$, [20] reports 3 800 bytes of intermediate values which excludes the non-reduced result polynomial of 1 022 bytes[4]. Our polynomial multiplication is entirely in place.

In comparison to the performance presented in [4], our NTT is more than a factor of 1.8 faster (when applying the same scaling to accommodate for the different dimension that was also used in [4]). Most of the techniques we present also apply to the NewHope parameters targeted in [4], but some of the speedup we achieve is specific to the smaller value of q (NewHope uses $q = 12289$).

5.2   Kyber.CCA

Table 2 presents the cycle counts for all our implementations in comparison to the existing speed records [5]. By just turning on -flto, we achieve speedups of 4–7% mainly caused due to in-lining modular reductions. The speed-ups achieved by applying our speed optimizations are 14–23% and, thus, go far beyond what the compiler achieves. Our implementation of the round one variants of Kyber achieve the lowest cycle counts reported.

As a result of the optimizations described in Sect. 4, we were able to reduce the stack usage of all Kyber variants significantly (see Table 3). Prior to our optimizations $k^2 + 3k$, $k^2 + 4k + 3$, and $2k + 2$ polynomials were used by key generation, encryption, and decryption respectively. Our optimizations were able to reduce this to $k+1$ for all. Therefore, we notice a more considerable reduction for the higher security levels of Kyber.

Kyber v2. With our optimizations applied to the round two versions of Kyber, the cycle counts are comparable to round 1 if not faster. Similarly, stack size reductions are very comparable with the reductions made in round 1. The exception is the key generation procedure which uses $k+2$ polynomials instead of $k+1$ as described in Sect. 4.

---

[4] $2n - 1$ coefficients of 2 bytes each.

Table 2. Cycle counts for all three security levels of Kyber compared to [5]. Link time optimization does benefit Kyber consistently, but our optimizations go far beyond. Kyber v2 is even faster, mainly due to algorithmic changes.

Scheme	Impl.	KeyGen	Encaps	Decaps
		Cycles	Cycles	Cycles
Kyber-512 (v1)	[5]	$666k$	$904k$	$934k$
	lto[a]	$637k$ (-4.3%)	$866k$ (-4.1%)	$881k$ (-5.6%)
	This work	$575k$ (-13.7%)	$763k$ (-15.6%)	$730k$ (-21.8%)
Kyber-512 (v2)	This work	$499k$	$634k$	$597k$
Kyber-768 (v1)	[5]	$1\,098k$	$1\,384k$	$1\,417k$
	lto[a]	$1\,048k$ (-4.6%)	$1\,325k$ (-4.3%)	$1\,339k$ (-5.5%)
	This work	$946k$ (-13.9%)	$1\,167k$ (-15.7%)	$1\,117k$ (-21.1%)
Kyber-768 (v2)	This work	$947k$	$1\,113k$	$1\,059k$
Kyber-1024 (v1)	[5]	$1\,730k$	$2\,083k$	$2\,134k$
	lto[a]	$1\,630k$ (-5.8%)	$1\,970k$ (-5.4%)	$1\,994k$ (-6.6%)
	This work	$1\,483k$ (-14.2%)	$1\,753k$ (-15.8%)	$1\,698k$ (-20.4%)
Kyber-1024 (v2)	This work	$1\,525k$	$1\,732k$	$1\,653k$

[a]Only adding the compiler flag `-flto`.

Table 3. Stack usage for all three security levels of Kyber comparing our optimized implementations to [5]. For our stack-optimized implementation we notice a significant decrease of stack usage across all variants. The stack use of key generation of version 2 is roughly one polynomial (512 bytes) larger than in version 1. This is due to choice of Kyber's authors to represent the public key in the NTT domain.

Scheme	Impl.	KeyGen	Encaps	Decaps
		Bytes	Bytes	Bytes
Kyber-512 (v1)	[5]	$6\,448$	$9\,112$	$9\,920$
	This work	$2\,632$ (-59%)	$2\,672$ (-71%)	$2\,736$ (-72%)
Kyber-512 (v2)	This work	$3\,136$	$2\,720$	$2\,744$
Kyber-768 (v1)	[5]	$10\,544$	$13\,720$	$14\,880$
	This work	$3\,072$ (-71%)	$3\,120$ (-77%)	$3\,176$ (-79%)
Kyber-768 (v2)	This work	$3\,648$	$3\,232$	$3\,248$
Kyber-1024 (v1)	[5]	$15\,664$	$19\,352$	$20\,864$
	This work	$3\,520$ (-78%)	$3\,568$ (-82%)	$3\,624$ (-83%)
Kyber-1024 (v2)	This work	$4\,160$	$3\,752$	$3\,776$

5.3 Profiling

Table 4 contains the profiling information of our implementations for all parameter sets of Kyber v1 and Kyber v2. We observe the following:

Dominance of Hashing. Note that in the original implementation already 54% to 69% of execution time are spent in highly hand-optimized assembly implementation of the Keccak. This limits the speed-ups to be obtained since there is nothing or very little to be gained for this large fraction of the execution time. Our implementations spend the same time in hashing as the previous implementation, but this accounts for 64% to 81% of the total cycle counts. This confirms what previous work concluded [20,29]: Post-quantum key encapsulation schemes are vastly dominated by hashing and having a hardware-accelerated Keccak permutation would speed-up the majority of schemes significantly. Kyber v2 spends significantly less time in Keccak which is due to the change of the

Table 4. Profiling of Kyber before and after applying all our optimizations. The runtime is vastly dominated by hashing. The cycles spent in NTT reduced notably. Only a small portion of the run-time is still spent in non-optimized code.

	Impl.		Total	Keccak		NTT		NTT $^{-1}$	
Kyber-512 (v1)	[5]	K:	666k	453k	(68%)	44k	(7%)	47k	(7%)
		E:	904k	596k	(66%)	87k	(10%)	71k	(8%)
		D:	934k	506k	(54%)	131k	(14%)	95k	(10%)
	This work	K:	575k	453k	(79%)	19k	(3%)	21k	(4%)
		E:	763k	596k	(78%)	38k	(5%)	31k	(4%)
		D:	730k	506k	(69%)	57k	(8%)	42k	(6%)
Kyber-512 (v2)	This work	K:	499k	354k	(71%)	31k	(6%)	0	(0%)
		E:	634k	472k	(74%)	15k	(2%)	28k	(4%)
		D:	597k	381k	(64%)	31k	(5%)	37k	(6%)
Kyber-768 (v1)	[5]	K:	1 098k	754k	(69%)	66k	(6%)	71k	(6%)
		E:	1 384k	922k	(67%)	131k	(9%)	95k	(7%)
		D:	1 417k	794k	(56%)	197k	(14%)	118k	(8%)
	This work	K:	946k	754k	(80%)	28k	(3%)	31k	(3%)
		E:	1 167k	922k	(79%)	57k	(5%)	42k	(4%)
		D:	1 117k	794k	(71%)	85k	(8%)	52k	(5%)
Kyber-768 (v2)	This work	K:	947k	680k	(72%)	46k	(5%)	0	(0%)
		E:	1 113k	836k	(75%)	23k	(2%)	37k	(3%)
		D:	1 059k	708k	(67%)	46k	(4%)	47k	(4%)
Kyber-1024 (v1)	[5]	K:	1 730k	1 197k	(69%)	87k	(5%)	95k	(5%)
		E:	2 083k	1 403k	(67%)	175k	(8%)	118k	(6%)
		D:	2 134k	1 249k	(59%)	262k	(12%)	142k	(7%)
	This work	K:	1 483k	1 197k	(81%)	38k	(3%)	42k	(3%)
		E:	1 753k	1 403k	(80%)	76k	(4%)	52k	(3%)
		D:	1 698k	1 249k	(74%)	113k	(7%)	62k	(4%)
Kyber-1024 (v2)	This work	K:	1 525k	1 112k	(73%)	62k	(4%)	0	(0%)
		E:	1 732k	1 305k	(75%)	31k	(2%)	47k	(3%)
		D:	1 653k	1 139k	(69%)	62k	(4%)	56k	(3%)

Table 5. Performance results of Kyber-768 in comparison to other round two candidates of NISTPQC optimized for the Cortex-M4. Prior to this work the fasted scheme in terms of encapsulation was NTRU-HRSS-KEM, whereas key generation is (still) fastest for Saber. The best memory footprints were achieved by R5ND_3PKEb and the memory optimized variant of Saber. Note that Saber, R5ND_3PKEb, and NTRU-KEM-743 are claiming NIST security level 3, whereas NTRU-HRSS-KEM claims NIST security level 1.

Scheme	Impl.	Runtime		Stack usage	
			Cycles		Bytes
Kyber-768 (v1)	This work	K:	946k	K:	3072
		E:	1167k	E:	3120
		D:	1117k	D:	3176
Kyber-768 (v2)	This work	K:	947k	K:	3648
		E:	1113k	E:	3232
		E:	1059k	E:	3248
Frodo-AES128	[10]	K:	41681k	K:	31116
		E:	45758k	E:	51444
		D:	46720k	D:	61820
Frodo-cSHAKE128	[10]	K:	81300k	K:	26272
		E:	86255k	E:	41472
		D:	87212k	D:	51848
Saber	[20][a]	K:	902k	K:	13248
		E:	1173k	E:	15528
		D:	1217k	D:	16624
	[23][b]	K:	1165k	K:	6931
		E:	1530k	E:	7019
		D:	1635k	D:	8115
R5ND_3PKEb	[29][c]	K:	1032k	K:	6796
		E:	1510k	E:	8908
		D:	1913k	D:	4296
NewHope1024CCA	[4,21][a,d]	K:	1221k	K:	11152
		E:	1902k	E:	17448
		D:	1926k	D:	19648
NTRU-HRSS-KEM	[20][a]	K:	145986k	K:	23396
		E:	406k	E:	19492
		D:	827k	D:	22140
NTRU-KEM-743	[20][a]	K:	5203k	K:	25320
		E:	1603k	E:	23808
		D:	1884k	D:	28472

[a] Re-benchmarked in SRAM1 (see beginning of Sect. 5)
[b] Optimized for stack consumption
[c] Since R5ND_3PKEb does not report any stack usage, we report the numbers from https://github.com/mupq/pqm4/pull/16
[d] NTT assembly implementation from [4] with reference implementation in pqm4 [21]

parameters q and η. Both allow for a more efficient sampling routine that uses less SHAKE output and, thus, less Keccak permutations.

NTT. Prior to our optimizations 10% to 24% were spent in the NTT and NTT^{-1}. We speed-up those parts of the code by more than a factor of two and, consequently, they only account for 5% to 14% of the cycles in our optimized implementations.

5.4   Comparison to Other PQC Schemes on Cortex-M4

Compared to other implementations of NIST PQC KEM candidates on the ARM Cortex-M4 (Table 5), our Kyber implementation has both the smallest memory footprint and lowest cycle count for the sum of key generation, encapsulation and decapsulation. Both our stack-optimized implementations of Kyber-768 outperform all other implementations by large margins in terms of stack usage. We also note a performance gap between the fastest implementation of Saber, reported in [20], and the stack-optimized implementation [23], whereas our implementations do not suffer any slow-down due to our stack optimizations.

Acknowledgments. The authors would like to thank Pedro Massolino, Joost Rijneveld, and Ko Stoffelen for their help with obtaining reasonable cycle counts on the ARM Cortex-M4.

References

1. Alagic, G., et al.: Status report on the first round of the NIST post-quantum cryptography standardization process. National Institute of Standards and Technology Internal Report 8240 (2019). https://doi.org/10.6028/NIST.IR.8240
2. Alkim, E., et al.: NewHope: algorithm specification and supporting documentation. Submission to the NIST Post-Quantum Cryptography Standardization Project (2017). https://cryptojedi.org/papers/#newhopenist
3. Alkim, E., Ducas, L., Pöppelmann, T., Schwabe, P.: Post-quantum key exchange – a new hope. In: Holz, T., Savage, S. (eds.) Proceedings of the 25th USENIX Security Symposium. USENIX Association (2016). https://eprint.iacr.org/2015/1092
4. Alkim, E., Jakubeit, P., Schwabe, P.: NEWHOPE on ARM cortex-M. In: Carlet, C., Hasan, M.A., Saraswat, V. (eds.) SPACE 2016. LNCS, vol. 10076, pp. 332–349. Springer, Cham (2016). https://doi.org/10.1007/978-3-319-49445-6_19. http://cryptojedi.org/papers/#newhopearm
5. Avanzi, R., et al.: ARM Cortex-M4 optimized implementation of Kyber. https://github.com/pq-crystals/kyber/tree/cm4/cm4. Accessed 07 Mar 2019
6. Avanzi, R., et al.: CRYSTALS-Kyber: algorithm specification and supporting documentation. Submission to the NIST Post-Quantum Cryptography Standardization Project (2017). https://pq-crystals.org/kyber
7. Avanzi, R., et al.: CRYSTALS-Kyber: algorithm specification and supporting documentation (version 2.0). Submission to the NIST Post-Quantum Cryptography Standardization Project (2019). https://pq-crystals.org/kyber

8. Bertoni, G., Daemen, J., Peeters, M., Assche, G.V.: The Keccak reference. Submission to the NIST SHA-3 competition (round 3) (2011). https://keccak.team/files/Keccak-reference-3.0.pdf

9. Bos, J.W., et al.: CRYSTALS – kyber: A cca-secure module-lattice-based KEM. In: 2018 IEEE European Symposium on Security and Privacy (EuroS&P), pp. 353–367. IEEE (2018). https://eprint.iacr.org/2017/634

10. Bos, J.W., Friedberger, S., Martinoli, M., Oswald, E., Stam, M.: Fly, you fool! Faster Frodo for the ARM Cortex-M4. Cryptology ePrint Archive, Report 2018/1116 (2018). https://eprint.iacr.org/2018/1116

11. de Clercq, R., Roy, S.S., Vercauteren, F., Verbauwhede, I.: Efficient software implementation of ring-LWE encryption. In: Design, Automation & Test in Europe Conference & Exhibition, DATE 2015, pp. 339–344. EDA Consortium (2015). http://eprint.iacr.org/2014/725

12. Cook, S.: On the Minimum Computation Time of Functions. Ph.D. thesis, Harvard University (1966)

13. Cooley, J.W., Tukey, J.W.: An algorithm for the machine calculation of complex fourier series. Math. Comput. **19**(90), 297–301 (1965). https://www.jstor.org/stable/2003354

14. Daemen, J., Hoffert, S., Peeters, M., Assche, G.V., Keer, R.V.: eXtended Keccak Code Package. https://github.com/XKCP/XKCP. Accessed 07 Mar 2019

15. Fujisaki, E., Okamoto, T.: Secure integration of asymmetric and symmetric encryption schemes. In: Wiener, M. (ed.) CRYPTO 1999. LNCS, vol. 1666, pp. 537–554. Springer, Heidelberg (1999). https://doi.org/10.1007/3-540-48405-1_34

16. Goldstine, H.H.: A History of Numerical Analysis from the 16th through the 19th Century. Springer, New York (1977). https://doi.org/10.1007/978-1-4684-9472-3

17. Güneysu, T., Oder, T., Pöppelmann, T., Schwabe, P.: Software speed records for lattice-based signatures. In: Gaborit, P. (ed.) PQCrypto 2013. LNCS, vol. 7932, pp. 67–82. Springer, Heidelberg (2013). https://doi.org/10.1007/978-3-642-38616-9_5. Document ID: d67aa537a6de60813845a45505c313, http://cryptojedi.org/papers/#lattisigns

18. Heideman, M.T., Johnson, D.H., Burrus, C.S.: Gauss and the history of the fast fourier transform. IEEE ASSP Mag. **1**(4) (1984). http://www.cis.rit.edu/class/simg716/Gauss_History_FFT.pdf

19. Hülsing, A., Rijneveld, J., Schanck, J.M., Schwabe, P.: NTRU-KEM-HRSS: algorithm specification and supporting documentation. Submission to the NIST Post-Quantum Cryptography Standardization Project (2017). https://ntru-hrss.org

20. Kannwischer, M.J., Rijneveld, J., Schwabe, P.: Faster multiplication in $\mathbb{Z}_{2^m}[x]$ on Cortex-M4 to speed up NIST PQC candidates (2018). https://eprint.iacr.org/2018/1018

21. Kannwischer, M.J., Rijneveld, J., Schwabe, P., Stoffelen, K.: PQM4: post-quantum crypto library for the ARM Cortex-M4. https://github.com/mupq/pqm4. Accessed 07 Mar 2019

22. Karatsuba, A., Ofman, Y.: Multiplication of multidigit numbers on automata. Sov. Phys. Dokl. **7**, 595–596 (1963). Translated from Doklady Akademii Nauk SSSR, vol. 145, no. 2, pp. 293–294, July 1962. Scanned version on http://cr.yp.to/bib/1963/karatsuba.html

23. Karmakar, A., Mera, J.M.B., Roy, S.S., Verbauwhede, I.: Saber on ARM CCA-secure module lattice-based key encapsulation on ARM. IACR Trans. Cryptogr. Hardw. Embed. Syst. **2018**(3), 243–266 (2018). https://eprint.iacr.org/2018/682

24. Lyubashevsky, V., Seiler, G.: NTTRU: Truly fast NTRU using NTT. Cryptology ePrint Archive, Report 2019/040 (2019). https://eprint.iacr.org/2019/040

25. Montgomery, P.L.: Modular multiplication without trial division. Math. Comput. **44**(170), 519–521 (1985). http://www.ams.org/journals/mcom/1985-44-170/S0025-5718-1985-0777282-X/S0025-5718-1985-0777282-X.pdf

26. National Institute for Standards and Technology: Submission requirements and evaluation criteria for the post-quantum cryptography standardization process (2017). https://csrc.nist.gov/csrc/media/projects/post-quantum-cryptography/documents/call-for-proposals-final-dec-2016.pdf

27. Oder, T., Pöppelmann, T., Güneysu, T.: Beyond ECDSA and RSA: lattice-based digital signatures on constrained devices. In: 2014 51st ACM/EDAC/IEEE Design Automation Conference (DAC), pp. 1–6. ACM (2014). https://www.sha.rub.de/media/attachments/files/2014/06/bliss_arm.pdf

28. Pöppelmann, T., Oder, T., Güneysu, T.: High-performance ideal lattice-based cryptography on 8-bit ATxmega microcontrollers. In: Lauter, K., Rodríguez-Henríquez, F. (eds.) LATINCRYPT 2015. LNCS, vol. 9230, pp. 346–365. Springer, Cham (2015). https://doi.org/10.1007/978-3-319-22174-8_19. Extended version, https://eprint.iacr.org/2015/382

29. Saarinen, M.J.O., Bhattacharya, S., Garcia-Morchon, O., Rietman, R., Tolhuizen, L., Zhang, Z.: Shorter messages and faster post-quantum encryption with Round5 on Cortex M. Cryptology ePrint Archive, Report 2018/723 (2018). https://eprint.iacr.org/2018/723

30. Seiler, G.: Faster AVX2 optimized NTT multiplication for Ring-LWE lattice cryptography. Cryptology ePrint Archive, Report 2018/039 (2018). https://eprint.iacr.org/2018/039

31. Reference manual for STM32F405/415, STM32F407/417, STM32F427/437, and STM32F429/439 advanced ARM-based 32-bit MCUs (2019). https://www.st.com/resource/en/reference_manual/dm00031020.pdf

32. Toom, A.L.: The complexity of a scheme of functional elements realizing the multiplication of integers. Sov. Math. Dokl. **3**, 714–716 (1963). www.de.ufpe.br/~toom/my-articles/engmat/MULT-E.PDF

33. Zhang, Z., Chen, C., Hoffstein, J., Whyte, W.: NTRUEncrypt: algorithm specification and supporting documentation. Submission to the NIST Post-Quantum Cryptography Standardization Project (2017). https://csrc.nist.gov/projects/post-quantum-cryptography/round-1-submissions

Reducing the Cost of Authenticity with Leakages: a CIML2-Secure AE Scheme with One Call to a Strongly Protected Tweakable Block Cipher

Francesco Berti[✉], Olivier Pereira, and François-Xavier Standaert

ICTEAM/ELEN/Crypto Group, Université catholique de Louvain,
B-1348, Louvain-la-Neuve, Belgium
{francesco.berti,olivier.pereira,fstandae}@uclouvain.be

Abstract. This paper presents CONCRETE (*Commit − Encrypt − Send − the − Key*) a new Authenticated Encryption mode that offers CIML2 security, that is, ciphertext integrity in the presence of nonce misuse and side-channel leakages in both encryption and decryption.

CONCRETE improves on a recent line of works aiming at *leveled implementations*, which mix a strongly protected and energy demanding implementation of a single component, and other weakly protected and much cheaper components. Here, these components all implement a tweakable block cipher TBC.

CONCRETE requires the use of the strongly protected TBC only once while supporting the leakage of the full state of the weakly protected components – it achieves CIML2 security in the so-called *unbounded leakage model*.

All previous works need to use the strongly protected implementation at least twice. As a result, for short messages whose encryption and decryption energy costs are dominated by the strongly protected component, we halve the cost of a leakage-resilient implementation. CONCRETE additionally provides security when unverified plaintexts are released, and confidentiality in the presence of simulatable leakages in encryption and decryption.

Keywords: Leakage-resilience · Authenticated encryption · Leveled implementation · Ciphertext integrity with misuse and leakage (CIML2)

1   Introduction

Authenticated encryption (AE) provides in a single scheme both confidentiality and authenticity. Nowadays AE is a standard primitive [8, 26] (e.g., it is the only one accepted in TLS 1.3 [23]). Although these schemes are deemed secure in the black box model (that is, when adversaries have access only to the inputs and

© Springer Nature Switzerland AG 2019
J. Buchmann et al. (Eds.): AFRICACRYPT 2019, LNCS 11627, pp. 229–249, 2019.
https://doi.org/10.1007/978-3-030-23696-0_12

outputs), they may not be secure when implemented, because their implementation secrets leak via side-channels. For example, the computation time, the power consumption, or the electromagnetic radiation of an implementation may reveal information about its manipulated secrets [1,27,29–31]. These attacks have a broad applicability, especially in contexts where cryptographic implementations can be under adversarial control (e.g., in IoT applications). As a result, various types of countermeasures have been introduced in the literature.

A first approach is to embed protections directly at the (hardware or software) implementation level. Examples include the addition of noise, masking or hiding: these solutions aim to reduce the information leaked by the implementation, but they are expensive and depend on technological assumptions, which may be hard to enforce [30]. For example, compared to an unprotected implementation, a good masking scheme typically implies factors of overheads ranging from tenths to hundreds, depending on the desired security level [19].

A complementary approach is to design schemes (typically, modes of operation) which are inherently more secure against side-channel attacks (for example, by manipulating the plaintext and the key as little as possible, and by using a key only a few number of times before changing it) [18]. This general idea, which we will denote as the leakage-resilient approach, can be instantiated in two main manners. One option is to rely on underlying primitives (like PRPs, PRFs and hash functions) that are all protected with the same level of security: we will denote this option as *uniform implementations*. Alternatively, one can rely on the very strong (and therefore expensive) protection of the implementations of a few blocks (we will call them leak free implementations for simplicity) and try to minimize their use. Such *leveled implementations* are expected to bring significant performance gains for implementations with high physical security levels as soon as the messages' length is beyond a few blocks [11,32].

We insist that despite no implementation is perfectly leak free in practice, we support this concept because (i) we may have reasonable instantiations of close to leak free components by using very high-order masking [24], (ii) this approach anyway indicates hardware designers where their efforts should be concentrated for security against side-channel attacks, and (iii) we may hope for more graceful degradations in the future, which is an interesting scope for further research.

We note also that although leakage affects the two goals of *leakage-resilient authenticated encryption* (LRAE) (i.e., confidentiality and authenticity), this paper is focused on authenticity (for privacy we reuse previous works [11,32]). Based on this premise, we aim to achieve CIML2, that is, *Ciphertext Integrity with coin Misuse and Leakage in encryption and decryption*, in the *unbounded leakage model*.

CIML2, introduced by Berti et al. [13], assumes that the adversary receives the leakage of every encryption and decryption query he does. Moreover, the adversary has taken control of the random source used by the AE scheme. In the *unbounded leakage model*, everything computed by the scheme is leaked apart from the key used in the leak free primitive (that is, all inputs and outputs of every primitive and all the keys used by non leak free components).

In particular, this implies that, to have CIML2 in this model, the correct authentication tag *cannot* be recomputed during decryption, because, otherwise, it would be leaked [11,13]. As a result, most standard AE modes do not achieve CIML2 in this model. By now, all modes achieving CIML2 use at least 2 calls to the leak free primitive per encryption or decryption query [10,13,20]. Therefore, if c_{LF} is the cost of a call to a leak free primitive which, in our case, is a tweakable block cipher, c_{wp} is the cost of a call to a weakly protected primitive which, in our case, is a block cipher with the same block size, the best cost to process an l-block message is $2c_{LF} + 4lc_{wp}$ [10] (since all modes uses a hash function, to do a fair comparison, we suppose that it is always done according to the Hirose construction, which cost 2 calls per block [22]). Typically, c_{LF} will be within the range of tens or hundred times c_{wp}. For short messages, this cost is dominated by the cost of the leak free primitive. Our goal in this paper is to improve results on this front in order to extend the benefits of leveled implementations to shorter message lengths. For this purpose, we reduce the number of calls to the leak free block to one. We also design a mode that allows the Release of Unverified Plaintexts (RUP), which is a convenient feature for devices with little secure memory (see for example the discussions in [2,3,5]).

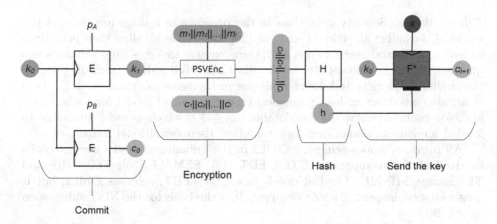

Fig. 1. The scheme CONCRETE *Commit − Encrypt − Send − the − Key*. We use red for long term secrets, orange for ephemeral ones and green for outputs. The gray shadowed primitive, F^*, is the leak free one. The key k_0 is randomly picked. It uses the PSV encryption scheme [32], described in Sect. 3. For decryption, first k_0 is recomputed $k_0 = F_k^{*,-1}(h, c_{l+1})$, then c_0 is recomputed and checked. From k_0 decryption proceeds in the natural way. p_A and p_B are two n-bit constants, with $p_A \neq p_B$.

Our Contribution. We provide a new mode of operation which is CIML2-secure and uses only one leak free call per execution in both encryption and decryption: CONCRETE (for COmmit-eNCRypt-sEnd-The-kEy), see Fig. 1. The cost for l-block message is $c_{LF} + 4(l + 1)c_{wp}$. Thus, compared to [10], we approximately halve the cost when the message is short and the leak free component is much more expensive than the weakly protected primitive. Previous modes proceed by deriving an ephemeral key from the long term key and a leak free component, and use that ephemeral key to encrypt the message. Our main idea is to avoid this key derivation step and to encrypt the message with a fresh random key k_0, obtaining $c_1, ..., c_l$. That key k_0 is then encrypted with the long term key, obtaining c_{l+1} so that it can be recovered by the receiver. To provide authenticity, first we put a commitment of k_0, c_0, then, we make c_{l+1} depend on all $c_1, ..., c_l$ and c_0. Thus, k_0 may be seen as the IV of the mode which is kept secret. The idea to put the IV secret is already present in [11], while Bellare [6] realises that encrypting the nonce (an IV which is not picked randomly, but only not repeated) improves the security of a scheme and prevents some protocol attacks. As the previous modes achieving CIML2 (for example [13]), the leak free primitive is a strong tweakable pseudorandom permutation (STPRP), which is inverted during the decryption. CONCRETE is the first AE scheme achieving CIML2 in the unbounded leakage model without using a range-oriented preimage-resistant hash function.

In addition, our mode is an AE scheme which is secure even when unverified plaintexts are released (i.e., it is a RUPAE) and it provides privacy in the presence of leakage (i.e., CPAL and CCAL [20]).

Related Works. Security definitions in the presence of leakage are given in the works of Barwell et al. [4] and Guo et al. [20]. Barwell et al. allow their primitives to leak in a limited manner (precisely, they exclude leakages from the challenge queries). The definitions of Guo et al. rather allow full leakage (including during the challenge queries) and nonce-resilience in the sense of Ashur et al. [3]. Guo et al. also use different leakage models (the unbounded model for authenticity and, for confidentiality, the simulatable one [33]), which is more amenable to leveled implementations. Therefore, we follow their definitional framework.

All previous modes achieving CIML2 in the unbounded model uses two calls to the leak free component: DTE2, EDT [13], FEMALE [20], TEDT [10] and TETSponge/S1P [21]. The last one is based on TEDT, achieves CIML2, but it uses a sponge, instead of PSV to encrypt. It is the basis for the NIST submission Spook [9].

Dobraunig et al. [16] and Bertoni et al. [15] propose two LRAE designs based on a sponge construction. Although their solutions are interesting and elegant, both lack a detailed analysis of the leakage-resilient properties (the recent works [17,21] do steps in this direction). Moreover, CIML2 in the unbounded model seems unachievable with a construction based only on sponges, since it seems impossible not to recompute the tag during decryption (differently from what it is done in all CIML2 secure modes).

Finally, Barwell et al. [4] also propose an LRAE mode which supports strong composability results, but contrary to the previous ones, it is based on an uniform implementation, protecting everything in the same way. In practice, their concrete instances requires evaluating a pairing for each message block.

Structure of the Paper. We review in Sect. 2, the main definitions and notations used in the paper. Then, in Sect. 3 we present the specifications for our mode and the structure of previous constructions. After that, we present the rationale of the design of CONCRETE. The security statements of CIML2, AE, RUPAE, CPAL2 and CCAL2 security conclude the paper. Due to space constraints, only the sketchs of these proofs are provided.

In the extended version [14], the complete proofs can be found with all the details. Moreover, an extended background, a detailed analysis of previous works and the extension to associated data can be found.

2 Background

Notations. We use $(q_1, ..., q_d, t)$- bounded adversaries, who have access to the oracles $\mathcal{O}_1, ..., \mathcal{O}_d$, can make at most q_i queries to oracle $\mathcal{O}_i$ and who runs in time bounded by t. If $\mathcal{O}$ is an oracle, $\mathcal{O}L$ is its leaking variant.

Given a string x, we denote with $|x|$ its length. With $\{0,1\}^n$ we denote the set of all n bits long strings, with $\{0,1\}^{\leq n}$ (resp. $\{0,1\}^*$) the set of all at most n bits long strings (resp. all finite strings) (that is, $\{0,1\}^{\leq n} = \overset{n}{\underset{i=1}{\cup}} \{0,1\}^i$ [resp. $\{0,1\}^* = \overset{\infty}{\underset{i=1}{\cup}} \{0,1\}^i$]). 0^n denotes the n zero string.

$x \overset{\$}{\leftarrow} \mathcal{X}$ denotes that the element x is picked uniformly at random from the set $\mathcal{X}$.

Given a probabilistic algorithm Alg, we call the support of Alg(x) the set
$\mathsf{supp}(\mathsf{Alg}(x)) := \{y \in \{0,1\}^* \text{ s.t. } \Pr[\mathsf{Alg}(x) = y] > 0\}$, that is, the set of the possible outputs y from an input x.

A value is *fresh* if it has never appeared before in the history of the game.

2.1 Primitives: Hash Functions, PRFs and STPRPs

A *hash function* is a mapping $\mathsf{H} : \mathcal{S} \times \mathcal{M}' \longmapsto \mathcal{B}$. We suppose that hash functions are (t, ϵ)-*collision resistant*: any t-bounded adversary has a probability at most ϵ to produce a collision, that is, given the key s, which is randomly picked, of the hash function, to output distinct $m_0, m_1 \in \mathcal{M}'$ s.t. $\mathsf{H}_s(m_0) = \mathsf{H}_s(m_1)$. From now on, since the adversary knows the key of the hash functions, we omit the key s. Thus, for simplicity we refer to the hash function H_s as H. To simplify cost comparison, we assume that the hash is implemented with the Hirose construction [22], costing 2 block cipher calls per n-bit message block processed.

A (q, t, ϵ)-*pseudorandom function* (PRF) is a mapping $\mathsf{E} : \mathcal{K} \times \mathcal{M} \longmapsto \mathcal{T}$ s.t. there is no (q, t)-adversary able to distinguish with probability better than ϵ whether he is interacting with an $\mathsf{E}_k(\cdot)$ oracle, for a random key k, or with a random function $\mathsf{f}(\cdot)$ with the same signature as $\mathsf{E}_k(\cdot)$.

A (q, t, ϵ)- *strong tweakable pseudorandom permutation* (STPRP) is a mapping $\mathsf{F} : \mathcal{K} \times \mathcal{TW} \times \mathcal{M} \longmapsto \mathcal{T}$ s.t. $\forall (k, tw) \in \mathcal{K} \times \mathcal{TW}$, $\mathsf{F}_k^{tw}(\cdot)$ is a permutation and there is no (q, t)-adversary able to distinguish with probability better than ϵ, if he is interacting with $\mathsf{F}_k(\cdot, \cdot)$ and $\mathsf{F}_k^{-1}(\cdot, \cdot)$ for a random key k or with a random tweakable permutation $\mathsf{f}(\cdot, \cdot)$ (that is, for every tw, $\mathsf{f}(tw, \cdot)$ is an independent random permuation) and its inverse $\mathsf{f}^{-1}(\cdot, \cdot)$, with the same signature as $\mathsf{F}_k(\cdot, \cdot)$ [28].

2.2 Authenticated Encryption (AE)

For authenticated encryption (AE) schemes we use the syntax introduced in Katz and Lindell [25] and also used in many works about AE, e.g., [7,26].

Definition 1. *An* authenticated encryption scheme AE *is a triple of algorithms* $\Pi = (\mathcal{K}, \mathsf{Enc}, \mathsf{Dec})$ *s.t. the keyspace* $\mathcal{K}$ *is a nonempty set, the encryption algorithm* Enc *is a probabilistic algorithm which takes as input the tuple* $(k, m) \in \mathcal{K} \times \mathcal{ME}$ *and outputs a string* $c \leftarrow \mathsf{Enc}_k(m)$. *The decryption algorithm* Dec *is a deterministic algorithm which takes as input the tuple* $(k, c) \in \mathcal{K} \times \mathcal{C}$ *and outputs a string* $m \leftarrow \mathsf{Dec}_k(c)$ *which is either a string in* $\mathcal{ME}$ *or the symbol* "$\perp$ '" *(invalid).*

We require that the algorithms Enc *and* Dec *are the inverse of each other, asking the correctness* $(\forall m, k : m = \mathsf{Dec}_k(\mathsf{Enc}_k(m)))$ *and tidiness (if* $m = \mathsf{Dec}_k(c)$ *and* $m \neq \perp$ *then* $c \in \mathrm{supp}(\mathsf{Enc}_k(m)))$ *property. If* $m \leftarrow \mathsf{Dec}_k(c)$ *with* $m \neq \perp$ *we say that* c *is* valid, *otherwise it is* invalid.

We suppose that, to be probabilistic, Enc has internally access to a random source (for example, a (pseudo)random generator).

2.3 Security for Authenticated Encryption

The security guarantee that we expect from AE schemes is the following:

Definition 2. *An authenticated encryption* AE *scheme* $\Pi = (\mathcal{K}, \mathsf{Enc}, \mathsf{Dec})$ *is* (q_E, q_D, t, ϵ)-AE *secure if the following advantage is bounded by* ϵ:

$$\mathsf{Adv}_{\Pi, \mathsf{A}}^{\mathsf{AE}} := \left| \Pr\left[\mathsf{A}^{\mathsf{Enc}_k(\cdot), \mathsf{Dec}_k(\cdot)} \Rightarrow 1 \right] - \Pr\left[\mathsf{A}^{\$(\cdot), \perp(\cdot)} \Rightarrow 1 \right] \right| \leq \epsilon$$

for any (q_E, q_D, t)-adversary A, *where the key* k *is picked uniformly at random, the algorithm* $\$(m)$ *answers a random string of length* $|c|$ *with* $c \leftarrow \mathsf{Enc}_k(m)$, *and* $\perp(\cdot)$ *is an algorithm which answers always* $\perp$ *("invalid"). The adversary* A *may ask* q_E *encryption queries (to the left oracle) and* q_D *decryption queries (to the right oracle). If he receives* c *as an answer of the first oracle, [that is,* $c \leftarrow \mathsf{Enc}_k(m)$ *(or* $c \leftarrow \$(m)$*)], he is not allowed to query the second oracle on input* c.

This property provides both confidentiality and authenticity in the absence of leakages.

2.4 Ciphertext Integrity with Misuse and Leakage in Encryption and Decryption (CIML2)

Berti et al. [13] introduced the notion of ciphertext integrity with misuse and leakage in encryption and decryption (CIML2). Originally intended for nAE schemes, we adjust it to the syntax introduced in Definition 1.

A specific point here is that we require protection against corrupted sources of randomness used by the encryption oracle, hence offering a guarantee of randomness misuse resistance. To this purpose, in the definition below, we suppose that the adversary has control of the source of randomness used by Enc. In effect, in the game below, the adversary chooses and provides the randomness to the encryption oracle, which is now deterministic.

Definition 3. *An authenticated encryption (AE) scheme $\Pi = (\mathcal{K}, \mathsf{Enc}, \mathsf{Dec})$ is (q_E, q_D, t, ϵ)-ciphertext integrity with misuse and leakage in encryption and decryption (CIML2)-secure if, for every (q_E, q_D, t)-bounded adversary controlling the randomness used in the encryption process by the EncL oracle, we have*

$$\Pr\left[\mathsf{A}^{\mathsf{EncL}(\cdot), \mathsf{DecL}(\cdot)} \Rightarrow c^* \ s.t. \ c^* \ is \ fresh \ and \ valid \right] \leq \epsilon$$

(c^* fresh means that it was not previously returned by the EncL oracle)

Without leakage, it is mostly irrelevant if the adversary has or not has access to the decryption oracle [12,25]. This is not the case in the presence of leakage [11].

Leakage Model: The Unbounded Model. The definition above has leaking encryption and decryption oracles. We obviously need to define some limitations on what those leaking oracles leak.

We use a liberal model of leakages that seeks implementations with two levels of component protection. Our leakage model then distinguishes between:

- a strongly protected STPRP F^*, of which we make minimal use, and which we assume to not leak anything about its key, and
- a PRF and a hash function, which we assume to completely leak their internal state.

Following [11], we call this the *unbounded leakage model*.

2.5 Security When Unverified Plaintexts Are Released (RUPAE)

For this section, we follow [5] adapting their definitions to our AE syntax.

First, we observe that many decryption algorithms can be split in two: one part, SDec which decrypts, the other, SVer which verifies the authenticity. This is called *separated syntax* and a *separated* AE-scheme is $\Pi = (\mathcal{K}, \mathsf{Enc}, \mathsf{SDec}, \mathsf{SVer})$.

Now we can define the RUPAE security definition:

Definition 4 ([5]). *A separated* AE *scheme* $\Pi = (\mathcal{K}, \mathsf{Enc}, \mathsf{SDec}, \mathsf{SVer})$ *is* $(q_E,$ $q_D, t, \epsilon)$-RUPAE *secure if for any* (q_E, q_D, t)-*adversary* A *the following advantage*

$$\mathsf{Adv}_{\Pi,\mathsf{A}}^{\mathsf{RUPAE}} := \left| \Pr\left[\mathsf{A}^{\mathsf{Enc}_k(\cdot),\mathsf{SDec}_k(\cdot),\mathsf{SVer}_k(\cdot)} \Rightarrow 1\right] - \Pr\left[\mathsf{A}^{\$_E(\cdot),\$_D,\perp(\cdot)} \Rightarrow 1\right] \right| \leq \epsilon$$

where the key k *is picked uniformly at random, the algorithm* $\$_E(m)$ *answers a random string of length* $|c|$ *with* $c \leftarrow \mathsf{Enc}_k(m)$, *the algorithm* $\$_D(c)$ *outputs a random string of length* $|m|$ *with* $m \leftarrow \mathsf{SDec}_k(c)$ *and* $\perp(\cdot)$ *is an algorithm which answers always* $\perp$ *("invalid"). The adversary* A *is granted to* q_E *encryption query (to the left oracle) and* q_D *decryption query (to the right oracle). If he receives* c *as an answer of the first oracle, that is* $c \leftarrow \mathsf{Enc}_k(m)$ *(or* $c \leftarrow \$(m)$) *he is not allowed to query the second or third oracle on input* c.

A more detailed treatment can be found in [14].

Our focus in this paper is on authenticity. In the [14] of this document, we provide definitions of confidentiality with leakage (CPAL2 and CCAL2).

3   Design Specifications and Previous Solutions

Notations. For the leak free STPRP F^*, the PRF E and the hash function H, we assume $\mathcal{K} = \mathcal{M} = \mathcal{TW} = \mathcal{T} = \mathcal{B} = \{0,1\}^n$, $\mathcal{M}' = \{0,1\}^*$ and $\mathcal{ME} = \{0,1\}^{\leq Ln}$. A n-bit string is a *block*. Given a message m, we parse it in $(m_1, ..., m_l)$ with $|m_1| = ... = |m_{l-1}| = n$ and $1 < |m_l| \leq n$ (we sometimes also call m_l a block, regardless of its length).

The design goals of our proposed mode are as follows:

– AE secure in the black box model,
– CIML2 secure in the unbounded leakage model,
– CPAL and CCAL secure with some hypothesis about the leakage,
– only one call to the leak free component per execution,
– RUPAE (optional).

To reduce the possibility of leakage attacks via DPA (differential power analysis), the PRF E should not be used with more than two different plaintexts for any key. There is such an encryption mode, called PSV (see Sect. 3) [32] and some AE modes [10,11,13,20] (based on PSV which is based on the PRG proposed by Standaert et al. [33], which uses a PRF E and which is based on *rekeying*). The challenge of this PRG-based rekeying process lies in the choice of the first ephemeral key, on which we may repeatedly leak. Usually, LRAE modes based on PSV may be divided in three parts, not necessarily in this order:

1 Generation of the first ephemeral key (for us k_1), using a call to the leak free component;
2 Encryption, using PSV starting from k_1, using weakly/non protected components;
3 Authentication, again using a call to the leak free component.

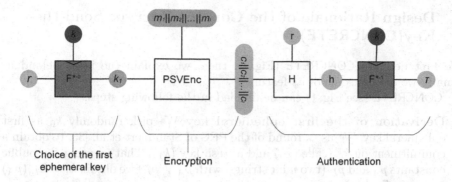

Choice of the first
ephemeral key   Encryption   Authentication

Fig. 2. The CIML2-secure scheme EDT [13] divided in the three parts.

Our goal in this paper is essentially to get rid of the leak free component used in the first part. An example of a construction divided in this three parts, can be found in Fig. 2.

PSV. [32] creates a (pseudo)random stream of block $y_1, ..., y_l$ which is XORed to $m_1, ..., m_l$. From an ephemeral key k_i, a new key $k_{i+1} = \mathsf{E}_{k_i}(p_A)$ and a new stream block $y_i = \mathsf{E}_{k_i}(p_B)$ are obtained. (p_A and p_B are two n bit strings with $p_A \neq p_B$)

A detailed analysis of various modes following this design pattern can be found in [14].

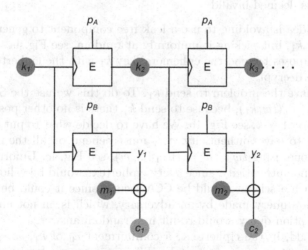

Fig. 3. The PSV encryption algorithm, presented at CCS 2015 by Pereira et al. [32].

4   Design Rationale of the Commit-Encrypt-Send-the-Key(**CONCRETE**)

We first describe CONCRETE (Fig. 1), then, we explain the ideas behind it. Finally we discuss some of its features.

CONCRETE (see Fig. 1) can be divided in the following steps:

- **Derivation of the first ephemeral key** We pick randomly k_0 as first ephemeral key. We use a round of the PRG of Standaert et al. [33] to obtain a commitment on k_0 (called c_0) and a fresh key (k_1). That is, using the public constants p_A and p_B (two n bit strings, with $p_A \neq p_B$) we obtain $k_1 = \mathsf{E}_{k_0}(p_A)$ and $c_0 = \mathsf{E}_{k_0}(p_B)$.
- **Encryption** From k_1 the PSV [32] (see Sect. 3) encryption algorithm is used to encrypt m, using the constants p_A and p_B, obtaining $c_1, ..., c_l$. We denote the algorithm in this part enc.
- **Sending the key** k_0 Since k_0 is picked uniformly at random, it must be recomputed by the decryption algorithm Dec from the ciphertext c. Thus, we send $c_{l+1} = \mathsf{F}_k^*(tw, k_0)$. Now, we need to choose tw.
- **Authenticity** To have it, we use for the tweak tw, the hash of the commitment c_0 and the output of the encryption part $c_1, ..., c_l$ obtaining $tw = h = \mathsf{H}(c_0\|c_1\|...\|c_l)$ and we encrypt k_0 obtaining $c_{l+1} = \mathsf{F}_k^*(h, k_0)$. The ciphertext is $c := (c_0, c_1, ..., c_l, c_{l+1})$.
- **Decryption** First $h = \mathsf{H}(c_0\|...\|c_l)$, then, k_0 is retrieved, with $k_0 = \mathsf{F}_k^{*,-1}(h, c_{l+1})$ and $\tilde{c}_0 = \mathsf{E}_{k_0}(p_B)$ is computed. If $c_0 = \tilde{c}_0$, the ciphertext is deemed valid and decryption proceeds in the natural way; otherwise, the ciphertext is deemed invalid.

The main idea is avoiding to use a leak free component to generate the first ephemeral key k_1, but picking it uniformly at random, see Fig. 4a.

But this imposes to send the ephemeral key k_1 with the ciphertext, to allow the receiver to decrypt.

Next, we have the problem to send k_1. To do this we use the STPRP F^* to generate $c_{l+1} = \mathsf{F}_k^*(tw, k_1)$, because to send k_1 there is no other possibility than to use the master key k, see Fig. 4b. We have to decide what to put as tweak tw. Since we want to have authenticity, c_{l+1} must depend on all the other blocks. This can be done using $tw = h' = \mathsf{H}(c_1\|...\|c_l)$, see Fig. 4c. Unfortunately this solution gives no authenticity, since every ciphertext would be valid. It could be argued that such a scheme would be CCA-secure, since it could be proved that every decryption query made by an adversary, which is an not answer from a previous encryption query, would result in a random answer.

Thus, we add, in the ciphertext, a commitment c_0 of k_1, as $c_0 = \mathsf{E}_{k_1}(p_C)$ for a certain constant p_C (p_C must be different from p_B [and p_A], otherwise, the first block of plaintext would be leaked, or k_2). Thus, $h = \mathsf{H}(c_0\|...\|c_l)$ (see Fig. 4d). This scheme is CIML2 secure, when we recompute $\tilde{c}_0$ and check it.

But in this last scheme, k_1 is used three times with three different plaintexts as key of E. Thus, to avoid this, we pick randomly k_0, we compute its commit $c_0 = \mathsf{E}_{k_0}(p_B)$ and we do a rekeying to obtain $k_1 = \mathsf{E}_{k_0}(p_A)$ (see Fig. 4e).

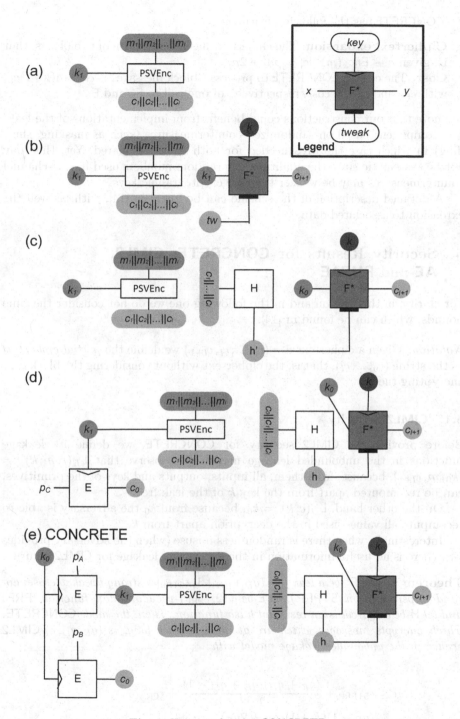

Fig. 4. How we designe CONCRETE.

CONCRETE has the following features:

- **Ciphertext expansion.** The ciphertext has an expansion of two blocks, that is, given $c \leftarrow \mathsf{Enc}_k(m)$, $|c| = |m| + 2n$.
- **Cost.** The cost of CONCRETE to process l block messages is $c_{\mathsf{F}^*} + 4(l+1)c_{\mathsf{E}}$, with c_{F^*} and c_{E} the cost, respectively, of one call to F^* and E.

We note that our constructions could benefit from implementations of the leak-free component based on randomized countermeasures (such as masking, shuffling) in which case the PRG needed for both could be shared. Yet, this may not be systematic since the quality of the random numbers used in side-channel countermeasures may be weaker than for cryptographic keys.

A detailed description of the scheme can be found in [14], with, as well the extension to associated data.

5 Security Results for CONCRETE: CIML2, AE and RUPAE

For clarity, in this section and in the following one we do not consider the time bounds, which can be found in [14].

Notation. Given a ciphertext $c = (c_0, ..., c_l, c_{l+1})$ we define the *partial ciphertext* as the string $(c_0, ..., c_l)$, that is, the ciphertext without considering the block c_{l+1} encrypting the key.

5.1 CIML2 Security

Before proving the CIML2 security for CONCRETE, we define its leakage functions in the unbounded leakage model. We observe that $\mathsf{L}_E(r, m; k) := (k_0, m, c_{l+1})$, because, from them, all inputs, outputs and keys of the primitives, can be recomputed apart from the key k of the leak free F^*.

On the other hand, $\mathsf{L}_D(c; k) := k_0$, because from k_0 the adversary is able to recompute all values used in the decryption apart from k.

Interestingly, when there is randomness misuse (when the adversary provides k_0), there is no useful information in the encryption leakage for CIML2 security.

Theorem 1. *Let F^* be a leak free $(q_D + q_E + 1, \epsilon_{\mathsf{STPRP}})$-strong tweakable pseudorandom permutation (STPRP), let E be a $(2, \epsilon_{\mathsf{PRF}})$-pseudorandom function (PRF) and let H be a ϵ_{CR}-collision resistant hash function. Then, the mode CONCRETE, which encrypts messages which are at most L-block long, is (q_E, q_D, ϵ)-CIML2 secure in the unbounded leakage model with*

$$\epsilon \leq \epsilon_{\mathsf{STPRP}} + \frac{(q_E + q_D)(q_E + q_D - 1)}{2^{n+1}} + \epsilon_{\mathsf{CR}}$$

$$+ \frac{(q_D + 1)(L + 1)(q_D + 2q_E)}{2^{n+1}} + \frac{q_D + 1}{2^n} + (q_D + 1)\epsilon_{\mathsf{PRF}}.$$

Observation on the Bound. We want to discuss some terms of the bound:

- $\epsilon_{\mathsf{STPRP}} + \frac{(q_E+q_D)(q_E+q_D-1)}{2^{n+1}}$ because F^* is a STPRP and not a PRF.
- ϵ_{CR} because, if there is a collision, the mode is trivially broken: given $c_0 = \mathsf{E}_{k_0}(p_B)$ if there is a collision $((c_0, c_1, ..., c_l), (c_0, c'_1, ..., c'_l))$ we observe that $c_{l+1} = c'_{l+1}$ if they both encrypt k_0,
- $(q_D + 1)\epsilon_{\mathsf{PRF}}$, because we do not check k_0, but $\mathsf{E}_{k_0}(p_B)$.[1]
- $\frac{(q_D+1)(L+1)(q_D+2q_E)}{2^{n+1}}$ because we need that, in every decryption query, k_0 must have never been used before as ephemeral key; otherwise, c_0 would not be random anymore. It may be improved to $\frac{(q_D+1)(q_D+2q_E)}{2^{n+1}}$ if E is not used in PSV, [for example, we may use a different PRF, but this choice would require one more primitive to be implemented].

Proof (Sketch). In the proof, first, we replace F^* with a random tweakable permutation, then, we suppose that all the hash outputs are different (provided that their inputs are different). For fresh decryption queries, on input $c = (c_0, c_1, ..., c_l, c_{l+1})$ we observe the following:

1. If the partial ciphertext $(c_0, ..., c_l)$ is fresh, then, its hash h is fresh. Thus, k_0 is random. Consequently, the probability that $c_0 = \mathsf{E}_{k_0}(p_B)$ is $\leq \epsilon_{\mathsf{PRF}}$.
2. If the partial ciphertext $(c_0, ..., c_l)$ is not fresh and comes from an encryption query, then, the couple $((c_0, ..., c_l), c_{l+1})$ must be fresh; otherwise, either the decryption query is not fresh [not possible by hypothesis] or it is the repetition of a previous decryption query [so, its validity has already been established]. Thus, $k_0 = \mathsf{F}_k^{*,-1}(h, c_{l+1})$ is still random. Then, again, the probability that $c_0 = \mathsf{E}_{k_0}(p_B)$ is $\leq \epsilon_{\mathsf{PRF}}$.

To prove that $\Pr[c_0 = \mathsf{E}_{k_0}(p_B)]$ is negligible, we use that E is a PRF, thus, we must assume that k_0 is fresh.

The complete proof can be found in [14] as well with the theorem with the time bounds (Thm. 6).

5.2 AE Security

After having proved the authenticity, we want to prove the confidentiality, which is based on the security of the PSV encryption scheme. We start studying confidentiality in the blackbox model:

Theorem 2. *Let F^* be a $(q_D + q_E, \epsilon_{\mathsf{STPRP}})$-strong tweakable pseudorandom permutation (STPRP), let E be a $(2, \epsilon_{\mathsf{PRF}})$-pseudorandom function (PRF) and let H be a ϵ_{CR}-collision resistant hash function. Then, the mode CONCRETE, which encrypts messages which are at most L-block long, is (q_E, q_D, ϵ)-AE secure with*

$$\epsilon \leq \epsilon_{\mathsf{STPRP}} + \epsilon_{\mathsf{CR}} + \frac{q_D(L+1)(q_D-1+2q_E)}{2^{n+1}} + \frac{q_D}{2^n}$$
$$(q_E(L+1) + q_D)\epsilon_{\mathsf{PRF}} + \frac{q_E(L+1)[q_E(L+1)-1]}{2^{n+1}} + \frac{(q_D+q_E)(q_D+q_E-1)}{2^{n+1}}.$$

---

[1] If we had checked k_0 and put it into the ciphertext, i.e., $c_0 = k_0$, we would have obtained a better CIML2 bound, but no AE security.

Observation on the Bound. In addition to the bound due to the $(q_E, q_D - 1)$-CIML2 security[2] (which is the same as for the ciphertext integrity) we have:

- $(q_E(L + 1))\epsilon_{\mathsf{PRF}} + \frac{q_E(L+1)[q_E(L+1)-1]}{2^{n+1}}$ is due to PSV because we want that every ciphertext block is random,
    - in particular, $\frac{q_E(L+1)[q_E(L+1)-1]}{2^{n+1}}$ because we need that, in every encryption query, all keys used by E are different.

Proof (Sketch). First, we note that $c_0, ..., c_l$ can be seen as $(c_0, ..., c_l) = \mathsf{PSV}_{k_0}$ $(0^n\|m)$. After that, we observe that the scheme is ciphertext-integrity secure (since it is CIML2 secure), then, we observe that all the ciphertext blocks can be replaced by random ones since either they are obtained via a STPRP with a different input (c_{l+1}) or via the PSV encryption scheme using a different key k_0 per encryption query.

The theorem with the time bounds (Thm. 7), its proof and a discussion of what happens if PSV is replaced with another scheme can be found in [14].

5.3 The RUPAE Security

Even if unverified plaintexts are released, CONCRETE remains secure:

Theorem 3. *Let* F* *be a* $(Q, \epsilon_{\mathsf{STPRP}})$-*strong tweakable pseudorandom permutation (STPRP), let* E *be a* $(2, \epsilon_{\mathsf{PRF}})$-*pseudorandom function (PRF) and let* H *be a* ϵ_{CR}-*collision resistant hash function. Then, the mode* CONCRETE, *which encrypts at most L-block long messages, is* (q_E, q_D, ϵ)-RUPAE *secure with* $Q = q_E + q_D$ *and* ϵ *bounded by:*

$$\epsilon_{\mathsf{STPRP}} + \epsilon_{\mathsf{CR}} + Q(L+1)\epsilon_{\mathsf{PRF}} + \frac{q_D}{2^n} + \frac{(L+1)Q[(L+1)Q-1]}{2^{n+1}} + \frac{q_E(q_E-1)}{2^{n+1}}.$$

Observation on the Bound. In addition to bounds due to the previous theorems, we have

- $Q(L+1)\epsilon_{\mathsf{PRF}}$ due to PSV, since, if k_1 is random, PSV in decryption outputs a random string,
- $\frac{(L+1)Q[(L+1)Q-1]}{2^{n+1}}$, because we suppose that every ephemeral key used in an encryption or decryption query is different from all the others,
- $\epsilon_{\mathsf{STPRP}} + \frac{q_E(q_E-1)}{2^{n+1}}$ because F* is a STPRP and not a PRF (a part of the bound is in the previous term)

Proof (Sketch). We have already proved the CIML2 (thus, the ciphertext integrity) and the AE security. To prove the RUPAE, it is enough to observe that, for invalid ciphertexts, the k_0 obtained is random. Moreover, from a random k_0, PSV gives a random decryption.

The theorem with the time bounds (Thm. 8), its proof and a discussion of what happens if PSV is replaced with another scheme can be found in [14].

---

[2] Observe that in the AE security definition, there is no more the final decryption query granted in the CIML2 security game.

6   Confidentiality with Leakage of CONCRETE

First, we introduce the leakage assumption we do on E: *simulatability*. Then, we discuss the security with leakage of PSV [32], in particular to what it is reduced to: the eavesdropper security with leakage (EavLDs) of an idealized single round variant of PSV called $PSVs^I$. Finally, we prove the CPAL2 and CCAL2 security of CONCRETE.

6.1   Leakage Model: Simulatability

For confidentiality it is necessary to bound the amount of information leaked by E, since $c_i = y_i \oplus m_i$ with $y_i = E_{k_i}(p_B)$. To do this, we use the *simulatability* assumption: that is, let $y = E_k(x)$, it is possible to create a simulator $\mathcal{S}^L$, which has access only to x and y (not to k) and to the leakage function L. This simulator outputs a simulated leakage $\mathcal{S}(x, y, k')$ for a random k' which should be indistinguishable from the real one $L_E(x; k)$. This is captured by the following definition (Table 1):

Table 1. The q–sim experiment of Standaert et al. [33].

Game q-sim$(A, PRF, L, \mathcal{S}, b)$ [33, Section 2.1].		
The challenger selects two random keys $k, k^* \xleftarrow{\$} \mathcal{K}$. The output of the game is a bit b' computed by A^L based on the challenger responses to a total of at most q adversarial queries of the following type:		
Query	Response if $b = 0$	Response if $b = 1$
$E \setminus \$(x)$	$E_k(x), L(k, x)$	$E_k(x), \mathcal{S}^L(k^*, x, E_k(x))$
and one query of the following type:		
Query	Response if $b = 0$	Response if $b = 1$
Gen-$\mathcal{S}(z, x)$	$\mathcal{S}^L(z, x, k)$	$\mathcal{S}^L(z, x, k^*)$

Definition 5 [*q-simulatable leakages* [33, Def. 1]]. *Let E be a PRF whose implementation has leakage function L. Then E has $(q_{\mathcal{S}}, t_{\mathcal{S}}, q_A, t_A, \epsilon_{q\text{-sim}})$ q-simulatable leakages if there is a $(q_{\mathcal{S}}, t_{\mathcal{S}})$-bounded simulator $\mathcal{S}^L$ such that, for every (q_L, t)-bounded adversary A^L, we have*

$$| \Pr[\text{q-sim}(A, E, L, \mathcal{S}^L, 1) = 1] - \Pr[\text{q-sim}(A, E, L, \mathcal{S}^L, 0) = 1]| \leq \epsilon_{q\text{-sim}}.$$

We observe that A is granted q_L queries to the leakage oracle. This queries are different from the queries done by the challenger. In fact for the queries done by A, he chooses the key and the plaintext, thus, they are intended to profile the leakage of the implementation E.

Moreover, he has access to a special query, the Gen-$\mathcal{S}$, because, since E is used in PSV, which is a scheme based on rekeying, the leakage of a previous round involves also the key used in the following round.

This assumption is useful to reduce the leakage security of the whole PSV encryption scheme to the leakage security of the encryption of a single block.

6.2   Other Leakage Assumptions

In addition, with respect to the PSV model [32], we need some additional hypothesis on the leakage of E and F*. We start giving the reason why we need these additional hypothesis: k_0 has an additional source of leakage; $c_{l+1} := F_k^*(h, k_0)$. Moreover, it is randomly picked and not output by E.

Thus, we need to simulate the leakage also of the STPRP $F_k^*(\cdot, \cdot)$:

Definition 6. *The leak free implementation of the STPRP* $F^*(\cdot, \cdot)$ *has* $(q, q_{\mathcal{S}'},$ $t, t_{\mathcal{S}'})$-*indistinguishable leakage if for any* (q, t) *adversary, there exists a* $(q_{\mathcal{S}'}, t_{\mathcal{S}'})$-*simulator such that the leakage* $\mathsf{L}_{F^*}(x, y; k)$ *of the computation* $z \leftarrow F_k^*(x, y)$ *is indistinguishable from the simulated leakage* $\mathcal{S}_{F^*}^{\mathsf{L}_{F^*}}(x, y, z, k^*)$ *for a random key* k^*.

This hypothesis is given by the leak free assumption. Anyway, it is reasonable to believe that the adversary if he were able distinguish them, he would not be able to use this difference.

Thus, we are able to define the q–sim$'$ experiment, which models the leakage of k_0:

Definition 7 [q-simulatable leakages']. *Let* E *be a PRF having leakage function* L *and let* F* *be a STPRP having* $(q_{\mathcal{S}'}, t_{\mathcal{S}'})$-*indistinguishable leakage (see Definition 6). Then* E *has* $(q_\mathsf{L}, q_\mathcal{S}, q_{\mathcal{S}'}, t, t_\mathcal{S}, t_{\mathcal{S}'}, \epsilon_{\mathsf{q\text{-}sim}})$ *q-simulatable' leakage if there is a* $(q_\mathcal{S}, t_\mathcal{S})$-*bounded simulator* $\mathcal{S}^\mathsf{L}$ *such that, for every* (q_L, t)-*bounded adversary* A^L, *we have*

$$| \Pr[\mathsf{q\text{-}sim}'(\mathsf{A}, \mathsf{E}, \mathsf{L}, \mathcal{S}^\mathsf{L}, 1) = 1] - \Pr[\mathsf{q\text{-}sim}'(\mathsf{A}, \mathsf{E}, \mathsf{L}, \mathcal{S}^\mathsf{L}, 0) = 1]| \leq \epsilon_{\mathsf{q\text{-}sim}}.$$

The q–sim$'$ experiment is the q–sim with the following two modifications:

- first, the Gen-$\mathcal{S}$ query is replaced by the Gen-$\mathcal{S}'$ query which is answered by $\mathsf{L}_\$(k)$ if $b = 0$; otherwise, by $\mathsf{L}_\$(k^*)$.
- second, the adversary is allowed to an additional Key-Send(h) query, which may be asked after having received the answer to the previous queries. If $b = 0$, A receives $\mathcal{S}_{F^*}^{\mathsf{L}_{F^*}}(h, k, k^+, w)$; otherwise $\mathcal{S}_{F^*}^{\mathsf{L}_{F^*}}(h, k^*, k^+, w)$.

This models well the situation for k_0

6.3   The Eavesdropper Security with Leakage (EavLDs) Security of a Single Round Idealized Version of PSV

Similarly to what was done for PSV [32], we reduce the whole security of the scheme to the EavLDs security of an ideal version of PSVs^I, where the PRF $\mathsf{E}_{k_i^j}$

and its leakage are replaced with a random function and the simulated leakage, which encrypts only one block messages (see Table 2).

The EavLDs game (see Table 2) is a game where the adversary chooses two different one block message and receives the encryption and the leakage of one of them, and he has to guess what message has been encrypted. (A scheme is (q_L, t, ϵ)-EavLD secure if the probability a (q_L, t)-adversary correctly guesses the bit b is bounded by $\frac{1}{2} + \epsilon$).

Table 2. The EavLDs experiment and the idealized single block version PSV^I. $\mathcal{S}$ is a simulator for the leakage of the PRF E. Note that k_1 is given as output for composability (see [14]).

The EavLDs game and the idealized variant of PSV which encrypts a single block, PSVs^I	
EavLDs	PSVs^I
Initialization:	Gen^I :
$\quad k_0 \xleftarrow{\$} \mathcal{K}, \ p_A, p_B \in \{0,1\}^n, \ p_A \neq p_B$	$\quad k_0 \xleftarrow{\$} \{0,1\}^n$
$\quad b \xleftarrow{\$} \{0,1\}$	
	$\mathsf{encs}^I_{k_0}(m)$:
	$\quad y \xleftarrow{\$} \{0,1\}^n$
Challenge output:	$\quad c = y \oplus m$
$\quad (m^{*,0}, m^{*,1}) \leftarrow \mathsf{A}^L(p_A, p_B)$	$\quad k_1 \xleftarrow{\$} \{0,1\}^n$
$\quad (c, k_1, \mathsf{L}_{\mathsf{PSVs}^I}) \leftarrow \mathsf{encsL}_{k_0}(m^{*,b})$	$\quad$ Return (c, k_1)
Finalization:	
$\quad b' \leftarrow \mathsf{A}^L(c, k_1, \mathsf{L}_{\mathsf{PSVs}^I})$	$\mathsf{decs}^I_{k_0}(c)$ proceeds in the natural way.
$\quad$ If $|m_0| \neq |m_1| \vee |m_0| \neq n$, Return 0	
$\quad$ If $b = b'$, Return 1, Else, Return 0	
The leakage resulting from $\mathsf{encs}^I(m)$ is defined as $\mathsf{L}_{\mathsf{encs}^I}(m, k_1, y; k_0) :=$ $(\mathcal{S}^L(k_0, p_A, k_1), \mathcal{S}^L(k_0, p_B, y), \mathsf{L}_\oplus(m, y), \mathcal{S}^L(k^-, p_A, k_0), k^-)$ with $k^- \xleftarrow{\$} \{0,1\}^n$.	

For PSV the EavLD security (EavLDs for multiple block messages) is given by the following proposition:

Proposition 1 ([32]). *Let E be a $(2, \epsilon_{\mathsf{PRF}})$-PRF, whose implementation has $(q_L, q_S, \epsilon_{2\text{-sim}})$-2-simulatable leakage then, PSV, if it encrypts at most L block messages, is ϵ-EavLD-secure with $\epsilon \leq L(\epsilon_{\mathsf{PRF}} + \epsilon_{2\text{-sim}} + \epsilon_{\mathsf{EavLDs}})$.*

6.4   CPAL2

Theorem 4. *Let F^* be a leak free $(q_E + 1, \epsilon_{\mathsf{STPRP}})$-STPRP whose implementation has $(q_E + 1, q_{S'})$-indistinguishable leakage, let E be a $(2, \epsilon_{\mathsf{PRF}})$-PRF, whose implementation has $(q_L, q_S, \epsilon_{2\text{-sim}})$-2-simulatable leakage and*

$(q_L, q_S, q_{S'}, \epsilon_{2\text{-sim}'})$-2-simulatable leakage', let PSVs^I be $(q_l, \epsilon_{\mathsf{EavLDs}})$-EavLDs-secure, then, CONCRETE, if it encrypts at most L block messages, is (q_E, ϵ)-CPAL2-secure with

$$\epsilon \leq \epsilon_{\mathsf{STPRP}} + \frac{q_E}{2^n} + \epsilon_{2\text{-sim}'} + (L+1)\epsilon_{\mathsf{PRF}} + L(\epsilon_{2\text{-sim}} + \epsilon_{\mathsf{EavLDs}})$$

About the bound we can observe:

- $L(\epsilon_{2\text{-sim}} + \epsilon_{\mathsf{EavLDs}} + \epsilon_{\mathsf{PRF}})$ is the EavLD-security of PSV [32].

The theorem with the time bounds (Thm. 9) and its proof can be found in [14].

Proof (Sketch). First, we reduce the EavLD security of CONCRETE to the EavLDs security of PSVs^I, using the same argument as Pereira et al. [32] (we have to do a little tweak in their proof to consider the additional leakage source of c_0 and c_{l+1}).

Then, we replace the STPRP F^* with a random function, and we replace its leakage $\mathsf{L}_{\mathsf{F}^*}(\cdot, \cdot; \cdot)$ with the simulated one $\mathcal{S}^{\mathsf{L}_{\mathsf{F}^*}}(\cdot, \cdot, \cdot, \cdot)$; after that, observing that, since, k_0 is randomly picked, the leakage of other encryption queries do not give any more information about the challenge query, we reduce the CPAL2 adversary to an EavLD adversary.

6.5   CCAL2

Moreover, CONCRETE is CCAL2 secure:

Theorem 5. *Let F^* be a leak free $(q_E + q_D + 1, \epsilon_{\mathsf{STPRP}})$-STPRP whose implementation has $(q_E + 1, q_{S'})$-indistinguishable leakage, let E be a $(2, \epsilon_{\mathsf{PRF}})$-PRF, whose implementation has $(q_L, q_S, \epsilon_{2\text{-sim}})$-2-simulatable leakage and $(q_L, q_S, q_{S'}, \epsilon_{2\text{-sim}'})$-2-simulatable leakage', let H be a ϵ_{CR}-collision resistant hash function, let PSVs^I be $(q_L, \epsilon_{\mathsf{EavLDs}})$-EavLD-secure, then, CONCRETE, if encrypts at most L block messages, is (q_E, q_D, ϵ)-CCAL2-secure with*

$$\epsilon \leq \epsilon_{\mathsf{STPRP}} + \epsilon_{\mathsf{CR}} + \frac{q_E + q_D}{2^n} + \frac{q_D(L+1)(q_D + 2q_E)}{2^{n+1}} +$$

$$(q_D + L + 1)\epsilon_{\mathsf{PRF}} + \epsilon_{2\text{-sim}'} + L(\epsilon_{2\text{-sim}} + \epsilon_{\mathsf{EavLDs}})$$

This bound is the CIML2 bound + the CPAL2 one ($\epsilon_{\mathsf{STPRP}}$ is not added twice because both proof shares the replacement of the STPRP F^* with a random tweakable permutation).

Proof (Sketch). We reuse the proof of the CPAL2 security (Thm. 4). We add only that, due to the CIML2-security in the unbounded model, the adversary can only ask invalid decryption queries and invalid decryption queries may not give any information about the challenge query, because the ephemeral k_0^* picked during the challenge query is independent from the ephemeral key k_0 recomputed during their decryptions.

The theorem with the time bounds (Thm. 10) and its complete proof can be found in [14].

7   Conclusion

With CONCRETE we have provided the first AE scheme achieving CIML2 in the unbounded model with the leak free is used only once. It provides also RUPAE and CPAL2 and CCAL2 [20]. This brings significant performance improvements, especially for short messages.

The leakage-resilience of this scheme crucially relies on the security of the leak free component. It would then be an interesting future challenge to investigate whether a weaker assumption could be made about this component: for instance, we may wonder whether an assumption of unpredictability could be sufficient.

Acknowledgments. François-Xavier Standaert is a senior research associate of the Belgian Fund for Scientific Research (F.R.S.-FNRS). This work has been funded in parts by the European Union (EU) and the Walloon Region through the FEDER project USERMedia (convention number 501907-379156) and the ERC project SWORD (convention number 724725).

References

1. Albrecht, M.R., Paterson, K.G.: Lucky Microseconds: A Timing Attack on Amazon's *s2n* Implementation of TLS. In: Fischlin, M., Coron, J.-S. (eds.) EUROCRYPT 2016, Part I. LNCS, vol. 9665, pp. 622–643. Springer, Heidelberg (2016). https://doi.org/10.1007/978-3-662-49890-3_24

2. Andreeva, E., Bogdanov, A., Luykx, A., Mennink, B., Mouha, N., Yasuda, K.: How to securely release unverified plaintext in authenticated encryption. In: Sarkar, P., Iwata, T. (eds.) ASIACRYPT 2014, Part I. LNCS, vol. 8873, pp. 105–125. Springer, Heidelberg (2014). https://doi.org/10.1007/978-3-662-45611-8_6

3. Ashur, T., Dunkelman, O., Luykx, A.: Boosting authenticated encryption robustness with minimal modifications. In: Katz, J., Shacham, H. (eds.) CRYPTO 2017, Part III. LNCS, vol. 10403, pp. 3–33. Springer, Cham (2017). https://doi.org/10.1007/978-3-319-63697-9_1

4. Barwell, G., Martin, D.P., Oswald, E., Stam, M.: Authenticated encryption in the face of protocol and side channel leakage. In: Takagi, T., Peyrin, T. (eds.) ASIACRYPT 2017, Part I. LNCS, vol. 10624, pp. 693–723. Springer, Cham (2017). https://doi.org/10.1007/978-3-319-70694-8_24

5. Barwell, G., Page, D., Stam, M.: Rogue decryption failures: reconciling AE robustness notions. In: Groth, J. (ed.) IMACC 2015. LNCS, vol. 9496, pp. 94–111. Springer, Cham (2015). https://doi.org/10.1007/978-3-319-27239-9_6

6. Bellare, M.: Symmetric ecryption revised. Technical report (2018). https://spotniq.files.wordpress.com/2018/07/spotniq18-se-revisited.pdf

7. Bellare, M., Desai, A., Pointcheval, D., Rogaway, P.: Relations among notions of security for public-key encryption schemes. In: Krawczyk, H. (ed.) CRYPTO 1998. LNCS, vol. 1462, pp. 26–45. Springer, Heidelberg (1998). https://doi.org/10.1007/BFb0055718

8. Bellare, M., Namprempre, C.: Authenticated encryption: relations among notions and analysis of the generic composition paradigm. In: Okamoto, T. (ed.) ASIACRYPT 2000. LNCS, vol. 1976, pp. 531–545. Springer, Heidelberg (2000). https://doi.org/10.1007/3-540-44448-3_41

9. Bellizia, D., Berti, F., Bronchain, O., Cassiers, G., Duval, S., Guo, C., Leander, G., Leurent, G., Levi, I., Momin, C., Pereira, O., Peters, T., Standaert, F.-X., Wiemer, F.: Spook: sponge-based leakage-resilient authenticated encryption with a masked tweakable block cipher (2019). https://csrc.nist.gov/CSRC/media/Projects/Lightweight-Cryptography/documents/round-1/spec-doc/Spook-spec.pdf

10. Berti, F., Guo, C., Pereira, O., Peters, T., Standaert, F.-X.: TEDT, a leakage-resilient AEAD mode for high (physical) security applications. Cryptology ePrint Archive, Report 2019/137 (2019)

11. Berti, F., Koeune, F., Pereira, O., Peters, T., Standaert, F.-X.: Ciphertext integrity with misuse and leakage: definition and efficient constructions with symmetric primitives. In: AsiaCCS 2018, pp. 37–50 (2018)

12. Berti, F., Pereira, O., Peters, T.: Reconsidering generic composition: the tag-then-encrypt case. In: Chakraborty, D., Iwata, T. (eds.) INDOCRYPT 2018. LNCS, vol. 11356, pp. 70–90. Springer, Cham (2018). https://doi.org/10.1007/978-3-030-05378-9_4

13. Berti, F., Pereira, O., Peters, T., Standaert, F.-X.: On leakage-resilient authenticated encryption with decryption leakages. IACR Transactions on Symmetric Cryptology 2017(3), pp. 271–293 (2017)

14. Berti, F., Pereira, O., Standaert, F.-X.: Reducing the cost of authenticity with leakages: a CIML2-secure AE scheme with one call to a strongly protected tweakable block cipher. Cryptology ePrint Archive, Report 2019/451 (2019).https://eprint.iacr.org/2019/451

15. Bertoni, G., Daemen, J., Peters, M., Van Assche, G., Van Keer, R.: CAESAR submission: Ketje v2. Technical report (2016)

16. Dobraunig, C., Eichlseder, M., Mangard, S., Mendel, F., Unterluggauer, T.: ISAP - towards side-channel secure authenticated encryption. Transactions on Symmetric Cryptology 2017(1), pp. 80–105 (2017)

17. Dobraunig, C., Mennink, B.: Leakage resilience of the duplex construction. IACR Cryptology ePrint Archive 2019, p. 225 (2019)

18. Dziembowski, S., Pietrzak, K.: Leakage-resilient cryptography. In: FOCS 2008, pp. 293–302 (2008)

19. Goudarzi, D., Rivain, M.: How fast can higher-order masking be in software? In: Coron, J.-S., Nielsen, J.B. (eds.) EUROCRYPT 2017. LNCS, vol. 10210, pp. 567–597. Springer, Cham (2017). https://doi.org/10.1007/978-3-319-56620-7_20

20. Guo, C., Pereira, O., Peters, T., Standaert, F.-X.: Leakage-resilient authenticated encryption with misuse in the leveled leakage setting: Definitions, separation results, and constructions. Cryptology ePrint Archive, Report 2018/484 (2018)

21. Guo, C., Pereira, O., Peters, T., Standaert, F.-X.: Towards lightweight side-channel security and the leakage-resilience of the duplex sponge (2019)

22. Hirose, S.: Some plausible constructions of double-block-length hash functions. In: Robshaw, M. (ed.) FSE 2006. LNCS, vol. 4047, pp. 210–225. Springer, Heidelberg (2006). https://doi.org/10.1007/11799313_14

23. IETF: The transport layer security (TLS) protocol version 1.3 draft-ietf-tls-tls13-28. Technical report (2018). https://tools.ietf.org/html/draft-ietf-tls-tls13-28

24. Journault, A., Standaert, F.-X.: Very high order masking: efficient implementation and security evaluation. In: Fischer, W., Homma, N. (eds.) CHES 2017. LNCS, vol. 10529, pp. 623–643. Springer, Cham (2017). https://doi.org/10.1007/978-3-319-66787-4_30

25. Katz, J., Lindell, Y.: Introduction to Modern Cryptography, 2nd edn. CRC Press, Boca Raton (2014)

26. Katz, J., Yung, M.: Unforgeable encryption and chosen ciphertext secure modes of operation. In: Goos, G., Hartmanis, J., van Leeuwen, J., Schneier, B. (eds.) FSE 2000. LNCS, vol. 1978, pp. 284–299. Springer, Heidelberg (2001). https://doi.org/10.1007/3-540-44706-7_20

27. Kocher, P., Jaffe, J., Jun, B.: Differential power analysis. In: Wiener, M. (ed.) CRYPTO 1999. LNCS, vol. 1666, pp. 388–397. Springer, Heidelberg (1999). https://doi.org/10.1007/3-540-48405-1_25

28. Liskov, M., Rivest, R.L., Wagner, D.: Tweakable block ciphers. In: Yung, M. (ed.) CRYPTO 2002. LNCS, vol. 2442, pp. 31–46. Springer, Heidelberg (2002). https://doi.org/10.1007/3-540-45708-9_3

29. Longo, J., De Mulder, E., Page, D., Tunstall, M.: SoC it to EM: electromagnetic side-channel attacks on a complex system-on-chip. In: Güneysu, T., Handschuh, H. (eds.) CHES 2015. LNCS, vol. 9293, pp. 620–640. Springer, Heidelberg (2015). https://doi.org/10.1007/978-3-662-48324-4_31

30. Mangard, S., Oswald, E., Popp, T.: Power Analysis Attacks. Springer, Boston, MA (2007). https://doi.org/10.1007/978-0-387-38162-6

31. Mangard, S., Oswald, E., Standaert, F.-X.: One for all - all for one: unifying standard differential power analysis attacks. IET Inf. Secur. 5(2), 100–110 (2011)

32. Pereira, O., Standaert, F.-X., Vivek, S.: Leakage-resilient authentication and encryption from symmetric cryptographic primitives. In: ACM CCS 2015, pp. 96–108 (2015)

33. Standaert, F.-X., Pereira, O., Yu, Y.: Leakage-resilient symmetric cryptography under empirically verifiable assumptions. In: Canetti, R., Garay, J.A. (eds.) CRYPTO 2013. LNCS, vol. 8042, pp. 335–352. Springer, Heidelberg (2013). https://doi.org/10.1007/978-3-642-40041-4_19

An Improvement of Correlation Analysis for Vectorial Boolean Functions

Youssef Harmouch[1](✉), Rachid El Kouch[1], and Hussain Ben-Azza[2]

[1] Department of Mathematics, Computing and Networks,
National Institute of Posts and Telecommunications, Rabat, Morocco
{harmouch,elkouch}@inpt.ac.ma
[2] Moulay Ismail University, ENSAM-Meknès, Meknes, Morocco
hbenazza@yahoo.com

Abstract. This paper investigates the correlation of n-bit to m-bit vectorial Boolean functions denoted by F. At Crypto 2000, Zhang and Chan showed that the maximum of linear approximations for F with Boolean functions g have a higher bias than those based on the usual correlation attack. The correlation for this linear approximation has been named the maximum correlation and has been shown to be a useful tool for correlation attack resistance. In this work, we deal with two issues. Firstly, we show that combining F with any g does not always increase the bias as stated by several works. To justify such results, we demonstrate the exact correlation link between F, g and the combination of F by g. Secondly, we provide the exact condition in which the correlation coefficients for this approximation are maximum.

Keywords: Correlation attack · Vectorial boolean function · Bias · Maximum correlator · Stream cipher

1 Introduction

This work focuses on n to m bit vectorial Boolean functions often called S-boxes and denoted by $F : \mathbb{F}_2^n \to \mathbb{F}_2^m$. For instance, stream cipher based on LFSR "linear feedback shift registers" uses F as a nonlinear filter or as a nonlinear combiner [16] because these functions offer a high throughput compared to Boolean functions, i.e. instead of having one binary information, we have a vector of m bits. Namely, if a correlation attack for F has a probability close to $1/2$, the attacker can retrieve secret LFSR bits when enough keystream bits are known.

At Crypto 2000, Zhang and Chan [17] improved correlation attacks by defining a new term called the maximum correlation that considers the linear approximation based on a Boolean function $g : \mathbb{F}_2^m \to \mathbb{F}_2$ to $F(x)$ instead of a linear combination of $F(x)$, i.e. instead of studying $F(x)$ we study the composition of g and F, that is, $g \circ F(x) = g(F(x))$. This new concept offers a choice of 2^{n+2^m} of linear approximations instead of 2^{n+m} in the usual approach, which increase the chances of selecting a linear approximation with a higher bias,

© Springer Nature Switzerland AG 2019
J. Buchmann et al. (Eds.): AFRICACRYPT 2019, LNCS 11627, pp. 250–269, 2019.
https://doi.org/10.1007/978-3-030-23696-0_13

i.e. where probability $Pr\Big(g \circ F(x) = a \cdot x\Big)$ is further away from $1/2$. The Boolean function g that gives the maximum bias for $g \circ F$ to all $g : \mathbb{F}_2^m \to \mathbb{F}_2$ is called the maximum correlator.

In general, it is difficult to determine this maximum correlator since there are 2^{2^m} functions in $\mathbb{F}_2^m$. Moreover, a number of researchers claim that the use of any g for F (except when g is a constant function) has a greater correlation coefficients than that of F alone. This statement is built on several experimental results.

In this work, we show that $g \circ F$ with any Boolean function g does not always give a higher correlation coefficient than F, i.e. any g does not increase the bias for F. In order to understand such results, we determine the condition on g that leads to increase the bias for F. This condition presents a very interesting result because now we reduced the number of g by removing all the Boolean functions g, which does not increase the bias. Therefore, the probability of selecting a Boolean function g that increases the bias for F is now much higher. Furthermore, in this work, we prove the exact condition in which the maximum correlator can be found.

The rest of the paper is organized as follows. Section 2 presents the preliminaries, while Sect. 3 presents the related work. In Sect. 4 we show the motivation and the aim of this work. In Sect. 5, we prove the link between F, g and $g \circ F$ in order to determine the condition for which the bias increases when composing F by g. In Sect. 6, we further analyze the proved theorems in this work. Section 7 concerns a discussion about the maximum correlator, while Sect. 8 concludes the paper.

2   Preliminaries and Notations

Let $\mathbb{F}_2$ denote the finite field with two elements, $\mathbb{F}_2^n$ denote the $\mathbb{F}_2$-vector space of dimension n, '+'denote the addition in $\mathbb{F}_2^n$ and let $x \cdot y$ denote the scalar product of vectors x and y defined as $x \cdot y = \sum_{i=1}^{n} x_i \times y_i$. A Boolean function is a map from $\mathbb{F}_2^n$ to $\mathbb{F}_2$. A vectorial Boolean function $F : \mathbb{F}_2^n \to \mathbb{F}_2^m$ is a map from $\mathbb{F}_2^n$ to $\mathbb{F}_2^m$ i.e.$F(x) = (f_1(x), f_2(x), \ldots, f_m(x))$ where the Boolean functions $(f_1, \ldots, f_m)$ are called the coordinate functions of F and $x = (x_1, \ldots, x_n) \in \mathbb{F}_2^n$.

We denote the set of (n, m) vectorial Boolean functions or $\mathbb{F}_2^n \to \mathbb{F}_2^m$ by $\mathcal{B}_{n,m}$. In the case of Boolean functions $(m = 1)$ we write $\mathcal{B}_n$ instead of $\mathcal{B}_{n,1}$. Moreover, we denote by $\mathcal{B}_n^*$ the set of non-constant Boolean functions.

The Hamming weight of a vector x is the number of '1'in x. The Hamming weight $wt(f)$ of a function f is the number of vectors $x \in \mathbb{F}_2^n$ such that $f(x) = 1$. A function $f \in \mathcal{B}_n$ is said to be balanced if $wt(f) = wt(f \oplus 1) = 2^{n-1}$, i.e. all the output values have exactly the same number of occurrence.

The correlation coefficient of two Boolean functions f and g, denoted by $c(f, g)$, is defined in terms of probabilities Pr as follows [17]:

$$c(f, g) = \Pr\Big(f(x) = g(x)\Big) - \Pr\Big(f(x) \neq g(x)\Big). \tag{1}$$

The correlation coefficient of a Boolean function f and the set of all Boolean affine functions is of special interest in the analysis and design of f because it is linked to the correlation attacks used against stream cipher, and to the nonlinearity, hence to the linear cryptanalysis for block cipher. The correlation coefficient of f to the nearest affine Boolean function $\ell_a : \mathbb{F}_2^n \to \mathbb{F}_2$, $\ell_a(x) = a \cdot x$ describes the statistical dependency between f and ℓ_a with $a \in \mathbb{F}_2^n$ and it is defined as [7]:

$$c_f(a) = c(f, \ell_a) = \frac{\#\{x \in \mathbb{F}_2^n | f(x) = \ell_a(x)\} - \#\{x \in \mathbb{F}_2^n | f(x) \neq \ell_a(x)\}}{2^n}. \quad (2)$$

As for the Hamming distance $d(f, \ell_a)$ between f and the set of affine functions ℓ_a, it is related to the correlation coefficient by [15]:

$$c(f, \ell_a) = 1 - 2^{-n+1} d(f, \ell_a). \quad (3)$$

In order to perform a correlation attack on the stream cipher, we try to find an approximation of a linear combination of output bits by a linear combination of input bits i.e. $\max_{a \in \mathbb{F}_2^n} \Pr(f = \ell_a)$. The minor correlation if found, indicates that all linear approximations have small bias [2]:

$$\varepsilon_f = \left| \max_{a \in \mathbb{F}_2^n} \Pr(f = \ell_a) - \frac{1}{2} \right| = \frac{\max_{a \in \mathbb{F}_2^n} |c(f, \ell_a)|}{2} = \frac{1}{2} \max_{a \in \mathbb{F}_2^n} |c_f(a)|. \quad (4)$$

A useful tool for studying $c_f(a)$ is the Walsh transform $W_f : \mathbb{F}_2^n \to \mathbb{Z}$ [1]:

$$W_f(a) = \sum_{x \in \mathbb{F}_2^n} (-1)^{\ell_a(x) + f(x)} = \sum_{x \in \mathbb{F}_2^n} (-1)^{a \cdot x + f(x)}. \quad (5)$$

The value $W_f(a)$ is called the Walsh coefficient of f at point a and the multiset composed of all Walsh coefficients of f is called the Walsh spectrum of f. The Walsh spectrum of f corresponds to the biases of all approximations of f by a linear function. This quantity, especially its maximum, plays an important role in linear cryptanalysis [2] and correlation attack.

The correlation c_f of a Boolean function f can also be expressed through the Walsh Transform as [12]:

$$c_f(a) = c(f, \ell_a) = \frac{W_f(a)}{2^n}. \quad (6)$$

In case of an S-box $F \in \mathcal{B}_{n,m}$, the Walsh transform is taken over all linear masks in the output of F, hence

$$W_F(a, b) = \sum_{x \in \mathbb{F}_2^n} (-1)^{a \cdot x + b \cdot F(x)}. \quad (7)$$

Thus the correlation of $F \in \mathcal{B}_{n,m}$ is expressed by

$$c_F(a, b) = c(b \cdot F, \ell_a) = \frac{W_F(a, b)}{2^n}, \quad (8)$$

while the bias is given by

$$\varepsilon_F = \left| \max_{a \in \mathbb{F}_2^n, b \in \mathbb{F}_2^m - \{0\}} \Pr(b \cdot F = \ell_a) - \frac{1}{2} \right| = \frac{1}{2} \max_{a \in \mathbb{F}_2^n, b \in \mathbb{F}_2^m - \{0\}} |c_F(a,b)|. \qquad (9)$$

3   Related Work

At Crypto 2000, Zhang and Chan [17] observed that instead of taking linear combination of the output bit functions $b \cdot F(x)$ with $b \in \mathbb{F}_2^m$, we can compose $F(x)$ with a Boolean function $g \in \mathcal{B}_m^*$ and consider the probability $\Pr[a \cdot x = g \circ F(x)]$, because, the approximation of $b \cdot F(x)$ is a particular case of the approximation of $g \circ F(x)$ and since $F(x)$ corresponds to the output which is known, then $g \circ F(x)$ is also known. It is easier to get a better linear approximation for $\Pr[g \circ F = \ell_a]$ further away from $1/2$ than $\Pr[b \cdot F = \ell_a]$. Therefore $g \circ F(x) = \ell_a(x)$ is a linear approximation that can be used in correlation attacks with the bias of such approximation is equal to:

$$\varepsilon_{g \circ F} = \left| \max_{a \in \mathbb{F}_2^n} \Pr\left(g \circ F = \ell_a\right) - \frac{1}{2} \right| = \frac{1}{2} \max_{a \in \mathbb{F}_2^n} |c(g \circ F, \ell_a)|. \qquad (10)$$

In this work [17], Zhang and Chan define a new correlation value named the maximum correlation by $\max_{g \in \mathcal{B}_m^*} c_{g \circ F}(a) = \max_{g \in \mathcal{B}_m^*} c(g \circ F, \ell_a)$ and then they proved the following theorem:

Theorem 1. (Theorem 4. in [17]). *Let F be a function in $\mathcal{B}_{n,m}$ and g be a function in $\mathcal{B}_m$. For any $a \in \mathbb{F}_2^n$ we have:*

$$\max_{g \in \mathcal{B}_m^*} c_{g \circ F}(a) \leq 2^{m/2} \max_{b \in \mathbb{F}_2^m} |c_F(a,b)|. \qquad (11)$$

This maximum correlation was later used by Carlet and Prouff in [6] to define a new nonlinearity term called the unrestricted nonlinearity which was soon further developed to a new term called the generalized nonlinearity [4]. The terms mentioned encompass today's correlation study for the Boolean and vectorial Boolean functions.

Further studies were developed during time to correlation analysis for Boolean function such as [11] who improved the lower bound for the unrestricted and generalized nonlinearity. Several researchers studied the correlation to improve and/or to evolve the correlation immunity for Boolean functions such as [13], while many of them analyze Boolean function nonlinearity. It must be mentioned that the linearity, the nonlinearity, the linear cryptanalysis and the correlation attacks are all correlated, which means that improving one of them directly affects others.

However, until now and to the best of our knowledge, no work had been done before to complete the work of Zhang and Chan. All the works cited use or approximate the methods of Zhang and Chan from different perspectives.

Since we believe that Zhang and Chan approximation is the key to improve the correlation study for Boolean functions, this work attempts to complete, with proofs and experiments, the maximum correlation by linking the correlation of F, g and $g \circ F$.

4   Aim and Motivation

Several works such as [4,5] state that "linear approximations based on composing the vector output with any Boolean functions have higher bias than those based on the usual correlation attack". In this work, we present a counterexample of some balanced S-boxes such as $\Gamma_1, \Gamma_2 \in \mathcal{B}_{8,8}$ with a Boolean function $g \in \mathcal{B}_8^*$, and we show that combining the output of these S-boxes with g do not increase the bias but it actually decreases it. The method describing how Γ_1 and Γ_2 are constructed is not mentioned in this work. Γ_1 and Γ_2 are illustrated in Appendix-A while g is given by $\forall x \in \mathbb{F}_2^8$, $x = (x_1, x_2, x_3, x_4, x_5, x_6, x_7, x_8)$:

$$g(x) = x_1 x_2 + x_3 x_4 + x_5 x_6 + x_7 x_8 + x_1 x_2 x_3 x_4 + x_5 x_6 x_7 x_8.$$

The logic circuit of g is presented in Fig. 1.

Table 1 shows that $\varepsilon_F > \varepsilon_{g \circ F}$ for Ed Dawson S-box example, Γ_1, Γ_2 and the 8×8 S-box used in the stream cipher Turing. This result contradicts the statement that $\varepsilon_F \leq \varepsilon_{g \circ F}$ for any $g \in \mathcal{B}_8^*$. Table 1 gives a clear evidence that "it is not always true that composing F by any g increases the bias".

This result is quite interesting because now we are certain that the set of all the Boolean functions $g \in \mathcal{B}_m^*$ is combined of two subsets: the first subset does not decreases the bias and the second subset decreases the bias. Therefore, the search for the maximum correlation as defined by Zhang and Chan $\max_{g \in \mathcal{B}_m^*} c(g \circ F, \ell_a)$ will be now much faster because the search is going now to focus on the

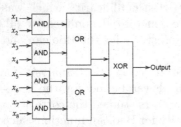

Fig. 1. The logic circuit of the boolean function g used to approach F.

Table 1. ε_F and $\varepsilon_{g \circ F}$ calculated for multiple 8×8 S-boxes. The column on the right indicates the value of the input mask a for which the correlation $c_{g \circ F}$ is maximal. If there is more than one value of a, we use a semicolon to separate the values.

S-box	ε_F	$\varepsilon_{g \circ F}$	a in Hex
AES	0,0625	0,1015	$F4$
GA2 [9]	0,0703	0,1016	$1E$
Kazymyrov [10]	0,0938	0,1016	ED
Ed Dawson [8]	0,1015	0,0937	$6E;F4$
Γ_1	0,1328	0,0859	64
Γ_2	0,1406	0,0896	$42;4B;7F$
Turing [14]	0,1328	0,0859	$71;74;E9$

first subset only i.e. the complexity time to find the maximum correlator will be less than $2^{2^m} - 2$.

In order to determine the first subset, we develop the walsh transformation for $g \circ F$ to get the condition for F and g for which $\varepsilon_F \leq \varepsilon_{g \circ F}$ (see the following section).

5   The Correlation Link Between F, g and $g \circ F$

Here we present a Theorem giving the correlation link of $g \circ F$ to both F and g.

Theorem 2. *Let F be any balanced function in $\mathcal{B}_{n,m}$ and let g bet any function in $\mathcal{B}_m^*$. The correlation $c_F(a,b)$ for F, $c_g(b)$ for g and $c_{g \circ F}(a)$ for $g \circ F$ satisfy $\forall a \in \mathbb{F}_2^n - \{0\}$ and $\forall b \in \mathbb{F}_2^m - \{0\}$:*

$$\frac{1}{2}\Big(c_F(a,b) + c_g(b)\Big)^2 - 1 \leq c_{g \circ F}(a) \leq 1 - \frac{1}{2}\Big(c_F(a,b) - c_g(b)\Big)^2. \qquad (12)$$

In order to prove Theorem 2, Lemmas 1, 2 and 3 will be used.

Remark 1. If $a = 0$ in equation (12), then it does not involve the input x and if $b = 0$, then the linear combination of $F(x)$ is missing in $c_F(a,b)$, therefore, these two cases are not useful for correlation attack.

Lemma 1. *For any functions $F \in \mathcal{B}_{n,m}$, $g \in \mathcal{B}_m^*$ and for any $a \in \mathbb{F}_2^n$ and $b \in \mathbb{F}_2^m$, we have:*

$$W_{g \circ F}(a) = \sum_{x \in \mathbb{F}_2^n} (-1)^{a \cdot x + b \cdot F(x)}(-1)^{b \cdot F(x) + g(F(x))}. \qquad (13)$$

Proof. According to (5), it is clear that

$$W_{g \circ F}(a) = \sum_{x \in \mathbb{F}_2^n} (-1)^{a \cdot x + b \cdot F(x)}(-1)^{b \cdot F(x) + g(F(x))}(-1)^{-2b \cdot F(x)}.$$

To any $F(x) \in \mathbb{F}_2^m$ and $b \in \mathbb{F}_2^m$ we have $(-1)^{-2b \cdot F(x)} = 1$, thus

$$W_{g \circ F}(a) = \sum_{x \in \mathbb{F}_2^n} (-1)^{a \cdot x + b \cdot F(x)}(-1)^{b \cdot F(x) + g(F(x))}.$$

Lemma 2. *For any balanced $F \in \mathcal{B}_{n,m}$ and for any $g \in \mathcal{B}_m^*$, and for any $a \in \mathbb{F}_2^n$ and $b \in \mathbb{F}_2^m$, we have:*

$$\frac{1}{2^{n+1}}\Big(W_F(a,b) + 2^{n-m}W_g(b)\Big)^2 - 2^n \leq W_{g \circ F}(a). \qquad (14)$$

Proof. Let $A_F : \mathbb{F}_2^n \times \mathbb{F}_2^m \times \mathbb{F}_2^n \to \mathbb{Z}$ and $A_g : \mathbb{F}_2^m \times \mathbb{F}_2^m \to \mathbb{Z}$ be

$$\begin{cases} A_F(a, b, x) = (-1)^{a \cdot x + b \cdot F(x)}, \\ A_g\big(b, F(x)\big) = (-1)^{b \cdot F(x) + g\big(F(x)\big)}. \end{cases}$$

Based on the remarkable identity-Square of an addition, we know that $\forall u_i, v_i \in \mathbb{Z}$,

$$\sum_i u_i v_i = \frac{1}{2}\left[\sum_i (u_i + v_i)^2 - \sum_i u_i^2 - \sum_i v_i^2\right].$$

According to Lemma 1, we have

$$W_{g \circ F}(a) = \sum_{x \in \mathbb{F}_2^n} A_F(a, b, x) \times A_g\big(b, F(x)\big)$$

$$= \frac{1}{2}\left[\sum_{x \in \mathbb{F}_2^n}\left(A_F(a, b, x) + A_g\big(b, F(x)\big)\right)^2 - \sum_{x \in \mathbb{F}_2^n} A_F(a, b, x)^2 - \sum_{x \in \mathbb{F}_2^n} A_g\big(b, F(x)\big)^2\right].$$

It is easy to see that

$$\sum_{x \in \mathbb{F}_2^n} A_F(a, b, x)^2 = \sum_{x \in \mathbb{F}_2^n} A_g\big(b, F(x)\big)^2 = \sum_{x \in \mathbb{F}_2^n} 1 = 2^n,$$

hence

$$W_{g \circ F}(a) = \frac{1}{2}\sum_{x \in \mathbb{F}_2^n}\left(A_F(a, b, x) + A_g\big(b, F(x)\big)\right)^2 - 2^n.$$

According the Cauchy-Schwarz inequality

$$\left(\sum_{i=1}^n u_i\right)^2 = \left(1 \times \sum_{i=1}^n u_i\right)^2 \leq \left(\sum_{i=1}^n 1^2\right) \times \left(\sum_{i=1}^n u_i^2\right) = n \times \left(\sum_{i=1}^n u_i^2\right),$$

we can write

$$\frac{1}{2^n}\left(\sum_{x \in \mathbb{F}_2^n}\left(A_F(a, b, x) + A_g\big(b, F(x)\big)\right)\right)^2 \leq \sum_{x \in \mathbb{F}_2^n}\left(A_F(a, b, x) + A_g\big(b, F(x)\big)\right)^2.$$

By multiplying both sides of the inequality by $1/2$ and subtracting 2^n, we get

$$\frac{1}{2^{n+1}}\left(\sum_{x \in \mathbb{F}_2^n} A_F(a, b, x) + \sum_{x \in \mathbb{F}_2^n} A_g\big(b, F(x)\big)\right)^2 - 2^n \leq \frac{1}{2}\sum_{x \in \mathbb{F}_2^n}\left(A_F(a, b, x) + A_g\big(b, F(x)\big)\right)^2 - 2^n.$$

Notice that the right side of the above inequality is $W_{g \circ F}(a)$. Thanks to the balancedness of F we have

$$\sum_{x \in \mathbb{F}_2^n} A_g\big(b, F(x)\big) = 2^{n-m}\sum_{z \in \mathbb{F}_2^m} A_g(b, z),$$

with $z = F(x)$ is a variable over $\mathbb{F}_2^m$. Thus

$$\frac{1}{2^{n+1}} \left(\sum_{x \in \mathbb{F}_2^n} A_F(a, b, x) + 2^{n-m} \sum_{z \in \mathbb{F}_2^m} A_g(b, z) \right)^2 - 2^n \leq W_{g \circ F}(a).$$

Notice that $\sum_{x \in \mathbb{F}_2^n} A_F(a, b, x)$ and $\sum_{z \in \mathbb{F}_2^m} A_g(b, z)$ are the Walsh transform for F and the Walsh transform for g respectively. Therefore

$$\frac{1}{2^{n+1}} \left(W_F(a, b) + 2^{n-m} W_g(b) \right)^2 - 2^n \leq W_{g \circ F}(a).$$

Lemma 3. *For any balanced $F \in \mathcal{B}_{n,m}$ and $g \in \mathcal{B}_m^*$, and for any $a \in \mathbb{F}_2^n$ and $b \in \mathbb{F}_2^m$, we have:*

$$W_{g \circ F}(a) \leq 2^n - \frac{1}{2^{n+1}} \left(W_F(a, b) - 2^{n-m} W_g(b) \right)^2. \tag{15}$$

Proof. This inequality can be easily found following the same steps in the previous proof of Lemma 2 with the use of the remarkable identity-Square of a subtraction $\forall u_i, v_i \in \mathbb{Z}$

$$\sum_i u_i v_i = -\frac{1}{2} \left[\sum_i (u_i - v_i)^2 - \sum_i u_i^2 - \sum_i v_i^2 \right]. \qquad \square$$

Lemma 2 and 3 reveal that the Walsh transform of approximating F by g is linked to a simple addition or subtraction of the Walsh transform for F and the Walsh transform for g.

The Proof of Theorem 2 is easily obtained by multiplying the two sides of Lemma 2 and 3 by 2^{-n} and with the use of (6) and (8). Since Theorem 2 is valid for any $b \in \mathbb{F}_2^m$, the quantity $c_{g \circ F}(a)$ is tightly bounded by :

$$\frac{1}{2} \max_b \left(c_F(a, b) + c_g(b) \right)^2 - 1 \leq c_{g \circ F}(a) \leq 1 - \frac{1}{2} \max_b \left(c_F(a, b) - c_g(b) \right)^2. \tag{16}$$

The inequalities in (16) can become equalities by considering the case where F and g are affine.

Example 1. Let $x \in \mathbb{F}_2^8$, $x = (x_1, x_2, x_3, x_4, x_5, x_6, x_7, x_8)$ with $x_i \in \mathbb{F}_2$ and $b \in \mathbb{F}_2^8$. For $F \in \mathcal{B}_{8,8}$ and $g \in \mathcal{B}_8^*$ such that $F(x) = x + e$ ($e \in \mathbb{F}_2^8$) and $g(x) = x_1 + x_2 + x_3 + x_4 + x_5 + x_6 + x_7 + x_8$. For a given $a \in \mathbb{F}_2^8$ ($a = 2^8 - 1$), we have :

$$\frac{1}{2} \max_b \left(c_F(255, b) + c_g(b) \right)^2 - 1 = c_{g \circ F}(255) = 1 - \frac{1}{2} \max_b \left(c_F(255, b) - c_g(b) \right)^2 = \pm 1.$$

6   The Correlation Analysis

Theorem 2 provides a useful formula for determining the subset that maximizes the bias. We denote such subset by $\mathcal{B}_m^+(F)$ $(\mathcal{B}_m^+(F) \subset \mathcal{B}_m^*)$. Theorem 2 helps also to determine the probability of finding a function g that maximizes the bias for F and determines where the maximum correlation for $g \circ F$ is reached.

Definition 1. The set of F-linearizer functions is defined by :

$$g \text{ is an } F\text{-linearizer} \Leftrightarrow \{g \in \mathcal{B}_m^* | \; \varepsilon_F \leq \varepsilon_{g \circ F}\}.$$

Theorem 3. *Let F be any balanced function in $\mathcal{B}_{n,m}$. If g is an F-linearizer, then for any $b \in \mathbb{F}_2^m - \{0\}$, the correlations c_F and c_g satisfy :*

$$|c_g(b)| \leq \min\left\{1, \left|2\sqrt{\left(\frac{1}{2} - \varepsilon_F\right)} - \min_{a \in \mathbb{F}_2^n - \{0\}}|c_F(a,b)|\right|\right\}. \tag{17}$$

Proof. Theorem 2 gives:

$$-\left(1 - \frac{1}{2}\left(c_F(a,b) + c_g(b)\right)^2\right) \leq c_{g \circ F}(a) \leq 1 - \frac{1}{2}\left(c_F(a,b) - c_g(b)\right)^2.$$

That is to say:

$$0 \leq |c_{g \circ F}(a)| \leq \max\left\{1 - \frac{1}{2}\left(c_F(a,b) - c_g(b)\right)^2, 1 - \frac{1}{2}\left(c_F(a,b) + c_g(b)\right)^2\right\}.$$

The function g is an F-linearizer, therefore $\max_{a,b}|c_F(a,b)| \leq \max_a|c_{g \circ F}(a)|$, hence

$$\max_{a,b}|c_F(a,b)| \leq \max_a \max\left\{1 - \frac{1}{2}\left(c_F(a,b) - c_g(b)\right)^2, 1 - \frac{1}{2}\left(c_F(a,b) + c_g(b)\right)^2\right\}$$

$$\leq \max_a \max\left\{1 - \frac{1}{2}\left(c_F(a,b) - c_g(b)\right)^2, 1 - \frac{1}{2}\left(c_F(a,b) + c_g(b)\right)^2\right\}$$

$$\leq \max\left\{1 - \frac{1}{2}\min_a\left(c_F(a,b) - c_g(b)\right)^2, 1 - \frac{1}{2}\min_a\left(c_F(a,b) + c_g(b)\right)^2\right\}.$$

This inequality gives, according to the above maximum,

$$\min_a\left|c_F(a,b) \pm c_g(b)\right| \leq \sqrt{2\left(1 - \max_{a,b}|c_F(a,b)|\right)},$$

with $\pm$ denotes either $+$ or $-$. Besides, it is easy to see that

$$\begin{cases} \min_a|c_F(a,b)| - |c_g(b)| \leq \min_a|c_F(a,b) - c_g(b)|, & (*) \\ \min_a|c_F(a,b) + c_g(b)| = \min_a|c_F(a,b)| + |c_g(b)|, & \text{if } c_F(a,b) \times c_g(b) \geq 0 \; (**) \\ \min_a|c_F(a,b) + c_g(b)| = \min_a\left||c_F(a,b)| - |c_g(b)|\right| \geq \min_a|c_F(a,b)| - |c_g(b)|. \; \text{if } c_F(a,b) \times c_g(b) < 0 \; (*) \end{cases}$$

As a result, (*) gives

$$\min_a |c_F(a,b)| - \sqrt{2\left(1 - \max_{a,b} |c_F(a,b)|\right)} \leq |c_g(b)|,$$

while (**) gives

$$|c_g(b)| \leq \sqrt{2\left(1 - \max_{a,b} |c_F(a,b)|\right)} - \min_a |c_F(a,b)|.$$

Thus we deduce that

$$|c_g(b)| \leq \left| \sqrt{2\left(1 - \max_{a,b} |c_F(a,b)|\right)} - \min_a |c_F(a,b)| \right|.$$

Example 2. Let $F \in \mathcal{B}_{n,m}$ be any balanced function. Theorem 3 says that if g is an F-linearizer then :

1. In case of F is a perfect nonlinear function PN ($n \geq 2m$), the equation (17) gives

$$\max_{b \in \mathbb{F}_2^m - \{0\}} |W_g(b)| \leq 2^{m-n/2} \left[2^{(n+1)/2} \sqrt{1 - 2^{-n/2}} - 1 \right]. \qquad (18)$$

It is easy to see that the following inequality holds for $n > 4$

$$2^{n/2} \leq \left[2^{(n+1)/2} \sqrt{1 - 2^{-n/2}} - 1 \right].$$

Therefore the upper bound in (18) is always minimized by 2^m, and since the maximum that can have a Walsh coefficient for any Boolean function g is 2^m, we deduce that

$$\max_{b \in \mathbb{F}_2^m} |W_{\text{PN-linearizer}}(b)| \leq 2^m,$$

which means that all the Boolean functions $g \in \mathcal{B}_m^*$ are an PN-linearizer. If $2 < n \leq 4$ then

$$\max_{b \in \mathbb{F}_2^m} |W_{\text{PN-linearizer}}(b)| \leq 2^{m-0,352}.$$

2. In case of F is an affine function, the Eq. (17) gives

$$\max_{b \in \mathbb{F}_2^m - \{0\}} |W_g(b)| \leq 2^{m-n} \max_{b \in \mathbb{F}_2^m - \{0\}} \min_{a \in \mathbb{F}_2^n - \{0\}} |W_F(a,b)|.$$

In general for $n \geq m$, the quantity in (19) is small, which implies that only few Boolean functions can be affine-linearizer.

$$2^{m-n} \max_{b \in \mathbb{F}_2^m - \{0\}} \min_{a \in \mathbb{F}_2^n - \{0\}} |W_F(a,b)|. \qquad (19)$$

As it is well known that if $g \circ F$ and F are linear, then g is linear. Therefore we deduce that only affine functions can be affine-linearizer.

The aim of these two examples is to show that the number of F-linearizers decreases when the linearity of F increases. This can be justified by studying the Hamming distance of g. In terms of Hamming distance, Theorem 3 shows that if g is an F-linearizer, then the minimum of Hamming distance between g and the set of all affine functions satisfy (for $a \in \mathbb{F}_2^n, b \in \mathbb{F}_2^m$):

$$\min_b d(g, \ell_b) \geq 2^m - 2^{m-n} \left(\max_{a,b} d(b \cdot F, \ell_a) + 2^{n/2} \sqrt{\min_{a,b} d(b \cdot F, \ell_a)} \right). \tag{20}$$

Let us denote the quantity $\left(\max_{a,b} d(b \cdot F, \ell_a) + 2^{n/2} \sqrt{\min_{a,b} d(b \cdot F, \ell_a)} \right)$ by α_F. Then (20) can be written as :

$$2^m - 2^{m-n} \alpha_F \leq \min_b d(g, \ell_b) \leq 2^m, \quad \text{with} \quad \alpha_F \geq 0. \tag{21}$$

The quantity α_F is a positive variable describing the linearity of F, i.e., the increase of α_F implies a decrease in the linearity of F and vice versa. It is easy to see from (21) that the range for $\min_b d(g, \ell_b)$ increases as α_F increases, which means that the number of F-linearizers increases as the linearity of F decreases. This explains the results obtained in the two previous examples.

By using Theorems 2 and 3, we can determine according to the linearity of any balanced function F, the approximate number of F-linearizers denoted by $\#\mathcal{B}_m^+(F)$ and the range for the F-linearizers bias denoted by $\Re$. This will decrease the search time of the maximum correlator defined by Zhang and Chan since $\#\mathcal{B}_m^+(F) < 2^{2^m} - 2$. Table 2 illustrates, based on ε_F, the approximated number of $\#\mathcal{B}_m^+(F)$ and Pr_g that denotes the probability of finding an F-linearizer.

Table 2. The number of F-linearizer denoted by $\#\mathcal{B}_m^+(F)$, the bias-range for F-linearizers denoted by $\Re$ and the probability Pr_g of finding a boolean function $g \in \mathcal{B}_m^*$ that is an F-linearizer.

ε_F	$\Re$	Pr_g	$\#\mathcal{B}_m^+(F)$
0	0,5	0,8325	$0,8325 \times (2^{2^m} - 2)$
0,05	0,5	0,7275	$0,7275 \times (2^{2^m} - 2)$
0,1	0,5	0,6125	$0,6125 \times (2^{2^m} - 2)$
0,15	0,4416	0,4921	$0,4921 \times (2^{2^m} - 2)$
0,2	0,3477	0,3805	$0,3805 \times (2^{2^m} - 2)$
0,25	0,25	0,2806	$0,2806 \times (2^{2^m} - 2)$
0,3	0,1472	0,1935	$0,1935 \times (2^{2^m} - 2)$
0,35	0,0372	0,1201	$0,1201 \times (2^{2^m} - 2)$
0,4	0,08377	0,0615	$0,0615 \times (2^{2^m} - 2)$
0,45	0,22639	0,0199	$0,0199 \times (2^{2^m} - 2)$
0,5	0	0	0

Note 1. The computing of Pr_g is explained in Appendix-B.

Theorem 4. *Let F be any balanced function in $\mathcal{B}_{n,m}$ with $a \in \mathbb{F}_2^n - \{0\}$ and $b \in \mathbb{F}_2^m - \{0\}$ are the input mask and the output mask, respectively. Let $h \in \mathcal{B}_m^*$ be the maximum correlator for F to $\ell_a = a \cdot x$. Then*

$$\max_{g \in \mathcal{B}_m^*, a} \left| c_{g \circ F}(a) \right| = \max_a \left| c_{h \circ F}(a) \right| \leq 1 - \frac{\gamma}{2}. \tag{22}$$

Moreover, the bias for this maximum correlator satisfies

$$\varepsilon_h \leq \varepsilon_F + \sqrt{\gamma}/2, \tag{23}$$

with $\gamma \in \mathbb{R}^+$ is given by

$$\gamma = \min\left(\min_a \max_b \left(c_F(a,b) - c_h(b)\right)^2, \min_a \max_b \left(c_F(a,b) + c_h(b)\right)^2 \right).$$

Proof. Theorem 2 gives

$$\max_a \left| c_{g \circ F}(a) \right| \leq \max\left\{ 1 - \tfrac{1}{2} \min_a \max_b \left(c_F(a,b) - c_g(b)\right)^2, 1 - \tfrac{1}{2} \min_a \max_b \left(c_F(a,b) + c_g(b)\right)^2 \right\}.$$

Let $h \in \mathcal{B}_m^*$ be the Boolean function that reaches the maximum for $\max_a \left| c_{g \circ F}(a) \right|$ over g, i.e. h is the maximum correlator $(\max_{g,a} \left| c_{g \circ F}(a) \right| = \max_a \left| c_{h \circ F}(a) \right|)$. Hence

$$\max_a \left| c_{h \circ F}(a) \right| \leq \max\left\{ 1 - \tfrac{1}{2} \min_a \max_b \left(c_F(a,b) - c_h(b)\right)^2, 1 - \tfrac{1}{2} \min_a \max_b \left(c_F(a,b) + c_h(b)\right)^2 \right\}.$$

Furthermore, let $\delta_b \in \mathbb{R}^+$ and $\theta_b \in \mathbb{R}^+$ be two variables that present the minimum over $a \in \mathbb{F}_2^n$ for $\left(c_F(a,b) - c_h(b)\right)^2$ and $\left(c_F(a,b) + c_h(b)\right)^2$ respectively. Also, let $\gamma \in \mathbb{R}^+$ be the minimum between $\max_b \delta_b$ and $\max_b \theta_b$ $\left(\gamma = \min\{\max_b \delta_b, \max_b \theta_b\} \right)$. We have

$$\min_a \left(c_F(a,b) - c_h(b)\right)^2 = \delta_b \implies \min_a \max_b \left(c_F(a,b) - c_h(b)\right)^2 = \max_b \delta_b.$$

$$\min_a \left(c_F(a,b) + c_h(b)\right)^2 = \theta_b \implies \min_a \max_b \left(c_F(a,b) + c_h(b)\right)^2 = \max_b \theta_b.$$

Therefore

$$\max_{g,a} \left| c_{g \circ F}(a) \right| = \max_a \left| c_{h \circ F}(a) \right| \leq 1 - \frac{\gamma}{2}.$$

Besides, we have

$$\sqrt{\delta_b} = \min_a \left| c_h(b) - c_F(a,b) \right| \geq \left| c_h(b) \right| - \max_a \left| c_F(a,b) \right|. \tag{24}$$

$$\begin{aligned} \sqrt{\theta_b} = \min_a \left| c_h(b) + c_F(a,b) \right| &= \min_a \left| c_h(b) - (-c_F(a,b)) \right| \\ &\geq \left| c_h(b) \right| - \max_a \left| -c_F(a,b) \right| \\ &\geq \left| c_h(b) \right| - \max_a \left| c_F(a,b) \right|. \end{aligned} \tag{25}$$

From (24) we have

$$\max_{b}\left|c_h(b)\right| \leq \max_{a,b}\left|c_F(a,b)\right| + \max_{b}\sqrt{\delta_b}.$$

From (25) we have

$$\max_{b}\left|c_h(b)\right| \leq \max_{a,b}\left|c_F(a,b)\right| + \max_{b}\sqrt{\theta_b}.$$

Hence

$$\max_{b}\left|c_h(b)\right| \leq \max_{a,b}\left|c_F(a,b)\right| + \min\left\{\max_{b}\sqrt{\delta_b}, \max_{b}\sqrt{\theta_b}\right\} = \max_{a,b}\left|c_F(a,b)\right| + \sqrt{\gamma}.$$

Thus

$$\varepsilon_h \leq \varepsilon_F + \sqrt{\gamma}/2.$$

Corollary 1. *Let F be any balanced function in $\mathcal{B}_{n,m}$ and let $h \in \mathcal{B}_m^*$ be the maximum correlator for F to $\ell_a = a \cdot x$ with $(a \neq 0)$. Then*

$$\varepsilon_{h \circ F} \leq \frac{1}{2} - (\varepsilon_h - \varepsilon_F)^2. \tag{26}$$

Proof. Equation (23) gives

$$(\varepsilon_h - \varepsilon_F)^2 \leq \gamma/4,$$

hence (22) can be written as

$$\frac{\max_a\left|c_{h \circ F}(a)\right|}{2} = \varepsilon_{h \circ F} \leq \frac{1}{2} - \frac{\gamma}{4} \leq \frac{1}{2} - (\varepsilon_h - \varepsilon_F)^2.$$

Corollary 1 shows that the correlation for $g \circ F$ is maximal only when the bias of g is equal to the bias of F. During crypto 2000, Zhang and Chan gave the algebraic equation to determine the maximum correlator. In this work, we have succeeded in showing that the maximum correlator is the one where γ is the smallest, that is, the one closest to zero. So, the maximum correlator is the Boolean function with the bias closest to that of F.

7   A Discussion About the Maximum Correlator

The approximation of F by g does increase the bias in some cases which was illustrated in this work. However, even by determining the number of Boolean function in $\mathcal{B}_m^+(F)$, the number of test required to find the maximum correlator is high. For instance, if $g \in \mathcal{B}_4^*$ and $F \in \mathcal{B}_{4,4}$ with $\varepsilon_F = 0.2$ the approximate number of Boolean function in $\mathcal{B}_4^+(F)$ is 21476. By increasing m linearly, the approximate number of Boolean function in $\mathcal{B}_m^+(F)$ increases exponentially.

During their work, Zhang and Chan gave a method for calculating the maximum correlator. Here we recall the Theorem as defined by Zhang and Chan to compute the maximum correlator.

Theorem 5. (Theorem 1. in [17]). *Let F be a function in $\mathcal{B}_{n,m}$ and let X be a uniformly distributed variable over $\mathbb{F}_2^n$. For $a \in \mathbb{F}_2^n$ and $z \in \mathbb{F}_2^m$, let $e_a(z)$ denote the conditional probability difference between $a \cdot X = 1$ and $a \cdot X = 0$ under the condition $F(X) = z$, namely:*

$$e_a(z) = \Pr(a \cdot X = 1 | F(X) = z) - \Pr(a \cdot X = 0 | F(X) = z). \qquad (27)$$

Then

$$\max_{g \in \mathcal{B}_m^*} c_{g \circ F}(a) = \Sigma_{z \in \mathbb{F}_2^m} |e_a(z)| \Pr(F(X) = z). \qquad (28)$$

Moreover, the function $g(z) = sgn(e_a(z))$ is the maximum correlator of F to ℓ_a where

$$sgn(x) = \begin{cases} 1, & x > 0, \\ 0 \text{ or } 1, & x = 0, \\ 0, & x < 0. \end{cases}$$

Now, let us begin the analysis of Theorem 5. When F is a permutation, (27) can be written as :

$$e_a(z) = \Pr(a \cdot F^{-1}(z) = 1 | F(X) = z) - \Pr(a \cdot F^{-1}(z) = 0 | F(X) = z),$$

or better :

$$e_a(z) = \Pr(a \cdot F^{-1}(z) = 1) - \Pr(a \cdot F^{-1}(z) = 0).$$

F is a bijective function, hence the output of the conditional probability difference $e_a(z)$ has only two values $\{1,-1\}$. This means that g can be written as:

$$g(z) = a \cdot F^{-1}(z). \qquad (29)$$

Since $|e_a(z)| = 1$ to any z and a, (28) gives

$$\max_{g \in \mathcal{B}_m^*} c_{g \circ F}(a) = \Sigma_{z \in \mathbb{F}_2^m} \Pr(F(X) = z) = 1.$$

Our Theorem 4 showed that $\max_{a,g} |c_{g \circ F}(a)| \le 1 - \gamma/2$, while Theorem 5 shows that $\max_{a,g} c_{g \circ F}(a) = 1$ which means that $\gamma = 0$ when F is a permutation. Moreover, it is known that bijective functions $(n = m)$ and their inverse have the same bias [3], hence the bias for the maximum correlator in (29) is the same as F. This result is consistent with Corollary 1 (the bias for maximum correlator is equal to ε_F because $\varepsilon_{h \circ F} = 1/2$). As a result, Theorems 4, 5 and Corollary 1 show that the permutation function is weak in front of Zhang and Chan attack.

In case of $F \in \mathcal{B}_{n,m}$ is a surjective function, the conditional probability difference may have a null output i.e. $e_a(z) = 0$. Therefore $g(z)$ will be equal either to 0 or 1, because the condition for $sgn(0)$ is not clearly fixed. If n and m are big, then $e_a(z) = 0$ will occur many times. It is true that the choice of 0 or 1 does not affect the construction of the maximum correlator of F to ℓ_a as the conditional probability is balanced,

$$e_a(z) = 0 \Leftrightarrow \Pr(a \cdot X = 1 | X = F^{-1}(z)) = \Pr(a \cdot X = 0 | X = F^{-1}(z)),$$

but when $\varGamma$ is studied to all ℓ_a (the maximum is over $a \in \mathbb{F}_2^n - \{0\}$), then the choice becomes relevant because it plays an important role in ε_g.

Let assume that the function $F \in \mathcal{B}_{n,m}$ is a surjective balanced function and $e_a(z) = 0$ occur many/few times. As a result, (28) can be written as

$$\max_{g \in \mathcal{B}_m^*} c_{g \circ F}(a) = 2^{m-n} \Sigma_{z \in \mathbb{F}_2^m} |e_a(z)|, \tag{30}$$

because $\Pr(F(X) = z) = 2^{m-n}$. Since $e_a(z) = 0$ occurs, then (30) gives

$$\max_{g \in \mathcal{B}_m^*} c_{g \circ F}(a) < 1. \tag{31}$$

Therefore

$$\max_{g \in \mathcal{B}_m^*} \varepsilon_{g \circ F} \neq 1/2. \tag{32}$$

That is, according to (26)

$$\varDelta = \min_{g \in \mathcal{B}_m^*} (\varepsilon_g - \varepsilon_F), \tag{33}$$

with $\varDelta \in \mathbb{R}$ is a non-zero variable ($\varDelta \neq 0$). Therefore, the maximum correlator is only the function that has a bias close to ε_F by $\varDelta$ (close in the sense of greater or smaller than ε_F by $\varDelta$). Based on an experimental calculation (see the example below), the choice of the sign function changes ε_g, especially when the constructed functions g are quite different. For instance and by randomly placing 1 and 0 when $e_a(z) = 0$, we got several functions g that have a different bias, hence the difficulty to figure out the good maximum correlator.

By increasing the number of $e_a(z) = 0$, our work will help to determine the exact maximum correlator, since it is proved in this paper that the bias for the maximum correlator is the closest to ε_F.

Example 3. Let x and z be a random variable over $\mathbb{F}_2^8$ and $\mathbb{F}_2^4$ respectively. We have $x = (x_1, x_2, x_3, x_4, x_5, x_6, x_7, x_8)$ with $x_i \in \mathbb{F}_2$ and $z = (z_1, z_2, z_3, z_4)$ with $z_i \in \mathbb{F}_2$. Let us define the surjective balanced function $F \in \mathcal{B}_{8,4}$ as $F(x) = z = H\big(AES(x)\big)$ with $AES(x)$ is the output of AES S-box for the input x and $H \in \mathcal{B}_{8,4}$ is a surjective balanced function given by :

$$H(x) = (x_2, x_3, x_4, x_1) + (x_8, x_5, x_6, x_7) = (x_2 + x_8, x_3 + x_5, x_4 + x_6, x_1 + x_7).$$

In the Table 3, we show according to each input mask $a \in \mathbb{F}_2^8 - \{0\}$, the number of times that the conditional probability difference $e_a(Z)$, defined in Theorem 5, is zero. For instance, for $a = 0xFC$ we have $e_a(z)$ is null seven times, i.e. seven variable z from $\mathbb{F}_2^4$ gave $e_a(z) = 0$, which yields to 2^7 possible maximum correlators for F to $\ell_{0xFC} = (0xFC) \cdot x$. For the function F defined in this example (F has the same nonlinearity as AES which is 112), the method of Zhang and Chan gives many Boolean functions $g \in \mathcal{B}_4^*$ (to all $a \in \mathbb{F}_2^8 - \{0\}$). Based on experimental calculations after randomly placing 0 and 1 when $e_a(Z) = 0$, the Boolean functions g constructed showed a different ε_g. If we change the function $F : \mathbb{F}_2^n \to \mathbb{F}_2^m$ (especially when the number n increases), the obtained number of maximum correlators can be increased even more, which makes our Corollary 1 very useful, since it allows us to determine with certainty the correct maximum correlator $\max_{a, g \in \mathcal{B}_m^*} c_{g \circ F}(a)$ (it is the one that has the closest bias to that of F).

Table 3. The count of $e_a(z) = 0$ to each $a \in \mathbb{F}_2^8 - \{0\}$ (a in Hex format).

	0	1	2	3	4	5	6	7	8	9	A	B	C	D	E	F
0	-	2	3	4	4	1	2	2	1	4	4	2	2	3	6	6
1	2	4	3	2	4	1	1	2	4	2	6	5	4	7	3	3
2	1	4	1	4	3	5	6	5	2	4	2	2	4	3	2	1
3	3	2	3	3	4	2	2	5	5	5	3	2	4	4	4	6
4	1	3	3	2	5	4	1	4	1	3	3	3	5	4	2	5
5	3	7	5	3	1	3	3	3	3	3	3	1	3	2	2	2
6	1	1	1	1	1	4	3	3	7	1	2	4	3	1	3	4
7	4	2	5	3	4	2	3	3	4	6	3	3	1	3	4	4
8	3	5	7	4	2	1	4	5	3	2	3	2	2	3	3	2
9	0	4	3	3	2	2	4	3	1	4	0	3	0	3	3	5
A	4	4	3	2	4	6	4	3	5	5	1	4	5	2	4	3
B	1	4	3	3	4	2	3	3	5	2	5	1	3	4	2	4
C	4	3	2	6	5	3	5	4	4	3	4	1	6	4	3	3
D	2	5	5	5	4	3	3	2	3	0	5	1	1	3	2	2
E	2	2	1	0	3	5	3	3	4	2	2	4	0	3	1	3
F	6	3	3	5	2	1	3	6	5	4	5	6	7	2	5	2

8   Conclusion

The current paper analyzed Zhang and Chan method (combining F by g) to maximize the bias. In this work, we showed that the statement "for any g, the bias for $g \circ F$ is bigger than the bias of F" is not correct. Moreover, our proofs showed that the maximum correlator that is the function g that reaches the maximum bias for $g \circ F$ has the closest bias to that of F. In addition, the analysis of the maximum correlator presented by Zhang and Chan showed that the computing method coincide with our results when F is a permutation. When F is a surjective function, the method of constructing the maximum correlator can generate several functions. Our experience has shown that the functions obtained by the proposed method can have different bias. Accordingly, our work will help to determine the exact maximum correlator by removing all the computed functions g which have a bias far from ε_F.

A   Appendix-A

See Tables 4 and 5

- Γ_1

Table 4. Hexadecimal Representation for Γ_1

	0	1	2	3	4	5	6	7	8	9	A	B	C	D	E	F
0	6B	72	36	BD	BB	AD	1F	CC	FB	52	89	B4	DF	EF	63	08
1	70	80	56	A0	1C	48	9B	A9	1B	C0	32	A3	B1	03	28	58
2	C3	14	8B	DE	5E	82	88	EE	33	59	27	78	9C	B2	77	30
3	E4	16	4C	86	AE	A7	AB	E1	F0	B9	8C	17	F3	E9	99	F1
4	A6	EC	25	D7	CE	A8	35	AF	DB	2D	AA	D5	DA	2B	7B	D4
5	3E	E8	53	6E	7F	D3	F6	29	38	40	8E	3B	D9	BF	57	C5
6	55	04	A1	01	96	A2	4D	66	5A	CB	49	94	FF	07	46	1E
7	CF	AC	09	98	B3	A5	75	06	0E	3A	05	1A	91	CA	12	20
8	B5	E6	24	54	44	6C	A4	19	43	65	23	8F	DC	FA	69	92
9	6D	71	90	74	0C	D8	D1	DD	F7	93	9E	C7	D2	0F	61	60
A	B0	ED	2C	2F	C6	13	81	EB	BA	18	4F	34	F2	F8	7C	4E
B	73	8D	F5	F9	6A	F4	51	8A	9F	E3	64	D6	E7	CD	E2	50
C	9A	4A	11	4B	5B	BE	FC	C2	76	BC	FD	0D	7D	0B	83	02
D	3D	79	E0	7E	D0	FE	E5	37	21	5D	95	97	6F	22	5C	5F
E	00	3F	2A	B7	15	85	9D	EA	1D	39	C1	2E	B8	31	62	87
F	42	47	B6	68	41	C4	26	7A	84	C8	C9	0A	3C	45	10	67

• Γ_2

Table 5. Hexadecimal Representation for Γ_2

	0	1	2	3	4	5	6	7	8	9	A	B	C	D	E	F
0	4F	F0	16	B8	11	62	D4	EC	89	33	41	4E	C7	40	A8	93
1	67	34	82	D6	7B	69	94	0A	AF	D1	21	E7	A0	3E	EF	F3
2	8C	FE	F7	6C	1B	90	BC	70	39	07	C8	C0	D0	84	BD	17
3	68	5D	A9	87	0E	5C	F5	FB	77	10	AA	47	0D	6D	53	65
4	61	27	02	3C	25	66	C9	79	DF	F6	B4	A6	5F	BA	9D	2B
5	97	1C	9E	72	A1	06	D3	3B	74	83	DC	C5	9A	7D	AB	AD
6	55	7F	49	78	43	C1	2D	1A	A7	60	3A	E8	D5	1E	E0	73
7	F4	EB	BB	8A	05	6A	E2	63	92	00	80	BF	F1	4C	9C	9F
8	75	6B	35	A3	9B	4A	3F	5A	7A	38	85	CE	6E	B5	D9	DD
9	96	B0	A2	EE	24	D8	AC	15	B6	DA	C6	E9	4D	64	2C	5B
A	D2	98	FC	51	57	C3	8E	7C	30	B9	0B	42	88	8D	13	59
B	6F	4B	20	DB	F9	D7	DE	37	14	91	E6	EA	45	23	52	09
C	C2	3D	44	26	04	03	99	56	2E	46	32	B1	CF	36	E3	ED
D	FF	31	01	E5	AE	29	B2	86	B3	FD	0F	76	BE	B7	54	A4
E	28	1D	1F	5E	0C	C4	E4	A5	22	71	E1	CD	8F	CC	58	FA
F	2F	50	8B	19	2A	95	81	F8	CB	12	48	08	CA	7E	F2	18

B   Appendix-B

As Theorem 2 is linked to $\max_b(c_F(a,b) \pm c_g(b))^2$, we fix $\max_b c_F(a,b)$ and we vary $c_g(b)$. The y-axis indicates $c_{g \circ F}(a)$ and the x-axis indicates $\max_b c_g(b)$. By computing the white area surface ($|\varepsilon_F| \leq |\varepsilon_{g \circ F}|$), the probability Pr_g is determined as the ratio of white area surface over the rectangle area surface (Fig. 2).

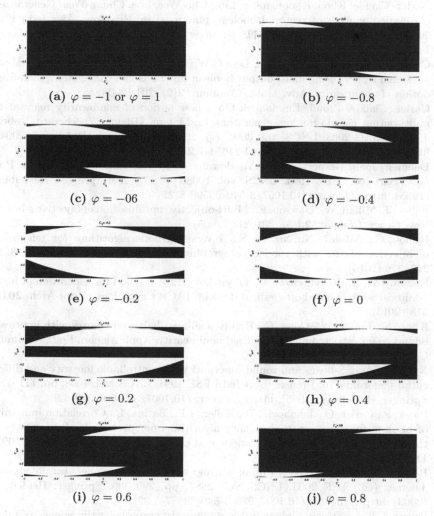

(a) $\varphi = -1$ or $\varphi = 1$ (b) $\varphi = -0.8$

(c) $\varphi = -06$ (d) $\varphi = -0.4$

(e) $\varphi = -0.2$ (f) $\varphi = 0$

(g) $\varphi = 0.2$ (h) $\varphi = 0.4$

(i) $\varphi = 0.6$ (j) $\varphi = 0.8$

Fig. 2. Computing Pr_g methods where φ denotes the fixed $\max_b c_F(a,b)$, i.e. $\max_b(c_F(a,b) \pm c_g(b))^2 = \max_b(\varphi \pm c_g(b))^2$

References

1. Braeken, A.: Cryptographic properties of boolean functions and S-boxes. Ph.D. thesis, phd thesis-2006 (2006)
2. Canteaut, A., Naya-Plasencia, M.: Correlation attacks on combination generators. Crypt. Commun. **4**(3–4), 147–171 (2012)
3. Carlet, C.: Boolean methods and models, ch. boolean functions for cryptography and error correcting codes (2009)
4. Carlet, Claude, Khoo, Khoongming, Lim, Chu-Wee, Loe, Chuan-Wen: Generalized correlation analysis of vectorial boolean functions. In: Biryukov, Alex (ed.) FSE 2007. LNCS, vol. 4593, pp. 382–398. Springer, Heidelberg (2007). https://doi.org/10.1007/978-3-540-74619-5_24
5. Carlet, C., Khoo, K., Lim, C.W., Loe, C.W.: On an improved correlation analysis of stream ciphers using multi-output boolean functions and the related generalized notion of nonlinearity. Adv. Math. Commun. **2**(2), 201 (2008)
6. Carlet, Claude, Prouff, Emmanuel: On a new notion of nonlinearity relevant to multi-output pseudo-random generators. In: Matsui, Mitsuru, Zuccherato, Robert J. (eds.) SAC 2003. LNCS, vol. 3006, pp. 291–305. Springer, Heidelberg (2004). https://doi.org/10.1007/978-3-540-24654-1_21
7. Daemen, Joan, Govaerts, René, Vandewalle, Joos: Correlation matrices. In: Preneel, Bart (ed.) FSE 1994. LNCS, vol. 1008, pp. 275–285. Springer, Heidelberg (1995). https://doi.org/10.1007/3-540-60590-8_21
8. Fuller, J., Millan, W., Dawson, E.: Multi-objective optimisation of bijective s-boxes. New Gener. Comput. **23**(3), 201–218 (2005)
9. Ivanov, G., Nikolov, N., Nikova, S.: Reversed genetic algorithms for generation of bijective s-boxes with good cryptographic properties. Crypt. Commun. **8**(2), 247–276 (2016)
10. Kazymyrov, O., Kazymyrova, V., Oliynykov, R.: A method for generation of high-nonlinear s-boxes based on gradient descent. IACR Cryptology ePrint Arch. **2013**, 578 (2013)
11. Khoo, K., Lim, C.W., Gong, G.: Highly nonlinear balanced s-boxes with improved bound on unrestricted and generalized nonlinearity. Appl. Algebra Eng., Commun. Comput. **19**(4), 323–338 (2008)
12. Nyberg, Kaisa: S-boxes and round functions with controllable linearity and differential uniformity. In: Preneel, Bart (ed.) FSE 1994. LNCS, vol. 1008, pp. 111–130. Springer, Heidelberg (1995). https://doi.org/10.1007/3-540-60590-8_9
13. Picek, S., Carlet, C., Jakobovic, D., Miller, J.F., Batina, L.: Correlation immunity of boolean functions: an evolutionary algorithms perspective. In: Proceedings of the 2015 Annual Conference on Genetic and Evolutionary Computation. pp. 1095–1102. ACM (2015)
14. Rose, Gregory G., Hawkes, Philip: Turing: a fast stream cipher. In: Johansson, Thomas (ed.) FSE 2003. LNCS, vol. 2887, pp. 290–306. Springer, Heidelberg (2003). https://doi.org/10.1007/978-3-540-39887-5_22
15. Rueppel, R.A.: Stream ciphers, in\contemporary cryptology: the science of information integrity. Simmons, G.J. (ed.) (1991)

16. Tarannikov, Yuriy, Korolev, Peter, Botev, Anton: Autocorrelation coefficients and correlation immunity of boolean functions. In: Boyd, Colin (ed.) ASIACRYPT 2001. LNCS, vol. 2248, pp. 460–479. Springer, Heidelberg (2001). https://doi.org/10.1007/3-540-45682-1_27

17. Zhang, Muxiang, Chan, Agnes: Maximum correlation analysis of nonlinear s-boxes in stream ciphers. In: Bellare, Mihir (ed.) CRYPTO 2000. LNCS, vol. 1880, pp. 501–514. Springer, Heidelberg (2000). https://doi.org/10.1007/3-540-44598-6_31

Block Ciphers

On MILP-Based Automatic Search
for Differential Trails Through Modular
Additions with Application to Bel-T

Muhammad ElSheikh, Ahmed Abdelkhalek, and Amr M. Youssef[✉]

Concordia Institute for Information Systems Engineering,
Concordia University, Montréal, QC, Canada
youssef@ciise.concordia.ca

Abstract. Using modular addition as a source of nonlinearity is frequently used in many symmetric-key structures such as ARX and Lai–Massey schemes. At FSE'16, Fu *et al.* proposed a Mixed Integer Linear Programming (MILP)-based method to handle the propagation of differential trails through modular additions assuming that the two inputs to the modular addition and the consecutive rounds are independent. However, this assumption does not necessarily hold. In this paper, we study the propagation of the XOR difference through the modular addition at the bit level and show the effect of the carry bit. Then, we propose a more accurate MILP model to describe the differential propagation through the modular addition taking into account the dependency between the consecutive modular additions. The proposed MILP model is utilized to launch a differential attack against Bel-T-256, which is a member of the Bel-T block cipher family that has been adopted recently as a national standard of the Republic of Belarus. In particular, we employ the concept of partial Differential Distribution Table to model the 8-bit S-Box of Bel-T using a MILP approach in order to automate finding a differential characteristic of the cipher. Then, we present a $4\frac{1}{7}$-round (out of 8) differential attack which utilizes a 3-round differential characteristic that holds with probability 2^{-111}. The data, time and memory complexities of the attack are 2^{114} chosen plaintexts, $2^{237.14}$ $4\frac{1}{7}$-round encryptions, and 2^{224} 128-bit blocks, respectively.

Keywords: Differential cryptanalysis · MILP · Modular addition · ARX · Bel-T

1 Introduction

Differential cryptanalysis, which was introduced by Biham and Shamir [4], is one of the most powerful attacks that are used to evaluate the security of symmetric-key primitives. For an n-bit primitive, the crucial step of the differential attack is to find a distinguisher $(\Delta P \rightarrow \Delta C)$ where an XOR difference of two plaintexts (ΔP) gives, after some rounds, another XOR difference (ΔC) with probability

© Springer Nature Switzerland AG 2019
J. Buchmann et al. (Eds.): AFRICACRYPT 2019, LNCS 11627, pp. 273–296, 2019.
https://doi.org/10.1007/978-3-030-23696-0_14

higher than 2^{-n}, independent of the secret key. Using this distinguisher, a key recovery attack can be performed by appending (prepending) some rounds after (before) the distinguisher and guessing the round keys.

Different optimization techniques such as Mixed Integer Linear Programming (MILP) attracted the attention of many cryptanalysis researchers. The first attempt to utilize MILP technique in symmetric-key cryptanalysis was developed by Mouha et al. [17] in which they applied a MILP technique to prove security bounds against both differential and linear cryptanalysis. Later, Cui et al. [6] proposed a MILP model for both impossible differential and zero-correlation attacks. Sasaki and Todo [19] developed a new search tool for impossible differential using MILP. Recently, Xiang et al. [25] defined systematic rules for constructing integral distinguishers using MILP. Then, Sun et al. complemented this work by handling ARX-based ciphers (`modulo` operations) [21] and ciphers with non-bit-permutation linear layer [22]. One of the downsides of these MILP models was the inability to efficiently describe the Difference Distribution Table (DDT) of large (8-bit) S-boxes which was tackled by Abdelkhalek et al. [2]. Regarding ARX-based block ciphers, Fu et al. [10] represented the conditions developed by Lipmaa and Moriai [15] (hereafter referred to as Lipmaa's conditions) by a set of MILP constraints in order to automate the search for the best differential trail through the modular addition. In this representation, the authors assume that the two inputs to modular addition and the consecutive component of the cipher's round function are independent. However, this assumption is very often not satisfied, especially with round functions that have two or more consecutive modular operations, see [24]. In the same context, Leurent [14] provides a tool based on finite state machines to automate the search for differential characteristics through the modular addition considering the constraints due to several consecutive bits of the modular addition inputs. However, the complexity of this analysis is linear in the number of states, and the number of states can be exponential in the size of the system, which according to the authors, makes this approach suitable only to study systems with a limited number of states.

In this work, we revisit the conditions stated by Lipmaa and Moriai [15] to verify the possibility of an XOR difference of two inputs of addition modulo 2^n to produce a specific XOR difference at the output. In particular, we deduce the conditions on the bits of the inputs and the output of addition modulo 2^n that have to be satisfied in order to propagate an XOR difference of the inputs to a particular XOR difference at the output. Using these conditions, we describe some examples showing that using Lipmaa's conditions with the independence assumption between the consecutive components of a block cipher is not enough to ensure the validity of the derived differential characteristic. To address this problem, we propose a new MILP model considering the dependency between two or more successive modular additions.

To illustrate the effectiveness of our approach, we apply our method to attack the block cipher Bel-T, which is a family of block ciphers that has been approved as the national standard of the Republic of Belarus [1], formerly known by its Russian name Belorussia. The Bel-T family includes three block ciphers, denoted as Bel-T-k, all of them have the same block size of 128 bits and a variable key length (k) of 128, 192 or 256 bits. The designers of Bel-T combined a Lai-Massey scheme [12] with a Feistel network [9] to build a complex round function with 7 S-box layers per round. The round function is iterated 8 times to construct the whole cipher. Concretely, we employ our MILP approach beside a Hamming weight-based partial DDT to search for a differential distinguisher for Bel-T. Then, we mount a $4\frac{1}{7}$-round differential attack on round-reduced Bel-T-256 which, up to our knowledge, is the best published attack against this cipher in the single-key setting. Moreover, we show that the Bel-T block cipher is not a Markov cipher [13] *i.e.*, the validity of the differential characteristic depends on the used secret key. In this context, we also provide a systematic method to define the set of keys that can be attacked using our differential characteristic.

Few cryptanalysis results on Bel-T block ciphers have been published including fault-based attacks [11] and the related-key differential attack on round-reduced Bel-T-256 [3]. Recently, ElSheikh *et al.* [8] presented two integral attacks on ($3\frac{2}{7}$ and $3\frac{6}{7}$)-round reduced Bel-T-256 in the single-key setting. It should be noted that in the related-key differential attack presented in [3], the modular addition is modeled using the method proposed by Fu *et al.* [10] with the independency assumption. We verified the distinguisher presented in [3] and found it to be invalid as it involves two modular additions that share the same input and have conflicting condition. Table 1 contrasts our attack with the integral attacks in [8].

The rest of this paper is organized as follows. In Sect. 2, we briefly revisit the XOR differential characteristic of modular addition. The developed MILP-based method, which is used to search for the differential characteristic, is explained in Sect. 3. In Sect. 4, we describe how we apply the new MILP model to find a differential distinguisher for Bel-T. Then, the details of our attack are presented in Sect. 5. Finally, the paper is concluded in Sect. 6.

Table 1. Attack results on Bel-T-256

Model	Attack	#Rounds	Data	Time	Memory	Reference
Single Key	Integral	$3\frac{2}{7}$	2^{13}	$2^{199.33}$	-	[8]
		$3\frac{6}{7}$	2^{33}	$2^{254.61}$	-	[8]
	Differential	$4\frac{1}{7}$	2^{114}	$2^{237.14}$	2^{224}	Sect. 5

2   XOR-Differential Characteristics of Modular Addition

Definition 1. *Let α, β and γ be fixed n-bit XOR differences. The XOR-differential probability (DP) of addition modulo 2^n (xdp^+) is the probability with which α and β propagate to γ through the modular addition operation, computed over all pairs of n-bit inputs (x,y):*

$$xdp^+(\alpha, \beta \to \gamma) = 2^{-2n} \times \#\{(x,y) : ((x \oplus \alpha) \boxplus (y \oplus \beta)) \oplus (x \boxplus y) = \gamma\}.$$

Lipmaa and Moriai [15] stated the following two conditions that have to be satisfied in order for the XOR input differences (α, β) to propagate to an output difference (γ) through the addition modulo 2^n:

1. The bit-wise XOR of the least significant bit of the inputs and output differences must be 0, i.e., $\alpha_0 \oplus \beta_0 \oplus \gamma_0 = 0$ which is equivalent to $\gamma_0 = \alpha_0 \oplus \beta_0$.
2. If the three bits α_i, β_i, and γ_i are equal, then the XOR of the subsequent bits $\alpha_{i+1}, \beta_{i+1}$, and γ_{i+1} must equal these bits as well, i.e., $\alpha_{i+1} \oplus \beta_{i+1} \oplus \gamma_{i+1} = \alpha_i = \beta_i = \gamma_i$ for $0 \le i \le n - 2$.

If these two conditions above are satisfied, then the probability of the differential characteristic (xdp^+) can be calculated as:

$$xdp^+(\alpha, \beta \to \gamma) = 2^{-\sum_{i=0}^{n-2} \neg eq(\alpha_i, \beta_i, \gamma_i)}$$

where $\neg eq$ is 0 when $(\alpha_i, \beta_i, \gamma_i)$ are the same, and 1 otherwise. By using these conditions, we can determine if a differential characteristic $(\alpha, \beta \to \gamma)$ is a valid one or not. For example, the characteristic $(\alpha, \beta \to \gamma) = (0001, 0001 \to 0001)$ is impossible because it breaks the first condition.

In the remaining of this section, we show our interpretation of these two conditions by deriving the relationship between the input and output differences at the bit level.

Let $x = (x_{n-1}, x_{n-2}, \dots, x_1, x_0)^1$, $y = (y_{n-1}, y_{n-2}, \dots, y_1, y_0)$, and $z = (z_{n-1}, z_{n-2}, \dots, z_1, z_0)$ be n-bit vectors where $z = x \boxplus y$. Then, z_i can be iteratively expressed as follows:

$$z_0 = x_0 \oplus y_0 \oplus c_0, \qquad c_0 = 0, \tag{1}$$

$$z_{i+1} = x_{i+1} \oplus y_{i+1} \oplus c_{i+1}, \quad c_{i+1} = x_i y_i \oplus x_i c_i \oplus y_i c_i \quad \forall i = 0, 1, \dots, n - 2. \tag{2}$$

It is obvious that the Lipmaa's conditions are based on Eqs. (1) and (2). Consider that we have two pairs (x, x^*) and (y, y^*) such that $\Delta x = x \oplus x^*$, and $\Delta y = y \oplus y^*$. The relation between the XOR input differences $\Delta x, \Delta y$ and the XOR output difference $\Delta z = z \oplus z^*$ can be derived as follows: Let $\Delta x = (\delta x_{n-1}, \delta x_{n-2}, \dots, \delta x_1, \delta x_0)$, $\Delta y = (\delta y_{n-1}, \delta y_{n-2}, \dots, \delta y_1, \delta y_0)$, and $\Delta z = (\delta z_{n-1}, \delta z_{n-2}, \dots, \delta z_1, \delta z_0)$ be the XOR difference where $\delta x_i = x_i \oplus x_i^*$, $\delta y_i = y_i \oplus y_i^*$, and $\delta z_i = z_i \oplus z_i^*$, respectively. The Lipmaa's first condition comes from Eq. (1) in which $\delta z_0 = \delta x_0 \oplus \delta y_0 \oplus \delta c_0$, but $\delta c_0 = 0$ as $c_0 = c_0^* = 0$. Therefore, for $(\Delta x, \Delta y \to \Delta z)$ to be a possible differential characteristic, the relation $(\delta z_0 = \delta x_0 \oplus \delta y_0)$ must be satisfied.

For given input and output differences at two successive bits $((\delta x_i, \delta y_i, \delta z_i)$ and $(\delta x_{i+1}, \delta y_{i+1}, \delta z_{i+1}))$, we can use Eq. (2) to calculate the XOR difference at the carry bit δc_{i+1} using the following two equations:

$$\delta c_{i+1} = c_{i+1} \oplus c_{i+1}^*$$
$$= x_i y_i \oplus x_i c_i \oplus y_i c_i \oplus x_i^* y_i^* \oplus x_i^* c_i^* \oplus y_i^* c_i^*, \tag{3}$$
$$\delta c_{i+1} = \delta z_{i+1} \oplus \delta x_{i+1} \oplus \delta y_{i+1} \tag{4}$$

---

[1] We use little-endian representation where x_0 is the least significant bit.

To have a valid differential characteristic, the value of δc_{i+1} evaluated from these two equations must be consistent. For example, if we have $\delta x_i = \delta y_i = \delta z_i = 0$, this implies that $\delta c_i = 0$, *i.e.*, if $x_i^* = x_i$, $y_i^* = y_i$, $z_i^* = z_i$ then $c_i^* = c_i$. Therefore, from equation (3), $\delta c_{i+1} = 0$. Consequently, $\delta z_{i+1} \oplus \delta x_{i+1} \oplus \delta y_{i+1} = 0$ must hold with probability 1.

As another example, let us consider the following XOR differences: $\delta x_i = \delta y_i = 0$, and $\delta z_i = 1$, this implies that $\delta c_i = 1$, *i.e.*, if $x_i^* = x_i$, $y_i^* = y_i$ and $z_i^* = \bar{z}_i$ then $c_i^* = \bar{c}_i$ where $\bar{z}_i, \bar{c}_i$ are the bit-wise NOT of z_i, c_i, respectively. As a result, the value of δc_{i+1} from Eq. (3) will depend on the relation between x_i and y_i as follows: $\delta c_{i+1} = x_i \oplus y_i$. If δc_{i+1} is 0, then the condition $x_i = y_i$ must be satisfied. In this case, from Eq. (2), the output bit z_i will equal to c_i and the carry bit c_{i+1} will be equal to x_i.

By iterating over all possible values of $\delta x_i, \delta y_i, \delta z_i$ and δc_{i+1}, we can drive the conditions on the bits x_i, y_i, z_i, c_i and c_{i+1} to have a valid differential characteristic. We summarize these conditions in Table 2, in which the condition column is divided into three sub-columns: the first one is the direct condition similar to the one we derived in the previous examples. The second and third sub-columns are the values of z_i and c_{i+1} in case the direct condition, the first sub-column, is satisfied.

It should be noted that Lipmaa's second condition is specified by the first two rows and last two rows of Table 2, *i.e.*, if $\delta x_i, \delta y_i$ and δz_i are equal, then $\delta c_{i+1} = \delta z_{i+1} \oplus \delta x_{i+1} \oplus \delta y_{i+1}$ has to equal them.

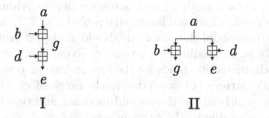

Fig. 1. Examples of incompatible conditions

2.1 Examples of Incompatible Conditions

In this section, we show some examples in which using Lipmaa's conditions with the independency assumption between the consecutive components of the block cipher is not enough to ensure the validity of the differential characteristic.

Example 1. Consider the two cascaded modular operations shown in Fig. 1(I) and the following XOR differences:

$$\Delta a = 00000001 \qquad g = a \boxplus b \qquad\qquad e = g \boxplus d$$
$$\Delta b = 00000000 \qquad \Delta g = 00001111 \qquad \Delta d = 00000000 \qquad \Delta e = 00001101$$

Table 2. Relation between $\delta x_i, \delta y_i, \delta z_i$ and δc_{i+1}

δz_i	δy_i	δx_i	δc_i	δc_{i+1}	Condition		
0	0	0	0	0	No condition		
0	0	0	0	1	Invalid		
0	0	1	1	0	$x_i = \bar{c}_i$	$z_i = \bar{y}_i$	$c_{i+1} = y_i = \bar{z}_i$
0	0	1	1	1	$x_i = c_i$	$z_i = y_i$	$c_{i+1} = x_i = c_i$
0	1	0	1	0	$y_i = \bar{c}_i$	$z_i = \bar{x}_i$	$c_{i+1} = x_i = \bar{z}_i$
0	1	0	1	1	$y_i = c_i$	$z_i = x_i$	$c_{i+1} = y_i = c_i$
0	1	1	0	0	$x_i = \bar{y}_i$	$z_i = \bar{c}_i$	$c_{i+1} = c_i = \bar{z}_i$
0	1	1	0	1	$x_i = y_i$	$z_i = c_i$	$c_{i+1} = x_i = y_i$
1	0	0	1	0	$x_i = y_i$	$z_i = c_i$	$c_{i+1} = x_i = y_i$
1	0	0	1	1	$x_i = \bar{y}_i$	$z_i = \bar{c}_i$	$c_{i+1} = c_i = \bar{z}_i$
1	0	1	0	0	$y_i = c_i$	$z_i = x_i$	$c_{i+1} = y_i = c_i$
1	0	1	0	1	$y_i = \bar{c}_i$	$z_i = \bar{x}_i$	$c_{i+1} = x_i = \bar{z}_i$
1	1	0	0	0	$x_i = c_i$	$z_i = y_i$	$c_{i+1} = x_i = c_i$
1	1	0	0	1	$x_i = \bar{c}_i$	$z_i = \bar{y}_i$	$c_{i+1} = y_i = \bar{z}_i$
1	1	1	1	0	Invalid		
1	1	1	1	1	No condition		

When looking at each modular addition operation individually, each one satisfies the Lipmaa's conditions and holds with probability 2^{-4}. Assuming independency, the whole differential characteristic should hold with probability 2^{-8}, however, it is actually an impossible characteristic. To explain, using Table 2, we can show that if the characteristic holds for the first operation, $g = (g_{n-1}, \cdots, g_1, g_0)$ will have a specific pattern ($g_1 = g_0$) due to the carry effect. On the other hand, the characteristic will hold for the second modular addition if g has a specific pattern ($g_1 = \bar{g}_0$), also due to the carry effect.

To further explain this carry effect, consider for the first operation the differences of the first three bits $(\delta g_0, \delta b_0, \delta a_0) = (1, 0, 1)$, $(\delta g_1, \delta b_1, \delta a_1) = (1, 0, 0)$ and $(\delta g_2, \delta b_2, \delta a_2) = (1, 0, 0)$. We access Table 2 twice with $(\delta z_i, \delta y_i, \delta x_i, \delta c_i, \delta c_{i+1})$ $= (\delta g_0, \delta b_0, \delta a_0, \delta c_0, \delta c_1) = (1,0,1,0,1)$ where the carry $\delta c_0 = \delta g_0 \oplus \delta b_0 \oplus \delta a_0$ and the carry $\delta c_1 = \delta g_1 \oplus \delta b_1 \oplus \delta a_1$, and with $(\delta z_i, \delta y_i, \delta x_i, \delta c_i, \delta c_{i+1}) = (\delta g_1, \delta b_1, \delta a_1, \delta c_1, \delta c_2) = (1,0,0,1,1)$ where the carry $\delta c_2 = \delta g_2 \oplus \delta b_2 \oplus \delta a_2$. From the first access, we get the following condition:

$$b_0 = \bar{c}_0 \Rightarrow g_0 = \bar{a}_0 \text{ and } c_1 = a_0 = \bar{g}_0 \tag{5}$$

And from the second access, we get the condition:

$$a_1 = \bar{b}_1 \Rightarrow g_1 = \bar{c}_1 \text{ and } c_2 = c_1 = \bar{g}_1 \tag{6}$$

From Eq. (5), if the characteristic is valid for the first bit, the carry bit c_1 will equal to $\bar{g}_0$. Also, if the characteristic is valid for the second bit, the same carry bit c_1 will have a relation with g_1 as determined by equation (6). By combining these two relations, we prove that the output g has the pattern $(g_1 = g_0)$.

Using the same methodology, we can also prove that the characteristic will hold for the second operation if the input g has the pattern $(g_1 = \bar{g}_0)$ which contradicts with the output of the first operation. All these patterns have also been verified experimentally.

Example 2. Let us consider another ordering of two modular operations as shown in Fig. 1(II) and the following XOR differences:

$$\Delta a = 00001111 \qquad g = a \boxplus b \qquad\qquad\qquad e = a \boxplus d$$
$$\Delta b = 00000001 \qquad \Delta g = 00010000 \qquad \Delta d = 00000001 \qquad \Delta e = 00000000$$

Again, the two operations individually satisfy the Lipmaa's conditions. However, the first operation requires the input a to be in a specific pattern $(a_0 = a_1 = a_2 = a_3)$ and the second operation requires the input a to be in another contradicting pattern $(a_0 = a_1 = a_2 = \bar{a}_3)$.

3 New MILP Model for Differential Characteristics of Modular Addition

Fu et al. [10] represent Lipmaa's conditions by a set of MILP constraints in order to automate the search for the best differential trail through the modular addition. As explained in the previous section, Lipmaa's conditions are not enough to ensure the validity of the derived differential characteristic especially when the block cipher structure has two or more consecutive modular additions. We propose a more accurate MILP model to automate the search for differential characteristics through modular additions taking into account the dependency between two consecutive modular additions that put more constraints on the values of input and output bits.

In order to represent the relation between two consecutive bits i and $i - 1$ on a variable x, we define a new variable called $x_i^{\oplus} = x_i \oplus x_{i-1}$ which can take a value of $\{0, 1, ?\}$; it is set to 0 if the condition $x_i = x_{i-1}$ is required and set to 1 if the condition $x_i = \bar{x}_{i-1}$ is required. Also, $x_i^{\oplus}$ can be kept undetermined (?) which means it can be 0 or 1 if there is no restriction on the relation between x_i and x_{i-1}.

Evaluation of $(z_i^{\oplus}, y_i^{\oplus}, x_i^{\oplus})$ for a Modular Addition. The relation between the bits x_i and x_{i-1}, for the input x in a modular addition comes through the carry bit c_i. Therefore the variable $x_i^{\oplus}$ can be evaluated as:

$$x_i^{\oplus} = (x_i \oplus c_i) \oplus (c_i \oplus x_{i-1})$$

where $x_i \oplus c_i$ and $c_i \oplus x_{i-1}$ can take a value of $\{0, 1, ?\}$ like $x_i^{\oplus}$ and the bit-wise XOR of ? with any value equals to ?. Based on Table 2, the values of $(x_i \oplus c_i)$ and

$(c_i \oplus x_{i-1})$ reflect the situation where there are conditions that should be satisfied to get the XOR differences $(\delta z_i, \delta y_i, \delta x_i, \delta c_{i+1})$ and $(\delta z_{i-1}, \delta y_{i-1}, \delta x_{i-1}, \delta c_i)$, respectively. Thus, the values of $(z_i^\oplus, y_i^\oplus, x_i^\oplus)$ will be determined based on the XOR differences $(\delta z_{i-1}, \delta y_{i-1}, \delta x_{i-1}, \delta z_i, \delta y_i, \delta x_i, \delta c_{i+1})$. We develop Algorithm 1 to determine these values. The input of our proposed algorithm is a general-purpose data structure dictionary $\mathbb{D}$ which is obtained by reformatting the valid rows in Table 2 where the relations between the current bits (z, y, x) with the current carry bit c and the subsequent carry bit c_{+1} are derived from the condition column in Table 2 and indexed by the value of the XOR difference of these bits, see Table 3. The output of Algorithm 1 is the truth table $\mathbb{T}$ of $(z_i^\oplus, y_i^\oplus, x_i^\oplus)$ as a function of the possible XOR differences $(\delta z_{i-1}, \delta y_{i-1}, \delta x_{i-1}, \delta z_i, \delta y_i, \delta x_i, \delta c_{i+1})$. Out of $2^7 = 128$ values of these bits, there are only 98 values that can be used as possible differences. Table 4 shows part of the derived truth table $\mathbb{T}$.

MILP Constraints for Modular Addition. To automate the process of the search for the differential characteristic using MILP technique, we have to transform the truth table $\mathbb{T}$ into a set of linear constraints. To this end, we represent the rows of $\mathbb{T}$ combined with the value of $\neg eq(\delta z_i, \delta y_i, \delta x_i)$ as a set of points in 11-dimensional binary vector space by substituting ? with all possible values e.g., the row $(0010010??1)$ associated with $\neg eq(0,0,1) = 1$ will be described by 4 binary vectors: $(00100100011, 00100100111, 00100101011, 00100101111)$. After this step, we have 640 binary vectors which have a convex hull. We use the `inequality_generator()` function in Sage[2] to obtain the H-Representation which is a set of linear inequalities that describe the vectors of this convex hull. We can use this set of inequalities as MILP constraints to present the possible XOR differences in two successive bits $(\delta z_{i-1}, \delta y_{i-1}, \delta x_{i-1}, \delta z_i, \delta y_i, \delta x_i)$ and the carry of the third bits (δc_{i+1}) combined with the conditions on the value of these bits represented as $(z_i^\oplus, y_i^\oplus, x_i^\oplus)$. In our case, the number of generated inequalities is 313, which is very large to be handled by any MILP optimizer. Therefore, we employ the Greedy algorithm proposed by Sun *et al.* in [23] to reduce this set to only 24 inequalities. In order to link the current bit with the following bits, we encoded Eq. (4), which is a bit-wise XOR of three inputs and one output, by 8 linear inequalities utilizing the truth table of the bit-wise XOR and `inequality_generator()` function in Sage. In this manner, we have represented the relation between three successive bits using $24 + 8 = 32$ inequalities and this representation is repeated for $i = 1, 2, \ldots, n - 2$. In order to complete the MILP modeling for the modular addition, we describe the condition on the first bit $(i = 0)$ $\delta z_0 \oplus \delta y_0 \oplus \delta x_0 = 0$ associated with $\neg eq(\delta z_0, \delta y_0, \delta x_0)$ by 4 linear inequalities. Accordingly, we can represent the difference propagation through the addition modulo 2^n taking into account the relation between the value of two successive bits using $32 \times (n - 2) + 4$ inequalities. The objective function of the MILP optimizer would minimize $\sum_{i=0}^{n-2} \neg eq(\delta z_i, \delta y_i, \delta x_i)$, which denotes the log_2 probability of the underlying characteristic.

---

[2] http://www.sagemath.org/.

Algorithm 1. Truth table generator

Input : The Dictionary $\mathbb{D}$.
Output: The truth table $\mathbb{T}$ of $(z_i^{\oplus}, y_i^{\oplus}, x_i^{\oplus})$ as a function of the possible XOR
  differences $(\delta z_{i-1}, \delta y_{i-1}, \delta x_{i-1}, \delta z_i, \delta y_i, \delta x_i, \delta c_{i+1})$

begin
$\quad$ $\mathbb{T} = \emptyset$
$\quad$ **for** 2^7 possible values of $(\delta z_{i-1}, \delta y_{i-1}, \delta x_{i-1}, \delta z_i, \delta y_i, \delta x_i, \delta c_{i+1})$ **do**
$\quad\quad$ $\delta c_{i-1} \leftarrow \delta z_{i-1} \oplus \delta y_{i-1} \oplus \delta x_{i-1}$
$\quad\quad$ $\delta c_i \leftarrow \delta z_i \oplus \delta y_i \oplus \delta x_i$
$\quad\quad$ **if** $(\delta z_{i-1}, \delta y_{i-1}, \delta x_{i-1}, \delta c_{i-1}, \delta c_i)$ in $\mathbb{D}$.keys AND $(\delta z_i, \delta y_i, \delta x_i, \delta c_i, \delta c_{i+1})$
$\quad\quad$ in $\mathbb{D}$.keys **then**
$\quad\quad\quad$ RCarry1 $\leftarrow \mathbb{D}[(\delta z_i, \delta y_i, \delta x_i, \delta c_i, \delta c_{i+1})][0]$
$\quad\quad\quad$ RCarry2 $\leftarrow \mathbb{D}[(\delta z_{i-1}, \delta y_{i-1}, \delta x_{i-1}, \delta c_{i-1}, \delta c_i)][1]$
$\quad\quad\quad$ $(z_i^{\oplus}, y_i^{\oplus}, x_i^{\oplus}) \leftarrow$ RCarry1 $\oplus$ RCarry2
$\quad\quad\quad$ $\mathbb{T} \leftarrow \mathbb{T} \cup \{(\delta z_{i-1}, \delta y_{i-1}, \delta x_{i-1}, \delta z_i, \delta y_i, \delta x_i, \delta c_{i+1}, z_i^{\oplus}, y_i^{\oplus}, x_i^{\oplus})\}$
$\quad\quad$ **end**
$\quad$ **end**
$\quad$ **return** $\mathbb{T}$
end

---

4 Application on Bel-T

4.1 Bel-T Specification

Since the official Bel-T specification is available only in Russian, we rely on the
English version of the specification that is provided by Jovanovic and Polian,
who presented fault-based attacks on the Bel-T block cipher family [11]. Bel-T
has a 128-bit block size and a variable key length of 128, 192 or 256 bits. The
128-bit plaintext P is split into 4 32-bit words, *i.e.*, $P = A_0^0 || B_0^0 || C_0^0 || D_0^0$. The
round function of Bel-T consists of 7 S-box layers in which a 32-bit mapping
function (G_r) is combined with one or two modulo operations as illustrated in
Fig. 2. Then, this round function is repeated 8 times for all versions of Bel-T. The
function G_r (G-box) maps a 32-bit word $w = w_1 || w_2 || w_3 || w_4$, with $w_i \in \{0,1\}^8$,
as follows: $G_r(w) = (H(w_1) || H(w_2) || H(w_3) || H(w_4)) \lll r$. Here, H is an 8-bit
S-box and $\lll r$ denotes left shift rotation by r positions ($r \in \{5, 13, 21\}$). The
specification of the 8-bit S-box can be found in [11].

Key Schedule. In all versions of Bel-T, the 128-bit plaintext block P is
encrypted using a 256-bit encryption key denoted as $K_1 || \ldots || K_8$, where K_i is a
32-bit word for $1 \leq i \leq 8$. The encryption key is distributed among the round
keys as shown in Table 5. The encryption key is extracted from the master key
as follows:

- Bel-T-256: the encryption key is identical to the master key.
- Bel-T-192: the master key is formatted as $K_1 || \ldots || K_6$ and K_7, K_8 are set to
  $K_7 := K_1 \oplus K_2 \oplus K_3$ and $K_8 := K_4 \oplus K_5 \oplus K_6$.

– Bel-T-128: the master key is formatted as $K_1 \| \ldots \| K_4$ and K_5, K_6, K_7, K_8 are set to $K_5 := K_1$, $K_6 := K_2$, $K_7 := K_3$ and $K_8 := K_4$.

Table 3. The dictionary $\mathbb{D}$.

D.keys					$\mathbb{D}[*][0]$	$\mathbb{D}[*][1]$
δz	δy	δx	δc	δc_{+1}	$c \oplus (z,y,x)$	$c_{+1} \oplus (z,y,x)$
0	0	0	0	0	$(?, ?, ?)$	$(?, ?, ?)$
0	0	1	1	0	$(?, ?, 1)$	$(1, 0, ?)$
0	0	1	1	1	$(?, ?, 0)$	$(?, ?, 0)$
0	1	0	1	0	$(?, 1, ?)$	$(1, ?, 0)$
0	1	0	1	1	$(?, 0, ?)$	$(?, 0, ?)$
0	1	1	0	0	$(1, ?, ?)$	$(1, ?, ?)$
0	1	1	0	1	$(0, ?, ?)$	$(?, 0, 0)$
1	0	0	1	0	$(0, ?, ?)$	$(?, 0, 0)$
1	0	0	1	1	$(1, ?, ?)$	$(1, ?, ?)$
1	0	1	0	0	$(?, 0, ?)$	$(?, 0, ?)$
1	0	1	0	1	$(?, 1, ?)$	$(1, ?, 0)$
1	1	0	0	0	$(?, ?, 0)$	$(?, ?, 0)$
1	1	0	0	1	$(?, ?, 1)$	$(1, 0, ?)$
1	1	1	1	1	$(?, ?, ?)$	$(?, ?, ?)$

Table 4. Part of the truth table $\mathbb{T}$.

δz_{i-1}	δy_{i-1}	δx_{i-1}	δz_i	δy_i	δx_i	δc_{i+1}	$z_i^\oplus$	$y_i^\oplus$	$x_i^\oplus$
...									
0	0	1	0	0	1	0	?	?	1
0	0	1	0	0	1	1	?	?	0
0	0	1	0	1	1	0	0	?	?
0	0	1	0	1	1	1	1	?	?
0	0	1	1	0	1	0	?	0	?
0	0	1	1	0	1	1	?	1	?
0	1	0	0	1	0	0	?	1	?
0	1	0	0	1	0	1	?	0	?
0	1	0	0	1	1	0	0	?	?
0	1	0	0	1	1	1	1	?	?
0	1	0	1	1	0	0	?	?	0
0	1	0	1	1	0	1	?	?	1
0	1	1	0	0	1	0	?	?	1
0	1	1	0	0	1	1	?	?	0
0	1	1	0	1	0	0	?	1	?
0	1	1	0	1	0	1	?	0	?
0	1	1	0	1	1	0	0	?	?
...									

4.2 MILP-Based Search for Differential Characteristic of Bel-T

To search for differential characteristics in a block cipher using MILP, the difference propagation through its components is described using a set of linear constraints. In Bel-T, this means generating a set of linear inequalities to describe how an XOR difference would propagate through a bit-wise XOR, an addition/subtraction modulo 2^{32}, and an 8-bit S-box. As the difference propagates with probability through the non-linear components, its associated probability is incorporated in the corresponding linear inequalities. The objective function of the MILP model would be to maximize this probability, which we do by minimizing the negative of the base-2 logarithm of this probability.

Bit-Wise XOR. If $\delta x_i, \delta y_i$ and δz_i represent the bit-level differences, then the difference propagation through the bit-wise XOR operation $\delta x_i \oplus \delta y_i = \delta z_i$ can be represented by 5 linear inequalities [23]. Using the truth table of the XOR operation, these can be further reduced to the following 4 linear inequalities:

$$\delta x_i + \delta y_i - \delta z_i \geq 0, \ \ \delta x_i - \delta y_i + \delta z_i \geq 0, \ \ -\delta x_i + \delta y_i + \delta z_i \geq 0, \ \ -\delta x_i - \delta y_i - \delta z_i \geq -2.$$

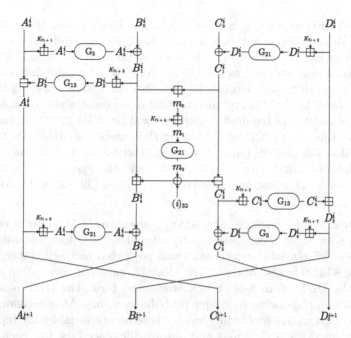

Fig. 2. Bel-T round function. $\oplus, \boxplus, \boxminus$ denote bit-wise XOR, arithmetic addition and subtraction modulo 2^{32} respectively, and $(i)_{32}$ denotes the round number represented as 32-bit word.

Table 5. Encryption Key schedule of Bel-T, where i and K_{7i+j} denote the round number and the round key, respectively.

i	K_{7i+1}	K_{7i+2}	K_{7i+3}	K_{7i+4}	K_{7i+5}	K_{7i+6}	K_{7i+7}
0	K_1	K_2	K_3	K_4	K_5	K_6	K_7
1	K_8	K_1	K_2	K_3	K_4	K_5	K_6
2	K_7	K_8	K_1	K_2	K_3	K_4	K_5
3	K_6	K_7	K_8	K_1	K_2	K_3	K_4
4	K_5	K_6	K_7	K_8	K_1	K_2	K_3
5	K_4	K_5	K_6	K_7	K_8	K_1	K_2
6	K_3	K_4	K_5	K_6	K_7	K_8	K_1
7	K_2	K_3	K_4	K_5	K_6	K_7	K_8

Modular Addition and Subtraction. We use the new MILP model described in Sect. 3 to propagate the input differences ($\Delta x, \Delta y$) to an output difference (Δz) through the addition modulo 2^{32} such that $x \boxplus y = z$ using $32 \times (32-2) + 4 = 964$ inequalities. Since the subtraction modulo 2^n, $x \boxminus y = z$ is equivalent to $x = y \boxplus z$, the difference propagation through modular subtraction can be described in a similar way as that used to describe modular addition.

Modular Addition with a Secret Key. The Bel-T round function encompasses a modular addition with a secret key which has zero difference in a single-key differential attack. This operation can then be expressed as $x \boxplus k = z$ and the differential characteristic as $(\Delta x, 0) \rightarrow \Delta z$. Therefore, the difference propagation through this operation can be described in a similar way as that used to describe modular addition by inserting 32 more constraints to explicitly set $\Delta y = 0$. The number of required constraints will be $964 + 32 = 996$. Indeed, we can improve this description by decreasing the number of MILP constraints to roughly half as follows. We repeat the steps described in Sect. 3 using the rows of the truth table $\mathbb{T}$ that have $\delta y_{i-1} = \delta y_i = 0$ and also $\delta y_{i+1} = 0$. Consequently, the number of MILP constraints decreases to $(13 + 4)(32 - 2) + 2 = 512$.

8-Bit S-Box. Using the Sage `inequality_generator()` function to model the DDT of an 8-bit S-box is computationally infeasible. Therefore, the use of MILP to search for differential characteristics was restricted to block ciphers that do not include 8-bit S-boxes. Abdelkhalek et al. [2] have put forward an approach to model the DDT of an 8-bit S-box efficiently. First, the DDT is split into several tables corresponding to unique probability values. After assigning binary variables to each unique probability value, these binary variables are represented as Boolean functions in the input and output difference bits, i.e., each Boolean function is 1 when the input difference is propagated to the output difference with the corresponding probability value, and 0 otherwise. Next, the Quine-McCluskey algorithm [16,18] was used to transform the Boolean functions to their reduced Product of Sum (PoS) which can then be described by a set of linear inequalities. To describe the deterministic propagation of the zero-difference, an additional binary variable was used as a sort of flag, i.e., when it is 0, the S-box is inactive and therefore both the input and output differences are set to 0. When it is 1, the S-box is active and one probability value along with input difference and corresponding output difference are chosen. As in ARX block ciphers, the probability of the differential characteristic gets lower when more bits are active, we decided to follow the approach in [3] in which we do not use the high probability entries in the DDT, but rather the entries with low Hamming weight in the input and output differences. Throughout our experiments, we have limited the Hamming weight of the input and output difference not to exceed 3. However, the partial DDT was still too large to be handled directly using the `inequality_generator()` function and hence we augmented our approach with the approach proposed by Abdelkhalek et al. for handling the DDT of large S-boxes to describe the partial DDT using linear inequalities. Based on our implementation, 1,660 linear inequalities are needed to describe this Hamming weight-based partial DDT.

Lai-Massey Scheme. Since the Lai-Massey scheme is invertible, the following constraints are added to our model to enforce the output of the Lai-Massey scheme (B_4^i, C_2^i) to be non-zero when its input (B_1^i, C_1^i) is non-zero, see Fig. 2.

$$\sum_{j=0}^{n-1} B_{1,j}^i + \sum_{j=0}^{n-1} C_{1,j}^i + LM_i \geq 1,$$

$$\sum_{j=0}^{n-1} B_{4,j}^i + \sum_{j=0}^{n-1} C_{2,j}^i + 2n \times LM_i \leq 2n,$$

$$\sum_{j=0}^{n-1} B_{1,j}^i + \sum_{j=0}^{n-1} C_{1,j}^i + 2n \times LM_i \leq 2n,$$

$$\sum_{j=0}^{n-1} B_{4,j}^i + \sum_{j=0}^{n-1} C_{2,j}^i + LM_i \geq 1.$$

In these constraints, LM_i is a dummy binary variable. If the input difference is zero, the first equation enforces LM_i to be 1 which enforces the output difference to be zero in the second equation. If the input difference is non-zero, the third equation enforces LM_i to be 0 which enforces the output difference to be non-zero in the fourth equation.

4.3   3-round Differential Characteristic

Using the above derived MILP model of the different components of the Bel-T, we are able to build a model of the whole round of Bel-T using $55,641$ linear inequalities and $2,647$ binary variables. Then, we used the Gurobi[3] optimizer on a server of two Xeon Processors E5-2697 ($2 \times 12 = 24$ cores in total) with 125 GB RAM to search for a differential characteristic of Bel-T. Consequently, we found a 2-round differential characteristic with probability 2^{-54} after about 4.5 hours. We use this characteristic as an initial solution for the optimizer in order to extend the characteristic to 3 rounds. After running the search process for 36 days, we were not able to find a 3-round differential characteristic better than the one that holds with probability 2^{-111}. The 3-round differential characteristic we use in our attack is shown in Fig. 3 in which 0 denotes a 32-bit difference of all zeros, e_i, e_{i-j} and $e_{i,j,k,\dots}$ denote 32-bit difference of all 0's and 1 at bit i, bits i to j, and bits $i, j, k, \cdots$, respectively.

4.4   Validity of the Differential Characteristic

In this section, we show that Bel-T block cipher is not a Markov cipher and the differential characteristic depends on the used secret key. Consequently, we propose a systematic way to obtain the ratio of the keys that can be attacked using our distinguisher.

Recall that a Markov cipher [13] is an iterated block cipher in which the probability of the difference e.g., the XOR difference through the individual operations of the round function is independent of the corresponding plaintext values of its input, if the round keys applied to each round are independent

---

[3] http://www.gurobi.com/.

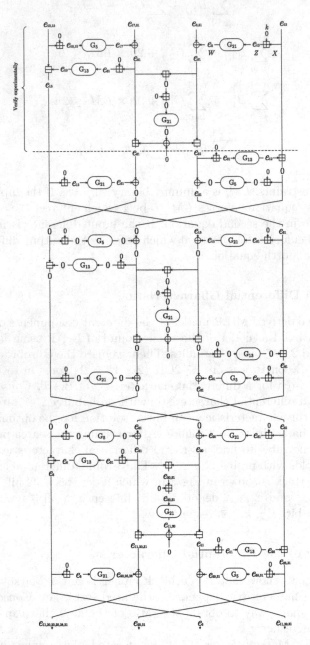

Fig. 3. 3-round differential characteristic of Bel-T with probability 2^{-111}. 0 denotes a 32-bit difference of all zeros, e_i, e_{i-j} and $e_{i,j,k}$ denote a 32-bit difference of 0's and 1 at bit i, bits i to j, and bits i, j, and k, respectively

and chosen in a uniformly random manner. In the case of Bel-T, the secret key is mixed via modular addition operations, therefore the XOR difference propagation through these operations is probabilistic and depends on the used key. Additionally, the hypothesis of independent round keys does not hold due to the simple key schedule of Bel-T. Moreover, there are many two or more successive modular additions, which are not independent as shown in Sect. 2. For these reasons, we can conclude that Bel-T is not a Markov cipher.

Since the secret key is mixed via modular addition operations, Bel-T is not a *key-alternating* cipher [7] and the probability of the XOR difference of these modular operations may drop to zero due to the used key [5] and we therefore cannot use our distinguisher in this case. In the remaining of this section, we obtain the ratio of the keys (valid keys) which we can use the distinguisher with. We define the S-box layer to include the modular addition with a key followed by the G-box mapping (G_r). We consider a 32-bit key as an invalid key when the probability of the XOR difference through its S-box layer drops to zero independent of the other input of the modular addition.

Let us consider, *e.g.*, the S-box layer of K_2 in round 0 (see Fig. 3) in which the key K_2 has a specific value k, $Z = X \boxplus k$ and $W = G_{21}(Z)$ where $\Delta X = \Delta Z = 0x00001000$, $\Delta k = 0x00000000$ and $\Delta W = 0x00000008$. Therefore, we are looking for the values of k that cannot give the output difference ΔW for any value of X.

For each value of k, we can exhaustively search over all possible values of the pair $(X, X \oplus \Delta X)$ to check if there is a value of X that leads to the output difference ΔW. If there is no such value, we consider k as invalid. The complexity of search for all possible values of K_2 will be roughly $\mathcal{O}(2^{64})$ which is computationally hard because we will repeat this search for all modular additions with keys.

Alternatively, we can obtain from Table 2 that the condition $k_{12} = c_{12}$, where k_{12} and c_{12} are the bit number 12 of the key and the carry respectively, is the only constraint that has to be checked to verify whether the key k is an invalid key or not. Also from the DDT of the G-box, the second byte of Z (bits from Z_8 to Z_{15}) in hexadecimal has to be one of $\{0x02, 0x12, 0x4C, 0x5C\}$ to satisfy the output difference ΔW. Accordingly, the following constraints have to be satisfied:

$$k_{12} = c_{12}, \quad Z_8 = 0, \quad Z_{13} = 0, \quad Z_{15} = 0, \quad \bar{Z}_9 = Z_{10} = Z_{11} = Z_{14}.$$

For each value of k, there is a value X that gives $Z_8 = 0$ with probability 1 because there are no conditions on k nor Z from bit 0 to 7. Given this fact and by using Eqs. (1) and (2), we can prove that the carry bits $c_9 = c_{10} = c_{11} = c_{12} = 0$ if the key bits $k_8 = 1$ and $k_9 = k_{10} = k_{11} = 0$ independently of the corresponding bits of X. Therefore, if the key bit $k_{12} = 1$, the condition $k_{12} = c_{12}$ will be impossible. As a result, if the key k has the pattern $k_8 = k_{12} = 1$ and $k_9 = k_{10} = k_{11} = 0$, it will be an invalid key irrespective of the value X due to the contradiction between the two constraints $Z_8 = 0$ and $k_{12} = c_{12}$. We can manually search for such patterns but this process is very difficult, time-consuming, and error-prone.

Observation 1. *Consider a modular addition $z = x \boxplus y$ where the bit z_i has a specific value. Then, the carry bit c_j (for $j > i$) depends on the input bits from i to $j - 1$ and is independent of the input bits from 0 to $i - 1$.*

The dependency between a carry bit c_j and the input bits from 0 to $j - 1$ is due to the carry chain (see Eq. 2). If we know that the output bit z_i has a specific value, we can evaluate the carry bit c_i as $c_i = z_i \oplus x_i \oplus y_i$ instead of evaluating it using the value of x_{i-1}, y_{i-1} and c_{i-1}. Thus, the carry chain and dependency are broken. Back to our example, given that $Z_8 = 0$, the carry bit c_{12} will depend on the bits from 8 to 11 of the inputs X and k based on the observation. Therefore, considering the key k as an invalid will depend on its bits from 8 to 12. In general, given a key k, if we exhaustively search over all possible values of the pair $(X, X \oplus \Delta X)$ and there is no value X that can lead to the difference ΔW, then the byte of the key containing the conditional bits is the reason for invalidating ΔW. We therefore can repeat the search for all possible value of these bytes. Consequently, the exhaustive search complexity in our example will be reduced roughly to $\mathcal{O}(2^{40})$ which is feasible.

The above approach can be generalized to determine the set of the byte values $\mathbb{K}$ leading to invalid keys as shown in Procedure (Obtain Invalid Key Set).

Table 6 summarizes the ratio of valid keys of each key K_i that has conditions in our distinguisher. It should be noted that the key K_2 is used in two rounds but the bytes that have the conditions are in different positions. Accordingly, the total ratio of the valid keys can be evaluated as the multiplication of all ratios of the valid keys which will be $2^{-3.8}$ corresponding to $2^{252.2}$ keys. In order to validate this result, we have experimentally verified the differential characteristic. In particular, we have opted the first four S-box layers of the differential characteristic of probability 2^{-24} (see Fig. 3) and have found that the experimental probability matches on average the theoretical one for 4426 of 10000 randomly generated keys. Comparing with Table 6, this ratio is very close to the ratio of the valid keys for this part of the distinguisher.

5   Differential Attack on $4\frac{1}{7}$-Round Reduced Bel-T-256

In this section, we present a differential attack on $4\frac{1}{7}$-round reduced Bel-T-256 by appending one round and one S-box layer on the above derived differential distinguisher as illustrated in Fig. 4. Our differential characteristic ends at A_0^3, B_0^3, C_0^3 and D_0^3 with values $e_{11,20,23,25,28,31}$, $e_{25,31}$, e_5 and $e_{11,29,31}$, respectively. Therefore, by propagating the differences at A_0^3 and D_0^3 through the S-box layers, we obtain the corresponding 32-bit difference at B_1^3 and C_1^3. Table 7 summarizes the difference in Binary at some points that we will use during the attack. Our attack has two phases: pre-computation phase and an online phase.

5.1   Pre-computation Phase

In this phase, we create 4 hash tables (H_1, H_2, H_3, H_4) corresponding to the S-box layers shown in Fig. 4 as follows:

Procedure Obtain Invalid Key Set

```
Input  : ΔX, ΔW
Output: K
begin
   K = ∅
   Determine PosOfBytes and NBytes which are the position and the number
      of bytes that have XOR difference in ΔX
   for 2^(8×NBytes) possible values of Bytes do
      Generate k randomly such that the concatenation of the bytes in the
         position PosOfBytes has the value Bytes
      invalid = True
      for 2^32 possible values of X do
         if G(X ⊞ k) ⊕ G((X ⊕ ΔX) ⊞ k) = ΔW then
            invalid = False
            break
         end
      end
      if invalid then
         K ← K ∪ {Bytes}
      end
   end
   return K
end
```

Table 6. Ratio of valid keys

Round	Key	Ratio of valid keys
0	K_1	136/256
	K_2	216/256
	K_6	129/256
2	K_2	216/256
	K_3	144/256
	K_4	228/256
	K_5	192/256

Table 7. The difference at the points used in the attack

Point label	The difference in Binary			
A_0^3	10010010	10010000	00001000	00000000
B_0^3	10000010	00000000	00000000	00000000
C_0^3	00000000	00000000	00000000	00100000
D_0^3	10100000	00000000	00001000	00000000
B_1^3	???00000	000?????	????????	????????
C_1^3	????????	????????	???00000	000?????

H_1: For all $2^{5×32=160}$ possible values of $x, \Delta x, y, \Delta y$ and K_2, we obtain the corresponding values of z and Δz such that $z = y \boxminus G_{13}(x \boxplus K_2)$. If the value of Δz is equal to the difference at D_0^3, we store the values of K_2 and z in the hash table H_1 indexed by the values of $x, \Delta x, y$ and Δy. The probability that the value of Δz is equal to the difference at D_0^3 is equal to 2^{-32}. Therefore, Table H_1 has on average $2^{160} \times 2^{-32} = 2^{128}$ entries. As a result, we have, on average, $\frac{2^{128}}{2^{4×32}} = 1$ value for K_2 per row.

H_2: For the value of Δx equal to the difference at D_0^3 and all 2^{24} possible value of Δy in form of the difference at C_1^3 combined with all $2^{3×32=96}$ possible values of x, y and K_7, we obtain the corresponding values of z and Δz such that $z = y \oplus G_{21}(x \boxplus K_7)$. Then, we store the value of K_7 in the hash table H_2 indexed by the values of x, y and Δy, if the value of Δz is equal to the difference at C_0^3 which has a probability equal to 2^{-24}. Therefore, Table H_2 has on average $2^{96+24} \times 2^{-24} = 2^{96}$ entries. Thus, we have, on average, $\frac{2^{96}}{2^{2 \times 32 + 24}} = 2^8$ value for K_7 per row.

H_3: For all 2^{24} possible value of Δx in form of the difference at B_1^3 combined with all $2^{4 \times 32 = 128}$ possible values of $x, y, \Delta y$ and K_8, we obtain the corresponding values of z and Δz such that $z = y \boxplus G_{13}(x \boxplus K_8)$. If the value of Δz is in the form of the difference at A_0^3, we store the values of K_8 and z in the hash table H_3 indexed by the values of $x, \Delta x, y$ and Δy. The probability that the value of Δz is in the form of the difference at A_0^3 is equal to 2^{-32}. Therefore, Table H_3 has on average $2^{128+24} \times 2^{-32} = 2^{120}$ entries. As a result, we have, on average, $\frac{2^{120}}{2^{3 \times 32 + 24}} = 1$ values for K_8 per row.

H_4: Initialize a hash table of $2^{3 \times 32 + 24 = 120}$ rows with binary value 0. Then, for the value of Δx equal to the difference at A_0^3 and all 2^{24} possible values of Δy in the form of the difference at B_1^3 combined with all $2^{3 \times 32 = 96}$ possible values of x, y, and K_6, we obtain the corresponding values of z and Δz such that $z = y \oplus G_5(x \boxplus K_6)$. If the value of Δz is equal to the difference at B_0^3, we store a binary value 1 in the hash table H_4 indexed by the values of $x, y, \Delta y$ and K_6. Here, the binary values 1 and 0 denote a valid entry and an invalid entry. The probability of finding a valid entry in H_4, equivalent to the probability that the value Δz is equal to the difference at B_0^3, is equal to 2^{-24}. Consequently, we have one valid entry for every 2^{24} accesses to H_4.

Table 8 summarizes the time and memory complexities of the pre-computation phase. It should be noted that the memory required by the tables H_1 and H_4 can be slightly reduced to $2^{128.51}$ and $2^{119.01}$ 32-bit words respectively, if we store only the valid candidates of K_2 and K_6 based on the ratio of the valid keys form Table 6.

5.2   Online Phase

In this phase, we collect a set of plaintext/ciphertext pairs. Then, we utilize the pre-computation tables and key guessing to obtain right candidate keys and then recover the correct master key.

Table 8. The time and memory complexities of the pre-computation phase

Table	Time (S-box layer Encryption)	Memory (32-bit word)
H_1	2^{160}	$2^{160} \times 2^{-32} \times 2 = 2^{129}$
H_2	2^{120}	$2^{120} \times 2^{-24} \times 1 = 2^{96}$
H_3	2^{152}	$2^{152} \times 2^{-32} \times 2 = 2^{121}$
H_4	2^{120}	2^{120}[a]

[a] For simplicity, we store the binary values 0 and 1 as 32-bit words.

Data Collection. We select a set of 2^m 128-bit plaintexts that can take any arbitrary values then we compute another set of 2^m plaintexts by XORing each plaintext in the first set with the input of the differential distinguisher (*i.e.*, $A_0^0||B_0^0||C_0^0||D_0^0$). After that, we query the encryption oracle and compute the corresponding ciphertext difference. Here, we use 2^{m+1} plaintexts to generate 2^m plaintext/ciphertext pairs satisfying the input difference of our differential distinguisher (the value of m will be determined below).

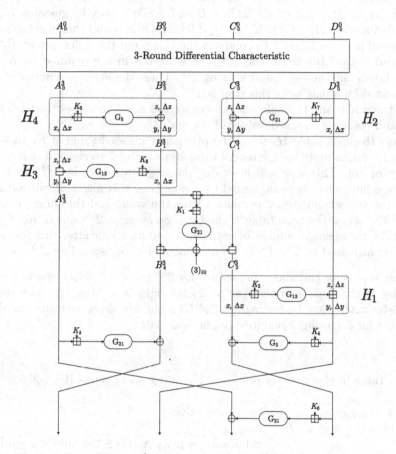

Fig. 4. $4\frac{1}{7}$-Round Attack on Bel-T-256

Key Recovery. We first prepare $2^{7 \times 32} = 2^{224}$ counters corresponding to the 2^{224} keys involved in the analysis. After that, for each ciphertext pair in 2^m pairs obtained in the data collection phase, we apply the following procedure:

1. Guess K_4 and partially decrypt the ciphertext to get the value and the difference at C_2^3. The average number of keys suggested by a pair after this step is 2^{32}.

2. Access the hash table H_1 to get, on average, 1 value of K_2 and D_0^3.
3. Guess K_6 and partially decrypt the ciphertext to get the value and the difference at A_3^3. The average number of keys suggested by a pair after this step will increase to 2^{64}.
4. Guess K_3 and partially decrypt the ciphertext combined with the value and the difference from the previous step to get the value and the difference at B_4^3. The average number of keys suggested by a pair after this step is 2^{96}.
5. Recall that $B_1^3 = B_4^3 \boxminus G_{21}(B_1^3 \boxplus C_1^3 \boxplus K_1) \oplus (3)_{32}$ and $C_1^3 = C_2^3 \boxplus G_{21}(B_1^3 \boxplus C_1^3 \boxplus K_1) \oplus (3)_{32}$. Hence $B_1^3 \boxplus C_1^3 = B_4^3 \boxplus C_2^3$. Therefore, by guessing K_1, we can deduce $G_{21}(B_1^3 \boxplus C_1^3 \boxplus K_1) = G_{21}(B_4^3 \boxplus C_2^3 \boxplus K_1)$ and then use the values obtained in steps 1 and 4 to compute the value and the difference at B_1^3 and C_1^3 and discard the key if the differences are not in the required form. This step filters out the suggested keys by 2^{16}. Thus, the average number of keys suggested by a pair after this step is 2^{112}.
6. Use the values and the differences form steps 3 and 5 to access the hash table H_3 and get, on average, 1 values of K_8 and A_0^3.
7. Access the hash table H_4 using the previously guessed value of K_6 in step 3 and the values and the differences from steps 5 and 7 to check if it is a valid entry or not. This step will filter out the suggested keys by 2^{24}. Thus, the average number of keys suggested by a pair after this filtration will be 2^{88}.
8. Use the value from step 2 combined with the value and the difference from step 5 to access the hash table H_2 and get, on average, 2^8 value of K_7. Consequently, the average number of keys suggested by a pair after this procedure will be increased to 2^{96}. Thus, we increment the corresponding 2^{96} counters.

After repeating the above procedure for 2^m pairs, we select the key corresponding to the highest counter as a 224-bit right key. After that, we recover the 256-bit master key by testing the 224-bit right key along with the remaining 2^{32} values for K_5 using 2 plaintext/ciphertext pairs.

Table 9. Key recovery process of the attack on $4\frac{1}{7}$-round Bel-T-256

Step	# of suggested keys by a pair	Time complexity	
		32-bit word memory Access	S-box layer Encryption
1	2^{32}	-	$2^m \times 2^{32} \times 2 = 2^{m+33}$
2	$2^{32} \times 1 = 2^{32}$	$2^m \times 2^{32} \times 2 = 2^{m+33}$	-
3	$2^{32} \times 2^{32} = 2^{64}$	-	$2^m \times 2^{64} \times 2 = 2^{m+65}$
4	$2^{64} \times 2^{32} = 2^{96}$	-	$2^m \times 2^{96} \times 2 = 2^{m+97}$
5	$2^{96} \times 2^{32} \times 2^{-16} = 2^{112}$	-	$2^m \times 2^{128} \times 2 = 2^{m+129}$
6	$2^{112} \times 1 = 2^{112}$	$2^m \times 2^{112} \times 2 = 2^{m+113}$	-
7	$2^{112} \times 2^{-24} = 2^{88}$	$2^m \times 2^{112} \times 1 = 2^{m+112}$	-
8	$2^{88} \times 2^8 = 2^{96}$	$2^m \times 2^{96} \times 1 = 2^{m+96}$	-

Table 9 summarizes the above steps, whereas the second column presents the average number of keys suggested by a pair after each step. The third and fourth columns present the time complexity of each step in form of memory accesses and single S-box layer encryption in terms of m.

5.3   Attack Complexity and Success Probability

In this section, we present the complexity analysis of our attack in order to determine the required number of chosen plaintexts and the memory required to launch this attack. Also, we compute the success probability of the attack. Finally, we calculate its time complexity to compare our attack against the exhaustive search attack.

Data Complexity. For the differential attack to succeed with a high probability, we have to determine an appropriate value for the number of required plaintext/ciphertext pairs. To do so, we utilize the concept of signal-to-noise ratio (S/N) [4], which is calculated using the following formula:

$$S/N = \frac{2^k \times p}{\alpha \times \beta}$$

where k is the number of key bits involved in the analysis, p is the probability of the differential characteristic, α is the number of guessed keys by a pair, and β is the ratio of the pairs that are not discarded. In our analysis, $k = 224$, $p = 2^{-111}$, $\alpha = 2^{96}$ from Table 9, and $\beta = 1$. Therefore, we have $S/N = \frac{2^{224} \times 2^{-111}}{2^{96} \times 1} = 2^{17}$. Due to this high S/N, we can use the recommendation of Biham and Shamir [4] that 3–4 right pairs are sufficient enough to mount a successful differential attack. Therefore, we select the number of plaintext/ciphertext pairs (2^m) equal to $4 \times p^{-1} = 2^{113}$. Consequently, the data complexity will be 2^{114} chosen plaintexts.

According to [20] and due to the high S/N, the success probability of the attack (P_s) can be calculated as $P_s \approx \Phi(\sqrt{p \times 2^m})$ where Φ is the cumulative distribution function of the standard normal distribution. Therefore, our differential attack will succeed with probability $P_s \approx 0.9772$.

Time Complexity. During the attack procedure, we make 32-bit word memory accesses in some steps and partially decrypt single S-box layers in other steps. Each S-box layer can be considered as a 32-bit big S-box with one or two modulo operations. Therefore, the time of single S-box layer will be slightly higher than the time of 32-bit word memory access. For simplicity, we assume that the time of 32-bit word memory access is the same as the time of a single S-box layer lookup which is roughly equal to $\frac{1}{7}$ of the time of one round encryption.

From Table 8, the time complexity of the pre-computation phase is dominated by the time required to construct the hash table H_1 which is equal to $\frac{1}{7} \times \frac{1}{4\frac{4}{7}} \times 2^{160} \approx 2^{155.14}$ $4\frac{1}{7}$-round encryptions. Similarly, from Table 9, the dominant part of the time complexity in the online phase comes from steps 5 which is

$\frac{1}{7} \times \frac{1}{4\frac{1}{7}} \times (2^{m+129}) = 2^{m+124.14}$ $4\frac{1}{7}$-round encryptions. Therefore, the total time complexity of the online phase will be $2^{113+124.14} + 2 \times 2^{32} = 2^{237.14}$ $4\frac{1}{7}$-round encryptions.

Memory Complexity. The memory complexity of the pre-computation phase can be determined from Table 8 in which we need $2^{129} + 2^{96} + 2^{121} + 2^{120} \approx 2^{129}$ 32-bit word $= 2^{127}$ 128-bit blocks of memory. During the online phase, we have prepared 2^{224} counters corresponding to 2^{224} keys involved in the analysis. Since the upper limit of each counter depends on the number of plaintext/ciphertext pairs $(2^m = 2^{113})$, we can declare each counter as an unsigned 128-bit integer variable. Consequently, we need 2^{224} 128-bit blocks of memory in total.

6   Conclusion

In this paper, we studied the propagation of the XOR difference through modular addition. We showed that the independency assumption between two or more consecutive modular addition operations does not necessarily hold, and we constructed a more accurate MILP model for the differential trail through the modular addition taking into account the dependency between the consecutive modular additions. Then, we utilized the developed MILP model to automate the search process for the differential characteristics for Bel-T cipher. Up to the authors' knowledge, this is the best published theoretical attack against Bel-T-256 in the single-key setting.

References

1. Preliminary State Standard of Republic of Belarus (STBP 34.101.312011) (2011). http://apmi.bsu.by/assets/files/std/belt-spec27.pdf
2. Abdelkhalek, A., Sasaki, Y., Todo, Y., Tolba, M., Youssef, A.: MILP modeling for (large) s-boxes to optimize probability of differential characteristics. IACR Trans. Symmetric Cryptology **2017**(4), 99–129 (2017)
3. Abdelkhalek, A., Tolba, M., Youssef, A.M.: Related-key differential attack on round-reduced Bel-T-256. IEICE Trans. Fundam. Electron. Commun. Comput. Sci. **101**(5), 859–862 (2018)
4. Biham, E., Shamir, A.: Differential Cryptanalysis of the Data Encryption Standard. Springer, New York (1993). https://doi.org/10.1007/978-1-4613-9314-6
5. Biryukov, A., Velichkov, V.: Automatic search for differential trails in ARX ciphers. In: Benaloh, J. (ed.) CT-RSA 2014. LNCS, vol. 8366, pp. 227–250. Springer, Cham (2014). https://doi.org/10.1007/978-3-319-04852-9_12
6. Cui, T., Jia, K., Fu, K., Chen, S., Wang, M.: New automatic search tool for impossible differentials and zero-correlation linear approximations. Cryptology ePrint Archive, Report 2016/689 (2016). https://eprint.iacr.org/2016/689
7. Daemen, J., Rijmen, V.: Probability distributions of correlation and differentials in block ciphers. J. Math. Cryptology JMC **1**(3), 221–242 (2007)

8. ElSheikh, M., Tolba, M., Youssef, A.M.: Integral Attacks on Round-Reduced Bel-T-256. In: Cid, C., Jacobson Jr., M. (eds.) Selected Areas in Cryptography - SAC 2018. LNCS, vol. 11349, pp. 73–91. Springer, Cham (2019). https://doi.org/10.1007/978-3-030-10970-7_4

9. Feistel, H., Notz, W.A., Smith, J.L.: Some cryptographic techniques for machine-to-machine data communications. Proc. IEEE 63(11), 1545–1554 (1975)

10. Fu, K., Wang, M., Guo, Y., Sun, S., Hu, L.: MILP-based automatic search algorithms for differential and linear trails for speck. In: Peyrin, T. (ed.) FSE 2016. LNCS, vol. 9783, pp. 268–288. Springer, Heidelberg (2016). https://doi.org/10.1007/978-3-662-52993-5_14

11. Jovanovic, P., Polian, I.: Fault-based attacks on the Bel-T block cipher family. In: Proceedings of the 2015 Design, Automation & Test in Europe Conference & Exhibition, pp. 601–604. EDA Consortium (2015)

12. Lai, X., Massey, J.L.: A proposal for a new block encryption standard. In: Damgård, I.B. (ed.) EUROCRYPT 1990. LNCS, vol. 473, pp. 389–404. Springer, Heidelberg (1991). https://doi.org/10.1007/3-540-46877-3_35

13. Lai, X., Massey, J.L., Murphy, S.: Markov ciphers and differential cryptanalysis. In: Davies, D.W. (ed.) EUROCRYPT 1991. LNCS, vol. 547, pp. 17–38. Springer, Heidelberg (1991). https://doi.org/10.1007/3-540-46416-6_2

14. Leurent, G.: Analysis of differential attacks in ARX constructions. In: Wang, X., Sako, K. (eds.) ASIACRYPT 2012. LNCS, vol. 7658, pp. 226–243. Springer, Heidelberg (2012). https://doi.org/10.1007/978-3-642-34961-4_15

15. Lipmaa, H., Moriai, S.: Efficient algorithms for computing differential properties of addition. In: Matsui, M. (ed.) FSE 2001. LNCS, vol. 2355, pp. 336–350. Springer, Heidelberg (2002). https://doi.org/10.1007/3-540-45473-X_28

16. McCluskey Jr., E.J.: Minimization of boolean functions. Bell Syst. Tech. J. 35(6), 1417–1444 (1956)

17. Mouha, N., Wang, Q., Gu, D., Preneel, B.: Differential and linear cryptanalysis using mixed-integer linear programming. In: Wu, C.-K., Yung, M., Lin, D. (eds.) Inscrypt 2011. LNCS, vol. 7537, pp. 57–76. Springer, Heidelberg (2012). https://doi.org/10.1007/978-3-642-34704-7_5

18. Quine, W.V.O.: A way to simplify truth functions. Am. Math. Monthly 62(9), 627–631 (1955). http://www.jstor.org/stable/2307285

19. Sasaki, Y., Todo, Y.: New impossible differential search tool from design and cryptanalysis aspects. In: Coron, J.-S., Nielsen, J.B. (eds.) EUROCRYPT 2017. LNCS, vol. 10212, pp. 185–215. Springer, Cham (2017). https://doi.org/10.1007/978-3-319-56617-7_7

20. Selçuk, A.A.: On probability of success in linear and differential cryptanalysis. J. Cryptology 21(1), 131–147 (2008)

21. Sun, L., Wang, W., Liu, R., Wang, M.: MILP-aided bit-based division property for ARX-based block cipher. Cryptology ePrint Archive, Report 2016/1101 (2016). https://eprint.iacr.org/2016/1101

22. Sun, L., Wang, W., Wang, M.: MILP-aided bit-based division property for primitives with non-bit-permutation linear layers. Cryptology ePrint Archive, Report 2016/811 (2016). https://eprint.iacr.org/2016/811

23. Sun, S., et al.: Towards Finding the Best Characteristics of Some Bit-oriented Block Ciphers and Automatic Enumeration of (Related-key) Differential and Linear Characteristics with Predefined Properties (2014). https://eprint.iacr.org/2014/747

24. Wang, G., Keller, N., Dunkelman, O.: The delicate issues of addition with respect to XOR differences. In: Adams, C., Miri, A., Wiener, M. (eds.) SAC 2007. LNCS, vol. 4876, pp. 212–231. Springer, Heidelberg (2007). https://doi.org/10.1007/978-3-540-77360-3_14

25. Xiang, Z., Zhang, W., Bao, Z., Lin, D.: Applying MILP method to searching integral distinguishers based on division property for 6 lightweight block ciphers. In: Cheon, J.H., Takagi, T. (eds.) ASIACRYPT 2016. LNCS, vol. 10031, pp. 648–678. Springer, Heidelberg (2016). https://doi.org/10.1007/978-3-662-53887-6_24

Practical Attacks on Reduced-Round AES

Navid Ghaedi Bardeh[1(✉)] and Sondre Rønjom[1,2]

[1] Department of Informatics, University of Bergen, Bergen, Norway
{navid.bardeh,sondre.ronjom}@uib.no
[2] Nasjonal sikkerhetsmyndighet, Oslo, Norway

Abstract. In this paper we investigate the security of 5-round AES against two different attacks in an adaptive setting. We present a practical key-recovery attack on 5-round AES with a secret s-box that requires 2^{32} adaptively chosen ciphertexts, which is as far as we know a new record. In addition, we present a new and practical key-independent distinguisher for 5-round AES which requires $2^{27.2}$ adaptively chosen ciphertexts. While the data complexity of this distinguisher is in the same range as the current best 5-round distinguisher [14], it exploits new structural properties of 5-round AES.

Keywords: AES · Zero-difference · Secret-key distinguisher · Differential · Secret s-box

1 Introduction

Block ciphers are typically designed by iterating an efficiently computable round function many times in the hope that the resulting composition behaves like a randomly drawn permutation. The designer is typically constrained by various practical criterion, e.g. security target, implementation boundaries, and specialized applications, that might lead the designer to introduce symmetries and structures in the round function as a compromise between efficiency and security. In the compromise, a round function is iterated enough times to make sure that any symmetries and structural properties that might exist in the round function vanish. Thus, a round function is typically designed to increasingly de-correlate with structure and symmetries after several rounds. Low data- and computational-complexity distinguishers and key-recovery attacks on round-reduced block ciphers have recently gained renewed interest in the literature. There are several reasons for this. In one direction cryptanalysis of block ciphers has focused on maximizing the number of rounds that can be broken without exhausting the full codebook and key space. This often leads to attacks marginally close to that of pure brute-force. These are attacks that typically have been improved over time based on many years of cryptanalysis. The most successful attacks often become de-facto standard methods of cryptanalysis for a particular block cipher and might discourage anyone from pursuing new directions in cryptanalysis that do not reach the same number of rounds. This in itself

© Springer Nature Switzerland AG 2019
J. Buchmann et al. (Eds.): AFRICACRYPT 2019, LNCS 11627, pp. 297–310, 2019.
https://doi.org/10.1007/978-3-030-23696-0_15

might hinder new breakthroughs, thus it can be important to investigate new promising ideas that might not have reached its full potential yet. New methods of cryptanalysis that break or distinguish fewer rounds faster but with lower complexity than established cryptanalysis is therefore interesting in this process. Many constructions employ reduced round AES as part of their design. On the other hand, reduced versions of AES have nice and well-studied properties that can be favorable as components of larger designs (see for instance Simpira [13]).

The security of Rijndael-type block cipher [5] designs is believed to be a well-studied topic and has been in the focus of a large group of cryptanalysts during the last 20 years (see e.g. [1–4,6–9,12,14]). Several distinguisher attacks exists against reduced-round of AES. The aim of a distinguisher attack is to distinguish the cipher from a sufficiently generic permutation i.e. the aim is to find some properties of the cipher that allows to set up a test for an unusual event with sufficiently different probability of happening in comparison to random (e.g. finding certain collision-events in a set of ciphertexts when restricted to structured sets of plaintexts). At Crypto 2016, Sun et al. [15] presented the very first 5-round key-dependent distinguisher for AES. They extend a 4-round integral property to 5-rounds by exploiting properties of the AES MixColumn matrix. Although their distinguisher requires the whole codebook, it spawned a series of new fundamental results for AES. It was later improved to $2^{98.2}$ chosen plaintexts with 2^{107} computations by extending a 4-round impossible differential property to a 5-round property. Then, at Eurocrypt 2017, Grassi et al. [12] proposed the first 5-round key-independent chosen plaintext distinguisher which requires 2^{32} chosen plaintexts with a computational cost of $2^{36.6}$ look-ups into memory of size 2^{36} bytes. They showed that by encrypting cosets of certain subspaces of the plaintext space the number of times the difference of ciphertext pairs lie in a particular subspace of the state space always is a multiple of 8. Later, at Asiacrypt 2017, Rønjom et al. [14] presented new fundamental properties for Rijndael-type block cipher designs leading to new types of 3- to 6-round key-independent distinguishers for AES that beats all previous records. They showed that zero-differences of encrypted plaintext (or decrypted ciphertext) pairs are left invariant by encrypting new pairs formed by exchanging ciphertext/plaintext-dependent values between already observed pairs. Using this property they present the first 6-round distinguisher which requires $2^{122.83}$ adaptively chosen ciphertexts and which has computational cost of $2^{121.83}$ XORs. Note that their result is in the adaptive setting where the adversary can actively query the encryption and decryption function depending on observed values, while the previous distinguishers are in the chosen plaintext or ciphertext setting.

The security of AES with a secret s-box has been investigated in several papers. In this case, when the choice of s-box is made uniformly at random from all 8-bit s-boxes, the size of the secret information increases from 128− and 256-bit keys to 1812− and 1940-bits of secret key material. In FSE 2015, Tiessen et al. [16] proposed the first 5-round key recovery attack on AES with a secret s-box based on integral cryptanalysis, which requires 2^{40} chosen plaintexts with a computational cost of $2^{38.7}$ encryptions. In their attack, they first derive an affine equivalent s-box before they recover the secret key. Then at FSE 2016, Grassi et al. [11] proposed a key recovery attack which exploits a particular property of the AES MixColumn matrix. They then combine this with impossible differential cryptanalysis to derive the secret key. Their attack requires 2^{102} chosen plaintexts with $2^{100.4}$ computations. It was later improved to $2^{53.25}$ chosen plaintexts and $2^{52.6}$ computations in [10] by using a similar approach, but instead of using impossible differential cryptanalysis, they apply multiple-n cryptanalysis.

1.1   Our Contribution

So far, various 5-round key recovery attacks on AES with a secret s-box have been presented based on integral, impossible differential and multiple-n cryptanalysis. In this paper, we raise the question whether it is possible to set up a 5-round key recovery attack on AES with a secret s-box based on recently developed attack techniques called *zero-difference cryptanalysis*. In this paper we present an efficient key-recovery attack on 5-round AES with a secret s-box based on zero-difference cryptanalysis that requires 2^{32} adaptively chosen ciphertexts and that has computational complexity consisting of 2^{31} XORs. We also present a new key-independent distinguisher for 5-round AES which requires $2^{27.2}$ adaptively chosen ciphertexts and which has computational complexity consisting of $2^{26.2}$ XORs. The latter distinguisher exploits new structural properties in 5-round AES.

1.2   Overview of this Paper and Main Results

In Sect. 2 we briefly recall some results and notation that we use in the rest of this paper. In Sect. 3, we describe a new 5-round distinguisher for AES. Then in Sect. 4 we present a new key-recovery attack for AES with a secret s-box. The current best secret key distinguishers for 5-round AES and best key-recovery attacks for 5-round AES-128 with a secret s-box are presented in Tables 1 and 2. We adopt that data complexity is measured in a minimum number of chosen plaintexts/ciphertexts CP/CC or adaptively chosen plaintexts/ciphertexts ACP/ACC. Time complexity is measured in equivalent number of AES encryptions (E), memory access (M) and/or XOR operations (XOR).

Table 1. Secret-key distinguishers for 5-round AES

Property	Rounds	Data	Cost	Key-independent	Ref.
Multiple-8	5	2^{32} CP	$2^{36.6}$ M	✓	[12]
Zero difference	5	$2^{27.2}$ ACC	$2^{26.2}$XOR	✓	**Sect. 3**
Zero difference	5	$2^{26.8}$ ACC	$2^{25.8}$ XOR	✓	[14]

Table 2. Comparison of key-recovery on 5-round AES with a secret s-box

Attack	Rounds	Data	Computation	Memory	Ref.
Imp. diff	5	$2^{76.37}$ CP	$2^{74.09}$ E	2^8	[10]
Multiple of n	5	$2^{53.25}$ CP	$2^{52.6}$ E	2^{16}	[10]
Integral	5	2^{40} CP	$2^{38.7}$ E	2^{40}	[16]
Zero difference	5	$2^{29.19}$CP $+ 2^{32}$ ACC	2^{31} XOR	small[3]	**Sect. 4**

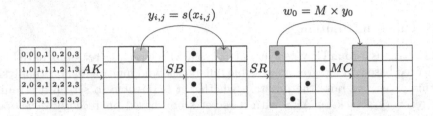

Fig. 1. Description of one AES round

2   Preliminaries

2.1   A Short Description of AES

The AES internal state is typically represented as a 4 by 4 matrix over the finite field $\mathbb{F}_{2^8}$. The state is sometimes also represented as a vector of length 4 over $\mathbb{F}_{2^8}^4$ typically formed by concatenating the columns of the matrix state from left to right. This is the view typically taken in SuperBox cryptanalysis. One full round of AES consists of SubBytes (SB), ShiftRows (SR), MixColumns (MC) and AddKey (AK), $R = AK \circ MC \circ SR \circ SB$ (depicted in Fig. 1). The SB-layer applies a fixed 8-bit to 8-bit s-box independently to each byte of the state, the SR-layer cyclically shift the i-th row by i positions, while the MC-layer applies a fixed linear transformation to each column. The key addition simply XORs a secret round-dependent value to the state. Also, $R^n(x)$ means n rounds of AES. We omit the last $MC \circ SR$ operations to simplify the presentation of our attacks (our attacks work as well in the case in which the final linear layer is omitted).

2.2   Subspace Trail on AES

In [11], Grassi et al. present subspace trail cryptanalysis on AES. They define two different subspaces related to AES. If we let $\{e_{0,0}, ..., e_{3,3}\}$ form the unit vectors of $\mathbb{F}_{2^8}^{4 \times 4}$, we have the following.

Definition 1. *(Diagonal spaces) The diagonal spaces $\mathcal{D}_i$ are defined as*

$$\mathcal{D}_i = < e_{0,i}, e_{1,i+1}, e_{2,i+2}, e_{3,i+3} >$$

where $i + j$ is computed modulo 4. For instance, the diagonal space $\mathcal{D}_0$ corresponds to the symbolic matrix:

$$\mathcal{D}_0 = \left\{ \begin{bmatrix} x_1 & 0 & 0 & 0 \\ 0 & x_2 & 0 & 0 \\ 0 & 0 & x_3 & 0 \\ 0 & 0 & 0 & x_4 \end{bmatrix} \middle| \forall x_1, x_2, x_3, x_4 \in \mathbb{F}_{2^8} \right\}.$$

Definition 2. *(Column spaces)* *The column spaces* $\mathcal{C}_i$ *are defined as*

$$\mathcal{C}_i = <e_{0,i}, e_{1,i}, e_{2,i}, e_{3,i}>.$$

For instance, the columns space $\mathcal{C}_0$ corresponds to the symbolic matrix

$$\mathcal{C}_0 = \left\{ \begin{bmatrix} x_1 & 0 & 0 & 0 \\ x_2 & 0 & 0 & 0 \\ x_3 & 0 & 0 & 0 \\ x_4 & 0 & 0 & 0 \end{bmatrix} \middle| \forall x_1, x_2, x_3, x_4 \in \mathbb{F}_{2^8} \right\}.$$

Definition 3. *Let* $I \subseteq \{0, 1, 2, 3\}$. *Let* $\mathcal{D}_I$ *and* $\mathcal{C}_I$ *be defined as*

$$\mathcal{D}_I = \bigoplus_{i \in I} \mathcal{D}_i, \qquad \mathcal{C}_I = \bigoplus_{i \in I} \mathcal{C}_i.$$

The dimension of the subspaces $\mathcal{D}_I$ and $\mathcal{C}_I$ are both $4 \cdot |I|$. The following theorem describes the deterministic mapping between these two subspaces.

Theorem 1. *[11] For* $I \subset \{0, 1, 2, 3\}$ *and for each* $a \in \mathcal{D}_I^{\perp}$ *(orthogonal complement of* $\mathcal{D}_I$*), there exists one and only one* $b \in \mathcal{C}_I^{\perp}$ *(orthogonal complement of* $\mathcal{C}_I$*) such that:*

$$R(\mathcal{D}_I \oplus a) = \mathcal{C}_I \oplus b.$$

Lemma 1. *[11] For all* $x, y \in \mathbb{F}_{2^8}^{4 \times 4}$ *and for all* $I \subseteq \{0, 1, 2, 3\}$*, it follows that*

$$Pr(R(x) \oplus R(y) \in \mathcal{C}_I | x \oplus y \in \mathcal{D}_I) = 1.$$

In the other word, we can deduce that for each $c \in \mathcal{C}_I^{\perp}$, there exists exactly one $d \in \mathcal{D}_I^{\perp}$ such that

$$R^{-1}(\mathcal{C}_I \oplus c) = \mathcal{D}_I \oplus d$$

and in general

$$Pr(R^{-1}(x) \oplus R^{-1}(y) \in \mathcal{D}_I | x \oplus y \in \mathcal{C}_I) = 1.$$

Lemma 2. *[11] For any* $\mathcal{C}_I$ *and* $\mathcal{D}_J$*, we have that*

$$Pr(x \in (\mathcal{C}_I \cap \mathcal{D}_J) | x \in \mathcal{C}_I) = (2^{-8})^{4 \cdot |I| - |I| \cdot |J|}$$

$$Pr(x \in (\mathcal{C}_J \cap \mathcal{D}_I) | x \in \mathcal{D}_I) = (2^{-8})^{4 \cdot |I| - |I| \cdot |J|}.$$

This means that if two elements belong to the same coset of $\mathcal{D}_I$ (respectively $\mathcal{C}_I$), then they also belong to the same coset of $\mathcal{C}_J$ (respectively $\mathcal{D}_J$) with probability $(2^{-8})^{4 \cdot |I| - |I| \cdot |J|}$. More precisely, when we encrypt two plaintexts from the same coset of D_I for one round, then they belong to the same coset of $\mathcal{C}_I \cap \mathcal{D}_J$ with probability $(2^{-8})^{4 \cdot |I| - |I| \cdot |J|}$. We use this lemma to compute most of the probabilities in our attacks.

2.3 Zero-Difference for 4-Round AES

In [14], Rønjom et al. present zero-difference cryptanalysis against generic Substitution Permutation Networks (SPNs). In the following, we recall the basic zero-difference properties for 4-rounds of AES.

Definition 4. *[14] For a vector $v \in \mathbb{F}_2^4$ and a pair of states $\alpha, \beta \in \mathbb{F}_{2^8}^{4 \times 4}$ define a new state*

$$\rho^v(\alpha, \beta) = (\alpha_i v_i \oplus \beta_i(v_i \oplus 1) \mid 0 \le i < n).$$

where α_i and β_i are ith columns of α and β

The new pair $(\alpha', \beta') = (\rho^v(\alpha, \beta), \rho^v(\beta, \alpha))$ is formed by exchanging individual words between α and β according to the binary coefficients of v.

Zero-difference cryptanalysis exploits a fundamental property of the SLS construction (S is a non-linear layer and L is a linear transformation) which is encapsulated in the following theorem originally presented in [14].

Theorem 2. *[14] Let $\alpha, \beta \in \mathbb{F}_{2^8}^{4 \times 4}$ and $\alpha' = \rho^v(\alpha, \beta), \beta' = \rho^v(\beta, \alpha)$ then*

$$\nu(S \circ L \circ S(\alpha) \oplus S \circ L \circ S(\beta)) = \nu(S \circ L \circ S(\alpha') \oplus S \circ L \circ S(\beta'))$$

where $\nu(x)$ denotes the indicator vector which is 1 if the word i of x is zero and 0 otherwise.

Due to the symmetry of SLS, we get exactly the same result in the decryption direction. Note that the SLS construction essentially corresponds to 4 full rounds of AES. In [14], the authors fix plaintexts with fixed zero diagonals and decrypt the exchanged ciphertext pairs to a new plaintext pair which with probability 1 have exactly the same zero diagonals.

We can represent Theorem 2 in terms of subspace cryptanalysis. Consider two plaintexts in the same coset of a diagonal space $\mathcal{D}_I$, $p^0, p^1 \in \mathcal{D}_I + a$. Then let $c^0 = R^4(p^0)$, $c^1 = R^4(p^1)$, $p'^0 = R^{-4}(\rho^v(c^0, c^1)))$ and $p'^1 = R^{-4}(\rho^v(c^1, c^0)))$. Then with probability one, we also have that $p'^0 \oplus p'^1 \in \mathcal{D}_I$ (different coset than $\mathcal{D}_I + a$). In the next two sections, we present two practical different attacks based on this 4-round property. We have practically verified the attacks on full-scale AES in C/C++[1].

---

[1] https://github.com/Kryptoraphy/practical-attacks.

3   5-Round Key-Independent Distinguisher

In this section we extend the 4-round distinguisher mentioned in the previous section to a 5-round distinguisher by adding one round at beginning. We encrypt a plaintext set and expect that some of them follow the 4-round property after one round encryption. Thus, we present a new 5-round key-independent distinguisher which requires $2^{27.2}$ adaptively chosen ciphertexts. The idea for setting up a 5-round distinguisher is as follows. We pick a plaintext set P from a coset of a diagonal space $\mathcal{D}_0$, $P \subset \mathcal{D}_0 + a$, and encrypt them. Then from the set of all possible ciphertext pairs we form 7 new ciphertext pairs by exchanging mixed values between the original pairs. Then we decrypt the set of these newly generated ciphertext pairs and expect to observe one such pair belonging to the same coset of $\mathcal{D}_L$ with $|L| = 3$.

We know that each coset of $\mathcal{D}_I$ is mapped into a coset of $\mathcal{C}_I$ with probability one, and diagonal and column spaces always have an intersection with a certain probability (Lemma 2). So, when we encrypt the plaintexts set P, one of following cases may happen after one round encryption.

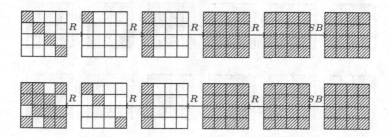

Fig. 2. 5-round truncated differential characteristic used in case 1

First case. After one round encryption, then according to Lemma 2, with probability $4 \cdot 2^{-24}$ (a single byte can be active in 4 different positions in a column) we have that

$$R(p^i) \oplus R(p^j) \in D_K \cap C_0$$

where $|K| = 1$. If we swap word(s) between the ciphertexts and decrypt them, we have, according to the 4-round property mentioned in Sect. 2.3, that

$$R^{-4}(\rho^v(c^i, c^j)) \oplus R^{-4}(\rho^v(c^j, c^i)) \in D_K$$

and

$$R^{-4}(\rho^v(c^i, c^j)) \oplus R^{-4}(\rho^v(c^j, c^i)) \in D_K \cap C_L$$

where $|L| = 3$ with probability $4 \cdot 2^{-8}$ (there are 4 possible choices for choosing L). It means that after one more round of decryption, according to Theorem 1, the two new plaintexts, p'^i and p'^j, are in same coset of a diagonal space $\mathcal{D}_L$

where $|L| = 3$. Thus, it happens with a probability $4 \cdot 2^{-24} \cdot 4 \cdot 2^{-8}$. The truncated differential characteristic used in this case is depicted in Fig. 2.

Second case. In this case, $R(p^i) \oplus R(p^j)$ differ in only two bytes with probability $6 \cdot 2^{-16}$. In other words:

$$R(p^i) \oplus R(p^j) \in D_K \cap C_0$$

where $|K| = 2$. Then, according to the 4-round property, we have that

$$R^{-4}(\rho^v(c^i, c^j)) \oplus R^{-4}(\rho^v(c^j, c^i)) \in D_K,$$

and with probability $4 \cdot 2^{-16}$ we have that

$$R^{-4}(\rho^v(c^i, c^j)) \oplus R^{-4}(\rho^v(c^j, c^i)) \in D_K \cap C_L$$

so $R^{-5}(\rho^v(c^i, c^j)) \oplus R^{-5}(\rho^v(c^j, c^i))$ is zero in a diagonal with probability $6 \cdot 2^{-16} \cdot 4 \cdot 2^{-16}$. Figure 3 depicts the truncated differential characteristic used in this case.

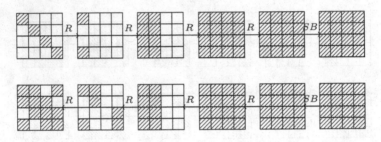

Fig. 3. 5-round truncated differential characteristic used in case 2

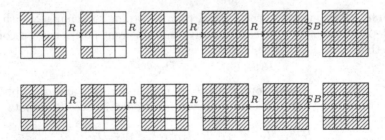

Fig. 4. 5-round truncated differential characteristic used in case 3

Third case. There is also a case that $R(p^i) \oplus R(p^j)$ is zero in all bytes except three bytes, which happens with probability $4 \cdot 2^{-8}$. It means that

$$R(p^i) \oplus R(p^j) \in D_K \cap C_0$$

where $|K| = 3$. Thus, this pair follows the 4-round property

$$R^{-4}(\rho^v(c^i, c^j)) \oplus R^{-4}(\rho^v(c^j, c^i)) \in D_K,$$

and with probability $4 \cdot 2^{-24}$, we also have that

$$R^{-4}(\rho^v(c^i, c^j)) \oplus R^{-4}(\rho^v(c^j, c^i)) \in D_K \cap C_L.$$

Then after one more round of decryption, it follows that $p'^i \oplus p'^j \in \mathcal{D}_L$ where $|L| = 3$. In total, we expect this event happens with probability $4 \cdot 2^{-8} \cdot 4 \cdot 2^{-24}$. In Fig. 4, the truncated differential characteristic used in this case is depicted.

In total, the probability that there is a plaintext pair such that $p'^i \oplus p'^j \in C_L$ is $16 \cdot 2^{-24} \cdot 2^{-8} + 24 \cdot 2^{-16} \cdot 2^{-16} + 16 \cdot 2^{-8} \cdot 2^{-24} = 2^{-26.19}$. In order to set up a distinguisher, we encrypt $2^{12.2}$ plaintexts from a coset of D_0. We generate all $2^{23.4}$ possible ciphertext pairs and for each pair we generate all 7 possible new ciphertext pairs by swapping words between them. Then we decrypt all $7 \cdot 2^{23.4}$ ciphertext pairs and expect that there is at least one plaintext pair such that $p'^0 \oplus p'^1 \in D_L$ with $|L| = 3$. At random, the probability that two plaintexts belong to the same coset of D_L is 2^{-30}. For AES, the probability of having a plaintext pair with our desired difference pattern is $1 - (1 - 2^{-26.2})^{2^{26.2}} = 0.63$ after decrypting $2^{26.2}$ ciphertext pairs, while for a random permutation, this probability is $1 - (1 - 2^{-30})^{2^{26.2}} = 0.07$. Thus, the probability of success is 0.58. So, we can distinguish 5-round AES from a random permutation using $2^{12.2}$ chosen plaintext and $2 \cdot 2^{26.2} = 2^{27.2}$ adaptively chosen ciphertext. The algorithm for this distinguisher is presented in Algorithm 1.

The data complexity of this distinguisher is in the same range as the data complexity of the best 5-round adaptive distinguisher presented in [14]. Both distinguishers extend on the 4-round distinguisher mentioned in Sect. 2.3 to a 5-round distinguisher by adding a round at the begining. In the distinguisher presented in [14], the aim is to find plaintext pairs such that all of them have a certain property (a certain zero-byte set). To achieve this, attacker needs to generate new pairs of plaintexts and ciphertexts adaptively from the original pairs. To set up our distinguisher, we just need to generate new ciphertext pairs adaptively. Our distinguisher exploits another structural properties over 5-round.

4   Key Recovery Attack on 5-Round AES with a Single Secret S-Box

In this section we present a new key-recovery attack on 5-round AES with a secret s-box. The idea is to turn the 4-round distinguisher mentioned in Sect. 2.3 to a key recovery attack by adding a round at beginning using a property of the MixColumn operation in AES. The MixColumns matrix M in AES is defined by

$$M = \begin{bmatrix} \alpha & \alpha+1 & 1 & 1 \\ 1 & \alpha & \alpha+1 & 1 \\ 1 & 1 & \alpha & \alpha+1 \\ \alpha+1 & 1 & 1 & 1 \end{bmatrix}.$$

Algorithm 1. 5-round key-independent distinguisher

Input: Set $\mathcal{P}$ contains $2^{12.2}$ plaintext p^i where bytes in first diagonal takes a
     random values and others are constant
Output: 1 for an AES, -1 otherwise.
for i *from* 0 *to* $2^{12.2}$ **do**
    $c^i \leftarrow enc_k(p^i)$
end
for i *from* 0 *to* $2^{12.2}$ **do**
    for j *from* $i+1$ *to* $2^{12.2} - 1$ **do**
        for r *from* 1 *to* 7 **do**
            $c'^i \leftarrow \rho^{v_r}(c^i, c^j)$, $c'^j \leftarrow \rho^{v_r}(c^j, c^i)$
            $p'^i \leftarrow dec_k(c'^i)$, $p'^j \leftarrow dec_k(c'^j)$
            if $p'^i \oplus p'^j \in D_L$ *where* $|L| = 3$ **then**
                return 1
            end
        end
    end
end

We pick two pairs of plaintexts p^0 and p^1 where the first diagonal is given by
$SR^{-1}(p_0^0) = SR^{-1}(0, i, j, 0)$ and $SR^{-1}(p_0^1) = SR^{-1}(z, z+i, z+j, 0)$ and where
z is a random non-zero element of $\mathbb{F}_{2^8}$. Let $k_0 = (k_{0,0}, k_{1,1}, k_{2,2}, k_{3,3})$ denote the
key-bytes XORed with the first diagonal of the plaintext. Then the difference
between the first column after one encryption of the two plaintexts becomes

$$\alpha \Delta x_0 \oplus (\alpha + 1)\Delta x_1 \oplus \Delta x_2 = y_0$$
$$\Delta x_0 \oplus \alpha \Delta x_1 \oplus (\alpha + 1)\Delta x_2 = y_1$$
$$\Delta x_0 \oplus \Delta x_1 \oplus \alpha \Delta x_2 = y_2$$
$$(\alpha + 1)\Delta x_0 \oplus \Delta x_1 \oplus \Delta x_2 = y_3.$$

where $\Delta x_0 = s(k_{0,0}) \oplus s(z \oplus k_{0,0})$, $\Delta x_1 = s(k_{1,1} \oplus z \oplus i) \oplus s(k_{1,1} \oplus i)$, $\Delta x_2 = s(k_{2,2} \oplus z \oplus j) \oplus s(k_{2,2} \oplus j)$ and where $s(x)$ is the AES-sbox. Since the plaintexts
are equal in the last byte, this part cancels out in the difference. In particular, if
we look at the first two equations, it is not hard to see that they are zero when
$\Delta x_0 = \Delta x_1 = \Delta x_2$,

$$s(k_{0,0}) \oplus s(z \oplus k_{0,0}) = s(k_{1,1} \oplus z \oplus i) \oplus s(k_{1,1} \oplus i) = s(k_{2,2} \oplus z \oplus j) \oplus s(k_{2,2} \oplus j)$$

This happens when $i \in \{k_{0,0} \oplus k_{1,1}, z \oplus k_{0,0} \oplus k_{1,1}\}$ and $j \in \{k_{0,0} \oplus k_{2,2}, z \oplus k_{0,0} \oplus k_{2,2}\}$. Thus, if we let i and j run through all values of $\mathbb{F}_{2^8}$, we are guaranteed
that there are at least four values for which the first two equations are zero.

We prepare a set $\mathcal{P}$ of plaintext pairs as follows. For each i and j, we
generate a pair of plaintexts p^0 and p^1 where the first diagonal of p^0 is
$SR^{-1}(p_0^0) = SR^{-1}(0, i, j, 0)$ while the first diagonal in the second text is
$SR^{-1}(p_0^1) = SR^{-1}(z, z \oplus i, z \oplus j, 0)$. We then encrypt this pair five rounds
to a pair of ciphertexts c^0 and c^1. We then pick all 7 new ciphertext pairs

$c'^0, c'^1 = (\rho^v(c^0, c^1), \rho^v(c^1, c^0))$ and return the corresponding plaintexts p'^0 and p'^1. Now we know that there are 28 pairs in the set such that

$$R^{-4}(\rho^v(c^0, c^1)) \oplus R^{-4}(\rho^v(c^1, c^0)) \in D_K$$

where $|K| = 2$, since for each of the pair satisfy $R(p^0) \oplus R(p^1) \in D_K$. Thus, according to Lemma 2, with probability $4 \cdot 2^{-16}$ we have that

$$R^{-4}(\rho^v(c^0, c^1)) \oplus R^{-4}(\rho^v(c^1, c^0)) \in D_K \cap C_L$$

where $|L| = 3$. This means that $p'^0 \oplus p'^1 \in D_L$. Thus, for this pair, we can deduce the values of i and j which corresponds to $k_{0,0} \oplus k_{1,1}$ ($z \oplus k_{0,0} \oplus k_{1,1}$) and $k_{0,0} \oplus k_{2,2}$ ($z \oplus k_{0,0} \oplus k_{2,2}$) respectively. The truncated differential characteristic used in the attack is depicted in Fig. 5. Since there are 28 right pairs in the set $\mathcal{P}$, the probability that there is a new plaintext pair such that $p'^0 \oplus p'^1 \in C_L$ is $1 - (1 - 2^{-14})^{28} = 2^{-9.19}$. Then we need to encrypt $2^{9.19}$ sets $\mathcal{P}$ (by picking different constants for the last three diagonals). Thus, to find two bytes of the key, the attacker needs $2 \cdot 2^{9.19} \cdot 2^{16} = 2^{26.19}$ chosen plaintexts and $2 \cdot 7 \cdot 2^{9.19} \cdot 2^{16} = 2^{29}$ adaptively chosen ciphertexts. Then the attacker can repeat the attack for other diagonals (two times for each diagonal) and guess one byte of the key for each diagonal. In total the attacker needs $2^{29.19}$ chosen plaintexts and 2^{32} adaptively chosen ciphertexts to form an attack with success rate of 0.63. The algorithm for this key recovery attack is presented in Algorithm 2.

Algorithm 2. Key recovery attack on 5-round AES with a single secret s-box

---

    Input: $2^{9.12}$ different sets $\mathcal{P}$ where each contains 2^{16} plaintext pairs
    Output: Candidates for $k_{0,0} \oplus k_{1,1}$ ($1 \oplus k_{0,0} \oplus k_{1,1}$) and $k_{0,0} \oplus k_{2,2}$
        ($1 \oplus k_{0,0} \oplus k_{2,2}$)
for c *from* 0 *to* $2^{9.12}$ **do**
    for i *from* 0 *to* 2^8 **do**
        for j *from* 0 *to* 2^8 **do**
            $p_0^0 \leftarrow (0, i, j, 0)$, $p_0^1 \leftarrow (1, 1 \oplus i, 1 \oplus j, 0)$
            $p_l^0 = p_l^1 = Random - value$ for $l = 1, 2, 3$
            $c^0 \leftarrow enc_k(p^0)$, $c^1 \leftarrow enc_k(p^1)$
            for r *from* 1 *to* 7 **do**
                $c'^0 \leftarrow \rho^{v_r}(c^0, c^1)$, $c'^1 \leftarrow \rho^{v_r}(c^1, c^0)$
                $p'^0 \leftarrow dec_k(c'^0)$, $p'^1 \leftarrow dec_k(c'^1)$
                if $p'^0 \oplus p'^1 \in D_L$ *where* $|L| = 3$ **then**
                    (i, j) is a candidate for two bytes of key.
            end
        end
    end
end

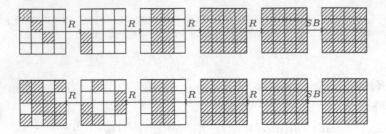

Fig. 5. 5-round truncated differential characteristic used in key recovery attack AES

The key-recovery attacks on 5-round AES with a secret s-box presented in [10] are based on impossible and multiple-n cryptanalysis, while our attack is based on zero-difference cryptanalysis. Since our attack exploits a probability one 4-round property, it requires less texts than others which exploit probabilistic 4-round properties. Also, the best 5-round key recovery attacks in adaptive setting [14] and non-adaptive setting [1] require $2^{11.3}$ adaptively chosen ciphertexts and 2^{22} chosen plaintext respectively (with a known s-box), so compared to our attack, and despite the increased size of the secret information, the required data is increased, at most, by a factor of 2^{21}.

5   Conclusion

In this paper we have introduced a new 5-round key-independent distinguisher which requires $2^{12.2}$ chosen plaintexts and $2^{27.2}$ adaptively chosen ciphertexts. In addition, we present a new key recovery attack against 5-round AES with a secret s-box based on zero-difference cryptanalysis. The attack requires $2^{29.19}$ chosen plaintexts and 2^{32} adaptively chosen ciphertexts. Both attacks mentioned in this paper are practical and have been verified experimentally on a standard laptop.

Acknowledgments. We thank the anonymous reviewers for their valuable comments and suggestions. This Research was supported by the Norwegian Research Council.

References

1. Bar-On, A., Dunkelman, O., Keller, N., Ronen, E., Shamir, A.: Improved key recovery attacks on reduced-round AES with practical data and memory complexities. In: Advances in Cryptology - CRYPTO 2018–38th Annual International Cryptology Conference, Santa Barbara, CA, USA, 19–23 August 2018, Proceedings, Part II, pp. 185–212 (2018). https://doi.org/10.1007/978-3-319-96881-0_7

2. Biryukov, A., Khovratovich, D.: Related-key cryptanalysis of the full AES-192 and AES-256. In: Advances in Cryptology - ASIACRYPT 2009, 15th International Conference on the Theory and Application of Cryptology and Information Security, Tokyo, Japan, 6–10 December 2009, Proceedings, pp. 1–18 (2009). https://doi.org/10.1007/978-3-642-10366-7_1

3. Biryukov, A., Khovratovich, D., Nikolic, I.: Distinguisher and related-key attack on the full AES-256. In: Advances in Cryptology - CRYPTO 2009, 29th Annual International Cryptology Conference, Santa Barbara, CA, USA, 16–20 August 2009, Proceedings, pp. 231–249 (2009). https://doi.org/10.1007/978-3-642-03356-8_14

4. Bouillaguet, C., Derbez, P., Dunkelman, O., Fouque, P., Keller, N., Rijmen, V.: Low-data complexity attacks on AES. IEEE Trans. Inf. Theor. **58**(11), 7002–7017 (2012). https://doi.org/10.1109/TIT.2012.2207880

5. Daemen, J., Rijmen, V.: The block cipher rijndael. In: Smart Card Research and Applications, This International Conference, CARDIS 1998, Louvain-la-Neuve, Belgium, 14–16 September 1998, Proceedings, pp. 277–284 (1998). https://doi.org/10.1007/10721064_26

6. Derbez, P., Fouque, P., Jean, J.: Improved key recovery attacks on reduced-round AES in the single-key setting. In: Advances in Cryptology - EUROCRYPT 2013, 32nd Annual International Conference on the Theory and Applications of Cryptographic Techniques, Athens, Greece, 26–30 May 2013, Proceedings, pp. 371–387 (2013). https://doi.org/10.1007/978-3-642-38348-9_23

7. Dunkelman, O., Keller, N., Shamir, A.: Improved single-key attacks on 8-round AES-192 and AES-256. In: Advances in Cryptology - ASIACRYPT 2010–16th International Conference on the Theory and Application of Cryptology and Information Security, Singapore, 5–9 December 2010, Proceedings, pp. 158–176 (2010). https://doi.org/10.1007/978-3-642-17373-8_10

8. Ferguson, N., et al.: Improved cryptanalysis of rijndael. In: Fast Software Encryption, 7th International Workshop, FSE 2000, New York, NY, USA, 10–12 April 2000, Proceedings, pp. 213–230 (2000). https://doi.org/10.1007/3-540-44706-7_15

9. Gilbert, H., Minier, M.: A collision attack on 7 rounds of rijndael. In: AES Candidate Conference, pp. 230–241 (2000)

10. Grassi, L.: Mixcolumns properties and attacks on (round-reduced) AES with a single secret s-box. In: Topics in Cryptology - CT-RSA 2018 - The Cryptographers' Track at the RSA Conference 2018, San Francisco, CA, USA, 16–20 April 2018, Proceedings, pp. 243–263 (2018). https://doi.org/10.1007/978-3-319-76953-0_13

11. Grassi, L., Rechberger, C., Rønjom, S.: Subspace trail cryptanalysis and its applications to AES. IACR Trans. Symmetric Cryptol. **2016**(2), 192–225 (2016). 10.13154/tosc.v2016.i2.192-225

12. Grassi, L., Rechberger, C., Rønjom, S.: A new structural-differential property of 5-round AES. In: Advances in Cryptology - EUROCRYPT 2017–36th Annual International Conference on the Theory and Applications of Cryptographic Techniques, Paris, France, 30 April - 4 May 2017, Proceedings, Part II, pp. 289–317 (2017). https://doi.org/10.1007/978-3-319-56614-6_10

13. Gueron, S., Mouha, N.: Simpira v2: A family of efficient permutations using the AES round function. In: Advances in Cryptology - ASIACRYPT 2016–22nd International Conference on the Theory and Application of Cryptology and Information Security, Hanoi, Vietnam, 4–8 December 2016, Proceedings, Part I, pp. 95–125 (2016). https://doi.org/10.1007/978-3-662-53887-6_4

14. Rønjom, S., Bardeh, N.G., Helleseth, T.: Yoyo tricks with AES. In: Advances in Cryptology - ASIACRYPT 2017–23rd International Conference on the Theory and Applications of Cryptology and Information Security, Hong Kong, China, 3–7 December 2017, Proceedings, Part I, pp. 217–243 (2017). https://doi.org/10.1007/978-3-319-70694-8_8

15. Sun, B., Liu, M., Guo, J., Qu, L., Rijmen, V.: New insights on aes-like SPN ciphers. In: Advances in Cryptology - CRYPTO 2016–36th Annual International Cryptology Conference, Santa Barbara, CA, USA, 14–18 August 2016, Proceedings, Part I, pp. 605–624 (2016). https://doi.org/10.1007/978-3-662-53018-4_22

16. Tiessen, T., Knudsen, L.R., Kölbl, S., Lauridsen, M.M.: Security of the AES with a secret s-box. In: Fast Software Encryption - 22nd International Workshop, FSE 2015, Istanbul, Turkey, 8–11 March 2015, Revised Selected Papers, pp. 175–189 (2015). https://doi.org/10.1007/978-3-662-48116-5_9

Six Shades of AES

Fatih Balli[(✉)] and Subhadeep Banik

LASEC, École Polytechnique Fédérale de Lausanne, Lausanne, Switzerland
{fatih.balli,subhadeep.banik}@epfl.ch

Abstract. Recently there have been various attempts to construct light
weight implementations of the AES-128 encryption and combined encryp-
tion/ decryption circuits [2,13]. However no known lightweight circuit
exists for AES-192 and AES-256, the variants of AES that use longer
keys. Investing in lightweight implementations of these ciphers is important as we enter the post quantum era in which security is, by a rule of
the thumb, scaled down to the square-root of the size of the keyspace.
In this paper, we propose a single circuit that is able to offer functionalities of both encryption and decryption for AES-128/192/256. Our circuit
operates on an 8-bit datapath and occupies around 3672 GE of area in
silicon. We outline the challenges that presented themselves while performing the combinatorial optimization of circuit area and the methods
we used to solve them.

1 Introduction

In the past few years, lightweight cryptography has become a popular research
discipline. A number of lightweight block ciphers have been proposed over the
years. Among them Clefia [17] and Present [6] are well-studied with respect
to their security and implementation. Both ciphers have been standardized in
ISO/IEC 29192 "Lightweight Cryptography". Very recently the Simon and Speck
family of block ciphers [5] was proposed by the NSA with the goal of reducing
hardware area. While the above ciphers have mostly targeted optimization of
hardware area, there have been other block ciphers aimed at optimizing other
lightweight design metrics. For instance, the block cipher Prince [7] was designed
for low latency applications like memory encryption. Another example is Midori
[4] which was designed to optimize energy consumption. However, AES still
remains the de-facto encryption standard worldwide for a number of sectors like
banking and e-commerce. It is a part of several internet protocols like HTTPS,
FTPS, SFTP, WebDAVS, OFTP, and AS2.

There have been several lightweight implementations of AES proposed in
literature. In [16], the authors propose a 32-bit serial architecture with optimized
tower field implementation of the S-box and a combinatorial optimization of the
Mix Columns circuit. The size of this implementation was around 5400 GE (gate
equivalents, i.e. are occupied by an equivalent number of 2-input NAND gates).
The "Grain of Sand" implementation [12] by Feldhofer et al. constructs an 8-bit
serialized architecture with circuit size of around 3400 GE but a latency of over

© Springer Nature Switzerland AG 2019
J. Buchmann et al. (Eds.): AFRICACRYPT 2019, LNCS 11627, pp. 311–329, 2019.
https://doi.org/10.1007/978-3-030-23696-0_16

1000 cycles for both encryption and decryption. The implementation by Moradi et al. [15] with size equal to 2400 GE and encryption latency of 226 cycles is one of the smallest known architectures for AES. In [14], the authors report an 8-bit serial implementation that takes 1947/2090 GE for the encryption/decryption circuits respectively. This implementation makes use of intermediate register files that can be synthesized in the ASIC flow using memory compilers.

Very recently two further serial architectures have been proposed for AES-128. The first, named Atomic AES [2], which was followed up by Atomic AES v2.0. [3] uses the basic architecture of [15] along with a few tweaks to achieve encryption and decryption functionalities in the same circuit. The circuit takes around 2060 GE of area. [13] takes the design one step further, but proposing the first bit serial architecture for AES in less than 1600 GE. However since the architecture advances data one bit every clock cycle, it is around 8 times slower than byte serial architectures.

1.1 Motivation and Challenges

One important thing to note is that the all papers [2,3,13,15] assume that the key and data are input to the circuit arranged in a **row-major** fashion, i.e. bytes of each individual rows are input to the circuit together. This is slightly odd as AES specifications explicitly recommend **column-major** ordering and hence implementing AES in the proper columnwise ordering of bytes is an important challenge.

Secondly, there have surprisingly been no attempts made to implement AES-192 and AES-256 in a lightweight fashion. These are the variants of AES that use longer keys. Investing in lightweight implementations of these ciphers is important as we enter the post quantum era in which security is, by a rule of the thumb, scaled down to the square-root of the size of the keyspace, due to Grover's algorithm. Lightweight implementation of AES-192 and AES-256 is of added importance as AES-256 is a core component of a number of candidates in the NIST Post-quantum project for standardization of a quantum-secure public key cryptosystem [1]. NIST targets three level of security in this standardization: Level 1/3/5 respectively equivalent to AES-128/192/256 bit security. Out of 17 second round post quantum KEM candidate constructions, 9 candidates employ AES in their construction: 8 of these use AES-256 in counter mode, making it a preferred choice for generating pseudorandomness. Few candidates also propose 3 designs for 3 different security levels, therefore using all AES-128/192/256 instances at the same time. For signatures schemes, 2 out of 9 schemes make use of AES-256.

However designing serial implementations of AES-192 and AES-256 is slightly challenging due to reasons as outlined follows. One of the main reasons it is comparatively easy to implement AES-128 in a serial fashion is that the round function and key update operations are synchronized, which is to say that after every round, the state and the current key are updated. Thus every round involves executing the same operations on the state (except the last round MixColumns) and key registers which can be iterated 10 times to get the encryption/decryption functionality. This is however **not** the case with either AES-192 or AES-256. Since AES-192 uses a 192 bit key but only a 128 bit state, it requires only 8 full key update operations, to produce sufficient key material for the 12 rounds recommended by the designers. In fact, in AES-192 state and key operations become synchronized after 3 round functions and 2 key update operations. AES-256 uses a 256 bit key and requires only 7 full key updates for 14 executions of the round function. The key update operation of this cipher is also slightly different as each key update requires S-box operation to be applied on 2 columns of the current key instead of 1 in both AES-128 and AES-192. This asymmetry in the round and key schedule operations make serial implementation of AES-192 and AES-256 slightly more difficult.

A final challenge is implementing the functionalities of encryption and decryption on the same circuit. Various modes of operations like CBC [11] and EℓMD [10], that use block ciphers as the underlying primitive, require access to both its encryption and decryption functionalities. Thus it is useful to have an implementation that achieves both functionalities of a block cipher with minimal overhead.

1.2   Contribution and Organization

In this paper we present an 8-bit serial architecture that performs all encryption and decryption operations of three instances AES-128, AES-192, AES-256. The circuit thus supports six functionalities. We remove the requirement that bytes be ordered in row-first fashion, and construct our circuit so that it can support inputs when they are arranged in a column first fashion. The circuit occupies area of around 3672 GE when synthesized with the standard cell library of the STM 90 nm CMOS logic process.

The paper is organized in the following manner. Section 2 gives some background on AES and some necessary definitions required to read the paper. Section 3 describes the architecture and functioning of our circuit in detail and we describe explicitly how we overcome some of the challenges presented in Sect. 1.1. Section 4 tabulates all implementation results and compares synthesis results for various standard cell libraries.

2   Background and Preliminaries

2.1   Encryption/Decryption Overview

Let r denote the number of rounds in the encryption/decryption function, n denote the number of key expansion rounds, ℓ denote the byte size of the key for a given AES instance. Note that, r, n, $\ell = (10, 10, 16)$, $(12, 8, 24)$, and $(14, 7, 32)$ for AES-128, AES-192, and AES-256 respectively.

The encryption algorithm consists of multiple calls to AddRoundKey$(\cdot, \cdot)$, SubBytes$(\cdot)$, ShiftRows$(\cdot)$ and MixColumns$(\cdot)$ layers where each input denoted with '$\cdot$', as well as each output, is a 4×4 byte matrix. AddRoundKey takes the state information St and the round key K_i and returns the byte-wise XOR of them. With SubBytes, each byte is substituted according to AES S-box. ShiftRows rotates the i-th row by i position to the left (for $i = 0, 1, 2, 3$). During MixColumns, each column $[s_{4i}, s_{4i+1}, s_{4i+2}, s_{4i+3}]^T$ of input sequence s is multiplied with a fixed 4×4 byte matrix M, where byte values are treated as elements of $GF(2^8)$. An important property of M is $M^4 = I$, where I denotes the identity matrix. We skip further details of these four layers, and refer the reader to [9].

Even though the block size in all 6 instances of AES is exactly 4×4 bytes and thereby matches exactly with the input and output of the aforementioned layers, the same cannot be said for the key. Namely, in AES-192, the key is arranged in a 4×6 byte matrix and in AES-256 it is arranged in a 4×8 byte matrix. As a consequence, the iterations of the key expansion algorithm, whose task is to generate fresh 4×4 bytes of round key for each AddRoundKey operation, desynchronize with the round operations performed on the state and it leads to a great deal of complexity in our design. We briefly remind the details of the key expansion algorithm below.

2.2 Key Expansion

Let S denote the AES S-box. Let $RC_1, \ldots, RC_{10}$ denote a sequence of round constant bytes[1]. The key expansion generates a sequence of key bytes $k_0, \ldots, k_{16r+15}$ given the bytes $k_0, \ldots, k_{\ell-1}$ as input. At each iteration of key expansion, ℓ bytes of *fresh* key is produced by XORing the original matrix with an additional offset. For instance, with AES-128, the very first round of key expansion generates key bytes $k_{16}, \ldots, k_{31}$ from $k_0, \ldots, k_{15}$ according to:

$$\begin{bmatrix} k_{16}, & k_{20}, & k_{24}, & k_{28} \\ k_{17}, & k_{21}, & k_{25}, & k_{29} \\ k_{18}, & k_{22}, & k_{26}, & k_{30} \\ k_{19}, & k_{23}, & k_{27}, & k_{31} \end{bmatrix} \leftarrow \begin{bmatrix} k_0, & k_4, & k_8, & k_{12} \\ k_1, & k_5, & k_9, & k_{13} \\ k_2, & k_6, & k_{10}, & k_{14} \\ k_3, & k_7, & k_{11}, & k_{15} \end{bmatrix} \oplus \begin{bmatrix} S(k_{13}) \oplus RC_1, & k_{16}, & k_{20}, & k_{24} \\ S(k_{14}), & k_{17}, & k_{21}, & k_{25} \\ S(k_{15}), & k_{18}, & k_{22}, & k_{26} \\ S(k_{12}), & k_{19}, & k_{23}, & k_{27} \end{bmatrix}$$

Similarly, with AES-192, the very first round of key expansion is:

$$\begin{bmatrix} k_{24}, & k_{28}, & k_{32}, & k_{36}, & k_{40}, & k_{44} \\ k_{25}, & k_{29}, & k_{33}, & k_{37}, & k_{41}, & k_{45} \\ k_{26}, & k_{30}, & k_{34}, & k_{38}, & k_{42}, & k_{46} \\ k_{27}, & k_{31}, & k_{35}, & k_{39}, & k_{43}, & k_{47} \end{bmatrix} \leftarrow \begin{bmatrix} k_0, & k_4, & k_8, & k_{12}, & k_{16}, & k_{20} \\ k_1, & k_5, & k_9, & k_{13}, & k_{17}, & k_{21} \\ k_2, & k_6, & k_{10}, & k_{14}, & k_{18}, & k_{22} \\ k_3, & k_7, & k_{11}, & k_{15}, & k_{19}, & k_{23} \end{bmatrix} \oplus \begin{bmatrix} S(k_{21}) \oplus RC_1, & k_{24}, & k_{28}, & k_{32}, & k_{36}, & k_{40} \\ S(k_{22}), & k_{25}, & k_{29}, & k_{33}, & k_{37}, & k_{41} \\ S(k_{23}), & k_{26}, & k_{30}, & k_{34}, & k_{38}, & k_{42} \\ S(k_{20}), & k_{27}, & k_{31}, & k_{35}, & k_{39}, & k_{43} \end{bmatrix}$$

However, AES-256 contains a slight tweak (denoted with blue):

$$\begin{bmatrix} k_{32}, & k_{36}, & k_{40}, & k_{44}, & k_{48}, & k_{52}, & k_{56}, & k_{60} \\ k_{33}, & k_{37}, & k_{41}, & k_{45}, & k_{49}, & k_{53}, & k_{57}, & k_{61} \\ k_{34}, & k_{38}, & k_{42}, & k_{46}, & k_{50}, & k_{54}, & k_{58}, & k_{62} \\ k_{35}, & k_{39}, & k_{43}, & k_{47}, & k_{51}, & k_{55}, & k_{59}, & k_{63} \end{bmatrix} \leftarrow \begin{bmatrix} k_0, & \ldots, & k_{28} \\ k_1, & \ldots, & k_{29} \\ k_2, & \ldots, & k_{30} \\ k_3, & \ldots, & k_{31} \end{bmatrix} \oplus \begin{bmatrix} S(k_{29}) \oplus RC_1, & k_{32}, & k_{36}, & k_{40}, & S(k_{44}), & k_{48}, & k_{52}, & k_{56} \\ S(k_{30}), & k_{33}, & k_{37}, & k_{41}, & S(k_{45}), & k_{49}, & k_{53}, & k_{57} \\ S(k_{31}), & k_{34}, & k_{38}, & k_{42}, & S(k_{46}), & k_{50}, & k_{54}, & k_{58} \\ S(k_{28}), & k_{35}, & k_{39}, & k_{43}, & S(k_{47}), & k_{51}, & k_{55}, & k_{59} \end{bmatrix}$$

The same operation is repeated for 10, 8, 7 times for AES-128/192/256 respectively. Later, regardless of the instance and the initial key size, the subsequence $k_{16i}, \ldots, k_{16i+15}$ will act as the round key K_i for the i-th round. A key expansion round can be seen as a proper combination of the following unit operations, each of which processes one byte per clock cycle.

---

[1] Since at most 10 elements of this sequence is used, we consider it as a lookup table.

- ke0 (key expand 0) takes the byte from the second row and the last column of the current key, applies S-box, and XORs with the round constant RC_j. The result is added to the key byte in the first row and column e.g. $k_{16} \leftarrow k_0 \oplus S(k_{13}) \oplus RC_1$ is computed in AES-128. Each key expansion round contains exactly one ke0 operation.
- ke1 (key expand 1) takes the byte (from the next row) from last column and applies S-box, and XORs with the next key byte in the first column, e.g. $k_{17} \leftarrow k_1 \oplus S(k_{14})$ is computed in AES-128. Each key expansion round contains exactly three ke1 operations.
- ke2 (key expand 2) takes the byte from the last column and the same row, applies S-box, and XORs with the original value, e.g. $k_{48} \leftarrow k_{16} \oplus S(k_{44})$ is computed in AES-256. This operations is specific to AES-256 and is used exactly four times for each round of key expansion.
- kxor (key xor) XORs the current key byte with the $(\ell-4)$th previous keybyte, e.g. $k_{20} \leftarrow k_4 \oplus k_{16}$. Each key expansion round contains 12, 20, 24 kxor operations in AES-128, AES-192, AES-256 respectively.

The combination ke0, ke1, k1, ke1 performed for 4 consecutive clock cycles helps complete the first stage of the key expansion in which the last column of the current key is rotated, passed through the AES S-box, added to a round constant and thereafter added to the 1st column of the key. For AES-128 a keyschedule round consists of the following sequence of operations ke0, ke1^3, kxor^{12}, where op^i denotes i successive executions of the operation op. For AES-192 the sequence is ke0, ke1^3, kxor^{20} and for AES-256 the sequence is ke0, ke1^3, kxor^{12}, ke2^4, kxor^{12}. As already mentioned, the key expansion round and the encryption/decryption rounds are perfectly synchronized in AES-128, however the same cannot be said for AES-192 and AES-256. This was one of the primary challenges we had to overcome when designing a circuit that can perform all six instances together.

3 One Circuit to Rule Them All

3.1 Input, Output Formats

Our AES architecture is a sequential (clocked) one with 8-bit datapath. 8-bit KeyIn for key, 8-bit DataIn for the plaintext (resp. ciphertext) data, 3-bit selector Ins to choose among six instances (AES-128/192/256 encryption/decryption), a reset signal Rst and a clock signal Clk are wired as input. Its output consists of a 8-bit DataOut for the result (for the computed ciphertext or plaintext) and a ready signal Rdy indicating the completion of the operation. Loading the input values takes upto 16, 24, 32 cycles for AES-128/192/256 respectively, and the reception of the output takes 16 cycles; whereas the encryption/decryption operation takes on the order of few hundreds cycles.

We denote the data (i.e. the input plaintext/ciphertext) as a byte sequence $d_0, \ldots, d_{15}$. We denote the original key with $k_0, \ldots, k_{\ell-1}$ where ℓ is 16, 24, 32 for AES-128/192/256 respectively. Lastly, we denote the last ℓ bytes of round keys used in AddRoundKey with $k'_0, \ldots, k'_{\ell-1}$. Namely, these are the byte sequences $k_{160}, \ldots, k_{175}$ in AES-128; $k_{184}, \ldots, k_{207}$ in AES-192; and $k_{208}, \ldots, k_{239}$ in AES-256.

Loading Cycles. In AES-128, the key and the data has the same size, therefore loading the both can be synchronized, i.e. k_i (resp. k'_i) and d_i are loaded at the same clock cycle for encryption (resp. decryption). However, in AES-192/256, the key is larger than the data, therefore we should clarify which bytes of the key and the data are loaded at which cycles. For encryption, the data and the first 16 bytes of key are loaded during the first 16 cycles. The remaining bytes of the key, i.e. $k_{16}, \ldots, k_{\ell-1}$, are loaded in the following 8 (resp. 16) cycles in AES-192 (resp. AES-256). For decryption, first $\ell - 16$ bytes of the last used round key bytes (the sequence $k'_0, \ldots, k'_{\ell-17}$) are loaded. Namely, first 8 (resp. 16) cycles are used to load $k'_0, \ldots, k'_7$ (resp. $k'_0, \ldots, k'_{15}$) in AES-192 (resp. AES-256). Then, the following 16 cycles are used to load $k'_{\ell-16}, \ldots k'_{\ell-1}$ and $d_0, \ldots, d_{15}$ simultaneously.

Input Format. For encryption, the key $k_0, \ldots, k_{\ell-1}$ and the data $d_0, \ldots, d_{15}$ are loaded. For decryption, the key byte sequence (see Sect. 2.2) $k'_0, \ldots, k'_{\ell-1}$ is loaded instead of the original key $k_0, \ldots, k_{\ell-1}$.

Result Cycles. The result data sequence $c_0, \ldots, c_{15}$ (ciphertext for encryption or plaintext for decryption) is observed at DataOut in the correct order. The signal Rdy is also set to '1' during the 16 cycles this result is available.

3.2 Components

- *Enabled byte flip flop* (henceforth referred as EFF) is a byte storage unit that preserves its output during many cycles when enable signal is unset, i.e. its value is frozen. When enable signal is set, its value (and thereby output) is updated with the first rising edge of the clock signal. They are denoted with shadowed white squares in Fig. 1, and used in the key pipeline.
- *Enabled byte scan flip flop* (henceforth referred as SEFF) is an EFF combined with a multiplexer. Two separate bytes are wired as input, and its next value is assigned to either one of them based on an additional selection signal. Its value is updated on the next rising edge, if the enable signal is set. If enable signal is unset, its value is preserved. They are denoted with grayed and shadowed squares in Fig. 1, and used mostly in the state pipeline.
- *Control Logic* is a finite-state machine which activates with the release of the reset signal Rst, and computes either one of the six AES instances based on Ins signal. It controls all flip flop enable signals, scan flip flop selectors, mux selectors, mask AND selectors, S-box direction signal and Rdy.
- *Mix Column* takes 4-byte column $[s_{4i}, s_{4i+1}, s_{4i+2}, s_{4i+3}]^T$ as input and computes $M \times [s_{4i}, s_{4i+1}, s_{4i+2}, s_{4i+3}]^T$ over $\mathsf{GF}(2^8)$, where M denotes the AES mixcolumn matrix [9]. Since $M^4 = I$ where I is the identity matrix, we can use the same circuit to do InvMixColumns by performing MixColumns three times. It outputs the 4-byte result.

- We use the Canright S-box architecture [8] that performs both the *S-box/S-box-inverse* operation and has a very low hardware footprint. S-box S, as well as its inverse S^{-1}. The direction of the operation is determined with an additional selection signal.
- *RC lookup table* contains ten round constant bytes used in all three instances. A 4-bit counter is also attached to choose the correct value from the table.

In order to minimize number of gates, we limit our design to a single two-directional S-box (shared between SubBytes and KeyExpand), a single mix column circuit (used for both MixColumns and InvMixColumns) and a series of EFF and SEFF as two pipelines: one for the state and another for the key. Since the keysize in AES-256 is 32-bytes, the key pipeline contains 32 byte flip flops.

3.3   High Level Description of the Design

Our design is fully described in Fig. 1. Below, we refer to EFF/SEFF directly though their two-digit addresses: for EFF/SEFF in the key pipeline we use 00, and for SEFF in the state pipeline we employ the italic font *00*.

State Pipeline. 16 SEFF are arranged in a upward-moving serial fashion, where a byte value enters into the pipeline from *33*, moves in the upwards direction to *30*, then moves to *23*, etc. and finally reaches to *00* in 16 clock cycles during normal operation. This is done via vertical connections in the pipeline which permit loading the state information in one-byte-per-clock fashion into the bus for executing AddRoundKey and SubBytes operations simultaneously in 16 cycles. Moreover, alternative lateral connections (e.g. from *30* to *00*) allow each column to be loaded into Mix Column circuit for MixColumns operation in 4 cycles. The same lateral connections in the left direction allows us to do ShiftRows operation, by carefully enabling and disabling rows in harmony in 3 cycles. With the help of muxes connected to *30, 31, 32, 33*, we can choose between ShiftRows and MixColumns operations. Notice that the control logic determines the direction of the flow by the select signals and whether or not some EFF/SEFFs are frozen by enable signals. Partially or fully freezing is useful for ShiftRows or when another operation is stalling the key pipeline.

Key Pipeline. It consists of 31 EFF and 1 SEFF to store the 32 byte key in AES-256. The connections of the pipeline are tweaked through muxes 5, 6 in such a way that:

- During AES-128 operations, from 20 to 53 are bypassed (disabled) and the output of 60 is wired to 13 through mux 5. Therefore the key pipeline effectively shrinks to 16 byte flip flops.
- During AES-192 operations, from 40 to 53 are bypassed (disabled) and the output of 60 is wired to 33 through mux 6. The output of 20 is wired to 13 through mux 5. The key pipeline shrinks to 24 flip flops.
- During AES-256 operations, no EFF in the key pipeline is disabled and 40 is wired to 33 through mux 6 and 20 is wired to 13 through mux 5.

In order to work in harmony with the state pipeline, the task of the key pipeline is to provide the particular byte of key to the bus, so that AddRoundKey can be performed correctly with the byte coming from the state. This key byte from the pipeline can be fetched from 00, 20 or 40 based on the selection signal of mux 10, whereas the pipeline supports rotation through connections 00 → 73 through mux 12. As before, enable signals are configured by the control logic and can freeze the pipeline when another operation is stalling the state pipeline.

Main Bus. Consists of two muxes 10, 7 to choose the source of key and data bytes to be loaded into the bus. The crucial component in the bus is the S-box, whose input and output is complemented with two byte XOR gates. The XOR gate before S-box is useful for encryption, as the key addition precedes the S-box, and the XOR gate after S-box is useful for decryption. The choice of S-box/S-box-inverse functionality and the select signals of muxes are configured by the control logic.

Key Expansion Logic. The most challenging part of our design by far is the computation of proper round key for AddRoundKey operation for 6 different instances on the same circuit. For this reason, a combination of XOR/AND gates is connected to the key pipeline to execute KeyExpand on-the-fly (while the pipeline is moving to perform another operation). The gates highlighted with lightgray background in Fig. 1 connected to 00, 10 (positioned above key pipeline) enables key expansion for the encryption and decryption, and the gates connected to 13, 23, 33, 63, 73 (positioned below the key pipeline) enable key expansion during decryption.

3.4 Elementary Operations of Layers

In order to simplify the explanation of how our circuit operates, we conceptually divide the control of the circuit into various operations. We also explain their connection to four different layers (plus KeyExpand). Some of the operations described below are computed on completely independent parts of the circuit, hence they can be performed simultaneously by our hardware. We will squeeze them into same cycles as much as possible. Each of the following instructions sets particular control bits for given cycle to perform its corresponding operation. If an operation does not explicitly mandate how a certain SEFF/EFF should behave, then it is **frozen** by setting the enable signal to '0'. As before, 00 refers to the top-left EFF of the key pipeline and *00* refers to the top-left SEFF in the state pipeline.

add Both the key and the state pipelines are fully active, and two bytes from each are loaded into the bus. The state byte is fetched from *00* of the state pipeline. On the other hand, the key byte can be fetched either from 00, 20 or 60 of the key pipeline (note that key bytes are fetched from 20 and 60 during AES-192 decryption). Exception to this is the initialization where the key and the data are being loaded to the circuit: then, two bytes must come from DataIn and KeyIn but not from the pipelines. If the chosen functionality

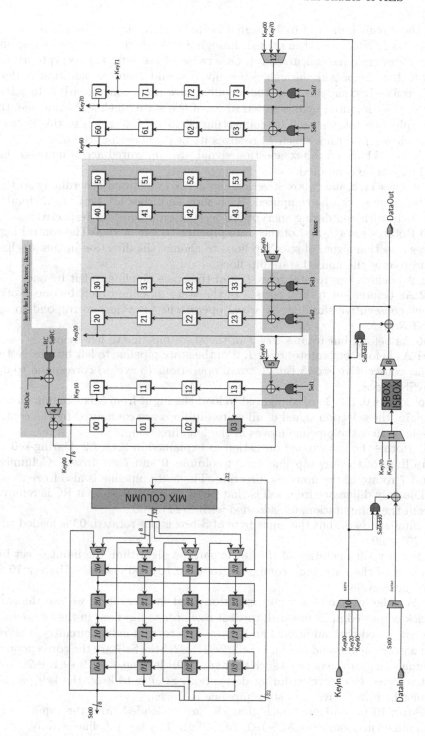

Fig. 1. Circuit diagram for the 6AES architecture

of the circuit indicated by Ins signal is encryption, the two bytes on the bus are first XORed, and then passed through S-box (therefore AddRoundKey and SubBytes are done concurrently). Otherwise (if Ins indicates decryption), the state byte is passed through S-box-inverse, and then the addition is done (therefore InvSubBytes and AddRoundKey are done concurrently). In either case, the computed byte is stored to 33 of the state pipeline. Meanwhile, the key pipeline rotates itself by connecting 00 to 73. Exception to this is again initialization, during which 73 receives its next value from the bus.

sbox Muxes 11, 8 and S-box selection signal are configured accordingly so that S-box can be computed.

isbox Muxes 11, 8 and S-box selection signal are configured accordingly so that S-box-inverse can be computed. Both sbox and isbox are performed simultaneously with add during encryption/decryption operations respectively.

srow0 Rotates rows 1, 2, 3 of the state pipeline to left by one. The control logic uses selection signal of scan flip flops to change the direction in the pipeline, and freezes the unused state flip flops.

srow1 As before, but rotates rows 1, 2 of the state pipeline to left by one.

srow2 As before, but rotates rows 3 of the state pipeline to left by one. Notice that consecutive srow0, srow1, srow2 operations (3 cycles) correspond to one ShiftRows.

isrow0 As before, but rotates row 1 of the state pipeline to left by one.

isrow1 As before, but rotates rows 1, 2 of the state pipeline to left by one. Notice that consecutive isrow0, isrow1, srow0 operations (3 cycles) correspond to one InvShiftRows.

mixcol Muxes 0, 1, 2, 3 are configured to load the input from Mix Column circuit. Again, the selection signal of all state flip flops are configured by the control logic so that the pipeline moves in the left direction.

ke0 Performs the key expand operation as explained in Sect. 2.2. During ke0, all flip flops of the key pipeline except columns 0 and 7 are frozen. Columns 0 and 7 rotate in the upwards direction. The state pipeline is also frozen.

ke1 The only difference from ke0 is that SelRC is set to 0, so that RC is removed from the computation, 03 is loaded with $S(71) \oplus 00$.

0ke2 Similar to ke0, but the input byte of S-box is not rotated, 03 is loaded with $S(70) \oplus 00$.

kxor For key xor operation of the key expansion algorithm, the input select bits of 03 and the mux 4 are configured to store $10 \oplus 00$ instead of barely 10 for the next cycle.

ikxor For the inverse of key xor operation used in decryption we use the same trick employed in [2] in which the last row of byte flip-flops in the key register is controlled with additional and gates. The corresponding circuitry is shown in a gray background in Fig. 1. Sel1, Sel2, Sel3, Sel6, Sel7 are the corresponding signals that are configured such that key XOR is done, e.g. $13 \leftarrow 10 \oplus 20$, only at selected clock cycles during decryption. Similar to kxor, the key pipeline must be fully active, and state pipeline is frozen.

load Mux 10 is configured such that the key is loaded from the input to the pipeline (necessary for AES-192, AES-256). The key pipeline is fully active, and the state pipeline is frozen.

rot The key is rotated in the pipeline, where the exiting byte 00 is fed back into
73. The key pipeline is fully active.

rxor Pseudonym for combination of rot and kxor. Therefore the key is updated
on the pipeline with key xor operation, as it rotates.

In the following two subsections, we will separate encryption/decryption
round functions performed on the state, completely from key expansion. Encryption and decryption round function operations are straightforward to implement
with the design given in Fig. 1 and remains quite similar through six different
instances. However, the key expansion becomes a major challenge and due to its
instance-specific nature, requires significant effort.

3.5   Generic Encryption/Decryption Overview

First, for the sake of argument, suppose that the key pipeline always contains the
necessary round key K_i at round i, with which AddRoundKey is being done. Then
we can readily convert the encryption algorithm into a sequence of operations.
AddRoundKey and SubBytes can be done simultaneously through add and sbox
operations in 16 cycles. Then for ShiftRows, it suffices to run srow0, srow1, srow2
subsequently in 3 cycles. Then, in 4 cycles of mixcol, we complete MixColumns.
This sequence corresponds to one round of operation in the encryption algorithm, and can be repeated as many times as necessary, as long as the key
pipeline handles the key expansion and provides the correctly aligned key bytes
during AddRoundKey. The same line of reasoning also applies to decryption,
where InvSubBytes and AddRoundKey can be done with isbox and add simultaneously in 16 cycles, InvShiftRows can be done with isrow0, isrow1, srow0 in 3
cycles; and InvMixColumns can be done in 12 cycles of mixcol (as explained before
InvMixColumns is 3 repetitions of MixColumns).

Therefore, what remains is to continuously *refresh* the key in the pipeline, by
removing *dirty* key bytes (i.e. already used with AddRoundKey), and replacing
with *fresh* bytes (not yet used) of key. By refreshing we mean computing the next
round key in encryption, and previous round key in decryption (since decryption
starts with the last ℓ key bytes of the last round and computes the round keys
in the reverse direction). In the following section we describe how key bytes are
managed in the key pipeline, and how its operations are interleaved with the
four layers of encryption and decryption.

3.6   Key Expansion Details

AES-128 Encryption: The detailed chronology of operations is given in Fig. 2.
During the first 16 cycles, muxes 7, 10 are configured such that the key and
the data are loaded to the bus through inputs DataIn, KeyIn, instead of the
pipelines. At the same time, AddRoundKey and SubBytes operations are done
simultaneously, where the computed state is loaded into the state pipeline, and
the key is loaded into 00–13, 60–73.

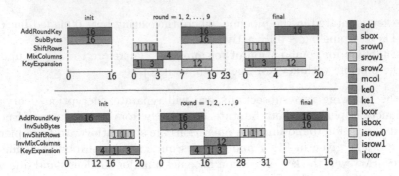

Fig. 2. The chronology of operations in AES-128 encryption (on top) and AES-128 decryption (below). The numbers in the boxes indicate the number of cycles over which the operation is executed.

A round takes 23 cycles to complete. At the beginning of the round, all the keys in the pipeline are dirty. Therefore, we use the first 4 cycles to refresh the key bytes in column 0 with running ke0, ke1, ke1, ke1 sequentially. ShiftRows and MixColumns are also performed in parallel, since they have no effect on the key pipeline. At the end of 7 cycles (after ke0, ke1^3 and waiting for 3 cycles), the key pipeline still contains 12 dirty key bytes contained in 10–13, 60–73. These bytes are refreshed in 12 cycles with kxor as the pipeline moves, as they are loaded into 03. Therefore, it is merged with add and sbox, which takes 16 cycles. At the end of a round, all bytes in the key pipeline are again dirty. In the final round, MixColumns is skipped, and the ciphertext is available during the very last 16 cycles.

AES-128 Decryption: We remind that for decryption, KeyIn loads the very last 16 bytes of key used with the last AddRoundKey, but not the original key used for encryption. The rounds can be seen as the symmetrically opposite versions of encryption.

A round takes 31 cycles to complete. At the beginning, all bytes in the key pipeline are fresh. At the end of 12 cycles, the key pipeline contains only 4 fresh bytes. Then, ikxor is enabled through 13, 63, 73 (by setting Sel13, Sel63, Sel73 to '1') for 4 cycles. Therefore at cycle 16, the key pipeline contains exactly 12 bytes of fresh key contained in 10–13, 60–73. The remaining dirty key column is refreshed by ke0, ke1, ke1, ke1 operations are in the next 4 cycles. Therefore, at the end of the round, all bytes in the key pipeline are fresh. As before, the output of decryption, i.e. the plaintext becomes available during the last 16 cycles.

AES-192 Encryption: The detailed chronology of operations is given in Fig. 3. Performing the key expansion in AES-192 becomes quite challenging given the fact that each key expansion round generates 24 bytes of new round key, whereas only 16 of them are used for each encryption round. This leads to misalignment and desynchronization issues between the state pipeline and the key pipeline.

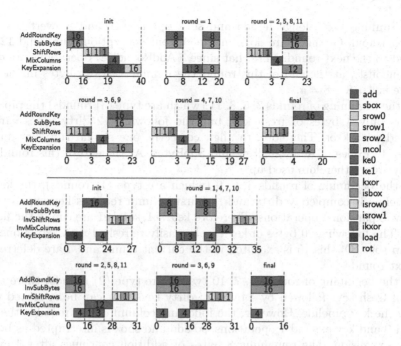

Fig. 3. The chronology of operations in AES-192 encryption (on top) and AES-192 decryption (below). The numbers in the boxes indicate the number of cycles over which the operation is executed.

We overcome them by interrupting AddRoundKey and SubBytes operations and running key expansion algorithm in the middle. This leads to three different types of rounds: (1) first type of round has no fresh key byte in the pipeline at the beginning and has to run a key expansion round algorithm before addition, (2) the second type of round has 4 leftover fresh bytes in 00–03 and 4 dirty bytes in 10–13 that can be refreshed with kxor as the pipeline moves. This means that AddRoundKey and SubBytes have to run for 8 cycles, then pause for key expansion, and later resume for 8 more cycles (3) third type of round has 4 fresh bytes in 00–03, and 12 dirty bytes in 10–33 that can be refreshed with kxor as the pipeline moves.

During the first 16 cycles, AddRoundKey and SubBytes is simultaneously performed as before. The next 8 cycles are used to load the rest of the key into the key pipeline. Then, in order to align the key properly, the key pipeline is rotated for 16 cycles with rot. Thereby, at the end, 8 fresh bytes are located at 00–13, and the dirty bytes are at 20–33, 60–73.

During round 1, we have to interrupt AddRoundKey and SubBytes after 8 cycles, at which point all the bytes in the key pipeline are dirty. The 4 bytes of key that requires to be updated by key expand 0 and key expand 1 operations are located at 00–03, therefore we run ke0, ke1, ke1, ke1 in the following four cycles. The remaining 20 dirty key bytes are refreshed as they are loaded into

03, by running kxor alongside add and sbox operations, and it overflows into the next round. Of this 8 are done in the current encryption round and 12 are deferred to the next round. Note that since 8 AddRoundKey operations are done simultaneously, at the end of this round the number of fresh bytes in the key pipeline is $4 + 8 - 8 = 4$.

At the beginning of rounds 2, 5, 8, 11 (which are type (3) rounds) the pipeline contains only 4 bytes of fresh key, but the following 12 dirty bytes can be refreshed with kxor. Therefore, to align correctly, one should run kxor during the first 12 cycles of AddRoundKey and SubBytes. At the end of this round, all fresh bytes are therefore used up.

At the beginning of rounds 3, 6, 9 (which are type (1) rounds); the key in the pipeline is completely dirty and the first column requires key expansion 0 and key expansion 1 operations. Therefore ke0, ke1, ke1, ke1 are run in the first 4 cycles. The following 20 bytes of key can be easily refreshed with kxor alongside add and sbox. Of this 16 is executed in the current round and 4 are deferred to the next round.

At the beginning of rounds 4, 7, 10 (which are type (2) rounds) there are 4 bytes of fresh keys followed by 4 bytes of dirty keys that can be refreshed with kxor in the key pipeline. However, the following column of key requires the key expand 0 and key expand 1 operations, so add and sbox is interrupted as before for key expansion. The remaining 8 bytes of addition continues after 4 cycles of ke0, ke1, ke1, ke1. The ciphertext is available in DataOut during the last 16 cycles.

AES-192 Decryption: A second obstacle that arises during the decryption is that fresh bytes in the key pipeline are not necessarily always start from 00. Recall that for decryption, the last 24 bytes of used round keys are loaded initially, therefore we have to run the key expansion algorithm in the reverse order. Therefore, we have to start refreshing key columns starting with the highest index, i.e. whichever column of key was used last in the encryption should be removed first. At the same time, due to flow direction of the pipeline, the lowest indexed key column occupies 00–03, whereas during various stages of operation the key columns to be used in key addition are located at 20–23 or 60–63. Our solution is to connect pipeline exits Key20, Key60 to mux 10, so that even if the next fresh key byte is misaligned in the key pipeline, we can continue AddRoundKey, InvSubBytes operations without requiring additional cycles for rotation. This irregular exit of key bytes from the pipeline is only necessary for AES-192 decryption.

Since the last 24 bytes of round key is loaded into the circuit (k_{184} to k_{207}), 8 cycles are used for loading the first 8 bytes of this key. Then the following 16 cycles are used for add. During the last four cycles of add, ikxor is also performed through 33, 63, 73 (but not 03, 13, 23). Therefore, at cycle 24, the key pipeline contains 20 fresh bytes (8 unused from the initial load and 12 from ikxor), where the 4 dirty bytes are stored in 20–23 and they can only be refreshed with ke0, ke1, ke1, ke1. Therefore, we will wait until this key moves into 00–03.

At the beginning of rounds 1, 4, 7, 10; the key pipeline contains 20 fresh bytes. However the next 8 fresh bytes to be used for add are located at 60–73, whereas the remaining 8 bytes required for add are located at 00–13. Therefore we fetch the next byte key into the bus from Key60, and at the same time rotate the pipeline by connecting 00 → 73. After 8 cycles, we interrupt isbox and add because the dirty column of key that requires the key expand 0/1 operations to update now reaches 00–03, so we can perform ke0, ke1, ke1, ke1. After refreshing this column of keys in 4 cycles, we resume fetching key bytes from 60 for AddRoundKey and InvSubBytes. Concurrently, at the last 4 cycles, we do ikxor with 03, 13, 23, 33 to obtain 16 fresh bytes for the next round. All the 24 bytes in the pipeline after this are completely fresh.

At the beginning of rounds 2, 5, 8, 11; the key pipeline is completely fresh. However the next 16 bytes of key to be used with add are located at 20–33 and 60–73. Therefore, key bytes are fetched from Key20 into the pipeline, and the pipeline is rotated as before. During the last 4 cycles of add, ikxor is performed over 13. After the 16 add cycles, the bytes of key that require update by key expand 0/1 arrive at 00–03, and therefore ke0, ke1, ke1, ke1 is executed to generate 4 fresh bytes. At the end, the key pipeline contains 16 fresh key bytes in 00–33.

At the beginning of rounds 3, 6, 9; the key pipeline contains 16 fresh bytes starting from 00, and they are aligned with the state pipeline for add. In order to arrange future key bytes, we still perform ikxor on 33, 63 for the first 4 cycles, and 33, 63, 73 for the last 4 cycles. At the end, the key pipeline contains 4 dirty bytes located at 20–23.

AES-256 Encryption: The detailed chronology of operations is given in Fig. 4. AES-256 remains simpler to achieve than AES-192, because each key expansion round produces enough keys for two AddRoundKey operations. During the first 16 cycles, add, sbox is performed. We spend other 16 cycles to load the rest of the key. Then the key expansion is performed with ke0, ke1, ke1, ke1, and key is rotated for 16 cycles to move the fresh key bytes to 00–33. During the first 12 cycles of this period, we also enable kxor (named rxor for convenience) so that old keys are refreshed as they rotate through the pipeline.

At the beginning of round 1, the key pipeline is completely fresh, therefore there are sufficient bytes of keys for round 2 as well. Therefore, no key expansion operation is done during the first two rounds.

At the beginning of rounds 3, 5, 7, 9, 11, 13; the key pipeline is completely dirty, and the bytes at 00–03 require 4 cycles of ke2. Then at the first 12 cycles of add, kxor is also enabled so that the following 12 dirty bytes can be refreshed.

The rounds 4, 6, 8, 10,12 work exactly same, except the special key column requires ke0, ke1, ke1, ke1 rather than 4 cycles of ke2. The ciphertext is available in the last 16 rounds of the final round.

AES-256 Decryption: Since the last 32 used bytes of key are loaded into the circuit, we use first 16 cycles to load the first half of this key. The next 16 cycles receives the data and the second half of the key at the same time, therefore performs the add operation.

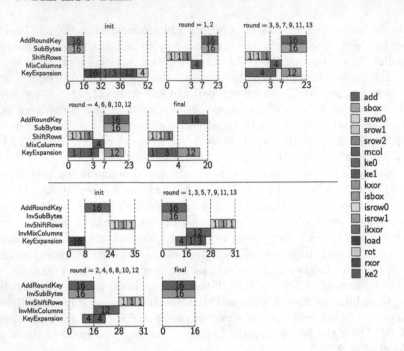

Fig. 4. The cycle arrangement of AES-256 encryption (on top) and AES-128 decryption (below). The numbers in the boxes indicate the number of cycles over which the operation is executed.

At the beginning of rounds 1, 3, 5, 7, 9, 11, 13; the first 16 bytes of the key pipeline are fresh and the rest is dirty. At the last 4 cycles of add, ikxor is performed through 13, 23, 33 so that 12 bytes are refreshed. The following 4 bytes are also refreshed with ke0, ke1, ke1, ke1.

The rounds 2, 4, 6, 8, 10, 12 work exactly same except the key column requiring update by key expand 2 is refreshed with 4 cycles of ke2 instead of ke0, ke1, ke1, ke1. The plaintext is available in the last 16 rounds of the final round.

4 Performance Evaluation and Conclusion

In order to perform a fair performance evaluation, we implemented the circuit using VHDL. Thereafter the following design flow was adhered to for all the circuits: a functional verification at the RTL level was first done using Mentor Graphics Modelism software. The designs were synthesized using the standard cell libraries of the CMOS logic processes listed in Table 1, with the Synopsys Design Compiler, with the compiler being specifically instructed to optimize the circuit for area. A timing simulation was done on the synthesized netlist to confirm the correctness of the design, by comparing the output of the timing simulation with known test vectors. The switching activity of each gate of

Table 1. Performance comparison of 6AES architecture (E: Encryption, D: Decryption). Power is reported at a clock frequency of 10 MHz. TP$_{max}$ denotes the maximum throughput achievable on the circuit.

Library	Area (GE)	Power (μW)	Variant	Latency (cycles)	Energy (nJ)	TP$_{max}$ (Mbps)	Variant	Latency (cycles)	Energy (nJ)	TP$_{max}$ (Mbps)
STM 90 nm	3672	189.5	AES-128E	243	4.605	75.8	AES-128D	315	5.969	58.5
			AES-192E	322	6.102	57.2	AES-192D	400	7.580	46.0
			AES-256E	371	7.030	49.6	AES-256D	454	8.603	40.6
TSMC 90 nm	4760	95.4	AES-128E	243	2.318	71.8	AES-128D	315	3.005	55.4
			AES-192E	322	3.072	54.2	AES-192D	400	3.816	43.7
			AES-256E	371	3.539	47.1	AES-256D	454	4.331	38.5
UMC 90 nm	5009	192.9	AES-128E	243	4.687	101.3	AES-128D	315	6.076	78.1
			AES-192E	322	6.211	76.4	AES-192D	400	7.716	61.5
			AES-256E	371	7.157	66.3	AES-256D	454	8.758	54.2
TSMC 180 nm	4680	1209.9	AES-128E	243	29.400	71.5	AES-128D	315	38.112	55.1
			AES-192E	322	38.959	53.9	AES-192D	400	48.396	43.4
			AES-256E	371	44.887	46.8	AES-256D	454	54.929	38.2

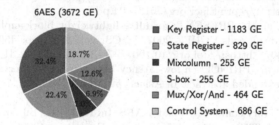

6AES (3672 GE)

■ Key Register - 1183 GE
□ State Register - 829 GE
■ Mixcolumn - 255 GE
□ S-box - 255 GE
■ Mux/Xor/And - 464 GE
□ Control System - 686 GE

Fig. 5. Area requirements of the individual components

the circuit was collected while running post-synthesis simulation. The average power was obtained using *Synopsys Power Compiler*, using the back annotated switching activity.

We outline some of the essential lightweight metrics of the 6AES architecture in Table 1. In Fig. 5, we present a component-wise breakdown of the circuit size when synthesized with the STM 90 nm logic process. A significant area is required for generating the control signals, as accommodating 6 different functionalities in a single circuit requires more fine-grained control over specific circuit components. This is because both the structure (wrt sequence of operations) and duration (wrt number of clock cycles) of a single round shows a wide range of variations as the size of the key changes. To the best of our knowledge, this is the first work that aims to minimize the size of the circuit while implementing all the 3 versions of the AES circuit. The circuit offers flexibility to designers who want to move to higher levels of security in the near future, and implement modes of operation that would require simultaneous access to block cipher encryption/decryption circuits.

Acknowledgments. Subhadeep Banik is supported by the Ambizione Grant PZ00P2_179921, awarded by the Swiss National Science Foundation (SNSF).

References

1. NIST Post-Quantum Cryptography Project. Available at https://csrc.nist.gov/ Projects/Post-Quantum-Cryptography
2. Banik, S., Bogdanov, A., Regazzoni, F.: Atomic-AES: a compact implementation of the aes encryption/decryption core. In: Dunkelman, O., Sanadhya, S.K. (eds.) INDOCRYPT 2016. LNCS, vol. 10095, pp. 173–190. Springer, Cham (2016). https://doi.org/10.1007/978-3-319-49890-4_10
3. Banik, S., Bogdanov, A., Regazzoni, F.: Atomic-AES v 2.0. In IACR eprint archive. Available at https://eprint.iacr.org/2016/1005.pdf
4. Banik, S., et al.: Midori: a block cipher for low energy. In: Iwata, T., Cheon, J.H. (eds.) ASIACRYPT 2015. LNCS, vol. 9453, pp. 411–436. Springer, Heidelberg (2015). https://doi.org/10.1007/978-3-662-48800-3_17
5. Beaulieu, R., Shors, D., Smith, J., Treatman-Clark, S., Weeks, B., Wingers, L.: The simon and speck families of lightweight block ciphers. In IACR eprint Archive. Available at https://eprint.iacr.org/2013/404.pdf
6. Bogdanov, A., et al.: PRESENT: an ultra-lightweight block cipher. In: Paillier, P., Verbauwhede, I. (eds.) CHES 2007. LNCS, vol. 4727, pp. 450–466. Springer, Heidelberg (2007). https://doi.org/10.1007/978-3-540-74735-2_31
7. Borghoff, J., et al.: PRINCE - a low-latency block cipher for pervasive computing applications - extended abstract. In Asiacrypt 2012, LNCS, vol. 7658, pp. 208–225 (2012)
8. Canright, D.: A very compact S-box for AES. In: Rao, J.R., Sunar, B. (eds.) CHES 2005. LNCS, vol. 3659, pp. 441–455. Springer, Heidelberg (2005). https://doi.org/ 10.1007/11545262_32
9. Daemen, J., Rijmen, V.: The Design of Rijndael: AES - The Advanced Encryption Standard. Springer-Verlag, Berlin (2002)
10. Datta, N., Nandi, M.: ELmD v1.0. Submission to the Caesar compedition. Available at https://competitions.cr.yp.to/round1/elmdv10.pdf
11. Dworkin, M.: Recommendation for Block Cipher Modes of Operation. NIST Special Publication 800–38A. Available at http://csrc.nist.gov/publications/nistpubs/ 800-38a/sp800-38a.pdf
12. Feldhofer, M., Wolkerstorfer, J., Rijmen, V.: AES implementation on a grain of sand. IEEE Proc. Inf. Secur. **152**(1), 13–20 (2005)
13. Jean, J., Moradi, A., Peyrin, T., Sasdrich, P.: Bit-sliding: a generic technique for bit-serial implementations of spn-based primitives. In: Fischer, W., Homma, N. (eds.) CHES 2017. LNCS, vol. 10529, pp. 687–707. Springer, Cham (2017). https:// doi.org/10.1007/978-3-319-66787-4_33
14. Mathew, S., et al.: 340 mV-1.1V, 289 Gbps/W, 2090-gate nanoAES hardware accelerator with area-optimized encrypt/decrypt $GF(2^4)^2$ polynomials in 22 nm tri-gate CMOS. IEEE J. Solid-State Circ. **50**, 1048–1058 (2015)
15. Moradi, A., Poschmann, A., Ling, S., Paar, C., Wang, H.: Pushing the limits: a very compact and a threshold implementation of AES. In: Paterson, K.G. (ed.) EUROCRYPT 2011. LNCS, vol. 6632, pp. 69–88. Springer, Heidelberg (2011). https://doi.org/10.1007/978-3-642-20465-4_6

16. Satoh, A., Morioka, S., Takano, K., Munetoh, S.: A compact rijndael hardware architecture with S-Box optimization. In: Boyd, C. (ed.) ASIACRYPT 2001. LNCS, vol. 2248, pp. 239–254. Springer, Heidelberg (2001). https://doi.org/10.1007/3-540-45682-1_15

17. Shirai, T., Shibutani, K., Akishita, T., Moriai, S., Iwata, T.: The 128-bit Block-cipher CLEFIA(Extended Abstract). In FSE 2007, LNCS, vol. 4593, pp. 181–195 (2007)

Side-Channel Attacks and Countermeasures

Revisiting Location Privacy from a Side-Channel Analysis Viewpoint

Clément Massart[(⊠)] and François-Xavier Standaert

ICTEAM - Crypto Group, Université Catholique de Louvain, Louvain-la-Neuve,
Belgium
clement.massart@uclouvain.be

Abstract. Inspired by the literature on side-channel attacks against cryptographic implementations, we describe a framework for the analysis of location privacy. It allows us to revisit (continuous) re-identification attacks with a combination of information theoretic and security metrics. Our results highlight conceptual differences between re-identification attacks exploiting leakages that are internal or external to a pseudonymised database. They put forward the amount of data to collect in order to estimate a predictive model as an important – yet less discussed – dimension of privacy assessments. They finally leverage recent results on the security evaluations/certification of cryptographic implementations to connect information theoretic and security metrics, and to formally bound the risk of re-identification with external leakages.

1 Introduction

Location privacy has become an important concern with the advent of pervasive computing: we refer to [2] for one of the first studies motivating this active line of research. In this paper, we are interested in the quantification of location privacy in a setting where an adversary can access a database with location information about different users, together with their pseudonyms. We focus in particular on the risks of re-identification attacks, where an adversary tries to exploit leakages (i.e., the location data of some individuals supposedly in the pseudonymized database) to re-identify users. Such re-identification attacks are continuous (i.e., it is possible for the adversary to accumulate leakages for the same user). In this context, our starting observation is that leakages can be internal (i.e., part of the data collected in the database) or external (i.e., fresh observations).

Our first contribution is a consolidating one. We revisit re-identification attacks with a combination of information theoretic and security metrics, as usually considered in the evaluation of leaking cryptographic implementations against side-channel attacks [20]. We put forward that re-identification attacks with internal leakages can be captured with information theoretic metrics similar to Diaz et al.'s anonymity degree [7], and that re-identification attacks with external leakages can be captured with security metrics (similar to Maouche et al.'s re-identification rate [15]). We consolidate these results by connecting both

© Springer Nature Switzerland AG 2019
J. Buchmann et al. (Eds.): AFRICACRYPT 2019, LNCS 11627, pp. 333–351, 2019.
https://doi.org/10.1007/978-3-030-23696-0_17

types of metrics thanks to established results in the worst-case evaluation of cryptographic implementations [8], which prove that the success rate of a worst-case side-channel attack is (under some assumptions) proportional to the mutual information between its target key and the leakages it exploits.

We then show that this consolidating effort can lead to both new observations/refined intuitions and technical advances in the analysis of location privacy.

A first novel observation is that the database size has opposite effects on attacks using internal and external leakages: attacks with internal (resp., external) leakages become more challenging (resp., easier) when the database grows.

A second novel observation is that most existing location privacy metrics tailored for the evaluation of external leakages quantify (to some extent) the success of an attack given a statistical model for the collected data. We argue that the convergence of the model is also interesting to analyze since it determines the amount of data needed to infer something about a user's behavior.

Based on these observations, we conclude that evaluating the risks of re-identifications with external leakages is in general more challenging since they increase when collecting more data (or merging databases). In this respect, our third and most important contribution is to show that such risks can be formally bounded. For this purpose, we leverage a recent result in the leakage certification of cryptographic implementations [3], which shows that our information theoretic metrics evaluated with internal leakages are (in expectation) an upper bound of these metrics evaluated with external observations. As a result, we can bound the risk of re-identification attacks with external leakages independent of the database size (with the bound becoming tight as this size increases).

In the extended version of this work, we show that localization attacks where an adversary tries to predict the position of a user (as in [19]) can be captured in a similar framework, and critically depends on the time dimension of the observations which determines the adversary's efforts to intercept a user.

2   Definitions and Framework

In this section, we specify the location data that we aim to analyze and the estimation tools used to characterize statistical distributions.

Data Specification. The location data we consider is based on spatial coordinates: longitude x and latitude y (possibly with a time component t). In general, we will consider two types of observations. First, "independent observations" where every triple (x, y, t) is analyzed independently.[1] These could for example correspond to the location data of a mobile phone application (where consecutive observations are distant in space and time), as pictured in Fig. 1 (left). We will next refer to this data as "positions" and denote them as $\boldsymbol{p} = (x, y, t)$. Second, correlated observations for which the joint analysis is expected to lead to

---

[1] The word "independent" does not refer to the fact that these observations are truly independent, but only to the fact that such observations are exploited assuming it.

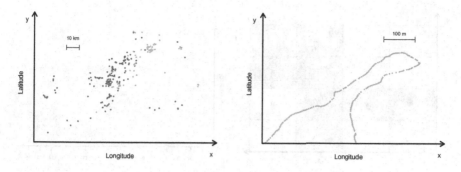

Fig. 1. Left: positions for two users. Right: route for a single user.

improved characterization. It could for example correspond to the GPS data of a jogger (where consecutive observations are close in space and time), as pictured in Fig. 1 (right). We will denote them as "routes" in the following.

More formally, we first define a set of n users:

$$\mathcal{U} = \{u_1, u_2, \ldots, u_n\}.$$

Assuming that some location data has been collected for each of the users, we denote the jth route of user i as:

$$r_{ij} = \{p_{ij}^1, p_{ij}^2, \ldots, p_{ij}^k, \ldots, p_{ij}^{N_p^{ij}}\},$$

with N_p^{ij} the number of positions in the route, and denote the number of routes collected for a user i as N_r^i. Note that independent observations can be considered as single-position routes. In the latter case, the number of routes collected per user equals the number of positions collected per user, next denoted as N_p^i.

The collection of location data is then formalized as follows. We first assume that the routes are sampled from an unknown statistical distribution that reflects the true users' behavior. This true distribution can be continuous, in which case we denote its Probability Density Function (PDF) as $f(r|u)$, or discrete, in which case we denote its Probability Mass Function (PMF) as $g(r|u)$. Next, the sampling process giving rise to a set of N_r^i routes for user i is written as:

$$\mathcal{S}_i \xleftarrow{N_r^i} f(r|u_i) \text{ or } \mathcal{S}_i \xleftarrow{N_r^i} g(r|u_i),$$

for the continuous and discrete cases, respectively.

Eventually, even if routes can be sampled from a continuous distribution, their storage is generally discrete. Besides, it is usually convenient for exploitation purposes (or necessary for privacy purposes) to further truncate the data. We reflect this process with a discretization function. Ignoring the time component for simplicity, it decomposes the location space into Δ ($=\delta_1 \times \delta_2$) cells, illustrated in Fig. 2 (left) and denoted as $D_1 : \mathcal{R} \rightarrow \{0,1\}^\Delta$, with $\mathcal{R}$ the set of all possible routes. In the basic setup of this section, it is computed by assigning a one to each cell where at least one observation of the route falls.

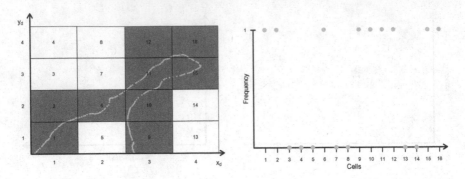

Fig. 2. Left: discretization of a route with D_1 & $\Delta = 16$. Right: D_1-discretized route $\boldsymbol{d}$.

Based on this discretization function, we represent a discretized route as in Fig. 2 (right), which we define as $\boldsymbol{d} = D_1(\boldsymbol{r})$. For conciseness, we only consider the case where the true (unknown) user distribution is continuous and then discretized. Directly discrete user distributions can be formalized identically.

Types of Estimations. Given a set of N_r^i discretized routes $\mathcal{D}_i$ obtained for a user i denoted as: $\mathcal{D}_i \xleftarrow{N_r^i} D_1(f(\boldsymbol{r}|u_i))$, the evaluation of our metrics will be based on the estimation of a model for the true (unknown) distribution. We will consider two types of modeling phases. The first one, next denoted as the direct (DI) estimation process, uses all the samples in the set $\mathcal{D}_i$ and is written as:

$$\tilde{f}(\boldsymbol{d}|u_i) \xleftarrow{\text{di}} \mathcal{D}_i \text{ or } \tilde{g}(\boldsymbol{d}|u_i) \xleftarrow{\text{di}} \mathcal{D}_i,$$

for continuous and discrete models. In the following, we will always refer to "DI-estimated" models with the tilde notation. Note that independent of the nature of the true distribution (i.e., continuous or discrete), it is always possible to model it as continuous and discrete. In the second type of modeling, next denoted as the (k-fold) cross–validated (CV) estimation process, the set $\mathcal{D}_i$ is first split into k non-overlapping sets $\mathcal{D}_i^{(j)}$ with $1 \leq j \leq k$. We then define k model building sets $\mathcal{B}_i^{(j)} = \mathcal{D}_i \setminus \mathcal{D}_i^{(j)}$ and the corresponding test sets $\mathcal{T}_i^{(j)} = \mathcal{D}_i^{(j)}$ so that we write the model estimation for all (j)'s as:

$$\left\{ \hat{f}^{(1:k)}(\boldsymbol{d}|u_i), \mathcal{T}_i^{(1:k)} \right\} \xleftarrow{\text{cv}} \mathcal{D}_i,$$

or:

$$\left\{ \hat{g}^{(1:k)}(\boldsymbol{d}|u_i), \mathcal{T}_i^{(1:k)} \right\} \xleftarrow{\text{cv}} \mathcal{D}_i,$$

where the hat notation is for "CV-estimated" models. As usual in statistics, the difference between these estimations is that direct estimation may suffer from overfitting (i.e., the characterization of features that are specific to the collected data $\mathcal{D}_i$ rather than the distribution $f(\boldsymbol{r}|u_i)$), which cross-validation aims to limit. In this work, we will need both types of estimation in order to capture both internal and external leakages (details are given in Sect. 3).

Estimation Tools. For both types of estimation, we then need to define how the models are built. In the basic setup of this section, we will exploit two (discrete) estimation tools: an exhaustive one and a simplifying one.

The exhaustive model, denoted as $\tilde{g}_{ex}(d|u_i)$ for the discrete and direct estimation case (the variant with cross–validation is referred to with the hat notation): it corresponds to a histogram with 2^Δ bins corresponding to all the routes. Note that despite the support of this model grows exponentially in Δ, its memory complexity (and the time needed to evaluate it) is bounded by the amount of collected data (i.e., we only need to store routes with non-zero probabilities).

The 1st-order independent model, denoted as $\tilde{g}_1(d|u_i)$ for the discrete and direct estimation case (the variant with cross–validation is denoted with the hat notation): it corresponds to the independent estimation of $\tilde{g}_1(d(c)|u_i)$ for the Δ cells, with $d(c)$ a cell of the discretized route d. More precisely, for each cell c, this model is computed as follows:

$$\tilde{g}_1(d(c)|u_i) = \frac{1}{N_r^i} \sum_{d' \in \mathcal{D}_i} d'(c).$$

In the case of the exhaustive model, the probability of a user u_i given a discretized route d is directly obtained thanks to Bayes' formula, assuming a uniform distribution for the users. For example, in the DI estimation case it yields:

$$\tilde{Pr}_{ex}[u_i|d] = \frac{\tilde{g}_{ex}(d|u_i)}{\sum_{j=1}^{n} \tilde{g}_{ex}(d|u_j)}.$$

In the 1st-order independent case, it is derived similarly by first computing the 1st-order likelihood as follows:

$$\tilde{q}_1(d|u_i) = \prod_{c \in d} \tilde{g}_1(d(c)|u_i) \cdot \prod_{c \notin d} \left(1 - \tilde{g}_1(d(c)|u_i)\right),$$

where $c \in d$ denotes the cells that are part of the route d and $c \notin d$ the ones that are not. The probability $\tilde{Pr}_1[u_i|d]$ is derived thanks to Bayes as:

$$\tilde{Pr}_1[u_i|d] = \frac{\tilde{q}_1(d|u_i)}{\sum_{j=1}^{n} \tilde{q}_1(d|u_j)}.$$

In this case, the probability of a route is estimated by assuming the independence of the observations in each cell, which is obtained by multiplying the probabilities of all the cells in the route. Summarizing, we so far defined models estimated directly and with cross–validation, that correspond to an exhaustive characterization of the routes, or are based on a 1st-order independence assumption. Other options could be considered. For example, Gambs et al. used a modeling based on Markov chains which could also be analyzed with the following tools [13].

In the extended version of this work, we detail how this 1st-order independent model can be generalized to an *oth-order independent model* which can capture higher-order correlations in the distribution by first "extending" the data towards higher-orders and then using estimation tools similar to the ones described in this section. In this respect, we note that an oth-order independent model is not equivalent to the exhaustive model since the knowledge of a statistical distribution is not equivalent to the knowledge of its moments. So while increasing o can be used to characterize higher-order dependencies of the user's behavior, it cannot lead to an optimal model.

3   Threat Models and Metrics

Our threat model is depicted in Fig. 3 and formalized as follows.

First, as in Sect. 2, we have a number of users (i.e., Alice, Bob, Carol, David, ... on the figure). For each of them, a number of routes have been collected and stored in a database under different pseudonyms. Pseudonyms are user IDs reorganized according to a secret permutation. Other data may be collected (e.g., performance data for sport applications, preferences for cultural applications, ...). Second, we mostly (yet, as will be clear next, not only) consider an open data scenario where the collected data is anonymized thanks to pseudonyms, and then made public, e.g., to facilitate the investigations of social scientists. Third, we assume that the adversary can have access to two types of leakages. The first one is an "internal leakage". That is, the adversary learns that some route(s) in the database correspond(s) to a user. This typically happens by spying on a user while data is collected. The second one is an "external leakage". That is, the adversary learns that some fresh route(s) correspond(s) to a user. This typically happens by spying on a user after data has been collected.

Concretely, there are two important quantities that impact privacy in this threat model. First, the size of the anonymized database, which we will denote with a number of routes collected per user N_r^i (as in Sect. 2). Second, the number of leakages obtained per user, that we will next denote as M_r^i. In general, we expect that the number of leakages collected is significantly smaller than the size of the anonymized database.

Based on this setup, the goal of the adversary is to re-identify the users thanks to their leakages, which may for example allow him to gain access to other sensitive data. This can be achieved both with internal and external leakages. Yet, the meaning of successful re-identification with these two types of leakages is quite different. In the latter case (i.e., with external leakages), it implies that the collected data is representative of the true users' distributions. That is, external leakages can only be linked to the collected data of their originating user if this data can be used to predict fresh routes to some extent. By contrast re-identification with internal leakages does not imply anything regarding the representativity of the collected data. That is, since the leakages come from the database, they are guaranteed to be linkable to their originating user (possibly with other users if they are found in the observations of multiple users).

In statistical terms, these two types of leakages therefore directly correspond to our two types of estimations. Internal leakages can be captured with the

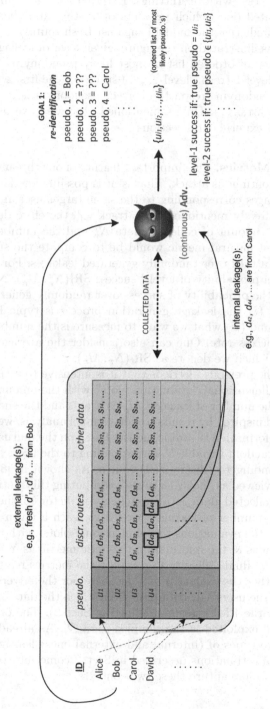

Fig. 3. Re-identification attack threat model.

direct estimation process (with overfitting). External leakages can be captured with the cross-validated one (which prevents overfitting and therefore can be used to assess how predictive the model is against fresh routes).

Eventually, and as illustrated on the figure, given a set of leakages for a user, the adversary outputs an ordered list of most likely pseudonyms. We then say that the attack is a level-1 (resp., level-2, ...) success if the first element of this list is the correct pseudonym (resp., the correct pseudonym is among the first two elements of the list, ...). Unless mentioned otherwise, we assume level-1 successes in the next experimental sections.

Re-Identification Metrics. One important feature of our threat model is that it corresponds to a continuous attack. That is, it is possible for the adversary to obtain multiple leakages corresponding to the same target user and to combine these leakages. As already mentioned, the attack will therefore depend on two main quantities: the amount of collected data N_r^i and the number of leakages M_r^i. Therefore, a first natural metric would be to compute the success rate of the re-identification attack over randomly generated leakages. For each user u_i, this corresponds to a probability of level-l success $\mathrm{SR}_l^i(N_r^i, M_r^i)$. Note that it is natural to consider the probability of success over randomly generated leakages in our setting since (i) the leakage generation process is typically not under adversarial control, and (ii) what we want to measure is the number of leakages leading to a high success rate. One can also consider the average success rate (over all the users), which we denote as $\mathrm{SR}_l(N_r, M_r)$.

A limitation of the previous metric is that it is intensive to estimate, since it requires building 3-dimensional "evaluation plots" with the amount of collected data N_r^i as X axis, the number of leakages M_r^i as Y axis and the success rate as Z axis. As a result, and inspired by results in side-channel analysis, we will consider easier-to-estimate information theoretic metrics based on the mutual information between the target random variable U corresponding to the users and a random variable D corresponding to (discretized) routes. As shown in [8], in case the observations can be viewed as "noisy leakages", computing this metric in function of the amount of collected data is an excellent predictor of the attack data complexity (i.e., the number of leakages needed to reach a given success rate). It allows simplifying the evaluations to 2-dimensional plots, with the amount of collected data as X axis & the information theoretic metric as Y axis.

In this respect, the final difficulty to compute the metrics relates to the fact that in practice, neither the evaluator of a database nor the adversary trying to exploit it know the true users's distributions from which the data originates (i.e., the PDFs $f(r|u_i)$ or the PMFs $g(r|u_i)$ defined in Sect. 2). The only thing that can be analyzed and exploited is the sampled data $\mathcal{D}_i$. As already mentioned, this is where the two types of (internal and external ones) leakages considered and the two types of estimations described in Sect. 2 come into play and allow defining metrics that can capture these two contexts.

Internal Leakages Evaluation. In this setting, we use the direct estimation process of Sect. 2 to obtain discrete models $\tilde{g}(d|u_i)$ and the probabilities $\tilde{\Pr}[u_i|d]$ and compute the Hypothetical Information (HI):

$$\tilde{\text{HI}}(U; D) = \text{H}[U] + \sum_{u_i \in \mathcal{U}} \Pr[u_i] \cdot \sum_{d \in \mathcal{D}} \tilde{g}(d|u_i) \cdot \log_2 \tilde{\Pr}[u_i|d],$$

where we use the short notation $\Pr[X = x] := \Pr[x]$ and we assume uniform users (i.e., $\text{H}[U] = \log_2(n)$). As discussed in [9], the HI corresponds to the amount of information that would be extracted from the observations of (hypothetical) users behaving exactly according to the models $\tilde{g}(d|u_i)$. The higher the HI, the more different are the model distributions of the users and the easier the re-identification attack will be. Intuitively, the word hypothetical is used to make explicit that we do not know the true users' distributions. Concretely, it corresponds to the context of internal leakages since in this case, the collected data exactly defines the PDFs and PMFs that the adversary exploits. Note that when considering internal leakages, the adversary has no incentive to exploit a simplified model (since this model is guaranteed to be correct by definition). Hence, in the following, we will only consider the HI with exhaustive model.

External Leakages Evaluation. In this setting, the situation significantly differs since in order to be successful, the adversary has to build from the collected data a model that can be used to predict fresh routes. In order to capture this goal, we will therefore use the cross–validation estimation process of Sect. 2. Indeed, it typically reflects situations where a part of the observations are used to build a model that is then tested with another part of the observations (which actually corresponds to the leakages in an actual attack).

Importantly, successful attacks in this setting require that the true distributions are stationary to some extent (i.e., that $f(d|u_i)$ or $g(d|u_i)$ do not vary too much over time), so we need a metric that captures this requirement. For this purpose, we compute the Perceived Information (PI) as described next. First, we use the cross–validated estimation process in order to generate the models and test samples as in Sect. 2:

$$\left\{ \hat{g}^{(1:k)}(d|u_i), \mathcal{T}_i^{(1:k)} \right\} \xleftarrow{\text{cv}} \mathcal{D}_i,$$

where any model $\hat{g}^{(j)}(d|u_i)$ can be used to define probabilities $\hat{\Pr}^{(j)}[u_i|d]$. We next evaluate the models by using the test samples and deriving the estimates:

$$\hat{\text{PI}}^{(j)}(U; D) = \text{H}[U] + \sum_{u_i \in \mathcal{U}} \Pr[u_i] \tag{1}$$

$$\cdot \sum_{d' \in \mathcal{T}_i^{(j)}} \frac{1}{|\mathcal{T}_i^{(j)}|} \cdot \log_2 \hat{\Pr}^{(j)}[u_i|d'].$$

The latter equation actually corresponds to an estimation by sampling, where we assign a probability $\frac{1}{|\mathcal{T}_i^{(j)}|}$ to each test sample which (by definition) directly originates from the true user distribution. The k outputs of this process (for a k-fold cross-validation) are finally averaged in order to obtain a more precise estimate $\hat{\text{PI}}(U; D)$. As discussed in [10], the PI corresponds to the amount of information that is extracted from the observations of actual users, by using models that are potentially biased by estimation and assumption errors. The PI is related to the success rate of an adversary using the same models. Intuitively, a positive PI means that the collected data reflects the differences between the true users' distributions to some extent. Incidentally, it also means that the user's distributions have been somewhat stationary during the data collection. The more positive the PI, the more successful are re-identification attacks with external leakages. By contrast, a negative PI means that the collected data is not sufficiently reflective of the true user's distribution (i.e., the models built from the collected data are not sufficiently predictive, due to insufficient data, wrong assumptions or strong model drift). Eventually, the PI converges towards Shannon's standard definition of Mutual Information (MI) if the models $\hat{g}(d|u_i)$ are perfect (i.e., if they are equal to the true $g(d|u_i)$).

Note that when considering external leakages, the adversary has incentives to exploit simplified models (such as a 1st-order independent model). Indeed, the PI is a tradeoff between estimation and assumption errors, i.e., between the speed of convergence and the asymptotic informativeness of a model. This tradeoff will be discussed in the experimental sections.

Remark. As the amount of collected data increases, it reflects more and more the true users' distributions. Hence, if both the HI and the PI metrics are estimated with the same model family and based on data discretized with the same function (and Δ), they both converge towards the same value. In case an exhaustive model is used, they additionally converge towards the true mutual information $\text{MI}(U; D)$. Based on this intuition, it was demonstrated in [3] that the HI is (in expectation) an upper bound of the MI and PI.

Besides, we note that the HI and PI metrics are averages over the users. Yet, it can happen that the success rate of the re-identification attacks highly vary in function of the users. The latter is easily analyzed by computing those metrics for fixed users, i.e., by evaluating $\tilde{\text{HI}}(U = u; D)$ or $\hat{\text{PI}}(U = u; D)$.

Links to Other Metrics. We now discuss the links between the HI and PI metrics and related metrics introduced in the privacy literature.

k-**Anonymity and Related Metrics.** The re-identification threat model _with internal leakages_ (where the collected data is available to the adversary) shares similarities with the problem of privacy-preserving data publishing for which various metrics have been introduced, some of them surveyed in [12]. In this setting, the k-anonymity is among the simplest (and most popular) solutions [17]. Informally, k-anonymity guarantees that a leakage does not allow to (strictly) distinguish (i.e., with probability one) a user from at least $k - 1$ other users. As discussed in [14], this may not be enough to prevent all types of linking attacks. A typical example is the case where all the users that remain indistinguishable have the same "sensitive data" that the linking attack aims to recover (i.e., referred to as "other data" in Fig. 3). In other words, a lack of diversity in the sensitive data may allow the adversary to deduce private information for a database that ensures k-anonymity. The main limitation of the k-anonymity and refinements such as the l-diversity in our context is that they only consider the strict indistinguishability of the users, and ignore the possibility that the list of users for which a leakage is possible may have different conditional probabilities. The latter possibility is particularly relevant in a continuous attack setting (since these probabilities may be combined in maximum likelihood attacks).

Other Information Theoretic Metrics. In order to mitigate the previous limitation, a usual solution is to consider information theoretic metrics, for example such as the anonymity degree introduced by Diaz et al. [7] or variations thereof [18]. The anonymity degree can be viewed as similar to the HI metric, since it is also computed from a model built thanks to a direct estimation process. The only differences are that (i) the anonymity degree considers the normalized conditional entropy rather than the mutual information for the HI (hence its link with the success rate is less direct), and (ii) as already mentioned, the HI metric makes explicit that it is based on a hypothetical model.

Location Privacy Metrics. By contrast, neither the k-anonymity nor the anonymity degree can be used to evaluate re-identification attacks *with external leakages*. This was argued in a paper by Shokri et al. [19] (yet, for a different attack goal than re-identification, namely the localization attacks that we discuss in the extended version of this work). The authors identified three types of metrics (namely the uncertainty, accuracy and correctness) and argued that correctness is the appropriate way to quantify attacks aiming at predicting new events. Informally, the correctness is correlated to the probability of error of an adversary trying to predict fresh positions. In our re-identification context, it therefore captures a similar intuition as the success rate of an attack exploiting external leakages, the data complexity of which being itself correlated with the PI metric. The accuracy then measures the convergence of the model estimate and can be analyzed based on the convergence of the PI metric (thanks to estimation plots or confidence intervals). We will argue next that it is also relevant to the evaluation of re-identification attacks with external leakages. Eventually, the uncertainty corresponds to the HI metric and is indeed irrelevant to analyze attacks using external leakages. Even closer to our framework, the attacks described in [15] consider re-identification with external leakages quantified with a re-identification rate (which is directly equivalent to our success rate).

Unicity. In yet another line of papers, de Montjoye et al. introduced the concept of unicity, which captures re-identification attacks based on location data [5,6]. Their analysis uses a direct estimation process and is therefore linked to the HI. Informally, assuming independent leakages so that each observation reduces $H[U]$ by $\tilde{HI}(U; D)$, unicity corresponds to a case where the number of leakages is such that users have no entropy left.

Differential Privacy. Eventually, we mention that preventing re-identification attacks could be achieved thanks to differential privacy [11], yet in a different setting. Namely, in differential privacy, one aims to guarantee that a few queries made to a database do not reveal private information. In our setting, we rather make this database fully available to the adversary and allow multiple leakages. As will be clear in the experimental sections, obtaining privacy in this setting is extremely challenging (if possible at all). Our quantitative tools can therefore be viewed as a motivation for differential privacy (or similar frameworks aiming at restricting the adversary's power in a relevant manner). See for example the discussion about geo-indistinguishability in [1,16].

4   Experimental Validation and Discussion

The following experiments are based on 4 different data sets (all of them discretized thanks to the D_1 process). Our first data set is a simulated one where the space is discretized into $\Delta = 128$ cells and we generated 1000 routes for 5 users according to chosen distributions. The experiments additionally consider a more discretized process with only $\Delta = 16$ cells. This setting is only used in order to put forward the general intuitions of the metrics (since it allows generating sufficient number of observations from stable distributions so that all metrics perfectly converge). Our second data set comes from *Brightkite*, an application enabling to share visited places with friends. It provides global coordinates that we reduce in two steps [4]. First we only consider the San Francisco Area. Second, we discretize the space into $\Delta = 16$ cells. It then remained 302 users with at least 50 single-position routes.[2] Our third data set is based on *jogging records* obtained with smart watches. We followed 7 users with at least 100 routes, discretized in respectively 16, 32 and 121 cells.[3] Eventually, our last data set comes from the *BikeShare* stations (also in the San Francisco area), publicly available for a contest about data visualization.[4] We consider 27 groups of users (since the database has been anonymized by grouping users according to their ZIP code) and $\Delta = 33$ cells which correspond to different BikeShare stations.

We start by evaluating the simulated data set to put forward general intuitions that can be extracted from our framework and metrics. We then analyze the different real-life data sets and discuss their interpretation.

General Metric Intuitions. The metrics estimated from our simulated data set are given in Fig. 4. The left plot reports information theoretic metrics in function of the number of collected routes per user N. The right plot reports the success rate in function of the number of (external) leakages obtained by the adversary M, for various N values. They lead to the next observations.

Starting with the IT metrics, a first noticeable fact is that the HI decreases with N while the PI increases with N. This is theoretically expected in both

---

[2] https://snap.stanford.edu/data/loc-brightkite.html (4/2008 - 10/2010).
[3] This data set is not publicly available (1/2010 - 2/2016).
[4] https://www.fordgobike.com/system-data (8/2013 - 8/2016).

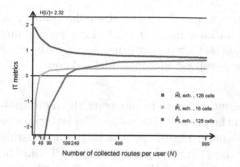 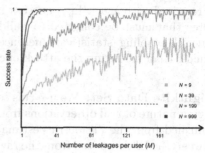

Fig. 4. Simulated data. Left: IT metrics. Right: success rate of attacks with external leakages (with the collected routes discretized in $\Delta = 128$ cells).

cases. For the HI, the reduction intuitively depends on the number of collisions in a data set (just as would be observed with the k-anonymity metric). As a result, larger numbers of routes per user N imply more risks of collisions for our data set (where some routes are possible for all users). For the PI, it reflects the fact that by increasing N, one builds more accurate models, with less estimation errors, saturating when N is sufficient to perfectly estimate the model.

A second observation (specific to the PI and the evaluation of external leakages) is that the level of discretization brings a tradeoff between the speed of convergence of the model and the informativeness of the (fully characterized) model. For example, the model estimated with 16 cells converges faster (and is more rapidly informative) than the one with 128 cells, but less informative for $N = 999$. The latter suggests that the speed of convergence of a model is a relevant evaluation metric since it determines the amount of observations that a malicious adversary would require to build a database that is sufficient to infer something about a user. This could for example be useful in a (non open data) scenario where routes are maliciously collected.

Eventually, a third observation is that since we only consider exhaustive models in this simulated setting, the HI and the PI with 128 cells converge towards the same value (equal to the MI), as expected [3].

An Open Source Tool in R language allowing the generation of HI/PI plots to confirm these intuitions is available in complement to this work.

As for the success rate plots, we first observe that the number of leakages M required to reach high success rates is proportional to the value of the PI for the corresponding N value, as theoretically predicted in [8]. This makes it an interesting alternative to the success rate since it is typically easier to sample, as reflected by the less smooth success rate curves when M increases (since there are less sets of M traces based on which we can estimate the success rate). Also, the PI plots allow easy comparisons between two models (e.g., the ones with 16 and 128 cells) in order to determine the number of collected traces such that one becomes more informative than the other, which happens when their respective PI curves intersect. Besides, we also note that the number of leakages

M required to reach a high success rate is usually lower than the number of routes that must be collected to build an informative model. That is, building a model enabling statistical inference attacks with external leakages is more difficult than mounting the attack once a well estimated model is known.

Brightkite Data Set. We use this second data set to illustrate the more challenging nature of real observations from the privacy viewpoint. The latter can be confirmed from the IT metrics estimations in Fig. 5, and the large gap existing between the HI computed from the raw data (from which no positive PI could be extracted) and the HI and PI computed after discretization. It reflects the general fact that location privacy rarely comes for free (i.e., without sanitization). For example, the high HI value for the raw data suggests that re-identification with internal leakages is trivial (i.e., successful after a couple of raw leakages). Since this value bounds the PI for a larger database, it means that with the amount of collected data, we can only bound the risks of re-identification with external leakages very conservatively with the raw HI value. We also notice that by discretizing the data we can reduce the HI while enabling the estimation of predictive models, as witnessed by the PI curve that converges to positive values. The latter values ($> \frac{1}{10}$) suggest that a handful of external leakages is sufficient for re-identification. Indeed, a simple bound for the re-identification complexity is given by $\frac{c}{PI}$ [8].[5] Stronger discretizations (e.g., with 16 cells) show a faster convergence of the PI at the cost of a reduction of its asymptotic value (i.e., a speed of convergence vs. informativeness tradeoff).

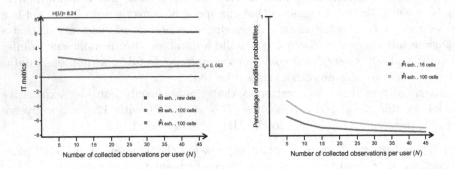

Fig. 5. Left: Brightkite data, IT analysis. Right: outliers correction

Another observation of interest is that in the case of real data, it frequently happens that the modeling phase is made more difficult due to outliers (i.e., user's observations that only happen rarely, possibly once). Those can lead to prohibitively low probabilities (e.g., zero probabilities that make the estimation

---

[5] With c a small constant depending on H[U] and the target success rate (e.g., $c =$ H[U] is a usual heuristic that corresponds to a success rate of approximately 80%).

of the PI impossible). We deal with these outliers by "correcting" the observations for which the probability is lower than $\frac{1}{N}$ and setting them to this minimum value, while also counting the fraction of corrected probabilities. This fraction f_o is always given for the final value of our PI estimates in the figures (e.g., $f_o = 0.063$ in the left part of Fig. 5). As illustrated the right part of the figure, it generally decreases with the size of the profiling set.

Jogging Data Set. We use this third data set and the results in (the left part of) Fig. 6 to illustrate a case where a simplified modeling exploiting an independence assumption does not allow a better model convergence. The figure clearly shows that the PI extracted by using an exhaustive model (with sufficiently discretized routes) is significantly higher than the PI extracted by using a 1st-order independent model. It corresponds to the intuition that in the case of jogging data (e.g., the ones in right part of Fig. 1), the consecutive observations of a route are highly correlated and therefore an independence assumption during the modeling is unlikely to bring any significant gain.

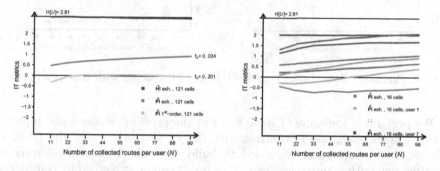

Fig. 6. Jogging data. Left: IT analysis. Right: IT analysis per user.

Another observation of interest in this context is that the routes of the joggers we analyzed are (on average) very discriminating, both with respect to internal leakages (with an HI value stuck to H[U]) and external leakages (with a PI value close to $\frac{H[U]}{4}$). We further use this context to put forward the differences that can occur in the characterization of the models for different users, as illustrated in the right part of Fig. 6. The latter recalls that the HI and PI are average metrics and are handy to have a quick "privacy overview" of a data set. However, a rigorous analysis of the leakages' informativeness has to be performed at the user level. For example, the aforementioned connection between information theoretic metrics and the success rate only holds per user [8].

BikeShare Data Set. We finally use this fourth data set to illustrate a case where a simplified modeling exploiting an independence assumption is needed for re-identification with external leakages, and to discuss the addition of the time component of the observation's in our reasoning.

Starting with the modeling issue, we first provide some additional intuition about the BikeShare data set based on Fig. 8 (given in Appendix A). It represents the daily usage of different bike stations by different users with different ZIP codes (i.e., 100% means the station is used everyday by the user). More precisely, it corresponds to the daily usage of sets of users living in the same area, which have been grouped in order to preserve their anonymity. We will denote these sets as users for simplicity. One can clearly see that depending on the area a user lives in, his most used BikeShare stations vary significantly.

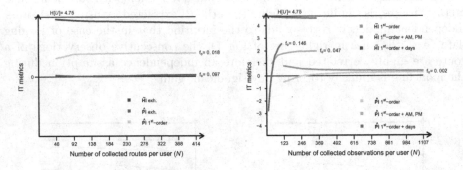

Fig. 7. BikeShare data. Left: IT analysis. Right: IT analysis with time component.

We performed the same IT analysis as in the previous sections and report it in Fig. 7. This time, and in contrast with the jogging case study, the 1st-order independence assumption is needed to build a predictive model allowing re-identification with external leakages. This result can be explained by considering the nature of the data represented in Fig. 8. Namely, contrary to the case of the jogging data where the consecutive observations in a route are very correlated, the use of BikeShare can be interleaved with other public or private transports, hence creating a good level of independence between the observations in a route. Based on this conclusion, our following analyzes of the BikeShare data set will systematically split all the routes into several independent observations. Note that contrary to the case of jogging data, the definition of a route is more difficult in the BikeShare context. In Fig. 7 we arbitrarily defined it as the consecutive observations of one day.

This analysis leads to important conclusions from a risk assessment view-point. Indeed, it highlights that the possibility to mount re-identification attacks exploiting external leakages against the privacy of some users in a database does not only depend on the amount of data collected but also on the assumptions that an adversary can make about them. In this respect, the possibility to bound this risk thanks to the HI estimated with an exhaustive model is a useful tool for privacy assessments. As already observed, for many real-world data sets, this bound is unlikely to be tight due to a lack of data (since for an infinite amount of data, it is proven to be tight). For example, in the simple case of Fig. 7, we tested a 1st-order independent model which leads to a better PI than the exhaustive model, but still falls far away from the HI bound. This gap captures the risk that some non-obvious assumption about the data set (or simply more data in case a malicious database owner is hiding a part of the collected data) would significantly improve the model informativeness and/or convergence: combined with the previous experimental observation that building a model is usually more data consuming than exploiting it, it implies that the risks of statistical inference attacks are in general hard to bound tightly, unless some specific mechanisms prevent the unrestricted use of the data.

Including the Time Component. We conclude the paper by showing that the time component of location observations can be used to further improve the attacks with external leakages. This fact is illustrated by the information theoretic analysis in the right part of Fig. 7 where the PI is estimated with and without time component, considering two granularities: AM/PM (in which case the total number of bins of the independent model is doubled) and daily (in which case this total number of bins is multiplied by seven).

Two preliminary remarks resulting from the figure are: (i) that the value of the PI without time component in the left part of Fig. 7 is reduced compared to the one in the right plot. The latter derives from the fact that we now estimate $PI(U; P)$ (since, as mentioned earlier, we split all the routes in independent observations) rather than $PI(U; D)$, and routes contain several positions: roughly, the average number of observations per route can be approximated by the ratio between the two PI values on these figures; and (ii) that the maximum size of the profiling set decreases when considering the time component (since we now need a sufficient amount of observations for all time values).

The figure highlights the significant gain of information that is obtained by characterizing the time component of the users' observations, hence revealing that their biking habits differ depending on the days and time of the days. It also confirms the aforementioned fact that the HI bound becomes tighter when a large database with more observations is available.[6]

Acknowledgments. François-Xavier Standaert is a Senior Research Associate of the Belgian Fund for Scientific Research (FNRS-F.R.S.). This work has been funded in parts by the ERC project SWORD (Consolidator Grant 724725).

---

[6] Note that the bound is here given for 1st-order independent models, as shown in the left part of the figure, the bound for the exshaustive models is stuck at $H[U]$.

A   Additional Figure

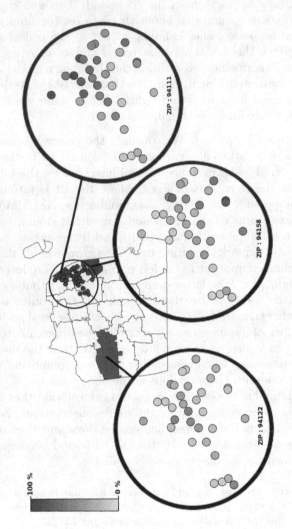

Fig. 8. Daily usage of BikeShare stations for three users (ZIP codes).

References

1. Andrés, M.E., Bordenabe, N.E., Chatzikokolakis, K., Palamidessi, C.: Geo-indistinguishability: differential privacy for location-based systems. In: Sadeghi, A.-R., Gligor, V.D., Yung, M. (eds.), ACM SIGSAC, pp. 901–914. ACM (2013)
2. Beresford, A.R., Stajano, F.: Location privacy in pervasive computing. IEEE Pervasive Comput. **2**(1), 46–55 (2003)

3. Bronchain, O., Hendrickx, J.M., Massart, C., Olshevsky, A., Standaert, F.-X.: Leakage certification revisited: Bounding model errors in side-channel security evaluations. IACR Cryptology ePrint Archive 2019:132 (2019)
4. Cho, E., Myers, S.A., Leskovec, J.: Friendship and mobility: user movement in location-based social networks. In: Apté, C., Ghosh, J., Smyth, P. (eds.) ACM SIGKDD, pp. 1082–1090. ACM (2011)
5. de Montjoye, Y.-A., Hidalgo, C.A., Verleysen, M., Blondel, V.: Unique in the crowd: the privacy bounds of human mobility. Nat. Sci. Rep. **3**(1376), 5 (2013)
6. de Montjoye, Y.-A., Radaelli, L., Singh, V.K., Pentland, A.S.: Unique in the shopping mall: on the reidentifiability of credit card metadata. Science **347**(6221), 536–539 (2015)
7. Díaz, C., Seys, S., Claessens, J., Preneel, B.: Towards measuring anonymity. In: Dingledine, R., Syverson, P. (eds.) PET 2002. LNCS, vol. 2482, pp. 54–68. Springer, Heidelberg (2003). https://doi.org/10.1007/3-540-36467-6_5
8. Duc, A., Faust, S., Standaert, F.-X.: Making masking security proofs concrete. In: Oswald, E., Fischlin, M. (eds.) EUROCRYPT 2015. LNCS, vol. 9056, pp. 401–429. Springer, Heidelberg (2015). https://doi.org/10.1007/978-3-662-46800-5_16
9. Durvaux, F., Standaert, F.-X., Pozo, S.M.D.: Towards easy leakage certification: extended version. J. Cryptographic Engineering **7**(2), 129–147 (2017)
10. Durvaux, F., Standaert, F.-X., Veyrat-Charvillon, N.: How to certify the leakage of a chip? In: Nguyen, P.Q., Oswald, E. (eds.) EUROCRYPT 2014. LNCS, vol. 8441, pp. 459–476. Springer, Heidelberg (2014). https://doi.org/10.1007/978-3-642-55220-5_26
11. Dwork, C.: Differential privacy: a survey of results. In: Agrawal, M., Du, D., Duan, Z., Li, A. (eds.) TAMC 2008. LNCS, vol. 4978, pp. 1–19. Springer, Heidelberg (2008). https://doi.org/10.1007/978-3-540-79228-4_1
12. Fung, B.C.M., Wang, K., Chen, R., Yu, P.S.: Privacy-preserving data publishing: a survey of recent developments. ACM Comput. Surv. **42**(4), 1–53 (2010)
13. Gambs, S., Killijian, M.-O., del Prado Cortez, M.N.: Next place prediction using mobility markov chains. In: Proceedings of the First Workshop on Measurement, Privacy, and Mobility, MPM 2012, pp. 3:1–3:6 (2012)
14. Machanavajjhala, A., Kifer, D., Gehrke, J., Venkitasubramaniam, M.: L-diversity: privacy beyond k-anonymity. TKDD **1**(1), 3 (2007)
15. Maouche, M., Ben Mokhtar, S., Bouchenak, S.: Ap-attack: a novel re-identification attack on mobility datasets. In: Kaafar, D., Zhou, G. (eds.) MobiQuitous. ACM (2017)
16. Oya, S., Troncoso, C., Pérez-González, F.: Is geo-indistinguishability what you are looking for? In: Thuraisingham, B.M., Lee, A.J. (eds.) Proceedings of the 2017 on Workshop on Privacy in the Electronic Society, pp. 137–140. ACM (2017)
17. Samarati, P., Sweeney, L.: Generalizing data to provide anonymity when disclosing information (abstract). In: Mendelzon, A.O., Paredaens, J. (eds.) ACM SIGACT-SIGMOD-SIGART, p. 188. ACM Press (1998)
18. Serjantov, A., Danezis, G.: Towards an information theoretic metric for anonymity. In: Dingledine, R., Syverson, P. (eds.) PET 2002. LNCS, vol. 2482, pp. 41–53. Springer, Heidelberg (2003). https://doi.org/10.1007/3-540-36467-6_4
19. Shokri, R., Theodorakopoulos, G., Le Boudec, J.-Y., Hubaux, J.-P.: IEEE s&p. pp. 247–262. IEEE Computer Society (2011)
20. Standaert, F.-X., Malkin, T.G., Yung, M.: A unified framework for the analysis of side-channel key recovery attacks. In: Joux, A. (ed.) EUROCRYPT 2009. LNCS, vol. 5479, pp. 443–461. Springer, Heidelberg (2009). https://doi.org/10.1007/978-3-642-01001-9_26

Side Channel Analysis of SPARX-64/128: Cryptanalysis and Countermeasures

Sumesh Manjunath Ramesh[1,2,3](✉) and Hoda AlKhzaimi[1,2,3]

[1] Center for Cyber Security, New York University Abu Dhabi, Abu Dhabi, UAE
{r.sumesh.manjunath,hoda.alkhzaimi}@nyu.edu
[2] Division of Engineering, New York University Abu Dhabi, Abu Dhabi, UAE
[3] Tandon School of Engineering, New York University, New York, USA

Abstract. SPARX family of lightweight block cipher was introduced in Asiacrypt 2016. The family consists of three variants (a) SPARX-64/128, (b) SPARX-128/128 and (c) SPARX-128/256. In this work, first, we propose a technique to perform Correlation Power Analysis (CPA) on the SPARX-64/128 cipher. Our technique uses a combination of first-order, second-order and modulo addition CPA methods. Using our proposed technique we extract 128 key bits of SPARX-64/128 cipher with low complexities in general; key guess complexity of 2^{12} and $65000 \approx 2^{16}$ power traces. We initially propose a countermeasure of SPARX-64/128 block cipher against side-channel attacks in terms of power analysis, a threshold implementation based on a serialized design of SPARX-64/128 core. The serialized design of SPARX-64/128 core is implemented in hardware and occupies 60 slices in FPGA. As a countermeasure, this serialized implementation is extended to propose a provably secure threshold implementation of SPARX-64/128 core (TI-SPARX). The TI-SPARX core occupies 131 slices in FPGA and runs at 144 MHz thus, giving a throughput of 9 Mbps. To the best of our knowledge, this is the first side channel attack and countermeasure result on SPARX-64/128 cipher.

Keywords: Side channel analysis · Lightweight cryptography · SPARX · Correlation Power Analysis · Threshold implementation

1 Introduction

Cryptographic primitives such as stream ciphers, block ciphers and hash functions are essential building blocks for various security applications and protocols such as SSL, TLS, etc. In the past years, the focus on lightweight designs in the community has been increasing in order to build efficient and secure cryptographic primitives that can be utilized in extreme restricted physical environments such as embedded systems, Internet of Things devices, sensors, RFID tags, energy harvesting devices, and many others.

The designed primitives have been initiated to exhibit optimal criteria for specific metrics as in optimized performance, lower power/energy consumption, reduced area size, increased throughput, and security, among many others.

© Springer Nature Switzerland AG 2019
J. Buchmann et al. (Eds.): AFRICACRYPT 2019, LNCS 11627, pp. 352–369, 2019.
https://doi.org/10.1007/978-3-030-23696-0_18

PRESENT and CLEFIA are lightweight block ciphers proposed as ISO standard for lightweight applications [1]. SIMON and SPECK block ciphers are proposed by the NSA [7]. SPARX [13] is a lightweight block cipher which comes with security bound against differential and linear characteristics. These are a The-few block ciphers introduced specifically for lightweight applications both in hardware as well as software. Many of these ciphers are based on Substitution-Permutation Network, Feistel Network or Addition-Rotation-Xor (ARX) design methodology.

Every proposed design of cryptographic primitives is associated with certain security rationale and needs a thorough analysis against proposed security margins. Normally, this is achieved through classical statistical and non-statistical cryptanalysis techniques, as well as physical hardware cryptanalysis techniques embodied in side-channel analysis approaches. The primitives which are resistant to valid cryptanalysis techniques are highly recommended. In some cases, even if such primitives are resistant to classical cryptanalysis techniques, and they come with a strong provable security model, they might be vulnerable to certain Side Channel Analysis (SCA) approaches. These approaches facilitate the extraction of secret information from the measured leakage data. Power leakage analysis [19], Fault analysis [14], Electro-Magnetic leakage analysis [24], Acoustic leakage analysis [11] and Timing analysis [23] are a few examples on the exploitation of leakage information to get the secret key. Therefore, SCA is equally important because (a) Cryptographic Primitives ultimately gets implemented in hardware and/or software, and (b) Hardware/Software may exhibit a physical leakage of information about the internal processing values with the secret key while executing a cryptographic primitive.

Masking is one of the techniques proposed to prevent Side Channel Attack [17,21]. Many variants of masking schemes were proposed to reduce leakage information. Threshold Implementation [26] is a claimed provably secure approach to protect the implementation of ciphers from side channels. This is based on secret sharing and multi-party computation techniques.

Related Work: In [12], authors retrieved 64-bit key of SIMON-32/64 block cipher using differential power analysis, thus making it vulnerable in hardware applications. In [3], authors proposed a Threshold implementation for SIMON and gave a side channel secure implementation of SIMON which can be used in hardware. Similarly, unprotected Present block cipher is vulnerable to Correlation Power analysis [5,20] protects the cipher against first-order side-channel attacks. In [10], the authors gave a secure Speck core and the methodology to secure ARX based ciphers.

Contribution: Our contribution in this research is that we analyze SPARX-64/128 block cipher against power leakage. First-Order Correlation Power Analysis (CPA) and Second-Order CPA techniques are combined to recover the complete secret key of SPARX-64/128 using 2^{12} key guesses and $65000 \approx 2^{16}$ power traces. We implement an area optimized hardware design of SPARX–64/128 and compare with round-based design, for performance based on area, speed, and throughput. Finally, we propose a secure threshold implementation of SPARX-64/128 as a countermeasure for the proposed side channel attacks.

Organization: The document is organized into seven main sections. The background information on power analysis, threshold implementation and SPARX family algorithm are given in Sect. 2. Correlation Power Analysis (CPA) technique to recover all 128 bit key of round-based SPARX-64/128 cipher is given in Sect. 3. After the attack description, SPARX-64/128 serialized implementation is proposed in Sect. 4. Based on this serialized design, we propose as a threshold implementation in Sect. 5. The CPA attack details and results and the analysis of threshold implementation results are exhibited in Sect. 6. Finally, the conclusion of the analysis is presented in Sect. 7.

2   Background

In this section, we introduce the SPARX Family of Block Cipher along with the basic understanding of First-Order and Second-Order Correlation Power Analysis. In addition to that, CPA technique on n-bit addition modulo 2^n is explained. Finally, Threshold Implementation and its properties are described.

2.1   Preliminaries to Power Analysis (CPA)

A brief introduction to First-Order and Second-Order Correlation Power Analysis (CPA) and CPA for n-bit modulo addition 2^n is given in this section. We assume the power model for our attack to be Hamming Distance model.

Pearson Correlation Coefficient and CPA. Pearson Correlation Coefficient (PCC) gives the measure of linear relationship (correlation) between two data sets. This is used in CPA to retrieve the secret key. The power traces of N encryption forms one data set and the *hamming distance* between one round function with a given hypothesis key for the same N plaintexts form another data set. The PCC is calculated for each hypothesis key. Say, for n-bit hypothesis key has total 2^n keys. The highest PCC among all hypothesis keys is the potential candidate secret key.

First-Order CPA. In 1999, Kocher et al. [19] introduced simple and differential power analysis. In these methods mostly single bit of secret key is retrieved and the experiment needs to be repeated for more bits. In [16], Correlation Power Analysis method uses Pearson Correlation Coefficient to retrieved more bits at a time. Usually, either first round or last round of the cipher is considered to extract the corresponding round key.

Let us consider a toy block cipher A which takes 16-bit plaintext, X, and 16-bit secret key, K, and output 16-bit ciphertext, Y. The encryption function using AES S-Box [18] is mentioned below.

$$\left.\begin{array}{ll} X = X_0 \| X_1, & K = K_0 \| K_1, \\ S_0 = X_0 \oplus K_0, & S_1 = X_1 \oplus K_1, \\ Y_0 = sbox(S_0), & Y_1 = sbox(S_1), \\ Y = Y_0 \| Y_1. \end{array}\right\} \tag{1}$$

First, power traces of N random plaintext encryption function is captured. Next, retrieve 8-bit K_0 of secret key and then the remaining 8-bit, K_1 of secret key K using CPA method. As in Eq. 1, X_0 is known plaintext and K_0 is unknown 8-bit of secret key. The total possible value for K_0 is 256. Therefore, by taking each possible value for K_0, say hypothesis key, evaluate only a part of the encryption function on the same N plaintexts and calculate the hamming distance between X_0 and Y_0. Now, find the correlation coefficient (PCC) between the power trace and calculated hamming distance for each hypothesis key. The candidate key for K_0 is the hypothesis key with maximum PCC value. The key guess complexity is 2^8. The same process is repeated for K_1. Therefore with 2^9 key guess complexity 16-bit secret key is retrieved whereas the brute force takes 2^{16} key guess complexity.

Second-Order CPA. One way to resist first-order CPA attack is by using random mask with the input [17,21]. This countermeasure can be thwarted, when the attacker is able to correlate between the points (sample) in a power trace for random mask generation and usage of mask with the input. The attacker can retrieve secret key as described in [15,27], but it requires a large number of traces to be successful.

CPA on Addition Modulo 2^n. Unlike in the first-order CPA method, where K_0 and K_1 can be retrieved independently, the CPA on addition modulo 2^n function dependents on carry bit from previous bit addition. Hence, the secret bits must be extracted in certain order only. Therefore, first Least Significant Byte (8-bit) is retrieved and then second Least Significant Byte is retrieved till Most Significant Byte, using correlation method.

2.2 Threshold Implementation

Threshold Implementation (TI) [26] is a provably secure countermeasure to side channel attacks. TI uses secret sharing techniques on the input such as plaintext and secret key. It is assumed that the attacker will not be able to measure leakage information of all share at the same time, thus making it a good counter measure against side channel. In TI, the number of shares (n) for each variable is based on number of variables (s) (i.e $n \geq s + 1$) [26]. For secure implementation of linear transformation, each share must be processed independently, whereas for non-linear transformation it is complex. For non-linear transformation, three properties must be satisfied for a secure Threshold Implementation. First: *Non-Completeness*, which makes each sub function independent of at least one share of all inputs, thus the attacker cannot see the complete output of the function. Second. *Correctness*, which provides the correct result once the output of each sub-function is combined together, thereby the output is not modified. Third: the *Balance* property, which says that the if the input shares are uniformly distributed then the output shares are also uniformly distributed. This is to ensure that there is no leakage because of the differences in the distribution between input and output shares. In [9], the authors showed TI methods to counter higher order side channel attacks. Threshold Implementation is a popular countermeasure used to protect many ciphers including TI-AES [8], TI-Simon [3,4], TI-Speck [10] and TI-Present [5].

2.3 Description of SPARX

In 2016, Daniel et al. proposed a SPARX family of ciphers, which is based on Long Trail Strategy method, to bound the cipher against differential and linear characteristics [13]. The SPARX has three variants based on block and key size: SPARX-64/128, SPARX-128/128 and SPARX-128/256. Each block in SPARX-n/k consist of $w = n/32$ words of 32 bits and key is divided into $v = k/32$ words.

The encryption algorithm consist of n_s steps. Each step consist of r_a round function and one linear-mix layer. In each round, there are two operations (1) Round Key addition, (2) Addition Box (A-Box) operation, which consist of Addition Rotation and Xor operations. The parameters for each variant of SPARX is given in Table 1.

Table 1. Parameters of SPARX-64/128

Parameters	SPARX-64/128	SPARX-128/128	SPARX-128/256
State word (w)	2	4	4
Key word (v)	4	4	8
Steps (n_s)	8	8	10
Rounds/Step (r_a)	3	4	4
Total rounds	24	32	40

The Round function for all variant of SPARX is same, whereas the linear-mix layer between SPARX-64/128 and other two variants are different. Similarly, step structure between SPARX-64/128 and other two variants are different. Finally, key scheduling algorithm is different for all the three variants.

Hereafter, SPARX-64/128 and SPARX are used interchangeably and it refers to SPARX-64/128 variant unless otherwise specified. SPARX block size is 64 bit and key size is 128 bit. The state at step s and round r is represented as $X_{r,s}^0 \| X_{r,s}^1 \| X_{r,s}^2 \| X_{r,s}^3$, where size of $X_{r,s}^i$ is 16-bit. The initial state is loaded with plaintext and represented as $X_{0,0}^0 \| X_{0,0}^1 \| X_{0,0}^2 \| X_{0,0}^3$. After one round function the state is $X_{1,0}^0 \| X_{1,0}^1 \| X_{1,0}^2 \| X_{1,0}^3$. At the end of one step (i.e.) after linear-mix layer, the state is $X_{0,1}^0 \| X_{0,1}^1 \| X_{0,1}^2 \| X_{0,1}^3$. The ith round key is $K_L^{0,i} \| K_R^{0,i}$, $K_L^{1,i} \| K_R^{1,i}$, $K_L^{2,i} \| K_R^{2,i}$, $K_L^{3,i} \| K_R^{3,i}$, where $K_L^{j,i}, K_R^{j,i}, (0 \le j \le 3)$ are 16-bit each. The 128-bit master key is $K_L^{0,0} \| K_R^{0,0}$, $K_L^{1,0} \| K_R^{1,0}$, $K_L^{2,0} \| K_R^{2,0}$, $K_L^{3,0} \| K_R^{3,0}$.

In 2017, Abdelkhalek et al. in [2], proposed an impossible differential distinguisher for 13 round to attack 16 round of SPARX-64/128. Recently in 2018, Ankele et al. in [25], proposed a chosen ciphertext differential attacks on 16 round

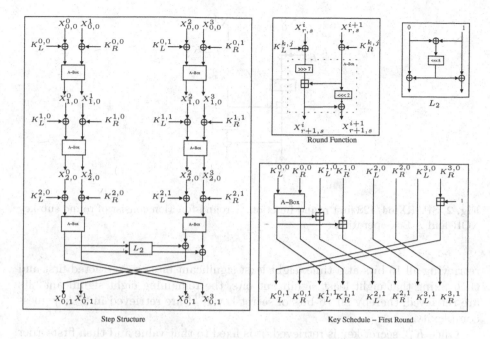

Fig. 1. One step of SPARX-64/128, One round function with A-Box, Linear Mix Layer and one round of Key scheduling algorithm

of SPARX-64/128. Until now there has been no work on side channel analysis of SPARX block cipher.

3 CPA on SPARX-64/128: Full Key Recovery

The first-order and second-order CPA attack described in Sect. 2.1 is combined to retrieve secret key bits used in a round function. Thereby, complete 128-bit key bits are extracted using the secret key bits from 4 round functions and key scheduling algorithm which is explained in detail below.

3.1 Attack on SPARX Round Function

Let us assume that one input to the round function $X_{r,s}^0 \| X_{r,s}^1$ is known, another input $K_L^{0,i} \| K_R^{0,i}$ is unknown. SPARX round function after key addition and A-Box operation it output $X_{r+1,s}^0 \| X_{r+1,s}^1$. The first round function is shown in Fig. 2.

It is noteworthy that, only first order CPA techniques cannot be used to retrieve either $K_L^{0,i}$ or $K_R^{0,i}$ because each act as mask to other in the operation. In contrast, by using second-order CPA technique, $X_{1,0}^0$ is removed from $X_{1,0}^1$, thereby revealing $K_R^{0,i}$, 16-bit secret by hypothesis keys. Here instead of

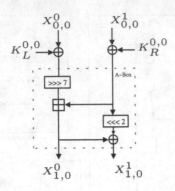

Fig. 2. SPARX-64/128 first round function. A round function consist of round sub-key XOR and A Box operation

retrieving all 16 bits at a time, eight least significant bits are extracted first and then fixing that eight least significant bits, the remaining eight significant bits are retrieved, thereby all 16-bits of secret key $K_R^{0,i}$ are retrieved in 2^9 key guess complexity.

Once $K_R^{0,i}$ secret key is retrieved, it is fixed to that value and then first-order CPA for addition modulo 2^{16} technique is applied to retrieve 16-bit $K_L^{0,i}$ secret key. This takes 2^9 key guess complexity. Thereby, 32-bit secret key $K_L^{0,i} \| K_R^{0,i}$ used in the first round function is extracted in 2^{10} key guess complexity.

Extract 16-bit Secret Key $K_R^{0,i}$: The following operations occur different time instance.

- At T_1: $X_{r+1,s}^0 = \left(X_{r,s}^0 \oplus K_L^{0,i}\right)_7 + \left(X_{r,s}^1 \oplus K_R^{0,i}\right) \bmod 2^{16}$,
- At T_2: $X_{r+1,s}^1 = X_{r+1,s}^0 \oplus \left(X_{r,s}^1 \oplus K_R^{0,i}\right)_{-2}$.

For second-order DPA attack, power measurement at two time instance is subtracted to get modified power measurement of a trace.

As in Eq. (2), $X_{r,s}^1$ is known and using first-order CPA technique, $K_R^{0,i}$ is extracted. To reduce the key guess complexity, first, eight least significant bits (lsb) is targeted. Hence, total hypothesis keys are $2^8 = 256$. The round function is simulated with these hypothesis keys keeping the eight most significant bits (msb) to zero. The hamming distance between output from the simulated hypothesis key and input is correlated with $P(t = T_1) - P(t = T_2)$ from power traces. The hypothesis key which gives maximum correlation coefficient is the correct 8-bit lsb of $K_R^{0,i}$. Fixing the 8 lsb and repeating the simulation for 8 msb position. In this way, $K_R^{0,i}$ is extracted with $2^8 + 2^8 = 2^9$ hypothesis key guesses.

$$\left.\begin{aligned}
P(t = T_1) - P(t = T_2) &\approx HD\left(X^0_{r+1,s}\right) - HD\left(X^1_{r+1,s}\right), \\
&\approx HW\left(X^0_{r+1,s} \oplus X^1_{r+1,s}\right), \\
&\approx HW\left(X^0_{r+1,s} \oplus \left(X^0_{r+1,s} \oplus \left(X^1_{r,s} \oplus K^{0,i}_R\right)_{-2}\right)\right), \\
&\approx HW\left(X^0_{r+1,s} \oplus X^0_{r+1,s} \oplus X^1_{r,s} \oplus K^{0,i}_R\right), \\
&\approx HW\left(X^1_{r,s} \oplus K^{0,i}_R\right).
\end{aligned}\right\}$$

$$(2)$$

Extract 16-bit secret key $K^{0,i}_L$: 16-bit $K^{0,i}_R$ is fixed to the above extracted value. $X^0_{r,s}$ and $X^1_{r,s}$ is also known. Therefore, the modular addition is given in Eq. (3)

$$\left.\begin{aligned}
P(t = T_1) &\approx HD\left(X^0_{r+1,s}, X^0_{r,s}\right), \\
&\approx HD\left(\left(\left(X^0_{r,s} \oplus K^{0,i}_L\right)_7 + \left(X^1_{r,s} \oplus K^{0,i}_R\right)\right) \bmod 2^{16}, X^0_{r,s}\right), \\
&\approx HD\left(\left((known \oplus K^{0,i}_L)_7 + (known \oplus known)\right) \bmod 2^{16}, known\right).
\end{aligned}\right\}$$

$$(3)$$

As per the Eq. (3), only $K^{0,i}_L$ is unknown. Therefore, using CPA technique on Addition Modulo 2^n, we extract $K^{0,i}_L$. Thus, $K^{0,i}_L$ is extracted with $2^8 + 2^8 = 2^9$ hypothesis key guesses from Modular addition CPA technique.

Total Key Guess Complexity: To guess the correct value for $K^{0,i}_R$ sub-key, 2^9 key guesses are required and for $K^{0,i}_L$ sub-key, 2^9 key guesses are required. Therefore the total number of key guess complexity for one round function is 2^{10}, whereas the brute force for the same is 2^{32}.

3.2   Full Key Recovery on SPARX-64/128

The technique to retrieve 32-bit secret key from a round function and one round key scheduling algorithm are used to extract complete 128-bit master key. First, key scheduling algorithm is explained with few observations. The 128-bit master key is $K^{0,0}_L \| K^{0,0}_R \| K^{1,0}_L \| K^{1,0}_R \| K^{2,0}_L \| K^{2,0}_R \| K^{3,0}_L \| K^{3,0}_R$. After one round of key scheduling algorithm the second round key is $K^{0,1}_L \| K^{0,1}_R \| K^{1,1}_L \| K^{1,1}_R \| K^{2,1}_L \| K^{2,1}_R \| K^{3,1}_L \| K^{3,1}_R$ as shown in Fig. 1.

Observation 1. $K^{0,1}_L$ *of second round key is same as* $K^{3,0}_L$ *of first round key.*

$$K^{3,0}_L = K^{0,1}_L$$

Observation 2. *The relationship between* $K^{0,1}_R$ *of second round key and* $K^{3,0}_R$ *of first round key is*

$$K^{3,0}_R = \left(K^{0,1}_R - 1\right) \bmod 2^{16}$$

Let's explain the full key recovery. The plaintext is loaded into the state $X^0_{0,0}\|$ $X^1_{0,0}\| X^2_{0,0}\| X^3_{0,0}$ and the first round key is $K^{0,0}_L\|K^{0,0}_R\| K^{1,0}_L\|K^{1,0}_R\| K^{2,0}_L\|K^{2,0}_R\|$ $K^{3,0}_L\|K^{3,0}_R$.

For the first round function, the inputs are $X^0_{0,0}\|X^1_{0,0}$ and $K^{0,0}_L\|K^{0,0}_R$ and after key addition and A-Box operation the output is $X^0_{1,0}\|X^1_{1,0}$. By our proposed CPA technique as explained in Sect. 3.1, 32-bit secret key, $K^{0,0}_L\|K^{0,0}_R$, is extracted. Since, key and the plaintext known, the output of first round function, $X^0_{1,0}\|X^1_{1,0}$, is also known.

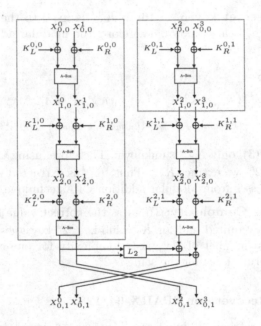

Fig. 3. SPARX-64/128 one step function. The four round functions used to retrieve 128-bit secret key is highlighted

For second round function, one input, $X^0_{1,0}\|X^1_{1,0}$, is known and the key input $K^{1,0}_L\|K^{1,0}_R$ is unknown. Using the similar technique, $K^{1,0}_L\|K^{1,0}_R$ is extracted, thereby the output of second round function, $X^0_{2,0}\|X^1_{2,0}$ is known. By following the same way, $K^{2,0}_L\|K^{2,0}_R$ secret key is extracted. So far, 96-bits of secret key is extracted which are $K^{0,0}_L\|K^{0,0}_R$, $K^{1,0}_L\|K^{1,0}_R$, $K^{2,0}_L\|K^{2,0}_R$. Now 32-bit, $K^{3,0}_L\|K^{3,0}_R$, secret key is not used in any of the round functions.

Let us retrieve 32-bit $K^{0,1}_L\|K^{0,1}_R$ second round key. As shown in Fig. 3, the input to the right side round function is 32-bit of plaintext, $X^2_{0,0}\|X^3_{0,0}$ which is known and using our proposed technique, $K^{0,1}_L\|K^{0,1}_R$, 32-bit second round key is extracted. Now, using Observation 1 and 2, $K^{3,0}_L\|K^{3,0}_R$ is retrieved from $K^{0,1}_L\|K^{0,1}_R$. Therefore, all 128-bit secret key is retrieved.

Complexity: For extracting 32-bit secret key from one round function is 2^{10}. To retrieve complete 128-bit secret key, we need to retrieve 32-bit secret key from four round functions, therefore the total time complexity is $2^{10}+2^{10}+2^{10}+2^{10} = 2^{12}$ key guesses.

4   SPARX Hardware Implementation

The SPARX algorithm is a lightweight block cipher and its potential uses will be in embedded devices, IoT devices where optimized hardware implementation of the cipher is important. Optimization means with respect to area, throughput and speed are required based on the applications. In this work, we optimize the area and propose as serialized implementation of SPARX core. The round function of SPARX is similar to the round function of SPECK with the difference in the key XOR operation, therefore our proposed serialized implementation is inspired from [10].

The block size for SPARX-64/128 is 64-bit. The SPARX algorithm have round function which takes only 32-bit inputs whereas linear-mix layer needs 64-bit input to process. First, serialized implementation of round function will be explained and then implementation of linear-mix layer and finally, complete step structure of SPARX is optimized.

4.1   Serialized Round Function

The round function of SPARX comprises key addition and A-Box operations. The input to the round function is 32-bit state and 32-bits of round key. The 32-bit state is split into two 16-bit data and stored in X and Y registers. The main operations are XOR, cyclic shift and modulo addition. XOR operation is linear and implemented bit-wise. Splitting the registers eliminates the need for implementing cyclic shift operations. Modulo addition of 16-bit input is implemented as 16 serialized one-bit full adder by storing the carry from previous one-bit addition. This takes less area in the hardware. Since the new values are stored in the same registers, there are two feedback functions: One for the X register and another for Y register as shown in Fig. 4.

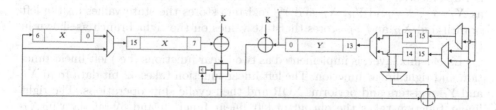

Fig. 4. Serialized implementation of round function of SPARX-64/128

The X register in the left is split into two parts such as $X[6:0]$ and $X[15:7]$, thereby exposing eighth bit position of X register to the left feedback function and the first bit position of Y register is sent to the left feedback function. In the feedback function, corresponding key bits are XORed with eighth and first bit positions of X and Y registers, respectively. After key XOR, one-bit full addition is performed. The new carry is stored and the left feedback function output the sum. For the first seven clock cycles in each round, the output of left feedback function is fed into $X[6:0]$ part of register as new value and at the same time the old values in $X[6:0]$ are feed into $X[15:7]$ so that it can be processed in the left feedback function. After seven clock cycles, the sum is directly fed into $X[15:7]$ part of register, thereby exposing 8th bit of new value in X register for next round as shown in Fig. 4.

The values in Y register are processed twice, one in left feedback function and another in right feedback function. Hence, we need to duplicate values in Y register. Since the right feedback function consist of two cyclic shift operation and XOR operation, duplicate of two bits is sufficient instead of all 16 bits of Y register. One copy stores the old values for right feedback function and another copy stores new values for next round. Hence, the Y register is split into $Y[13:0]$ and $Y[14:15]$ and two copies of $Y[14:15]$ is maintained. The right feedback function performs XOR between output of left feedback function and fourteenth bit in Y register. The output is fed back into fifteenth bit position of Y register as new value for next round. After sixteen clock cycles, one round function is completed. At this instance, one copy of $Y[14:15]$ register has old values and another copy has new value. The register having new value is valid and the register having old value is invalid for next round function. So the valid register is used for next round and invalid register is used to store new values from the new round. Thus, the role of each registers are reverse at the start of each round. One round function takes sixteen clock cycles.

4.2   Serialized Linear-Mix Layer

Linear-mix layer of SPARX-64/128 takes 64-bit input and after mixing it gives 64-bit output as shown in the Fig. 1. The linear-mix layer is implemented in two steps. In first step, the output of the linear function is processed without the cyclic shift operation. In second step, cyclic left shift of output by 32 bits is implemented. The 64-bit input state are stored in four 16-bit registers such as X_L, Y_L, X_R and Y_R. X_L and Y_L registers stores the state values on the left branch and X_R and Y_R stores the state values on the right branch as shown in the Fig. 5.

Linear-mix layer, is implemented as two linear functions (i.e.) left linear function and right linear function. The left linear function takes 32-bit data from X_L and Y_L registers and performs XOR and then cyclic shift operations. The right linear function takes the output of left linear function and 32-bit data in X_R and Y_R registers as input and performs XOR operation.

In the left linear function, cyclic shift is implemented by directly exposing eighth bit position of X_L and Y_L registers, respectively, such as $X_L[7:0]$, $X_L[15:8]$, $Y_L[7:0]$ and $Y_L[15:8]$. The eighth bit of X_L and Y_L registers are XORed and the value is again XORed with first bit of X_L and Y_L separately (i.e. two XOR) and these two bits, say, b_x, b_y, are the output of left linear function. Meanwhile, eighth bit of X_L is fed back into seventh bit position of X_L and at same time zeroth bit X_L is feed into fifteenth bit position of X_L. The similar feedback operations are performed for Y_L as well.

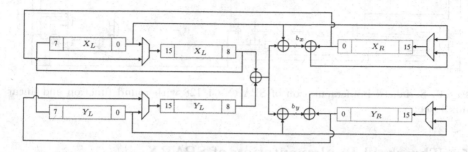

Fig. 5. Serialized implementation of linear mix layer of SPARX-64/128

In the right linear function, the output bit, b_x of left linear function is XORed with first bit of X_R. The XORed bit value is feedback into fifteenth bit position of X_R. Similarly, the output bit, b_y of left linear function is XORed with first bit position of Y_R and the XORed bit value is feedback into fifteenth bit position of Y_R. After sixteen clock cycles, the values in X_L, Y_L, X_R and Y_R registers are new values.

Now the rotation step is implemented. The values in X_L and X_R registers are swapped. Similarly, the values in Y_L and Y_R registers are also swapped. The swap values are taken from zeroth bit position and feed into fifteenth bit position.

Since X_L and Y_L registers are split to expose eighth bit position, while feeding new value at fifteenth position, eighth bit is fed into seventh bit position as shown in Fig. 5. The rotation step takes sixteen clock cycles to complete. Therefore the linear mix layer takes 32 clock cycles to complete.

4.3 Serialized SPARX

In Sects. 4.1 and 4.2, serialized implementation of round function and linear mix layer are proposed independently. Now, we combine both the design to implement one step structure of SPARX-64/128. Four 16-bit registers such as X_L, Y_L, X_R and Y_R are loaded with 64 bit plaintext sequentially. X_L and X_R registers are split into three, to expose required bits for round and linear mix layer functions. In the same way, Y_L and Y_R registers are split into three and corresponding bits are duplicated as shown in Fig. 6.

Appropriate registers are selected for the round functions. For three rounds in a step, first X_L and Y_L registers are selected and executed with first round key bits, and once it is done, X_R and Y_R registers are now selected and again three rounds are executed with second round key bits. Finally, linear-mix layer is executed on all four registers simultaneously as shown in Fig. 6.

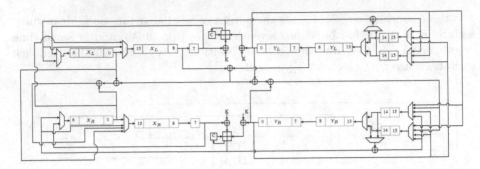

Fig. 6. Serialized implementation of SPARX-64/128 with round function and linear mix layer

5   Threshold Implementation of SPARX

The Threshold Implementation proposed in this work inspires TI implementation of Speck proposed in [10], because the round function in the SPARX is similar to the round function of SPECK expect the key addition operation. This similarity allows us to utilize the TI of Speck with little modification.

For a secure threshold implementation, *Correctness, Non-Completeness* and *Balance* properties needs to be satisfied. There are two variables: plaintext and secret key. Therefore, minimum three shares are required for TI for the reason as given in [26]. So, plaintext P is split as P_1, P_2, and P_3 shares, similarly key K into K_1, K_2, and K_3 shares. These shares are generated as shown in Eq. 4.

$$P_1 \xleftarrow{\$} \{0,1\}^{64}; P_2 \xleftarrow{\$} \{0,1\}^{64}; P_3 = P \oplus P_1 \oplus P_2$$
$$K_1 \xleftarrow{\$} \{0,1\}^{64}; K_2 \xleftarrow{\$} \{0,1\}^{64}; K_3 = K \oplus K_1 \oplus K_2$$

(4)

The shares generated are random and the correctness is verified as given in Eq. 4. SPARX round function consist of XOR, cyclic shift and modulo addition operations; and linear-mix layer consist of XOR and cyclic shift operations. Since, XOR and cyclic operation are linear operations, they operate on each share independently without exposing other shares. Therefore, non-completeness property is achieved on these operations. Modulo addition is the only non linear operation in round function. It is implemented using 1-bit full adder. The threshold implementation for 1-bit addition used in this work is inspired from [28].

At each clock cycle, one bit of two inputs are added. Therefore, for a given two n-bit inputs, starting from least significant bit to the most significant bit of two inputs, each bit are added using one-bit adder circuit, hence n clock cycles are required to complete the addition. Therefore, at i^{th} clock cycle, i^{th} bit is added, where $i \in \{0, 1, \ldots 15\}$.

Let us explain how TI is achieved in one-bit full adder. One-bit full adder takes two input bits and input carry bit from previous bit addition and output sum bit and output carry bit. For 16-bit addition, the input bits comes from two 16-bit data, let us say a and b, where a_i, b_j represents i^{th}, j^{th} bit of a and

b, respectively. The carry bit is denoted as c, where least significant bit of c is zero ($c_1 = 0$). In threshold implementation, a and b are split into three shares and their corresponding carry bit also contains three shares as shown below.

$$a_i = a_{i,1} \oplus a_{i,2} \oplus a_{i,3}$$
$$b_i = b_{i,1} \oplus b_{i,2} \oplus b_{i,3} \tag{5}$$
$$c_i = c_{i,1} \oplus c_{i,2} \oplus c_{i,3}$$

Now, the three shares of sum bit s_i and output carry bit c_{i+1} is given below

$$s_{i,1} = a_{i,1} \oplus b_{i,1} \oplus c_{i,1}$$
$$s_{i,2} = a_{i,2} \oplus b_{i,2} \oplus c_{i,2} \tag{6}$$
$$s_{i,3} = a_{i,3} \oplus b_{i,3} \oplus c_{i,3}$$

$$
\begin{aligned}
c_{i+1,1} &= (a_{i,2} \cdot b_{i,2}) \oplus (a_{i,2} \cdot b_{i,3}) \oplus (a_{i,3} \cdot b_{i,2}) \\
&\quad (a_{i,2} \cdot c_{i,2}) \oplus (a_{i,2} \cdot c_{i,3}) \oplus (a_{i,3} \cdot c_{i,2}) \\
&\quad (b_{i,2} \cdot c_{i,2}) \oplus (b_{i,2} \cdot c_{i,3}) \oplus (b_{i,3} \cdot c_{i,2}) \\
c_{i+1,2} &= (a_{i,3} \cdot b_{i,3}) \oplus (a_{i,3} \cdot b_{i,1}) \oplus (a_{i,1} \cdot b_{i,3}) \\
&\quad (a_{i,3} \cdot c_{i,3}) \oplus (a_{i,3} \cdot c_{i,1}) \oplus (a_{i,1} \cdot c_{i,3}) \\
&\quad (b_{i,3} \cdot c_{i,3}) \oplus (b_{i,3} \cdot c_{i,1}) \oplus (b_{i,1} \cdot c_{i,3}) \\
c_{i+1,3} &= (a_{i,1} \cdot b_{i,1}) \oplus (a_{i,1} \cdot b_{i,2}) \oplus (a_{i,2} \cdot b_{i,1}) \\
&\quad (a_{i,1} \cdot c_{i,1}) \oplus (a_{i,1} \cdot c_{i,2}) \oplus (a_{i,2} \cdot c_{i,1}) \\
&\quad (b_{i,1} \cdot c_{i,1}) \oplus (b_{i,1} \cdot c_{i,2}) \oplus (b_{i,2} \cdot c_{i,1})
\end{aligned}
\tag{7}
$$

By XORing each shares, gives the correctness property. As given in Eqs. 6 and 7, each share of sum and carry is independent of at least one share of each input, thus non-completeness property is also satisfied. As given in [28], the sum and carry shares are uniformly distributed. Thus, all three properties of threshold implementation are satisfied.

6   Results

We performed CPA attack on SPARX-64/128 using SAKURA-G board and also proposed a provably secure threshold implementation of SPARX in Spartan 3.

6.1   Full Key Recovery Results

We implemented SPARX-64/128 cipher in SAKURA-G FPGA board and captured the power traces using Tektronix MSO5204B oscilloscope. SAKURA-G board consist of two Spartan-6 FPGA where one is controller FPGA and another is the main FPGA. SPARX design is implemented in main FPGA. The board is connected with a laptop to send plaintext for encryption and receive the corresponding ciphertext. At the same time, an oscilloscope is connected with the board to sample the power consumption during the encryption process. These sampled power measurements are called power traces and it is stored in the PC via the oscilloscope. Once the power traces are collected, our proposed technique is applied and full 128-bit secret key is recovered. To recover 128-bit secret key, $65000 \approx 2^{16}$ power traces are used and the number of key guess complexity is 2^{12}. Due to the limitation of the space, the PCC of all hypothesis keys for the $K_L^{0,0}$ only is shown in Fig. 7. The actual key used to encrypt 65000 random plaintexts is $0x0001\ 0x0203\ 0x0405\ 0x0607\ 0x0809\ 0x0A0B\ 0x0C0D\ 0x0E0F$. The key used in first round function is $0x0001\ 0x0203$. $K_L^{0,0} = 0x0001$ is extracted successfully, as the PCC for hypothesis keys $0x00$ and $0x01$ in MSB and LSB position are maximum, respectively as shown in Fig. 7.

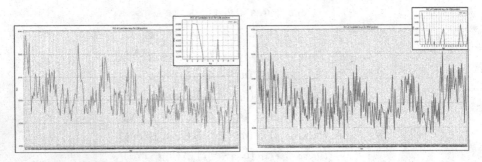

Fig. 7. PCC of all 256 hypothesis keys for LSB and MSB of $K_L^{0,0}$

6.2   FPGA Implementation of SPARX-64/128

We implemented the SPARX design as given in Sects. 4 and 5 in Verilog on Xilinx Spartan 3 FPGA using Xilinx ISE 14.7. The serialized implementation of SPARX requires 32 Flip-Flops and 114 LUTs occupying 60 slices and the maximum speed achieved is 173 MHz. For TI-SPARX 64/128, the addition circuit of serialized implementation is modified and three individual serialized circuit for each share are required. The TI-SPARX 64/128 requires 69 Flip-Flops and 231 LUTs occupying 131 slices and it runs at 144 MHz. SPARX round based design is used in the side channel attack and is also used for comparison. Round based means one step structure of SPARX (three rounds and one linear-mix layer) runs in one clock cycle. Serialized SPARX occupies the least area of all three implementation and the round based occupies the most because round based need large area to implement one step in one clock cycle. The TI-SPARX which is based on serialized implementation occupies lesser area compared to round based, whereas it needs more area than serialized to preserve three properties of threshold implementation. The results are given in Table 2.

Serialized implementation of SPARX is compared with Speck 128/128, Simon 128/128 and PRESENT lightweight ciphers as they are NSA and ISO standard lightweight block ciphers, respectively. SPARX occupies almost 50% less area compared to PRESENT at the expense of lower throughput by 17.59 Mbps.

Table 2. Resource utilization of different implementations of SPARX 64/128. Flip-flops are used as registers, LUT for logic and shift registers. Slice contains certain number of LUTs, flip-flops and multiplexers

Implementation	Flip-Flops	LUTs	Slices	Speed (MHz)	Throughput (Mbps)
Round based SPARX	2671	4299	2370	204	22.9
Serialized SPARX	32	114	60	173	10.81
TI-SPARX	69	231	131	144	9

At the same time, SPARX has almost three times higher throughput than Simon 128/128 but 1.7 times the area requirement of Simon 128/128. This is expected because Simon is proposed mainly for hardware. SPARX occupies almost 1.4 times the area required for Speck 128/128. The increase in the area is due to extra linear layer design in SPARX which is not present in Speck 128/128 (Table 3).

Table 3. Comparison of SPARX-64/128 with other ciphers on area and throughput

Cipher	Slices	Throughput (Mbps)	FPGA
TI-SPARX 64/128	**131**	**9**	**xc3s50**
TI Speck 128/128 [10]	99	9.68	xc3s50
TI Simon 128/128 [3]	87	3.0	xc3s50
SPARX-64/128	**60**	**10.81**	**xc3s50**
Speck 128/128 [10]	43	10.05	xc3s50
Simon 128/128 [6]	36	3.6	xc3s50
PRESENT [22]	117	28.4	xc3s50-5

7   Conclusion and Future Work

Although, SPARX design has a provable security bounds against differential and linear cryptanalysis, there is still a margin of analysis to be performed when it comes to side channel cryptanalysis. In this research, we successfully demonstrated that SPARX-64/128 cipher is vulnerable to first order and second order power side channel analysis. We are able to recover full 128-bit secret key of SPARX-64/28 implemented in SAKURA-G board using 2^{12} key guess and $65000 \approx 2^{16}$ power traces. The attack mentioned for SPARX-64/128 worked for two other variants SPARX-128/128 and SPARX-128/256. As a countermeasure to secure SPARX-64/128, we proposed Threshold Implementation to improve the security of the initial SPARX core. First, a serialized implementation of SPARX is given. Then, a first-order side-channel-resilient threshold implementation for SPARX-64/128 is proposed using the previously given serialized implementation. As shown in Sect. 5, Non-Completeness, Correctness and Balance properties are preserved in the proposed secure TI design to indicate resiliency to side channel analysis. This provides a slower, yet a provably secure version of SPARX. For the future work, we will investigate a generalized model that would extend the threshold implementation to other variants of SPARX cipher. This model would be used to study the complexity analysis and the effectively of using threshold implementations on different lightweight design methodologies.

Acknowledgement. This work is supported by Center of Cyber Security Abu Dhabi in NYUAD. The authors would like to acknowledge the support of Dr. K. K. Soundra Pandian and Mohammed Nabeel Thari Moopan.

References

1. https://www.iso.org/standard/56552.html
2. Abdelkhalek, A., Tolba, M., Youssef, A.M.: Impossible differential attack on reduced round SPARX-64/128. In: Joye, M., Nitaj, A. (eds.) AFRICACRYPT 2017. LNCS, vol. 10239, pp. 135–146. Springer, Cham (2017). https://doi.org/10.1007/978-3-319-57339-7_8
3. Shahverdi, A., Taha, M., Eisenbarth, T.: Silent Simon: a threshold implementation under 100 slices. In: IEEE International Symposium on Hardware Oriented Security and Trust, HOST 2015, Washington, DC, USA, pp. 1–6 (2015)
4. Shahverdi, A., Taha, M., Eisenbarth, T.: Lightweight side channel resistance: threshold implementations of SIMON. IEEE Trans. Comput. **66**(4), 661–671 (2017)
5. Poschmann, A., Moradi, A., Khoo, K., Lim, C.-W., Wang, H., Ling, S.: Side-channel resistant crypto for less than 2, 300 GE. J. Cryptol. **24**(2), 322–345 (2011)
6. Aysu, A., Gulcan, E., Schaumont, P.: SIMON says: break area records of block ciphers on FPGAs. Embed. Syst. Lett. **6**(2), 37–40 (2014)
7. Beaulieu, R., Shors, D., Smith, J., Treatman-Clark, S., Weeks, B., Wingers, L.: The SIMON and SPECK families of lightweight block ciphers. Cryptology ePrint Archive, Report 2013/404 (2013)
8. Bilgin, B., Gierlichs, B., Nikova, S., Nikov, V., Rijmen, V.: A more efficient AES threshold implementation. In: Pointcheval, D., Vergnaud, D. (eds.) AFRICACRYPT 2014. LNCS, vol. 8469, pp. 267–284. Springer, Cham (2014). https://doi.org/10.1007/978-3-319-06734-6_17
9. Bilgin, B., Gierlichs, B., Nikova, S., Nikov, V., Rijmen, V.: Higher-order threshold implementations. In: Sarkar, P., Iwata, T. (eds.) ASIACRYPT 2014. LNCS, vol. 8874, pp. 326–343. Springer, Heidelberg (2014). https://doi.org/10.1007/978-3-662-45608-8_18
10. Chen, C., İnci, M.S., Taha, M., Eisenbarth, T.: SpecTre: a tiny side-channel resistant speck core for FPGAs. In: Lemke-Rust, K., Tunstall, M. (eds.) CARDIS 2016. LNCS, vol. 10146, pp. 73–88. Springer, Cham (2017). https://doi.org/10.1007/978-3-319-54669-8_5
11. Genkin, D., Shamir, A., Tromer, E.: Acoustic cryptanalysis. J. Cryptol. **30**(2), 392–443 (2017)
12. Chakraborty, R.S., Matyas, V., Schaumont, P. (eds.): SPACE 2014. LNCS, vol. 8804. Springer, Cham (2014). https://doi.org/10.1007/978-3-319-12060-7
13. Dinu, D., Perrin, L., Udovenko, A., Velichkov, V., Großschädl, J., Biryukov, A.: Design strategies for ARX with provable bounds: SPARX and LAX. In: Cheon, J.H., Takagi, T. (eds.) ASIACRYPT 2016. LNCS, vol. 10031, pp. 484–513. Springer, Heidelberg (2016). https://doi.org/10.1007/978-3-662-53887-6_18

14. Biham, E., Shamir, A.: Differential fault analysis of secret key cryptosystems. In: Kaliski, B.S. (ed.) CRYPTO 1997. LNCS, vol. 1294, pp. 513–525. Springer, Heidelberg (1997). https://doi.org/10.1007/BFb0052259

15. Oswald, E., Mangard, S., Herbst, C., Tillich, S.: Practical second-order DPA attacks for masked smart card implementations of block ciphers. In: Pointcheval, D. (ed.) CT-RSA 2006. LNCS, vol. 3860, pp. 192–207. Springer, Heidelberg (2006). https://doi.org/10.1007/11605805_13

16. Brier, E., Clavier, C., Olivier, F.: Correlation power analysis with a leakage model. In: Joye, M., Quisquater, J.-J. (eds.) CHES 2004. LNCS, vol. 3156, pp. 16–29. Springer, Heidelberg (2004). https://doi.org/10.1007/978-3-540-28632-5_2

17. Goubin, L., Patarin, J.: DES and differential power analysis the "Duplication" method. In: Koç, Ç.K., Paar, C. (eds.) CHES 1999. LNCS, vol. 1717, pp. 158–172. Springer, Heidelberg (1999). https://doi.org/10.1007/3-540-48059-5_15

18. Daemen, J., Rijmen, V.: The Design of Rijndael: AES - The Advanced Encryption Standard. Information Security and Cryptography. Springer, Heidelberg (2002). https://doi.org/10.1007/978-3-662-04722-4

19. Kocher, P., Jaffe, J., Jun, B.: Differential power analysis. In: Wiener, M. (ed.) CRYPTO 1999. LNCS, vol. 1666, pp. 388–397. Springer, Heidelberg (1999). https://doi.org/10.1007/3-540-48405-1_25

20. Lo, O., Buchanan, W.J., Carson, D.: Correlation power analysis on the PRESENT block cipher on an embedded device. In: Proceedings of the 13th International Conference on Availability, Reliability and Security, ARES 2018. ACM (2018)

21. Messerges, T.S.: Securing the AES finalists against power analysis attacks. In: Goos, G., Hartmanis, J., van Leeuwen, J., Schneier, B. (eds.) FSE 2000. LNCS, vol. 1978, pp. 150–164. Springer, Heidelberg (2001). https://doi.org/10.1007/3-540-44706-7_11

22. Yalla, P., Kaps, J.-P.: Lightweight cryptography for FPGAs. In: 2009 International Conference on Reconfigurable Computing and FPGAs, Cancun, Quintana Roo, Mexico, ReConFig 2009 (2009)

23. Kocher, P.C.: Timing attacks on implementations of diffie-hellman, RSA, DSS, and other systems. In: Koblitz, N. (ed.) CRYPTO 1996. LNCS, vol. 1109, pp. 104–113. Springer, Heidelberg (1996). https://doi.org/10.1007/3-540-68697-5_9

24. Quisquater, J.-J., Samyde, D.: ElectroMagnetic analysis (EMA): measures and counter-measures for smart cards. In: Attali, I., Jensen, T. (eds.) E-smart 2001. LNCS, vol. 2140, pp. 200–210. Springer, Heidelberg (2001). https://doi.org/10.1007/3-540-45418-7_17

25. Ankele, R., List, E.: Differential cryptanalysis of round-reduced Sparx-64/128. In: Preneel, B., Vercauteren, F. (eds.) ACNS 2018. LNCS, vol. 10892, pp. 459–475. Springer, Cham (2018). https://doi.org/10.1007/978-3-319-93387-0_24

26. Nikova, S., Rechberger, C., Rijmen, V.: Threshold implementations against side-channel attacks and glitches. In: Ning, P., Qing, S., Li, N. (eds.) ICICS 2006. LNCS, vol. 4307, pp. 529–545. Springer, Heidelberg (2006). https://doi.org/10.1007/11935308_38

27. Messerges, T.S.: Using second-order power analysis to attack DPA resistant software. In: Koç, Ç.K., Paar, C. (eds.) CHES 2000. LNCS, vol. 1965, pp. 238–251. Springer, Heidelberg (2000). https://doi.org/10.1007/3-540-44499-8_19

28. Schneider, T., Moradi, A., Güneysu, T.: Arithmetic addition over boolean masking. In: Malkin, T., Kolesnikov, V., Lewko, A.B., Polychronakis, M. (eds.) ACNS 2015. LNCS, vol. 9092, pp. 559–578. Springer, Cham (2015). https://doi.org/10.1007/978-3-319-28166-7_27

Analysis of Two Countermeasures Against the Signal Leakage Attack

Ke Wang[1,2]($\boxtimes$) and Haodong Jiang[1,3]

[1] TCA Laboratory, State Key Laboratory of Computer Science,
Institute of Software Chinese Academy of Sciences, Beijing, China
wangke@tca.iscas.ac.cn, hdjiang13@gmail.com
[2] University of Chinese Academy of Sciences, Beijing, China
[3] State Key Laboratory of Mathematical Engineering and Advanced Computing,
Zhengzhou, Henan, China

Abstract. In 2017, a practical attack, referred to as signal leakage attack, against reconciliation-based RLWE key exchange protocols was proposed. In particular, this attack can recover a long-term private key if a key pair is reused.

Directly motivated by this attack, recently, Ding et al. proposed two countermeasures against the attack. One is the RLWE key exchange protocol with reusable keys (KERK), which is included in the Ding Key Exchange, a NIST submission; the other is the practical randomized RLWE key exchange (PRKE) (TOC'18). Meanwhile, there exits another key reuse attack on RLWE key exchange (ACISP'18 and Africacrypt'18), which is called key mismatch attack.

In this paper, we find that KERK and PRKE are vulnerable to key mismatch attack. In particular, we propose a simpler key mismatch attack and apply it to KERK and PRKE, respectively. In fact, key mismatch attack shares the same idea with the signal leakage attack, which is one of the communicators chooses a RLWE sample with special structure as his/her public key. In order to resist key mismatch attack, we extend KERK and give an improved one, where any party can construct a new "public key" of the other party. And we also extend PRKE by increasing randomization further. Finally, by comparison, we get that the improved PRKE is more practical.

Keywords: RLWE · Key exchange · Post-quantum · Key reuse ·
Key mismatch · Active attacks · Countermeasures

1 Introduction

Key exchange is an important cryptography primitive. It allows two or more parties to agree on the same key, which is used in symmetric ciphers to encrypt and decrypt traffic data. Since the groundbreaking work of Diffie-Hellman key exchange [1], various key exchange protocols following this idea have been designed, implemented and deployed in real-world applications.

© Springer Nature Switzerland AG 2019
J. Buchmann et al. (Eds.): AFRICACRYPT 2019, LNCS 11627, pp. 370–388, 2019.
https://doi.org/10.1007/978-3-030-23696-0_19

In 1994, Shor proposed a quantum algorithm in [2], which can break most current public key cryptosystems based on integer factoring problem, discrete logarithm problem etc. Cryptographic algorithms designed based on these hard problems are no longer secure when large quantum computers are implemented. Fortunately, there are several approaches that can defeat such attacks, including lattice-based, multivariate-based, hash-based, code-based, and others. In particular, lattice-based cryptography is regarded as a very promising one because construction based on lattice problems are extremely hard to solve, even against quantum computers. It also enjoys strong provable security and very high efficiency. An important line of lattice-based cryptography is constructions based on the Ring-Learning with Error (RLWE) problem [4].

RLWE key exchange protocol was introduced in 2012 (denoted as DING12) [5], which gave RLWE variant of Diffie-Hellman key exchange. Following the idea of this work, various RLWE key exchange protocols have been designed and implemented, including [6–9,11,12]. One common approach to achieve RLWE key exchange is error reconciliation. In particular, DING12, PKT14 [6], NewHope [9] and HILA5 [26] belong to reconciliation-based RLWE key exchange protocol.

Recently, a practical attack, referred to as signal leakage attack, against reconciliation-based RLWE key exchange protocols was proposed [13]. This attack could recover a long-term private key if a key pair is reused. It is known that in the real world, key reuse is commonly adopted in applications like the SSH and TLS protocol to improve performance. In TLS v1.2, the resumption mode allows key reuse, and this reduces online computations significantly. Another instance of key reuse appears in the Internet Key Exchange (IKE). Currently with classical DH, some implementations of IKE do reuse the keys for improved computational efficiency and latency. If RLWE key exchange protocols that are vulnerable to key reuse attack are adopted in TLS and IKE with reused keys, the security of communication is compromised.

Directly motivated by this attack, Ding et al. constructed two countermeasures against the attack. One is called the RLWE key exchange protocol with reusable keys (KERK), which was proposed in the Ding Key Exchange, a NIST submission [3]. However, there are few descriptions of KERK in the submission. The other is the practical randomized RLWE key exchange (PRKE) [15]. It extends DING12 and incorporates an additional ephemeral public error term into key exchange materials so that the practical signal leakage attack does not work.

In addition, Ding et al. [19] proposed a new attack on DING12 using key mismatch, and Bernstein et al. [18] demonstrated a key-recovery attack on HILA5 using an active attack on reused keys. These two attacks both follow the method in [17] and we call such attacks key mismatch attack. However, there are some differences between [18] and [19]. The attack in [18] can adopt the method in [17] directly while the attack in [19] can't. The reason is that the method in [17] only works on the RLWE key exchange that derives the shared secret from the most significant bits of the approximately equal keys computed by both parties. Therefore, in [19], Ding et al. make some modifications to make the attack work on DING12, but the modified attack is relatively complex.

In fact, key mismatch attack shares the same idea with the signal leakage attack. Specifically, in key mismatch attack, Alice is an honest participant who reuses her secret key s_A and her public key $p_A = as_A + e_A$, Bob is an active adversary who initiates many connections with Alice and tries to learn s_A; while in the signal leakage attack, Bob is an honest participant who reuses his secret key s_B and his public key $p_B = as_B + e_B$, Alice is an active adversary who constructs her public key p_A as to learn information about s_B.

1.1 Related Work

In 2015, Kirkwood et al. from National Security Agency(NSA) revealed an issue in reconciliation-based key exchange protocols [16]. They suggested that if a public and private key pairs is reused, current reconciliation-based LWE and RLWE key exchange protocols may suffer from an attack that can reveal a private key with multiple key exchange executions.

In 2016, Fluhrer [17] gave cryptanalysis on RLWE key exchange protocols. This work gave the basic structure of the attack and showed that RLWE key exchange can be broken when a key pair is reused. In 2017, Ding et al. [13] presented a signal leakage attack. In 2017, Bernstein et al. [18] demonstrated a key-recovery attack on HILA5 using an active attack on reused keys.

In December 2017, Ding et al. [3] submitted their post-quantum cryptosystem, Ding Key Exchange, to NIST, which is based on DING12. In their scheme, KERK was included, which can achieve secure key reuse. In 2018, Ding et al. [19] described a new attack on DING12's one pass case without relying on the signal function output but using only the information of whether the final key of both parties agree. In 2018, Gao et al. [15] constructed a new randomized RLWE key exchange protocol against the signal leakage attack. In particular, they incorporated an additional ephemeral public error term into key exchange materials.

Recently, D'Anvers et al. [28] investigated the impact of decryption failures on the chosen-ciphertext security of (Ring/Module)-Learning With Errors and (Ring/Module)-Learning with Rounding based primitives. In particular, they introduced a technique to increase the failure rate of these schemes and examined the amount of information that an adversary can derive from failing ciphertexts. Bauer et al. [30] studied the security of NewHope when an active adversary accesses a key establishment and is given access to an key mismatch oracle. This attack model turns out to be relevant in key reuse situations.

1.2 Our Contributions

In this work, our contributions are as follows:

– First, we find that two countermeasures, KERK and PRKE, are vulnerable to key mismatch attack. In particular, we extend the method in [17], propose a simpler key mismatch attack and apply it to KERK and PRKE, respectively.

- Next, we find that key mismatch attack shares the same idea with the signal leakage attack. In order to resist key mismatch attack, we extend KERK and PRKE and develop improved KERK and PRKE. Finally, by comparison, we get that the improved PRKE is more practical.
- In addition, we further elaborate on KERK and explain why it can resist the signal leakage attack.

1.3 Organization

In Sect. 2, we introduce some notations, background on RLWE and the error reconciliation mechanism from DING12. In Sect. 3, we revisit the signal leakage attack on DING12 and its two countermeasures: KERK and PRKE. In Sect. 4, we revisit key mismatch attack, propose a simpler key mismatch attack and apply it to KERK and PRKE. In Sect. 5, we develop two measures to deal with key mismatch attack and they are extensions of KERK and PRKE, respectively. In addition, some discussions and comparison are also included in Sect. 5. In Sect. 6, we make a conclusion.

2 Preliminaries

Notation. Let n be an integer and a power of 2. Define $f(x) = x^n + 1$ and consider the ring $R := \mathbb{Z}[x]/\langle f(x) \rangle$. For the prime integer q, we define $R_q = R/qR \cong \mathbb{Z}_q[x]/\langle f(x) \rangle$ analogously, where the ring of polynomials over $\mathbb{Z}$ (respectively $\mathbb{Z}_q = \mathbb{Z}/q\mathbb{Z}$) we denote by $\mathbb{Z}[x]$ (respectively $\mathbb{Z}_q[x]$)). For any polynomial $p \in R$ (or R_q), let $p[i]$ denote the i-th coefficient of p. In particular, there is a map between a polynomial $c_0 + c_1 x + c_2 x^2 + ... + c_{n-1} x^{n-1}$ and a vector $(c_0, c_1, c_2, ..., c_{n-1})$.

Discrete Gaussian Distribution. For any positive real $\sigma \in \mathbb{R}$, and vector $c \in \mathbb{R}^n$, the continuous Gaussian distribution over $\mathbb{R}^n$ with standard deviation σ centered at c is defined by the probability function $\rho_{\sigma,c}(x) = (\frac{1}{\sqrt{2\pi\sigma^2}})^n exp(\frac{-\|x-c\|^2}{2\sigma^2})$. For integer vectors $c \in \mathbb{Z}^n$, let $\rho_{\sigma,c}(\mathbb{Z}^n) = \sum_{x \in \mathbb{Z}^n} \rho_{\sigma,c}(x)$. Then, we define the discrete Gaussian distribution over $\mathbb{Z}^n$ as $D_{\mathbb{Z}^n,\sigma,c}(x) = \frac{\rho_{\sigma,c}(x)}{\rho_{\sigma,c}(\mathbb{Z}^n)}$, where $x \in \mathbb{Z}^n$. The subscripts σ and c are taken to be 1 and 0 (respectively) when omitted. In particular, we will use a bound of the norm of the Gaussian distribution as follows.

Lemma 1. ([29]). For any $\sigma \geq \omega(\sqrt{\log n})$, then we have

$$Pr[\|x\| > \sigma\sqrt{n} | x \leftarrow D_{\mathbb{Z}^n,\sigma}] \leq 2^{-n}. \tag{1}$$

Ring Learning with Errors(RLWE). A Lattice $L(b_1, ..., b_n) = \{\sum_{i=1}^{n} x_i b_i | x_i \in \mathbb{Z}\}$ is formed by integer linear combinations of n linearly independent vectors $b_1, ..., b_n \in \mathbb{R}^n$ called the Lattice Basis. In 1996, Ajtai's seminal result [21] heralded the use of lattices for constructing cryptographic systems, with the security based on hardness of problems such as the Shortest Vector Problem (SVP) and Closest Vector Problem (CVP). The Learning with Errors (LWE) problem introduced by Oded Regev in 2005 [4] is a generalization of the parity-learning problem. The reduction from solving hard problems in lattices in the worst case to solving LWE in the average case provides strong security guarantees for LWE based cryptosystems, yet it is not efficient enough for practical applications due to its large key sizes of $O(n^2)$. Ring-Learning with Errors(RLWE) is the version of LWE in the ring setting, that overcomes the efficiency disadvantages of LWE. The search version of RLWE is to find a secret s in R_q given $(a, as + e)$ for polynomial number of samples, where a is sampled uniform from R_q and e is sampled according to the error distribution $D_{\mathbb{Z}^n, \sigma}$. An equivalent problem of the search version is the decision version which is commonly used for security proof of cryptographic algorithms based on RLWE. Let $A_{s, D_{\mathbb{Z}^n, \sigma}}$ denote the distribution of the pair $(a, as + e)$, where a, s is sampled uniformly from R_q and e is sampled according to the error distribution $D_{\mathbb{Z}^n, \sigma}$. The decision version of the RLWE problem is to distinguish $A_{s, D_{\mathbb{Z}^n, \sigma}}$ from the uniform distribution on $R_q \times R_q$ with polynomial number of samples. The *normal form* [22,23] of the RLWE problem is by modifying the definition above by choosing s from the error distribution $D_{\mathbb{Z}^n, \sigma}$ rather than uniformly. It has been proven that the ring-LWE assumption still holds even with this variant [4,24].

Reconciliation-Based Key Exchange. It is an approach to construct a passively secure lattice-based Key Exchange scheme [11]. In particular, we take DING12 (Table 1) as an example. In the protocol, Alice and Bob each compute a noisy version of the shared secret. In order to agree on a common value, one

Table 1. DING12

Alice		Bob
Public key: $p_A = as_A + 2e_A \in R_q$		Public key: $p_B = as_B + 2e_B \in R_q$
Private key: $s_A \in R_q$		Private key: $s_B \in R_q$
where $s_A, e_A \leftarrow D_{\mathbb{Z}^n, \sigma}$		where $s_B, e_B \leftarrow D_{\mathbb{Z}^n, \sigma}$
	$\xrightarrow{\quad p_A \quad}$	
		$k_B = p_A s_B + 2e'_B$
		where $e'_B \leftarrow D_{\mathbb{Z}^n, \sigma}$
		$w = \text{Cha}(k_B) \in \{0,1\}^n$
	$\xleftarrow{\quad p_B, w \quad}$	
$k_A = p_B s_A + 2e'_A$		$\sigma_B = \text{Mod}_2(k_B, w) \in \{0,1\}^n$
where $e'_A \leftarrow D_{\mathbb{Z}^n, \sigma}$		$sk_B = \text{SHA2} - 256(\sigma_B)$
$\sigma_A = \text{Mod}_2(k_A, w) \in \{0,1\}^n$		
$sk_A = \text{SHA2} - 256(\sigma_A)$		

party additionally sends a signal of his value so that both parties can recover the exact key from their respective noisy versions.

The Error Reconciliation Mechanism from DING12. The error reconciliation mechanism in DING12 mainly consists of a signal function and a robust extractor.

Signal Function. For the Key Exchange from RLWE presented in [5], the signal function is required for the two parties in the key exchange to derive a final shared secret. The signal function is usually sent by the responding party to the initiator of the key exchange, which gives additional information about whether the responder's key computed lies in a specific region.

For prime $q > 2$, hint functions $\sigma_0(x), \sigma_1(x)$ from $\mathbb{Z}_q$ to $\{0, 1\}$ are defined as:

$$\sigma_0(x) = \begin{cases} 0, & x \in [-\lfloor \frac{q}{4} \rfloor, \lfloor \frac{q}{4} \rfloor] \\ 1, & \text{otherwise} \end{cases}$$

$$\sigma_1(x) = \begin{cases} 0, & x \in [-\lfloor \frac{q}{4} \rfloor + 1, \lfloor \frac{q}{4} \rfloor + 1] \\ 1, & \text{otherwise} \end{cases}$$

Signal function Cha() is defined as: For any $y \in \mathbb{Z}_q$, $\mathrm{Cha}(y) = \sigma_b(y)$, where $b \xleftarrow{\$} \{0, 1\}$.

Robust Extractor. Informally, a robust extractor enables two parties to extract an identical information from two close elements with some additional hint. The robust extractor is defined as:

$$\mathrm{Mod}_2(x, w) = (x + w \cdot \frac{q-1}{2} \bmod q) \bmod 2.$$

3   Revisit the Signal Leakage Attack on DING12 and Its Countermeasures

3.1   The Signal Leakage Attack on DING12

In this section, we briefly recall the signal leakage attack [13] on DING12 (Table 2). In the attack, honest communicator Bob reuses key pair (s_B, p_B), active adversary Alice (boxed out in Table 2) tries to recover Bob's private key s_B within multiple queries by choosing p_A with special structure.

In the attack, malicious Alice chooses $p_A = k$, then, at the Bob side,

$$w = \mathrm{Cha}(k_B) = \mathrm{Cha}(p_A s_B + 2e'_B) = \mathrm{Cha}(k s_B + 2e'_B), \tag{2}$$

In particular,

$$w[i] = \mathrm{Cha}(k_B[i]) = \mathrm{Cha}(p_A s_B[i] + 2e'_B[i]) = \mathrm{Cha}(k s_B[i] + 2e'_B[i]), \tag{3}$$

where k loops from 0 to $q - 1$ in every communication and is used to reveal the value of $s_B[i]$.

Table 2. Signal leakage attack on DING12

Alice	Bob
Public key: $\boxed{p_A = k} \in R_q$	Public key: $p_B = as_B + 2e_B \in R_q$
	Private key: $s_B \in R_q$
	where $s_B, e_B \leftarrow D_{\mathbb{Z}^n, \sigma}$

$$\xrightarrow{\quad p_A \quad}$$

$$k_B = p_A s_B + 2e'_B$$
$$\text{where } e'_B \leftarrow D_{\mathbb{Z}^n, \sigma}$$
$$w = \text{Cha}(k_B) \in \{0, 1\}^n$$

$$\xleftarrow{\quad p_B, w \quad}$$

$k_A = p_B s_A + 2e'_A$	$\sigma_B = \text{Mod}_2(k_B, w) \in \{0, 1\}^n$
where $e'_A \leftarrow D_{\mathbb{Z}^n, \sigma}$	$sk_B = \text{SHA2} - 256(\sigma_B)$
$\sigma_A = \text{Mod}_2(k_A, w) \in \{0, 1\}^n$	
$sk_A = \text{SHA2} - 256(\sigma_A)$	

According to the definition of signal function Cha, signal value $w[i]$ flips when $ks_B[i] + 2e'_B[i]$ enters or exits inner region $[-q/4, q/4]$. Error $2e'_B[i]$ is relatively small and can be ignored. When k loops from 0 to $q - 1$, signal value $w[i]$ flips exactly $2s_B[i]$ times. Therefore, by communicating with Bob with k looping from 0 to $q - 1$, Alice can get the value of $s_B[i]$ based on the number of times that signal $w[i]$ changes.

3.2   Two Countermeasures Against the Signal Leakage Attack

Next, we revisit two countermeasures against the signal leakage attack. The first one is KERK, which is based on the authentication protocol proposed in [27], where they firstly designed a zero knowledge-based authentication protocol. The other is PRKE, which mixes more randomization [15].

Table 3. KERK

Alice	Bob
Public key: $p_A = as_A + 2e_A \in R_q$	Public key: $p_B = as_B + 2e_B \in R_q$
Private key: $s_A \in R_q$	Private key: $s_B \in R_q$
where $s_A, e_A \leftarrow D_{\mathbb{Z}^n, \sigma}$	where $s_B, e_B \leftarrow D_{\mathbb{Z}^n, \sigma}$

$$\xrightarrow{\quad p_A \quad}$$

	Sample $e'_B, e''_B \leftarrow D_{\mathbb{Z}^n, \sigma}$
	$\text{Samp}(\text{H}(p_A)) \leftarrow D_{\mathbb{Z}^n, \sigma}$
	$\overline{p_A} = a \cdot \text{Samp}(\text{H}(p_A)) + 2e'_B + p_A$
Sample $e'_A \leftarrow D_{\mathbb{Z}^n, \sigma}$	$k_B = \overline{p_A} s_B + 2e''_B$
$\text{Samp}(\text{H}(p_A)) \leftarrow D_{\mathbb{Z}^n, \sigma}$	$w = \text{Cha}(k_B) \in \{0, 1\}^n$

$$\xleftarrow{\quad p_B, w \quad}$$

$k_A = p_B \cdot (s_A + \text{Samp}(\text{H}(p_A))) + 2e'_A$	$sk_B = \text{Mod}_2(k_B, w) \in \{0, 1\}^n$
$sk_A = \text{Mod}_2(k_A, w) \in \{0, 1\}^n$	

KERK. As shown in Table 3, KERK can resist the signal leakage attack effectively. In particular, if malicious Alice chooses $p_A = k$, then, at the Bob side,

$$
\begin{aligned}
w = \mathrm{Cha}(k_B) &= \mathrm{Cha}(\overline{p_A} s_B + 2e_B'') \\
&= \mathrm{Cha}((a \cdot \mathrm{Samp}(\mathrm{H}(p_A)) + 2e_B' + p_A)s_B + 2e_B'') \\
&= \mathrm{Cha}((a \cdot \mathrm{Samp}(\mathrm{H}(k)) + 2e_B' + k)s_B + 2e_B''), \quad\quad (4)
\end{aligned}
$$

where H is a hash function, Samp() is a function which generates polynomial in R_q using output of H according to distribution $D_{\mathbb{Z}^n, \sigma}$, and e_B' is chosen by Bob according to distribution $D_{\mathbb{Z}^n, \sigma}$. Although Alice can manipulate k, she can't control the value of $a \cdot \mathrm{Samp}(\mathrm{H}(k)) + 2e_B'$. Therefore, by looping k from 0 to $q-1$, Alice can't get the value of $s_B[i]$ based on the number of times that signal $w[i]$ changes.

Table 4. Regular mode

Alice	Bob
Public key: $p_A = as_A + 2e_A \in R_q$	Public key: $p_B = as_B + 2e_B \in R_q$
Private key: $s_A \in R_q$	Private key: $s_B \in R_q$
where $s_A, e_A \leftarrow D_{\mathbb{Z}^n, \sigma}$	where $s_B, e_B \leftarrow D_{\mathbb{Z}^n, \sigma}$
$\xrightarrow{\quad p_A \quad}$	
	$k_B = (p_A s_B + 2e_p) \cdot e_p + 2e_B'$
	where $e_p, e_B' \leftarrow D_{\mathbb{Z}^n, \sigma}$
	$w = \mathrm{Cha}(k_B) \in \{0, 1\}^n$
$\xleftarrow{\quad p_B, w, e_p \quad}$	
$k_i = (p_B s_A + 2e_p) \cdot e_p + 2e_A'$	$\sigma_B = \mathrm{Mod}_2(k_B, w) \in \{0, 1\}^n$
where $e_A' \leftarrow D_{\mathbb{Z}^n, \sigma}$	$sk_B = \mathrm{SHA2} - 256(\sigma_B)$
$\sigma_A = \mathrm{Mod}_2(k_A, w) \in \{0, 1\}^n$	
$sk_A = \mathrm{SHA2} - 256(\sigma_A)$	

PRKE. As shown in Tables 4 and 5, PRKE has two modes: regular mode and key reuse mode, which share the same structure. Regular mode is designed for common key exchange between two parties without reused keys. Key reuse mode is designed for both parties wanting to reuse a key pair and it is directly derived from the regular mode. The main motivation for key reuse is for better performance because generating the key pair is somewhat expensive.

The key exchange in key reuse mode can prevent malicious Alice from implementing the signal leakage attack. In particular, if malicious Alice chooses $p_A = k$, then, at the Bob side,

$$
\begin{aligned}
w = \mathrm{Cha}(k_B) &= \mathrm{Cha}((p_A s_B + 2e_p) \cdot e_p + 2e_B') \\
&= \mathrm{Cha}((ks_B + 2e_p) \cdot e_p + 2e_B') \\
&= \mathrm{Cha}(ks_B e_p + 2e_p^2 + 2e_B'), \quad\quad (5)
\end{aligned}
$$

Table 5. Key reuse mode

Alice	Bob
Reused public key: $p_A = as_A + 2e_A$	Reused public key: $p_B = as_B + 2e_B$
Reused private key: s_A	Reused private key: s_B

$$\xrightarrow{\quad Session\ ID \quad}$$

$$k_B = (p_A s_B + 2e_p) \cdot e_p + 2e'_B$$
$$\text{where } e_p, e'_B \leftarrow D_{\mathbb{Z}^n, \sigma}$$
$$w = \text{Cha}(k_B) \in \{0,1\}^n$$

$$\xleftarrow{\quad w, e_p \quad}$$

$$k_A = (p_B s_A + 2e_p) \cdot e_p + 2e'_A \qquad\qquad \sigma_B = \text{Mod}_2(k_B, w) \in \{0,1\}^n$$
$$\text{where } e'_A \leftarrow D_{\mathbb{Z}^n, \sigma} \qquad\qquad\qquad sk_B = \text{SHA2} - 256(\sigma_B)$$
$$\sigma_A = \text{Mod}_2(k_A, w) \in \{0,1\}^n$$
$$sk_A = \text{SHA2} - 256(\sigma_A)$$

where e_p is chosen by Bob to mix more randomization. By looping k from 0 to $q-1$, Alice can't get the value of $s_B[i]$ based on the number of times that signal $w[i]$ changes. In fact, the approach of mixing more randomization is a common and practical solution, for example, using public random one-time initialization vector (IV) in encryption, nonce in various cryptography protocols, long and random salt in password-based key derivation function.

4   Key Mismatch Attack on KERK and the PRKE in Key Reuse Mode

Different from the signal leakage attack, key mismatch attack considers the scene where Alice is an honest participant who reuses her public key, Bob is an active adversary who initiates many connections with Alice and tries to learn corresponding private key. The countermeasures above can resist the signal leakage attack effectively, but they are vulnerable to key mismatch attack.

4.1   Revisit Key Mismatch Attack

In [17], Fluhrer analyzed RLWE key exchange with key reused, where Alice reuses the same public key and Bob uses a fresh public key each time. Each time after Alice and Bob have performed the key exchange protocol, Alice will derive her shared secret and Bob can be able to generate one guess of Alice's shared secret. Then Bob verifies his guess by communicating with Alice. In RLWE key exchange, shared secret is usually used to generate symmetric keys that Alice and Bob would use to communicate. Bob can generate his symmetric keys based on his guess; if Alice is able to decrypt (and respond) based on those keys, then (with high probability) Bob's guess was correct; if Alice rejects, then Bob's guess was not correct.

In particular, Fluhrer gave a attack, where adversary Bob chooses a public key with special structure each time and Alice's shared secret will leak the information about Alice's private key. However, the attack has limitations. It only works on the RLWE key exchange that derives the shared secret from the most significant bits of the approximately equal keys computed by both parties, and does not work on DING12 that uses the least significant bits to derive a shared secret.

Therefore, Ding et al. [19] proposed a specific attack on DING12. However, compared with [17], the attack in [19] is relatively complex. In [19], when Bob chooses public key, he needs to determine j satisfying $s_A[j] = 1$ and he uses a method of hypothesis and verification. In particular, Bob first assumes $s_A[0] = 1$, then recover s_A to verify the hypothesis. If fails, Bob assumes $s_A[1] = 1$ and like this until j is found. As s_A is sampled from the error distribution with standard deviation σ, determining one coefficient of s_A needs at most $t\sigma$ connections, where t is a constant. Thus, the attack complexity to recover s_A is $tn\sigma \approx O(n\sigma)$. Therefore, the complexity depends on the position of j. If $s_A[0] = 1$, then the complexity is $O(n\sigma)$; if $s_A[n-1] = 1$, then the complexity is $O(n^2\sigma)$.

Next, we extend the method in [17] such that it can work on the RLWE key exchange that uses the least significant bits to derive a shared secret. In particular, the attack is simper and the complexity is $O(n\sigma)$. Next, we apply it to KERK and PRKE, respectively.

4.2   Key Mismatch Attack on KERK

Main Idea. In the attack, Alice is an honest participant who reuses her public key, Bob is an active adversary who initiates many connections with Alice. In every connection, Bob uses a fresh public key and tries to learn Alice's private key.

Table 6. Key mismatch attack on KERK

Alice	Bob
Public key: $p_A = as_A + 2e_A \in R_q$	Public key: $\boxed{p_B = j(kas_B + e_B) \in R_q}$
Private key: $s_A \in R_q$	Private key: $s_B \in R_q$
where $s_A, e_A \leftarrow D_{\mathbb{Z}^n,\sigma}$	where $\boxed{s_B}$, $\boxed{e_B} \leftarrow D_{\mathbb{Z}^n,\sigma}$

$$\xrightarrow{\quad p_A \quad}$$

Sample $e'_B, e''_B \leftarrow D_{\mathbb{Z}^n,\sigma}$
Samp(H(p_A))$\leftarrow D_{\mathbb{Z}^n,\sigma}$
$\overline{p_A} = a \cdot$ Samp(H(p_A)) $+ 2e'_B + p_A$
$\boxed{k_B - jk\overline{p_A}s_B + 2e''_B}$
$\boxed{w} = \text{Cha}(k_B) \in \{0,1\}^n$

Sample $e'_A \leftarrow D_{\mathbb{Z}^n,\sigma}$
Samp(H(p_A))$\leftarrow D_{\mathbb{Z}^n,\sigma}$

$$\xleftarrow{\quad p_B, w \quad}$$

$k_A = p_B \cdot (s_A + \text{Samp}(\text{H}(p_A))) + 2e'_A$ $sk_B = \text{Mod}_2(k_B, w) \in \{0,1\}^n$
$sk_A = \text{Mod}_2(k_A, w) \in \{0,1\}^n$

As shown on in Table 6, Bob and his malicious operations are boxed out. For convenience, we denote $(s_A + \text{Samp}(\text{H}(p_A)))$ by $\overline{s_A}$. In order to recover s_A, Bob needs to recover $\overline{s_A}$ first. when recovers $\overline{s_A}[i]$, $i \in [0, n-1]$, Bob construct p_B with special structure and modifies $w[0]$ so as to the value of $sk_A[0]$ can reveal the value of $\overline{s_A}[i]$.

Meanwhile, the correctness of the protocol, $sk_A = sk_B$, make sure that Bob can compute the value sk_A, except for index 0. In order to identify the value of $sk_A[0]$, Bob can guess a $sk_A[0] = 0$ and communicate with Alice to see if his guess is correct. If he guesses correctly, then $sk_A[0] = 0$, otherwise, $sk_A[0] = 1$.

Attack Details. When recovers $\overline{s_A}[i]$, $i \in [0, n-1]$, malicious Bob chooses $p_B = j(kas_B + e_B)$, where

- s_B satisfies that $(as_B\overline{s_A})[0] = 1^1$
- e_B satisfies that $(e_B\overline{s_A})[0] = \overline{s_A}[i]^2$.
- j and k are small integers, which vary in every connection and are used to reveal the information of value $\overline{s_A}[i]$.

In this way, at the Alice side, $k_A = p_B\overline{s_A}$, which results in

$$
\begin{aligned}
k_A[0] &= (p_B\overline{s_A})[0] \\
&= j((kas_B\overline{s_A})[0] + (e_B\overline{s_A})[0]) \\
&= j(k + \overline{s_A}[i]).
\end{aligned} \tag{6}
$$

Next, Bob performs the protocol honestly, except that he deliberately flips bit $w[0]$ to be 1, thus, at the Alice side,

$$
\begin{aligned}
sk_A[0] &= \text{Mod}_2(k_A[0], w[0]) \\
&= k_A[0] + w[0] \cdot \frac{q-1}{2} \bmod q \bmod 2 \\
&= j(k + \overline{s_A}[i]) + \frac{q-1}{2} \bmod q \bmod 2.
\end{aligned} \tag{7}
$$

Notice that, for the same k, if $sk_A[0] = 0$ for different $j's$, then $k + \overline{s_A}[i] = 0 \bmod q$ with overwhelming probability[3]. Thus, the k value reveals the value of $\overline{s_A}[i]$.

---

[1] [17] proposed an off-line method to search for s_B and here we adopt the same method. in particular, Bob can do this by searching for values s_B such that $(s_B\overline{p_A})[0]$ is a small value, where s_B consists of at most three coefficients are $[1, -1]$ and the rest 0. As $s_B\overline{p_A} = s_B(a\overline{s_A} + 2e_A + 2e'_B) = as_B\overline{s_A} + 2s_B(e_A + e'_B)$ where e_A and e'_B are known to be small, such a s_B has a nontrivial probability of meeting the criteria. What's more, p_A is Alice's public key, this computation can be done off-line. In fact, $(as_B\overline{s_A})[0] = -1$ also works and we just consider the case $(as_B\overline{s_A})[0] = 1$.

[2] Specifically, he can choose $e_B = x^{n-i}$, namely, $e_B[t] = 0$ for all $t = 0, ..., n-1$ except $t = n - i$ and $e_B[n-i] = 1$.

[3] Since the addition of $\frac{q-1}{2}$ to a positive value will changes its parity by the representation of $\mathbb{Z}_q$ to be $\{-\frac{q-1}{2} ... \frac{q-1}{2}\}$.

Meanwhile, as Bob performs the protocol mostly honestly, Bob can compute the value sk_A, except for index 0, for which he flips the signal bit. Bob can guess a $sk_A[0] = 0$ and communicate with Alice to see if his guess is correct. If he guesses correctly, then $sk_A[0] = 0$, otherwise, $sk_A[0] = 1$.

Correctness of the Protocol and Choice of j and k. The correctness of the protocol can guarantee that if Bob performs the protocol mostly honestly, he can compute the value sk_A, except for index 0. The correctness of the protocol mainly depends on the difference between k_B and k_A: $|k_A - k_B|$. If the difference $|k_A - k_B|$ is small enough, then $sk_A = sk_B$ with overwhelming probability. In particular, Bob chooses $k_B = jk\overline{p_A}s_B + 2e_B''$, and

$$
\begin{aligned}
k_A - k_B &= p_B\overline{s_A} + 2e_A' - (jk\overline{p_A}s_B + 2e_B'') \\
&= jkas_B\overline{s_A} + je_B\overline{s_A} + 2e_A' - jka\overline{s_A}s_B - 2jk(e_A + e_B')s_B - 2e_B'' \\
&= je_B\overline{s_A} + 2e_A' - 2jke_As_B - 2jke_B's_B - 2e_B''.
\end{aligned}
\tag{8}
$$

As $\overline{s_A} = (s_A + \mathrm{Samp}(\mathrm{H}(p_A)))$, where $\mathrm{Samp}()$ is a function which generates polynomial in R_q using output of H according to distribution $D_{\mathbb{Z}^n,\sigma}$, from Lemma 1, we have that

$$
|je_B\overline{s_A} + 2e_A' - 2jke_As_B - 2jke_B's_B - 2e_B''| \leq 12|jk| \cdot (\sigma\sqrt{n}) \cdot (\sigma\sqrt{n}) \leq 12|jk|\sigma^2 n.
$$

If $sk_A = sk_B$ with overwhelming probability when $|k_A - k_B| \leq \theta$, then j and k need to satisfy that $|jk| \leq \frac{\theta}{12\sigma^2 n}$. According to [15], the error reconciliation mechanism in DING12 can tolerance error $\theta = \frac{q}{4} - 2$, then $|jk| \leq \frac{q-8}{48\sigma^2 n}$. As $s_A[i]$ and $\mathrm{Samp}(\mathrm{H}(p_A))[i]$ are sampled form the error distribution with the standard deviation σ, then $\overline{s_A}[i]$ satisfies a error distribution with the standard deviation 2σ and $\overline{s_A}[i] \in [-6\sigma, 6\sigma]$ with about probability 99.7%. Therefore, we can first choose a k such that $|k| \leq 6\sigma$, then choose a j such that $|jk| \leq \frac{q-8}{48\sigma^2 n}$.

Generally, when $k_A = p_B\overline{s_A} + 2e_A'$, the number of connections required to recover $\overline{s_A}[i]$ increases, due to the complexity involved in eliminating the effect of the noise $2e_A'$. Similarly, we adopt the strategy in [19], which is to run the attack on the same coefficient $\overline{s_A}[i]$ multiple times[4] and look at the distribution[5] of k.

Analysis of the Complexity. Bob can adopt the technology in [17] to choose s_B and e_B, which can be done off-line. Therefore, the complexity of the attack is to query $\overline{s_A}[i]$ for each i. As $\overline{s_A}[i]$ is sampled from the error distribution with standard deviation 2σ, determining a coefficient value $\overline{s_A}[i]$ needs at most $t\sigma$ queries, where t is a constant. Thus, the attack complexity to recover $\overline{s_A}$ is $tn\sigma \approx O(n\sigma)$.

---

[4] The number of times is chosen to derive a reasonable number of samples for analyzing the distribution of $\overline{s_A}[i]$ with a certain confidence level. For a confidence level of 95%, the number of samples is estimated to be 1000 with margin of error 3%.

[5] Since $e_A'[i]$ is sampled from an error distribution (Discrete Gaussian) centered at 0, the obtained value of $\overline{s_A}[i]$ with perturbation will be centered at $\overline{s_A}[i]$.

4.3   Key Mismatch Attack on the PRKE in Key Reuse Mode

Using the same idea, the attack also works on the PRKE in Key Reuse Mode. As shown in Table 7, Alice is an honest party and active adversary Bob constructs p_B, w, and e_p so as to recover the private key s_A of Alice.

Table 7. Key mismatch attack on the PRKE in key reuse mode

Alice	Bob
Reused public key: $p_A = as_A + 2e_A$	Reused public key: $\boxed{p_B} = as_B + 2e_B$
Reused private key: s_A	Reused private key: s_B

$$\xrightarrow{\quad Session\ ID \quad}$$

$$k_B = (p_A s_B + 2e_p) \cdot e_p + 2e'_B$$
$$\text{where } \boxed{e_p}, e'_B \leftarrow D_{\mathbb{Z}^n, \sigma}$$
$$\boxed{w} = \mathrm{Cha}(k_B) \in \{0,1\}^n$$

$$\xleftarrow{\quad w, e_p \quad}$$

$k_A = (p_B s_A + 2e_p) \cdot e_p + 2e'_A$
where $e'_A \leftarrow D_{\mathbb{Z}^n, \sigma}$
$\sigma_A = \mathrm{Mod}_2(k_A, w) \in \{0,1\}^n$
$sk_A = \mathrm{SHA2} - 256(\sigma_A)$

$\sigma_B = \mathrm{Mod}_2(k_B, w) \in \{0,1\}^n$
$sk_B = \mathrm{SHA2} - 256(\sigma_B)$

In order to recover coefficient $s_A[i], i \in [0, n-1]$, Bob chooses small integer pair (c, k), $p_B = 2c$ and $e_p = kx^i c$, flips bit $w[2i]$ to be 0, then, at the Alice side, $k_A = (p_B s_A + 2e_p) \cdot e_p$ will result in

$$k_A = (p_B s_A + 2e_p) \cdot e_p = (2cs_A + 2kx^i c) \cdot kx^i c$$
$$= (s_A + kx^i) \cdot 2kx^i c^2$$
$$= [(\sum_{j=0, j \neq i}^{n-1} s_A[j] x^j) + (s_A[i] + k) x^i] \cdot 2kx^i c^2. \quad (9)$$

In particular,

$$k_A[2i] = (s_A[i] + k) \cdot 2kc^2, \quad (10)$$

Next, Bob performs the protocol honestly, except that he deliberately flips bit $w[2i]$ to be 1, thus, at the Alice side,

$$\sigma_A[2i] = \mathrm{Mod}_2(k_A[2i], w[2i]) = (k_A[2i] + w[2i] \cdot \frac{q-1}{2} \bmod q) \bmod 2$$
$$= (((s_A[i] + k) \cdot 2kc^2) + w[2i] \cdot \frac{q-1}{2} \bmod q) \bmod 2$$
$$= (((s_A[i] + k) \cdot 2kc^2) + \frac{q-1}{2} \bmod q) \bmod 2. \quad (11)$$

Notice that, for the same k, if $\sigma_A[2i] = 0$ for different c's, then $s_A[i] + k = 0 \bmod q$ with overwhelming probability[6]. Thus, k reveals the value of $s_A[i]$.

---

[6] Since the addition of $\frac{q-1}{2}$ to a positive value will changes its parity by the representation of $\mathbb{Z}_q$ to be $\{-\frac{q-1}{2} ... \frac{q-1}{2}\}$.

Meanwhile, as Bob performs the protocol mostly honestly, Bob can compute the value σ_A, except for index $2i$, for which he flips the signal bit. Bob can guess $\sigma_A[2i] = 0$ and communicate with Alice to see if his guess is correct. If he guesses correctly, then $\sigma_A[2i] = 0$, otherwise, $\sigma_A[2i] = 1$.

5 Countermeasures Against Key Mismatch Attack

In fact, the idea behind the signal attack and key mismatch attack is the same, which is one of the communicators for key exchange can manipulate his/her public key or ciphertext so that he/she can obtain the private key of the other. Therefore, the countermeasures against the signal leakage will also work on key mismatch attack.

5.1 An Improved KERK

In the signal leakage attack, Alice chooses a RLWE sample with special structure as her public key. As a countermeasure, Bob constructs a new "public key" of Alice in KERK. In this section, we develop an improved KERK (Table 8) where Alice also constructs a new "public key" of Bob, which can further resist key mismatch attack.

Table 8. Improved KERK

Alice	Bob
Public key: $p_A = as_A + 2e_A \in R_q$	Public key: $p_B = as_B + 2e_B \in R_q$
Private key: $s_A \in R_q$	Private key: $s_B \in R_q$
where $s_A, e_A \leftarrow D_{\mathbb{Z}^n,\sigma}$	where $s_B, e_B \leftarrow D_{\mathbb{Z}^n,\sigma}$

$$\xrightarrow{\quad p_A \quad}$$

Bob:
Sample $e'_B, e''_B \leftarrow D_{\mathbb{Z}^n,\sigma}$
$\mathrm{Samp}(\mathrm{H}(p_A)), \mathrm{Samp}(\mathrm{H}(p_B)) \leftarrow D_{\mathbb{Z}^n,\sigma}$
$\overline{s_B} = s_B + \mathrm{Samp}(\mathrm{H}(p_B))$
$\overline{p_A} = a \cdot \mathrm{Samp}(\mathrm{H}(p_A)) + 2e'_B + p_A$
$k_B = \overline{p_A} \cdot \overline{s_B} + 2e''_B$
$w = \mathrm{Cha}(k_B) \in \{0,1\}^n$

Alice:
Sample $e'_A, e''_A \leftarrow D_{\mathbb{Z}^n,\sigma}$
$\mathrm{Samp}(\mathrm{H}(p_A)), \mathrm{Samp}(\mathrm{H}(p_B)) \leftarrow D_{\mathbb{Z}^n,\sigma}$
$\overline{s_A} = s_A + \mathrm{Samp}(\mathrm{H}(p_A))$

$$\xleftarrow{\quad p_B, w \quad}$$

$\overline{p_B} = a \cdot \mathrm{Samp}(\mathrm{H}(p_B)) + 2e'_A + p_B$
$k_A = \overline{p_B} \cdot \overline{s_A} + 2e''_A$
$sk_A = \mathrm{Mod}_2(k_A, w) \in \{0,1\}^n$

$sk_B = \mathrm{Mod}_2(k_B, w) \in \{0,1\}^n$

Similar to the original KERK, after receiving Bob's public key p_B, Alice computes a new "public key"

$$\overline{p_B} \leftarrow a \cdot \mathrm{Samp}(\mathrm{H}(p_B)) + 2e'_A + p_B = a \cdot \mathrm{Samp}(\mathrm{H}(p_B)) + 2e'_A + as_B + 2e_B$$
$$= a \cdot (\mathrm{Samp}(\mathrm{H}(p_B)) + s_B) + 2e'_A + 2e_B,$$

where a is public parameter, H is a hash function, Samp() is a function which generates polynomial in R_p using output of H according to distribution $D_{\mathbb{Z}^n\sigma}$, and e'_A is chosen by Alice according to distribution $D_{\mathbb{Z}^n\sigma}$.

The new "public key" $\overline{p_B}$ consists of "secret" $\overline{s_B} = \text{Samp}(\text{H}(p_B)) + s_B$ and "error" $2e'_A + 2e_B$. Although Bob can control s_B and e_B, $\text{Samp}(\text{H}(p_B))$ and e'_A are out of control, which can deal with the case where malicious Bob chooses a bad p_B. Next, Alice operates $\overline{p_B}$ instead of p_B, $\overline{s_A}$ instead of s_A. At the side of Bob, Bob operates $\overline{p_A}$ instead of p_A, $\overline{s_B}$ instead of s_B.

What's more, these operations above hardly affect the correctness of the protocol. In particular,

$$
\begin{aligned}
k_B &= \overline{p_A} \cdot \overline{s_B} + 2e''_B \\
&= a \cdot (\text{Samp}(\text{H}(p_A)) + s_A)\overline{s_B} + (2e'_B + 2e_A)\overline{s_B} + 2e''_B \\
&= a \cdot \overline{s_A} \cdot \overline{s_B} + (2e'_B + 2e_A)\overline{s_B} + 2e''_B,
\end{aligned}
\tag{12}
$$

$$
\begin{aligned}
k_A &= \overline{p_B} \cdot \overline{s_A} + 2e''_A \\
&= a \cdot (\text{Samp}(\text{H}(p_B)) + s_B)\overline{s_A} + (2e'_A + 2e_B)\overline{s_A} + 2e''_A \\
&= a \cdot \overline{s_B} \cdot \overline{s_A} + (2e'_A + 2e_B)\overline{s_A} + 2e''_A,
\end{aligned}
\tag{13}
$$

$$
\begin{aligned}
k_B - k_A &= (2e'_B + 2e_A)\overline{s_B} + 2e''_B - (2e'_A + 2e_B)\overline{s_A} - 2e''_A \\
&= (2e'_B + 2e_A)(\text{Samp}(\text{H}(p_B)) + s_B) + 2e''_B \\
&\quad - (2e'_A + 2e_B)(\text{Samp}(\text{H}(p_A)) + s_A) - 2e''_A
\end{aligned}
$$

where $e'_B, e_A, e'_A, e_B, \text{Samp}(\text{H}(p_A)), \text{Samp}(\text{H}(p_B)), s_B, s_A, e''_A, e''_B \leftarrow D_{\mathbb{Z}^n,\sigma}$.

From Lemma 1, we have that

$$
|k_B - k_A| \leq 20 \cdot (\sigma\sqrt{n}) \cdot (\sigma\sqrt{n}) \leq 20\sigma^2 n.
\tag{14}
$$

Therefore, if the error reconciliation mechanism in protocol can handle the case where $|k_B - k_A| \leq 20\sigma^2 n$, then sk_A matches sk_B with overwhelming probability.

5.2 An Improved PRKE in Key Reuse Mode

Recalling the attack in Sect. 4.3, the key to the attack is that Bob can obtain information about s_A by manipulating p_B and e_p. Therefore, in order to resist the attack, Alice should hide as much information about s_A as possible. In particular, we extend the PRKE in key reuse mode such that Alice also chooses e'_p according to distribution $D_{\mathbb{Z}^n\sigma}$ and sends it with Session ID to Bob (Table 9). Then Bob computes $k_B = (p_A s_B + 2e_p + 2e'_p) \cdot e_p \cdot e'_p + 2e'_B$ and Alice computes $k_A = (p_B s_A + 2e_p + 2e'_p) \cdot e_p \cdot e'_p + 2e'_A$. Although Bob can control p_B and e_p, he can't control e'_p, which brings more randomness to the calculation of k_A, thus it effectively resists key mismatch attack.

Table 9. Improved PRKE in key reuse mode

Alice	Bob
Reused public key: $p_A = as_A + 2e_A$	Reused public key: $p_B = as_B + 2e_B$
Reused private key: s_A	Reused private key: s_B
$e_p' \leftarrow D_{\mathbb{Z}^n, \sigma}$	

$$\xrightarrow{\quad Session\ ID, e_p' \quad}$$

$$k_B = (p_A s_B + 2e_p + 2e_p') \cdot e_p \cdot e_p' + 2e_B'$$
$$\text{where } e_p, e_B' \leftarrow D_{\mathbb{Z}^n, \sigma}$$
$$w = \text{Cha}(k_B) \in \{0,1\}^n$$

$$\xleftarrow{\quad w, e_p \quad}$$

$$k_A = (p_B s_A + 2e_p + 2e_p') \cdot e_p \cdot e_p' + 2e_A'$$
$$\text{where } e_A' \leftarrow D_{\mathbb{Z}^n, \sigma}$$
$$\sigma_A = \text{Mod}_2(k_A, w) \in \{0,1\}^n$$
$$sk_A = \text{SHA2} - 256(\sigma_A)$$

$$\sigma_B = \text{Mod}_2(k_B, w) \in \{0,1\}^n$$
$$sk_B = \text{SHA2} - 256(\sigma_B)$$

5.3 Discussion

As mentioned in introduction, key exchange becomes efficient when we are able to reuse the public keys. However, DING12 with key reuse becomes vulnerable. Therefore, corresponding countermeasures are proposed. In other words, the proposed countermeasures are important only when they are more efficient than DING12 without key reuse.

Table 10. Major time-consuming operation for various schemes

	DING12	KERK	PRKE[a]	IKERK[b]	IPRKE[c]
Gaussian sampling	6	9	3	12	4
NTT	4	6	1	10	2
Inverse NTT	2	2	2	2	2
Polynomial multiplication	4	5	4	6	6

[a] the PRKE in key reuse mode
[b] the improved KERK
[c] the improved PRKE in key reuse mode

As shown in Table 10, we compare major time-consuming operations. In DING12, both Alice and Bob have to perform 3 Gaussian sampling, 2 NTT, 1 Inverse NTT, and 2 polynomial multiplication. In the improved PRKE in key reuse mode, both Alice and Bob have to perform 2 Gaussian sampling, 1 NTT, 1 Inverse NTT, and 3 polynomial multiplication. Thus, the improved PRKE in key reuse mode is a little efficient than DING12 and it is practical.

As for the improved KERK, the major time-consuming operations are significantly more than that in DING12. Thus, the improved KERK is less efficient than DING12 and it is not practical. However, it doesn't change the communication between Alice and Bob, while the improved PRKE in key reuse mode does due to the introduction of e_p and e_p'.

In addition, compared with DING12, the improved KERK doesn't change the communication between Alice and Bob. Therefore, the security analysis of DING12 also works for the improved KERK. In [15], Gao et al. analysed the security of PRKE in Sect. 4.3 and the method can also be applied to the improved PRKE.

6 Conclusion

In this work, we have proposed a simpler key mismatch attack and apply it to KERK and PRKE, respectively. In response to key mismatch attack, we improve KERK such that Alice also constructs a new "public key" of Bob and develop an improved KERK. As s result, the improved KERK can both resist the signal leakage and key mismatch attack. In addition, the PRKE in key reuse mode can also be extended to resist key mismatch attack and we develop an improved PRKE, which is more practical.

Acknowledgements. This work is supported by the National Key Research and Development Program of China (No. 2017YFB0802000), the National Natural Science Foundation of China (No. U1536205, 61802376).

References

1. Diffie, W., Hellman, M.: New directions in cryptography. IEEE Trans. Inf. Theory **22**(6), 644–654 (1976)
2. Shor, P.W.: Algorithms for quantum computation: discrete logarithms and factoring. In: Proceedings of 35th Annual Symposium on Foundations of Computer Science 1994, pp. 124–134. IEEE (1994)
3. National Institute of Standards and Technology: Round 1 Submissions (2017). https://csrc.nist.gov/projects/post-quantum-cryptography/round-1-submissions
4. Lyubashevsky, V., Peikert, C., Regev, O.: On ideal lattices and learning with errors over rings. In: Gilbert, H. (ed.) EUROCRYPT 2010. LNCS, vol. 6110, pp. 1–23. Springer, Heidelberg (2010). https://doi.org/10.1007/978-3-642-13190-5_1
5. Ding, J., Xie, X., Lin, X.: A Simple Provably Secure Key Exchange Scheme Based on the Learning with Errors Problem. IACR Cryptology EPrint Archive, Report 2012/688 (2012)
6. Peikert, C.: Lattice cryptography for the internet. In: Mosca, M. (ed.) PQCrypto 2014. LNCS, vol. 8772, pp. 197–219. Springer, Cham (2014). https://doi.org/10.1007/978-3-319-11659-4_12
7. Bos, J.W., Costello, C., Naehrig, M., et al.: Post-quantum key exchange for the TLS protocol from the ring learning with errors problem. In: 2015 IEEE Symposium on Security and Privacy (SP) 2015, pp. 553–570. IEEE (2015)
8. Zhang, J., Zhang, Z., Ding, J., Snook, M., Dagdelen, Ö.: Authenticated key exchange from ideal lattices. In: Oswald, E., Fischlin, M. (eds.) EUROCRYPT 2015. LNCS, vol. 9057, pp. 719–751. Springer, Heidelberg (2015). https://doi.org/10.1007/978-3-662-46803-6_24
9. Alkim, E., Ducas, L., Pöppelmann, T., et al.: Post-quantum key exchange-a new hope. In: USENIX Security Symposium 2016 (2016)

10. Bos, J., Costello, C., Ducas, L., et al.: Frodo: take off the ring! practical, quantum-secure key exchange from LWE. In: Proceedings of the 2016 ACM SIGSAC Conference on Computer and Communications Security, pp. 1006–1018. ACM (2016)
11. Alkim, E., Ducas, L., Pöppelmann, T., et al.: NewHope without reconciliation. IACR Cryptology ePrint Archive Report 2016/1157 (2016)
12. Ding, J., Alsayigh, S., Lancrenon, J., RV, S., Snook, M.: Provably secure password authenticated key exchange based on rlwe for the post-quantum world. In: Handschuh, H. (ed.) CT-RSA 2017. LNCS, vol. 10159, pp. 183–204. Springer, Cham (2017). https://doi.org/10.1007/978-3-319-52153-4_11
13. Ding, J., Alsayigh, S., Saraswathy, R.V., et al.: Leakage of signal function with reused keys in RLWE key exchange. In: 2017 IEEE International Conference on Communications (ICC), pp. 1–6. IEEE (2017)
14. Rescorla, E.: The transport layer security (TLS) protocol version 1.3. (2018)
15. Gao, X., Ding, J., Li, L., et al.: Practical randomized RLWE-based key exchange against signal leakage attack. IEEE Trans. Comput. 1, 1–1 (2018)
16. Kirkwood, D., Lackey, B.C., McVey, J., et al.: Failure is not an option: standardization issues for post-quantum key agreement. In: Talk at NIST Workshop on Cybersecurity in a Post-Quantum World, vol. 2 (2015). http://www.nist.gov/itl/csd/ct/post-quantum-crypto-workshop-2015.cfm
17. Fluhrer, S.R.: Cryptanalysis of ring-LWE based key exchange with key share reuse. IACR Cryptology ePrint Archive Report 2016/85 (2016)
18. Bernstein, D.J., Groot Bruinderink, L., Lange, T., Panny, L.: HILA5 pindakaas: on the CCA security of lattice-based encryption with error correction. In: Joux, A., Nitaj, A., Rachidi, T. (eds.) AFRICACRYPT 2018. LNCS, vol. 10831, pp. 203–216. Springer, Cham (2018). https://doi.org/10.1007/978-3-319-89339-6_12
19. Ding, J., Fluhrer, S., Rv, S.: Complete attack on RLWE key exchange with reused keys, without signal leakage. In: Susilo, W., Yang, G. (eds.) ACISP 2018. LNCS, vol. 10946, pp. 467–486. Springer, Cham (2018). https://doi.org/10.1007/978-3-319-93638-3_27
20. Gao, X., Ding, J., Liu, J., Li, L.: Post-quantum secure remote password protocol from RLWE problem. In: Chen, X., Lin, D., Yung, M. (eds.) Inscrypt 2017. LNCS, vol. 10726, pp. 99–116. Springer, Cham (2018). https://doi.org/10.1007/978-3-319-75160-3_8
21. Ajtai, M.: Generating hard instances of lattice problems. In: Proceedings of the Twenty-Eighth Annual ACM Symposium on Theory of Computing, pp. 99–108. ACM (1996)
22. Brakerski, Z., Gentry, C., Vaikuntanathan, V.: (Leveled) fully homomorphic encryption without bootstrapping. ACM Trans. Comput. Theory (TOCT) 6(3), 13 (2014)
23. Brakerski, Z., Vaikuntanathan, V.: Fully homomorphic encryption from ring-LWE and security for key dependent messages. In: Rogaway, P. (ed.) CRYPTO 2011. LNCS, vol. 6841, pp. 505–524. Springer, Heidelberg (2011). https://doi.org/10.1007/978-3-642-22792-9_29
24. Applebaum, B., Cash, D., Peikert, C., Sahai, A.: Fast cryptographic primitives and circular-secure encryption based on hard learning problems. In: Halevi, S. (ed.) CRYPTO 2009. LNCS, vol. 5677, pp. 595–618. Springer, Heidelberg (2009). https://doi.org/10.1007/978-3-642-03356-8_35
25. Gao, X., Ding, J., Li, L., et al.: Efficient Implementation of Password-Based Authenticated Key Exchange from RLWE and Post-Quantum TLS. Cryptology ePrint Archive, Report 2017/1192 (2017). http://eprint.iacr.org/2017/1192

26. Saarinen, M.-J.O.: HILA5: on reliability, reconciliation, and error correction for ring-LWE encryption. In: Adams, C., Camenisch, J. (eds.) SAC 2017. LNCS, vol. 10719, pp. 192–212. Springer, Cham (2018). https://doi.org/10.1007/978-3-319-72565-9_10

27. Ding, J., Saraswathy, R.V., Alsayigh, S., et al.: How to validate the secret of a Ring Learning with Errors (RLWE) key. IACR Cryptology ePrint Archive, Report 2018/81 (2018)

28. D'Anvers, J.P., Vercauteren, F., Verbauwhede, I.: On the impact of decryption failures on the security of LWE/LWR based schemes. Cryptology ePrint Archive, Report 2018/1089 (2018). https://eprint.iacr.org/2018/1089

29. Micciancio, D., Regev, O.: Worst-case to average-case reductions based on Gaussian measures. SIAM J. Comput. **37**(1), 267–302 (2007)

30. Bauer, A, Gilbert, H., Renault, G., Rossi, M.: Assessment of the Key-Reuse Resilience of NewHope. Cryptology ePrint Archive, Report 2019/075 (2019). https://eprint.iacr.org/2019/075

Signatures

Handling Vinegar Variables to Shorten Rainbow Key Pairs

Gustavo Zambonin[✉], Matheus S. P. Bittencourt, and Ricardo Custódio

Departamento de Informática e Estatística,
Universidade Federal de Santa Catarina,
Florianópolis 88040-900, Brazil
gustavo.zambonin@posgrad.ufsc.br, matheus.spb@grad.ufsc.br,
ricardo.custodio@ufsc.br

Abstract. Multivariate quadratic equations are the basis of one of the main mathematical techniques for the creation of digital signatures that are quantum-resistant. In these schemes, the creation and verification of signatures is highly efficient. However, key sizes are quite impractical and orders of magnitude greater than conventional schemes. One of the best-known signature schemes built upon multivariate equations is called Rainbow, which is based on the Oil-Vinegar principle. We observe that the reuse of vinegar variables in the signature generation step of the Rainbow scheme leads to a shorter representation of its central map, and thus, of the entire private key. We analyse the security implications of this strategy and present a modification to the Rainbow scheme, enabling a private key size reduction of up to 85% with secure parameters. Additionally, this framework can be applied on top of already existing schemes that shorten either private or public keys, spawning derivatives that reduce the total key pair size by a factor of 3.5.

Keywords: Multivariate cryptography · Digital signatures · Rainbow

1 Introduction

Secure exchange of messages is nowadays treated as a requirement in digital systems, instead of a privilege. It is often mandatory that data is not altered in transit, that its sender is uniquely identifiable and that it cannot deny having sent the message. These notions, known as integrity, authenticity and non-repudiation, are achieved through the use of cryptographic foundations known as digital signatures. Data protected with such a method is adequate to prevent forgery and ensure confidentiality, according to Goldreich [13].

Conventional digital signature schemes are predominantly bound to one of two mathematical problems, namely integer factorisation and discrete logarithm. The most common examples are the RSA and ECDSA signature schemes [12], respectively. Nonetheless, in the wake of possible quantum adversaries, these problems are provably solvable in polynomial time, due to Shor's

© Springer Nature Switzerland AG 2019
J. Buchmann et al. (Eds.): AFRICACRYPT 2019, LNCS 11627, pp. 391–408, 2019.
https://doi.org/10.1007/978-3-030-23696-0_20

algorithm [26]. Ergo, the design of quantum-resistant, or post-quantum digital signature schemes, is indispensable to preserve secure communications in a scenario with quantum computers.

The creation of post-quantum digital signatures can be achieved through several approaches, one of which is based on systems of multivariate quadratic equations. Due to this fact, it is named multivariate cryptography, and schemes derived from this mathematical foundation are based on problems not known to be more efficiently solved by quantum computers [2]. Moreover, their signature generation and verification procedures are extremely efficient [7], since most computations rely only on simple finite field arithmetic.

It is known that multivariate cryptography hosts distinct schemes with several combinations of security parameters, signature and key pair lengths, as summarised by the authors of [8]. A balanced choice lies in the Rainbow signature scheme [9], itself a generalisation of the classic Unbalanced Oil and Vinegar (UOV) scheme [16]. It is a popular scheme, with several improvements featured in the literature, and multiple hardware implementations, *e.g.* [5,27,34]. Furthermore, it is currently featured in the second round of the standardisation process organised by the National Institute of Standards and Technology (NIST) [1].

One major drawback of multivariate cryptography, including Rainbow, is the size of private and public keys. While conventional signature schemes have key sizes that are a few bytes long, schemes based on multivariate equations feature keys that are dozens of kilobytes long. Hence, it is desired to reduce these by means of novel mathematical strategies, without decreasing the security of the scheme. Various strategies are applied to shorten keys, such as generating systems of equations represented by sparse matrices, or elements produced by cyclic recurrences. However, the security implications of such modifications are often obscure and possibly harmful.

Our Contributions. We present a general framework that can be applied to any Rainbow-like signature scheme, with the final intent of reducing private key sizes. It manipulates vinegar variables that are originally chosen randomly to successfully invert the central map. These variables are now locked into the private key, thus reducing the degree of all monomials that feature such variables, lowering the total number of field elements used to represent it by up to a factor of 6.25. To sustain our proposal, we analyse the relation between signatures and the choice of vinegar variables, security implications of this strategy and experiment on known Rainbow variants. To the best of our knowledge, Rainbow variants proposed in the literature allow the reduction of private or public keys, but not both simultaneously. We show that our proposal allows for a shorter private key without preventing modifications to the public key. Thus, by making use of known proposals to reduce public keys, we create the first Rainbow variants that reduce the total size of the key pair.

Notation. We will use the following symbols throughout this work. The symbol $\xleftarrow{\$}$ is read as "chosen randomly from", and $\approx_\varepsilon$ means that two numbers are equal within a precision of ε. A finite field $\mathbb{F}$ with order q and elements as vectors of length n is represented as $\mathbb{F}_q^n$, with q and n omitted for brevity if appropriate. The cardinality of a set S is given by $|S|$. This notation may also be used as the absolute value of an integer, if applicable. The usual function composition is given by the symbol $\circ$, and the inverse of a function f is given by f^{-1}. The usual standard deviation and mean functions for a set of elements S are respectively given by $\sigma(S)$ and $\mu(S)$.

Organisation. The next sections are organised as follows. Section 2 succinctly describes the theoretical background needed to assimilate our proposal, with a definition of the Rainbow signature scheme in Subsect. 2.1 and a review of works that already reduce keys for this scheme in Subsect. 2.2. Section 3 presents the rationale for our proposal and a formal description, alongside a security analysis. Section 4 shows the impact of our proposal when applied to the original Rainbow and variants. Finally, Sect. 5 offers our final considerations.

2 Preliminaries

2.1 Original Rainbow Signature Scheme

We will present below a description of the Rainbow signature scheme, a generalised version of the UOV scheme that reduces the length of keys and signatures. It consists of several "oil and vinegar" layers, that are combined to create a "rainbow". Consider a finite field $\mathbb{F}_q$ and $u, n \in \mathbb{N}$ where $u \leq n$. Choose a sequence of integers $v_1, \ldots, v_u$ such that $0 = v_0 < v_1 < \cdots < v_u < v_{u+1} = n$. Take the usual set $V = \{1, \ldots, n\}$ and define the vinegar variables as $V_l = \{1, \ldots, v_l\}$ for all $l \in \{1, \ldots, u\}$. Observe that $v_l = |V_l|$ and $V_1 \subset \cdots \subset V_u = V$. Oil variables are given by $O_l = \{v_l + 1, \ldots, v_{l+1}\}$. Note that $o_l = |O_l|$ and $O_l = V_{l+1} - V_l$. Let $m = n - v_1$. Now, we define vector spaces spanned by quadratic Oil-Vinegar polynomials of the form

$$P_l = \sum_{i,j \in V_l} \alpha_{ij} \cdot x_i \cdot x_j + \sum_{i \in V_l, j \in O_l} \beta_{ij} \cdot x_i \cdot x_j + \sum_{i \in V_l \cup O_l} \gamma_i \cdot x_i + \delta. \tag{1}$$

Key Generation. The central map of Rainbow is defined as $\mathcal{F} : \mathbb{F}^n \longrightarrow \mathbb{F}^m$, with the following construction: for each layer l, $F_l = (F_l^1, \ldots, F_l^{o_l}) \xleftarrow{\$} P_l$, and $\mathcal{F} = (F_1, \ldots, F_l)$. Since each sequence of vinegar variables in a layer contains all variables from the previous layer, this allows for the inversion of this map. Further, let $\mathcal{S} : \mathbb{F}^m \longrightarrow \mathbb{F}^m$ and $\mathcal{T} : \mathbb{F}^n \longrightarrow \mathbb{F}^n$ be two affine invertible maps, used as the trapdoor to this construction. Let $\mathcal{P} : \mathbb{F}^n \longrightarrow \mathbb{F}^m$ as $\mathcal{P} = \mathcal{S} \circ \mathcal{F} \circ \mathcal{T}$. Coefficients $\alpha_{ij}, \beta_{ij}, \gamma_i, \delta \in \mathbb{F}$ are chosen randomly. The private key is the triple $(\mathcal{S}, \mathcal{F}, \mathcal{T})$ and the public key is the map $\mathcal{P}$.

Signature Generation. To sign a message M, consider a cryptographic hash function $\mathcal{H} : \{0,1\}^* \longrightarrow \mathbb{F}^m$, and obtain the message digest $d = \mathcal{H}(M)$. The signature will be the set of variables which yield the solution to the equation $\mathcal{P}(x_1, \ldots, x_n) = d$. Compute $x = \mathcal{S}^{-1}(d)$. To generate $y = \mathcal{F}^{-1}(x)$, every layer must be inverted recursively. Start by randomly choosing values for $x_1, \ldots, x_{v_1}$ and inserting them into the first layer. This will bring forth a system of o_1 linear equations in $x_{v_1+1}, \ldots, x_{v_2}$. It can be solved with an algorithm such as Gaussian elimination. If the system does not have a solution, new vinegar variables have to be chosen. These solutions can then be substituted into the next layer, which will create a system of o_2 linear equations, that can be solved analogously. This procedure is repeated until all layers are solved. Finally, we compute $\sigma = \mathcal{T}^{-1}(y)$.

Signature Verification. To verify a signature, compute $d' = \mathcal{P}(\sigma)$. If $d = d'$, then the signature is valid, and invalid otherwise.

Finally, denote an instance of the scheme by Rainbow $(\mathbb{F}_q, v_1, o_1, \ldots, o_u)$. Note that when $u = 1$, we get the UOV scheme. Measured in field elements, the size of a private key is

$$|\mathcal{K}_{Pr}| = m^2 + m + n^2 + n + \sum_{k=1}^{u} o_k \cdot \left(\frac{v_k \cdot (v_k + 1)}{2} + v_k \cdot o_k + v_{k+1} + 1 \right), \quad (2)$$

whereas the size of a public key is

$$|\mathcal{K}_{Pu}| = m \cdot \frac{(n+1) \cdot (n+2)}{2}. \quad (3)$$

Further details on the construction of Rainbow may be found on [7, Section 3.3].

2.2   Related Works

Schemes based on multivariate cryptography with modifications that enable the reduction of private key sizes have been suggested even before Rainbow was created. Tame transformation schemes, such as the ones listed by Wolf and Preneel in [29], feature sparseness in their maps, a common strategy used to shorten private keys. However, these schemes were either broken, as summarised by the authors in [10], or in the case of Enhanced TTS, new parameters were suggested, and it was subsequently found to be a special case of Rainbow [28].

Additionally, there have been several published variations of Rainbow with the same goal, making use of distinct approaches. A scheme called Lite-Rainbow-0 [25] makes use of a small pseudorandom number generator (PRNG) seed to replace the private key entirely. This shortens the private key by a factor of approximately 99.8%, but greatly increases the cost for signature generation. NC-Rainbow was proposed in [31] with a novel strategy based in non-commutative rings to reduce a private key by up to 75%. However, it was shown by independent researchers to be insecure [14, 28]. Other variants called MB-Rainbow [30] and NT-Rainbow [33] employ sparseness of maps to reduce the number of terms in the private key by up to 40%.

The authors merged MB- and NC-Rainbow into a single scheme called MNT-Rainbow [32], shortening private keys by up to 76%. Nevertheless, the original schemes were deemed insecure and new parameters were suggested in [18]. It also proposes a new scheme called Circulant Rainbow, which reduces the private key by up to 45% due to the concept of rotating relations. Yet, it was broken shortly after [15].

It is also relevant to cite the approach by the authors of [21], which is, to the best of our knowledge, the main method for public key reduction without compromises to the signature size. It is summarised in several publications [20,22,24]. However, these cannot be combined with the private key improvements previously cited. Furthermore, it appears that the introduction of structures in the private key is highly threatening to the overall security of a Rainbow scheme. We will subsequently present a novel approach to these issues.

3   Our Proposal

We will describe our improvement to Rainbow-like signature schemes below, as well as supporting research on its soundness. Subsections 3.1 and 3.2 give a formal description of our modifications. In Subsect. 3.3, we look into the probability of matrices with elements in finite fields being invertible. In Subsect. 3.4, we present a statistical analysis of the structure of signatures created by our method, and finish with a security overview in Subsect. 3.5.

3.1   Modification to the Original Scheme

Our approach consists of modifications to the key and signature generation steps of Rainbow-like signature schemes. We propose to reuse the first set of vinegar variables for several signatures and replace these only when necessary, *i.e.* situations where the central map cannot be inverted and creating a signature would fail. By locking such variables and substituting them on the central map $\mathcal{F}$ early in the key generation algorithm, we create a $\mathcal{F}'$ linear in v_1, thus reducing storage requirements. This approach does not modify the underlying structure of the private key, but rather of the central map preimages.

To induce lower storage requirements for key pairs of Rainbow-like schemes, we explore constructions given in the literature and suggest general alterations to use our proposal. As per Subsect. 2.2, most variants that shorten private keys are structural in nature, that is, the key space is limited by some heuristic with the intent of producing a compact private key. Moreover, the main approach to reduce public keys [19] prevents alterations to the private key, since it indirectly generates $\mathcal{F}$ from a partial public key through linear relations between the maps.

This division of improvements is blurred by our proposal. We present general methods based on different techniques that shorten private keys in all Rainbow-like schemes. We collectively denote these by Rainbow-η and use the same definitions as in Subsect. 2.1, further denoting the vinegar variables for the first layer as $\widetilde{V}_1 = (x_1, \ldots, x_{v_1})$.

Rainbow-η_1 Key Generation. We use the fact that a PRNG has the ability to regenerate the same sequence of numbers given a seed. The choice of such a generator is outside the scope of our work, and we assume that a cryptographically secure PRNG is chosen. This approach is similar to Lite-Rainbow-0, but it is not as costly, since the private key does not need to be regenerated before every signature generation. It is best suited to environments in which an efficient generator is previously supplied.

We bound the creation of the key pair to a seed **S**. We are not aware of any Rainbow variants that disallow this practice. Thus, $\mathcal{S}$, $\mathcal{F}$ and $\mathcal{T}$, as well as the public key $\mathcal{P} = \mathcal{S} \circ \mathcal{F} \circ \mathcal{T}$ are generated through the target scheme key generation algorithm, seeded by **S**. We set $\widetilde{V}_1 \xleftarrow{\$} \mathbb{F}$, and substitute these into $\mathcal{F}$, giving $\mathcal{F}'$. According to Subsect. 3.3, in the rare case that a failure occurs in the central map inversion algorithm, we use **S** to regenerate $\mathcal{F}$, choose other values for $\widetilde{V}_1$ and create a different $\mathcal{F}'$. The private key of Rainbow-η_1 is $(\mathbf{S}, \mathcal{S}, \mathcal{F}', \mathcal{T})$ and the public key is $\mathcal{P}$.

Rainbow-η_2 Key Generation. This approach is based on the fact that a private key owner is able to recover the original $\mathcal{F}$ through the possession of all other private maps and the public key. We make use of the linear relations given by the authors of [21] and applied in the definition of the well-known CyclicRainbow scheme. A short explanation is given below, with the full rationale available in [19, Chapter 7].

Consider the public key $\mathcal{P} = \mathcal{S} \circ \mathcal{F} \circ \mathcal{T}$ and let $\mathcal{Q} = \mathcal{F} \circ \mathcal{T}$. Denote $\widetilde{Q}$ as a matrix containing only coefficients of the quadratic monomials from $\mathcal{Q}$, and define $\widetilde{F}$ and $\widetilde{P}$ similarly. Further let $\widetilde{T}$ be the matrix representation of $\mathcal{T}$, with its coefficients $t_{ij}, i, j \in \{1, \ldots, n\}$, and define $\widetilde{S}$ analogously. By fixing t_{ij}, the composition of $\mathcal{P}$ actually represents a linear relation between coefficients q_{ij}^k, f_{ij}^k of the monomial $x_i \cdot x_j$ in the k-th component of, respectively, $\mathcal{Q}$ and $\mathcal{F}$, with the form

$$q_{ij}^k = \sum_{r=1}^{n} \sum_{s=r}^{n} \alpha_{ij}^{rs} \cdot f_{rs}^k, \quad \alpha_{ij}^{rs} = \begin{cases} t_{ri} \cdot t_{si} & \text{if } i = j, \\ t_{ri} \cdot t_{sj} + t_{rj} \cdot t_{si} & \text{otherwise,} \end{cases} \tag{4}$$

$$k \in \{v_1 + 1, \ldots, n\}.$$

This can be simplified, since $\mathcal{F}$ does not allow quadratic monomials with only oil variables, and results in

$$q_{ij}^k = \sum_{r=1}^{v_l} \sum_{s=r}^{v_{l+1}} \alpha_{ij}^{rs} \cdot f_{rs}^k, \quad k \in O_l, \quad l \in \{1, \ldots, u\}. \tag{5}$$

A square matrix of order $\frac{n^2+n}{2}$ is created to further streamline the previous equations. Given a particular monomial ordering, let $A = (\alpha_{ij}^{rs})$ such that $i, j, r, s \in \{1, \ldots, n\}$, where $i \leq j$ and $r \leq s$ denote row and column indices, respectively. Thus, we have that $\widetilde{P} = \widetilde{S} \cdot \widetilde{Q}$ and $\widetilde{Q} = \widetilde{F} \cdot A^{\mathrm{T}}$. We note that the performance of this method is lower than that of Rainbow-η_1. However, it is a general technique that works on all Rainbow-like schemes.

Observe that the central map may not feature any linear or constant terms, due to the use of the above relations. This does not lower the overall security of the scheme, due to the fact that they are not multiplied with quadratic terms. With this implication in mind, the usual key generation algorithm for the target scheme is employed, yielding $(\mathcal{S}, \mathcal{F}, \mathcal{T})$ and $\mathcal{P}$ at a marginally faster rate. Substitute the sequence $\widetilde{V_1} \xleftarrow{\$} \mathbb{F}$ into $\mathcal{F}$, giving $\mathcal{F}'$. By the relations above, one is able to reconstruct $\mathcal{F}$ with no additional mechanisms if the central map inversion algorithm fails. The private key of Rainbow-η_2 is $(\mathcal{S}, \mathcal{F}', \mathcal{T})$ and the public key is $\mathcal{P}$.

Signature Generation. A digest $d = \mathcal{H}(M)$ from a message M is signed with a similar procedure. Compute $x = \mathcal{S}^{-1}(d)$, and attempt to generate $y = \mathcal{F}'^{-1}(x)$ by inverting every layer recursively. The first layer already has $\widetilde{V_1}$ set, and the remaining linear system needs only to be solved by providing appropriate values of d. It will generate a new set of vinegar variables, that can be used on the next layer, until all layers are solved. If any of the transitory systems are not solvable, a new $\widetilde{V_1}$ is chosen and $\mathcal{F}'$ regenerated, according to one of the methods given above. We finish by computing $\sigma = \mathcal{T}^{-1}(y)$.

Signature Verification. This step does not change. If $d = \mathcal{P}(\sigma)$, then the signature is valid, and invalid otherwise.

By making the first layer linear and substituting the remaining variables, the size of the private key is now

$$|\mathcal{K}^{\eta}_{Pr}| = m^2 + m + n^2 + n + |\widetilde{V_1}|$$
$$+ \sum_{k=1}^{u} o_k \cdot \left(\frac{(v_k - v_1)(v_k - v_1 + 1)}{2} + (v_k - v_1) \cdot o_k + (v_{k+1} - v_1) + 1 \right),$$
$$(6)$$

plus the additional size of $\mathbf{S}$ if the Rainbow-η_1 method is used. One needs to store $\widetilde{V_1}$, since it is part of the central map preimage, used on further map applications. The public key size does not change.

3.2 Application to the EF-CMA Variant

The Rainbow submission to the NIST standardisation process [6] presents a scheme description that diverges from the original works. The authors introduce modifications that provide security against the existential forgery under chosen-message attack (EF-CMA) model, whereas the original scheme only offers security against universal forgery. These changes are built upon the introduction of a random salt. We will briefly describe this approach, with the intent of preventing the recalculation of $\mathcal{F}'$ in the case that $\widetilde{V_1}$ is not suitable. Let us denote this method as **Rainbow-η_3**.

Key Generation. Consider $w \in \mathbb{N}$ as the length of the aforementioned salt. Generate private and public keys as per Subsect. 3.1. The private key for this scheme is $(\mathcal{S}, \mathcal{F}', \mathcal{T}, w)$, with the addition of $\mathbf{S}$ in the case of Rainbow-η_1. The public key is $(\mathcal{P}, w)$.

Signature Generation. Let $r \xleftarrow{\$} \{0,1\}^w$. The digest value is calculated as $\mathbf{d} = \mathcal{H}(\mathcal{H}(M) \parallel r)$, where M is the message. The value $x = \mathcal{S}^{-1}(\mathbf{d})$ is obtained as usual. In the rare case that the $y = \mathcal{F}'^{-1}(x)$ preimage calculation does not succeed, new variables in $\tilde{V}_1$ are chosen. However, the addition of a random salt to the original message digest alters $\mathbf{d}$ completely, due to the cryptographic hash function application. Thus, it is only necessary to generate a new r and restart the signature generation process, such that $\tilde{V}_1$, and consequently $\mathcal{F}'$, are not modified. Alternatively, if the preimage is generated successfully, we finish by letting $z = \mathcal{T}^{-1}(y)$ and $\sigma = (z, r)$.

Signature Verification. Recalculate the digest value $\mathbf{d}$. If $\mathbf{d} = \mathcal{P}(z)$, the signature is valid, and invalid otherwise.

The size of the private and public keys increase in exactly one element due to the addition of w. Real implementations of Rainbow-η_3 are tested on Sect. 4.

3.3 Invertibility of $\mathcal{F}$

Recall that, to create a Rainbow signature, the central map $\mathcal{F}$ needs to be inverted. Random guessing of vinegar variables is done in order to create a solvable linear system. It is also known that the central map is expressed as multivariate systems of equations, which can be themselves interpreted as multidimensional matrices of coefficients. Observe that, to describe these in a clearer way, a given monomial ordering is used such that only usual matrices are needed. With this in mind, we first derive the probability that a random matrix with elements in $\mathbb{F}$ is invertible.

Assume a square matrix M of order n such that $m_{ij} \in \mathbb{F}_q, i, j \in \{1, \dots, n\}$. For M to be invertible, it must be composed entirely of vectors, *i.e.* its rows $m_i \in \mathbb{F}^n$, that are linearly independent. The zero vector $(0, \dots, 0) \in \mathbb{F}^n$ is linearly dependent of all other vectors. Thus, $m_1 \neq (0, \dots, 0)$, with all other $q^n - 1$ possible vectors eligible. m_2 must not feature any of the q multiples of m_1, and $q^n - q$ vectors remain. Without loss of generality, $m_k \neq c_1 v_1 + c_2 v_2 + \cdots + c_{k-1} v_{k-1}, c_k \in \mathbb{F}$, and $q^n - q^{k-1}$ vectors can be selected. Then, the probability that all vectors chosen are linearly independent is

$$\Pi(q, n) = \prod_{k=1}^{n} \frac{q^n - q^{k-1}}{q^{-n}}$$

$$= \prod_{k=1}^{n} 1 - q^{-k}. \tag{7}$$

In the context of Rainbow, the number of layers directly influences $\Pi(q, n)$, since it dictates how many linear systems have to be solved. In other words, all square matrices of size $v_i, i \in \{1, \ldots, u\}$ need to be invertible to achieve a preimage under $\mathcal{F}$. Thus, the probability

$$\Pi(q, n, u) = \prod_{i=1}^{u} \prod_{k=1}^{v_{i+1}} 1 - q^{-k} \tag{8}$$

more accurately represents the upper bound for these chances. In the literature, the usual number of layers for a Rainbow instance is two, and we will denote this common case as $\Pi(q, n, 2) = \widetilde{\Pi}(q, n)$. Note that $\Pi(q, n, 1) = \Pi(q, n)$. Hence, schemes with more layers have a slightly lower probability of success in the signature generation preimage step.

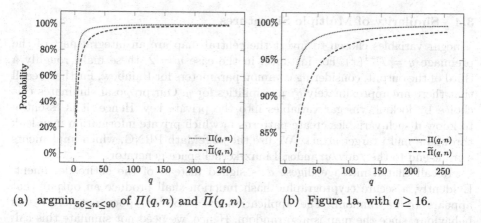

(a) $\mathrm{argmin}_{56 \leq n \leq 90}$ of $\Pi(q, n)$ and $\widetilde{\Pi}(q, n)$.   (b) Figure 1a, with $q \geq 16$.

Fig. 1. Probability of obtaining an invertible matrix, populated with field elements where $q \in \{2, \ldots 256\}$ and q is a prime power, given the quantity of layers of Rainbow.

Parameters for Rainbow are selected according to a number of restrictions, imposed by attacks that may harm the security of the scheme. Furthermore, note that the central map can be represented as square matrices of order n. Hence, we choose $n \in \{56, \ldots, 90\}$ from [19, Tables 6.4, 6.8, 6.13] and calculate the probability that a random matrix is invertible in finite fields of typical orders. For instance, $\Pi(16, 90) \approx 93.3594\%$ and $\Pi(256, 56) \approx 99.6078\%$. Figure 1 depicts the lowest probabilities computed for the appropriate range. To simulate layering, we set $v_i = i \cdot \lceil \frac{n}{u} \rceil$ and approximate to n when needed.

It is also useful to calculate $\lim_{n \to \infty} \Pi(q, n)$ to observe changes in the probability with the growth of m. Note that this is very similar to the Euler function $\phi(q)$. Ergo, we can use one of Euler's identities to redefine the above limit as

$$\Pi(q) = \sum_{k=-\infty}^{\infty} (-1)^k q^{\frac{-3 \cdot k^2 + k}{2}} \tag{9}$$

and obtain a fast approximation of the probability when n tends to infinity. We use the SageMath language arbitrary precision real numbers to obtain these values and find out that, when $n \geq 56$, $\Pi(q) \approx_{10^{-18}} \Pi(q, n)$ and $\widetilde{\Pi}(q) \approx_{10^{-8}} \widetilde{\Pi}(q, n)$. Thus, Fig. 1 also accurately reflects the behaviour of $\Pi(q)$, *i.e.*, current values of n already reach effective upper bounds for this probability.

If we consider that the two-dimensional coefficient matrix of $\mathcal{F}$ has an effective size of $\frac{n^2+n}{2}$ due to the aforementioned monomial ordering strategy, we note that the inversion event happens almost surely. This evidence shows that computing a preimage in order to sign a message happens at the first try with high probability in a wide range of Rainbow configurations. Therefore, the cost of a central map reconfiguration, in the case that chosen vinegar variables do not lead to an invertible central map, is amortised by the overwhelming probability that a signature is successfully generated.

3.4   Similarity of Multiple Signatures

Vinegar variables chosen to invert the central map are an integral part of the preimage $y = \mathcal{F}^{-1}(x)$. For instance, in the case $u = 2$, these make roughly a third of the output, considering common parameters for Rainbow. Further, recall that there are approximately q^v possibilities for y. Our proposal eliminates this choice by locking vinegar variables into the private key. Hence, it is essential to know if such variables create patterns in which private information may leak through a multi-target attack. We use the SageMath PRNG, which implements a front-end to the /dev/urandom Linux kernel space generator.

Recall that a message digest d is signed instead of the entire document. Evidently, a secure cryptographic hash function shall produce an output that appears to be random. The application $x = \mathcal{S}^{-1}(d)$ does not affect this behaviour, since the map is also random. Hence, we need not simulate this calculation in this analysis. According to Subsect. 3.3, the inversion $y = \mathcal{F}^{-1}(x)$ creates a valid preimage with overwhelming probability, where the first v_1 elements of any y will be the same.

We observe the distribution of field elements in vectors after the final function application, that is, $z = \mathcal{T}^{-1}(y)$. Let $Z'_t = (z_1, \ldots, z_t) \xleftarrow{\$} \mathbb{F}^n, t \in \mathbb{N}$ be a t-uple of "signatures". We build the sequence $Z_t = (z_1^1, z_1^2, \ldots, z_1^n, z_2^1, \ldots, z_t^{n-1}, z_t^n)$. When part of the vector y is fixed, we will instead denote these by $\widetilde{Z}'_t$ and $\widetilde{Z}_t$. Our hypothesis is that Z_t and $\widetilde{Z}_t$ will behave similarly to observations sampled from the discrete uniform distribution $\mathcal{U}\{0, q-1\}$. It is known that its standard deviation, where r values are observed in an equally likely manner, is equal to $\sqrt{\frac{r^2-1}{12}}$. For a finite field $\mathbb{F}$, we set $r = q$ and obtain the desired value. It is expected that

$$\lim_{t \to \infty} \sigma(\widetilde{Z}_t) = \sqrt{\frac{q^2 - 1}{12}}, \tag{10}$$

suggesting that greater values of n and t approximate faster to the theorised standard deviation.

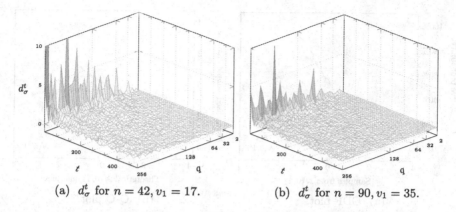

(a) d_σ^t for $n = 42, v_1 = 17$.   (b) d_σ^t for $n = 90, v_1 = 35$.

Fig. 2. Difference of standard deviations when $t \in \{1, \ldots, 1024\}$, and $q \in \{2, \ldots, 256\}$ with q as a prime power.

Let us denote the absolute difference between standard deviations for a value t as $d_\sigma^t = |\sigma(Z_t) - \sigma(\widetilde{Z}_t)|$. Figure 2 shows the amplitude of such values for various values of q and t. We note that the largest values of d_σ^t occur for finite fields of higher orders and lower t. For instance, given the finite field $\mathbb{F}_{223}^{42}$, we have $d_\sigma^1 \approx 8.25$, and for a slightly higher t, we obtain a much lower value $d_\sigma^{11} \approx 0.24$. This behaviour is also observed within absolute differences of means, defined analogously as d_μ^t. The field $\mathbb{F}_{191}^{42}$ gives the values $d_\mu^1 \approx 5.31$ and, comparatively, $d_\mu^9 \approx 1.14$.

The comparison of expected and obtained standard deviations and means in our experiments, gives positive results and confirms the law of large numbers. Still, it is interesting to look at the diffusion of values within $\widetilde{Z}_t$ and infer that it does not simply simulate the mean and standard deviation for a known discrete uniform. We count the amount of values for each class $k \in \{0, \ldots, q - 1\}$ and refer to them by $Z_{t,k}$ and $\widetilde{Z}_{t,k}$. By the central limit theorem, these counts should be normally distributed.

Figure 3 shows the cumulative distribution function (CDF) plot and the Q-Q (quantile-quantile) plot for such samples. The expected CDF, as well as examples for Z_t and $\widetilde{Z}_t$, show that all values are fairly distributed, with small variations due to the random generation of field elements. However, we note that this is due to the low number of classes, *i.e.* the order of the finite field, and experimentally confirm that such discrepancies are largely reduced with $q = 2^{10}$. This is further confirmed by the Q-Q plot created with rankits, where the points are sufficiently close to the $y = x$ expected line.

Our argument indicates that, even if part of the preimage created by the central map is fixed, the remaining affine map application disrupts this pattern with high efficacy. Hence, an attacker with possession of multiple signatures created by our method would not be more capable of forging a new signature or deducing private information.

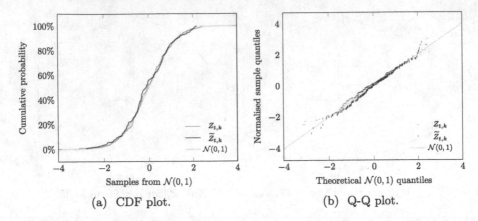

(a) CDF plot.   (b) Q-Q plot.

Fig. 3. Distribution of counts of elements in Z_t and $\widetilde{Z}_t$ such that $t = 2^{16}$ for $\mathbb{F}_{256}^{90}$.

3.5   Security Analysis

A variety of attacks currently thwart the security of Rainbow-like signature schemes if parameters are not chosen carefully. We will briefly state each of those, along with their estimated complexities [23], and argue that our methods do not facilitate such attacks.

Direct Attack. An attacker with possession of a digest d and the public key $\mathcal{P}$ tries to solve $\mathcal{P}(x) = d$. This is done by fixing some of the variables and applying an algorithm built upon the theory of Gröbner basis, such as the Hybrid approach [3]. While it is hard to pinpoint the exact running time of such methods, the authors give an estimation of its asymptotic complexity in Eq. 5 of the aforementioned work.

UOV Attack. The multi-layer approach of Rainbow does not hinder attacks that also work on the UOV signature scheme. This attack was originally created by Kipnis and Shamir [17] to break the Balanced Oil-Vinegar scheme. The objective of this attack is to obtain an equivalent private key by means of finding the preimage of a specific oil subspace under the map $\mathcal{T}$. The complexity of the generalised attack for unbalanced schemes [16] is $o_u^4 \cdot q^{n-1-2 \cdot o_u}$ field multiplications.

MinRank Attack. All systems of polynomials in the public key $\mathcal{P}$ may be individually represented as matrices. This attack consists in finding linear combinations of these, such that they have a lesser rank than v_2, in the case of Rainbow. This allows an attacker to isolate the central map polynomials from the first layer of Rainbow, and analogously recover the remaining layers with a much lower effort. In the context of Rainbow [4], its complexity is $q^{v_1+1} \cdot m \cdot \left(\frac{n^2}{2} - \frac{m^2}{6}\right)$ field multiplications.

HighRank Attack. In a similar way to MinRank, linear combinations of public key matrices are used to find the variables which appear the lowest number of times in the central map. This is used to identify the last Rainbow layer, and obtain the previous layers similarly. The complexity of the improved attack [11] is $q^{o_u} \cdot \frac{n^3}{6}$ field multiplications.

Rainbow-Band-Separation Attack. An extension of the UOV-Reconciliation attack by the same authors [11] that targets Rainbow, with the intent of producing an equivalent private key. It explores the fact that the central map matrix representation is composed of zeroes on its lower right corner. These yield quadratic equations which, if solved, lead to an alternative private key. The complexity of this attack is given by the hardness of solving a large system of equations, as seen above, is hard to estimate.

Side-Channel Attacks. It may be observed that none of the proposed Rainbow variants, as well as the original scheme, present constant time signature generation algorithms. Particularly, in Rainbow-η_2, a considerable amount of computation is added to the signature algorithm when one of the systems is not solvable. In a chosen message attack, one may observe the time spent on multiple signature generation steps and easily check if the linear systems are solvable, thus obtaining information about the central map. Although there are no known attacks that make use of this technique, it is possible that there may exist information leaks when applying our methods to Rainbow-like schemes.

We do not discard the possibility that specialised attacks exist, particularly ones that take in account multiple signatures, due to our fixing of vinegar variables. However, we have seen in Subsect. 3.4 that signatures generated by our method are comparably random with respect to conventional Rainbow signatures. Furthermore, we note that most attacks look for special structures within the private key. While our methods indeed modify the private key representation, it is still present in its entirety on the public key composition, which is the only information available to malicious entities that can be possibly used to forge signatures. We thus suggest that the right choice of parameters is made whenever our methods are applied, *e.g.* according to [23], to protect the scheme instance against these attacks.

4   Enhancement of Existing Schemes

Our method does not depend on special structures inserted on the private key. Consequently, it can be applied to all known Rainbow-like schemes. We experiment with several sets of parameters and observe the reduction of private keys. It is known that there are various limitations for the choice of parameters that lead to secure instances of Rainbow [23]. We implement several known guidelines and confirm that our proposal does indeed work for a large range of parameters. However, we only show results for known secure parameter sets to prevent accidental endorsement of untested, and possibly insecure, instances.

Table 1. Reduction of Rainbow key sizes, in bytes, for various instances of the scheme.

Instance	Parameters	n	m	$|\mathcal{K}_{Pr}|$	$|\mathcal{K}_{Pr}^{\eta}|$	Difference
I-a	$(\mathbb{F}_{16}, 32, 32, 32)$	96	64	100208	33152	-66.92%
I-b	$(\mathbb{F}_{31}, 36, 28, 28)$	92	56	114308	31676	-72.29%
I-c	$(\mathbb{F}_{256}, 40, 24, 24)$	88	48	143384	33024	-76.97%
III-b	$(\mathbb{F}_{31}, 64, 32, 48)$	144	80	409463	87628	-78.60%
III-c	$(\mathbb{F}_{256}, 68, 36, 36)$	140	72	537780	99656	-81.47%
IV-a	$(\mathbb{F}_{16}, 56, 48, 48)$	152	96	376140	103336	-72.53%
V-c	$(\mathbb{F}_{256}, 92, 48, 48)$	188	96	1274316	218984	-82.82%
VI-a	$(\mathbb{F}_{16}, 76, 64, 64)$	204	128	892078	233044	-73.88%
VI-b	$(\mathbb{F}_{31}, 84, 56, 56)$	196	112	1016868	217244	-78.64%
P-080	$(\mathbb{F}_{256}, 17, 17, 9)$	43	26	19208	5914	-69.21%
P-100	$(\mathbb{F}_{256}, 26, 22, 21)$	69	43	75440	23193	-69.26%
P-128	$(\mathbb{F}_{256}, 36, 28, 15)$	79	43	103704	22110	-78.68%
P-192	$(\mathbb{F}_{256}, 63, 46, 22)$	131	68	440638	71773	-83.71%
P-256	$(\mathbb{F}_{256}, 85, 63, 30)$	178	93	1086971	164721	-84.85%

We show results for the application of our method in Table 1, considering the following Rainbow instances. Conservative choices were made by the Rainbow submission authors [6] to fit security categories as requested by NIST. We apply our method to these recent proposals, and additionally choose parameters from Petzoldt [19, Table 6.12] for further comparison. The latter are named P-ℓ, where ℓ is the security level in bits. Indeed, the choice of v_1 remarkably affects the results. Moreover, a minimal value of o_u is also known to further reduce the private key size. Indeed, we suggest that $v_1 \geq o_u$ as much as possible to maximise the results of our method. However, we remark that one must set sufficient parameters for o_i such that the scheme still resists direct and UOV attacks.

The case of Rainbow variants is slightly more convoluted. Schemes claim optimisations of the private key often through the inclusion of inner structuring. To measure the impact of our method within the context of these schemes, it is imperative to understand such structures. For instance, it may be the case that a method introduces sparseness related to specific vinegar variables. Thus, the reduction would not be equally distributed over the private key elements and, as such, our method would have its efficiency reduced.

To the best of our knowledge, the schemes presented in Subsect. 2.2 feature changes that target the whole private key evenly. Hence, our method would yield similar results to those in Table 1 if this assumption is true. However, it is also the case that some variants were subsequently broken or new parameters were suggested. We will thus consider only schemes that reduce the public key size, *i.e.* CyclicRainbow [22] and RainbowLRS2 [19, Section 9.2].

Table 2. Total reduction of Rainbow key pairs, in bytes, for variants of the scheme.

Instance	Parameters	Variant	$|\mathcal{K}_{Pr}|$	$|\mathcal{K}_{Pr}^{\eta}|$	$|\mathcal{K}_{Pu}|$	Difference
P-080	$(\mathbb{F}_{256}, 17, 13, 13)$	Classic	19546	6524	25740	-28.76%
		Cyclic			10618	-62.15%
		LRS2			9789	-63.98%
P-100	$(\mathbb{F}_{256}, 26, 16, 17)$	Classic	46131	12474	60390	-31.60%
		Cyclic			22246	-67.41%
		LRS2			20662	-68.89%
P-128	$(\mathbb{F}_{256}, 36, 21, 22)$	Classic	105006	24924	139320	-32.78%
		Cyclic			48411	-69.98%
		LRS2			45547	-71.16%

We compare the total key pair sizes $|\mathcal{K}_{Pr}| + |\mathcal{K}_{Pu}|$ when our method is used alongside Rainbow variants that reduce the public key size. Table 2 shows the quantity of field elements for sets of parameters from Petzoldt [19, Table 9.8]. We calculate $|\mathcal{K}_{Pu}|$ for the variants according to Eqs. 9.2 and 9.4 of the same work, and as per its Remark 9.1, note that $q = 16$ and $q = 31$ are not considered due to a security restriction of RainbowLRS2. We obtain positive results, with key pair size reductions of up to factors of 3 and no security harm to the resulting scheme.

The use of CyclicRainbow or RainbowLRS2 with the Rainbow-η_2 method is recommended. These variants are based on the linear relations described in Subsect. 3.1, and resulting implementations may be effortlessly modified to use our proposal. Moreover, in the case that higher parameters are needed, *e.g.* a security level of 256 bits, we note that the key pair will be reduced more aggressively. Thus, our results reflect changes over a wide variety of platforms and possible Rainbow deployments that benefit from lower storage requirements.

We also briefly discuss the effect of these changes on the signature generation step overall performance. In the case of Rainbow-η_1, it does not vary greatly due to the fast regeneration of the central map elements from a given PRNG and $\mathbf{S}$. On the other hand, Rainbow-η_2 uses elaborate techniques to reconstruct the central map if vinegar variables are not suitable. This process is not without cost, and it may negatively affect the average signature generation time. Still, by making use of Rainbow-η_3, these computations are entirely avoided by choosing a new salt instead of new vinegar variables, reducing the inherent overhead.

5   Conclusion

Throughout this work, we have proposed general methods to lower private key sizes that can be applied to all known Rainbow variants. We suggest fixing the first sequence of vinegar variables and reuse it on the creation of signatures, reducing the static central map storage requirements, and thus obtaining a smaller private key. Our security analysis shows that this modification creates orderly signatures and does not harm the target scheme. Furthermore, we have also addressed the problem in which no scheme could reduce both keys in the key pair, by applying our proposal to known variants that reduce the public key size. We obtain gains of up to 85% on the private key size and 71% on the total key pair size.

We propose some topics to extend this work. Evidently, it is crucial for the security of our proposal that multiple signatures do not leak information for the chosen vinegar variables. Thus, we point out that further security analysis on multi-target and side-channel attacks is desirable. We also observe that our methods directly affect the signature generation performance, since the first layer computations are moved to the key generation step. As such, we suggest that measurements are made considering the average time for signature generation, in the case that the private key has to be recomputed due to a new choice of vinegar variables.

Acknowledgements. This study was financed in part by the Coordenação de Aperfeiçoamento de Pessoal de Nível Superior - Brasil (CAPES) - Finance Code 001. Additionally, we thank the anonymous referees for their suggestions.

References

1. Alagic, G., et al.: Status Report on the First Round of the NIST Post-Quantum Cryptography Standardization Process. Internal Report 8240, National Institute of Standards and Technology (NIST), January 2019. https://doi.org/10.6028/NIST.IR.8240
2. Bernstein, D.J., Buchmann, J., Dahmen, E.: Post Quantum Cryptography, 1st edn. Springer, Heidelberg (2008)
3. Bettale, L., Faugére, J.C., Perret, L.: Solving polynomial systems over finite fields: improved analysis of the hybrid approach. In: Proceedings of the 37th International Symposium on Symbolic and Algebraic Computation, pp. 67–74, July 2012. https://doi.org/10.1145/2442829.2442843
4. Billet, O., Gilbert, H.: Cryptanalysis of Rainbow. In: De Prisco, R., Yung, M. (eds.) SCN 2006. LNCS, vol. 4116, pp. 336–347. Springer, Heidelberg (2006). https://doi.org/10.1007/11832072_23
5. Czypek, W.: Implementing Multivariate Quadratic Public Key Signature Schemes on Embedded Devices. Master's thesis, Ruhr-Universität Bochum, April 2012
6. Ding, J., Chen, M.S., Petzoldt, A., Schmidt, D., Yang, B.Y.: Rainbow - Algorithm Specification and Documentation. Round 1 Submission, NIST Post-Quantum Cryptography Standardisation Process, December 2017
7. Ding, J., Gower, J., Schmidt, D.: Multivariate Public Key Cryptosystems, 1st edn. Springer, Boston (2006). https://doi.org/10.1007/978-0-387-36946-4
8. Ding, J., Petzoldt, A.: Current state of multivariate cryptography. IEEE Secur. Priv. **15**(4), 28–36 (2017). https://doi.org/10.1109/MSP.2017.3151328
9. Ding, J., Schmidt, D.: Rainbow, a new multivariable polynomial signature scheme. In: Ioannidis, J., Keromytis, A., Yung, M. (eds.) ACNS 2005. LNCS, vol. 3531, pp. 164–175. Springer, Heidelberg (2005). https://doi.org/10.1007/11496137_12

10. Ding, J., Schmidt, D., Yin, Z.: Cryptanalysis of the new TTS scheme in CHES 2004. Int. J. Inf. Secur. 5(4), 231–240 (2006). https://doi.org/10.1007/s10207-006-0003-9

11. Ding, J., Yang, B.-Y., Chen, C.-H.O., Chen, M.-S., Cheng, C.-M.: New differential-algebraic attacks and reparametrization of rainbow. In: Bellovin, S.M., Gennaro, R., Keromytis, A., Yung, M. (eds.) ACNS 2008. LNCS, vol. 5037, pp. 242–257. Springer, Heidelberg (2008). https://doi.org/10.1007/978-3-540-68914-0_15

12. von zur Gathen, J.: CryptoSchool, 1st edn. Springer, Heidelberg (2015). https://doi.org/10.1007/978-3-662-48425-8

13. Goldreich, O.: Foundations of Cryptography: Volume 2, Basic Applications, 1st edn. Cambridge University Press (2004)

14. Hashimoto, Y.: Cryptanalysis of the quaternion rainbow. In: Sakiyama, K., Terada, M. (eds.) IWSEC 2013. LNCS, vol. 8231, pp. 244–257. Springer, Heidelberg (2013). https://doi.org/10.1007/978-3-642-41383-4_16

15. Hashimoto, Y.: On the security of Circulant UOV/Rainbow. Cryptology ePrint Archive, Report 2018/847, October 2018. https://eprint.iacr.org/2018/947

16. Kipnis, A., Patarin, J., Goubin, L.: Unbalanced oil and vinegar signature schemes. In: Stern, J. (ed.) EUROCRYPT 1999. LNCS, vol. 1592, pp. 206–222. Springer, Heidelberg (1999). https://doi.org/10.1007/3-540-48910-X_15

17. Kipnis, A., Shamir, A.: Cryptanalysis of the oil and vinegar signature scheme. In: Krawczyk, H. (ed.) CRYPTO 1998. LNCS, vol. 1462, pp. 257–266. Springer, Heidelberg (1998). https://doi.org/10.1007/BFb0055733

18. Peng, Z., Tang, S.: Circulant rainbow: a new rainbow variant with shorter private key and faster signature generation. IEEE Access 5, 11877–11886 (2017). https://doi.org/10.1109/ACCESS.2017.2717279

19. Petzoldt, A.: Selecting and Reducing Key Sizes for Multivariate Cryptography. Ph.D. thesis, Technische Universität Darmstadt, July 2013

20. Petzoldt, A., Bulygin, S.: Linear recurring sequences for the UOV key generation revisited. In: Kwon, T., Lee, M.-K., Kwon, D. (eds.) ICISC 2012. LNCS, vol. 7839, pp. 441–455. Springer, Heidelberg (2013). https://doi.org/10.1007/978-3-642-37682-5_31

21. Petzoldt, A., Bulygin, S., Buchmann, J.: A multivariate signature scheme with a partially cyclic public key. In: Faugère, J.C., Cid, C. (eds.) International Conference on Symbolic Computation and Cryptography, pp. 229–235, June 2010

22. Petzoldt, A., Bulygin, S., Buchmann, J.: CyclicRainbow – a multivariate signature scheme with a partially cyclic public key. In: Gong, G., Gupta, K.C. (eds.) INDOCRYPT 2010. LNCS, vol. 6498, pp. 33–48. Springer, Heidelberg (2010). https://doi.org/10.1007/978-3-642-17401-8_4

23. Petzoldt, A., Bulygin, S., Buchmann, J.: Selecting parameters for the rainbow signature scheme. In: Sendrier, N. (ed.) PQCrypto 2010. LNCS, vol. 6061, pp. 218–240. Springer, Heidelberg (2010). https://doi.org/10.1007/978-3-642-12929-2_16

24. Petzoldt, A., Bulygin, S., Buchmann, J.: Linear recurring sequences for the UOV key generation. In: Catalano, D., Fazio, N., Gennaro, R., Nicolosi, A. (eds.) PKC 2011. LNCS, vol. 6571, pp. 335–350. Springer, Heidelberg (2011). https://doi.org/10.1007/978-3-642-19379-8_21

25. Shim, K.-A., Park, C.-M., Baek, Y.-J.: Lite-Rainbow: lightweight signature schemes based on multivariate quadratic equations and their secure implementations. In: Biryukov, A., Goyal, V. (eds.) INDOCRYPT 2015. LNCS, vol. 9462, pp. 45–63. Springer, Cham (2015). https://doi.org/10.1007/978-3-319-26617-6_3

26. Shor, P.W.: Polynomial-time algorithms for prime factorization and discrete logarithms on a quantum computer. SIAM J. Comput. **26**(5), 1484–1509 (1997). https://doi.org/10.1137/S0097539795293172

27. Tang, S., Yi, H., Ding, J., Chen, H., Chen, G.: High-speed hardware implementation of rainbow signature on FPGAs. In: Yang, B.-Y. (ed.) PQCrypto 2011. LNCS, vol. 7071, pp. 228–243. Springer, Heidelberg (2011). https://doi.org/10.1007/978-3-642-25405-5_15

28. Thomae, E., Wolf, C.: Cryptanalysis of enhanced TTS, STS and all its variants, or: why cross-terms are important. In: Mitrokotsa, A., Vaudenay, S. (eds.) AFRICACRYPT 2012. LNCS, vol. 7374, pp. 188–202. Springer, Heidelberg (2012). https://doi.org/10.1007/978-3-642-31410-0_12

29. Wolf, C., Preneel, B.: Taxonomy of Public Key Schemes based on the problem of Multivariate Quadratic equations. Cryptology ePrint Archive, Report 2005/077, March 2005. https://eprint.iacr.org/2005/077

30. Yasuda, T., Ding, J., Takagi, T., Sakurai, K.: A variant of rainbow with shorter secret key and faster signature generation. In: Chen, K., Xie, Q., Qiu, W., Xu, S., Zhao, Y. (eds.) ACM Workshop on Asia Public-Key Cryptography, pp. 57–62, May 2013. https://doi.org/10.1145/2484389.2484401

31. Yasuda, T., Sakurai, K., Takagi, T.: Reducing the key size of rainbow using non-commutative rings. In: Dunkelman, O. (ed.) CT-RSA 2012. LNCS, vol. 7178, pp. 68–83. Springer, Heidelberg (2012). https://doi.org/10.1007/978-3-642-27954-6_5

32. Yasuda, T., Takagi, T., Sakurai, K.: Efficient variant of Rainbow using sparse secret keys. J. Wirel. Mob. Netw. Ubiquitous Comput. Dependable Appl. **5**(3), 3–13 (2014)

33. Yasuda, T., Takagi, T., Sakurai, K.: Efficient variant of rainbow without triangular matrix representation. In: Mahendra, M.S., Neuhold, E.J., Tjoa, M.A., You, I. (eds.) Information and Communication Technology. LNCS, vol. 8407, pp. 532–541. Springer, Heidelberg (2014). https://doi.org/10.1007/978-3-642-55032-4_55

34. Yi, H., Tang, S.: Very small FPGA processor for multivariate signatures. Comput. J. **59**(7), 1091–1101 (2016). https://doi.org/10.1093/comjnl/bxw008

Further Lower Bounds
for Structure-Preserving Signatures
in Asymmetric Bilinear Groups

Essam Ghadafi[✉]

University of the West of England, Bristol, UK
essam.ghadafi@uwe.ac.uk

Abstract. Structure-Preserving Signatures (SPSs) are a useful tool for the design of modular cryptographic protocols. Recent series of works have shown that by limiting the message space of those schemes to the set of Diffie-Hellman (DH) pairs, it is possible to circumvent the known lower bounds in the Type-3 bilinear group setting thus obtaining the shortest signatures consisting of only 2 elements from the shorter source group. It has been shown that such a variant yields efficiency gains for some cryptographic constructions, including attribute-based signatures and direct anonymous attestation. Only the cases of signing a single DH pair or a DH pair and a vector from $\mathbb{Z}_p$ have been considered. Signing a vector of group elements is required for various applications of SPSs, especially if the aim is to forgo relying on heuristic assumptions.

An open question is whether such an improved lower bound also applies to signing a vector of $\ell > 1$ messages. We answer this question negatively for schemes existentially unforgeable under an adaptive chosen-message attack (EUF-CMA) whereas we answer it positively for schemes existentially unforgeable under a random-message attack (EUF-RMA) and those which are existentially unforgeable under a combined chosen-random-message attack (EUF-CMA-RMA). The latter notion is a leeway between the two former notions where it allows the adversary to adaptively choose part of the message to be signed whereas the remaining part of the message is chosen uniformly at random by the signer.

Another open question is whether strongly existentially unforgeable under an adaptive chosen-message attack (sEUF-CMA) schemes with 2-element signatures exist. We answer this question negatively, proving it is impossible to construct sEUF-CMA schemes with 2-element signatures even if the signature consists of elements from both source groups. On the other hand, we prove that sEUF-RMA and sEUF-CMA-RMA schemes with 2-element (unilateral) signatures are possible by giving constructions for those notions.

Among other things, our findings show a gap between random-message/combined chosen-random-message security and chosen-message security in this setting.

Keywords: Digital signatures · Bilinear groups · Structure-preserving

© Springer Nature Switzerland AG 2019
J. Buchmann et al. (Eds.): AFRICACRYPT 2019, LNCS 11627, pp. 409–428, 2019.
https://doi.org/10.1007/978-3-030-23696-0_21

1 Introduction

Structure-Preserving Signatures (SPSs) [4] are signature schemes over bilinear groups where the messages, the verification key and the signatures consist of only group elements from either/both source groups. Verification of signatures in those schemes only involves evaluating Pairing-Product Equations (PPEs) and checking group memberships. Such properties make them compatible with widely used constructs such as ElGamal encryption [22] and Groth-Sahai proofs [37]. Hence, they are an ideal building block for designing cryptographic protocols not relying on heuristic assumptions such as random oracles [25]. They have numerous applications which include group signatures, e.g [4,41], blind signatures, e.g. [4,27], attribute-based signatures, e.g. [24], tightly secure encryption, e.g. [3,38], malleable signatures, e.g. [12], anonymous credentials, e.g. [18,26], network coding, e.g. [12], oblivious transfer, e.g. [34], direct anonymous attestation, e.g. [15,31], and e-cash, e.g. [13].

Related Work. The notion was coined by Abe et al. [4] but earlier constructions conforming to the definition were given by [34,35]. The notion has been extensively studied. Constructions in the Type-3 setting (cf. Sect. 2.1) include [4,5,7,20,30,32,33,36]. Abe et al. [5] proved that signatures of schemes over Type-3 bilinear groups must contain at least 3 elements, which must include elements from both source groups, and require at least 2 PPEs for verification. This ruled out the existence of schemes with unilateral signatures, i.e. where all signature's components are from one of the source groups. Constructions relying on non-interactive assumptions were given by [2,3,9,17,19,29,39–41]. Abe et al. [6] proved that it is impossible to base the security of an optimal Type-3 scheme (i.e. with 3-element signatures) on non-interactive intractability assumptions. This in essence means that schemes based on non-interactive assumptions cannot be as efficient as their counterparts relying on interactive assumptions or those proven secure directly in the generic group model [44,45]. More recently, Abe et al. [1] proved lower bounds for schemes signing bilateral messages and based on non-interactive intractability assumptions.

Ghadafi [31] gave a randomizable scheme which can only sign a single Diffie-Hellman pair (cf. Sect. 2.1) yielding 3-element unilateral signatures and requiring the evaluation of 2 PPEs, excluding the cost for checking the well-formedness of the message, to verify signatures. More recently, Ghadafi [32] gave constructions for a single Diffie-Hellman pair yielding signatures consisting of only 2 elements from the shorter source group and requiring besides checking the well-formedness of the message, the evaluation of a single PPE for verification. He argued that restricting the message space to the set of Diffie-Hellman pairs does not restrict applicability of the schemes and used direct anonymous attestation [16], which is a protocol deployed in practice, and attribute-based signatures [42] as an example. Even though [32] gave a partially structure-preserving scheme which can sign a vector of field elements along the single Diffie-Hellman pair, it was left as an open problem to investigate the case of structure-preserving signatures for a vector of group elements. More recently, Ghadafi [33] gave EUF-CMA constructions for a vector of DH pairs with 2-element bilateral signatures.

Constructions in the Type-2 setting (where an efficiently computable unidirectional homomorphism between the source groups exists) were given in [1,8,14,20].

Fully structure-preserving schemes where even the secret key consists of only group elements from the source groups were recently given by [10,36,47].

Motivation and Contribution. Many applications of SPSs require signing a vector of group elements. For instance, consider the case when certifying the public keys of encryption or signature schemes. This is, for instance, required for constructing various variants of anonymous signatures, including group signatures [21], attribute-based signatures [42], proxy signatures [43], k-times anonymous authentication [46], and direct anonymous attestation [16]. This is particularly important when the aim is to dispense with relying on random oracles as in such cases one cannot use standard signature schemes which hinder the structure of the message, e.g. by hashing or requiring knowledge of their discrete logarithm. Therefore, the design of efficient SPS schemes for a vector of messages would have implications for various applications.

SPS schemes on Diffie-Hellman pairs have rendered themselves as a tool to get around the known lower bounds for SPS schemes thus improving efficiency without being too restrictive as they suffice for many applications of SPS schemes. Examples of where SPS schemes on Diffie-Hellman pairs provide better efficiency than optimal SPS schemes on unilateral messages include [23,32]. Also, as argued by [32], optimal SPS schemes on Diffie-Hellman pairs outperform some widely used non-structure-preserving schemes in terms of efficiency.

Note that the size of the elements of one of the source groups is twice as large as that of those from the other source group and hence having schemes with 2-element unilateral signatures from the shorter source group is desirable. A first intriguing open question is whether EUF-CMA SPS schemes for a vector of group elements with 2-element unilateral signatures are possible. We answer this question negatively by proving the impossibility of the existence of such schemes. However, we show that EUF-RMA and EUF-CMA-RMA (cf. Sect. 2.2) schemes are possible. The latter is a leeway between EUF-RMA and EUF-CMA where it allows the adversary to adaptively choose some part of the message whereas the remaining part of the message is chosen uniformly at random by the signer. While EUF-RMA and EUF-CMA-RMA are both weaker notions than EUF-CMA since unlike the latter, they restrict part of the message to being chosen uniformly at random, we envisage that EUF-CMA-RMA may suffice to replace EUF-CMA for some applications. Consider, for instance, κ-times anonymous authentication schemes [43], where an authority provides users with κ credentials which allow them to anonymously authenticate themselves κ times. The underlying idea for some of the existing constructions is that the credential is a signature by the authority on the user's public key/ID along with a random element chosen by the authority. EUF-CMA-RMA signature schemes may suffice to replace EUF-CMA schemes for such applications.

Another open question is whether strongly existentially unforgeable schemes under an adaptive chosen-message attack (sEUF-CMA) with 2-element (whether unilateral or bilateral) signatures exist. Strong unforgeability is essential for various applications, e.g. [11]. Optimal Type-3 sEUF-CMA schemes for unilateral messages, e.g. [7,20,36], have a lower bound of 3-element bilateral signatures, thus, investigating whether the improved lower bound that exploits a special structure of the message also applies to strong unforgeability would have implications for various applications of SPS schemes. We prove that sEUF-CMA schemes with 2-element signatures are not possible. This holds even if the signature is bilateral. On the other hand, we show that sEUF-RMA and sEUF-CMA-RMA schemes with 2-element (unilateral) signatures exist by giving constructions.

Our results highlight a gap between random-message/combined chosen-random-message security and chosen-message security in this setting.

Paper Organization. We provide some preliminary definitions in Sect. 2. In Sect. 3 we prove the impossibility of the existence of EUF-CMA schemes for a vector of $\ell > 1$ messages with 2-element unilateral signatures. In Sect. 4 we prove the impossibility of the existence of sEUF-CMA schemes with 2-element signatures regardless of whether the signatures are unilateral or bilateral. Finally, in Sect. 5 we construct a sEUF-CMA-RMA scheme for a vector of messages with 2-element unilateral signatures.

Notation. We write $y = A(x; r)$ when algorithm A on input x and randomness r outputs y. We write $y \leftarrow A(x)$ for the process of setting $y = A(x; r)$ where r is sampled at random. We also write $y \leftarrow S$ for sampling y uniformly at random from a set S. A function $\nu(.) : \mathbb{N} \rightarrow \mathbb{R}^+$ is negligible (in n) if for every polynomial $p(.)$ and all sufficiently large values of n, it holds that $\nu(n) < \frac{1}{p(n)}$. By PPT we mean running in probabilistic polynomial time in the relevant security parameter. We use $[k]$ to denote the set $\{1, \ldots, k\}$.

2 Preliminaries

In this section we provide some preliminary definitions.

2.1 Bilinear Groups

A bilinear group is a tuple $\mathcal{P} := (\mathbb{G}, \mathbb{H}, \mathbb{T}, p, G, \tilde{H}, e)$ where $\mathbb{G}$, $\mathbb{H}$ and $\mathbb{T}$ are groups of a prime order p, and G and $\tilde{H}$ generate $\mathbb{G}$ and $\mathbb{H}$, respectively. The function e is a non-degenerate bilinear map $e : \mathbb{G} \times \mathbb{H} \longrightarrow \mathbb{T}$. We refer to $\mathbb{G}$ and $\mathbb{H}$ as the source groups whereas we refer to $\mathbb{T}$ as the target group. We use multiplicative notation for all the groups. For clarity we will accent elements of $\mathbb{H}$ with $\tilde{\ }$. We let $\mathbb{G}^\times := \mathbb{G} \setminus \{1_\mathbb{G}\}$ and $\mathbb{H}^\times := \mathbb{H} \setminus \{1_\mathbb{H}\}$. We limit our attention to the efficient Type-3 setting [28], where $\mathbb{G} \neq \mathbb{H}$ and there is no efficiently computable homomorphism between the source groups in either direction. We assume there is an algorithm $\mathcal{BG}$ that on input a security parameter κ, outputs a description of bilinear groups.

The message space of the schemes we consider is the set of elements of the subgroup $\widehat{\mathbb{GH}}$ of $\mathbb{G} \times \mathbb{H}$ defined as the image of the map $\psi : x \longmapsto (G^x, \tilde{H}^x)$ for $x \in \mathbb{Z}_p$. One can efficiently test whether $(M, \tilde{N}) \in \widehat{\mathbb{GH}}$ by checking

$$e(M, \tilde{H}) = e(G, \tilde{N}) \cdot$$

Such pairs were called Diffie-Hellman (DH) pairs in [4]. We stress that we do not require that the signer knows the discrete logarithm of the message pair. In fact, in all of our proofs/constructions we assume a signer which does not know/does not exploit knowledge of such an exponent.

2.2 Digital Signatures

A digital signature scheme $\mathcal{DS}$ over a bilinear group $\mathcal{P}$ generated by $\mathcal{BG}$ for a message space $\mathcal{M}$ consists of the following algorithms:

KeyGen($\mathcal{P}$): On input $\mathcal{P}$, this outputs a pair of signing/verification keys (sk, vk).

Sign(sk, m): On input the secret signing key sk and a message $m \in \mathcal{M}$, this outputs a signature σ on m.

Verify(vk, m, σ): On input the verification key vk, a message $m \in \mathcal{M}$ and a signature σ, this outputs $0/1$ indicating the invalidity/validity of σ on m.

Definition 1 (Correctness). *A signature scheme $\mathcal{DS}$ over a bilinear group generator $\mathcal{BG}$ is (perfectly) correct if for all $\kappa \in \mathbb{N}$:*

$$\Pr \left[\begin{array}{c} \mathcal{P} \leftarrow \mathcal{BG}(1^\kappa); (\text{sk}, \text{vk}) \leftarrow \text{KeyGen}(\mathcal{P}); m \leftarrow \mathcal{M}; \sigma \leftarrow \text{Sign}(\text{sk}, m) \\ : \text{Verify}(\text{vk}, m, \sigma) = 1 \end{array} \right] = 1.$$

A signature scheme is said to be existentially unforgeable if it is hard to forge a signature on a new message that has not been signed before where the adversary may see signatures on other messages before outputting her forgery. We distinguish between adaptive chosen-message (EUF-CMA), random-message (EUF-RMA) and combined chosen-random-message (EUF-CMA-RMA) variants of existential unforgeability as defined below.

Definition 2 (EUF-CMA). *A signature scheme $\mathcal{DS}$ over a bilinear group generator $\mathcal{BG}$ is Existentially Unforgeable under an adaptive Chosen-Message Attack if for all $\kappa \in \mathbb{N}$ for all PPT adversaries $\mathcal{A}$, the following is negligible (in κ):*

$$\Pr \left[\begin{array}{c} \mathcal{P} \leftarrow \mathcal{BG}(1^\kappa); (\text{sk}, \text{vk}) \leftarrow \text{KeyGen}(\mathcal{P}); (\sigma^*, m^*) \leftarrow \mathcal{A}^{\text{Sign}(\text{sk}, \cdot)}(\mathcal{P}, \text{vk}) \\ : \text{Verify}(\text{vk}, m^*, \sigma^*) = 1 \wedge m^* \notin \mathcal{Q}_{\text{Sign}} \end{array} \right],$$

where $\mathcal{Q}_{\text{Sign}}$ is the set $\{m_i\}_{i=1}^q$ of messages queried to Sign.

Strong Existential Unforgeability under an adaptive Chosen-Message Attack (sEUF-CMA) is defined similarly and requires that the adversary cannot even output a new signature on a message that was queried to the sign oracle.

Definition 3 (EUF-RMA). *A signature scheme $\mathcal{DS}$ over a bilinear group generator $\mathcal{BG}$ is* Existentially Unforgeable under a Random-Message Attack *if for all $\kappa \in \mathbb{N}$ for all PPT adversaries $\mathcal{A}$, the following is negligible (in κ):*

$$\Pr \left[\begin{array}{c} \mathcal{P} \leftarrow \mathcal{BG}(1^\kappa); (\mathsf{sk}, \mathsf{vk}) \leftarrow \mathsf{KeyGen}(\mathcal{P}); (\sigma^*, m^*) \leftarrow \mathcal{A}^{\mathsf{Sign(sk)}}(\mathcal{P}, \mathsf{vk}) \\ : \mathsf{Verify}(\mathsf{vk}, m^*, \sigma^*) = 1 \wedge m^* \notin Q_{\mathsf{Sign}} \end{array} \right],$$

where Sign *uniformly samples a message m from $\mathcal{M}$ and returns m and a signature σ on it, and Q_{Sign} is the set $\{m_i\}_{i=1}^q$ of messages returned by* Sign.

Strong Existential Unforgeability under a Random-Message Attack (sEUF-RMA) is defined similarly and requires that the adversary cannot even output a new signature on a message that was chosen by Sign.

The following variant lies in between the two previous notions where it allows the adversary to adaptively choose some part of the message whereas the remaining part of the message is chosen uniformly at random by the sign oracle.

Definition 4 (EUF-CMA-RMA). *A signature scheme $\mathcal{DS}$ over a bilinear group generator $\mathcal{BG}$ for a message space $\mathcal{M} = \mathcal{M}_C \times \mathcal{M}_R$ is* Existentially Unforgeable under a combined Chosen-Random-Message Attack *if for all $\kappa \in \mathbb{N}$ for all PPT adversaries $\mathcal{A}$, the following is negligible (in κ):*

$$\Pr \left[\begin{array}{c} \mathcal{P} \leftarrow \mathcal{BG}(1^\kappa); (\mathsf{sk}, \mathsf{vk}) \leftarrow \mathsf{KeyGen}(\mathcal{P}); (\sigma^*, m^*, m'^*) \leftarrow \mathcal{A}^{\mathsf{Sign(sk, \cdot)}}(\mathcal{P}, \mathsf{vk}) \\ : \mathsf{Verify}(\mathsf{vk}, (m^*, m'^*), \sigma^*) = 1 \wedge (m^*, m'^*) \notin Q_{\mathsf{Sign}} \end{array} \right],$$

where when queried on a message $m_i \in \mathcal{M}_C$, Sign *uniformly samples a message m'_i from $\mathcal{M}_R$ and returns m'_i and a signature σ on (m_i, m'_i), and Q_{Sign} is the set $\{(m_i, m'_i)\}_{i=1}^q$ containing pairs on which signatures have been generated by* Sign.

Strong Existential Unforgeability under a combined Chosen-Random-Message Attack (sEUF-CMA-RMA) requires that the adversary cannot even output a new signature on a message pair on which she has obtained a signature from Sign.

2.3   Structure-Preserving Signatures

Structure-preserving signatures [4] are signature schemes defined over bilinear groups where the messages, the verification key and signatures are all group elements from either or both source groups, and verifying signatures only involves deciding group membership and evaluating PPEs of the form of Eq. (1).

$$\prod_i \prod_j e(A_i, \tilde{B}_j)^{c_{i,j}} = 1_{\mathbb{T}}, \tag{1}$$

where $A_i \in \mathbb{G}$ and $\tilde{B}_j \in \mathbb{H}$ are group elements appearing in $\mathcal{P}, m, \mathsf{vk}, \sigma$, whereas $c_{i,j} \in \mathbb{Z}_p$ are public constants.

Generic Signer. We refer to a signer that can only decide group membership, evaluate the bilinear map e, compute the group operations in groups $\mathbb{G}, \mathbb{H}$ and $\mathbb{T}$, and compare group elements as a *generic signer*.

3   Impossibility of Generic-Signer EUF-CMA SPS Schemes for a Vector of $\ell > 1$ Messages with 2-Element Unilateral Signatures

In this section we prove that generic-signer EUF-CMA SPS schemes for a vector of $\ell > 1$ messages with 2-element unilateral signatures cannot exist. We start by proving the following theorem which is a generalization of Lemma 1 from [8] for SPS schemes for unilateral messages.

Theorem 1. *A generic-signer EUF-RMA SPS scheme for a vector of $\ell \geq 1$ DH pairs must have for any message vector superpolynomially many potential signatures.*

Proof. Since the signer is generic, the signature $\sigma = (\boldsymbol{R}, \tilde{\boldsymbol{S}}) \in \mathbb{G}^n \times \mathbb{H}^{\tilde{n}}$ on the message vector $\left((M_i, \tilde{M}_i)\right)_{i=1}^{\ell}$ is computed via entry-wise exponentiation as $\sigma = (\boldsymbol{R}, \tilde{\boldsymbol{S}}) := (G^{\alpha} \prod_{i=1}^{\ell} M_i^{\alpha_i'}, \tilde{H}^{\beta} \prod_{i=1}^{\ell} \tilde{M}_i^{\beta_i'})$ for some vectors $(\boldsymbol{\alpha}, \boldsymbol{\alpha}_1', \ldots, \boldsymbol{\alpha}_{\ell}', \boldsymbol{\beta}, \boldsymbol{\beta}_1', \ldots, \boldsymbol{\beta}_{\ell}') \in \mathbb{Z}_p^{(\ell+1)n} \times \mathbb{Z}_p^{(\ell+1)\tilde{n}}$. Let's assume for contradiction that there is a scheme which has a polynomial number of potential signatures. This means there is a polynomial set $\{(\boldsymbol{\alpha}_i, \boldsymbol{\alpha}_{i,1}', \ldots, \boldsymbol{\alpha}_{i,\ell}', \boldsymbol{\beta}_i, \boldsymbol{\beta}_{i,1}', \ldots, \boldsymbol{\beta}_{i,\ell}')\}_{i=1}^{\text{poly}(\kappa)}$ for some polynomial ploy corresponding to the list of potential signatures. Now given signatures $\sigma_1 = (\boldsymbol{R}_1, \tilde{\boldsymbol{S}}_1)$ and $\sigma_2 = (\boldsymbol{R}_2, \tilde{\boldsymbol{S}}_2)$ on random DH message vectors $(\boldsymbol{M}_1, \tilde{\boldsymbol{M}}_1)$ and $(\boldsymbol{M}_2, \tilde{\boldsymbol{M}}_2)$, respectively, we have with probability $\frac{1}{\text{poly}(\kappa)^2}$ that those signatures were constructed using the same vector $(\boldsymbol{\alpha}_i, \boldsymbol{\alpha}_{i,1}', \ldots, \boldsymbol{\alpha}_{i,\ell}', \boldsymbol{\beta}_i, \boldsymbol{\beta}_{i,1}', \ldots, \boldsymbol{\beta}_{i,\ell}')$ for some $i \in [\text{ploy}(\kappa)]$. Thus, we have $\sigma^* = (\boldsymbol{R}^*, \tilde{\boldsymbol{S}}^*) = (\boldsymbol{R}_1^{1-\gamma} \boldsymbol{R}_2^{\gamma}, \tilde{\boldsymbol{S}}_1^{1-\gamma} \tilde{\boldsymbol{S}}_2^{\gamma})$ is a valid forgery on the message vector $(\boldsymbol{M}_1^{1-\gamma} \boldsymbol{M}_2^{\gamma}, \tilde{\boldsymbol{M}}_1^{1-\gamma} \tilde{\boldsymbol{M}}_2^{\gamma})$ for any $\gamma \leftarrow \mathbb{Z}_p^{\times}$. This means such a scheme is not EUF-RMA secure against an adversary which makes 2 (non-adaptive) signing queries. $\qquad\square$

We now proceed to proving the impossibility of the existence of generic-signer EUF-CMA (against $q > 1$ sign queries) SPS schemes for a vector of $\ell > 1$ messages with 2-element unilateral signatures. We prove that such schemes even for the simpler case where $\ell = 2$ cannot exist.

Theorem 2. *There is no generic-signer EUF-CMA (against $q > 1$ sign queries) SPS schemes for a vector of 2 DH pairs with 2-element unilateral signatures.*

Proof. We start by proving the following lemma regarding the number of verification equations required for schemes with 2-element signatures.

Lemma 1. *One verification equation (excluding the cost for verifying the well-formedness of the messages) is sufficient for a generic-signer SPS scheme with 2-element signatures.*

Proof. Assume a scheme has 2 verification equations. Both equations must pose non-trivial constraint on the signature components as otherwise we can reduce them to a single equation. Since each verification equation must involve at least 1 signature component, we have 3 cases:

- Both equations involve both signature components: This means we have 2 quadratic/linear equations in the discrete logarithm of the signature components. Such an equation system have at most 4 distinct solutions implying that there are at most 4 potential signatures for the message vector which contradicts the proof of Theorem 1.
- One equation involves both signature components whereas the other equation involves only one signature component: This means one equation is quadratic/linear involving both signature components, whereas the remaining equation is linear in one of the signature components. By substituting the value of the signature component in the linear equation into the other equation we end up with one verification equation that is sufficient for verifying the signature.
- Each verification equation involves a single signature component: Since the other constants (the verification key, the public parameters (if any) and the messages) are fixed, we have that each verification equation is a linear equation in one of the signature components, i.e. each equation is a linear equation in one unknown. Thus, there is exactly 1 potential signature for the message vector which contradicts the proof of Theorem 1. $\square$

Now let's assume WLOG that the signature is of the form $\sigma = (S_1, S_2) \in \mathbb{G}^2$, whereas the verification key is of the form $(\boldsymbol{X}, \tilde{\boldsymbol{Y}}) \in \mathbb{G}^n \times \mathbb{H}^{n'}$. The proof for the case where $\sigma = (\tilde{S}_1, \tilde{S}_2) \in \mathbb{H}^2$ is similar.

A generic signer computes the signature as $S_i := G^{\frac{\alpha_i(\boldsymbol{x},\boldsymbol{y})}{\alpha_i'(\boldsymbol{x},\boldsymbol{y})}} M_1^{\frac{\beta_{i,1}(\boldsymbol{x},\boldsymbol{y})}{\beta_{i,1}'(\boldsymbol{x},\boldsymbol{y})}} M_2^{\frac{\beta_{i,2}(\boldsymbol{x},\boldsymbol{y})}{\beta_{i,2}'(\boldsymbol{x},\boldsymbol{y})}}$ for some multivariate polynomials $\alpha_i, \alpha_i', \beta_{i,1}, \beta_{i,1}', \beta_{i,2}, \beta_{i,2}' \in \mathbb{Z}_p[\boldsymbol{x}, \boldsymbol{y}]$ for $i \in \{1, 2\}$. Note that none of those polynomials has a term in m_1 or m_2, i.e. they are independent of the messages. Thus, it is infeasible for a generic signer to compute a non-trivial signature component where its discrete logarithm s_i contains a message m_i (for any $i \in \{1, 2\}$) in a term in the denominator. This means that we must have that the verification equation does not contain the pairings $e(S_i, \tilde{M}_j)$ for all $j \in [2]$ and some $i \in [2]$, i.e. either S_1 or S_2 is independent of the messages as otherwise this would mean that m_i appears in the denominator of one of the signature components. Let's assume WLOG that S_1 is independent of the messages, i.e. the verification equation does not contain the pairings $e(S_1, \tilde{M}_i)$ for $i = 1, 2$. This means the scheme has a verification equation of the following form:

$$e(S_1, \prod_{i=1}^{n'} \tilde{Y}_i^{a_i}) \prod_{i=1}^{2} e(\prod_{j=1}^{n} X_j^{c_{i,j}}, \tilde{M}_i) \prod_{i=1}^{2} e(M_i, \prod_{j=1}^{n'} \tilde{Y}_j^{e_{i,j}} \prod_{j=1}^{2} \tilde{M}_j^{u_{i,j}})$$

$$e(S_2, \prod_{i=1}^{n'} \tilde{Y}_i^{b_i} \prod_{i=1}^{2} \tilde{M}_i^{d_i}) = \prod_{i=1}^{n} \prod_{j=1}^{n'} e(X_i, \tilde{Y}_j)^{t_{i,j}} \quad (2)$$

A generic signer cannot produce a signature component whose discrete logarithm has a term with any of the monomials: m_1^2, $m_1 m_2$, or m_2^2. Thus, WLOG we can also assume that the verification equation does not contain a pairing of the form $e(M_i, \tilde{M}_j)$ for all $i, j \in [2]$, i.e. $u_{i,j} = 0$ for all $i, j \in [2]$. This means the verification equation is of the following form:

$$e(S_1, \prod_{i=1}^{n'} \tilde{Y}_i^{a_i}) \prod_{i=1}^{2} e(\prod_{j=1}^{n} X_j^{c_{i,j}}, \tilde{M}_i) \prod_{i=1}^{2} e(M_i, \prod_{j=1}^{n'} \tilde{Y}_j^{e_{i,j}})$$

$$e(S_2, \prod_{i=1}^{n'} \tilde{Y}_i^{b_i} \prod_{i=1}^{2} \tilde{M}_i^{d_i}) = \prod_{i=1}^{n} \prod_{j=1}^{n'} e(X_i, \tilde{Y}_j)^{t_{i,j}} \quad (3)$$

Lemma 2 below proves that a scheme with a verification equation of the form of Eq. (3) is not secure against an adversary which makes 2 chosen-message sign queries, whereas Lemma 3 proves that even if we consider schemes with a verification equation of the form of Eq. (2) such schemes are not EUF-CMA secure against an adversary that makes 3 chosen-message sign queries, which concludes the proof of the theorem.

Lemma 2. *A SPS scheme for a vector of 2 DH pairs with a verification equation of the form of Eq. (3) is not EUF-CMA against 2 (non-adaptive) chosen-message sign queries.*

Proof. We have 2 cases as follows:

- Case $d_2 \neq 0$: Choose any 2 distinct messages $(M_{1,1}, \tilde{M}_{1,1}), (M_1^*, \tilde{M}_1^*)$ and set $(M_{1,2}, \tilde{M}_{1,2}) := (M_{1,1}, \tilde{M}_{1,1})^{\frac{-d_1}{d_2}}$, $(M_{2,1}, \tilde{M}_{2,1}) := (M_1^{*\frac{1}{\gamma}} M_{1,1}^{\frac{\gamma-1}{\gamma}}, \tilde{M}_1^{*\frac{1}{\gamma}} \tilde{M}_{1,1}^{\frac{\gamma-1}{\gamma}})$ and $(M_{2,2}, \tilde{M}_{2,2}) := (M_1^{*\frac{-d_1}{d_2\gamma}} M_{1,1}^{\frac{d_1(1-\gamma)}{d_2\gamma}}, \tilde{M}_1^{*\frac{-d_1}{d_2\gamma}} \tilde{M}_{1,1}^{\frac{d_1(1-\gamma)}{d_2\gamma}})$.
  After getting signatures $\sigma_1 = (S_{1,1}, S_{1,2})$ and $\sigma_2 = (S_{2,1}, S_{2,2})$ on the messages $((M_{1,1}, \tilde{M}_{1,1}), (M_{1,2}, \tilde{M}_{1,2}))$ and $((M_{2,1}, \tilde{M}_{2,1}), (M_{2,2}, \tilde{M}_{2,2}))$, respectively, we can compute a forgery $\sigma^* = (S_1^*, S_2^*) := (S_{1,1}^{1-\gamma} S_{2,1}^{\gamma}, S_{1,2}^{1-\gamma} S_{2,2}^{\gamma})$ on the message $((M_1^*, \tilde{M}_1^*), (M_2^*, \tilde{M}_2^*) := (M_1^*, \tilde{M}_1^*)^{\frac{-d_1}{d_2}})$. This is a valid signature and we have that $((M_1^*, \tilde{M}_1^*), (M_2^*, \tilde{M}_2^*)) \neq ((M_{1,1}, \tilde{M}_{1,1}), (M_{1,2}, \tilde{M}_{1,2}))$ and $((M_1^*, \tilde{M}_1^*), (M_2^*, \tilde{M}_2^*)) \neq ((M_{2,1}, \tilde{M}_{2,1}), (M_{2,2}, \tilde{M}_{2,2}))$ for any $\gamma \in \mathbb{Z}_p^\times \setminus \{1\}$.
- Case $d_2 = 0$: Choose random distinct messages $(M_{1,2}, \tilde{M}_{1,2}), (M_{2,2}, \tilde{M}_{2,2})$ and $(M_1^*, \tilde{M}_1^*)$ and set $(M_2^*, \tilde{M}_2^*) := (M_{1,2}^{1-\gamma} M_{2,2}^{\gamma}, \tilde{M}_{1,2}^{1-\gamma} \tilde{M}_{2,2}^{\gamma})$. Query the sign oracle on $((M_1^*, \tilde{M}_1^*), (M_{1,2}, \tilde{M}_{1,2}))$ and $((M_1^*, \tilde{M}_1^*), (M_{2,2}, \tilde{M}_{2,2}))$ to get signatures $\sigma_1 = (S_{1,1}, S_{1,2})$ and $\sigma_2 = (S_{2,1}, S_{2,2})$, respectively. We have that $\sigma^* = (S_1^*, S_2^*) := (S_{1,1}^{1-\gamma} S_{2,1}^{\gamma}, S_{1,2}^{1-\gamma} S_{2,2}^{\gamma})$ is a valid forgery on $((M_1^*, \tilde{M}_1^*), (M_2^*, \tilde{M}_2^*))$ for any $\gamma \leftarrow \mathbb{Z}_p^\times$. We have that $((M_1^*, \tilde{M}_1^*), (M_2^*, \tilde{M}_2^*)) \notin \{((M_1^*, \tilde{M}_1^*), (M_{1,2}, \tilde{M}_{1,2})), ((M_1^*, \tilde{M}_1^*), (M_{2,2}, \tilde{M}_{2,2}))\}$.

This concludes the proof.   □

Lemma 3. *A SPS scheme for a vector of 2 DH pairs with a verification equation of the form of Eq. (2) is not EUF-CMA against 3 (non-adaptive) chosen-message sign queries.*

Proof. We have 2 cases as follows:

- Case $d_2 \neq 0$: Choose any distinct messages: $(M_1^*, \tilde{M}_1^*)$, $(M_2^*, \tilde{M}_2^*)$ and $(M_{3,1}, \tilde{M}_{3,1})$. Set:

$$(M_{1,1}, \tilde{M}_{1,1}) := (M_1^{*\frac{\gamma-1}{2\gamma}} M_{3,1}^{\frac{\gamma+1}{2\gamma}}, \tilde{M}_1^{*\frac{\gamma-1}{2\gamma}} \tilde{M}_{3,1}^{\frac{\gamma+1}{2\gamma}})$$

$$(M_{1,2}, \tilde{M}_{1,2}) := (M_1^{*\frac{d_1(\gamma+1)}{2d_2\gamma}} M_{3,1}^{\frac{-d_1(\gamma+1)}{2d_2\gamma}} M_2^*, \tilde{M}_1^{*\frac{d_1(\gamma+1)}{2d_2\gamma}} \tilde{M}_{3,1}^{\frac{-d_1(\gamma+1)}{2d_2\gamma}} \tilde{M}_2^*)$$

$$(M_{2,1}, \tilde{M}_{2,1}) := (M_1^{*\frac{\gamma+1}{2\gamma}} M_{3,1}^{\frac{\gamma-1}{2\gamma}}, \tilde{M}_1^{*\frac{\gamma+1}{2\gamma}} \tilde{M}_{3,1}^{\frac{\gamma-1}{2\gamma}})$$

$$(M_{2,2}, \tilde{M}_{2,2}) := (M_1^{*\frac{d_1(\gamma-1)}{2d_2\gamma}} M_{3,1}^{\frac{d_1(1-\gamma)}{2d_2\gamma}} M_2^*, \tilde{M}_1^{*\frac{d_1(\gamma-1)}{2d_2\gamma}} \tilde{M}_{3,1}^{\frac{d_1(1-\gamma)}{2d_2\gamma}} \tilde{M}_2^*)$$

$$(M_{3,2}, \tilde{M}_{3,2}) := (M_1^{*\frac{d_1}{d_2}} M_{3,1}^{\frac{-d_1}{d_2}} M_2^*, \tilde{M}_1^{*\frac{d_1}{d_2}} \tilde{M}_{3,1}^{\frac{-d_1}{d_2}} \tilde{M}_2^*)$$

Now query the sign oracle on the messages $((M_{1,1}, \tilde{M}_{1,1}), (M_{1,2}, \tilde{M}_{1,2}))$, $((M_{2,1}, \tilde{M}_{2,1}), (M_{2,2}, \tilde{M}_{2,2}))$ and $((M_{3,1}, \tilde{M}_{3,1}), (M_{3,2}, \tilde{M}_{3,2}))$, to get the signatures $\sigma_1 = (S_{1,1}, S_{1,2})$, $\sigma_2 = (S_{2,1}, S_{2,2})$ and $\sigma_3 = (S_{3,1}, S_{3,2})$, respectively. We can now compute a forgery $\sigma^* = (S_1^*, S_2^*) := (S_{1,1}^{-\gamma} S_{2,1}^{\gamma} S_{3,1}, S_{1,2}^{-\gamma} S_{2,2}^{\gamma} S_{3,2})$ on the message $((M_1^*, \tilde{M}_1^*), (M_2^*, \tilde{M}_2^*))$. This is a valid signature and we have that $((M_1^*, \tilde{M}_1^*), (M_2^*, \tilde{M}_2^*)) \notin \{((M_{1,1}, \tilde{M}_{1,1}), (M_{1,2}, \tilde{M}_{1,2})), ((M_{2,1}, \tilde{M}_{2,1}), (M_{2,2}, \tilde{M}_{2,2})), ((M_{3,1}, \tilde{M}_{3,1}), (M_{3,2}, \tilde{M}_{3,2}))\}$ for any $\gamma \in \mathbb{Z}_p^{\times} \setminus \{-1, 1\}$.

- Case $d_2 = 0$: Choose any distinct messages: $(M_1^*, \tilde{M}_1^*)$, $(M_{2,2}, \tilde{M}_{2,2})$ and $(M_{3,2}, \tilde{M}_{3,2})$. Set

$$(M_{1,1}, \tilde{M}_{1,1}) = (M_{2,1}, \tilde{M}_{2,1}) = (M_{3,1}, \tilde{M}_{3,1}) := (M_1^*, \tilde{M}_1^*)$$

$$(M_2^*, \tilde{M}_2^*) := (M_{2,2}^{\frac{\gamma+1}{2}} M_{3,2}^{\frac{1-\gamma}{2}}, \tilde{M}_{2,2}^{\frac{\gamma+1}{2}} \tilde{M}_{3,2}^{\frac{1-\gamma}{2}})$$

$$(M_{1,2}, \tilde{M}_{1,2}) := (M_{2,2}^{\frac{1-\gamma}{2}} M_{3,2}^{\frac{\gamma+1}{2}}, \tilde{M}_{2,2}^{\frac{1-\gamma}{2}} \tilde{M}_{3,2}^{\frac{\gamma+1}{2}})$$

Now query the sign oracle on the messages $((M_{1,1}, \tilde{M}_{1,1}), (M_{1,2}, \tilde{M}_{1,2}))$, $((M_{2,1}, \tilde{M}_{2,1}), (M_{2,2}, \tilde{M}_{2,2}))$ and $((M_{3,1}, \tilde{M}_{3,1}), (M_{3,2}, \tilde{M}_{3,2}))$, to get the signatures $\sigma_1 = (S_{1,1}, S_{1,2})$, $\sigma_2 = (S_{2,1}, S_{2,2})$ and $\sigma_3 = (S_{3,1}, S_{3,2})$, respectively. We can now compute a forgery $\sigma^* = (S_1^*, S_2^*) := (S_{1,1} S_{2,1}^{\gamma} S_{3,1}^{-\gamma}, S_{1,2} S_{2,2}^{\gamma} S_{3,2}^{-\gamma})$ on the message $((M_1^*, \tilde{M}_1^*), (M_2^*, \tilde{M}_2^*))$. This is a valid signature and we have that $((M_1^*, \tilde{M}_1^*), (M_2^*, \tilde{M}_2^*)) \notin \{((M_{1,1}, \tilde{M}_{1,1}), (M_{1,2}, \tilde{M}_{1,2})), ((M_{2,1}, \tilde{M}_{2,1}), (M_{2,2}, \tilde{M}_{2,2})), ((M_{3,1}, \tilde{M}_{3,1}), (M_{3,2}, \tilde{M}_{3,2}))\}$ for any $\gamma \in \mathbb{Z}_p^{\times} \setminus \{-1, 1\}$.

This concludes the proof. □

The following corollary follows from Theorem 2.

Corollary 1. *There is no generic-signer EUF-CMA SPS scheme for a vector of $\ell > 1$ DH pairs with 2-element unilateral signatures.*

4   Impossibility of sEUF-CMA (Against $q > 1$ Sign Queries) SPS Schemes with 2-Element Signatures

In this section we prove the impossibility of the existence of sEUF-CMA SPS schemes with 2-element (unilateral/bilateral) signatures. However, in Sect. 5 we show that sEUF-RMA and sEUF-CMA-RMA with 2-element (unilateral) signatures are possible by giving concrete constructions.

Theorem 3. *There is no generic-signer sEUF-CMA (against $q > 1$ sign queries) SPS scheme with 2-element signatures.*

Proof. Lemma 1 proved that 1 PPE is sufficient for verifying 2-element signatures. The following 2 lemmata complete the proof, where the first deals with the case of bilateral signatures whereas the second deals with unilateral signatures.

Lemma 4. *There is no generic-signer sEUF-CMA (against $q > 1$ sign queries) SPS scheme with 2-element bilateral signatures.*

Proof. Let's WLOG assume that the signature is of the form $\sigma = (S_1, \tilde{S}_2) \in \mathbb{G} \times \mathbb{H}$, whereas the verification key (including any public parameters) is of the form $(\boldsymbol{X}, \tilde{\boldsymbol{Y}}) \in \mathbb{G}^n \times \mathbb{H}^{n'}$. The case where the signature is transposed is similar.

A generic signer computes the signature as $S_1 := M^{\frac{\alpha_1(x,y)}{\alpha_1'(x,y)}} G^{\frac{\beta_1(x,y)}{\beta_1'(x,y)}}$ and $\tilde{S}_2 := \tilde{M}^{\frac{\alpha_2(x,y)}{\alpha_2'(x,y)}} \tilde{H}^{\frac{\beta_2(x,y)}{\beta_2'(x,y)}}$ for some polynomials $\alpha_1, \alpha_1', \beta_1, \beta_1', \alpha_2, \alpha_2', \beta_2, \beta_2' \in \mathbb{Z}_p[\boldsymbol{x}, \boldsymbol{y}]$. Note that none of those polynomials has a term in m. Without knowledge of the discrete logarithm of the message m, it is infeasible for a generic signer to compute a non-trivial signature component where its discrete logarithm s_i contains the message m in a term in the denominator. Thus, we must have that either $e(S_1, \tilde{M})$ or $e(M, \tilde{S}_2)$ does not feature in the verification equation. WLOG let's assume that $e(S_1, \tilde{M})$ does not appear in the verification equation. The proof for the other case where $e(M, \tilde{S}_2)$ does not appear in the verification equation is similar.

Such a scheme would have a verification equation of the following form:

$$e(S_1, \prod_{i=1}^{n'} \tilde{Y}_i^{c_i} \tilde{S}_2^d) e(\prod_{i=1}^{n} X_i^{b_i}, \tilde{M}) e(M, \prod_{i=1}^{n'} \tilde{Y}_i^{e_i} \tilde{S}_2^f \tilde{M}^k)$$

$$e(\prod_{i=1}^{n} X_i^{a_i}, \tilde{S}_2) = \prod_{i=1}^{n} \prod_{j=1}^{n'} e(X_i, \tilde{Y}_j)^{t_{i,j}} \quad (4)$$

We have 3 cases as follows:

- Case for some $i \in [n']$, $c_i \neq 0$: After getting a signature $\sigma = (S_1, S_2)$ on a (random) message $(M, \tilde{M})$, fix any $i \in [n']$ where $c_i \neq 0$, we can compute a new signature $\sigma^* = (S_1^*, \tilde{S}_2^*)$ on the random message $(M, \tilde{M})$ as follows:

$$S_1^* := M^{\frac{-\gamma f}{c_i + \gamma d}} S_1^{\frac{c_i}{c_i + \gamma d}} \prod_{j=1}^{n} X_j^{\frac{-a_j \gamma}{c_i + \gamma d}} \qquad \tilde{S}_2^* := \tilde{S}_2^{\frac{c_i + \gamma d}{c_i}} Y_i^{\gamma} \prod_{j \neq i} Y_j^{\frac{c_j \gamma}{c_i}}$$

The new signature is a valid forgery and we have $\sigma^* \neq \sigma$ for any $\gamma \in \mathbb{Z}_p^\times$.

- Case $c_i = 0$ for all $i \in [n']$ but $d \neq 0$: After getting a signature $\sigma = (S_1, \tilde{S}_2)$ on a (random) message $(M, \tilde{M})$, we can compute a new signature $\sigma^* = (S_1^*, \tilde{S}_2^*)$ on the random message $(M, \tilde{M})$ as follows:

$$S_1^* := M^{\frac{f-\gamma f}{\gamma d}} S_1^{\frac{1}{\gamma}} \prod_{i=1}^{n} X_i^{\frac{a_i - a_i \gamma}{\gamma d}} \qquad\qquad \tilde{S}_2^* := \tilde{S}_2^\gamma$$

The new signature is a valid forgery and $\sigma^* \neq \sigma$ for any $\gamma \in \mathbb{Z}_p^\times \setminus \{1\}$.

- Case $c_i = 0$ for all $i \in [n']$ and $d = 0$: This means the verification equation does not involve the component S_1 and hence the signature consists of only 1 element and the equation is linear in s_2 (the discrete logarithm of $\tilde{S}_2$). This means for any message there is exactly 1 potential signature which contradicts Theorem 1.

This concludes the proof.   □

Lemma 5. *There is no generic-signer sEUF-CMA (against $q > 1$ sign queries) SPS scheme with 2-element unilateral signatures.*[1]

Proof. WLOG let's count any public parameters (if any) as part of the verification key vk. Such a scheme would have signatures of the form $\sigma = (S_1, S_2) \in \mathbb{G}^2$, a verification key of the form $(\boldsymbol{X}, \boldsymbol{Y}) \in \mathbb{G}^n \times \mathbb{H}^{n'}$, and a verification equation of the following form:

$$\prod_{i=1}^{2} e(S_i, \prod_{j=1}^{n'} \tilde{Y}_j^{c_{i,j}} \tilde{M}^{d_i}) e(\prod_{i=1}^{n} X_i^{a_i}, \tilde{M}) e(M, \prod_{i=1}^{n'} \tilde{Y}_i^{b_i} \tilde{M}^f) = \prod_{i=1}^{n} \prod_{j=1}^{n'} e(X_i, \tilde{Y}_j)^{t_{i,j}} \quad (5)$$

Theorem 1 proved that for a scheme to be EUF-RMA secure (against $q > 1$ sign queries), it must have superpolynomially many potential signatures. After obtaining any 2 distinct signatures $\sigma = (S_1, S_2)$ and $\sigma' = (S_1', S_2')$ on any message $(M, \tilde{M})$, we have that $\sigma^* = (S_1^*, S_2^*) := (S_1^\gamma S_1'^{1-\gamma}, S_2^\gamma S_2'^{1-\gamma})$ is with overwhelming probability a new valid signature on $(M, \tilde{M})$ for any $\gamma \in \mathbb{Z}_p^\times \setminus \{1\}$.   □

This concludes the proof.   □

5   sEUF-CMA-RMA Scheme for Diffie-Hellman Vectors

Here we construct a sEUF-CMA-RMA scheme with 2-element unilateral signatures for the message space $\mathcal{M} = \mathcal{M}_C \times \mathcal{M}_R$ where $\mathcal{M}_C = \widehat{\mathbb{GH}}$ and $\mathcal{M}_R = \widehat{\mathbb{GH}}^\eta$ for any $\eta \geq 1$. This also implies the existence of sEUF-RMA schemes with 2-element unilateral signatures.

Given the description of Type-3 bilinear groups $\mathcal{P}$ output by $\mathcal{BG}(1^\kappa)$, the scheme is as follows:

---

[1] Our result is stronger than that of [32] since we consider a bilateral verification key.

- KeyGen($\mathcal{P}$): Select $u, w_1, w_2, x, y_1, \ldots, y_\eta \leftarrow \mathbb{Z}_p$. Set $X := G^x$, $Y_i := G^{y_i}$ for all $i \in [\eta]$, $U := G^u$, $\tilde{W}_1 := \tilde{H}^{w_1}$ and $\tilde{W}_2 := \tilde{H}^{w_2}$. Set $\mathsf{sk} := (w_1, w_2, u, x, y_1, \ldots, y_\eta)$ and $\mathsf{vk} := (\tilde{W}_1, \tilde{W}_2, U, X, Y_1, \ldots, Y_\eta) \in \mathbb{H}^2 \times \mathbb{G}^{2+\eta}$.
- Sign($\mathsf{sk}, (M, \tilde{M}), ((M'_1, \tilde{M}'_1), \ldots, (M'_\eta, \tilde{M}'_\eta))$): To sign $((M, \tilde{M}), ((M'_1, \tilde{M}'_1),$ $\ldots, (M'_\eta, \tilde{M}'_\eta))) \in \widehat{\mathbb{GH}}^{1+\eta}$, select $r \leftarrow \mathbb{Z}_p$ and set $R := G^r$, and $S := (M^{r+x} \prod_{i=1}^{\eta} M_i'^{r+y_i} R^{w_1} U)^{\frac{1}{w_2}}$. Return $\sigma := (R, S) \in \mathbb{G}^2$.
- Verify $\left(\mathsf{vk}, \left((M, \tilde{M}), \left((M'_1, \tilde{M}'_1), \ldots, (M'_\eta, \tilde{M}'_\eta)\right)\right), \sigma = (R, S)\right)$: Return 1 only if $R, S \in \mathbb{G}$, $(M, \tilde{M}) \in \widehat{\mathbb{GH}}$, for all $i \in [\eta] : (M'_i, \tilde{M}'_i) \in \widehat{\mathbb{GH}}$, and

$$e(S, \tilde{W}_2) = e(R, \tilde{M} \prod_{i=1}^{\eta} \tilde{M}'_i \tilde{W}_1) e(X, \tilde{M}) \prod_{i=1}^{\eta} e(Y_i, \tilde{M}'_i) e(U, \tilde{H}),$$

otherwise, return 0.

Remark 1. We can set $Y_1 = G$ which reduces the size of the verification key by one group element.

Security of the Scheme. Correctness of the scheme follows by inspection and is straightforward to verify. We now prove the following theorem.

Theorem 4. *The scheme is sEUF-CMA-RMA secure in the generic group model.*

Proof. We show that no linear combinations representing Laurent polynomials (of degrees ranging from -1 to 2 after q sign queries) in the discrete logarithms of the group elements the adversary sees correspond to a forgery on a new message.

At the start of the game, the only elements in $\mathbb{H}$ the adversary sees are $\tilde{H}, \tilde{W}_1, \tilde{W}_2$ which correspond to the discrete logarithms $1, w_1, w_2$, respectively, whereas the only elements in $\mathbb{G}$ the adversary sees are $G, X, Y_1, \ldots, Y_\eta, U$ which correspond to the discrete logarithms $1, x, y_1, \ldots, y_\eta, u$, respectively.

Note that the only elements of $\mathbb{H}$ the q sign queries return are the uniformly random parts of the message $\{\tilde{M}'_{i,j}\}$ for $i \in [q]$ and $j \in [\eta]$. Thus, at the i-th sign query on the message $(M_i, \tilde{N}_i) \in \widehat{\mathbb{GH}}$, m_i and n_i the discrete logarithms of M_i and $\tilde{N}_i$, respectively, can only be linear combinations of the discrete logarithms of the elements in $\mathbb{G}$ and $\mathbb{H}$, respectively, the adversary sees up to that point of time. Thus, we have

$$m_i = a_{m_i} + b_{m_i} u + c_{m_i} x + \sum_{k=1}^{\eta} d_{m_{i,k}} y_k + \sum_{\ell=1}^{i-1} \sum_{k=1}^{\eta} e_{m_{i,\ell,k}} m'_{\ell,k} + \sum_{j=1}^{i-1} f_{m_{i,j}} r_j$$

$$+ \sum_{j=1}^{i-1} g_{m_{i,j}} \left(\frac{m_j(r_j + x) + \sum_{k=1}^{\eta} m'_{j,k}(r_j + y_k) + r_j w_1 + u}{w_2} \right)$$

$$n_i = a_{n_i} + b_{n_i} w_1 + c_{n_i} w_2 + \sum_{\ell=1}^{i-1} \sum_{k=1}^{\eta} d_{n_i,\ell,k} m'_{\ell,k}$$

Since for all $i \in [q]$, we must have that $(M_i, \tilde{N}_i) \in \widehat{\mathbb{GH}}$, i.e. $m_i = n_i$, we must have that $a_{m_i} = a_{n_i}$, $b_{m_i} = b_{n_i} = c_{m_i} = c_{n_i} = 0$, $d_{m_i,k} = 0$ for all $k \in [\eta]$, $f_{m_{i,j}} = g_{m_{i,j}} = 0$ for all $j \in [i-1]$, and $d_{n_i,\ell,k} = e_{m_i,\ell,k}$ for all $\ell \in [i-1]$ and $k \in [\eta]$. Thus, we have

$$m_i = n_i = a_{m_i} + \sum_{\ell=1}^{i-1} \sum_{k=1}^{\eta} e_{m_i,\ell,k} m'_{\ell,k}$$

If the message is well-formed, then at the i-th sign query, the adversary will receive a signature of the form $\sigma_i = (r_i, s_i)$, where s_i is of the following form:

$$s_i = \frac{m_i(r_i + x) + \sum_{j=1}^{\eta} m'_{i,j}(r_i + y_j) + r_i w_1 + u}{w_2}$$

At the end of the game (after at most q sign queries), we must have

$$m^* = n^* = a_m + \sum_{\ell=1}^{q} \sum_{k=1}^{\eta} e_{m_{\ell,k}} m'_{\ell,k}$$

$$m'^*_j = n'^*_j = a_{m'_j} + \sum_{\ell=1}^{q} \sum_{k=1}^{\eta} e_{m'_{j,\ell,k}} m'_{\ell,k} \quad \text{for all } j \in [\eta]$$

Similarly, since the adversary can only construct her forgery as linear combinations of the Laurent polynomials she sees in the game, we have at the end of the game that r^* and s^* must be linear combinations of the Laurent polynomials in $\mathbb{G}$. Thus, we have:

$$r^* = a_r + b_r u + c_r x + \sum_{i=1}^{\eta} d_{r_i} y_i + \sum_{i=1}^{q} \sum_{j=1}^{\eta} e_{r_{i,j}} m'_{i,j} + \sum_{i=1}^{q} f_{r_i} r_i$$

$$+ \sum_{i=1}^{q} g_{r_i} \left(\frac{m_i(r_i + x) + \sum_{j=1}^{\eta} m'_{i,j}(r_i + y_j) + r_i w_1 + u}{w_2} \right)$$

$$s^* = a_s + b_s u + c_s x + \sum_{i=1}^{\eta} d_{s_i} y_i + \sum_{i=1}^{q} \sum_{j=1}^{\eta} e_{s_{i,j}} m'_{i,j} + \sum_{i=1}^{q} f_{s_i} r_i$$

$$+ \sum_{i=1}^{q} g_{s_i} \left(\frac{m_i(r_i + x) + \sum_{j=1}^{\eta} m'_{i,j}(r_i + y_j) + r_i w_1 + u}{w_2} \right)$$

Since by the verification equation we must have that:

$$s^* w_2 = r^*(m^* + \sum_{j=1}^{\eta} m_j'^* + w_1) + m^* x + \sum_{j=1}^{\eta} m_j'^* y_j + u$$

Thus, we must have that:

$$a_s w_2 + b_s u w_2 + c_s x w_2 + \sum_{i=1}^{\eta} d_{s_i} y_i w_2 + \sum_{i=1}^{q} \sum_{j=1}^{\eta} e_{s_{i,j}} m_{i,j}' w_2 + \sum_{i=1}^{q} f_{s_i} r_i w_2$$

$$+ \sum_{i=1}^{q} g_{s_i} \left(m_i(r_i + x) + \sum_{j=1}^{\eta} m_{i,j}'(r_i + y_j) + r_i w_1 + u \right)$$

$$= \left(a_r + b_r u + c_r x + \sum_{i=1}^{\eta} d_{r_i} y_i + \sum_{i=1}^{q} \sum_{j=1}^{\eta} e_{r_{i,j}} m_{i,j}' + \sum_{i=1}^{q} f_{r_i} r_i \right.$$

$$\left. + \sum_{i=1}^{q} g_{r_i} \left(\frac{m_i(r_i + x) + \sum_{j=1}^{\eta} m_{i,j}'(r_i + y_j) + r_i w_1 + u}{w_2} \right) \right)$$

$$\left(m^* + \sum_{i=1}^{\eta} m_i'^* + w_1 \right) + m^* x + \sum_{i=1}^{\eta} m_i'^* y_i + u$$

There is no term of the form $\frac{u w_1}{w_2}$ on the LHS, so we must have that for all $i \in [q]$ that $g_{r_i} = 0$. Also, for all $i \in [\eta]$, there are no terms of the form $x w_1$, $y_i w_1$, $u w_1$ or w_1 on the LHS so we must have that $c_r = 0$, $d_{r_i} = 0$ for all $i \in [\eta]$, $b_r = 0$ and $a_r = 0$. Thus, we have:

$$a_s w_2 + b_s u w_2 + c_s x w_2 + \sum_{i=1}^{\eta} d_{s_i} y_i w_2 + \sum_{i=1}^{q} \sum_{j=1}^{\eta} e_{s_{i,j}} m_{i,j}' w_2 + \sum_{i=1}^{q} f_{s_i} r_i w_2$$

$$+ \sum_{i=1}^{q} g_{s_i} \left(m_i(r_i + x) + \sum_{j=1}^{\eta} m_{i,j}'(r_i + y_j) + r_i w_1 + u \right)$$

$$= \left(\sum_{i=1}^{q} \sum_{j=1}^{\eta} e_{r_{i,j}} m_{i,j}' + \sum_{i=1}^{q} f_{r_i} r_i \right) \left(m^* + \sum_{i=1}^{\eta} m_i'^* + w_1 \right) + m^* x + \sum_{i=1}^{\eta} m_i'^* y_i + u$$

There are no terms on the RHS with any of the monomials w_2, $u w_2$, $x w_2$, $y_i w_2$ for any $i \in [\eta]$, $r_i w_2$ for any $i \in [q]$, or $m_{i,j}' w_2$ for any $i \in [q]$ and $j \in [\eta]$. Thus, we must have that $a_s = 0$, $b_s = 0$, $c_s = 0$, $d_{s_i} = 0$ for all $i \in [\eta]$, $f_{s_i} = 0$ for all $i \in [q]$, and for all $i \in [q]$ and all $j \in [\eta]$ that $e_{s_{i,j}} = 0$. Thus, we have:

$$\sum_{i=1}^{q} g_{s_i} \left(m_i(r_i + x) + \sum_{j=1}^{n} m_{i,j}'(r_i + y_j) + r_i w_1 + u \right)$$

$$= \left(\sum_{i=1}^{q} \sum_{j=1}^{\eta} e_{r_{i,j}} m_{i,j}' + \sum_{i=1}^{q} f_{r_i} r_i \right) \left(m^* + \sum_{i=1}^{\eta} m_i'^* + w_1 \right) + m^* x + \sum_{i=1}^{\eta} m_i'^* y_i + u$$

There are no terms of the form $m'_{i,j}w_1$ for any $i \in [q]$ and any $j \in [\eta]$ on the LHS. Thus, we must have that $e_{r_{i,j}} = 0$ for all $i \in [q]$ and all $j \in [\eta]$ and hence we must have that:

$$\sum_{i=1}^{q} g_{s_i}\Big(m_i(r_i + x) + \sum_{j=1}^{\eta} m'_{i,j}(r_i + y_j) + r_i w_1 + u\Big)$$

$$= \sum_{i=1}^{q} f_{r_i} r_i m^* + \sum_{i=1}^{q} f_{r_i} r_i \sum_{i=1}^{\eta} m'^*_i + \sum_{i=1}^{q} f_{r_i} r_i w_1 + m^* x + \sum_{i=1}^{\eta} m'^*_i y_i + u$$

By the term u we have that $\sum_{i=1}^{q} g_{s_i} = 1$ and we must have that there is at least one value of $g_{s_i} \neq 0$. Also, by the term $r_i w_1$ we have that $g_{s_i} = f_{r_i}$ for all $i \in [q]$. Note that $m'_{i,j}$ for all $i \in [q]$ and all $j \in [\eta]$ on the LHS are all chosen uniformly at random by the sign oracle. Also, there is no term on the LHS containing the monomial $m_{i,j} r_k$ for any $k \neq i$. Thus, we cannot have for any $i, j \in [q]$ where $i \neq j$ that $f_{r_i} \neq 0$ and $f_{r_j} \neq 0$. This means we must have for some $i \in [q]$ that:

$$g_{s_i} m_i(r_i + x) + g_{s_i} \sum_{j=1}^{\eta} m'_{i,j}(r_i + y_j) + g_{s_i} r_i w_1 + g_{s_i} u$$

$$= f_{r_i} r_i m^* + f_{r_i} r_i \sum_{i=1}^{\eta} m'^*_i + f_{r_i} r_i w_1 + m^* x + \sum_{i=1}^{\eta} m'^*_i y_i + u$$

Since we must have that $\sum_{i=1}^{q} g_{s_i} = 1$ and for all $i \in [q]$ that $g_{s_i} = f_{r_i}$, we must have:

$$m_i(r_i + x) + \sum_{j=1}^{\eta} m'_{i,j}(r_i + y_j) + r_i w_1 + u$$

$$= r_i m^* + r_i \sum_{i=1}^{\eta} m'^*_i + r_i w_1 + m^* x + \sum_{i=1}^{\eta} m'^*_i y_i + u$$

By the monomial x, we must have that $m^* = m_i$, whereas by the monomial y_j we must have that $m'_{i,j} = m'^*_j$ for all $j \in [\eta]$. The above also means we have $r^* = r_i$ and $s^* = s_i$. This means (r^*, s^*) is not a valid forgery.

Remark 2. The proof holds even if we have that $y_1 = 1$ which means we can reduce the size of the verification key by eliminating 1 group element.

This concludes the proof.   □

References

1. Abe, M., Ambrona, M., Ohkubo, M., Tibouchi, M.: Lower bounds on structure-preserving signatures for bilateral messages. In: Catalano, D., De Prisco, R. (eds.) SCN 2018. LNCS, vol. 11035, pp. 3–22. Springer, Cham (2018). https://doi.org/10.1007/978-3-319-98113-0_1

2. Abe, M., Chase, M., David, B., Kohlweiss, M., Nishimaki, R., Ohkubo, M.: Constant-size structure-preserving signatures: generic constructions and simple assumptions. In: Wang, X., Sako, K. (eds.) ASIACRYPT 2012. LNCS, vol. 7658, pp. 4–24. Springer, Heidelberg (2012). https://doi.org/10.1007/978-3-642-34961-4_3

3. Abe, M., David, B., Kohlweiss, M., Nishimaki, R., Ohkubo, M.: Tagged one-time signatures: tight security and optimal tag size. In: Kurosawa, K., Hanaoka, G. (eds.) PKC 2013. LNCS, vol. 7778, pp. 312–331. Springer, Heidelberg (2013). https://doi.org/10.1007/978-3-642-36362-7_20

4. Abe, M., Fuchsbauer, G., Groth, J., Haralambiev, K., Ohkubo, M.: Structure-preserving signatures and commitments to group elements. In: Rabin, T. (ed.) CRYPTO 2010. LNCS, vol. 6223, pp. 209–236. Springer, Heidelberg (2010). https://doi.org/10.1007/978-3-642-14623-7_12

5. Abe, M., Groth, J., Haralambiev, K., Ohkubo, M.: Optimal structure-preserving signatures in asymmetric bilinear groups. In: Rogaway, P. (ed.) CRYPTO 2011. LNCS, vol. 6841, pp. 649–666. Springer, Heidelberg (2011). https://doi.org/10.1007/978-3-642-22792-9_37

6. Abe, M., Groth, J., Ohkubo, M.: Separating short structure-preserving signatures from non-interactive assumptions. In: Lee, D.H., Wang, X. (eds.) ASIACRYPT 2011. LNCS, vol. 7073, pp. 628–646. Springer, Heidelberg (2011). https://doi.org/10.1007/978-3-642-25385-0_34

7. Abe, M., Groth, J., Ohkubo, M., Tibouchi, M.: Unified, minimal and selectively randomizable structure-preserving signatures. In: Lindell, Y. (ed.) TCC 2014. LNCS, vol. 8349, pp. 688–712. Springer, Heidelberg (2014). https://doi.org/10.1007/978-3-642-54242-8_29

8. Abe, M., Groth, J., Ohkubo, M., Tibouchi, M.: Structure-preserving signatures from type II pairings. In: Garay, J.A., Gennaro, R. (eds.) CRYPTO 2014. LNCS, vol. 8616, pp. 390–407. Springer, Heidelberg (2014). https://doi.org/10.1007/978-3-662-44371-2_22

9. Abe, M., Hofheinz, D., Nishimaki, R., Ohkubo, M., Pan, J.: Compact structure-preserving signatures with almost tight security. In: Katz, J., Shacham, H. (eds.) CRYPTO 2017. LNCS, vol. 10402, pp. 548–580. Springer, Cham (2017). https://doi.org/10.1007/978-3-319-63715-0_19

10. Abe, M., Kohlweiss, M., Ohkubo, M., Tibouchi, M.: Fully structure-preserving signatures and shrinking commitments. In: Oswald, E., Fischlin, M. (eds.) EUROCRYPT 2015. LNCS, vol. 9057, pp. 35–65. Springer, Heidelberg (2015). https://doi.org/10.1007/978-3-662-46803-6_2

11. An, J.H., Dodis, Y., Rabin, T.: On the security of joint signature and encryption. In: Knudsen, L.R. (ed.) EUROCRYPT 2002. LNCS, vol. 2332, pp. 83–107. Springer, Heidelberg (2002). https://doi.org/10.1007/3-540-46035-7_6

12. Attrapadung, N., Libert, B., Peters, T.: Computing on authenticated data: new privacy definitions and constructions. In: Wang, X., Sako, K. (eds.) ASIACRYPT 2012. LNCS, vol. 7658, pp. 367–385. Springer, Heidelberg (2012). https://doi.org/10.1007/978-3-642-34961-4_23

13. Baldimtsi, F., Chase, M., Fuchsbauer, G., Kohlweiss, M.: Anonymous transferable E-cash. In: Katz, J. (ed.) PKC 2015. LNCS, vol. 9020, pp. 101–124. Springer, Heidelberg (2015). https://doi.org/10.1007/978-3-662-46447-2_5

14. Barthe, G., Fagerholm, E., Fiore, D., Scedrov, A., Schmidt, B., Tibouchi, M.: Strongly-optimal structure preserving signatures from type II pairings: synthesis and lower bounds. In: Katz, J. (ed.) PKC 2015. LNCS, vol. 9020, pp. 355–376. Springer, Heidelberg (2015). https://doi.org/10.1007/978-3-662-46447-2_16

15. Bernhard, D., Fuchsbauer, G., Ghadafi, E.: Efficient signatures of knowledge and DAA in the standard model. In: Jacobson, M., Locasto, M., Mohassel, P., Safavi-Naini, R. (eds.) ACNS 2013. LNCS, vol. 7954, pp. 518–533. Springer, Heidelberg (2013). https://doi.org/10.1007/978-3-642-38980-1_33

16. Brickell, E., Camenisch, J., Chen, L.: Direct anonymous attestation. In: ACM CCS 2004, pp. 132–145. ACM (2004)

17. Camenisch, J., Dubovitskaya, M., Haralambiev, K.: Efficient structure-preserving signature scheme from standard assumptions. In: Visconti, I., De Prisco, R. (eds.) SCN 2012. LNCS, vol. 7485, pp. 76–94. Springer, Heidelberg (2012). https://doi.org/10.1007/978-3-642-32928-9_5

18. Camenisch, J., Dubovitskaya, M., Haralambiev, K., Kohlweiss, M.: Composable and modular anonymous credentials: definitions and practical constructions. In: Iwata, T., Cheon, J.H. (eds.) ASIACRYPT 2015. LNCS, vol. 9453, pp. 262–288. Springer, Heidelberg (2015). https://doi.org/10.1007/978-3-662-48800-3_11

19. Chase, M., Kohlweiss, M.: A new hash-and-sign approach and structure-preserving signatures from DLIN. In: Visconti, I., De Prisco, R. (eds.) SCN 2012. LNCS, vol. 7485, pp. 131–148. Springer, Heidelberg (2012). https://doi.org/10.1007/978-3-642-32928-9_8

20. Chatterjee, S., Menezes, A.: Type 2 structure-preserving signature schemes revisited. In: Iwata, T., Cheon, J.H. (eds.) ASIACRYPT 2015. LNCS, vol. 9452, pp. 286–310. Springer, Heidelberg (2015). https://doi.org/10.1007/978-3-662-48797-6_13

21. Chaum, D., van Heyst, E.: Group signatures. In: Davies, D.W. (ed.) EUROCRYPT 1991. LNCS, vol. 547, pp. 257–265. Springer, Heidelberg (1991). https://doi.org/10.1007/3-540-46416-6_22

22. ElGamal, T.: A public key cryptosystem and a signature scheme based on discrete logarithms. IEEE Trans. Inf. Theor. **31**(4), 469–472 (1985)

23. El Kaafarani, A., Ghadafi, E.: Attribute-based signatures with user-controlled linkability without random Oracles. In: O'Neill, M. (ed.) IMACC 2017. LNCS, vol. 10655, pp. 161–184. Springer, Cham (2017). https://doi.org/10.1007/978-3-319-71045-7_9

24. El Kaafarani, A., Ghadafi, E., Khader, D.: Decentralized traceable attribute-based signatures. In: Benaloh, J. (ed.) CT-RSA 2014. LNCS, vol. 8366, pp. 327–348. Springer, Cham (2014). https://doi.org/10.1007/978-3-319-04852-9_17

25. Fiat, A., Shamir, A.: How to prove yourself: practical solutions to identification and signature problems. In: Odlyzko, A.M. (ed.) CRYPTO 1986. LNCS, vol. 263, pp. 186–194. Springer, Heidelberg (1987). https://doi.org/10.1007/3-540-47721-7_12

26. Fuchsbauer, G.: Commuting signatures and verifiable encryption. In: Paterson, K.G. (ed.) EUROCRYPT 2011. LNCS, vol. 6632, pp. 224–245. Springer, Heidelberg (2011). https://doi.org/10.1007/978-3-642-20465-4_14

27. Fuchsbauer, G., Hanser, C., Slamanig, D.: Practical round-optimal blind signatures in the standard model. In: Gennaro, R., Robshaw, M. (eds.) CRYPTO 2015. LNCS, vol. 9216, pp. 233–253. Springer, Heidelberg (2015). https://doi.org/10.1007/978-3-662-48000-7_12

28. Galbraith, S., Paterson, K., Smart, N.P.: Pairings for cryptographers. Discrete Appl. Math. **156**(2008), 3113–3121 (2008)

29. Gay, R., Hofheinz, D., Kohl, L., Pan, J.: More efficient (almost) tightly secure structure-preserving signatures. In: Nielsen, J.B., Rijmen, V. (eds.) EUROCRYPT 2018. LNCS, vol. 10821, pp. 230–258. Springer, Cham (2018). https://doi.org/10.1007/978-3-319-78375-8_8

30. Ghadafi, E.: Formalizing group blind signatures and practical constructions without random oracles. In: Boyd, C., Simpson, L. (eds.) ACISP 2013. LNCS, vol. 7959, pp. 330–346. Springer, Heidelberg (2013). https://doi.org/10.1007/978-3-642-39059-3_23

31. Ghadafi, E.: Short structure-preserving signatures. In: Sako, K. (ed.) CT-RSA 2016. LNCS, vol. 9610, pp. 305–321. Springer, Cham (2016). https://doi.org/10.1007/978-3-319-29485-8_18

32. Ghadafi, E.: More efficient structure-preserving signatures - or: bypassing the type-III lower bounds. In: Foley, S.N., Gollmann, D., Snekkenes, E. (eds.) ESORICS 2017. LNCS, vol. 10493, pp. 43–61. Springer, Cham (2017). https://doi.org/10.1007/978-3-319-66399-9_3

33. Ghadafi, E.: How low can you go? Short structure-preserving signatures for diffie-hellman vectors. In: O'Neill, M. (ed.) IMACC 2017. LNCS, vol. 10655, pp. 185–204. Springer, Cham (2017). https://doi.org/10.1007/978-3-319-71045-7_10

34. Green, M., Hohenberger, S.: Universally composable adaptive oblivious transfer. In: Pieprzyk, J. (ed.) ASIACRYPT 2008. LNCS, vol. 5350, pp. 179–197. Springer, Heidelberg (2008). https://doi.org/10.1007/978-3-540-89255-7_12

35. Groth, J.: Simulation-sound NIZK proofs for a practical language and constant size group signatures. In: Lai, X., Chen, K. (eds.) ASIACRYPT 2006. LNCS, vol. 4284, pp. 444–459. Springer, Heidelberg (2006). https://doi.org/10.1007/11935230_29

36. Groth, J.: Efficient fully structure-preserving signatures for large messages. In: Iwata, T., Cheon, J.H. (eds.) ASIACRYPT 2015. LNCS, vol. 9452, pp. 239–259. Springer, Heidelberg (2015). https://doi.org/10.1007/978-3-662-48797-6_11

37. Groth, J., Sahai, A.: Efficient non-interactive proof systems for bilinear groups. SIAM J. Comput. 41(5), 1193–1232 (2012)

38. Hofheinz, D., Jager, T.: Tightly secure signatures and public-key encryption. In: Safavi-Naini, R., Canetti, R. (eds.) CRYPTO 2012. LNCS, vol. 7417, pp. 590–607. Springer, Heidelberg (2012). https://doi.org/10.1007/978-3-642-32009-5_35

39. Jutla, C.S., Roy, A.: Improved structure preserving signatures under standard bilinear assumptions. In: Fehr, S. (ed.) PKC 2017. LNCS, vol. 10175, pp. 183–209. Springer, Heidelberg (2017). https://doi.org/10.1007/978-3-662-54388-7_7

40. Kiltz, E., Pan, J., Wee, H.: Structure-preserving signatures from standard assumptions, revisited. In: Gennaro, R., Robshaw, M. (eds.) CRYPTO 2015. LNCS, vol. 9216, pp. 275–295. Springer, Heidelberg (2015). https://doi.org/10.1007/978-3-662-48000-7_14

41. Libert, B., Peters, T., Yung, M.: Short group signatures via structure-preserving signatures: standard model security from simple assumptions. In: Gennaro, R., Robshaw, M. (eds.) CRYPTO 2015. LNCS, vol. 9216, pp. 296–316. Springer, Heidelberg (2015). https://doi.org/10.1007/978-3-662-48000-7_15

42. Maji, H.K., Prabhakaran, M., Rosulek, M.: Attribute-based signatures. In: Kiayias, A. (ed.) CT-RSA 2011. LNCS, vol. 6558, pp. 376–392. Springer, Heidelberg (2011). https://doi.org/10.1007/978-3-642-19074-2_24

43. Mambo, M., Usuda, K., Okamoto, E.: Proxy signatures for delegating signing operation. In: ACM CCS 1996, pp. 48–57. ACM (1996)

44. Maurer, U.: Abstract models of computation in cryptography. In: Smart, N.P. (ed.) Cryptography and Coding 2005. LNCS, vol. 3796, pp. 1–12. Springer, Heidelberg (2005). https://doi.org/10.1007/11586821_1

45. Shoup, V.: Lower bounds for discrete logarithms and related problems. In: Fumy, W. (ed.) EUROCRYPT 1997. LNCS, vol. 1233, pp. 256–266. Springer, Heidelberg (1997). https://doi.org/10.1007/3-540-69053-0_18

46. Teranishi, I., Furukawa, J., Sako, K.: k-times anonymous authentication (extended abstract). In: Lee, P.J. (ed.) ASIACRYPT 2004. LNCS, vol. 3329, pp. 308–322. Springer, Heidelberg (2004). https://doi.org/10.1007/978-3-540-30539-2_22
47. Wang, Y., Zhang, Z., Matsuda, T., Hanaoka, G., Tanaka, K.: How to obtain fully structure-preserving (automorphic) signatures from structure-preserving ones. In: Cheon, J.H., Takagi, T. (eds.) ASIACRYPT 2016. LNCS, vol. 10032, pp. 465–495. Springer, Heidelberg (2016). https://doi.org/10.1007/978-3-662-53890-6_16

A New Approach to Modelling Centralised Reputation Systems

Lydia Garms[✉] and Elizabeth A. Quaglia

Information Security Group, Royal Holloway University of London, Egham, UK
{Lydia.Garms.2015,Elizabeth.Quaglia}@rhul.ac.uk

Abstract. A reputation system assigns a user or item a reputation value which can be used to evaluate trustworthiness. Blömer, Juhnke and Kolb in 2015, and Kaafarani, Katsumata and Solomon in 2018, gave formal models for *centralised* reputation systems, which rely on a central server and are widely used by service providers such as AirBnB, Uber and Amazon. In these models, reputation values are given to items, instead of users. We advocate a need for shift in how reputation systems are modelled, whereby reputation values are given to users, instead of items, and each user has unlinkable items that other users can give feedback on, contributing to their reputation value. This setting is not captured by the previous models, and we argue it captures more realistically the functionality and security requirements of a reputation system. We provide definitions for this new model, and give a construction from standard primitives, proving it satisfies these security requirements. We show that there is a low efficiency cost for this new functionality.

1 Introduction

Reputation has always played a fundamental role in how we exchange products and services. While traditionally we have been used to trusting the reputation of established brands or companies, we are now facing a new challenge in the online world: determining the trustworthiness of a wide variety of possible exchanges. Whether we are selecting a restaurant, buying a product or getting a taxi, we are increasingly relying on scores and ratings to make our choice. For example, on Amazon, which in 2015 had over 2 million third party sellers worldwide [1], each seller is given a rating out of 5. Also Uber, with over 40 million monthly active users [2], allows drivers and passengers to rate each other.

A *reputation system* formalises this process of rating a user or service by associating with them a value representing their trustworthiness. A reputation is then built as the value gets updated over time, as a consequence of user interactions and service exchanges. Obviously, to form a reputation value for a specific user or service, their behaviour across interactions needs to be linked, but this may have privacy implications. For instance, a user could be deanonymised by linking all their interactions together in a profiling attack.

Given this, a cryptographic treatment of reputation systems has been considered necessary, and several models have been proposed in the literature so

© Springer Nature Switzerland AG 2019
J. Buchmann et al. (Eds.): AFRICACRYPT 2019, LNCS 11627, pp. 429–447, 2019.
https://doi.org/10.1007/978-3-030-23696-0_22

far [3,8,18]. Reputation Systems can be generally categorised into *distributed* or *centralised* systems. Distributed systems [23] have no central server and use local reputation values, i.e., reputation values created by users on other users. For example, a user may generate a reputation value based on feedback from querying other users, and their own interactions. This means a user does not have a unique reputation value, but many other users hold their own reputation value for them. For example privacy preserving decentralised reputation systems [25] are designed to maintain anonymity when answering queries from other nodes.

Centralised systems, on the other hand, have a central server that manages the network, performing tasks such as controlling communication between users, receiving feedback and evaluating reputation values. In this paper, we will focus on centralised systems since the reputation systems used by most service providers such as Airbnb, Uber and Amazon are of this type. A variety of centralised reputation system models and instantiations have been proposed in the literature, as we shall see in Sect. 2. While their applications and the used techniques vary greatly amongst them, all of the models have in common that reputations are assigned to each *item* or service, the object of the reputation, rather than each *user*, the provider of the service. To understand the limitations of this, let us consider the case of online shopping: in such a scenario, existing reputation systems would typically allocate a reputation to each product sold (item), and not to each seller (user), based on all their sold products.

In this paper, we advocate the need for a shift in how reputation systems are modelled, and we propose a new model for reputation systems in which a reputation value is given to each user, based on all their user behaviour or items. This is crucial in ensuring that a user's previous behaviour will contribute to their current reputation, instead of having separate reputations for each service provided. Clearly, if items belonging to a user could be linked together, the model which has been used so far could be transformed into our new one, by collating the reviews for each item belonging to a user to form a reputation value. However, if the user wishes to make their items unlinkable for privacy reasons, then this becomes more challenging.

1.1 Motivation and Contribution

Our contribution is to propose a new model for reputation systems so that reputation values are given to users instead of items, whilst guaranteeing that the user's behaviour is unlinkable, and that the central server does not have to be involved during every transaction. This means that users can have multiple unlinkable items, whilst a reputation value still reflects their entire behaviour. Therefore users can have the benefits of privacy, whilst still being held accountable for the previous behaviour.

A car pooling app is an example of the reputation systems we are modelling. A user may not want their trips (or items) to be linked together, as their movements could be tracked. However, a user's reputation should be based on their previous trips, so others can judge their reliability. In this context, reputations based on each journey are not useful, as they cannot be used for future journeys. This is why it is important to give reputation values to users instead of items.

The first challenge when developing such reputation systems, is to provide a mechanism for generating reputation values, whilst ensuring items cannot be linked by user. We model this with a ReceiveFB algorithm run by the Central Server (CS), the central server, which takes feedback, and links it to other feedback on items with the same author, updating their reputation. We define the security requirement, *Unlinkability of User Behaviour*, which defines the unlinkability of items by the same user achievable while reputations can still be updated using ReceiveFB. Our approach as described so far gives rise to a possible attack in which a user produces a valid item which will not contribute to this user's reputation, or will even unfairly affect another user ReceiveFB. We introduce the *Traceability* security requirement to mitigate against this attack. These security requirements are reminiscent of those for group signature schemes in [4].

The second challenge is to determine the reputation of a specific user, whose items are unlinkable. A naive solution could be for the user to simply attach their reputation to an item, but the user could lie about their reputation. To avoid this, we introduce the PostItem algorithm, with which the user posts their item, and proves they were given a reputation at a particular time, using a token generated by the CS. We further introduce the security requirement of *Unforgeability of Reputation* to ensure the user cannot lie about their reputation.

Finally, the standard security requirements of a centralised reputation system [8,18], namely Anonymity of Feedback, Soundness of Reputation and Non–frameability, still need to hold, and we adapt these naturally to our new model.

A reputation system satisfying our security requirements can be built using two standard primitives: Group Signature Schemes [16] for posting items, under the condition that they can be modified so that users can prove their reputation at a particular time with a token generated by the CS, and Direct Anonymous Attestation (DAA) [12] for sending feedback. In this paper we present a concrete construction using a modified version of the group signature scheme given in [17], which ensures the Unlinkability of User Behaviour, Traceability and Unforgeability of Reputation requirements described above. Our modification to [17], similarly to in [24], allows users to prove their reputation at a particular time. Our construction also makes use of the DAA scheme given in [15], which ensures anonymity of feedback, whilst multiple feedback on the same item can be detected, ensuring Soundness of Reputation. This is due to the user controlled linkability property of the DAA scheme, where only signatures with the same basenames can be linked, and we use this by setting the basename to be the item feedback is given on.

2   Related Work

While there exists an abundant literature on centralised reputation systems [3,7,19,24,26,28] the most relevant work to this paper are [8] and [18], due to their focus on formal models of reputation systems.

The model proposed in [8] is inspired by the security model for dynamic group signatures [6], and the authors provide an extra linkability feature to detect users giving multiple feedback on the same subject. In [18], the security requirements for this model are improved by giving more power to the adversary, (for example, in the public linkability security requirement the key issuer is no longer assumed to be honest), and introducing the requirement that an adversary cannot give feedback that will link to another user, invalidating their feedback. In [18] the model is also made fully dynamic [11], ie users can join or leave the scheme at any time, and a lattice-based instantiation satisfying this model is provided. To reduce complexity, our model is in the static setting, however the model and constuction could be converted to the dynamic case using [6], and due to the dynamic setting of our building blocks.

Crucially, in both [8] and [18] reputations are assigned to each *item*, the subject of feedback, not each *user*. By contrast, we propose a new model for reputation systems in which a reputation value is given to each user, based on all their user behaviour or items. This ensures a user's reputation reflects their entire past behaviour and so ensures they are accountable for their previous actions, modelling more accurately how such systems truly operate.

3   Defining a Reputation System

We define a reputation system, Π, as consisting of the following probabilistic polynomial time algorithms: Setup, AllocateReputation, PostItem, CheckItem, SendFB, VerifyFB, LinkFB, ReceiveFB. We illustrate our model in Fig. 1.

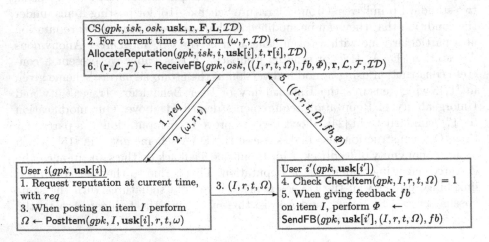

Fig. 1. Diagram modelling how entities interact in a centralised reputation system.

SendFB, VerifyFB, and LinkFB are equivalent to the Sign, Verify, Link algorithms in [8] and [18]. The additional algorithms, which we introduce in this paper, represent the key features of our new approach.

The entities involved are a set of users $\mathcal{U}$ and a Central Server (CS). The Central Server has two secret keys, isk and osk. The issuing secret key isk is necessary for allowing users to join the system and allocating them tokens to prove their reputation, whereas the opening secret key, osk, is necessary for forming reputations from feedback. For simplicity we give the CS both secret keys, but to reduce the power of one entity the role of the CS could be distributed.

The CS begins by running Setup. Users post items[1], which are the subject of feedback, while proving their reputation at a certain time using PostItem. After a request from a user, the CS runs AllocateReputation, which outputs tokens to allow a user to prove their current reputation at a specific time in PostItem. And other users verify that an item is a valid output of PostItem by running CheckItem. This ensures the item was authored by an enrolled user, the reputation alongside the item is correct for the given time, and the CS can use feedback on the item to form reputations. SendFB is run by a user when giving feedback on an item, and its output is sent to the CS. ReceiveFB is run by the Central Server when receiving the output of SendFB from a user. The CS updates their stored feedback and reputations, based on this. VerifyFB and LinkFB are used by ReceiveFB to check the feedback is valid and that there is no feedback by the same user on this item, otherwise ReceiveFB will abort.

In the car pooling example, whenever a driver wishes to update their reputation, they request the CS run AllocateReputation to obtain a token for their reputation. They are incentivised to do this by the fact the reputation is displayed alongside the time it was allocated. When they wish to give a ride, they use their most recent token to post an item with PostItem, which can be verified by passengers with CheckItem. The passenger can then pay using some anonymous payment system. After the ride, their passenger can then give feedback on this item to the CS using SendFB. The CS uses ReceiveFB to update their lists of feedback, and reputations for each user, if the feedback is valid.

Before describing in detail our new model, we provide, for ease of reading, an overview of our notation.

$\mathcal{R}$: The set of all possible reputation values.
$\hat{r}$: The initial reputation of every user at the system's setup.
$\mathcal{U}$: The set of all users in the scheme.
Aggr: A function that takes as input the new feedback fb, the user who's reputation is being updated i, the list of feedback already received $\mathcal{F}$, and the most recent reputation r, and outputs the new reputation r'.
$\mathbf{r}$: For the user $i \in \mathcal{U}$, $\mathbf{r}[i]$ is the user i's reputation held by the CS.
$\mathcal{L}$: A list of feedback that will contain entries in the form of a 6-tuple $((I, r, t, \Omega), fb, \Phi)$, where (fb, Φ) is feedback/proof pair, given on item I with reputation r, and time t, with the proof Ω. $\mathcal{L}$ is used by the CS to keep track of all feedback given, so that multiple feedback on the same item can be detected in ReceiveFB.

---

[1] A simple example of an item could be a product being sold.

$\mathcal{F}$: A list of feedback that will contain entries of the form (i, fb) where fb is feedback given to user i. $\mathcal{F}$ is used by the CS to keep track of all feedback given on user i to form reputations in ReceiveFB.

$\mathcal{ID}$: A list of identities for all users, this list will allow the CS to store information on users whilst running AllocateReputation for use in ReceiveFB.

We next formally define a centralised reputation system Π, consisting of the following probabilistic polynomial time algorithms: Setup, AllocateReputation, PostItem, CheckItem, SendFB, VerifyFB, LinkFB, ReceiveFB.

- Setup$(k, \mathcal{R}, \hat{r}, \mathcal{U}, \mathsf{Aggr})$ takes as input: a security parameter k, a set $\mathcal{R}$ of reputation values, $\hat{r} \in \mathcal{R}$, the initial reputation, a set of users $\mathcal{U}$, and the aggregation algorithm Aggr. The CS computes a public key gpk, the issuing secret key isk, which is used to issue new user secret keys, and in AllocateReputation, and the opening secret key osk, which is used in ReceiveFB to trace the author of an item to form reputations. The CS computes a secret key for each user, $\mathbf{usk} = \{\mathbf{usk}[i] : i \in \mathcal{U}\}$, and $\mathbf{r}$, the reputation for all users held by the CS, where $\forall i \in \mathcal{U}, \mathbf{r}[i] = \hat{r}$. The CS creates empty lists $\mathcal{L}, \mathcal{F}, \mathcal{ID}$ which are described above. It outputs $(gpk, isk, osk, \mathbf{usk}, \mathbf{r}, \mathcal{L}, \mathcal{F}, \mathcal{ID})$.
- AllocateReputation$(gpk, isk, i, \mathbf{usk}[i], t, \mathbf{r}[i], \mathcal{ID})$ takes as input the public key gpk, the issuing secret key isk, user i's secret key $\mathbf{usk}[i]$, the current time t, the current reputation of user i held by the CS $\mathbf{r}[i]$, and the list of identities for users $\mathcal{ID}$. It updates the list of identities $\mathcal{ID}$, and outputs $(\omega, \mathbf{r}[i], \mathcal{ID})$, where ω allows user i to prove they have reputation $\mathbf{r}[i]$.
- PostItem$(gpk, I, \mathbf{usk}[i], r, t, \omega)$ takes as input the public key gpk, an item I, user i's secret key $\mathbf{usk}[i]$, the last reputation r, time t and token ω received from the CS (r is not necessarily the reputation $\mathbf{r}[i]$ held by the CS). It outputs Ω, which proves the author is enrolled and has reputation r at time t, and is used in ReceiveFB to form a reputation for i.
- CheckItem(gpk, I, r, t, Ω) takes as input the public key gpk, an item I, a reputation r, a time t and Ω. It outputs 1 if Ω is a valid output of PostItem, given (I, r, t), and 0 otherwise.
- SendFB$(gpk, \mathbf{usk}[i], (I, r, t, \Omega), fb)$ takes as input the public key gpk, user i's secret key $\mathbf{usk}[i]$, the subject of their feedback, (I, r, t, Ω), and the feedback fb. It outputs Φ which is sent to the CS, to prove the author of Φ is enrolled, and also for the detection of multiple feedback.
- VerifyFB$(gpk, (I, r, t, \Omega), fb, \Phi)$ takes as input the public key gpk, an item (I, r, t, Ω), and feedback/proof pair on this item (fb, Φ). It outputs 1 if Φ is a valid output of SendFB, and 0 otherwise.
- LinkFB$(gpk, (I, r, t, \Omega), fb_0, \Phi_0, fb_1, \Phi_1)$ takes as input the public key gpk, an item (I, r, t, Ω), and two feedback/proof pairs on this item, (fb_0, Φ_0), (fb_1, Φ_1). It outputs 1 if Φ_0 and Φ_1 were generated by the same user with the same input of (I, r, t, Ω), and 0 otherwise.
- ReceiveFB$(gpk, osk, ((I, r, t, \Omega), fb, \Phi), \mathbf{r}, \mathcal{L}, \mathcal{F}, \mathcal{ID})$ takes as input the public key gpk, the opening secret key osk, a feedback/proof pair (fb, Φ) on item (I, r, t, Ω), the current reputations $\mathbf{r}$ held by the CS, the lists of feedback so

far $\mathcal{L}$ and $\mathcal{F}$, and the list of user identities $\mathcal{ID}$. If Φ is not valid, or the LinkFB algorithm finds multiple feedbacks in $\mathcal{L}$ then it outputs $\perp$. Otherwise, it uses the aggregation algorithm Aggr, and the list $\mathcal{F}$, to update $\mathbf{r}$, $\mathcal{L}$ and $\mathcal{F}$ to take into account the new feedback. It outputs $(\mathbf{r}, \mathcal{L}, \mathcal{F})$.

4 Security Requirements

As discussed earlier, we consider reputation systems satisfying the following requirements: Correctness, Unforgeability of Reputation, Traceability, Unlinkability of User Behaviour, Soundness of Reputation, Anonymity of Feedback, and Non–frameability. We begin with an informal discussion explaining the necessity for our security requirements and then follow up with formal definitions for the three security requirements original to this work.

We propose Unforgeability of Reputation, a new requirement that ensures a user cannot prove that they have a reputation for a certain time, which differs from the one they were allocated by the CS in AllocateReputation. This is necessary because when an item is unlinkable, the author's reputation cannot be determined. Therefore the reputation must be included alongside the item. This requirement ensures that the sender has not lied about their reputation.

Here we introduce Unlinkability of User Behaviour, which formalises our definition of unlinkable user behaviour, given that ReceiveFB can still form reputations, as well as Traceability, which ensures that all items generated by an adversary can be traced back to them when computing their reputation. This is necessary because, due to the Unlinkability of User Behaviour requirement, an attacker could attempt to subvert ReceiveFB. These requirements are reminiscent of the Full-Anonymity and Full-Traceability requirements [4] for group signature schemes, and have been adapted for reputation systems.

Soundness of Reputation ensures an adversary cannot give multiple feedback on the same item, undermining the integrity of reputation values. Anonymity of Feedback ensures that feedback cannot be traced to the user's identity and is unlinkable. We have adapted these two requirements from [8] to fit our notation[2]. Non–frameability, adapted from [18], ensures that an adversary cannot forge feedback that links to another user's feedback, so this feedback is unfairly disregarded. The Traceability requirement from [18] is not carried over, as we believe opening of feedback would add unnecessary complexity to the model.

We highlight that the issuing secret key is used by the Central Server for joining users to the scheme, and therefore for the Traceability and Soundness of Reputation requirements the adversary cannot corrupt the isk as otherwise they could cheat by creating unregistered users. The opening secret key is used by the Central Server to trace items, so that reputations can be updated with new feedback. Therefore in the Unlinkability of User Behaviour requirement the

---

[2] Soundness of Reputation is comparable to Public Linkability and Anonymity of Feedback is comparable to Anonymity.

adversary cannot corrupt the *osk* as otherwise they could trace signatures. This means the CS could be split into two separate entities with different secret keys.

In Fig. 2, we provide the oracles used in our security requirements: USK, POSTITEM, SENDFB, RECEIVEFB and ALLOCATEREP. USK allows the adversary to obtain users' secret keys. POSTITEM allows the adversary to obtain valid items of a user, without their secret key. SENDFB allows the adversary to obtain valid feedbacks of a user, without their secret key, storing outputs in the sets $\mathcal{G}_i$, for use in the Non–frameability requirement. RECEIVEFB allows the adversary to discover the output of ReceiveFB, without the opening secret key, *osk*. ALLOCATEREP allows the adversary to obtain outputs of the AllocateReputation algorithm, without the issuing secret key, *isk*.

USK(i):   **POSTITEM(I, i, r, t, ω):**

$\mathcal{C} \leftarrow \mathcal{C} \cup \{i\}$; **return** $\mathbf{usk}[i]$ **return** PostItem($gpk, I, \mathbf{usk}[i], r, t, \omega$)

SENDFB($i, fb, (I, r, t, \Omega)$):

$\Phi \leftarrow$ SendFB($gpk, \mathbf{usk}[i], (I, r, t, \Omega), fb$), $\mathcal{G}_i \leftarrow \mathcal{G}_i \cup \{((I, r, t, \Omega), fb, \Phi)\}$ **return** Φ

RECEIVEFB($(I, r, t, \Omega), fb, \Phi, \mathcal{ID}$):

return $(\mathbf{r}, \mathcal{L}, \mathcal{F}) \leftarrow$ ReceiveFB($gpk, osk, ((I, r, t, \Omega), fb, \Phi), \mathbf{r}, \mathcal{L}, \mathcal{F}, \mathcal{ID}$)

ALLOCATEREP(i, t, r):

return AllocateReputation($gpk, isk, i, \mathbf{usk}[i], t, r, \mathcal{ID}$)

Fig. 2. Oracles used in our security requirements

We next formally define our requirements. The full correctness conditions as well Soundness of Reputation Values, Anonymity of Feedback, and Non-Frameability are given in the full version [20] of this paper due to their similarities to existing work.

Correctness: There are five conditions for correctness. Condition 1 ensures that if AllocateReputation and PostItem are computed honestly then CheckItem will output 1. Condition 2 ensures that if SendFB is computed honestly then VerifyFB will output 1. Condition 3 ensures the LinkFB algorithm will output 1, with input valid outputs of SendFB on the same item of (I, r, t, Ω), using the same user secret key. Condition 4 ensures if an item and feedback were generated honestly in PostItem and SendFB, then ReceiveFB updates $\mathbf{r}, \mathcal{L}, \mathcal{F}$ correctly. Condition 5 ensures that ReceiveFB fails, if the feedback input is not valid according to VerifyFB, or links to other feedback in $\mathcal{L}$ according to LinkFB.

We first present our new security requirements, which are necessary as reputation values are assigned to users instead of their individual unlinkable items.

Unforgeability of Reputation: A user can only prove that they have reputation r at time t, if this was allocated to them by the CS in AllocateReputation.

Experiment: $\mathsf{Exp}_{\mathcal{A},\Pi}^{\text{anon-ub}}(k,\mathcal{R},\hat{r},\mathcal{U},\mathsf{Aggr})$

$b \leftarrow_\$ \{0,1\}; \quad (gpk, isk, osk, \mathbf{usk}, \mathbf{r}, \mathcal{L}, \mathcal{F}, \mathcal{ID}) \leftarrow_\$ \mathsf{Setup}(k, \mathcal{R}, \hat{r}, \mathcal{U}, \mathsf{Aggr})$

$(St, i_0, i_1, I, r, t, \mathcal{ID}) \leftarrow_\$ \mathcal{A}^{\text{RECEIVEFB}}(\text{choose}, gpk, isk, \mathbf{usk}, \mathbf{r}, \mathcal{L}, \mathcal{F}, \mathcal{ID})$

$\forall \tilde{b} \in \{0,1\} \quad (\omega_{\tilde{b}}, \mathcal{ID}) \leftarrow \mathsf{AllocateReputation}(gpk, isk, i, \mathbf{usk}[i_{\tilde{b}}], t, r, \mathcal{ID})$

$\Omega \leftarrow \mathsf{PostItem}(gpk, I, \mathbf{usk}[i_b], r, t, \omega_b)$

$d \leftarrow_\$ \mathcal{A}^{\text{RECEIVEFB}}(\text{guess}, St, \Omega, \mathcal{ID}); \quad d' \leftarrow_\$ 0, 1$

if $((I, r, t, \Omega), \cdot)$ queried to the RECEIVEFB oracle **return** $d \leftarrow d'$

if $d = b$ **return** 1;   **else return** 0

Experiment: $\mathsf{Exp}_{\mathcal{A},\Pi}^{\text{trace}}(k,\mathcal{R},\hat{r},\mathcal{U},\mathsf{Aggr})$

$(gpk, isk, osk, \mathbf{usk}, \mathcal{ID}) \leftarrow_\$ \mathsf{Setup}(k, \mathcal{R}, \hat{r}, \mathcal{U}, \mathsf{Aggr}); C \leftarrow \varnothing$

$(I, r, t, \Omega, fb, \Phi, \mathbf{r}, \mathcal{L}, \mathcal{F}) \leftarrow_\$ \mathcal{A}^{\text{USK,POSTITEM,SENDFB, ALLOCATEREP}}(gpk, osk, \mathcal{ID})$

if $\mathsf{CheckItem}(gpk, I, r, t, \Omega) = 0$ or $\mathsf{VerifyFB}(gpk, (I, r, t, \Omega), fb, \Phi) = 0$ **return** 0

if $\exists ((I, r, t, \Omega), fb', \Phi') \in \mathcal{L}$ with $\mathsf{LinkFB}(gpk, (I, r, t, \Omega), fb, \Phi, fb', \Phi') = 1$ **return** 0

$\forall i \in \mathcal{U}, \mathcal{ID} \leftarrow \mathsf{AllocateReputation}(gpk, isk, i, \mathbf{usk}[i], t, r, \mathcal{ID})$

if $\perp \leftarrow \mathsf{ReceiveFB}(gpk, osk, ((I, r, t, \Omega), fb, \Phi), \mathbf{r}, \mathcal{L}, \mathcal{F}, \mathcal{ID})$ **return** 1

else $(\mathbf{r}^*, \mathcal{L}^*, \mathcal{F}^*) \leftarrow \mathsf{ReceiveFB}(gpk, osk, ((I, r, t, \Omega), fb, \Phi), \mathbf{r}, \mathcal{L}, \mathcal{F}, \mathcal{ID})$

if $\mathcal{L}^* \neq ((I, r, t, \Omega), fb, \Phi) \cup \mathcal{L}$ **return** 1

if $\mathcal{F}^* = (i', fb) \cup \mathcal{F}$ for some $i' \in \mathcal{U}$ $i^* \leftarrow i'$ **else return** 1

if $\mathbf{r}^*[i^*] \neq \mathsf{Aggr}(fb, i^*, \mathcal{F}, \mathbf{r}[i^*])$, or $\exists \hat{i} \in \mathcal{U} \setminus \{i^*\}$ such that $\mathbf{r}^*[\hat{i}] \neq \mathbf{r}[\hat{i}]$ **return** 1

if $i^* \notin C$ and $(I, i^*, r, t, \cdot)$ was not queried to the POSTITEM oracle   **return** 1

else   **return** 0

Experiment: $\mathsf{Exp}_{\mathcal{A},\Pi}^{\text{unforge-rep}}(k,\mathcal{R},\hat{r},\mathcal{U},\mathsf{Aggr})$

$(gpk, isk, osk, \mathbf{usk}, \mathbf{r}, \mathcal{L}, \mathcal{F}, \mathcal{ID}) \leftarrow_\$ \mathsf{Setup}(k, \mathcal{R}, \hat{r}, \mathcal{U}, \mathsf{Aggr})$

$(I, r, t, \Omega) \leftarrow_\$ \mathcal{A}^{\text{USK,POSTITEM,ALLOCATEREP}}(gpk, osk, \mathcal{ID})$

if Ω returned by POSTITEM or if $\mathsf{CheckItem}(gpk, I, r, t, \Omega) = 0$ **return** 0

$j \leftarrow_\$ \mathcal{U}, fb \leftarrow 0, \Phi \leftarrow \mathsf{SendFB}(gpk, \mathbf{usk}[j], (I, r, t, \Omega), fb)$

$(\mathbf{r}^*, \mathcal{L}^*, \mathcal{F}^*) \leftarrow \mathsf{ReceiveFB}(gpk, osk, ((I, r, t, \Omega), fb, \Phi), \mathbf{r}, \mathcal{L}, \mathcal{F}, \mathcal{ID})$

if $\mathcal{F}^* \setminus \mathcal{F} = \{i', fb\}$ for some $i' \in \mathcal{U}$ $i^* \leftarrow i'$ **else return** 1

if $\mathcal{A}$ queried (i^*, t, r) to ALLOCATEREP oracle and $i^* \in C$ **return** 0 **else return** 1

Fig. 3. Experiments capturing our Unlinkability of User Behaviour, Traceability and Unforgeability of Reputation security requirements

In the context of car pooling, this security requirement means that a driver cannot lie about their reputation when requesting a passenger.

In our security game in Fig. 3, the adversary is given the opening secret key osk, the list of user identities $\mathcal{ID}$, the USK, POSTITEM, ALLOCATEREP oracles, but not isk, as they could run AllocateReputation. The adversary wins if they output a valid item, for reputation r, time t, tracing to a corrupted user i in ReceiveFB, without querying (i, r, t) to the ALLOCATEREP oracle, or it does not trace to any user.

A reputation system Π satisfies Unforgeability of Reputation if for all polynomial time adversaries $\mathcal{A}$, all sets $\mathcal{R}$ and $\mathcal{U}$ such that $|\mathcal{R}|$ and $|\mathcal{U}|$ are polynomially bounded in k, all $\hat{r} \in \mathcal{R}$, all Aggr functions, there exists a negligible function in k, $negl$, such that: $Pr[\mathsf{Exp}_{\mathcal{A}, \Pi}^{unforge-rep}(k, \mathcal{R}, \hat{r}, \mathcal{U}, \mathsf{Aggr}) = 1] \leq negl$.

Traceability of Users: This security requirement ensures that any valid item an adversary produces will contribute towards their own reputation in ReceiveFB. This also guarantees unforgeability. In the context of car pooling, this security requirement means that feedback on a driver's rides will always affect their own reputation and not another's.

In our security game in Fig. 3, the adversary is given the opening secret key osk, the list of user identities $\mathcal{ID}$, the USK oracle to corrupt users, and the POSTITEM, SENDFB, ALLOCATEREP oracles for uncorrupted user, but not isk, because they could cheat by generating the secret key of a new user. They must output a valid item and feedback, and $\mathbf{r}, \mathcal{L}, \mathcal{F}$, such that the feedback does not link to any in $\mathcal{L}$. If ReceiveFB fails, does not correctly update $\mathbf{r}, \mathcal{L}, \mathcal{F}$, or updates the reputation of a non corrupted user, then the adversary wins.

A reputation system Π satisfies Traceability if for all polynomial time adversaries $\mathcal{A}$, all sets $\mathcal{R}$ and $\mathcal{U}$ such that $|\mathcal{R}|$ and $|\mathcal{U}|$ are polynomially bounded in k, all $\hat{r} \in \mathcal{R}$, all Aggr functions, there exists a negligible funtion in k, $negl$, such that: $Pr[\mathsf{Exp}_{\mathcal{A}, \Pi}^{trace}(k, \mathcal{R}, \hat{r}, \mathcal{U}, \mathsf{Aggr}) = 1] \leq negl$.

Unlinkability of User Behaviour: This requirement ensures other users cannot link together the items authored by a particular user, while the CS can link items to form reputation values based on a user's entire behaviour. In the context of car pooling, this security requirement means that all rides a driver/user undertakes are unlinkable, so their movements cannot be tracked.

In our security game, given in Fig. 3, the adversary is given all user secret keys, the issuing secret key isk, $\mathbf{r}$, $\mathcal{L}$, $\mathcal{F}$, and $\mathcal{ID}$, but not the opening secret key osk, because otherwise they could run ReceiveFB, and then check which user's reputation changes. They are given the RECEIVEFB oracle, but its use is restricted so that the challenge signature cannot be queried, to avoid the attack above. This attack would not be practical in the real world, as reputations will be updated at intervals so that multiple users' reputations will change at once. Future work could consider specific Aggr algorithms that would allow this security requirement to be strengthened. In our work, to ensure our model is generic, we define security for all possible Aggr functions.

The adversary chooses an item I, a reputation r and a time t, an updated list of identities $\mathcal{ID}$, and two users i_0, i_1, they are then given Ω and must decide whether it was authored by i_0 or i_1.

A reputation system Π satisfies Unlinkability of User Behaviour if for all polynomial time adversaries $\mathcal{A}$, all sets $\mathcal{R}$ and $\mathcal{U}$ such that $|\mathcal{R}|$ and $|\mathcal{U}|$ are polynomially bounded in k, and all $\hat{r} \in \mathcal{R}$, all Aggr functions, there exists a negligible funtion in k, $negl$, such that: $Pr[\mathsf{Exp}_{\mathcal{A},\Pi}^{anon-ub}(k,\mathcal{R},\hat{r},\mathcal{U},\mathsf{Aggr}) = 1] - 1/2 \le negl$.

We now give an overview of the existing security requirements.

Soundness of Reputation Values: Users who are not enrolled should not be able to give feedback. Reputation values should be based on only one piece of feedback per item per user. In the context of car pooling, this security requirement would mitigate against an attack where a passenger repeatedly gives feedback on one ride, unfairly negatively influencing the driver's reputation.

In the security game, adapted from [8], given in the full version [20], the adversary is able to corrupt users with the USK oracle, and is given the opening secret key osk, but not the issuing key isk, as they could use this to cheat by generating a secret key for a new user. They can use the SENDFB, ALLOCATEREP and POSTITEM oracles for uncorrupted users. The adversary outputs a list of feedback on the same item. They win if they can output more valid unlinkable feedback than the number of corrupted users, without using the SENDFB oracle.

Anonymity of Feedback: Anonymity of Feedback captures the anonymity of feedback senders against the Central Server, and up to all but two colluding users. Unfortunately it is not possible for a reputation system to have anonymity against all colluding users, whilst still satisfying Soundness of Reputation. This is because an adversary could discover whether a user i authored some feedback $((I,r,t,\Omega),fb,\Phi)$ by running $\Phi' \leftarrow \mathsf{SendFB}(gpk,\mathbf{usk}[i],(I,r,t,\Omega),fb')$, then running $\mathsf{LinkFB}(gpk,(I,r,t,\Omega),fb,\Phi,fb',\Phi')$. If this outputs 1, then $((I,r,t,\Omega),fb,\Phi)$ must be authored by i. In the context of car pooling, this security requirement means that provided passengers never give multiple feedback on the same ride, their feedback will be unlinkable.

In the security game, adapted from [8], and given in the full version [20], the adversary is given isk, osk, and must choose two users i_0 and i_1, an item (I,r,t,Ω), and feedback fb. They then must decide which of these users authored the Φ returned to them. The adversary can corrupt users with USK, and use SENDFB, POSTITEM and ALLOCATEREP for uncorrupted users. We do not allow the adversary to query i_0 or i_1 to the USK oracle, or to query SENDFB with either i_0 or i_1 and (I,r,t,Ω), so that they cannot perform the above attack.

Non–frameability: This requirement, adapted from [18], ensures that an adversary, who has corrupted the Central Server and all users, cannot forge feedback that links to feedback of another user, meaning ReceiveFB detects multiple feedback by this user, and unfairly outputs $\perp$. In the context of car pooling, this security requirement means that a passenger cannot feedback on their own ride, linking to the driver involved, invalidating any feedback they give.

In the security game, given in the full version [20], the adversary is given isk, osk and can corrupt users using the USK oracle, and use the POSTITEM, SENDFB, ALLOCATEREP oracles for uncorrupted users. To win, they must output valid feedback not output by the SENDFB oracle, which links to feedback output by the SENDFB oracle, authored by an uncorrupted user.

5   A Centralised Reputation System with Unlinkable User Behaviour

We now give a construction for Π, a reputation system as defined in Sect. 3, satisfying the security requirements we defined in Sect. 4. Our construction makes use of two existing primitives: a Group Signature scheme [16], and Direct Anonymous Attestation (DAA) [12].

More specifically, we modify the group signature scheme XS [17], in XS*, similarly to what was done in [19,24], for posting items in PostItem, CheckItem, and AllocateReputation. The XS scheme satisfies Unlinkability of User Behaviour, whilst still allowing reputations to be formed in ReceiveFB, using the opening key ensuring Traceability. Furthermore our modification allows a user to prove they were allocated a reputation at a certain time by AllocateReputation.

We then adopt the DAA scheme in [15] for the feedback component of the reputation system in SendFB, VerifyFB, LinkFB. This perfectly fits our requirements, because of the user controlled linkability of the DAA scheme. Signatures are signed with respect to a basename, and are linkable only when they have the same author and basename. Therefore in the context of reputation systems, by setting the basename to be the subject of the feedback, multiple feedback on the same item can be detected, whilst still ensuring Anonymity of Feedback.

5.1   Binding Reputation to the XS Group Signature Scheme

Group Signatures [16] prove a user is a member of a group without revealing their identity, except to those with an opening key. Security requirements were defined for static groups [4], partially dynamic groups [6], and fully dynamic groups [11]. The XS scheme [17] satisfies the security requirements for partially dynamic groups [6], of Anonymity, Traceability and Non-Frameability, under the q-SDH [9] assumption and in the random oracle model [5].

q-Strong Diffie Hellman Assumption (q-SDH). There are two versions of the q-Strong Diffie Hellman Assumption. The first version, given by Boneh and Boyen in [9], is defined in a type-1 or type-2 pairing setting. We use their second version of that definition that supports type-3 pairings and was stated in the journal version of their paper [10].

Given $(g_1, g_1^\chi, g_1^{(\chi)^2}, ..., g_1^{(\chi)^q}, g_2, g_2^\chi)$ such that $g_1 \in \mathbb{G}_1, g_2 \in \mathbb{G}_2$, output $(g_1^{\frac{1}{\chi+x}}, x) \in \mathbb{G}_1 \times \mathbb{Z}_p \backslash \{-\chi\}$.

We present XS*, a modification of the XS scheme [17], to allow users to prove their reputation in PostItem. In this modification, we introduce an additional algorithm XSUpdate*, used in AllocateReputation, which outputs a token allowing a user to update their secret key, depending on their reputation r at time t. PostItem uses XSSign* to sign as in the original group signature scheme, but with this updated secret key as input. CheckItem uses XSVerify*, which is modified so that it takes (r, t) as input, and only outputs 1 if the secret key used to generate this signature has been updated correctly with (r, t).

The XS* signature scheme consists of the algorithms given in Fig. 4, and the group public parameters gpp_1 chosen as follows. Let $\mathbb{G}_1, \mathbb{G}_2, \mathbb{G}_3$ be multiplicative cyclic groups with large prime order p, with $|p| = k$, and with generators G_1 and G_2 respectively. Let $\hat{t} : \mathbb{G}_1 \times \mathbb{G}_2 \to \mathbb{G}_3$, be a bilinear map. The q-SDH assumption must hold in $(\mathbb{G}_1, \mathbb{G}_2)$. Select two hash functions: $\mathcal{H}_1 : \{0,1\}^* \to \mathbb{G}_1$ and $\mathcal{H}_2 : \{0,1\}^* \to \mathbb{Z}_p^*$. The group public parameters for XS* are: $gpp_1 = (\mathbb{G}_1, \mathbb{G}_2, \mathbb{G}_3, p, \hat{t}, G_1, G_2, \mathcal{H}_1, \mathcal{H}_2)$.

5.2 Direct Anonymous Attestation

Direct Anonymous Attestation (DAA) [12] allows users to prove they are members of a group. There is no opening key but there is user controlled linkability, as defined at the beginning of this section. In DAA, a signer consists of two separate entities: a trusted TPM and a host with higher computational power. A DAA scheme is secure if it is indistinguishable from the ideal functionality, given in [13]. The CDL scheme [15], is proved secure, assuming the LSRW [22], Discrete Logarithm (DL), and DDH assumptions. We use the CDL DAA scheme

---

XSKeyGen*(gpp_1)

$\xi_1, \xi_2 \leftarrow_\$ \mathbb{Z}_p; K \leftarrow_\$ \mathbb{G}_1 \setminus \{1_{\mathbb{G}_1}\}, H \leftarrow K^{\xi_1}, G \leftarrow K^{\xi_2}, \gamma \leftarrow_\$ \mathbb{Z}_p, W \leftarrow G_2^\gamma$
return $gpk_1 = (G_1, K, H, G, G_2, W), isk_1 = \gamma, osk = (\xi_1, \xi_2)$

XSJoin*(isk_1, i, gpk_1)   **XSUpdate*$(t, r, isk_1, (Z, x, y), gpk_1)$**

$x, y \leftarrow_\$ \mathbb{Z}_p; \quad Z \leftarrow (G_1 H^y)^{\frac{1}{\gamma+x}}$ $Q \leftarrow \mathcal{H}_1(r, t)$
return $usk_1[i] = (Z, x, y)$ **return** $(\omega \leftarrow Q^{\frac{1}{\gamma+x}}, Z \cdot \omega)$

XSSign*$(I, (\tilde{Z}, x, y), gpk_1, r, t)$

$\rho_1, \rho_2 \leftarrow_\$ \mathbb{Z}_p, T_1 \leftarrow K^{\rho_1}, T_2 \leftarrow \tilde{Z} H^{\rho_1}, T_3 \leftarrow K^{\rho_2}, T_4 \leftarrow \tilde{Z} G^{\rho_2}, r_{\rho_1}, r_{\rho_2}, r_x, r_z \leftarrow_\$ \mathbb{Z}_p$
$R_1 \leftarrow K^{r_{\rho_1}}, R_3 \leftarrow K^{r_{\rho_2}}, R_4 \leftarrow H^{r_{\rho_1}} G^{-r_{\rho_2}}, R_2 \leftarrow \hat{t}(T_2, G_2)^{r_x} \hat{t}(H, W)^{-r_{\rho_1}} \hat{t}(H, G_2)^{-r_z}$
$c \leftarrow \mathcal{H}_2(I, T_1, T_2, T_3, T_4, R_1, R_2, R_3, R_4, r, t), z \leftarrow x\rho_1 + y, s_{\rho_1} = r_{\rho_1} + c\rho_1, s_{\rho_2} = r_{\rho_2} + c\rho_2$
$s_x = r_x + cx, s_z = r_z + cz$ **return** $\Omega = (T_1, T_2, T_3, T_4, c, s_{\rho_1}, s_{\rho_2}, s_x, s_z)$

XSVerify*(I, r, t, Ω, gpk_1)

Let $\Omega = (T_1, T_2, T_3, T_4, c, s_{\rho_1}, s_{\rho_2}, s_x, s_z), \tilde{G}_1 = G_1 \cdot \mathcal{H}_1(r, t)$
$\tilde{R}_1 \leftarrow K^{s_{\rho_1}} T_1^{-c}, \tilde{R}_3 \leftarrow K^{s_{\rho_2}} T_3^{-c}, \tilde{R}_4 = H^{s_{\rho_1}} G^{-s_{\rho_2}} T_4^c T_2^{-c}$
$\tilde{R}_2 = \hat{t}(T_2, G_2)^{s_x} \hat{t}(H, W)^{-s_{\rho_1}} \hat{t}(H, G_2)^{-s_z} \left(\dfrac{\hat{t}(T_2, W)}{\hat{t}(\tilde{G}_1, G_2)} \right)^c$
if $c = \mathcal{H}_2(I, T_1, T_2, T_3, T_4, \tilde{R}_1, \tilde{R}_2, \tilde{R}_3, \tilde{R}_4, r, t)$ **return** 1   **else return** 0

XSOpen*$(I, r, t, \Omega, osk, gpk_1)$

if XSVerify*$(I, r, t, \Omega, gpk_1) = 0$ **return** $\perp$ **return** $\tilde{Z} \leftarrow T_2 T_1^{-\xi_1}$

Fig. 4. The algorithms of XS*, our modification to [17]

CDLKeyGen(gpp_2)

$\alpha, \beta \leftarrow\!\!\$\ \mathbb{Z}_p^*, X \leftarrow G_2{}^\alpha \in \mathbb{G}_2, Y = G_2{}^\beta \in \mathbb{G}_2$
return $gpk_2 = ((X, Y), isk_2 = (\alpha, \beta))$

CDLJoin(i, isk_2, gpk_2)

$f \leftarrow\!\!\$\ \mathbb{Z}_p; F \leftarrow G_1{}^f, r \leftarrow\!\!\$\ \mathbb{Z}_p$
$A \leftarrow G_1{}^r, B \leftarrow A^\beta; C \leftarrow (A^\alpha F^{r\alpha\beta}), D \leftarrow (F)^{r\beta}$
$cre \leftarrow (A, B, C, D)$ **return** $usk_2[i] \leftarrow (f, cre)$

CDLSign($msg, fb, (f, (A, B, C, D)), gpk_2$)

$a \leftarrow\!\!\$\ \mathbb{Z}_p, A' \leftarrow A^a, B' \leftarrow B^a, C' \leftarrow C^a, D' \leftarrow D^a, z \leftarrow\!\!\$\ \mathbb{Z}_p, J \leftarrow \mathcal{H}_1(msg)^f, M \leftarrow B'^z, N \leftarrow \mathcal{H}_1(msg)^z$
$c \leftarrow \mathcal{H}_2(B'||D'||J||M||N||msg||fb), s \leftarrow z - c \cdot f (\text{mod } p)$ **return** $\Phi = (A', B', C', D', J, c, s)$

CDLVerify(msg, fb, Φ, gpk_2)

Let $\Phi = (A', B', C', D', J, c, s), \tilde{M} \leftarrow B'^s D'^c, \tilde{N} \leftarrow \mathcal{H}_1(msg)^s J^c$
if $c \neq \mathcal{H}_2(B'||D'||J||\tilde{M}||\tilde{N}||msg||fb)$ or $A' = 1$ **return** 0
if $\hat{t}(A', Y) \neq \hat{t}(B', G_2)$ or $\hat{t}(A'D', X) \neq \hat{t}(C', G_2)$ **return** 0   **else return** 1

CDLLink($msg, (fb_0, \Phi_0), (fb_1, \Phi_1), gpk_2$)

if $\exists \iota \in \{0, 1\}$ with CDLVerify($msg_\iota, fb_\iota, \Phi_\iota, gpk_2$) = 0   **return** 0
For $\iota \in \{0, 1\}$, let $\Phi_\iota = (A'_\iota, B'_\iota, C'_\iota, D'_\iota, J_\iota, c_\iota, s_\iota)$
if $J_0 = J_1$ **return** 1   **else return** 0

Fig. 5. The algorithms of CDL [15]

in particular, because as shown in Table 1 of [14], it has the lowest estimated running time for signing out of the schemes proved secure under the more recent models. We prioritise efficiency of signing over verification, because in reputation systems verification is performed by a server with more computational power.

The CDL scheme, with the TPM and host merged, consists of the algorithms in Fig. 5, and the group public parameters gpp_2. Let $\mathbb{G}_1, \mathbb{G}_2, \mathbb{G}_3$ be multiplicative cyclic groups with large prime order p, with $|p| = k$, and with generators G_1 and G_2. Let $\hat{t} : \mathbb{G}_1 \times \mathbb{G}_2 \rightarrow \mathbb{G}_3$, be a bilinear map. The DDH and DL problem must be hard in $\mathbb{G}_1$, and the bilinear LRSW [22] problem must be hard in $(\mathbb{G}_1, \mathbb{G}_2)$. Select two hash functions: $\mathcal{H}_1 : \{0, 1\}^* \rightarrow \mathbb{G}_1$, $\mathcal{H}_2 : \{0, 1\}^* \rightarrow \mathbb{Z}_p^*$. The group public parameters for CDL are: $gpp_2 = (\mathbb{G}_1, \mathbb{G}_2, \mathbb{G}_3, p, \hat{t}, G_1, G_2, \mathcal{H}_1, \mathcal{H}_2)$.

5.3   Our Construction

In Fig. 6 we give our construction for a reputation system Π, as defined in Sect. 3, derived from the XS* scheme and the CDL scheme. We prove in the full paper that this satisfies the security requirements from Sect. 4.

6   Evaluation of Our Construction

We first analyse the security of our construction, and then evaluate the efficiency. We prove Theorems 1–6 and correctness in the full version of this paper [20].

In the proof of Theorem 1, we show that if an adversary $\mathcal{A}$ can break the Unforgeability of Reputation experiment for our construction then we can build

Setup$(k, \mathcal{R}, \hat{r}, \mathcal{U}, \mathsf{Aggr})$

Generate (gpp_1, gpp_2) as above , $(gpk_1, isk_1, osk) \leftarrow$ XSKeyGen$^*(gpp_1)$, $(gpk_2, isk_2) \leftarrow$ CDLKeyGen(gpp_2)
$gpk \leftarrow (gpk_1, gpk_2), isk \leftarrow (isk_1, isk_2)$
$\forall i \in \mathcal{U} \quad \mathbf{usk}_1[i] \leftarrow$ XSJoin$^*(isk_1, i, gpk_1)$, $\mathbf{usk}_2[i] \leftarrow$ CDLJoin(i, isk_2, gpk_2), $\mathbf{usk}[i] \leftarrow (\mathbf{usk}_1[i], \mathbf{usk}_2[i])$
$\mathcal{L} \leftarrow \varnothing, \mathcal{F} \leftarrow \varnothing, \mathcal{ID} \leftarrow \varnothing, \forall i \in \mathcal{U}, \mathbf{r}[i] \leftarrow \hat{r}$ return $(gpk, isk, osk, \mathbf{usk}, \mathbf{r}, \mathcal{L}, \mathcal{F}, \mathcal{ID})$

AllocateReputation$(gpk, isk, i, \mathbf{usk}[i], t, \mathbf{r}[i], \mathcal{ID})$ PostItem$(gpk, I, (Z, x, y), r, t, \omega)$

$(\omega, \tilde{Z}) \leftarrow$ XSUpdate$^*(t, \mathbf{r}[i], \mathbf{usk}_1[i], isk_1, gpk_1)$ if $\hat{t}(\omega, WG_2^x) \neq \hat{t}(\mathcal{H}_1(r, t), G_2)$ return $\perp$
$\mathcal{ID} \leftarrow \mathcal{ID} \cup (i, \mathbf{r}[i], t, \tilde{Z})$ return $(\omega, \mathbf{r}[i], \mathcal{ID})$ $\tilde{Z} \leftarrow Z \cdot \omega, u\tilde{s}k \leftarrow (\tilde{Z}, x, y)$

                                             return $\Omega \leftarrow$ XSSign$^*(I, u\tilde{s}k, gpk_1, r, t)$

CheckItem(gpk, I, r, t, Ω) SendFB$(gpk, \mathbf{usk}[i], (I, r, t, \Omega), fb)$

---

return $b \leftarrow$ XSVerify$^*(I, r, t, \Omega, gpk_1)$ return $\Phi \leftarrow$ CDLSign$((I, r, t, \Omega), fb, \mathbf{usk}_2[i], gpk_2)$

VerifyFB$(gpk, (I, r, t, \Omega), fb, \Phi)$ LinkFB$(gpk, (I, r, t, \Omega), fb_0, \Phi_0, fb_1, \Phi_1)$

---

return $b \leftarrow$ CDLVerify$((I, r, t, \Omega), fb, \Phi, gpk_2)$ return $b \leftarrow$ CDLLink$((I, r, t, \Omega), (fb_0, \Phi_0), (fb_1, \Phi_1), gpk_2)$

ReceiveFB$(gpk, osk, ((I, r, t, \Omega), fb, \Phi), \mathbf{r}, \mathcal{L}, \mathcal{F}, \mathcal{ID})$

---

if VerifyFB$(gpk, (I, r, t, \Omega), fb, \Phi) = 0$ return $\perp$
if $\exists (I, r, t, \Omega), fb', \Phi') \in \mathcal{L}$ s.t. LinkFB$(gpk, (I, r, t, \Omega), fb, \Phi, fb', \Phi') = 1$ return $\perp$
$\tilde{Z} \leftarrow$ XSOpen$^*(I, r, t, \Omega, osk, gpk_1)$, Find $(i, r, t, \tilde{Z}) \in \mathcal{ID}$, otherwise return $\perp$
$\mathbf{r}[i] \leftarrow$ Aggr$(fb, i, \mathcal{F}, \mathbf{r}[i])$, $\mathcal{L} \leftarrow ((I, r, t, \Omega), fb, \Phi) \cup \mathcal{L}, \mathcal{F} \leftarrow (i, fb) \cup \mathcal{F}$ return $(\mathbf{r}, \mathcal{L})$

Fig. 6. Our reputation system, Π

an adversary $\mathcal{A}'$ that breaks the q-SDH assumption. $\mathcal{A}'$ uses the q-SDH instance input to simulate $gpk, osk, \mathbf{usk}$ for $\mathcal{A}$ so that they are identically distributed to in the experiment, but γ in the isk is also the secret value in the problem instance. $\mathcal{A}'$ also simulates responses the AllocateRep oracle to $\mathcal{A}$ using the problem instance and by programming the random oracle. $\mathcal{A}'$ then uses the signature (I, r, t, Σ) output by $\mathcal{A}$ to output a valid solution to the q-SDH problem.

Theorem 1 (Unforgeability of Reputation). *Assuming the random oracle model, and the q-SDH assumption, our reputation system Π satisfies Unforgeability of Reputation.*

The proofs of the following Theorems 2 and 3, are similar to the proofs of Traceability/Non-Frameability and Anonymity for the XS scheme [17]. We have adapted these proofs due to the modification in XS*, and as our model is static (users do not join or leave after the scheme begins). The proofs of Theorems 4, 5 and 6 are similar to the simulation based proof of security of CDL [15]. It is clear due to the similarity of the security requirements for DAA schemes [15] and the security requirements of Soundness of Reputation, Anonymity of Feedback and Non-Frameability, that a reputation system that uses the CDL scheme will satisfy these requirements.

Theorem 2 (Traceability). *Assuming the random oracle model, and the joc q-SDH assumption, our reputation system Π satisfies Traceability.*

Theorem 3 (Unlinkability of User Behaviour). *Assuming the random oracle model, and the q-sdh assumption, our reputation system Π satisfies Unlinkability of User Behaviour.*

Theorem 4 (Soundness of Reputation). *Assuming the bilinear LRSW problem is hard in $(\mathbb{G}_1, \mathbb{G}_2)$, and the random oracle model, our reputation system Π satisfies Soundness of Reputation.*

Theorem 5 (Anonymity of Feedback). *Assuming the DDH assumption in $\mathbb{G}_1$, and the random oracle model, our reputation system Π satisfies Anonymity of Feedback.*

Theorem 6 (Non–frameability). *Assuming the DL assumption in $\mathbb{G}_1$, and the random oracle model, our reputation system Π satisfies Non–frameability.*

6.1 Efficiency

Computational Cost. We focus on PostItem, CheckItem, and SendFB, because these are performed by users with less computational power. We note that ReceiveFeedback only needs to check all feedback for the same item, to ensure Soundness of Reputation, not all feedback. SendFB requires 7 exponentiations in $\mathbb{G}_1$, and 2 hash computations which is a low computational cost.

There is an extra cost, compared to [8,18], required to achieve Unlinkability of user behaviour, in PostItem and CheckItem. We note that in [8,18] whenever a user posts an item they must receive a new secret key from the managing authority, which is not required by our reputation system. Assuming pre–computation, PostItem requires 8 exponentiations in $\mathbb{G}_1$, 3 exponentiations in $\mathbb{G}_3$, and 1 hash computation. CheckItem requires 2 computations of $\hat{t}$, 10 exponentiations in $\mathbb{G}_1$, 2 exponentiations in $\mathbb{G}_2$, 2 exponentiations in $\mathbb{G}_3$, 2 hash computations.

Communication Overhead. Using updated parameters for curves that give 128 bit security [27] and point compression, the XS* signature Ω has length 432 bytes and the CDL signature Φ has length 336 bytes. Therefore the communication overhead when sending feedback with our construction is 768 bytes, compared to 624 bytes in [8] using the same curves. This is a relatively small increase given the additional security of Unlinkability for user behaviour achieved. Our communication overhead compares well to [18] where signatures have length $\mathcal{O}(k \log(n))$, as shown in [21], compared to our signatures of length $\mathcal{O}(k)$.

6.2 Conventional Attacks on Reputation Systems

There are several attacks outside the scope of this work such as: On-Off attacks, where adversaries behave honestly/dishonestly alternatively, White-washing attacks, where adversaries leave and rejoin to shed a bad reputation, Sybil attacks, where users give dishonest feedback, and Self Rating attacks, where adversaries positively rate a large number of their own items.

Sybil attacks are partly mitigated by the Soundness of Reputation requirement. A solution for Whitewashing and Sybil attacks could be to make joining a scheme expensive. Self Rating attacks could be mitigated by making all users give the feedback "*" on their own items that could be used to link to self ratings, or be punished by the CS. The Central Server can also punish authors of items that do not represent a valid transaction.

7 Conclusion

We have introduced and formally defined a new security model for centralised reputation systems, where user behaviour is and unlinkable. This represents a shift from previous models which aims at more accurately capturing the real-world requirements of reputation systems, used by many on a daily basis.

We have provided a concrete construction which satisfies the new security requirements with a low additional efficiency cost. As a next step, we are considering the extension of our model to allow for dynamic join of users, similarly to [6], as well as a concrete implementation of the system to be used, for instance, by a car-pooling app.

References

1. Amazon's third-party sellers ship record-breaking 2 billion items in 2014, but merchant numbers stay flat. https://techcrunch.com/2015/01/05/amazon-third-party-sellers-2014/. Accessed 1 Apr 2019
2. Travis kalanick says uber has 40 million monthly active riders. https://techcrunch.com/2016/10/19/travis-kalanick-says-uber-has-40-million-monthly-active-riders/. Accessed 1 Apr 2019
3. Androulaki, E., Choi, S.G., Bellovin, S.M., Malkin, T.: Reputation systems for anonymous networks. In: Borisov, N., Goldberg, I. (eds.) PETS 2008. LNCS, vol. 5134, pp. 202–218. Springer, Heidelberg (2008). https://doi.org/10.1007/978-3-540-70630-4_13
4. Bellare, M., Micciancio, D., Warinschi, B.: Foundations of group signatures: formal definitions, simplified requirements, and a construction based on general assumptions. In: Biham, E. (ed.) EUROCRYPT 2003. LNCS, vol. 2656, pp. 614–629. Springer, Heidelberg (2003). https://doi.org/10.1007/3-540-39200-9_38
5. Bellare, M., Rogaway, P.: Random oracles are practical: a paradigm for designing efficient protocols. In: Ashby, V. (ed.) ACM CCS 93, 3–5 November 1993, pp. 62–73. ACM Press, Fairfax (1993)
6. Bellare, M., Shi, H., Zhang, C.: Foundations of group signatures: the case of dynamic groups. In: Menezes, A. (ed.) CT-RSA 2005. LNCS, vol. 3376, pp. 136–153. Springer, Heidelberg (2005). https://doi.org/10.1007/978-3-540-30574-3_11
7. Bethencourt, J., Shi, E., Song, D.: Signatures of reputation. In: Sion, R. (ed.) FC 2010. LNCS, vol. 6052, pp. 400–407. Springer, Heidelberg (2010). https://doi.org/10.1007/978-3-642-14577-3_35
8. Blömer, J., Juhnke, J., Kolb, C.: Anonymous and publicly linkable reputation systems. In: Böhme, R., Okamoto, T. (eds.) FC 2015. LNCS, vol. 8975, pp. 478–488. Springer, Heidelberg (2015). https://doi.org/10.1007/978-3-662-47854-7_29

9. Boneh, D., Boyen, X.: Short signatures without random oracles. In: Cachin, C., Camenisch, J.L. (eds.) EUROCRYPT 2004. LNCS, vol. 3027, pp. 56–73. Springer, Heidelberg (2004). https://doi.org/10.1007/978-3-540-24676-3_4

10. Boneh, D., Boyen, X.: Short signatures without random oracles and the SDH assumption in bilinear groups. J. Cryptol. **21**(2), 149–177 (2008)

11. Bootle, J., Cerulli, A., Chaidos, P., Ghadafi, E., Groth, J.: Foundations of fully dynamic group signatures. In: Manulis, M., Sadeghi, A.-R., Schneider, S. (eds.) ACNS 2016. LNCS, vol. 9696, pp. 117–136. Springer, Cham (2016). https://doi.org/10.1007/978-3-319-39555-5_7

12. Brickell, E.F., Camenisch, J., Chen, L.: Direct anonymous attestation. In: Atluri, V., Pfitzmann, B., McDaniel, P. (eds.) ACM CCS 2004, 25–29 October 2004, pp. 132–145. ACM Press, Washington (2004)

13. Camenisch, J., Chen, L., Drijvers, M., Lehmann, A., Novick, D., Urian, R.: One TPM to bind them all: fixing TPM 2.0 for provably secure anonymous attestation. In: 2017 IEEE Symposium on Security and Privacy, SP, pp. 901–920. IEEE (2017)

14. Camenisch, J., Drijvers, M., Lehmann, A.: Anonymous attestation using the strong Diffie Hellman assumption revisited. In: Franz, M., Papadimitratos, P. (eds.) Trust 2016. LNCS, vol. 9824, pp. 1–20. Springer, Cham (2016). https://doi.org/10.1007/978-3-319-45572-3_1

15. Camenisch, J., Drijvers, M., Lehmann, A.: Universally composable direct anonymous attestation. In: Cheng, C.-M., Chung, K.-M., Persiano, G., Yang, B.-Y. (eds.) PKC 2016. LNCS, vol. 9615, pp. 234–264. Springer, Heidelberg (2016). https://doi.org/10.1007/978-3-662-49387-8_10

16. Chaum, D., van Heyst, E.: Group signatures. In: Davies, D.W. (ed.) EUROCRYPT 1991. LNCS, vol. 547, pp. 257–265. Springer, Heidelberg (1991). https://doi.org/10.1007/3-540-46416-6_22

17. Delerablée, C., Pointcheval, D.: Dynamic fully anonymous short group signatures. In: Nguyen, P.Q. (ed.) VIETCRYPT 2006. LNCS, vol. 4341, pp. 193–210. Springer, Heidelberg (2006). https://doi.org/10.1007/11958239_13

18. Kaafarani, A.E., Katsumata, S., Solomon, R.: Anonymous reputation systems achieving full dynamicity from lattices. In: Twenty-Second International Conference on Financial Cryptography and Data Security (forthcoming)

19. Garms, L., Martin, K., Ng, S.-L.: Reputation schemes for pervasive social networks with anonymity. In: Proceedings of the fifteenth International Conference on Privacy, Security and Trust (PST 2017), IEEE (2017)

20. Garms, L., Quaglia, E.A.: A new approach to modelling centralised reputation systems. Cryptology ePrint Archive, Report 2019/453 (2019). https://eprint.iacr.org/2019/453

21. Ling, S., Nguyen, K., Wang, H., Xu, Y.: Lattice-based group signatures: achieving full dynamicity with ease. In: Gollmann, D., Miyaji, A., Kikuchi, H. (eds.) ACNS 2017. LNCS, vol. 10355, pp. 293–312. Springer, Cham (2017). https://doi.org/10.1007/978-3-319-61204-1_15

22. Lysyanskaya, A., Rivest, R.L., Sahai, A., Wolf, S.: Pseudonym systems. In: Heys, H., Adams, C. (eds.) SAC 1999. LNCS, vol. 1758, pp. 184–199. Springer, Heidelberg (2000). https://doi.org/10.1007/3-540-46513-8_14

23. Mármol, F.G., Pérez, G.M.: Security threats scenarios in trust and reputation models for distributed systems. Comput. Secur. **28**(7), 545–556 (2009)

24. Ng, S.-L., Martin, K., Chen, L., Li, Q.: Private reputation retrieval in public - a privacy-aware announcement scheme for vanets. IET Inf. Secur. (2016). https://doi.org/10.1049/iet-ifs.2014.0316

25. Pavlov, E., Rosenschein, J.S., Topol, Z.: Supporting privacy in decentralized additive reputation systems. In: Jensen, C., Poslad, S., Dimitrakos, T. (eds.) iTrust 2004. LNCS, vol. 2995, pp. 108–119. Springer, Heidelberg (2004). https://doi.org/10.1007/978-3-540-24747-0_9
26. Petrlic, R., Lutters, S., Sorge, C.: Privacy-preserving reputation management. In: Proceedings of the 29th Annual ACM Symposium on Applied Computing, SAC 2014, pp. 1712–1718. ACM, New York (2014)
27. Scott, M.: Pairing implementation revisited. Cryptology ePrint Archive, Report 2019/077 (2019). https://eprint.iacr.org/2019/077
28. Zhai, E., Wolinsky, D.I., Chen, R., Syta, E., Teng, C., Ford, B.: AnonRep: towards tracking-resistant anonymous reputation. In: 13th USENIX Symposium on Networked Systems Design and Implementation (NSDI 2016), pp. 583–596. USENIX Association (2016)

Author Index